# VACATIONING WITH YOUR PET!

*D0813448*

### Eileen's Directory
### Of Pet-Friendly Lodging

## By Eileen Barish

*Over 10,000 Listings of
Hotels, Motels, Inns, Ranches and B & B's
That Welcome Guests with Pets!*

Pet-Friendly Publications
P. O. Box 8459, Scottsdale, Az 85252
Tel: (800) 496-2665

Pet-Friendly Publications,
P. O. Box 8459, Scottsdale, Arizona 85252.
Tel: # (800) 496-2665

ISBN #1-884465-00-5
Library of Congress Catalog Card Number: 93-86759

ATTENTION: Clubs, Organizations, Travel Agencies, Animal Groups
and all interested parties; Contact the publisher for information on quantity discounts!
Every traveller who owns a pet should have this directory.

Printed and bound in the United States of America.

# TABLE OF CONTENTS

## DIRECTORY LISTINGS:

# Special Acknowledgements

Eileen's Directory would not have been possible without the help of my husband Harvey who guided me from beginning to end.

To Phyllis for her dedication to perfection, not to mention her flying fingers. To my children, Nona Sue, Kenny and Chris who accepted the newest additions to our family (Rosie and Maxwell) with little sibling rivalry, and to my mother Katie on her birthday.

In memory of Sam, the "best friend" who started it all.

Photograph of Eileen, Rosie and Maxwell by Ken Friedman.

# Travelling With Your Pet Can Be A Rewarding Experience.

## You and Your Pet Can:

- Explore the Northwest wilderness.
- Hike Colorado mountain trails.
- Window shop on New York's Fifth Avenue.
- Romp along lakeside paths in Minneapolis.

You never have to leave your best friend home or kenneled in a small cage while you vacation. Bring your four-legged friend along. Double your enjoyment and increase your safety. If your pet is a great companion at home, he can be an even better companion when you travel.

Whether you're a seasoned pet traveller or a first-time adventurer, EILEEN'S DIRECTORY OF PET-FRIENDLY LODGING will make travelling with your pet easier and more enjoyable. At a glance, you'll locate over 10,000 accommodations that welcome pets.

## What If I Travel Without Prior Reservations?

If you're travelling on a very loose itinerary, you need not worry. This directory provides the names of more than 10,000 lodgings.

In almost every area, you'll be able to locate lodging, even at the last minute. Of course, as with all travel during peak periods and holidays, your choices will be lessened.

# HOW TO USE THIS DIRECTORY.

You'll find the states listed alphabetically. Within each state, cities are also in alphabetical order. Accommodations include the name of the lodging, address and zip code. Also included is the phone number and approximate rate per night. Whenever available, 800 numbers for individual motels and hotels are provided, as well as 800 numbers for major hotel chains, state tourism departments and car rental agencies.

## Do Hotel and Motel Policies Differ Regarding Pets?

Yes. But all of the accommodations listed in EILEEN'S DIRECTORY OF PET-FRIENDLY LODGING allow pets, however, policies vary on charges and sometimes on pet size. Some might require a damage deposit (although most are refundable) and some combine their deposit with a daily and/or one-time charge. Some of the residence-type inns which cater to long-term guests, charge a long-term fee. Some restrict pets to the small variety while others only allow pets in specific rooms, perhaps only in cabins or cottages. Most though, do not charge a fee or place restrictions in any manner. At the time your reservations are made, determine the policy of your lodging choice.

# VACATION ACROSS AMERICA WITH YOUR PET

### The Newest Trend Is Bringing Families Closer.

Instead of embarking for foreign shores, more and more American vacationers are opting to remain on home soil rather than travelling abroad. The grandeur and wonder of our great country beckons like never before. Long appreciated by foreign visitors, Americans have returned to basics -- recognizing that there's more beauty in our own backyards than in all the castles and museums of faraway lands.

Americans are taking to the roads and skies in record numbers, exploring our vast mountain ranges, the majesty of our alpine forests, the serenity of our lake-side communities, the diversity of our ocean resorts, the excitement of our sophisticated cities. And not surprisingly, they're taking their pets along on their travels. Families are coming together more strongly. Family ties are becoming more precious. And those family ties include family pets. Long accepted as a part of life in America, pets have now become an accepted part of vacationing in America.

4

## Spot and Tabby Come Along.

Instead of leaving pets behind, sometimes subjecting them to traumatic and costly boarding experiences, families, couples, single men and women across the country have begun including their four-legged friends in vacation plans. And everyone's enjoyment has been increased.

## Money and Safety...Added Bonuses.

How often have you wondered whether your pet is well taken care of when you leave him at a kennel? How often have you returned from a vacation only to find that your healthy pet is now unhealthy -- perhaps he's been exposed to kennel cough or worse? How often have you fretted about finding a trustworthy person to come to your home as a pet caregiver? Taking your pet along eliminates the often expensive arrangements you once had to make. And think of the added enjoyment you'll experience, not to mention the safety of having a loyal defender as your constant companion. It dogs are regarded as the best deterrents to crime in your home, just imagine how much safer you'll feel when you travel.

5

## Become A Part Of This New Travel Phenomenon.

In a complicated world, it's good to return to the simpler things in life. Like an unpretentious stroll through a grassy field, lazy afternoons spent lakeside reading a good book, picnics in the cool shade of a pine forest. Whether you're enjoying family time or solitude -- those quiet moments can be even more pleasurable with your pet. Forget the chaos of the modern-day vacation, running from one amusement park to another, trying to cram each minute full of something, anything, yet missing out on what vacations once meant. Having your pet with you puts you more in touch with the people you'll encounter. You'll become more a part of every place you visit. This directory will lead you to lodgings where your pet is welcome. And it will help you discover a different kind of vacation.

## It's Easier Than You Think.

Without time consuming research, or wasted effort, you'll quickly and easily locate the type of accommodations that suit you with EILEEN'S DIRECTORY OF PET-FRIENDLY LODGING. Your choices are limitless. And you'll be surprised at some of the names you'll find listed. Whether you prefer city travel and enjoy being

6

pampered at a five star resort, or roaming the great outdoors looking for that rustic lakeside cabin or secluded cottage in the woods...this directory provides the information you need to find pet-friendly quality lodging in every price range.

## Accommodations Plus Much, Much More.

More than thirty introductory pages offer advice on how to travel with your pet -- from airline policies to car travel tips. Find out how to ease carsickness. Learn about "Kenneling Up." From food tips to what to bring along, this directory will answer most of the questions you might have on vacationing with your pet.

All that plus the only comprehensive listing of hotels, motels, and inns that welcome your pet.

There's even a selection of bed and breakfast places throughout the directory that are pet-friendly.

# INTRODUCTION:

# Eileen's U.S. Directory of Pet-Friendly Lodging

Let me begin by saying very clearly ... vacationing with your pet can be easy. Don't be intimidated. Don't think it takes special training or expertise. It doesn't. All it takes is a little planning and a little patience. Believe me, the rewards are worth the effort. This directory is filled with information that will make vacationing with your pet more pleasurable. From training tips to what to take along, to the do's and don'ts of travel, virtually all of your questions will be answered.

## Vacationing With Pets?

Not something I thought I'd ever do. But as the adage goes, necessity is the mother of invention. What began as a necessity for me turned into a new lifestyle. A lifestyle of travel that has improved every aspect of my vacation and travel time.

After planning a two-week vacation through California, with an ultimate destination of Lake Tahoe, my husband Harvey and I had our hearts stolen by two Golden Retriever puppies...Rosie and Maxwell. These additions to our family were ready to come home with us only weeks before our scheduled departure date. What to do? Kennel them? Hire a caretaker at our home? Neither solution felt right.

## Sooo...We Took Them Along.

Oh, the fun we had. And the friends we made. Both the two-legged and four-legged variety. Having our pets along made us more a part of the places we visited. Pets are natural conversation starters and they were the prime movers in some lasting friendships we made during our travels. Now when we revisit some of our favorite haunts, we have old friends to see as well as new ones to make. (I've actually been recognized by my dogs.)

Our travels have taken us to many distant places. We've visited alpine lakes, national forests, mountain resorts, seaside villages, island retreats, big cities and tiny hamlets. We've shared everything from luxury hotel rooms complete with balconies and indoor spas to rustic cabin getaways.

Our trip to Lake Tahoe, California and the many trips that followed proved so delightful that I decided to share my on-the-road adventures with other pet owners and lovers like you. That's how this directory was born. Conceived in love, it was nurtured by good times and interesting encounters.

## Just Ordinary Pets.

Rosie and Maxwell, my travelling companions, are not exceptional pets to anyone other than me. Their training was neither intensive nor professionally rendered.

They were trained with kindness, praise, consistency and love. And not all of their training came about when they were puppies. I too had a lot to learn. And as I learned what I wanted of them, their training continued. It was a sharing and growing experience. Old dogs (and humans too) can learn new tricks. Rosie and Maxwell never fail to surprise me. Their ability to adapt to new situations has never stopped. So don't think you have to start with a puppy. Every pet, young and old, can be taught to be travel-friendly.

As an animal lover, you'll be able to relate to this. Rosie and Maxwell know when I begin putting their things together that another holiday is about to begin. Their excitement mounts with every phase of preparation. They stick like glue -- remaining at my side as I organize their belongings. By the time I've finished, they can barely contain their joy. Rosie runs to grab her leash and prances about the kitchen holding it in her mouth while Max sits on his haunches, paws raised and begins to howl. If they could talk, they'd tell you how much they enjoy travelling. But since they can't, trust this directory to lead you to a different kind of experience. One that's filled with lots of love and an opportunity for shared adventure with your pet.

# TRIP TIPS ON VACATIONING WITH YOUR PET

## Is My Pet VACATION-FRIENDLY?

Most dogs and cats can be excellent travelling companions. Naturally, the younger they are when you accustom them to travelling with you, the more quickly they will adapt. But that doesn't mean that an older pet won't love vacationing with you. And it doesn't mean that the transition has to be a difficult one either.

When we began vacationing with Rosie and Max, some friends decided to join us on a few of our local outings. Their dog Brandy, a ten-year old Cocker Spaniel, had never travelled with them. Other than trips to the vet and groomers, she'd never been in the car. The question remained ... how would Brandy adjust? We needn't have worried. She took to the car immediately. Despite her small size, she quickly learned to jump in and out of the rear of their station wagon. She too ran through the forest with Rosie and Max, playing and frolicking as if she'd always had free run. To her owners and to Brandy, their world took on new meaning. Nature as seen through the eyes of their dog became a more intriguing place, a place of discovery.

Of course, every pet is different. And you know yours better than anyone. If you've never vacationed with your pet before, it might be a good idea to make your first voyage a short one. But you'll see. It won't be long until your pet will happily share travel and vacation times with you.

11

# VACATIONING BY CAR - "KENNEL UP"

"Kennel Up"...the magical, all-purpose command.
When I took Rosie and Maxwell for their puppy check-up, Dr. Rubano, my vet, offered a training tip which has been the basis of my dog training. He told me to use the command, "Kennel Up" whenever I put Rosie and Maxwell into their kennel in my home and whenever I wanted them to get into the car with me. There isn't a better tip I can pass along.

When Rosie and Maxwell's training began, I used a metal kennel which they regarded as their home, their sleeping place. When they were left alone during their housebreaking training, and then again when they were put to bed at night, I used the simple command, "Kennel Up," as I pointed to and tapped their kennel. They quickly learned the command and would immediately go to their special place. As they outgrew the kennel, the laundry room became their "Kennel Up" place. And when they were full grown, the entire kitchen took over as their "Kennel Up" location. Likewise, when they began accompanying me on car trips, I used the command each time I told them to jump into the car. The command was reinforced whenever I wanted them to go into their "place." There was no reason not to continue using this command during vacations. After checking into our lodging, I would find a cozy spot I thought would work best (usually on one side of the bed away from the flow of people traffic) and issue the command; "Kennel Up." It wasn't long before they knew what I wanted. Mindreaders. Now, they find their own "Kennel Up" spot before I have a chance to do it for them. "Kennel Up" continues to represent the command to remain quiet and behave themselves, whether at home, in my car or in a hotel room.

## Can My Pet Be Trained To Travel?

Of course it's ideal to begin training your pet to behave in the car at a young age. But most pets are quite adaptable and responsive and patience will definitely have its rewards. Pets love nothing more than to be with you. If it means behaving to have that privilege, they will respond.

Now that you've decided to travel and vacation with your pet, it's probably a good idea to get them started with short trips. Make travel times enjoyable. Stop every so often and do fun things. As you lengthen your travel times, don't think that you have to stop every hour or so. When you travel, just handle your pets as you would at home. They won't have to walk any more frequently whether they're at home or in the car. But when you do stop to let them out, leash them before you open the car doors. If you're vacationing with your cat, use a harness and leash for walking.

Most pets love an unexpected romp in a clearing, park, even a stroll on a city street. Keep a leash with you and leash your pet before you allow him out of the car. Also, as a consideration to others as well as our environment, carry plastic bags (supermarket vegetable bags are great) and paper towels so you can clean up after your pet.

And remember, always use the "Kennel Up" command each time you tell your pet to get into the car or back in its travelling kennel. Don't forget to use lots of praise every time they obey the command.

You'll find that your pet will most likely be lulled to sleep by the motion of the car. When I travel with Rosie and Maxwell, after less than fifteen minutes, they're both asleep. On long trips, I stop every few hours to give them water and "stretch my legs" while I let them "stretch their legs." They've become accustomed to these short stops and anticipate them. The moment the car motor is turned off and the hatch back popped open, they anxiously await their leashes. When our exercise time is over and we're back at the car, a simple "Kennel Up" gets them into their contented travel positions.

# TO KENNEL OR NOT TO KENNEL?

**Dogs:** Whether or not you use a kennel for car trips is a personal choice. The most important aspect of car travel is to make sure your pet doesn't interfere with your driving. His comfort should be your second concern. If you plan to use a kennel, line the bottom with an old blanket or towel or use shredded newspaper. When you're vacationing by car and not using a kennel, confine your dog to the back seat and command him to "Kennel Up." It's a good idea to cover the back seat with an old blanket to protect your upholstery. It will also make clean up at the end of your trip that much easier. To keep my car fresh smelling for the entire vacation, I use a small deodorizer tucked under the front seat.

**Cats:** Cats should be confined to a kennel -- for their safety and yours. Cats love to jump and perch and a kennel will eliminate the potential for accidents. Make your cat's kennel as comfortable as you can by including a small scratch post if that's what your cat likes or a favorite toy. Put some soft bedding on the floor of the kennel as well. You can use the same trick of getting your cat to eliminate as detailed in the plane travel section. Shortly before you plan to leave on your vacation, fill your cat's home litter box with fresh litter. Once she uses it, you can begin your trip knowing your cat has already voided.

15

## How Often Should I Stop?

Too many people think that when their pets are in the car, they have to "go" more often. Not true. Whenever you stop for yourself, you can let your pet have a drink and take a walk. But there's no need to make extra stops along the way unless your pet has a physical problem and must be walked more often. Always pull your car out of the flow of traffic so you can safely care for your pet. Never let your pet run free. Use a leash at all times. Since your pet is in unfamiliar territory, he can bolt into traffic, become lost or run away.

## What About Carsickness?

Some pets are queasier than others. Although both dogs and cats suffer from motion sickness, for some reason dogs and especially puppies suffer more frequently. It's best to wait a couple of hours after your pet has eaten before beginning your vacation. Or better yet, feed your pet after you arrive at your destination. Keep the windows open enough to allow in fresh air. If your pet has a tendency to be carsick, sugar can help. Give your dog a tablespoon of honey or a small piece of candy (no chocolate) before beginning your trip. That should help settle his stomach. If you notice that your pet looks sickly, stop and allow him some fresh air.

16

## Can My Pet Be Left Alone In The Car?

During the winter months, your pet can be left alone for short periods but make sure you lock your doors and leave your windows slightly open to circulate fresh air.

### *NEVER LEAVE YOUR PET UNATTENDED IN WARM WEATHER!*

Although you might only be gone a few minutes, that's all it takes for a pet to become dehydrated. When the outside temperature is only 85 degrees, the temperature in your car can reach 100 to 120 degrees in thirty minutes, even if all the windows are left open, even if your vehicle is parked in the shade. Exposure to high temperatures can cause brain damage and possibly death.

## What If My Pet Runs Off? - Pet Identification.

Vacationing is no different than staying at home as far as identification. Never allow your pet to be anywhere without proper identification. Tags should provide your pet's name, your name, address and phone number. Most states require pet owners to purchase a license every year. The tag includes, among other data, a license number that is registered with your state. Attach the license tag to your pet's collar. Should you become separated, your pet can be traced. There are also local organizations that help reunite lost pets and owners. The phone numbers of these organizations can be obtained from local police authorities.

# TRAVEL MANNERS

## Are There Lodging Guidelines For My Pets?

The lodgings listed are all pet-friendly. It's up to those of us who vacation with our pets to keep it that way. Treat the lodgings in a courteous manner and you'll continue to be welcomed. The following are some quick hints to make vacationing with your pet more enjoyable.

1. Don't allow your pet to sleep on the bed with you. If that's what your pet is accustomed to doing at home, take along an extra sheet and put that on top of the bedding provided by your lodging. If your pet has a favorite blanket, take it along on your vacation and let him sleep on that.

2. Bring a towel or small mat to use under your pet's food and water dishes. Feed your pet in the bathroom where clean-up is easier should accidents occur.

3. Try to keep pets off the furniture. Since that's particularly difficult with cats, a damp washcloth will remove most of your cat's hair from the furniture.

4. Keep your cat's litter box in the bathroom. Clean out the litter box every morning and flush waste down the toilet to keep the room smelling nice. It would also be considerate to rinse out cat food cans before placing them in the wastepaper basket.

5. When you walk your pet, carry plastic bags and/or paper towels for clean up.

6. Always keep your pet on a leash on the hotel/motel grounds.

## Can My Pet Be Left Alone In The Room?

Only you would know the answer to that. If your pet is not destructive, if your dog doesn't bark incessantly, then you might consider leaving your pet in the room for short periods of time — say for example when you dine out. If you do though, you should confine your cat to its travelling kennel and your dog to the bathroom. It would also be a good idea to put the "Do Not Disturb" sign on your door.

# WHAT AND HOW DO I PACK FOR MY PET?

To keep things simple from vacation to vacation, I use two packing bags which are restocked at the end of each vacation. That way, I'm always prepared for the next one.

## Large Mesh Bag:

I bought this mesh shopping bag while on vacation in Nogales, Mexico, but I've seen similar bags all over the country. It expands to hold any number of items. This bag usually holds:

1. The blanket I use to cover the back seat of my car.

2. Two to three old towels which I keep for emergencies. (I throw the blankets and towels in the wash when I return home and then store them in the bag -- that way they're always there and always clean.)

3. Two plastic bowls, one for water, the other for food.

4. A roll of plastic bags (for clean-up).

5. A roll of paper towels -- for clean-up and everything in between.

6. A long line of rope. You'll be surprised how often you'll use this very handy item.

7. An extra collar and lead.

## Canvas Zippered Bag:

This bag contains some of the smaller items I take along when vacationing with my pets. I keep a list (which my husband thoughtfully laminated and attached to the zipper) and just check off the contents as I pack. That prevents forgetting some little item I'll be sure to need the moment I pull away from the house. Of course, you'll have your own special list. Mine can be used as a guide in preparing your own.

1. An extra flea and tick collar.
2. Pet brush.
3. Small scissors.
4. Blunt end tweezers -- great for removing thorns and cacti.
5. Chew toys, balls, frisbees, treats -- whatever your pet prefers.
6. Can opener and spoon.
7. Food -- enough for a couple of days. Most brands are available throughout the country -- either at pet stores, supermarkets or veterinary offices. You'll want to take enough to eliminate having to find a place the first night or two of your vacation.
8. A package of pre-moistened towelettes. I keep an extra package in the glove compartment of my car as well. More than just handy for cleaning your hands, they serve a myriad of purposes.
9. A package of dry onion soup mix.

When I first began vacationing with Rosie and Maxwell, I took along both dry and wet dog food. After a while though, it became bothersome and messy to deal with the wet variety. I found the simplest solution. Now when we vacation together, I take along a package of onion soup mix. At dinnertime, I sprinkle a small amount of the onion mix on their dry food, moisten with warm water and voila. Not only do they have a tasty dinner but a great smelling one too. It's a treat that continues to appeal to both Rosie and Maxwell. Try it, I think you'll like it. I know your pet will. And readers, let me know about your pet's preference as well. Or some quick fix you've happened upon.

# MAKE VACATION TIME PLEASURABLE TIME

Some tips and suggestions to
increase your enjoyment.

1. Don't feed or water
your pet just before starting
on your trip. Feed and
water your pet approxi-
mately two hours before
you plan to depart. Or better still, if it's possible, wait
until you arrive at your destination.

2. Exercise your pet before you leave. A tired pet
will fall off to sleep more easily and adapt more readily.

3. Take along a large container of water. Your pet
will do better drinking from his own water supply for
the first day or so. And having water along will mean
you can stop wherever you like and not worry about
finding water.

4. Plan stops during your trip. Just like you, your pet
will enjoy short pauses. Along your route, there will be
many areas conducive to pet freedom. And if you
regard these stops as little rest periods and not chores,
you'll be surprised how satisfying they'll become. Make
the car ride a pleasant part of your trip and your
vacation will begin the moment you leave your house
not just when you reach your journey's end.

5. While you're driving, keep your windows open
enough to allow the circulation of fresh air but not
enough to allow your pet to jump out. If you have air
conditioning, that will keep your pet cool enough.

6. Vets advise against letting pets hang their head out of the window. Eyes, ears, and throats can become inflamed.

7. Use a short lead when walking your pet through public areas -- he'll be easier to control.

8. Take along your pet's favorite objects from home. If they entertain him there, they'll entertain him on vacation.

9. Before any trip, allow your pet to relieve himself.

10. Cover your back seat with an old blanket or towel to protect the upholstery.

11. Wedge your favorite air freshener under one of the seats. This will eliminate most animal odors throughout your vacation and keep your car fresh smelling.

12. If your pet has a tendency to carsickness, keep a small packet of honey (many restaurants offer them with toast) in the glove compartment or carry a roll of hard candy -- like Lifesavers -- with you. Either of these might help your pet with carsickness.

13. Use a flea and tick collar on your pet.

14. Brush your pet before you begin your vacation and as often as necessary to reduce the amount of hair in the car and in your room. Your pet will love the extra attention his brushing brings and he'll always look well groomed.

15. Keep a spray can of insect repellent in your car. Stopping in nature's playground can mean dealing with insects. If mosquitos or flies are about, the spray will come in handy for you and your pet. Cover your pet's face before spraying.

# TRAVELLING BY PLANE

### Pet Carriers/Kennels:

Most airlines require pets to be in specific carriers. Airline regulations vary and arrangements should be made in advance of travel. Some airlines allow very small pets to accompany their owners in the passenger cabins. In most cases, the carrier must fit under the passenger's seat. These regulations also vary and prior arrangements should be made. In addition, airlines also require that your pet remain in the carrier for the duration of the flight.

A number of airlines will not transport pets during the warm summer months. For the most part, pet travel in planes is relatively safe but there have been problems. Consult with an airline representative to determine individual policies.

### What About The Size Of The Carrier?

Your pet should have enough room to stand, lie down, sit and turn around comfortably. Larger than that doesn't equate to more comfort. If anything, larger quarters only increase the chances of your pet being hurt because of too much movement. Just as your cat likes to sleep curled up in a ball beneath your wing back chair and your dog's favorite place is under the kitchen desk area, a cozy, compact kennel will suit your pet much better than a spacious one.

## Should Anything Else Be In The Carrier?

Cover the bottom of the carrier with a fair amount of shredded paper. The paper will absorb any accidents and provide a soft, warm cushion for your pet. Toys, even favorite objects increase the risk of accidents so don't include them.

## How Will My Pet Feel About A Kennel?

Training and familiarization are the key elements in this area. Buy the kennel a couple of weeks before your trip (airlines as well as pet stores sell them). Leave it in your home, in the area where your pet spends most of his time. Let him become accustomed to its smell, feel and look. After a few days, your pet will become comfortable around the kennel. You might even try feeding him in the kennel to make it more like home. But keep all the associations friendly. Never use the kennel for punishment. Taking the time to accustom your pet with his travelling quarters will alleviate potential problems and make vacationing together more enjoyable.

## What About Identification?

The kennel should contain a tag identifying your pet and provide all pertinent information including the pet's name, age, feeding and water requirements, your name, address and phone number and your final destination. In addition, it should include the name and phone number of your vet.

This information can be provided on any "luggage-type" ID card. Securely fasten it to the kennel.

In addition, your pet should wear his state ID tag. Should your pet somehow become separated from his kennel, his ID will go along with him.

## How Can I Make Plane Travel Comfortable For My Pet?

If possible, make your travel plans for weekday rather than weekend travel. Travel during off hours. Direct and non-stop flights also reduce the potential for problems and delays. (Check with your airline to determine how much time they require before flight time for check in. It's usually one hour.) Limiting the amount of time your pet will be in the baggage compartment will make travel time that much more comfortable.

## Will There Automatically Be Room On Board For My Pet?

Airline space for pets is normally provided on a first-come, first-served basis. As soon as you know your travel plans, contact the airline and make your arrangements. Every airline has a different policy regarding the size of pets allowed in the cabin, the size and type of carrier required for travelling in the hold as well as the time required for check in.

## What Will Pet Travel Cost?

Prices vary depending on whether your pet travels with you in the cabin or whether a kennel must be provided in the hold. Check with the airlines to determine their pricing policies.

## Do Cats Require Special Planning?

In addition to the shredded newspaper in the travelling kennel, you'll want to include a small cardboard box of litter. And speaking of litter, let me pass along a cat tip from a friend who often travels with her cat.

Knowing how fussy her cat was about the cleanliness of her surroundings, my friend found a way to get her cat to eliminate before any trip. Just a short while before they begin their journey, my friend fills the litter box with fresh litter. Loving a clean box of litter, her cat invariably uses it and starts their trip with an empty bladder and bowel.

## What About Food and Water?

It's best not to feed your pet at least six hours before departure, water one hour before.

## What About Tranquilizers?

Opinions vary on this subject. You might want to discuss this with your vet. But don't give your pet any medication not prescribed by a vet. Dosages for animals and humans vary greatly.

## What About After We Land?

If your pet has not been in the passenger cabin with you, you'll be able to pick him up in the baggage claim area along with your luggage. Ask the baggage claim attendant where the kennels arrive. If your pet is a dog, it would be best to walk him as quickly as possible. Leash him before you let him out of the kennel. Since travelling in a kennel aboard a plane is an unusual experience, your dog may react strangely. Having his leash on will avoid possible problems. Give him a cool drink of water and then walk him.

If you're travelling with your cat, it's best to keep her in the kennel until you're in your car, preferably until you've arrived at your vacation spot. You wouldn't want to risk her running off. She'll probably be thirsty though, so provide water as soon as possible.

## Pets Who Shouldn't Fly.
Sickly, frail or pregnant animals should not be flown. In addition to the stress of flying, changes in altitude and cabin pressure might adversely effect these pets. Very young puppies, kittens (younger than two months) or females in heat shouldn't travel either.

## Health Certificates — Will I Need One?
Although I've never been asked to show a health certificate for Rosie or Maxwell, either by the airlines or lodging accommodations, it could happen. If you're concerned about this, your vet can supply a certificate indicating the innoculations your pet has received. Keep this information along with your travel papers and post a copy on the kennel. In most cases, the certificate must be dated within 30 days of your travel. In addition, your destination state may require current rabies tags on your pet.

# MY PET'S IDENTIFICATION:

In the event that your pet is lost or stolen, the following information will help in describing your animal. Before you leave on your first vacation, take a few minutes to fill out this form and then keep it handy.

Name of Pet:
Breed or Mix:
Sex:                     Age:                    Tag ID#:
Special Markings:                    Coloring:
Description of Hair (color, length and texture):

Indicate unusual markings, or scars:

TAIL:     ( ) Short  ( ) Long  ( ) Screw-type
          ( ) Bushy    ( ) Cut
EARS:  ( ) Clipped    ( ) Erect    ( ) Floppy

Collar Color:
Weight:                         Height:

If you have a recent photo of your pet, attach it to this form.

# "HEY EILEEN!
## HERE'S PET-FRIENDLY LODGING THAT YOU MISSED!"

When compiling this directory, every effort was made to be inclusive and provide the name of every accommodation that allows pets. If we missed any and you would like to see them included in the next edition of VACATIONING WITH YOUR PET! please furnish the names, addresses and phone numbers as well as the average rate per night's lodging.

If you have any comments or suggestions, pass them along as well. It's our desire to keep an open line of communication with our readers and provide them with the most informative pet-friendly directory. The special tips and hints that you share with us may be included in the next edition.

Your input is welcome and we appreciate the time you've taken to keep us current on vacationing and travelling with pets. Continued happy trails to you and your pet.

Send your suggestions, comments or additions to:

Eileen Barish
Pet-Friendly Publications
P.O. Box 8459
Scottsdale, Arizona 85252

# ALABAMA

## ANNISTON

**AMERICAN INN**
1015 Hwy 431 North (36201)
Rates: N/A;
Tel: (800) 467-2525

**HAMPTON INN-
ANNISTON/OXFORD**
Hwy 21S (36203)
Rates: $38-$51;
Tel: (205) 835-1492

**HOLIDAY INN-
ANNISTON/OXFORD**
P. O. Box 3308
(Oxford 36203)
Rates: $38-$55;
Tel: (205) 831-3410

**SAVE INN**
25 Elm St (Oxford 36203)
Rates: $21-$28;
Tel: (205) 831-9480

## ARDMORE

**THE COUNTRY INN**
I-65 AL53 Exit 365 (35620)
Rates: N/A;
Tel: (205) 423-6699

## ATHENS

**BEST WESTERN INN**
P. O. Box 816 (35611)
Rates: $32-$48;
Tel: (205) 233-4030

**DAYS INN**
Rt 11 (35611)
Rates: $35-$45;
Tel: (205) 233-7500

**WELCOME INN**
Box 1125 (35611)
Rates: N/A;
Tel: (205) 232-6944

## AUBURN

**AUBURN CONF CTR
& MOTOR LODGE**
P. O. Box 3467 (36830)
Rates: $41-$47;
Tel: (205) 821-7001

**AUBURN UNIVERSITY
HOTEL & CONF CTR**
241 S College St (36830)
Rates: $75-$85;
Tel: (205) 821-8200

**HEART OF
AUBURN MOTEL**
333 South College (36830)
Rates: N/A;
Tel: (205) 887-3462

## BESSEMER

**ECONO LODGE**
1021 9th Ave SW (35020)
Rates: $34-$45;
Tel: (205) 424-9780

## BIRMINGHAM
(and Vicinity)

**BIRMINGHAM MOTEL**
7905 Crestwood Blvd (35210)
Rates: $45-$80;
Tel: (800) 338-9275

**BUDGETEL INN**
513 Cahaba Park Cir (35242)
Rates: $35-$51;
Tel: (205) 995-9990

**COMFORT INN
PERIMETER SOUTHEAST**
4627 Hwy 280 (35242)
Rates: $46-$55;
Tel: (205) 991-9977

**DAYS INN AIRPORT**
5101 Airport Hwy (35212)
Rates: $45-$61;
Tel: (205) 592-6110

**HAMPTON INN-
MOUNTAIN BROOK**
2731 US Hwy 280 (35223)
Rates: $45-$55;
Tel: (205) 870-7822

**HOLIDAY INN-AIRPORT**
5000 10th Ave N (35212)
Rates: $59-$75;
Tel: (205) 591-6900

**HOLIDAY INN I-20 & 78E**
7941 Crestwood Blvd (35210)
Rates: $45-$47;
Tel: (205) 956-8211

**HOLIDAY INN-
GALLERIA SOUTH**
1548 Montgomery Hwy
(35216)
Rates: $55-$62;
Tel: (205) 822-4350

**HOWARD JOHNSON
MOTOR LODGE**
1485 Montgomery Hwy
(35216)
Rates: $40-$65;
Tel: (205) 823-4300

**LA QUINTA MOTOR INN**
905 11th Ct W (35204)
Rates: $46-$63;
Tel: (205) 324-4510

**PICKWICK HOTEL**
1023 20th St S (35205)
Rates: $105-$129;
Tel: (205) 933-9555

**RAMADA INN-AIRPORT**
5216 Airport Hwy (35212)
Rates: $53-$125;
Tel: (205) 591-7900

**RED MOUNTAIN INN**
400 Beacon Pkwy W (35209)
Rates: $39-$65;
Tel: (205) 942-2031

**RED ROOF INN**
151 Vulcan Rd (35209)
Rates: $33-$42;
Tel: (205) 942-9414

**RESIDENCE INN BY MARRIOTT**
3 Green Hill Pkwy at US 280
(35242)
Rates: $89-$99;
Tel: (205) 991-8686

**SHERATON PERIMETER
PARK SOUTH**
8 Perimeter Dr (35243)
Rates: $75-$280;
Tel: (205) 967-2700

**TRAVELODGE**
275 Oxmoor Rd (35209)
Rates: $32-$37;
Tel: (205) 942-0919

**TRAVELODGE-
CIVIC CENTER HOTEL**
2230 10th Ave N (35203)
Rates: $35-$64;
Tel: (205) 328-6320

**UAB UNIVERSITY INN**
951 18th St S (35205)
Rates: $43-$60;
Tel: (205) 933-7700

## BOAZ

**BEST WESTERN BOAZ
OUTLET CENTER**
751 US 431S (35957)
Rates: $37-$49;
Tel: (205) 593-8410

**BOAZ INN MOTEL**
Rt 5, Box 218 Hwy 431 N
(35957)
Rates: N/A;
Tel: (205) 593-2874

**KEY WEST INN**
410 E Mill Ave (35957)
Rates: $43-$53;
Tel: (205) 593-0800

## CLANTON

**ALABAMA LODGE-MOTEL**
2301 7th St (35045)
Rates: N/A;
Tel: (205) 755-4049

**HOLIDAY INN**
P. O. Box 2010 (35045)
Rates: $39-$55;
Tel: (205) 755-0510

**KEY WEST INN**
2045 7th St (35045)
Rates: $41-$46;
Tel: (205) 755-8500

**SHONEY'S INN**
946 Lake Mitchell Rd (35045)
Rates: $35-$48;
Tel: (205) 280-0306

## CULLMAN

**DAYS INN**
1841 4th St SW (35055)
Rates: $32-$42;
Tel: (205) 739-3800

**FRIENDLY VILLAGE MOTEL**
607 2nd Ave NW (35055)
Rates: N/A;
Tel: (205) 734-2770

**RAMADA INN**
P. O. Box 1204 (35056)
Rates: $40-$60;
Tel: (205) 734-8484

**TRAVEL-RITE INN**
1901 Carroll Dr (35055)
Rates: $24-$34;
Tel: (205) 734-8854

## DALEVILLE

**GREEN HOUSE INN
& LODGE**
501 S Daleville Ave (36322)
Rates: $29-$40;
Tel: (205) 598-1475

## DECATUR

**AMBERLEY SUITE**
807 Bank St NE (35601)
Rates: $49-$75;
Tel: (800) 288-7332

**DAYS INN**
P. O. Box 2063 (35602)
Rates: $39-$48;
Tel: (205) 355-3520

**ECONOMY INN**
3424 Hwy 31 South (35603)
Rates: N/A;
Tel: (205) 353-8194

**HOLIDAY INN-
DOWNTOWN**
1101 6th Ave NE (35601)
Rates: $49-$74;
Tel: (205) 355-3150

**QUALITY INN**
P. O. Box 1050 (35602)
Rates: $38-$46;
Tel: (205) 355-0190

**RAMADA INN**
1317 E Hwy 67 (35601)
Rates: $41-$46;
Tel: (205) 353-0333

## DEMOPOLIS

**BEST WESTERN-
MINT SUNRISE MOTEL**
1034 US 80 SE (36732)
Rates: $32-$38;
Tel: (205) 289-5772

**DAYS INN**
1005 Hwy 80E (36732)
Rates: $32-$36;
Tel: (205) 289-2500

**WINDWOOD INN**
628 US 80E (36732)
Rates: $28-$40;
Tel: (205) 233-0841

## DOTHAN

**COMFORT INN**
P. O. Box 1405 (36302)
Rates: $44-$62;
Tel: (205) 793-9090

**DAYS INN**
2841 Ross Clark Cir (36301)
Rates: $36-$45;
Tel: (205) 793-2550

**ECONO LODGE**
2901 Ross Clark Cir SW
(36301)
Rates: $31-$37;
Tel: (205) 793-5200

**HAMPTON INN**
3071 Ross Clark Cir (36301)
Rates: $39-$49;
Tel: (205) 671-3700

**HOLIDAY INN**
3053 Ross Clark Cir (36301)
Rates: $40-$62;
Tel: (205) 794-6601

**HOLIDAY INN-SOUTH**
2195 Ross Clark Cir SE
(36301)
Rates: $42-$56;
Tel: (205) 794-8711

**OLYMPIA SPA
GOLF RESORT**
P. O. Box 6108 (36302)
Rates: $39;
Tel: (205) 677-3321

**RAMADA INN**
P. O. Box 1761 (36302)
Rates: $46-$105;
Tel: (205) 692-0031

## ENTERPRISE

**COMFORT INN**
615 Hwy 84 Bypass (36330)
Rates: $39-$80;
Tel: (205) 393-2304

## EUFAULA

**BEST WESTERN
EUFAULA INN**
Hwy 431S (36027)
Rates: $32-$48;
Tel: (205) 687-3900

**HOLIDAY INN**
631 E Barbour St (36027)
Rates: $40-$48;
Tel: (205) 687-2021

## EVERGREEN

**ECONO LODGE**
P. O. Box 564 (36401)
Rates: $35-$42;
Tel: (205) 578-4701

## FAIRHOPE

**BARONS MOTEL**
701 S Mobile Ave (36532)
Rates: N/A;
Tel: (205) 929-8000

## FLORENCE

**BEST WESTERN
EXECUTIVE INN**
P.O. Box Q (35630)
Rates: $36-$43;
Tel: (205) 766-2331

**COMFORT INN**
400 S Court St (35630)
Rates: $37-$49;
Tel: (205) 760-8888

## FORT PAYNE

**BEST WESTERN-
FORT PAYNE**
1828 Gault Ave N (35967)
Rates: $36-$43;
Tel: (205) 845-0481

## FORT RUCKER

**ECONO LODGE**
241 Daleville Ave (36322)
Rates: $33-$37;
Tel: (205) 598-6304

## GADSDEN

**ECONO LODGE**
P. O. Box 571 (Attalla 35954)
Rates: $36-$42;
Tel: (205) 538-9925

**GADSDEN AIRPORT MOTEL**
1612 West Grand Ave
(35901)
Rates: N/A;
Tel: (800) 441-7344

**HOLIDAY INN**
801 Cleveland Ave (Attalla
35954)
Rates: $46-$58;
Tel: (205) 538-7861

**TRAVEL 8 MOTEL**
3909 West Meighan (35904)
Rates: N/A;
Tel: (205) 543-7261

**TRAVELER'S MOTOR INN**
421 E Broad St (35903)
Rates: N/A;
Tel: (205) 546-5211

## GAYLESVILLE

**LAKESHORE RESORT**
Hwy 68 N Weiss Lake Dr
(35973)
Rates: N/A;
Tel: (205) 422-3471

## GREENVILLE

**ECONO LODGE**
946 Fort Dale Rd (36037)
Rates: $40-$45;
Tel: (205) 382-3118

**HOLIDAY INN**
941 Fort Dale Rd (36037)
Rates: $40-$53;
Tel: (205) 382-2651

## GULF SHORES

**BEST WESTERN
ON THE BEACH**
P. O. Box 398 (36547)
Rates: $39-$135;
Tel: (205) 948-7047

**LIGHTHOUSE MOTEL**
P. O.Box 233 (36542)
Rates: $55-$110;
Tel: (205) 948-6188

**RAMADA INN**
610 W Beach Blvd (36542)
Rates: $28-$77;
Tel: (205) 948-8141

## GUNTERSVILLE

**MAC'S LANDING MOTEL**
7001 Val-Monte Dr (35976)
Rates: $47-$93;
Tel: (205) 582-1000

## HANCEVILLE

**MOTEL I-65**
14466 Hwy 91 (35077)
Rates: N/A;
Tel: (205) 287-1114

## HEFLIN

**SCOTTISH INNS**
Rt 2 (36264)
Rates: $29-$35;
Tel: (205) 463-2900

## HUNTSVILLE

**BUDGETEL**
4890 University Dr (35816)
Rates: $35-$51;
Tel: (205) 830-8999

**CARRIAGE INN HOTEL**
3911 University Dr (35816)
Rates: N/A;
Tel: (205) 722-0880

**DAYS INN-
HUNTSVILLE AIRPORT**
102 Arlington Dr
(Madison 35758)
Rates: $40-$46;
Tel: (205) 772-9550

**EXECUTIVE LODGE
SUITE HOTEL**
1535 Sparkman Dr (35816)
Rates: $39-$150;
Tel: (205) 830-8600

**HAMPTON INN**
4815 University Dr (35816)
Rates: $45-$50;
Tel: (205) 830-9400

**HOLIDAY INN-
SPACE CENTER**
3810 University Dr (35816)
Raters: $53-$61;
Tel: (205) 837-7171

**HOWARD JOHNSON
PARK SQUARE INN**
8721 Hwy 20W
(Madison 35758)
Rates: $39-$75;
Tel: (205) 772-8855

**HUNTSVILLE MARRIOTT**
5 Tranquility Base (35805)
Rates: $99-$120;
Tel: (205) 830-2222

**LA QUINTA HUNTSVILLE
RESEARCH PARK**
4870 Univeristy Dr (35816)
Rates: $43-$56;
Tel: (205) 830-2070

**LA QUINTA MOTOR INN-
SPACE CENTER**
3141 University Dr (35816)
Rates: $43-$56;
Tel: (205) 533-0756

**RADISSON SUITE HOTEL**
6000 Memorial Pkwy S
(35802)
Rates. $59-$62;
Tel: (205) 882-9400

**RED CARPET INN**
2700 Memorial Pkwy SW
(35801)
Rates: $25-$36;
Tel: (205) 536-6661

**THE RESIDENCE INN
BY MARRIOTT**
4020 Independence Dr
(35816)
Rates: $80-$100;
Tel: (205) 837-8907

**SAVE INN**
3100 University Dr (35816)
Rates: $25-$33;
Tel: (205) 533-0610

**SUPER 8 MOTEL**
3803 University Dr (35816)
Rates: $28-$38;
Tel: (205) 539-8881

## JASPER

**TRAVEL-RITE INN**
200 Mallway Dr (35501)
Rates: $23-$30;
Tel: (205) 221-1161

## LAFAYETTE

**HILL-WARE-
DOWDELL MANSION**
203 2nd Ave Southwest
(36862)
Rates: N/A;
Tel: (205) 864-7861

## LEEDS

**DAYS INN**
1835 Ashville Rd (35094)
Rates: $40-$45,
Tel: (205) 699-9833

## MOBILE

**DAYS INN I-65 AIRPORT**
3650 Airport Blvd (36608)
Rates: $34-$60;
Tel: (205) 344-3410

**DAYS INN OF MOBILE**
5550 I 10 Service Rd (36619)
Rates: $39-$45;
Tel: (205) 661-8181

**DRURY INN**
824 S Beltline Hwy (36609)
Rates: $50-$56;
Tel: (205) 344-7700

**ECONO LODGE-NORTH**
1 S Beltline Hwy (36606)
Rates: $34-$38;
Tel: (205) 479-5333

**FAMILY INNS OF AMERICA**
900 S Beltline Hwy (36609)
Rates: $29-$34;
Tel: (205) 344-5500

**HAMPTON INN**
930 S Beltline Hwy (36609)
Rates: $39-$54;
Tel: (205) 344-4942

**HOLIDAY INN I-65**
P. O. Box 16646 (36616)
Rates: $56-$71;
Tel: (205) 342-3220

## HOWARD JOHNSON LODGE
3132 Government Blvd (36606)
Rates: $40-$55;
Tel: (205) 471-2402

## HOWARD JOHNSON MOTOR HOTEL
6527 Hwy 90 W (36619)
Rates: $49-$76;
Tel: (205) 666-5600

## KNIGHTS INN
70 Hwy 90 (Daphne 36526)
Rates: $33-$46;
Tel: (205) 626-3500

## LA QUINTA MOTOR INN
816 Beltline Hwy S (36609)
Rates: $45-$60;
Tel: (205) 343-4051

## MALAGA INN
359 Church St (36602)
Rates: $48-$65;
Tel: (205) 438-4701

## OAK TREE INN
255 Church St (36602)
Rates: N/A;
Tel: (205) 433-6923

## OLSSON'S MOTEL
4137 Government Blvd (36693)
Rates: N/A;
Tel: (205) 661-5331

## RAMADA HOTEL BAY RESORT
P. O. Box 1626 (36633)
Rates: $39-$51;
Tel: (205) 626-7200

## RED ROOF INN-NORTH
33 S Beltline Hwy (36606)
Rates: $37-$40;
Tel: (205) 476-2004

## RED ROOF INN-SOUTH
5450 Coca Cola Rd (36619)
Rates: $30-$41;
Tel: (205) 666-1044

## SHONEY'S INN OF MOBILE
6556 US 90 (36619)
Rates: $38-$55;
Tel: (205) 660-1520

## STOUFFER RIVERVIEW PLAZA HOTEL
64 Water St (36602)
Rates: $79-$155;
Tel: (205) 438-4000

# MONROEVILLE

## MONROE MOTOR COURT
Hwy 21, 1 Mi N US 84 (36461)
Rates: N/A;
Tel: (205) 575-3177

# MONTEVALLO

## RAMSAY CONFERENCE CENTER
Station 6280 Vine St (35115)
Rates: N/A;
Tel: (205) 665-6280

# MONTGOMERY

## BEST WESTERN MONTGOMERY LODGE
977 W South Blvd (36105)
Rates: $34-$42;
Tel: (205) 288-5740

## BEST WESTERN PEDDLER'S INN
4231 Mobile Hwy (36108)
Rates: $30-$40;
Tel: (205) 288-0610

## BUDGETEL
5225 Carmichael Rd (36106)
Rates: $35-$45;
Tel: (205) 277-6000

## COLISEUM INN
1550 Federal Dr (36107)
Rates: N/A;
Tel: (800) 876-6835

## COMFORT INN
5175 Carmichael Blvd (36106)
Rates: $39-$58;
Tel: (205) 277-1919

## DAYS INN
2625 Zelda Rd (36107)
Rates: $40-$45;
Tel: (205) 269-9611

## DAYS INN-SOUTH
1150 South Blvd (36105)
Rates: $30-$40;
Tel: (205) 281-8000

## HAMPTON INN
1401 Eastern Blvd (36117)
Rates: $41-$48;
Tel: (205) 277-2400

## HOLIDAY INN AIRPORT I-65
1100 W South Blvd (36105)
Rates: $46-$57;
Tel: (205) 281-1660

## HOLIDAY INN-EAST
1185 Eastern Blvd (36117)
Rates: $67-$77;
Tel: (205) 272-0370

## HOLIDAY INN-PRATTVILLE
P. O. Box A (Millbrook 36054)
Rates: $39-$55;
Tel: (205) 285-3420

## INN SOUTH
4243 Inn South Ave (36105)
Rates: $29-$37;
Tel: (205) 288-7999

## LA QUINTA MOTOR INN
1280 East Blvd (36117)
Rates: $41-$54;
Tel: (205) 271-1620

## RAMADA INN-EAST
1355 Eastern Bypass (36117)
Rates: $48-$57;
Tel: (205) 277-2200

## RAMADA INN PRATTVILLE
P. O. Box 388 (Prattville 36067)
Rates: $49-$55;
Tel: (205) 365-3311

## RESIDENCE INN BY MARRIOTT
1200 Hilmar Ct (36117)
Rates: $59-$84;
Tel: (205) 270-3300

## RIVERFRONT INN
200 Coosa St (36104)
Rates: N/A;
Tel: (205) 834-4300

## SCOTTISH INN
7237 Troy Hwy (36064)
Rates: N/A;
Tel: (205) 288-1501

**STATEHOUSE INN**
924 Madison Ave (36104)
Rates: $40-$52;
Tel: (205) 265-0741

**SUPER 8 MOTEL**
1288 W South Blvd (36108)
Rates: $32-$39;
Tel: (205) 284-1900

**VILLAGER INN**
2750 Chestnut St (36107)
Rates: $34-$40;
Tel: (205) 834-4055

## MUSCLE SHOALS

**DAYS INN**
2700 Woodward Ave (35651)
Rates: $35-$47;
Tel: (205) 383-3000

## OPELIKA

**BEST WESTERN
MARINER INN**
1002 Columbus Pkwy (36801)
Rates: $29-$46;
Tel: (205) 749-1461

## ORANGE BEACH

**DAYS INN**
P. O. Box 1003 (36561)
Rates: $32-$145;
Tel: (205) 981-9888

**ISLAND DUNES RESORT**
P. O. Box 9 (36561)
Rates: N/A;
Tel: (205) 981-4255

## OXFORD

**HAMPTON INN**
1600 AL 21 S (36203)
Rates: $36-$46;
Tel: (205) 835-1492

**MOTEL 6**
202 Grace St (36203)
Rates: $18-$24;
Tel: (205) 831-5463

## OZARK

**BEST WESTERN
OZARK INN**
P. O. Box 1396 (36361)
Rates: $29-$35;
Tel: (205) 774-5166

**HOLIDAY INN**
151 US 231N (36360)
Rates: $41-$48;
Tel: (205) 774-7300

## PELL CITY

**BEST WESTERN
RIVERSIDE INN**
Rt 1, Box 1310 (35125)
Rates: $29-$49;
Tel: (205) 338-3381

## PHENIX CITY

**BEST WESTERN
AMERICAN MOTOR LODGE**
1600 Hwy 280 Bypass
(36867)
Rates: $35-$42;
Tel: (205) 298-8000

## ROGERSVILLE

**SECOND CREEK COUNTRY**
Rt 4, Box 341-B (35652)
Rates: N/A;
Tel: (205) 247-1183

## SCOTTSBORO

**DAYS INN**
1106 John T Reid Pkwy
(35768)
Rates: $39-$46;
Tel: (205) 574-1212

## SELMA

**HOLIDAY INN**
1806 US 80W (36701)
Rates: $39-$56;
Tel: (205) 872-0461

## SHEFFIELD

**HOLIDAY INN
OF SHEFFIELD**
4900 Hatch Blvd (35660)
Rates: $65-$75;
Tel: (205) 381-4710

**RAMADA INN**
4205 Hatch Blvd (35660)
Rates: $53-$60;
Tel: (205) 381-3743

## SHORTER

**DAYS INN**
P. O. Box 327 (36075)
Rates: $32-$49;
Tel: (205) 727-6034

## TROY

**DAYS INN-TROY**
P. O. Box 761 (36081)
Rates: $25-$45;
Tel: (205) 566-1630

**ECONO LODGE**
P. O. Box 1086 (36081)
Rates: $32-$38;
Tel: (205) 566-4960

**HOLIDAY INN OF TROY**
P. O. Box 564 (36081)
Rates: $40-$50;
Tel: (205) 566-1150

**SCOTTISH INNS**
P. O. Box 486 (36081)
Rates: N/A;
Tel: (205) 566-4090

## TUSCALOOSA

**BEST WESTERN
CATALINA INN**
2015 Hwy 82W
(Northport 35476)
Rates: $33-$38;
Tel: (205) 339-5200

**BEST WESTERN
UNIVERSITY INN**
1780 McFarland Blvd N
(35406)
Rates: $35-$54;
Tel: (205) 759-2511

**LA QUINTA MOTOR INN**
4122 McFarland Blvd E
(35405)
Rates: $42-$57;
Tel: (205) 349-3270

**RAMADA INN**
631 Skyland Blvd E (35405)
Rates: $34-$72;
Tel: (205) 759-4431

**SHONEY'S INN
OF TUSCALOOSA**
3501 McFarland Blvd E
(35405)
Rates: $41-$46;
Tel: (205) 556-7950

**TUSCUMBIA**

**KEY WEST INN**
1800 US 72 (35674)
Rates: $41-$46;
Tel: (205) 383-0700

# ALASKA

## ANCHORAGE

**ALASKA BED & BREAKFAST**
P. O. Box 110706 (99511)
Rates: N/A;
Tel: (907) 345-0923

**ALASKAN FRONTIER
GARDENS B & B**
1011 E Tudor Rd #160
(99503)
Rates: $85-$150;
Tel: (907) 561-1514

**ANCHORAGE
EAGLE NEST HOTEL**
4110 Spenard Rd (99517)
Rates: $50-$80;
Tel: (800) 848-7852

**BEST WESTERN-
BARRATT INN**
4616 Spenard Rd (99517)
Rates: $65-$140;
Tel: (907) 243-3131

**BIG TIMBER MOTEL**
2037 E 5th Ave (99501)
Rates: N/A;
Tel: (907) 272-2541

**BLACK ANGUS INN**
1430 Gambell St (99501)
Rates: N/A;
Tel: (907) 272-7503

**CHELSEA INN**
3836 Spenard Rd (99517)
Rates: $40-$100;
Tel: (800) 934-9106

**COMFORT INN-
HERITAGE SUITES**
111 W Warehouse Ave
(99501)
Rates: $50-$175;
Tel: (907) 277-6887

**DAYS INN**
321 5th Ave E (99501)
Rates: $49-$105;
Tel: (907) 276-7226

**8TH AVENUE HOTEL**
P. O. Box 200089 (99520)
Rates: $79-$135;
Tel: (907) 274-6213

**MERRILL FIELD MOTEL**
420 Sitka St (99501)
Rates: $50-$85;
Tel: (907) 276-4547

**REGAL ALASKAN HOTEL**
4800 Spenard Rd (99517)
Rates: $135-$225;
Tel: (907) 243-2300

**SIXTH & B
BED & BREAKFAST**
145 W Sixth Ave (99501)
Rates: $33-$88;
Tel: (907) 279-5293

**SOURDOUGH
VISITORS LODGE**
P. O. Box 200089 (99520)
Rates: $69-$125;
Tel: (907) 279-4148

**SUPER 8 MOTEL-ANCHORAGE**
3501 Minnesota Dr (99503)
Rates: $64-$87;
Tel: (800) 800-8000

**VALARIAN VISIT
BED & BREAKFAST**
1536 Valarian St (99508)
Rates: $50-$75;
Tel: (907) 274-5760

## BIG LAKE

**BIG LAKE MOTEL**
P. O. Box 520728 (99652)
Rates: $65-$75;
Tel: (907) 892-7976

## CANTWELL

**REINDEER MOUNTAIN LODGE**
MP 210 Parks Hwy (99729)
Rates: N/A;
Tel: (907) 768-2420

## CIRCLE SPRINGS

**CIRCLE HOT SPRINGS RESORT**
P. O. Box 254 (99730)
Rates: N/A;
Tel: (907) 520-5113

## COOPER LANDING

**GWIN'S LODGE**
Mile 52 Sterling Hwy (99572)
Rates: N/A;
Tel: (907) 595-1266

## DELTA JUNCTION

**ALASKA 7 MOTEL**
3548 Richardson Hwy (99737)
Rates: N/A;
Tel: (907) 895-4848

**BLACK SPRUCE LODGE**
2740 Old Richardson Hwy
(99737)
Rates: N/A;
Tel: (907) 895-4668

**DELTA INTERNATIONAL
HOSTEL**
Main St. USA North (99737)
Rates: N/A;
Tel: (907) 895-5074

**SUMMIT LAKE LODGE**
Mile 195 Richardson (99737)
Rates: N/A;
Tel: (907) 822-3969

**DENALI NATIONAL PARK
AND PRESERVE
BACKWOODS LODGE**
P. O. Box 32 (Cantwell 99729)
Rates: $70-$95;
Tel: (907) 683-2567

**DENALI GRIZZLY BEAR
CABINS & CAMPGROUND**
P. O. Box 7 (99755)
Rates: $50-$102;
Tel: (907) 683-2696

**DENALI WEST LODGE**
P. O. Box 40
(Lake Minchumina 99757)
Rates: $300;
Tel: (907) 276-5833

**DOME HOME
BED & BREAKFAST**
P. O. Box 262 (Healy 99743)
Rates: $35-$90;
Tel: (907) 683-1239

**MCKINLEY/DENALI
PRIVATE CABINS**
P. O. Box 90 (99755)
Rates: $35-$110;
Tel: (907) 683-2733

**MT. MCKINLEY MOTOR LODGE**
P. O. Box 77 (99755)
Rates: $98;
Tel: (907) 683-1240

## EAGLE RIVER

**MOUNTAIN AIR
BED & BREAKFAST**
HC83, Box 1652 (99577)
Rates: $40-$60;
Tel: (907) 696-3116

## FAIRBANKS

**A PIONEER BED & BREAKFAST**
1119 Second Ave (99701)
Rates: $55-$85;
Tel: (907) 452-5393

**A TASTE OF ALASKA LODGE**
551 Eberhardt Rd (99712)
Rates: $50-$80;
Tel: (907) 488-7855

**ALASKA MOTEL**
1546 Cushman St (99701)
Rates: $45-$70;
Tel: (907) 456-6393

**CAPTAIN BARTLETT INN**
1411 Airport Way (99701)
Rates: $70-$125;
Tel: (907) 452-1888

**CHENA HOT SPRINGS RESORT**
P. O. Box 73440 (99707)
Rates: $50-$110;
Tel: (907) 452-7867

**CHENA RIVER
BED & BREAKFAST**
1001 Dolly Varden Ln (99709)
Rates: $75-$90;
Tel: (907) 479-2532

**CHOCOLATE RUSH
BED & BREAKFAST**
P.O. Box 72296 (99707)
Rates: $55-$65;
Tel: (907) 474-8633

**FOX CREEK BED & BREAKFAST**
2498 Elliott Hwy (99712)
Rates: $54-$70;
Tel: (907) 457-5494

**HILLSIDE BED & BREAKFAST**
310 Rambling Road (99712)
Rates: $35-$55;
Tel: (907) 457-2664

**NORTH WOODS LODGE**
P. O. Box 83615 (99708)
Rates: $32-$75;
Tel: (907) 479-5300

**OLD F. E. GOLD CAMP**
5550 Old Steese Hwy N
(99712)
Rates: N/A;
Tel: (907) 389-2414

**REGENCY FAIRBANKS HOTEL**
95 Tenth Ave (99701)
Rates: N/A;
Tel: (907) 452-3200

**SOURDOUGH
BED & BREAKFAST**
P. O. Box 82730 (99708)
Rates: $55-$90;
Tel: (907) 479-6684

**SUCH A DEAL
BED & BREAKFAST**
P. O.Box 82527 (99708)
Rates: $45-$65;
Tel: (907) 474-8159

**SUPER 8 MOTEL-FAIRBANKS**
1909 Airport Rd (99701)
Rates: $62+;
Tel: (800) 800-8000

**TAMARAC INN MOTEL**
252 Minnie St (99701)
Rates: $54-$62;
Tel: (907) 456-6406

## GAKONA

**GAKONA JUNCTION VILLAGE**
P. O. Box 222 (99586)
Rates: $55-$98;
Tel: (800) 962-1933

## GLENNALLEN

**THE NEW CARIBOU HOTEL**
P. O. Box 329 (99588)
Rates: $69-$109;
Tel: (907) 822-3302

**GUSTAVUS (GLACIER BAY)
A PUFFIN'S BED & B & B**
Box 3 (1/4 Mile Logging Rd)
(99826)
Rates: N/A;
Tel: (907) 697-2260

**TRI BED & BREAKFAST**
P. O. Box 214 (99826)
Rates: $65;
Tel: (907) 697-2425

## HAINES

**CAPTAIN'S CHOICE MOTEL**
P. O. Box 392 (99827)
Rates: $75-$95;
Tel: (907) 766-3111

**EAGLE'S NEST MOTEL**
P. O. Box 250 (99827)
Rates: $54-$80;
Tel: (907) 766-2891

**FORT SEWARD LODGE
RESTAURANT & SALOON**
P. O. Box 307 (99827)
Rates: $40-$55;
Tel: (907) 766-2009

**FORT WM. H. SEWARD
BED & BREAKFAST**
P. O. Box 5 (99827)
Rates: $58-$125;
Tel: (907) 766-2856

**MOUNTAIN VIEW MOTEL**
P. O. Box 62 (99827)
Rates: $50-$69;
Tel: (907) 766-2900

**THUNDERBIRD MOTEL**
242 Dalton St (99827)
Rates: $58-$68;
Tel: (800) 327-2556

## HATCHER PASS

**HATCHER PASS LODGE**
P.O. Box 763 (99645)
Rates: $58-$85;
Tel: (907) 745-5897

## HOMER

**BEST WESTERN
BIDARKA INN**
575 Sterling Hwy (99603)
Rates: $78-$108;
Tel: (907) 235-8148

**DRIFTWOOD INN**
135 W Bunnell Ave (99603)
Rates: N/A;
Tel: (907) 235-8019

**HERITAGE HOTEL/LODGE**
147 E. Pioneer Ave (99603)
Rates: $50-$80;
Tel: (907) 235-7787

**HOME BED & BREAKFAST/
SEEKINS**
P. O. Box 1264 (99603)
Rates: $50-$80;
Tel: (907) 235-8996

**LAKEWOOD INN**
984 Ocean Dr #1 (99603)
Rates: N/A;
Tel: (907) 235-6144

**LAND'S END
HOTEL & RV PARK**
4786 Homer Spit Rd (99603)
Rates: $46-$140;
Tel: (907) 235-2500

**OCEAN SHORES MOTEL**
3500 Crittenden Dr (99603)
Rates: $45-$95;
Tel: (800) 770-7775

## JUNEAU

**BEST WESTERN
COUNTRY LANE INN**
9300 Glacier Hwy (99801)
Rates: $74-$120;
Tel: (907) 789-5005

**BLUEBERRY LODGE
BED & BREAKFAST**
9436 N Douglas Hwy (99801)
Rates: $65-$75;
Tel: (907) 463-5886

**THE DRIFTWOOD LODGE**
435 Willoughby Ave (99801)
Rates: $62-$78;
Tel: (800) 544-2239

**JAN'S VIEW
BED & BREAKFAST**
P. O. Box 32245 (99803)
Rates: $40-$65;
Tel: (907) 463-5897

**PROSPECTOR HOTEL**
375 Whittier St (99801)
Rates: $60-$120;
Tel: (800) 331-2711

**SUPER 8 MOTEL-JUNEAU**
2295 Trout St (99801)
Rates: $66-$82;
Tel: (800) 800-8000

## KENAI

**KENAI KINGS INN**
P. O. Box 1080 (99611)
Rates: $74-$104;
Tel: (907) 283-6060

**KENAI PENINSULA ANGLERS
LODGE & FISH CAMP**
P. O. Box 508 (Sterling 99672)
Rates: $50-$120;
Tel: (907) 262-1747

**KENAI WILDERNESS
LODGE**
3117 Commercial Dr
(Anchorage 99501)
Rates: $70;
Tel: (907) 262-4390

## KETCHIKAN

**BEST WESTERN-
THE LANDING**
3434 Tongass Ave (99901)
Rates: $75-$98;
Tel: (907) 225-5166

**INGERSOLL HOTEL**
303 Mission St (99901)
Rates: $59-$89;
Tel: (907) 225-2124

**SUPER 8 MOTEL-KETCHIKAN**
2151 Sea Level Dr (99901)
Rates: $66-$81;
Tel: (800) 800-8000

## KODIAK

**BUSKIN RIVER INN**
1395 Airport Way (99615)
Rates: N/A;
Tel: (800) 544-2202

**KALSIN BAY INN**
P. O. Box 1696 (99615)
Rates: N/A;
Tel: (907) 486-2659

**KODIAK
BED & BREAKFAST**
308 Cope St (99615)
Rates: $60-$72;
Tel: (907) 486-5367

## PALMER

**HATCHER PASS
BED & BREAKFAST**
HC01, Box 6797-D (99645)
Rates: $55;
Tel: (907) 745-4210

**MAT-SU BED & BREAKFAST
ASSOCIATION**
HC01, Box 6229-R (99645)
Rates: N/A;
Tel: (907) 376-7662

## PETERSBURG

**NARROWS INN**
P. O. Box 1048 (99833)
Rates: $70;
Tel: (907) 772-4284

**SCANDIA HOUSE**
110 Nordic Dr (99833)
Rates: N/A;
Tel: (907) 772-4281

**TIDES INN**
P. O. Box 1048 (99833)
Rates: $65-$75;
Tel: (907) 772-4288

## SALCHA

**SALCHA RIVER LODGE**
P. O. Box 111 (99714)
Rates: N/A;
Tel: (907) 488-2233

## SEWARD

**MURPHY'S MOTEL**
911 4th Ave (99664)
Rates: N/A;
Tel: (907) 224-8090

**"THE FARM"
BED & BREAKFAST**
P. O. Box 305 (99664)
Rates: $35-$100;
Tel: (907) 224-2300

## SKAGWAY

**GOLDEN NORTH HOTEL**
P. O. Box 431 (99840)
Rates: N/A;
Tel: (907) 983-2294

**WIND VALLEY LODGE**
P. O. Box 354 (99840)
Rates: N/A;
Tel: (907) 983-2236

## SOLDOTNA

**DENISE LAKE LODGE
BED & BREAKFAST**
P.O. Box 1050 (99669)
Rates: N/A;
Tel: (907) 262-1789

**KENAI PENINSULA APTS
& SUMMER RENTALS**
P.O. Box 3416 (99669)
Rates: $85-$115;
Tel: (907) 262-1383

**KENAI RIVER LODGE**
393 Riverside Dr (99669)
Rates: $50-$100;
Tel: (907) 262-4292

**RAVEN MT. FARM
BED & BREAKFAST**
P. O. Box 344 (Kasilof 99610)
Rates: $45-$76;
Tel: (907) 262-9186

**SOARING EAGLE LODGE**
HC01, Box 1203 (99669)
Rates: $50-$100;
Tel: (907) 337-1223

## TALKEETNA

**ALASKA LOG CABIN
BED & BREAKFAST**
#1A Beaver Rd (99676)
Rates: N/A;
Tel: (907) 733-2668

**LATITUDE 62 LODGE**
P. O. Box 478 (99676)
Rates: N/A;
Tel: (907) 733-2262

## TOK

**CLEFT OF THE ROCK
BED & BREAKFAST**
Sundog Trail Box 122 (99780)
Rates: $50-$110;
Tel: (907) 883-4219

**THE STAGE STOP
BED & BREAKFAST**
P. O. Box 69 (99780)
Rates: $40-$85;
Tel: (907) 883-5338

**TOK LODGE & TOK
LIQUOR MINI MART**
P. O. Box 135 (99780)
Rates: $55-$75;
Tel: (907) 883-2851

**YOUNG'S MOTEL**
Mile 1313 Alaska Hwy
(99780)
Rates: $50-$70;
Tel: (907) 883-4411

## TRAPPER CREEK

**MCKINLEY FOOTHILLS
BED & BREAKFAST**
P. O. Box 13089 (99683)
Rates: $80+;
Tel: (907) 773-1454

## WASILLA

**COUNTRY LAKES
FLYING SERVICE/B & B**
2651 E Palmer Wasilla Hwy
(99654)
Rates: $45-$65;
Tel: (907) 376-5868

# ARIZONA

## ASH FORK

**STAGECOACH MOTEL**
823 Park Ave (86320)
Rates: N/A;
Tel: (602) 637-2278

## BENSON

**BEST WESTERN
QUAIL HOLLOW INN**
P. O. Box 2107 (85602)
Rates: $38-$44;
Tel: (602) 586-3646

## BISBEE

**THE BISBEE INN
BED & BREAKFAST**
45 OK St (85603)
Rates: N/A;
Tel: (602) 432-5131

**THE GREENWAY HOUSE**
401 Cole Ave (85603)
Rates: N/A;
Tel: (602) 432-7170

## BULLHEAD CITY

**DESERT RANCHO MOTEL**
1041 Hwy 95 (86430)
Rates: N/A;
Tel: (602) 754-2578

**ECONO LODGE**
1717 Hwy 95 (86442)
Rates: $32-$58;
Tel: (602) 758-8080

**FIRST CHOICE INN**
2200 Karis Dr (86442)
Rates: $45-$55;
Tel: (602) 758-1711

**HOLIDAY INN
BULLHEAD CITY/LAUGHLIN**
839 Landon Dr (86430)
Rates: $35-$45;
Tel: (602) 754-4700

**LAKE MOHAVE RESORT**
At Katherine Landing (86430)
Rates: $60-$83;
Tel: (602) 754-3245

**SILVER CREEK INN**
1670 Hwy 95 (86442)
Rates: $44-$54;
Tel: (602) 763-8400

**TRAVELODGE**
2360 4th St (86430)
Rates: $35-$65;
Tel: (602) 754-3000

## CAREFREE

**THE BOULDERS**
34631 N Tom Darlington Rd (85377)
Rates: $240-$525;
Tel: (602) 488-9009

## CASA GRANDE

**BEST WESTERN
CASA GRANDE SUITES**
665 Via Del Cielo (85222)
Rates: $45-$66;
Tel: (602) 836-1600

**HOLIDAY INN**
777 N Pinal Ave (85222)
Rates: $58-$72;
Tel: (602) 426-3500

**FRANCISCO GRANDE
RESORT & GOLF CLUB**
26000 Gila Bend Hwy (85222)
Rates: $56-$196;
Tel: (602) 836-6444

**SE-TAY MOTEL**
901 North Pinal Ave (85222)
Rates: N/A;
Tel: (602) 836-7489

**SUNLAND INN**
7190 South Sunland Gin Rd (85222)
Rates: N/A;
Tel: (602) 836-5000

## CHAMBERS

**BEST WESTERN
CHIEFTAIN MOTEL**
P. O. Box 39 (86502)
Rates: $46-$61;
Tel: (602) 688-2754

## CHANDLER

**ALOHA MOTEL**
445 North Arizona Ave (85224)
Rates: N/A;
Tel: (602) 963-3403

**WYNDHAM GARDEN HOTEL**
7475 W Chandler Blvd (85226)
Rates: $73-$115;
Tel: (602) 961-4444

## COTTONWOOD

**BEST WESTERN
COTTONWOOD INN**
993 S Main (86326)
Rates: $47-$67;
Tel: (602) 634-5575

**THE VIEW MOTEL**
818 S Main (86326)
Rates: $30-$42;
Tel: (602) 634-7581

## EHRENBERG

**BEST WESTERN FLYING J MOTEL**
P. O. Box 778 (85334)
Rates: $39-$44;
Tel: (602) 923-9711

## ELOY

**SUPER 8 MOTEL**
3945 W Houser Rd (85231)
Rates: $34-$47;
Tel: (602) 466-7804

## FLAGSTAFF

**ARIZONA MOUNTAIN INN**
685 Lake Mary Rd (86001)
Rates: $60-$100;
Tel: (602) 774-8959

**BEST WESTERN
KINGS HOUSE MOTEL**
1560 E Route 66 (86001)
Rates: $30-$80;
Tel: (602) 774-7186

**COMFORT INN**
914 S Milton Rd (86001)
Rates: $46-$66;
Tel: (602) 774-7326

**DAYS INN**
2735 S Woodlands Village
Blvd (86001)
Rates: $36-$72;
Tel: (602) 779-1575

**DAYS INN**
1000 W Route 66 (86001)
Rates: $38-$79;
Tel: (602) 774-5221

**HOLIDAY INN FLAGSTAFF/
GRAND CANYON**
2320 E Lucky Ln (86004)
Rates: $49-$89;
Tel: (602) 526-1150

**MOTEL IN THE PINES**
P. O. Box 171, Munds Park
(86017)
Rates: $35-$65;
Tel: (602) 286-9699

**MOTEL 6**
2440 E Lucky Ln (86001)
Rates: $31-$37;
Tel: (602) 774-8756

**QUALITY INN**
2000 S Milton Rd (86001)
Rates: $59-$95;
Tel: (602) 774-8771

**RESIDENCE INN
BY MARRIOTT**
3440 N Country Club Dr
(86004)
Rates: $89-$135;
Tel: (602) 526-5555

**RODEWAY INN EAST**
2350 East Lucky Lane (86004)
Rates: N/A;
Tel: (602) 779-3614

**TRAVELODGE SUITES**
2755 Woodlands Village Rd
(86002)
Rates: $54-$79;
Tel: (602) 773-1111

## GILA BEND

**BEST WESTERN
SPACE AGE LODGE**
401 E Pima (85337)
Rates: $44-$65;
Tel: (602) 683-2273

**YUCCA MOTEL**
836 E Pima (85337)
Rates: N/A;
Tel: (602) 683-2211

## GLENDALE

**BEST WESTERN SAGE INN**
5940 NW Grand Ave (85301)
Rates: $55-$66;
Tel: (602) 939-9431

## GLOBE

**CLOUD NINE MOTEL**
1649 E Ash St (85502)
Rates: $44-$55;
Tel: (602) 425-5741

**COPPER MANOR MOTEL**
637 E Ash St (85501)
Rates: $36-$52;
Tel: (602) 425-7124

**EL REY MOTEL**
1201 East Ash St (85501)
Rates: N/A;
Tel: (602) 425-4427

## GOODYEAR

**BEST WESTERN PHOENIX
GOODYEAR INN**
1100 N Litchfield Rd (85338)
Rates: $39-$69;
Tel: (602) 932-3210

**SUPER 8 MOTEL**
1710 N Dysart Rd (85338)
Rates: $43-$48;
Tel: (602) 932-9622

## GRAND CANYON
## NATIONAL PARK

**BRIGHT ANGEL LODGE
& CABINS**
P. O. Box 699 (86023)
Rates: $47-$105;
Tel: (602) 638-2631

**EL TOVAR HOTEL**
P. O. Box 699 (86023)
Rates: $105-$160;
Tel: (602) 638-2631

**KACHINA LODGE**
P. O. Box 699 (86023)
Rates: $86-$97;
Tel: (602) 638-2631

**MASWIK LODGE**
P. O. Box 699 (86023)
Rates: $46-$95;
Tel: (602) 638-2631

**THUNDERBIRD LODGE**
P. O. Box 699 (86023)
Rates: $86-$97;
Tel: (602) 638-2631

**YAVAPAI LODGE**
P. O. Box 699 (86023)
Rates: $68-$78;
Tel: (602) 638-2631

# GREEN VALLEY

**QUALITY INN**
111 S La Canada Dr (85614)
Rates: $55-$93;
Tel: (602) 625-2250

# HOLBROOK

**BEST WESTERN
ADOBE INN**
615 W Hopi Dr (86025)
Rates: $36-$58;
Tel: (602) 524-3948

**BEST WESTERN
ARIZONIAN INN**
2508 E Navajo Blvd (86025)
Rates: $40-$68;
Tel: (602) 524-2611

**COMFORT INN**
2602 E Navajo Blvd (86025)
Rates: $44-$66;
Tel: (602) 524-6131

**RAINBOW INN**
2211 E Navajo Blvd (86025)
Rates: $30-$47;
Tel: (602) 524-2654

# KAYENTA

**GOULDING'S MONUMENT
VALLEY LODGE**
Box 1 (Monument Valley, UT
84536)
Rates: $52-$100;
Tel: (801) 727-3231

# KEARNY

**GENERAL KEARNY INN**
P. O. Box 188 (85237)
Rates: N/A;
Tel: (602) 363-5505

# KINGMAN

**BEST WESTERN
A WAYFARER'S INN**
2815 E Andy Devine (86401)
Rates: $36-$57;
Tel: (602) 753-6271

**BEST WESTERN KING'S INN**
2930 E Andy Devine (86401)
Rates: $33-$52;
Tel: (602) 753-6101

**DAYS INN EAST**
3381 E Andy Devine (86401)
Rates: $29-$50;
Tel: (602) 757-7337

**DAYS INN WEST**
3023 E Andy Devine (86401)
Rates: $29-$45;
Tel: (602) 753-7500

**HIGH DESERT INN**
2803 E Andy Devine (86401)
Rates: $19-$29;
Tel: (602) 753-2935

**HOLIDAY INN**
3100 E Andy Devine (86401)
Rates: $34-$49;
Tel: (602) 753-6262

**QUALITY INN**
1400 E Andy Devine (86401)
Rates: $36-$53;
Tel: (602) 753-4747

**RODEWAY INN**
411 W Beale St (86401)
Rates: $26-$45;
Tel: (602) 753-5521

**SILVER QUEEN MOTEL**
3285 E Andy Devine Ave
(86401)
Rates: $24-$34;
Tel: (602) 757-4315

# LAKE HAVASU CITY

**BEST WESTERN LAKE
PLACE INN**
31 Wing's Loop (86403)
Rates: $39-$79;
Tel: (602) 855-2146

**HOLIDAY INN**
245 London Bridge Rd (86403)
Rates: $45-$65;
Tel: (602) 855-4071

**ISLAND INN HOTEL**
1300 W McCulloch Blvd
(86403)
Rates: $65-$85;
Tel: (602) 680-0606

**RAMADA
LONDON BRIDGE RESORT**
1477 Queens Bay Rd (86403)
Rates: $75-$264;
Tel: (602) 855-0888

**SUPER 8 MOTEL**
305 London Bridge Rd (86403)
Rates: N/A;
Tel: (602) 855-8844

# LAKE MONTEZUMA

**BEAVER CREEK INN**
462 S Montezuma Ave
(86342)
Rates: $39-$48;
Tel: (602) 567-4475

# LAKESIDE

**LAKE OF THE WOODS**
2244 West White Mtn Blvd
(85929)
Rates: N/A;
Tel: (602) 368-5353

# LITCHFIELD PARK

**THE WIGWAM RESORT**
Indian School & N Litchfield Rds
(85340)
Rates: $80-$400;
Tel: (602) 935-3811

# MARBLE CANYON

**MARBLE CANYON LODGE**
Box 1 (86036)
Rates: $40-$90;
Tel: (800) 726-1789

# MESA

**ARIZONA GOLF RESORT
& CONFERENCE CENTER**
424 S Power Rd (85206)
Rates: $65-$155;
Tel: (602) 832-3202

**BEST WESTERN MESA INN**
1625 E Main St (85203)
Rates: $34-$65;
Tel: (602) 964-8000

**DAYS INN**
333 W Juanita (85210)
Rates: $54-$84;
Tel: (602) 844-8900

**HAMPTON INN**
1563 S Gilbert Rd (85204)
Rates: $55-$70;
Tel: (602) 926-3600

**HOLIDAY INN**
1600 S Country Club Dr
(85210)
Rates: $39-$99·
Tel: (602) 964-7000

**MARICOPA INN
MOTOR HOTEL**
3 E Main St (85201)
Rates: $28-$49;
Tel: (602) 834 6060

**QUALITY INN ROYAL MESA**
951 W Main St (85201)
Rates: $39 $109;
Tel: (602) 833-1231

## MIAMI

**BEST WESTERN
COPPER HILLS INN**
Rt 1, Box 506 (85539)
Rates: $47-$85;
Tel: (602) 425-7151

## NOGALES

**AMERICANA
MOTOR HOTEL**
639 N Grand Ave (85621)
Rates: $40-$65;
Tel: (602) 287-7211

**BEST WESTERN
SIESTA MOTEL**
673 N Grand Ave (85621)
Rates: $32-$48;
Tel: (602) 287-4627

**RIO RICO RESORT
& COUNTRY CLUB**
1069 Camino Caralampi
(Rio Rico 85648)
Rates: $50-$80;
Tel: (602) 281-1901

## PAGE

**EMPIRE HOUSE MOTEL**
Box 1747 (86040)
Rates: $46-$58;
Tel: (602) 645-2406

**HOLIDAY INN-PAGE**
287 N Lake Powell Blvd
(86040)
Rates: $52-$96;
Tel: (602) 645-8851

**INN AT LAKE POWELL**
716 Rim View Dr (86040)
Rates: $39-$92,
Tel: (602) 645-2466

**LAKE POWELL MOTEL**
P. O. Box 1597 (86040)
Rates: $40-$67;
Tel: (602) 645-2477

**WAHWEAP LODGE
& MARINA**
P. O. Box 1597 (86040)
Rates: $57-$106;
Tel: (602) 645-2433

## PARKER

**HOLIDAY KASBAH**
604 California Ave (85344)
Rates: $39-$63;
Tel: (602) 669-2133

**STARDUST MOTEL**
700 California Ave (85344)
Rates: N/A;
Tel: (602) 669-2278

## PATAGONIA

**STAGE STOP INN**
Box 777 (85624)
Rates: $49-$95;
Tel: (602) 394-2211

## PAYSON

**CHRISTOPHER CREEK
LODGE/MOTEL**
Star Rt Box 119 (85541)
Rates: N/A;
Tel: (602) 478-4300

**GREY HACKLE LODGE**
Star Route Box 145 (85541)
Rates: $40-$95;
Tel: (602) 478-4392

**KOHL'S RANCH RESORT**
East Hwy 260 (85541)
Rates: N/A;
Tel: (602) 478-4211

## PHOENIX

**BEST WESTERN
BELL MOTEL**
17211 N Black Canyon Hwy
(85023)
Rates: $30-$65;
Tel: (602) 993-8300

**BEST WESTERN INN SUITES
AT SQUAW PEAK**
1615 East Northern (85020)
Rates: N/A;
Tel: (602) 997-6285

**COACHMAN INN**
1520 N 84th Dr
(Tolleson, 85353)
Rates: $39-$59;
Tel: (602) 936-4667

**DAYS INN CAMELBACK**
502 W Camelback Rd (85013)
Rates: $56-$160;
Tel: (602) 264-9290

**DOUBLETREE SUITES/
PHOENIX GATEWAY CENTER**
320 N 44th St at Van Buren
(85008)
Rates: $48-$129;
Tel: (602) 225-0500

**EMBASSY SUITES HOTEL-
THOMAS RD/AIRPORT**
2333 E Thomas Rd (85016)
Rates: $59-$109;
Tel: (602) 957-1910

**EMBASSY SUITES-
WESTSIDE**
3210 NW Grand Ave (85017)
Rates: $59-$99;
Tel: (602) 279-3211

**E-Z 8 MOTEL**
1820 South 7th St (85034)
Rates: N/A;
Tel: (602) 254-9787

**FOUNTAINS SUITE HOTEL**
2577 W Greenway Rd
(85023)
Rates: $69-$129;
Tel: (602) 375-1777

**HAMPTON INN**
1563 South Gilbert Rd
(85204)
Rates: N/A;
Tel: (602) 926-3600

**HAMPTON INN I-17**
8101 Black Canyon Hwy
(85021)
Rates: $39-$68;
Tel: (602) 864-6233

**HOLIDAY INN**
1500 N 51st Ave (85043)
Rates: $56-$86;
Tel: (602) 484-9009

**HOLIDAY INN & HOLIDOME-
PHOENIX CORP CENTER**
2532 W Peoria Ave (85029)
Rates: $46-$110;
Tel: (602) 943-2341

**HOLIDAY INN
NORTH CENTRAL**
4321 N Central Ave (85012)
Rates: $50-$89;
Tel: (602) 277-6671

**HOTEL WESTCOURT**
10220 N Metro Pkwy East
(85051)
Rates: $59-$95;
Tel: (602) 997-5900

**LA QUINTA
MOTOR INN-COLISEUM**
2725 N Black Canyon Hwy
(85009)
Rates: $45-$72;
Tel: (602) 258-6271

**LOS OLIVOS
EXECUTIVE HOTEL**
202 E McDowell Rd (85004)
Rates: $59-$99;
Tel: (602) 258-6911

**OMNI ADAMS HOTEL**
P. O. Box 1000 (85001-1000)
Rates: $59-$164;
Tel: (602) 257-1525

**PREMIER INN**
10402 N Black Canyon Hwy
(85051)
Rates: $33-$89;
Tel: (602) 943-2371

**QUALITY INN-AIRPORT**
3541 E Van Buren St (85008)
Rates: $37-$64;
Tel: (602) 273-7121

**QUALITY HOTEL
CENTRAL PHOENIX**
3600 N 2nd Ave (85013)
Rates: $49-$84;
Tel: (602) 248-0222

**QUALITY INN-
SOUTH MOUNTAIN**
5121 E La Puente Ave (85044)
Rates: $39-$79;
Tel: (602) 893-3900

**PHOENIX SUNRISE MOTEL**
3644 East Van Buren (85008)
Rates: N/A;
Tel: (602) 275-7661

**RAMADA INN-
METRO CENTER**
12027 N 28th Dr (85029)
Rates: $40-$108;
Tel: (602) 866-7000

**RESIDENCE INN
BY MARRIOTT**
8242 N Black Canyon Hwy
(85051)
Rates: $99-$169;
Tel: (602) 864-1900

**RODEWAY INN-AIRPORT**
1202 S 24th St at Buckeye Rd
(85034)
Rates: $43-$62;
Tel: (602) 273-1211

**RODEWAY INN-
GRAND AVENUE**
3400 Grand Ave (85017)
Rates: $39-$49;
Tel: (602) 264-9164

**ROYAL PALMS INN**
5200 E Camelback Rd
(85018)
Rates: $40-$160;
Tel: (602) 840-3610

**SHERATON
GREENWAY INN**
2510 W Greenway Rd
(85023)
Rates: $42-$109;
Tel: (602) 993-0800

**SUPER 8 MOTEL
PHOENIX CENTRAL**
4021 N 27th Ave (85017)
Rates: $32-$54;
Tel: (602) 248-8880

**TRAVELODGE
METROCENTER**
8617 N Black Canyon Hwy
(85021)
Rates: $36-$61;
Tel: (602) 995-9500

**WYNDHAM
GARDEN HOTEL**
2641 W Union Hills Dr (85027)
Rates: $65-$105;
Tel: (602) 978-2222

# PINETOP

**BEST WESTERN INN
OF PINETOP**
P. O. Box 1005 (85935)
Rates: $59-$69;
Tel: (602) 367-6667

**ECONO LODGE**
P. O. Box 1226 (85935)
Rates: $46-$69;
Tel: (602) 367-3636

**MEADOW VIEW LODGE**
P. O. Box 325 (85935)
Rates: N/A;
Tel: (602) 367-4642

**MOUNTAIN
HACIENDA LODGE**
P. O. Box 713 (85935)
Rates: $31-$47;
Tel: (602) 367-4146

**NORTHWOODS RESORT**
P. O. Box 397A (85935)
Rates: $44-$97;
Tel: (602) 367-2966

# PRESCOTT

**BEST WESTERN
PRESCOTTONIAN MOTEL**
1317 E Gurley St (86301)
Rates: $44-$100;
Tel: (602) 445-3096

**COLONY INN
OF PRESCOTT**
1225 E Gurley St (86301)
Rates: $34-$75;
Tel: (602) 445-7057

**SHERATON PRESCOTT
RESORT & CONF CTR**
1500 Hwy 69 (86301)
Rates: $85-$120;
Tel: (602) 776-1666

# PRESCOTT VALLEY

**PRESCOTT VALLEY MOTEL**
8350 East Hwy 69 (86314)
Rates: N/A;
Tel: (602) 772-9412

# SAFFORD

**BEST WESTERN DESERT
INN OF SAFFORD**
1391 Thatcher Blvd (85546)
Rates: $50-$65;
Tel: (602) 428-0521

# SCOTTSDALE

**ADOBE
APARTMENT HOTEL**
3635 North 68th (85251)
Rates: N/A;
Tel: (602) 945-3544

**DAYS INN-SCOTTSDALE
FASHION SQ RESORT**
4710 N Scottsdale Rd (85251)
Rates. $66-$109;
Tel: (602) 947-5411

**HOLIDAY INN**
5101 N Scottsdale Rd (85250)
Rates: $50-$118;
Tel: (602) 945-4392

**HOLIDAY INN HOTEL
& CONF CTR/
SCOTTSDALE MALL**
7353 E Indian School Rd
(85251)
Rates: $53-$130;
Tel: (602) 994-9203

**MARRIOTT'S
CAMELBACK INN**
5402 E Lincoln Dr (85253)
Rates: $100-$290;
Tel: (602) 948-1700

**MARRIOTT'S MOUNTAIN
SHADOWS RESORT**
5641 E Lincoln Dr (85253)
Rates: $199-$310;
Tel: (602) 948-7111

**MARRIOTT
SUITES SCOTTSDALE**
7325 E 3rd Ave (85251)
Rates: $65-$145;
Tel: (602) 945-1550

**RAMADA HOTEL
VALLEY HO**
6850 Main St (85251)
Rates: $55-$137;
Tel: (602) 945-6321

**RED LION'S LA POSADA
RESORT HOTEL & INN**
4949 E Lincoln Dr (85253)
Rates: $85-$210;
Tel: (602) 952-0420

**RESIDENCE INN
BY MARRIOTT**
6040 N Scottsdale Rd (85253)
Rates: $129-$210;
Tel: (602) 948-8666

**SCOTTSDALE
EMBASSY SUITES**
5001 North Scottsdale Rd
(85250)
Rates: N/A;
Tel: (800) 528-1456

**SCOTTSDALE INN AT
EL DORADO PARK**
7707 E McDowell Rd (85257)
Rates: $39-$72;
Tel: (602) 941-1202

**SHANGRILA RESORT**
6237 North 59th Place
(85253)
Rates: N/A;
Tel: (602) 948-5930

**STOUFFER COTTON-
WOODS RESORT**
6160 N Scottsdale Rd (85253)
Rates: $89-$265;
Tel: (602) 991-1414

# SEDONA

**MATTERHORN
MOTOR LODGE**
230 Apple Ave (86336)
Rates: $44-$74;
Tel: (602) 282-7176

**QUALITY INN-KING'S
RANSOM MOTOR HOTEL**
P. O. Box 180 (86336)
Rates: $61-$119;
Tel: (602) 282-7151

**SKY RANCH LODGE**
P. O. Box 2579 (86336)
Rates: $45-$90;
Tel: (602) 282-6400

# SHOW LOW

**K C MOTEL**
60 W Deuce of Clubs (85901)
Rates: $34-$45;
Tel: (602) 537-4433

**KIVA MOTEL**
261 E Deuce of Clubs (85901)
Rates: $29-$42;
Tel: (602) 537-4542

# SIERRA VISTA

**RAMADA INN**
2047 S Hwy 92 (85635)
Rates: $58-$74;
Tel: (602) 459-5900

**SIERRA SUITES**
391 E Fry Blvd (85635)
Rates: $44-$76;
Tel: (602) 459-4221

**SUPER 8 MOTEL**
100 FAB Ave (85635)
Rates: N/A;
Tel: (602) 459-5380

**THUNDER MOUNTAIN INN**
1631 S Hwy 92 (85635)
Rates: $44;
Tel: (800) 222-5811

## SPRINGERVILLE

**REED'S MOTOR LODGE**
514 East Main Hwy 60
(85938)
Rates: N/A;
Tel: (602) 333-4323

## SUN CITY

**BEST WESTERN INN
OF SUN CITY**
11201 Grand Ave (85373)
Rates: $34-$62;
Tel: (602) 933-8211

**WINDMILL INN
AT SUN CITY WEST**
12454 W Bell Rd, Surprise
(85374)
Rates: $55-$88;
Tel: (602) 247-2333

## TAYLOR

**WHITING MOTOR INN**
825 North Highway 77
(85939)
Rates: N/A;
Tel: (602) 536-2600

## TEMPE

**THE BUTTES**
2000 Westcourt Way (85282)
Rates: $74-$205;
Tel: (602) 225-9000

**COMFORT INN**
5300 S Priest Dr (85283)
Rates: $35-$69;
Tel: (602) 820-7500

**FIESTA INN**
2100 S Priest Dr at Broadway
(85282)
Rates: $69-$115;
Tel: (602) 967-1441

**HOLIDAY INN**
915 E Apache Blvd (85281)
Rates: $56-$87;
Tel: (602) 968-3451

**HOWARD JOHNSON
HOTEL**
225 E Apache Blvd (85281)
Rates: $34-$81;
Tel: (602) 967-9431

**INNSUITES TEMPE/
PHOENIX AIRPORT**
1651 W Baseline Rd (85283)
Rates: $44-$92;
Tel: (602) 897-7900

**LA QUINTA MOTOR INN**
911 S 48th St (85281)
Rates: $47-$71;
Tel: (602) 967-4465

**QUALITY INN & SUITES**
1635 N Scottsdale Rd (85281)
Rates: $55-$105;
Tel: (602) 947-3711

**TEMPE/UNIVERSITY
TRAVELODGE**
1005 E Apache Blvd (85281)
Rates: $30-$48;
Tel: (602) 968-7871

**THE VAGABOND INN**
1221 E Apache Blvd (85281)
Rates: $36-$65;
Tel: (602) 968-7793

## TOMBSTONE

**LOOKOUT LODGE**
Hwy 80 (85638)
Rates: N/A;
Tel: (602) 457-2211

## TUBAC

**TUBAC GOLF RESORT**
P. O. Box 1297 (85646)
Rates: $79-$132;
Tel: (602) 398-2211

## TUCSON

**BEST WESTERN
EXECUTIVE INN**
333 W Drachman (85705)
Rates: $42-$150;
Tel: (602) 791-7551

**BEST WESTERN
GHOST RANCH LODGE**
801 W Miracle Mile (85705)
Rates: $31-$89;
Tel: (602) 791-7565

**BEST WESTERN
INNSUITES-CATALINA
FOOTHILLS**
6201 N Oracle Rd (85704)
Rates: $50-$94;
Tel: (602) 297-8111

**CANDLELIGHT SUITES**
1440 South Craycroft (85711)
Rates: N/A;
Tel: (602) 747-1440

**CHATEAU SUITES**
1402 North Alvernon (85712)
Rates: N/A;
Tel: (602) 323-7121

**CLARION HOTEL
TUCSON AIRPORT**
6801 S Tucson Blvd (85706)
Rates: $48-$99;
Tel: (602) 746-3932

**COUNTRY SUITES
BY CARLSON**
7411 N Oracle Rd (85704)
Rates: $49-$95;
Tel: (602) 575-9255

**DAYS INN-
TUCSON AIRPORT**
3700 E Irvington Rd (85714)
Rates: $40-$60;
Tel: (602) 571-1400

**DISCOVERY INN**
1010 S Freeway (85745)
Rates: $32-$45;
Tel: (602) 622-5871

**DOUBLETREE HOTEL**
445 S Alvernon Way (85711)
Rates: $49-$92;
Tel: (602) 881-4200

**EMBASSY SUITES
HOTEL & CONF CTR**
7051 S Tucson Blvd (85706)
Rates: $79-$119;
Tel: (602) 573-0700

**FRANCISCAN INN**
1165 N Stone Ave (85705)
Rates: $26-$60;
Tel: (602) 622-7763

**HAMPTON INN-AIRPORT**
6971 S Tucson Blvd (85706)
Rates: $42-$65;
Tel: (602) 889-5789

**HOLIDAY INN-BROADWAY**
181 W Broadway (85701)
Rates: $50-$160;
Tel: (602) 624 8711

**HOLIDAY INN-PALO VERDE**
4550 S Palo Verde Blvd
(85714)
Rates: $52-$128;
Tel: (602) 746-1161

**LA QUINTA INN-EAST**
6404 E Broadway (85710)
Rates: $48-$74;
Tel: (602) 747-1414

**LA QUINTA INN-WEST**
665 N Frwy (85745)
Rates: $46-$80;
Tel: (602) 622-6491

**THE LODGE
ON THE DESERT**
306 North Alvernon Way
(85711)
Rates: N/A;
Tel: (602) 325-3366

**PUEBLO INN**
350 South Freeway (85745)
Rates: N/A;
Tel: (602) 622-6611

**QUALITY INN-UNIVERSITY**
1601 N Oracle Rd (85705)
Rates: $45-$88;
Tel: (602) 623-6666

**RADISSON SUITE
HOTEL TUCSON**
6555 E Speedway Blvd
(85710)
Rates: $60-$125;
Tel: (602) 721-7100

**RAMADA INN FOOTHILLS**
6944 E Tanque Verde (85715)
Rates: $60-$99;
Tel: (602) 886-9595

**RESIDENCE INN
BY MARRIOTT**
6477 E Speedway Blvd
(85710)
Rates: $79-$150;
Tel: (602) 721-0991

**RODEWAY INN-BENSON
HWY & PARK**
810 E Benson Hwy (85713)
Rates: $30-$69;
Tel: (602) 884-5800

**RODEWAY INN I-10
& GRANT RD**
1365 W Grant Rd (85745)
Rates: $33-$97;
Tel: (602) 622-7791

**UNIVERSITY INN**
950 North Stone Ave (85705)
Rates: N/A;
Tel. (602) 791-7503

**WESTWARD LOOK RESORT**
245 E Ina Rd (85704)
Rates: $60-$110;
Tel: (602) 297-1151

**WINDMILL INN
AT ST. PHILLIP'S PLAZA**
4250 N Campbell Ave
(85718)
Rates: $49-$89;
Tel: (602) 577-0007

## WICKENBURG

**BEST WESTERN RANCHO
GRANDE MOTOR HOTEL**
293 E Wickenburg Way
(85358)
Rates: $47-$75;
Tel: (602) 684-5445

**WESTERNER MOTEL**
680 West Wickenburg Way
(85358)
Rates: N/A;
Tel: (602) 684-2493

## WILCOX

**BEST WESTERN
PLAZA INN**
1100 W Rex Allen Dr (85643)
Rates: $45-$80;
Tel: (602) 384-3556

**COMFORT INN**
724 N Bisbee Ave (85643)
Rates: $42-$52;
Tel: (602) 384-4222

**ROYAL WESTERN LODGE**
590 S Haskell Ave (85643)
Rates: $24-$38;
Tel: (602) 384-2266

## WILLIAMS

**BELAIR MOTEL**
620 West Bill Williams Ave
(86046)
Rates: N/A;
Tel: (602) 635-4415

**EL RANCHO MOTEL**
617 E Bill Williams Ave
(86046)
Rates: $22-$62;
Tel: (602) 635-2552

**GRAND-GATEWAY MOTEL**
234 East Bill Williams Ave
(86046)
Rates: N/A;
Tel: (602) 635-4601

**HIGHLANDER MOTEL**
533 W Bill Williams Ave
(86046)
Rates: $25-$48;
Tel: (602) 635-2541

**MOUNTAIN SIDE INN**
642 E Bill Williams Ave
(86046)
Rates: $65-$125;
Tel: (602) 635-4431

## WINSLOW

**BEST WESTERN
ADOBE INN**
1701 North Park Dr (86047)
Rates: $38-$62;
Tel: (602) 289-4638

BEST WESTERN
TOWN HOUSE LODGE
1914 W Third St (86047)
Rates: $32-$60;
Tel: (602) 289-4611

## YUMA

AIRPORTER STARDUST
711 East 32nd St (85365)
Rates: N/A;
Tel: (800) 835-1132

BEST WESTERN
CHILTON INN
300 E 32nd St (85364)
Rates: $65-$88;
Tel: (602) 344-1050

BEST WESTERN
CORONADO
233 4th Ave (85364)
Rates: $30-$79;
Tel: (602) 783-4453

BEST WESTERN
YUMA INNSUITES
1450 Castle Dome Ave
(85365)
Rates: $55-$89;
Tel: (602) 783-8341

HOLIDAY INN EXPRESS
3181 S 4th Ave at 32nd St
(85364)
Rates: $40-$75;
Tel: (602) 344-1420

SHILO INN
1550 S Castle Dome Rd
(85365)
Rates: $82-$98;
Tel: (602) 782-9511

# ARKANSAS

## ARKADELPHIA

BEST WESTERN-
CONTINENTAL INN
P. O. Box 296 (71923)
Rates: $38-$45;
Tel: (501) 246-5592

HOLIDAY INN
P. O. Box 450 (71923)
Rates: $57-$68;
Tel: (501) 246-5831

QUALITY INN
P. O. Box 420 (71923)
Rates: $38-$46;
Tel: (501) 246-5855

SIESTA MOTOR INN
137 Valley Dr (71923)
Rates: $28-$38;
Tel: (501) 246-3031

## BATESVILLE

RAMADA INN
OF BATESVILLE
1325 N St. Louis (72501)
Rates: $45-$51;
Tel: (501) 698-1800

## BENTON

BEST WESTERN INN
17036 I-30 (72015)
Rates: $34-$40;
Tel: (501) 778-9695

DAYS INN
1501 I-30 (72015)
Rates: $35-$46;
Tel: (501) 776-3200

ECONO LODGE
1221 Hot Springs Rd (72015)
Rates: $28-$33;
Tel: (501) 776-1515

RAMADA INN
16732 I-30 (72015)
Rates: $30-$45;
Tel: (501) 776-1900

## BENTONVILLE

BEST WESTERN
BENTONVILLE INN
2307 SE Walton Blvd (72712)
Rates: $39-$52;
Tel: (501) 273-9727

## BERRYVILLE

FAIRWAY MOTOR INN
RR 5, Box 106 (72616)
Rates: $25-$60;
Tel: (501) 423-3395

## BLYTHEVILLE

BEST WESTERN
COTTON INN
P. O. Box 1229 (72315)
Rates: $37-$50;
Tel: (501) 763-5220

COMFORT INN
OF BLYTHEVILLE
P. O. Box 1408 (72316)
Rates: $37-$45;
Tel: (501) 763-7081

DAYS INN
P. O. Box 1342 (72316)
Rates: $29-$39;
Tel: (501) 763-1241

DELTA K MOTEL
P. O. Box 1472 (72316)
Rates: $22-$29;
Tel: (501) 763-1410

**HOLIDAY INN**
P. O. Box 1408 (72316)
Rates: $46-$56;
Tel: (501) 763-5800

**THRIFTY INN**
201 N I-55 Service Rd (72315)
Rates: $33-$45;
Tel: (501) 763-2300

## BRINKLEY

**BEST WESTERN
FULLER MOTEL**
1306 Hwy 17N (72021)
Rates: $36-$48;
Tel: (501) 734-1650

**HERITAGE INN**
1507 Hwy 17N (72021)
Rates: $29-$42;
Tel: (501) 734-2121

## CAMDEN

**DAYS INN**
942 Adams Ave SW (71701)
Rates: $36-$42;
Tel: (501) 836-9372

## CARLISLE

**BEST WESTERN-
INTERSTATE INN CARLISLE**
P. O. Box 640 (72024)
Rates: $36-$52;
Tel: (501) 552-7566

## CLARKSVILLE

**BEST WESTERN
SHERWOOD MOTOR INN**
P. O. Box 146 (72830)
Rates: $34-$51;
Tel: (501) 754-7900

**DAYS INN**
Rt 1, Box 410 (72830)
Rates: $30-$38;
Tel: (501) 754-8555

**SUPER 8 MOTEL**
1238 Rogers Ave (72830)
Rates: $30-$35;
Tel: (501) 754-8800

## COLTER

**WHITE SANDS MOTEL**
P. O. Box 216 (72626)
Rates: N/A;
Tel: (501) 435-2244

## CONWAY

**BEST WESTERN KINGS
INN OF CONWAY**
P. O. Box 1619 (72032)
Rates: $34-$52;
Tel: (501) 329-9855

**HOLIDAY INN**
P. O. Box 998 (72032)
Rates: $47-$59;
Tel: (501) 329-2961

## CROSSETT

**RAMADA INN**
1400 Arkansas Hwy (71635)
Rates: $39-$56;
Tel: (501) 364-4101

## EUREKA SPRINGS

**COUNTRY
HOLIDAY MOTEL**
102 Kings Hwy (72632)
Rates: $29-$65;
Tel: (501) 253-8863

**DOGWOOD INN**
Rt 6, Box 20 (72632)
Rates: $18-$48;
Tel: (501) 253-7200

**FOUR RUNNER'S INN**
Rt 4, Box 206 (72632)
Rates: $38-$80;
Tel: (501) 253-6000

**SWISS VILLAGE INN**
Rt 6, Box 5 (72632)
Rates: $44-$60;
Tel: (501) 253-9541

## FAYETTEVILLE

**BEST WESTERN THE INN**
1000 Hwy 71 (72701)
Rates: $38-$44;
Tel: (501) 442-3041

**DAYS INN**
2402 N College Ave (72703)
Rates: $36-$40;
Tel: (501) 443-4323

**HOLIDAY INN EXPRESS**
1251 N Shiloh Dr (72701)
Rates: $39-$59;
Tel: (501) 444-6006

**INN AT THE MILL-
A CLARION
CARRIAGE HOUSE**
3906 Greathouse Springs Rd
(Johnson 72741)
Rates: $57-$69;
Tel: (501) 443-1800

**RAMADA INN**
3901 N College Ave (72703)
Rates: $42-$59;
Tel: (501) 443-3431

## FLIPPIN

**SPORTSMAN'S RESORT**
HCR 62, Box 96 (72634)
Rates: N/A;
Tel: (501) 453-2424

## FORREST CITY

**BEST WESTERN
COLONY INN**
2333 N Washington (72335)
Rates: $42-$58;
Tel: (501) 633-0870

**COMFORT INN**
115 Barrow Hill Rd (72335)
Rates: $33-$40;
Tel: (501) 633-0042

**HOLIDAY INN**
P. O. Box 790 (72335)
Rates: $41-$49;
Tel: (501) 633-6300

**LUXURY INN**
Rt 1, Box 9 (72335)
Rates: $32-$38;
Tel: (501) 633-8990

## FORT SMITH

**BEST WESTERN
KINGS ROW INN**
5801 Rogers Ave (72901)
Rates: $42-$48;
Tel: (501) 452-4200

**BEST WESTERN
TRADE WINDS INN**
101 N 11th St (72901)
Rates: $36-$49;
Tel: (501) 785-4121

**BUDGETEL INN**
2123 Burnham Rd (72903)
Rates: $36-$52;
Tel: (501) 484-5770

**HOLIDAY INN
FORT SMITH CIVIC CENTER**
700 Rogers Ave (72901)
Rates: $70-$88;
Tel: (501) 783-1000

**PARK INNS INTERNATIONAL**
301 N 11th St (72901)
Rates: $35-$40;
Tel: (501) 783-0271

**SHERATON INN-FORT SMITH**
5711 Rogers Ave (72901)
Rates: $65-$73;
Tel: (501) 452-4110

## HARRISON

**BEST WESTERN
OF HARRISON**
401 S Main Hwy 65B S
(72601)
Rates: $34-$55;
Tel: (501) 743-1000

**RAMADA INN**
1222 N Main (72601)
Rates: $36-$58;
Tel: (501) 741-7611

**ROCK CANDY MOUNTAIN**
Hwy 7 South (72601)
Rates: N/A;
Tel: (501) 743-1531

## HEBER SPRINGS

**LAKE AND RIVER INN**
2322 Hwy 25B (72543)
Rates: $30-$45;
Tel: (501) 362-3161

## HETH

**BEST WESTERN-
LAKE SIDE INN**
P. O. Box 151 (72346)
Rates: $30-$50;
Tel: (501) 657-2101

## HINDSVILLE

**FOXFIRE CAMP RESORT**
Rt 1, Box 198 (72738)
Rates: N/A;
Tel: (501) 789-2122

## HOPE

**BEST WESTERN
INN OF HOPE**
Jct I-30 & SR 4, exit 30
(71801)
Rates: $32-$50;
Tel: (501) 777-9222

**HOLIDAY INN**
I-30 & Hwy 4 (71801)
Rates: $32-$46;
Tel: (501) 777-8601

**QUALITY INN**
I-30 & Hwy 29 (71801)
Rates: $29-$40;
Tel: (501) 777-0777

## HOT SPRINGS
## NATIONAL PARK

**ARLINGTON RESORT
HOTEL & SPA**
Central Ave & Fountain St
(71901)
Rates: $42-$125;
Tel: (501) 623-7771

**BEST WESTERN
STAGECOACH INN**
2500 Central Ave (71901)
Rates: N/A;
Tel: (501) 624-2531

**LAKE HAMILTON RESORT**
2803 Albert Pike Rd (71913)
Rates: $65-$150;
Tel: (501) 767-5511

**MARGARETE MOTEL**
217 Fountain St (71901)
Rates: $24-$45;
Tel: (501) 623-1192

**QUALITY INN**
1125 E Grand Ave (71901)
Rates: $41-$46;
Tel: (501) 624-3321

**TRAVELLER
MOTOR LODGE**
1045 E Grand Ave (71901)
Rates: $27-$49;
Tel: (501) 624-4681

## JACKSONVILLE

**RAMADA INN**
200 Hwy 67N (72076)
Rates: $39-$46;
Tel: (501) 982-2183

## JONESBORO

**JONESBORO
BEST WESTERN**
2901 Phillips Dr (72401)
Rates: $39-$45;
Tel: (501) 932-6600

**PARK INN OF JONESBORO**
1421 S Caraway Rd (72401)
Rates: $39-$46;
Tel: (501) 935-8400

**SCOTTISH INN'S
COLONIAL MOTEL**
3116 Mead Dr (72401)
Rates: $29-$34;
Tel: (501) 972-8300

**SUPER 8 MOTEL**
2500 S Caraway Rd (72401)
Rates: $29-$35;
Tel: (501) 972-0849

**WILSON INN**
2911 Gilmore Dr (72401)
Rates: $32-$49;
Tel: (501) 972-9000

# LITTLE ROCK

**BEST WESTERN
INN TOWNE**
600 I-30 (72202)
Rates: $50-$100;
Tel: (501) 375-2100

**BUDGETEL INN**
1010 Breckenridge Rd (72205)
Rates: $35-$44;
Tel: (501) 225-7007

**COMFORT INN**
3200 Bankhead Dr (72206)
Rates: $40-$49;
Tel: (501) 490-2010

**DAYS INN SOUTH**
2600 W 65th St (72209)
Rates: $32-$44;
Tel: (501) 562-1122

**HAMPTON INN
LITTLE ROCK I-30**
6100 Mitchell Dr (72209)
Rates: $36-$50;
Tel: (501) 562-6667

**HOLIDAY INN
CITY CENTER**
617 S Broadway (72201)
Rates: $54-$59;
Tel: (501) 376-2071

**HOLIDAY INN EXPRESS**
I 440 at Airport exit (72206)
Rates: $58-$68;
Tel: (501) 490-4000

**HOLIDAY INN
OTTER CREST**
11701 I-30 (72209)
Rates: $49-$65;
Tel: (501) 455-2300

**HOLIDAY INN WEST**
201 S Shackelford (72211)
Rates: $70-$94;
Tel: (501) 223-3000

**LA QUINTA
MOTOR INN-FAIR PARK**
901 Fair Park Blvd (72204)
Rates: $42-$54;
Tel: (501) 664-7000

**LA QUINTA
MOTOR INN-SOUTH**
2401 W 65th St (72209)
Rates: $39-$52;
Tel: (501) 568-1030

**LA QUINTA
MOTOR INN-WEST**
200 Shackelford Rd (72211)
Rates: $43-$56;
Tel: (501) 224-0900

**LITTLE ROCK HILTON INN**
925 S University Ave (72204)
Rates: $69-$75;
Tel: (501) 664-5020

**RED ROOF INN**
7900 Scott Hamilton Dr
(72209)
Rates: $25-$37;
Tel: (501) 562-2694

**SUPER 8 LODGE**
7501 I-30 (72209)
Rates: $28-$35;
Tel: (501) 568-8888

# MAGNOLIA

**BEST WESTERN-
COACHMAN'S INN**
420 E Main St (71753)
Rates: $33-$43;
Tel: (501) 234-6122

# MALVERN

**TOWN HOUSE MOTEL**
304 E Page Ave (72104)
Rates: N/A;
Tel: (501) 332-5437

# MARION

**BEST WESTERN-
REGENCY MOTOR INN**
Rt 2, Box 398C (72364)
Rates: $32-$48;
Tel: (501) 739-3278

# MARKED TREE

**TRAVELAIR MOTEL**
201 Hwy 63S (72365)
Rates: $28-$40;
Tel: (501) 358-2700

# MORRILTON

**BEST WESTERN
CONFEDERATE INN**
Rt 1, Box 271 (72110)
Rates: $40-$52;
Tel: (501) 354-0181

# MOUNTAIN HOME

**BEST WESTERN-
CARRIAGE INN**
963 US 62E (72653)
Rates: $35-$47;
Tel: (501) 425-6001

**BLUE PARADISE RESORT**
Rt 6, Box 379 (72653)
Rates: $29-$46;
Tel: (501) 492-5113

**HOLIDAY INN**
1350 Hwy 62 SW (72653)
Rates: $42-$56;
Tel: (501) 425-5101

**RAMADA INN**
1127 Hwy 62 NE (72653)
Rates: $36-$50;
Tel: (501) 425-9191

**SILVER LEAF LODGE**
Rt 9, Box 544 (72653)
Rates: $35;
Tel: (501) 492-5187

**TEAL POINT RESORT**
Rt 6, Box 369 (72653)
Rates: $42-$90;
Tel: (501) 492-5145

# MOUNT IDA

**DENBY POINT
LODGE & MARINA**
SR 1, Box 241 (71957)
Rates: $35-$90;
Tel: (501) 867-3651

## NEWPORT

**PARK INN
INTERNATIONAL**
101 Olivia Dr (72112)
Rates: $37-$47;
Tel: (501) 523-5851

## NORTH LITTLE ROCK

**HAMPTON INN**
500 W 29th St (72114)
Rates: $38-$50;
Tel: (501) 771-2090

**HOLIDAY INN**
111 W Pershing Blvd (72114)
Rates: $55-$80;
Tel: (501) 758-1440

**LA QUINTA NORTH**
4100 E McCain Blvd (72117)
Rates: $41-$54;
Tel: (501) 945-0808

**MASTERS ECONOMY INN**
2508 Jacksonville Hwy
(72117)
Rates: $21-$31;
Tel: (501) 945-4167

**RAMADA INN**
120 W Pershing Rd (72115)
Rates: $38-$46;
Tel: (501) 758-1851

## OMAHA

**AUNT SHIRLEY'S
SLEEPING LOFT**
Rt 1, Box 84-D (72662)
Rates: N/A;
Tel: (501) 426-5408

## OSCEOLA

**BEST WESTERN INN**
P. O. Box 648 (72370)
Rates: $32-$42;
Tel: (501) 563-3222

## OZARK

**OZARK BUDGET
HOST MOTEL**
1711 W Commercial (72949)
Rates: $28-$34;
Tel: (501) 667-2166

## PINE BLUFF

**HOLIDAY INN**
2700 E Harding (71601)
Rates: $45-$55;
Tel: (501) 535-8640

**HOLIDAY INN PINE BLUFF
CONVENTION CTR**
2 Convention Center Plaza
(71601)
Rates: $47-$70;
Tel: (501) 535-3111

## PRESCOTT

**COMFORT INN**
Rt 5, Box 236 (71857)
Rates: $32-$43;
Tel: (501) 887-6641

## RUSSELLVILLE

**BUDGET INN**
2200 N Arkansas Ave (72801)
Rates: $25-$38;
Tel: (501) 968-4400

**HOLIDAY INN**
P. O. Box 460 (72801)
Rates: $48-$64;
Tel: (501) 968-4300

**THE MARINA INN**
504 W Birch St (72801)
Rates: $26-$37;
Tel: (501) 968-1450

**PARK MOTEL**
2615 W Main St (72801)
Rates: $23-$33;
Tel: (501) 968-4862

**SOUTHERN INN**
704 Dyke Rd (72801)
Rates: $27-$42;
Tel: (501) 968-5511

## SEARCY

**COMFORT INN**
107 S Rand St (72143)
Rates: $34-$45;
Tel: (501) 279-9100

## SILOAM SPRINGS

**HARTLAND LODGE**
1801 Hwy 412W (72761)
Rates: $34-$41;
Tel: (501) 524-2025

## SPRINGDALE

**HOLIDAY INN NORTHWEST
AR HOTEL/CONV CTR**
1500 S 48th St (72762)
Rates: $74-$89;
Tel: (501) 751-8300

## TEXARKANA

**BEST WESTERN KINGS
ROW INN**
4200 N State Line Ave
(75502)
Rates: $41-$46;
Tel: (501) 774-3851

**BUDGETEL INN**
5012 N State Line Ave
(75502)
Rates: $33-$49;
Tel: (501) 773-1000

**FOUR STATES INN**
4300 N State Line Ave
(75502)
Rates: $34-$42;
Tel: (501) 773-3144

**HOLIDAY INN EXPRESS**
5401 N State Line Ave
(75503)
Rates: $42-$49;
Tel: (501) 792-3366

**HOLIDAY INN TEXARKANA**
5100 N State Line Ave
(75502)
Rates: $61-$82;
Tel: (501) 774-3521

**LA QUINTA MOTOR
INN-TEXARKANA**
5201 State Line Ave (75503)
Rates: $39-$51;
Tel: (501) 794-1900

**RAMADA INN**
I-30 & Summerhill Rd (75503)
Rates: $36-$54;
Tel: (501) 794-3131

**SHONEY'S INN**
5210 State Line Ave (75504)
Rates: $38-$60;
Tel: (501) 772-0070

## VAN BUREN

**BEST WESTERN
BUTTERFIELD TRAIL INN**
P. O. Box 648 (72956)
Rates: $39-$45;
Tel: (501) 474-8001

## WHEATLEY

**COMFORT INN**
Rt 2, Box 107A (72392)
Rates: $33-$38;
Tel: (501) 457-2202

# CALIFORNIA

## ADELANTO

**DAYS INN**
11628 Bartlett Ave (92301)
Rates: $35-$55;
Tel: (619) 246-8777

## AGOURA HILLS

**RAMADA HOTEL**
30100 Agoura Rd (91301)
Rates: $59;
Tel: (818) 707-1220

## ALTURAS

**BEST WESTERN
TRAILSIDE INN**
343 N Main St (96101)
Rates: $36-$46;
Tel: (916) 233-4111

**HACIENDA MOTEL**
201 E 12th St (96101)
Rates: $26-$45;
Tel: (916) 233-3459

## ANAHEIM

**ANAHEIM HILTON
AND TOWERS**
777 Convention Way (92802)
Rates: $150-$230;
Tel: (714) 750-4321

**ANAHEIM
MARRIOTT HOTEL**
700 W Convention Way
(92802)
Rates: $160-$189;
Tel: (714) 750-8000

**BROADWAY MOTEL**
300 N Manchester Ave
(92801)
Rates: N/A;
Tel: (714) 535-3502

**ECONO LODGE-EAST**
871 S Harbor Blvd (92805)
Rates: $42-$62;
Tel: (714) 535-7878

**GRANADA INN**
2375 W Lincoln Ave (92801)
Rates: $45-$55;
Tel: (714) 774-7370

**HAMPTON INN**
300 E Katella Way (92802)
Rates: $55-$82;
Tel: (714) 772-8713

**JOLLY ROGER HOTEL/INN**
640 West Katella (92802)
Rates: N/A;
Tel: (714) 772-7621

**QUALITY HOTEL
& CONFERENCE CENTER**
616 Convention Way (92802)
Rates: $62-$85;
Tel: (714) 750-3131

**RAFFLES INN & SUITES**
2040 S Harbor Blvd (92802)
Rates: $54-$97;
Tel: (714) 750-6100

**RESIDENCE INN
BY MARRIOTT**
1700 S Clementine St (92802)
Rates: $159-$189;
Tel: (714) 533-3555

## ANDERSON

**BEST WESTERN
KNIGHTS INN**
2688 Gateway Dr (96007)
Rates: $40-$54;
Tel: (916) 365-2753

## ARCADIA

**EMBASSY SUITES**
211 E Huntington Dr (91006)
Rates: $107-$117;
Tel: (818) 445-8525

**HAMPTON INN**
311 E Huntington Dr (91006)
Rates: $60-$75;
Tel: (818) 574-5600

**HOLIDAY INN
OF MONROVIA**
924 W Huntington Dr
(Monrovia 91016)
Rates: $72-$200;
Tel: (818) 445-8525

**RESIDENCE INN
BY MARRIOTT**
321 E Huntington Dr (91006)
Rates: $109-$159;
Tel: (818) 446-6500

## ARCATA

**ARCATA SUPER 8**
4887 Valley West Blvd
(95521)
Rates: $32-$57;
Tel: (707) 822-8888

**BEST WESTERN
ARCATA INN**
4827 Valley West Blvd
(95521)
Rates: $52-$78;
Tel: (707) 826-0313

**HOTEL ARCATA**
708 9th St (95521)
Rates: $45-$120;
Tel: (707) 826-0217

**QUALITY INN-MAD RIVER**
3535 Janes Rd (95521)
Rates: $38-$76;
Tel: (707) 822-0409

## ARROYO GRANDE

**BEST WESTERN
CASA GRANDE INN**
850 Oak Park Rd (93420)
Rates: $58-$88;
Tel: (805) 481-7398

## AUBURN

**BEST WESTERN
GOLDEN KEY MOTEL**
13450 Lincoln Way (95603)
Rates: $46-$60;
Tel: (916) 885-8611

## BAKER

**BUN BOY MOTEL**
P. O. Box 130 (92309)
Rates: $29-$44;
Tel: (619) 733-4363

## BAKERSFIELD

**BEST WESTERN
HILL HOUSE**
700 Truxtun Ave at S St
(93301)
Rates: $46-$50;
Tel: (805) 327-4064

**BEST WESTERN INN**
2620 Pierce Rd (93308)
Rates: $47-$72;
Tel: (805) 327-9651

**BEST WESTERN OAK INN**
889 Oak St (93304)
Rates: $48-$56;
Tel: (805) 324-9686

**ECONOMY INNS
OF AMERICA**
6100 Knudsen Dr (93308)
Rates: $22-$37;
Tel: (805) 392-1800

**LA QUINTA MOTOR INN**
3232 Riverside Dr (93308)
Rates: $50-$62;
Tel: (805) 325-7400

**QUALITY INN**
1011 Oak St (93304)
Rates: $42-$62;
Tel: (805) 325-0772

**RED LION HOTEL**
3100 Camino Del Rio Ct
(93308)
Rates: $103-$138;
Tel: (805) 323-7111

**RESIDENCE INN
BY MARRIOTT**
4241 Chester Ln (93309)
Rates: $65-$114;
Tel: (805) 321-9800

**RIO MIRADA MOTOR INN**
4500 Pierce Rd (93308)
Rates: $48-$53;
Tel: (805) 324-5555

**SHERATON INN
BAKERSFIELD**
5101 California Ave (93309)
Rates: $65-$110;
Tel: (805) 325-9700

## BANNING

**DAYS INN**
2320 W Ramsey St (92220)
Rates: $44-$48;
Tel: (909) 849-0092

**SUPER 8 MOTEL**
1690 W Ramsey St (92220)
Rates: $31-$39;
Tel: (909) 849-6887

## BARSTOW

**ASTRO BUDGET MOTEL**
1271 E Main St (92311)
Rates: $22-$38;
Tel: (619) 256-2204

**BARSTOW INN**
1261 E Main St (92311)
Rates: $22-$40;
Tel: (619) 256-7581

**DESERT INN MOTEL**
1100 E Main St (92311)
Rates: $28-$38;
Tel: (619) 256-2146

**ECONO LODGE**
1230 E Main St (92311)
Rates: $24-$52;
Tel: (619) 256-2133

**ECONOMY INNS
OF AMERICA**
1590 Coolwater Ln (92311)
Rates: $24-$37;
Tel: (619) 256-1737

**GATEWAY MOTEL**
1630 E Main St (92311)
Rates: $22-$40;
Tel: (619) 256-8931

**QUALITY INN**
1520 E Main St (92311)
Rates: $46-$64;
Tel: (619) 256-6891

**VAGABOND INN**
1243 E Main St (92311)
Rates: $38-$63;
Tel: (619) 256-5601

## BEAUMONT

**GOLDEN WEST MOTEL**
625 E 5th St (92223)
Rates: $32-$40;
Tel: (909) 845-2185

**WINDSOR MOTEL**
1265 E 6th St (92223)
Rates: $26-$30;
Tel: (909) 845-1436

## BENICIA

**BEST WESTERN
HERITAGE INN**
1955 E 2nd St (94510)
Rates: $60-$65;
Tel: (707) 746-0401

**CAPTAIN
DILLINGHAM'S INN**
145 East D St (94510)
Rates: $70-$170;
Tel: (707) 746-7164

## BEVERLY HILLS

**BEVERLY HILLS COMSTOCK**
10300 Wilshire Blvd (90024)
Rates: $95-$290;
Tel: (800) 800-1234

**BEVERLY HILTON**
9876 Wilshire Blvd (90210)
Rates: $190-$250;
Tel: (310) 274-7777

## BIG BEAR LAKE

**BIG BEAR CABINS**
P. O. Box 1533 (92315)
Rates: $49-$99;
Tel: (909) 866-2723

**COZY HOLLOW LODGE**
P. O. Box 1288 (92315)
Rates: $49-$129;
Tel: (909) 866-8886

**EAGLE'S NEST
BED & BREAKFAST**
P. O. Box 1003 (92315)
Rates: $75-$140;
Tel: (909) 866-6465

**FRONTIER LODGE
& MOTEL**
P. O. Box 687 (92315)
Rates: $50-$132;
Tel: (909) 866-5888

**GREY SQUIRREL RESORT**
P. O. Box 5404 (92315)
Rates: $62-$88;
Tel: (909) 866-4335

**HAPPY BEAR VILLAGE**
P. O. Box 3939 (92315)
Rates: $70-$100;
Tel: (909) 866-2350

**SHORE ACRES LODGE**
40090 Lakeview Dr (92315)
Rates: N/A;
Tel: (909) 866-8200

## BIG PINE

**BIG PINE MOTEL**
370 S Main (93515)
Rates: $30-$42;
Tel: (619) 938-2282

## BISHOP

**BEST WESTERN
HOLIDAY SPA LODGE**
1025 N Main St (93514)
Rates: $54-$77;
Tel: (619) 873-3543

**BEST WESTERN
WESTERNER MOTEL**
150 E Elm St (93514)
Rates: $45-$65;
Tel: (619) 873-3564

**BISHOP INN**
805 N Main St (93514)
Rates: $47-$62;
Tel: (619) 873-4284

**SIERRA FOOTHILLS MOTEL**
535 S Main St (93514)
Rates: $33-$46;
Tel: (619) 872-1386

**THUNDERBIRD MOTEL**
190 W Pine St (93514)
Rates: $30-$50;
Tel: (619) 873-4215

**VAGABOND INN**
1030 N Main St (93514)
Rates: $44-$66;
Tel: (619) 873-6351

## BLYTHE

**BEST WESTERN
SAHARA MOTEL**
825 W Hobsonway (92225)
Rates: $49-$64;
Tel: (619) 922-7105

**COMFORT INN**
903 W Hobsonway (92225)
Rates: $38-$62;
Tel: (619) 922-4146

## BODEGA BAY

**BODEGA COAST INN**
P. O. Box 55 (94923)
Rates: $60-$180;
Tel: (707) 875-2217

## BORREGO SPRINGS

**PALM CANYON RESORT**
221 Palm Canyon Dr (92004)
Rates: $56-$99;
Tel: (619) 767-5341

## BRAWLEY

**TOWN HOUSE LODGE**
135 Main St (92227)
Rates: $43-$47;
Tel: (619) 344-5120

## BREA

**HYLAND MOTEL**
727 S Brea Blvd (92621)
Rates: $36-$40;
Tel: (714) 990-6867

## BRIDGEPORT

**BEST WESTERN RUBY INN**
P. O. Box 475 (93517)
Rates: $55-$90;
Tel: (619) 932-7241

**SILVER MAPLE INN**
P. O. Box 327 (93517)
Rates: $45-$80;
Tel: (619) 932-7383

**WALKER RIVER LODGE**
P. O. Box 695 (93517)
Rates: $45-$110;
Tel: (619) 932-7021

## BUENA PARK

**BEST WESTERN
BUENA PARK INN**
8580 Stanton Ave (90620)
Rates: $36-$52;
Tel: (714) 828-5211

## BURBANK

**HILTON-BURBANK AIRPORT
& CONVENTION CTR**
2500 Hollywood Way (91505)
Rates: $106-$171;
Tel: (818) 843-6000

**HOLIDAY INN-BURBANK**
150 E Angeleno (91510)
Rates: $96-$135;
Tel: (818) 841-4770

**RAMADA INN-BURBANK**
2900 N San Fernando Rd
(91504)
Rates: $75-$95;
Tel: (818) 843-5955

## BURNEY

**CHARM MOTEL**
P. O. Box 50 (96013)
Rates: $46-$74;
Tel: (916) 335-2254

## BUTTONWILLOW

**NICE INN**
20681 Tracy Ave (93206)
Rates: $26-$36;
Tel: (805) 764-5117

## CALIMESA

**CALIMESA INN MOTEL**
1205 Calimesa Blvd (92320)
Rates: $35-$47;
Tel: (909) 795-2536

## CALISTOGA

**BRANNAN COTTAGE INN**
109 Wapoo Ave (94515)
Rates: N/A;
Tel: (707) 942-4200

## CAMERON PARK

**BEST WESTERN
CAMERON PARK INN**
3361 Coach Ln (95682)
Rates: $54-$76;
Tel: (916) 677-2203

**SUPER 8 MOTEL**
3444 Coach Ln (95682)
Rates: $41-$49;
Tel: (916) 677-7177

## CAMPBELL

**CAMPBELL INN**
675 E Campbell Ave (95008)
Rates: $89-$175;
Tel: (408) 374-4300

**RESIDENCE INN
BY MARRIOTT-SAN JOSE**
2761 S Bascom Ave (95008)
Rates: $89-$149;
Tel: (408) 559-1551

## CARLSBAD

**ECONOMY INNS
OF AMERICA**
751 Raintree Dr (92209)
Rates: $29-$49;
Tel: (619) 931-1185

## CARMEL

**COACHMAN'S INN**
P. O. Box C-1 (93921)
Rates: $65-$150;
Tel: (408) 624-6421

**CYPRESS INN**
P. O. Box Y (93921)
Rates: $78-$185;
Tel: (408) 624-3871

**HIGHLANDS INN**
P. O. Box 1700 (93921)
Rates: $225-$650;
Tel: (408) 624-3801

**QUAIL LODGE RESORT
& GOLF CLUB**
8205 Valley Greens Dr
(93923)
Rates: $155-$295;
Tel: (408) 624-1581

**WAYSIDE INN**
P. O. Box 1900 (93921)
Rates: $75-$135;
Tel: (408) 624-5336

## CARMEL VALLEY

**BLUE SKY LODGE**
Flight Rd (93924)
Rates: N/A;
Tel: (408) 659-2935

**CARMEL VALLEY INN**
P. O. Box 115 (93924)
Rates: $49-$119;
Tel: (408) 659-3131

**VALLEY LODGE**
P. O. Box 93 (93924)
Rates: $95-$135;
Tel: (408) 659-2261

## CARNELIAN BAY

**LAKESIDE CHALETS**
5240 N Lake Blvd (96140)
Rates: N/A;
Tel: (916) 546-2369

## CASTAIC

**COMFORT INN**
31558 Castaic Rd (91384)
Rates: $40-$70;
Tel: (805) 295-1100

# CHICO

**HOLIDAY INN OF CHICO**
685 Manzanita Ci (95926)
Rates: $69-$85;
Tel: (916) 345-2491

**O'FLAHERTY HOUSE
BED & BREAKFAST**
1462 Arcadian (95926)
Rates: N/A;
Tel: (916) 893-5494

**SAFARI GARDEN MOTEL**
2352 Esplanade (95926)
Rates: $32-$44;
Tel: (916) 343-3201

**TOWN HOUSE MOTEL**
2321 Esplanade (95926)
Rates: $28-$42;
Tel: (916) 343-1621

# CHULA VISTA

**LA QUINTA INN**
150 Bonita Rd (91910)
Rates: $61-$76;
Tel: (619) 691-1211

**VAGABOND INN**
230 Broadway (91910)
Rates: $36-$55;
Tel: (619) 422-8305

# CLAREMONT

**GRISWOLD'S INN**
555 W Foothill Blvd (91711)
Rates: $75-$85;
Tel: (909) 626-2411

# CLEARLAKE

**WISEDA LAKESIDE RESORT**
14375 Lakeshore Dr (95422)
Rates: N/A;
Tel: (707) 994-2145

# COALINGA

**THE INN AT HARRIS RANCH**
Rt 1, Box 777 (93210)
Rates: $83-104;
Tel: (209) 935-0717

# COFFEE CREEK

**COFFEE CREEK RANCH**
Coffee Creek Rd (96091)
Rates: N/A;
Tel: (800) 624-4480

# COLEVILLE

**ANDRUSS MOTEL**
Walker Rte, Box 64 (96107)
Rates: $36-$42;
Tel: (916) 495-2216

**MEADOWCLIFF MOTEL**
Rte 1, Box 126 (96107)
Rates: $32-$45;
Tel: (916) 495-2255

# COLTON

**PATRIOT INN & SUITES**
2830 Iowa St (92324)
Rates: $44-$48;
Tel: (909) 788-9900

# COLUMBIA

**COLUMBIA INN MOTEL**
22646 Broadway (95310)
Rates: N/A;
Tel: (209) 533-0446

# COMMERCE

**WYNDHAM
GARDEN HOTEL**
5757 Telegraph Rd (90040)
Rates: $119-$129;
Tel: (213) 887-8100

# CONCORD

**BEST WESTERN
HERITAGE INN**
4600 Clayton Rd (94521)
Rates: $55-$60;
Tel: (510) 686-4466

**SHERATON HOTEL
& CONFERENCE CTR**
45 John Glenn Dr (94520)
Rates: $80-$100;
Tel: (510) 825-7700

**TREES INN**
1370 Monument Blvd (94520)
Rates. $49-$74;
Tel: (510) 827-8998

# CORCORAN

**BUDGET INN**
1224 Whitley Ave (93212)
Rates: $47-$60;
Tel: (209) 992-3171

# CORNING

**DAYS INN**
3475 Hwy 99W (96021)
Rates: $28-$60;
Tel: (916) 824-2000

**SHILO INN**
3350 Sunrise Way (96021)
Rates: $60-$67;
Tel: (916) 824-2940

# CORONADO

**EL CORDOVA MOTEL**
1351 Orange Ave (92118)
Rates: $70-$148;
Tel: (619) 435-4131

# COSTA MESA

**ANA MESA SUITES**
3597 Harbor Blvd (92626)
Rates: $51-$77;
Tel: (714) 662-3500

**LA QUINTA MOTOR INN**
1515 S Coast Dr (92626)
Rates: $45-$55;
Tel: (714) 957-5841

**RED LION HOTEL/ORANGE
COUNTY AIRPORT**
3050 Bristol St (92626)
Rates: $123-$172;
Tel: (714) 540-7000

**RESIDENCE INN
BY MARRIOTT**
881 W Baker St (92626)
Rates: $97-$132;
Tel: (714) 241-8800

**THE VAGABOND INN**
3205 Harbor Blvd (92626)
Rates: $40-$60;
Tel: (714) 557-8360

**THE WESTIN SOUTH
COAST PLAZA HOTEL**
686 Anton Blvd (92626)
Rates: $139-$164;
Tel: (714) 540-2500

## CRESCENT CITY

**PACIFIC MOTOR HOTEL**
440 Hwy 101 N (95531)
Rates: $37-$67;
Tel: (707) 464-4141

## DAVIS

**BEST WESTERN
UNIVERSITY LODGE**
123 B St (95616)
Rates: $50-$70;
Tel: (916) 756-7890

**ECONO LODGE**
221 D St (95616)
Rates: $45-$50;
Tel: (916) 756-1040

## DEATH VALLEY
## NATIONAL MONUMENT

**STOVE PIPE
WELLS VILLAGE**
SR 190 (92328)
Rates: $50-$69;
Tel: (619) 786-2387

## DELANO

**SHILO INN**
2231 Girard St (93215)
Rates: $80-$115;
Tel: (619) 755-9765

## DESERT HOT SPRINGS

**DESERT HOT SPRINGS
SPA HOTEL**
10805 Palm Dr (92240)
Rates: $39-$99;
Tel: (619) 329-6495

**STARDUST MOTEL**
66634 5th St (92240)
Rates: $37-$47;
Tel: (619) 329-5443

**TAMARIX MOTEL**
66185 Acoma (92240)
Rates: N/A;
Tel: (619) 329-6615

## DOWNEY

**EMBASSY SUITES HOTEL**
8425 Firestone Blvd (90241)
Rates: $89-$99;
Tel: (310) 861-1900

## DUNNIGAN

**BEST WESTERN COUNTRY**
P. O. Box 740 (95937)
Rates: $56-$68;
Tel: (916) 724-3471

**VALUE LODGE**
P. O. Box 740 (95937)
Rates: $39-$56;
Tel: (916) 724-3333

## DUNSMUIR

**CABOOSE MOTEL**
100 Railroad Park Rd (96025)
Rates: $45-$80;
Tel: (916) 235-4440

**CEDAR LODGE**
4201 Dunsmuir Ave (96025)
Rates: $28-$50;
Tel: (916) 235-4331

**DUNSMUIR TRAVELODGE**
5400 Dunsmuir Ave (96025)
Rates: $40-$60;
Tel: (916) 235-4395

## EL CAJON

**BUDGET HOST HACIENDA**
588 N Mollison Ave (92021)
Rates: $31-$36;
Tel: (619) 579-1144

**DAYS INN-LA MESA**
1250 El Cajon Blvd (92020)
Rates; $35-$49;
Tel: (619) 588-8808

**VILLA EMBASADORA**
1556 E Main St (92021)
Rates: $25-$42;
Tel: (619) 442-9617

## EL CENTRO

**BARBARA WORTH
COUNTRY CLUB & HOTEL**
2050 Country Club Dr
(Holtville 92250)
Rates: $48-$54;
Tel: (619) 356-2806

**BRUNNER'S MOTEL**
215 N Imperial Ave (92243)
Rates: $46-$55;
Tel: (619) 352-6431

**DEL CORONADO
CROWN MOTEL**
330 N Imperial Ave (92243)
Rates: $35-$60;
Tel: (619) 353-0030

**RAMADA INN**
1455 Ocotillo Dr (92243)
Rates: $46-$75;
Tel: (619) 352-5152

**SANDS MOTEL**
611 N Imperial Ave (92243)
Rates: $30-$44;
Tel: (619) 352-0715

## EL MONTE

**RAMADA SUITES**
1089 Santa Anita Ave
(S El Monte 91733)
Rates: $79-$107;
Tel: (818) 350-9588

## EMERYVILLE

**HOLIDAY INN-BAY BRIDGE**
1800 Powell St (94608)
Rates: $75-$130;
Tel: (510) 658-9300

## ESCONDIDO

**ESCONDIDO
ECONO LODGE**
1250 W Valley Pkwy (92029)
Rates: $44-$49;
Tel: (619) 741-7117

**LAWRENCE WELK RESORT**
8860 Lawrence Welk Dr
(92026)
Rates: $100-$110;
Tel: (619) 749-3000

## EUREKA

**EUREKA INN**
518 7th St (95501)
Rates: $85-$275;
Tel: (800) 862-4906

**NENDELS VALU INN**
2223 4th St (95501)
Rates: $40-$65;
Tel: (707) 442-3261

**RED LION MOTOR INN**
1929 4th St (95501)
Rates: $75-$135·
Tel: (707) 445-0844

**TOWN HOUSE MOTEL**
933 Fourth St (95501)
Rates: N/A;
Tel: (707) 443-4536

## FAIRFIELD

**BEST WESTERN
CORDELIA INN**
4373 Central Pl,
(Cordelia Vlge 94585)
Rates: $42-$54;
Tel: (707) 864-2029

**HOLIDAY INN
OF FAIRFIELD**
1350 Holiday Ln (94533)
Rates: $59-$86;
Tel: (707) 422-4111

**MOTEL 6**
1473 Holiday Ln (94533)
Rates: $25-$27;
Tel: (707) 425-4565

## FALLBROOK

**BEST WESTERN
FRANCISCAN INN**
1635 S Mission Rd (92028)
Rates: $45-$65;
Tel: (619) 728-6174

## FOSTER CITY

**HOLIDAY INN-
FOSTER CITY**
1221 Chess Dr (94404)
Rates: $65-$145;
Tel: (415) 570 5700

## FOUNTAIN VALLEY

**RESIDENCE INN
BY MARRIOTT**
9930 Slater Ave (92708)
Rates: $99-$127;
Tel: (714) 965 8000

## FREMONT

**LORD BRADLEY'S INN**
43344 Mission Blvd (94539)
Rates: $65-$75;
Tel: (510) 490-0520

**RESIDENCE INN
BY MARRIOTT**
5400 Farwell Pl (94536)
Rates: $104-$134;
Tel: (510) 794-5900

## FRESNO

**BROOKS RANCH INN**
4278 W Ashian Ave (93722)
Rates: $28-$42;
Tel: (209) 275-2727

**ECONOMY INNS
OF AMERICA**
2570 S East St (93706)
Rates: $24-$31;
Tel: (209) 486-1188

**FRESNO HILTON**
1055 Van Ness Ave (93721)
Rates: $65-$119;
Tel: (209) 485-9000

**HOLIDAY INN-AIRPORT**
5090 E Clinton Ave (93727)
Rates: $76-$105;
Tel: (209) 252-3611

**HOLIDAY INN
CENTRE PLAZA**
2233 Ventura St (93709)
Rates: $72-$86;
Tel: (209) 268-1000

**HOTEL VIRGINIA**
2125 Kern St (93721)
Rates: N/A;
Tel: (209) 268-8926

**HOWARD JOHNSON
HOTEL**
4071 N Blackstone Ave
(93726)
Rates: $36-$48;
Tel: (209) 222-5641

**PHOENIX LODGE**
2345 N Parkway Dr (93705)
Rates: $25-$33;
Tel: (209) 268-0711

**THE VAGABOND INN**
1101 N Parkway Dr (93728)
Rates: N/A;
Tel: (800) 522-1555

## FULLERTON

**FULLERTON MARRIOTT
HOTEL/CAL STATE UNIV**
2701 E Nutwood Ave (92631)
Rates: $79-$89;
Tel: (714) 738-7800

**HOLIDAY INN-FULLERTON**
222 W Houston Ave (92632)
Rates: $80-$100;
Tel: (714) 992-1700

## GARBERVILLE

**BENBOW INN**
445 Lake Benbow Dr (95542)
Rates: $88-$145;
Tel: (707) 923-2124

**BEST WESTERN
HUMBOLDT HOUSE**
701 Redwood Dr (95542)
Rates: $58-$78;
Tel: (707) 923-2771

**GARBERVILLE MOTEL**
948 Redwood Dr (95542)
Rates: $45-$60;
Tel: (707) 923-2422

**SHERWOOD FOREST MOTEL**
814 Redwood Dr (95542)
Rates: $50-$88;
Tel: (707) 923-2721

## GARDEN GROVE

**HIDDEN VILLAGE BED & BREAKFAST**
9582 Halekulani Dr (92641)
Rates: N/A;
Tel: (714) 636-8312

## GILROY

**LEAVESLEY INN**
8430 Murray Ave (95020)
Rates: $38-$50;
Tel: (408) 847-5500

**SUPER 8 MOTEL**
8435 San Ysidro (95020)
Rates: $39-$47;
Tel: (408) 848-4108

## GLEN AVON

**CIRCLE INN MOTEL**
9220 Granite Hill Dr (92509)
Rates: N/A;
Tel: (714) 360-1132

## GLENDALE

**HOLIDAY INN**
600 N Pacific Ave (91203)
Rates: $47-$57;
Tel: (818) 956-0202

**RED LION HOTEL/GLENDALE**
100 W Glenoaks Blvd (91203)
Rates: $125-$150;
Tel: (818) 956-5466

**THE VAGABOND INN**
120 W Colorado St (91204)
Rates: $61-$81;
Tel: (818) 240-1700

## GRASS VALLEY

**ALTA SIERRA RESORT MOTEL**
135 Tammy Way (95949)
Rates: $45-$85;
Tel: (916) 273-9102

**GOLDEN CHAIN RESORT MOTEL**
13363 SR 49 (95949)
Rates: $34-$70;
Tel: (916) 273-7279

**HOLIDAY LODGE**
1221 E Main St (95945)
Rates: $38-$50;
Tel: (916) 273-4406

## GROVELAND

**BUCK MEADOWS LODGE/ YOSEMITE WESTGATE**
7647 Hwy 120 (95321)
Rates: N/A;
Tel: (209) 962-5281

## HALF MOON BAY

**HOLIDAY INN EXPRESS**
230 Cabrillo Hwy (94019)
Rates: $61-$68;
Tel: (415) 726-3400

**ZABALLA HOUSE INN**
324 Main St (94019)
Rates: $50-$150;
Tel: (415) 726-9123

## HANFORD

**IRWIN STREET INN**
522 N Irwin (93230)
Rates: $69-$110;
Tel: (209) 583-8791

## HAYWARD

**EXECUTIVE INN**
20777 Hesperian Blvd (94541)
Rates: $68-$85;
Tel: (800) 553-5083

**THE VAGABOND INN**
20455 Hesperian Blvd (94541)
Rates: $50-$70;
Tel: (510) 785-5480

## HEMET

**COACH LIGHT MOTEL**
1640 W Florida Ave (92545)
Rates: $28-$40;
Tel: (909) 658-3237

**QUALITY INN**
800 W Florida Ave (92543)
Rates: $45-$55;
Tel: (909) 929-6366

**SUPER 8 MOTEL**
3510 W Florida Ave (92545)
Rates: $38-$46;
Tel: (909) 658-2281

## HESPERIA

**DAYS INN SUITES**
14865 Bear Valley Rd (92345)
Rates: $39-$69;
Tel: (619) 948-0600

## HIGHLAND

**SUPER 8 MOTEL**
26667 E Highland Ave (92346)
Rates: $36-$41;
Tel: (909) 864-0100

## HOLLISTER

**BEST WESTERN SAN BENITO INN**
660 San Felipe Rd (95023)
Rates: $40-$55;
Tel: (408) 637-9248

## HOLLYWOOD

**BEST WESTERN HOLLYWOOD MOTEL**
6141 Franklin Ave (90028)
Rates: $55-$80;
Tel: (213) 464-5181

**HOLIDAY INN**
1755 N Highland Ave (90028)
Rates: $94-$195;
Tel: (213) 462-7181

**OBAN HOTEL**
6364 Yucca St (90028)
Rates: N/A;
Tel: (213) 466-0524

## HOOPA

**BEST WESTERN
TSEWENALDIN INN**
P. O. Box 219 (95546)
Rates: $45-$70;
Tel: (916) 625-4294

## IDYLLWILD

**FIRESIDE INN**
P. O. Box 313 (92549)
Rates: $54-$78;
Tel: (909) 659-2966

## IMPERIAL BEACH

**HAWAIIAN GARDENS
SUITE-HOTEL**
1031 Imperial Beach Blvd
(91932)
Rates: $60-$125;
Tel: (619) 429-5303

## INDIAN WELLS

**STOUFFER
ESMERALDA RESORT**
44-400 Indian Wells Ln
(92210)
Rates: $119-$380;
Tel: (619) 773-4444

## INDIO

**BEST WESTERN
DATE TREE MOTOR HOTEL**
81-909 Indio Blvd (92201)
Rates: $42-$78;
Tel: (619) 347-3421

**RODEWAY INN
AT BIG AMERICA**
84-096 Indio Springs Dr
(92201)
Rates: $39-$76;
Tel: (619) 342-6344

**ROYAL PLAZA INN**
82-347 Hwy 111 (92201)
Rates: $36-$60;
Tel: (619) 347-0911

## IRVINE

**HOLIDAY INN-IRVINE/
ORANGE COUNTY AIRPORT**
17941 Von Karman Ave
(92714)
Rates: $85-$139;
Tel: (714) 863-1999

**HYATT REGENCY IRVINE**
17900 Jamboree Blvd (92714)
Rates: $89-$169;
Tel: (714) 975-1234

**IRVINE MARRIOTT HOTEL**
1800 Von Karman Ave
(92715)
Rates: $89-$139;
Tel: (714) 553-0100

**LA QUINTA INN**
14972 Sand Canyon Ave
(92718)
Rates: $56-$74;
Tel: (714) 551-0909

**RESIDENCE INN
BY MARRIOTT-IRVINE**
10 Morgan (92718)
Rates: $102-$160;
Tel: (714) 380-3000

## JACKSON

**AMADOR MOTEL**
12408 Kennedy Flat Rd
(95642)
Rates: $37-$42;
Tel: (209) 223-0970

**BEST WESTERN
AMADOR INN**
P. O. Box 758 (95642)
Rates: $46-$64;
Tel: (209) 223-0211

**JACKSON HOLIDAY
LODGE**
P. O. Box 1147 (95642)
Rates: $37-$60;
Tel: (209) 223-0486

## JULIAN

**PINE HILLS LODGE**
2960 La Posada, Box 2260
(92036)
Rates: N/A;
Tel: (619) 765-1100

## JUNE LAKE

**GULL LAKE LODGE**
P. O. Box 25 (93529)
Rates: $59-$75;
Tel: (619) 648) 7516

**JUNE LAKE
MOTEL & CABINS**
P. O. Box 98 (93529)
Rates: $48-$75;
Tel: (619) 648-7547

## KERNVILLE

**HI-HO RESORT LODGE**
11901 Sierra Way (93238)
Rates: $60-$80;
Tel: (619) 376-2671

**KERN LODGE MOTEL**
P. O.Box 66 (93238)
Rates: $47-$53;
Tel: (619) 376-2223

## KING CITY

**BEST WESTERN
KING CITY INN**
1190 Broadway (93930)
Rates: $42-$55;
Tel: (408) 385-6733

**COURTESY INN**
4 Broadway Cir (93930)
Rates: $42-$94;
Tel: (408) 385-4646

## LA JOLLA

**LA JOLLA PALMS INN**
6705 La Jolla Blvd (92037)
Rates: $49-$99;
Tel: (619) 454-7101

**MARRIOTT HOTEL**
4240 La Jolla Village Dr
(92037)
Rates: $149-$650;
Tel: (619) 587-1414

**RESIDENCE INN
BY MARRIOTT**
8901 Gilman Dr (92037)
Rates: $85-$139;
Tel: (619) 587-1770

**SCRIPPS INN**
555 Coast Blvd S (92037)
Rates: $90-$165;
Tel: (619) 454-3391

## LAKE ARROWHEAD

**ARROWHEAD
TREE TOP LODGE**
Box 186 (92352)
Rates: $55-$125;
Tel: (800) 358-8733

**LAKE ARROWHEAD
HILTON RESORT**
P. O. Box 1699 (92352)
Rates: $99-$239;
Tel: (909) 336-1511

## LAKE TAHOE

**ALDER INN & COTTAGES**
P. O. Box 5414
(S Lake Tahoe 96157)
Rates: $38-$95;
Tel: (916) 544-4485

**CAPTAIN'S ALPENHAUS**
P. O. Box 262 (Tahoma 96142)
Rates: $45-$100;
Tel: (916) 525-5000

**DAYS INN-
STATELINE/S LAKE TAHOE**
P. O. Box 6499
(S Lake Tahoe 96157)
Rates: $56-$92;
Tel: (916) 541-4800

**EMBASSY SUITES HOTEL**
4130 Lake Tahoe Blvd
(S Lake Tahoe 96150)
Rates: $139-$179;
Tel: (916) 544-5400

**HARRAH'S HOTEL
& CASINO**
P. O. Box 8
(Stateline, NV 89449)
Rates: $105-$175;
Tel: (702) 588-6611

**HIGH COUNTRY LODGE**
1227 Emerald Bay Rd
(S Lake Tahoe 96150)
Rates: $30-$70;
Tel: (916) 541-0508

**MATTERHORN MOTEL**
2187 Lake Tahoe Blvd
(S Lake Tahoe 96157)
Rates: $38-$58;
Tel: (916) 541-0367

**THE MONTGOMERY INN**
966 Modesto Ave
( S Lake Tahoe 96151)
Rates: N/A;
Tel: (916) 544-3871

**TAHOE SANDS INN**
P. O. Box 18692
(S Lake Tahoe 96151)
Rates: $53-$78;
Tel: (916) 544-3476

**TAHOE VALLEY MOTEL**
2241 Lake Tahoe Blvd
(S Lake Tahoe 96150)
Rates: $85-$150;
Tel: (916) 541-0353

## LA MIRADA

**RESIDENCE INN
BY MARRIOTT**
14419 Firestone Blvd (90638)
Rates: $115-$140;
Tel: (714) 523-2800

## LEE VINING

**MURPHEY'S MOTEL**
P. O. Box 57 (93541)
Rates: $32-$68;
Tel: (619) 647-6316

## LITTLE RIVER

**S S SEAFOAM LODGE**
6751 N Highway 1 (95460)
Rates: N/A;
Tel: (707) 937-1827

## LIVERMORE

**HOLIDAY INN-LIVERMORE**
720 Las Fores Rd (94550)
Rates: $53-$65;
Tel: (510) 443-4950

**RESIDENCE INN
BY MARRIOTT**
1000 Airway Blvd (94550)
Rates: $75-$113;
Tel: (510) 373-1800

**SPRINGTOWN MOTEL**
933 Bluebell Dr (94550)
Rates: N/A;
Tel: (510) 449-2211

## LODI

**BEST WESTERN
ROYAL HOST INN**
710 S Cherokee Ln (95240)
Rates: $45-$56;
Tel: (209) 369-8484

## LOMITA

**BEST WESTERN
ELDORADO INN**
2037 Pacific Coast Hwy
(90717)
Rates: $54-$61;
Tel: (310) 534-0700

## LOMPOC

**PORTO FINALE INN**
940 E Ocean Ave (93426)
Rates: $30-$50;
Tel: (805) 735-7731

**QUALITY INN
& EXECUTIVE SUITES**
1621 North H St (93436)
Rates: $46-$69;
Tel: (805) 735-8555

## REDWOOD MOTOR LODGE
1200 North H St (93436)
Rates: $40-$45;
Tel: (805) 735-3737

## TALLY HO MOTOR INN
1020 E Ocean Ave (93436)
Rates: $40-$45;
Tel: (805) 735-6444

## LONE PINE

### BEST WESTERN FRONTIER MOTEL
1008 S Main St (93545)
Rates: $46-$75;
Tel: (619) 876-5571

### DOW VILLA MOTEL
P. O. Box 205 (93545)
Rates: $52-$60;
Tel: (619) 876-5521

### NATIONAL 9 TRAILS MOTEL
633 S Main St (93545)
Rates: $32-$49;
Tel: (619) 876-5555

## LONG BEACH

### CLARION HOTEL EDGEWATER
6400 E Pacific Coast Hwy (90803)
Rates: $63;
Tel: (310) 434-8451

### HILTON-LONG BEACH AT WORLD TRADE CTR
Two World Trade Center (90831)
Rates: $99-$150;
Tel: (310) 983-3400

### HOLIDAY INN-LONG BEACH AIRPORT
2640 Lakewood Blvd (90815)
Rates: $104-$114;
Tel: (310) 597-4401

### RAMADA INN
5325 E Pacific Coast Hwy (90804)
Rates: $65-$95;
Tel: (310) 597-1341

### SHERATON LONG BEACH AT SHORELINE SQ
333 E Ocean Blvd (90802)
Rates: $135-$160;
Tel: (310) 436-3000

### TRAVELODGE/DOWNTOWN
80 Atlantic Ave (90802)
Rates: $49-$59;
Tel: (310) 435-2471

### THE VAGABOND INN
185 Atlantic Ave (90802)
Rates: N/A,
Tel: (800) 522-1555

## LOS ANGELES
(and Vicinity)

### BEST WESTERN CANOGA PARK MOTOR INN
20122 Vanowen St (Canoga Park 91305)
Rates: $49-$64;
Tel: (818) 883-1200

### BEST WESTERN HOLLYWOOD
6141 Franklin Ave (90028)
Rates: $54-$75.
Tel: (213) 464-5181

### BEST WESTERN THE MAYFAIR
1256 W 7th St (90017)
Rates: $75-$130;
Tel: (213) 484-9789

### BEVERLY HILLS COMSTOCK HOTEL
10300 Wilshire Blvd (90024)
Rates: $95-$290;
Tel: (310) 275-5575

### BRENTWOOD SUITES HOTEL
199 N Church Ln (90049)
Rates: $85-$105;
Tel: (310) 476-6255

### CENTURY PLAZA HOTEL & TOWER
2025 Avenue of the Stars (90067)
Rates: $175-$300;
Tel: (310) 277-2000

### CHATEAU MARMONT HOTEL
8221 Sunset Blvd (90046)
Rates: $145-$550;
Tel: (213) 656-1010

### CHECKERS HOTEL
535 S Grand Ave (90071)
Rates: $180-$190;
Tel: (213) 624-0000

### CROWN STERLING SUITES-LOS ANGELES
1440 E Imperial Ave (El Segundo 90245)
Rates: $99;
Tel: (310) 640-3600

### ECONO LODGE LAX
4123 W Century Blvd (Inglewood 90304)
Rates: $35-$50;
Tel: (310) 672-7285

### EMBASSY SUITES HOTEL-LAX/CENTURY
9801 Airport Blvd (90045)
Rates: $99;
Tel: (310) 214-1000

### HALLMARK HOTEL
7023 Sunset Blvd (90028)
Rates: $56-$75;
Tel: (213) 464-8344

### HAMPTON INN
10300 La Cienega Blvd (Inglewood 90304)
Rates: $65-$88;
Tel: (310) 337-1000

### HILTON & TOWERS-UNIVERSAL CITY
555 University Ter Pky (Universal City 91608)
Rates: $150-$1395;
Tel: (818) 506-2500

### HILTON WARNER CENTER
6360 Canoga Ave (Woodland Hills 91367)
Rates: N/A;
Tel: (818) 595-1000

### HOLIDAY INN CONVENTION CENTER
1020 S Figueroa St (90015)
Rates: $89-$129;
Tel: (213) 748-1291

**HOLIDAY INN-DOWNTOWN**
750 Garland Ave (90017)
Rates: $89-$99;
Tel: (213) 628-5242

**HOLIDAY INN-HOLLYWOOD**
1755 N Highland Ave (90028)
Rates: $85-$135;
Tel: (213) 462-7181

**HOLIDAY INN-WESTWOOD PLAZA**
10740 Wilshire Blvd (90024)
Rates: $120-$250;
Tel: (310) 475-8711

**HOLLYWOOD CELEBRITY HOTEL**
1775 Orchid Ave (90028)
Rates: $65-$83;
Tel: (213) 850-6464

**HOTEL SOFITEL MA MAISON**
8555 Beverly Blvd (90048)
Rates: $190-$230;
Tel: (310) 278-5444

**LAX HOTEL**
1804 E Sycamore St
(El Segundo 90245)
Rates: $45-$62;
Tel: (310) 615-1073

**LOS ANGELES AIRPORT HILTON & TOWERS**
5711 W Century Blvd (90045)
Rates: $135-$180;
Tel: (310) 410-4000

**LOS ANGELES AIRPORT MARRIOTT HOTEL**
5855 W Century Blvd (90045)
Rates: $119-$165;
Tel: (310) 641-5700

**MARRIOTT-WARNER CENTER**
21850 Oxnard St
(Woodland Hills 91367)
Rates: $139-$1500;
Tel: (818) 887-4800

**RADISSON HOTEL**
6300 E Telegraph (90040)
Rates: N/A;
Tel: (800) 333-3333

**RAMADA HOTEL**
6333 Bristol Pkwy
(Culver City 90230)
Rates: $85-$105;
Tel: (310) 670-3200

**SHERATON TOWN HOUSE**
2961 Wilshire Blvd (90010)
Rates: $95-$125;
Tel: (213) 382-7171

**SUMMERFIELD SUITES HOTEL**
21902 Lassen St
(Chatsworth 91311)
Rates: $80-$158;
Tel: (818) 773-0707

**THE VAGABOND INN**
20157 Ventura Blvd
(Woodland Hills 91364)
Rates: $45-$70;
Tel: (818) 347-8080

**THE VAGABOND INN FIGUEROA**
3101 S Figueroa St (90007)
Rates: $55-$75;
Tel: (800) 522-1555

**THE VAGABOND INN**
1904 W Olympic Blvd (90006)
Rates: N/A;
Tel: (800) 522-1555

**VISCOUNT HOTEL-LOS ANGELES**
9750 Airport Blvd (90045)
Rates: $75-$85;
Tel: (310) 645-4600

**WARNER CENTER MOTOR INN**
7132 DeSoto Ave
(Canoga Park 91303)
Rates: $40-$70;
Tel: (818) 346-5400

**THE WESTIN BONAVENTURE**
404 S Figueroa St (90071)
Rates: $89-$150;
Tel: (213) 624-1000

## LOS BANOS

**BONANZA MOTEL**
349 W Pacheco Blvd (93635)
Rates: $30-$42;
Tel: (209) 826-3871

**HOLIDAY INN MISSION DE ORO**
13070 S CA 33
(Santa Nella 95322)
Rates: $39-$64;
Tel: (209) 826-4444

## LOS GATOS

**LOS GATOS LODGE**
50 Saratoga Ave (95032)
Rates: $79-$89;
Tel: (408) 354-3300

## MADERA

**BEST WESTERN MADERA VALLEY INN**
217 North G St (93637)
Rates: $52-$66;
Tel: (209) 673-5164

**ECONOMY INNS OF AMERICA**
1855 W Cleveland Ave
(93637)
Rates: $26-$38;
Tel: (209) 661-1131

## MAMMOTH LAKES

**ECONOLODGE WILDWOOD INN**
P. O. Box 568 (93546)
Rates: $49-$89;
Tel: (619) 934-6855

**NORTH VILLAGE INN**
P. O. Box 1984 (93546)
Rates: $42-$69;
Tel: (619) 934-2525

**ROYAL PINES RESORT**
P. O. Box 348 (93546)
Rates: $44-$74;
Tel: (619) 934-2306

**SHILO INN**
P. O. Box 2179 (93546)
Rates: $74-$150;
Tel: (619) 934-4500

# CALIFORNIA

## MANHATTAN BEACH

**RESIDENCE INN
BY MARRIOTT**
1700 N Sepulveda Blvd
(90266)
Rates: $89-$189;
Tel: (310) 546-7627

## MARINA DEL REY/VENICE

**FOGHORN HARBOR INN**
4140 Via Marina (90292)
Rates: $80-$110;
Tel: (310) 823 4626

**MARINA DEL REY
MARRIOTT**
13480 Maxella Ave
(Marina del Rey 90291)
Rates: 139-$159;
Tel: (310) 822-8555

## MARIPOSA

**MARIPOSA LODGE**
5052 Hwy 140, Box 733
(95338)
Rates: N/A,
Tel: (209) 966-3607

## MENDOCINO

**BIG RIVER LODGE-
STANFORD INN
BY THE SEA**
P. O. Box 487 (95460)
Rates: $135-$250;
Tel: (707) 937-5615

## MIDPINES

**HOMESTEAD
GUEST RANCH**
P. O. Box 13 (95345)
Rates: N/A,
Tel: (209) 966-2820

## MILL VALLEY

**HOWARD JOHNSON
MOTOR LODGE**
160 Shoreline Hwy (94941)
Rates: $72-$86;
Tel: (415) 332-5700

## MILPITAS

**BROOKSIDE INN**
400 Valley Way (95035)
Rates: $39-$44;
Tel: (408) 265-5566

**ECONOMY INNS
OF AMERICA**
270 S Abbott Ave (95035)
Rates: $39-$49;
Tel: (408) 946-8889

## MIRANDA

**MIRANDA
GARDENS RESORT**
P. O. Box 186 (95553)
Rates: $45-$145;
Tel: (707) 943-3011

## MISSION VIEJO

**HAMPTON INN**
26328 Oso Pkwy (92691)
Rates: $57-$64;
Tel: (714) 582-7100

## MI-WUK VILLAGE

**MI-WUK MOTOR LODGE**
P. O. Box 70 (95346)
Rates: $41-$60;
Tel: (209) 586-3031

## MODESTO

**BEST WESTERN
TOWN HOUSE LODGE**
909 16th St (95354)
Rates: $44-$58;
Tel: (209) 524-7261

**RED LION HOTEL**
1150 9th St (95354)
Rates: $85-$127;
Tel: (209) 526-6000

**THE VAGABOND INN**
1525 McHenry Ave (95350)
Rates: $38-$57;
Tel: (209) 521-6340

## MOJAVE

**SCOTTISH INNS**
16352 Sierra Hwy (93501)
Rates: $35-$55,
Tel: (805) 824-9317

## MONROVIA

**HOLIDAY INN**
924 W Huntington Dr (91016)
Rates: $75-$79;
Tel: (818) 357-1900

## MONTE RIO

**HIGHLAND DELL INN**
P. O. Box 370 (95462)
Rates: $65-$225;
Tel: (707) 865-1759

## MONTEREY
(and MONTEREY PENINSULA)

**BAY PARK HOTEL**
1425 Munras Ave (93940)
Rates: $69-$129;
Tel: (408) 649-1020

**BEST WESTERN
VICTORIAN INN**
487 Foam St (93940)
Rates: $119-$189;
Tel: (408) 373-8000

**CALIFORNIAN MOTEL**
2042 Fremont St (93940)
Rates: $29-$99;
Tel: (408) 372-5851

**CYPRESS GARDENS INN**
1150 Munras Ave (93940)
Rates: $84-$225;
Tel: (408) 373-2761

<footer>67</footer>

**EL ADOBE INN**
936 Munras Ave (93940)
Rates: $54-$89;
Tel: (408) 372-5409

**HOLIDAY INN RESORT**
1000 Aquajito Rd (93940)
Rates: $112-$172;
Tel: (408) 373-6141

**MONTEREY BEACH HOTEL-
BEST WESTERN**
2600 Sand Dunes Dr (93940)
Rates: $89-$169;
Tel: (408) 394-3321

**MONTEREY
FIRESIDE LODGE**
1131 10th St (93940)
Rates: $55-$99;
Tel: (408) 373-4172

**MONTEREY MARRIOTT**
350 Calle Principal (93940)
Rates: $150-$170;
Tel: (408) 649-4234

**MONTEREY
MOTOR LODGE**
55 Camino Aquajito (93940)
Rates: $49-$110;
Tel: (408) 372-8057

**SAND DOLLAR INN**
755 Abrego St (93940)
Rates: $59-$109;
Tel: (408) 372-7551

## MORGAN HILL

**BEST WESTERN
COUNTRY INN**
16525 Condit Rd (95037)
Rates: $54-$76;
Tel: (408) 779-0447

## MORRO BAY

**BEST VALUE INN**
220 Beach St (93442)
Rates: $30-$72;
Tel: (805) 772-3333

**BEST WESTERN
EL RANCHO**
2460 Main St (93442)
Rates: $49-$89;
Tel: (805) 772-2212

**GOLD COAST**
670 Main ST (93442)
Rates: $30-$85;
Tel: (805) 772-7740

## MOUNTAIN VIEW

**BEST WESTERN
TROPICANA LODGE**
1720 El Camino Real W
(94040)
Rates: $55-$80;
Tel: (415) 961-0220

**RESIDENCE INN
BY MARRIOTT**
1854 El Camino Real (94040)
Rates: $134-$159;
Tel: (415) 940-1300

## MOUNT SHASTA

**ALPINE LODGE MOTEL**
908 S Mt. Shasta Blvd
(96067)
Rates: N/A;
Tel: (916) 926-3145

**MOUNTAIN AIR LODGE**
1121 S Mount Shasta Blvd
(96067)
Rates: $32-$56;
Tel: (916) 926-3411

**SWISS HOLIDAY LODGE**
2400 S Mount Shasta Blvd
(96067)
Rates: $32-$56;
Tel: (916) 926-3446

**THE TREE HOUSE
BEST WESTERN**
P. O. Box 236 (96067)
Rates: $56-$130;
Tel: (916) 926-3101

## NAPA

**BEST WESTERN INN**
100 Soscol Ave (94558)
Rates: $65-$150;
Tel: (707) 257-1930

**CHABLIS LODGE**
3360 Solano Ave (94558)
Rates: N/A;
Tel: (707) 257-1944

**CLARION INN
NAPA VALLEY**
3425 Solano Ave (94558)
Rates: $59-$119;
Tel: (707) 253-7433

## NEEDLES

**BEST MOTEL**
1900 W Broadway (92363)
Rates: $25-$30;
Tel: (619) 326-3824

**BEST WESTERN
COLORADO RIVER INN**
2271 W Broadway (92363)
Rates: $40-$60;
Tel: (619) 326-4552

**BEST WESTERN
OVERLAND MOTEL**
712 Broadway (92363)
Rates: $34-$60;
Tel: (619) 326-3821

**DAYS INN**
1111 Pashard St (92363)
Rates: $40-$65;
Tel: (619) 326-5660

**IMPERIAL 400 MOTEL**
644 Broadway (92363)
Rates: $22-$38;
Tel: (619) 326-2145

**RIVER VALLEY
MOTOR LODGE**
1707 W Broadway (92363)
Rates: $21-$34;
Tel: (619) 326-3839

## NEWARK

**WOODFIN SUITES**
39150 Cedar Blvd (94560)
Rates: $79-$84;
Tel: (510) 795-1200

## NEWPORT BEACH

**FOUR SEASONS HOTEL**
690 Newport Center Dr
(92660)
Rates: $195-$295;
Tel: (714) 759-0808

HYATT NEWPORTER
1107 Jamboree Rd (92660)
Rates: $119-$204;
Tel: (714) 729-1234

NEWPORT BEACH
MARRIOTT HOTEL
900 Newport Center Dr
(92660)
Rates: $144-$169;
Tel: (714) 640-4000

## NOVATO

RUSH CREEK
NOVATO TRAVELODGE
7600 Redwood Blvd (94945)
Rates: $55-$65;
Tel: (415) 892-7500

## OAKLAND

DAYS INN-OAKLAND AIRPORT
8350 Edes Ave (94621)
Rates: $59-$84;
Tel: (510) 568-1880

HAMPTON INN
OAKLAND AIRPORT
8485 Enterprise Way (94621)
Rates: $64-$75;
Tel: (510) 632-8900

HILTON
OAKLAND AIRPORT
P. O. Box 2549 (94614)
Rates: $120-$160;
Tel: (510) 635-5000

HOLIDAY INN-
OAKLAND AIRPORT
500 Hegenberger Rd (94621)
Rates: $79-$105;
Tel: (510) 562-5311

LAKE MERRITT HOTEL
1800 Madison (94612)
Rates: $79-$149;
Tel: (510) 832-2300

## OCCIDENTAL

NEGRI'S OCCIDENTAL LODGE
P. O. Box 84 (95465)
Rates: $38-$48;
Tel: (707) 874-3623

## OCEANSIDE

SANDMAN MOTEL
1501 Carmelo Dr (92054)
Rates: $36-$49;
Tel: (619) 722-76621

## OJAI

BEST WESTERN CASA OJAI
1302 E Ojai Ave (93023)
Rates: N/A;
Tel: (800) 255-8175

OJAI VALLEY INN
& COUNTRY CLUB
P. O. Box L (93023)
Rates: $190-$250;
Tel: (800) 422-6524

## ONTARIO

COUNTRY INN
2359 S Grove Ave (91761)
Rates: $39-$49;
Tel: (909) 923-1887

COUNTRY SUITES
BY CARLSON
231 N Vineyard Ave (91764)
Rates: $62-$72;
Tel: (909) 983-8484

HOLIDAY INN-
ONTARIO INTL AIRPORT
1801 East G St (91764)
Rates: $67-$80;
Tel: (909) 983-3604

HOWARD JOHNSON
LODGE-ONTARIO
AIRPORT SOUTH
2425 S Archibald Ave (91761)
Rates: $40-$72;
Tel: (909) 923-2728

INN SUITES
ONTARIO AIRPORT HOTEL
3400 Shelby St (91764)
Rates: $62-$76;
Tel: (909) 466-9600

RED LION HOTEL
222 N Vineyard Ave (91764)
Rates: $59-$79;
Tel: (909) 983-0909

RESIDENCE INN
BY MARRIOTT
2025 East D St (91764)
Rates: $99-$129;
Tel: (909) 983-6788

## ORANGE

DOUBLETREE HOTEL
AT THE CITY
100 The City Dr (92668)
Rates: $125-$155;
Tel: (714) 634-4500

THE RESIDENCE INN
BY MARRIOTT
201 N State College Blvd
(92668)
Rates: $89-$145;
Tel: (714) 978-7700

## ORLAND

ORLAND INN
1052 South St (95963)
Rates: $28-$40;
Tel: (916) 865-7632

## OROVILLE

BEST WESTERN
GRAND MANOR INN
1470 Feather River Blvd
(95965)
Rates: $53-$91;
Tel: (916) 533-9673

## OXNARD

FRIENDSHIP INN REGALODGE
1012 S Oxnard Blvd (93030)
Rates: N/A;
Tel: (805) 486-8383

THE VAGABOND INN
1245 N Oxnard Blvd (93030)
Rates: N/A;
Tel: (800) 522-1555

# PACIFIC GROVE

**BEST WESTERN
BUTTERFLY TREES LODGE**
1150 Lighthouse Ave (93950)
Rates: $59-$109;
Tel: (408) 372-0503

**BID-A-WEE MOTEL**
221 Asilomar Blvd (93950)
Rates: N/A;
Tel: (408) 372-2330

# PALMDALE

**THE VAGABOND INN**
130 E Palmdale Blvd (93550)
Rates: N/A;
Tel: (800) 522-1555

# PALM SPRINGS

**CAMBRIDGE INN**
1277 S Palm Canyon Dr
(92264)
Rates: $30-$42;
Tel: (619) 325-5574

**CASA CODY COUNTRY INN**
175 S Cahuilla Rd (92262)
Rates: $40-$160;
Tel: (619) 320-9346

**DOUBLETREE RESORT
AT DESERT PRINCESS**
CC 67-967 Vista Chino
(92263)
Rates: $50-$110;
Tel: (619) 322-7000

**DUESENBERG
MOTOR LODGE**
269 Chuckwalla Rd (92262)
Rates: $45-$65;
Tel: (619) 326-2567

**HILTON RESORT-
PALM SPRINGS**
400 E Tahquitz Canyon Way
(92262)
Rates: $80-$295;
Tel: (619) 320-6868

**HYATT REGENCY SUITES
PALM SPRINGS**
285 N Palm Canyon Dr
(92262)
Rates: $199-$229;
Tel: (619) 322-9000

**QUALITY INN**
1269 E Palm Canyon Dr
(92264)
Rates: $35-$119;
Tel: (619) 323-2775

# PALO ALTO

**DAYS INN**
4238 El Camino Real (94306)
Rates: $49-$100;
Tel: (415) 493-4222

**HAYTT PALO ALTO**
4290 El Camino Real (94306)
Rates: $75-$175;
Tel: (415) 493-0800

**HYATT RICKEYS**
4219 El Camino Real (94306)
Rates: $75-$170;
Tel: (415) 493-8000

# PARADISE

**PALOS VERDES MOTEL**
P. O. Box 458 (95967)
Rates: $35-$39;
Tel: (916) 877-2127

**PONDEROSA
GARDENS MOTEL**
7010 Skyway (95969)
Rates: $47-$65;
Tel: (916) 872-9094

# PASADENA

**HOLIDAY INN**
303 E Cordova St (91101)
Rates: $88-$125;
Tel: (818) 449-4000

**PASADENA HILTON**
150 S Los Robles Ave (91101)
Rates: $119-$175;
Tel: (818) 577-1000

**THE VAGABOND INN**
2863 E Colorado Blvd (91107)
Rates: $42-$62;
Tel: (800) 522-1555

# PASO ROBLES

**TRAVELODGE PASO ROBLES**
2701 Spring St (93446)
Rates: $34-$75;
Tel: (805) 238-0078

# PEBBLE BEACH

**THE LODGE AT PEBBLE BEACH**
P. O. Box 1128 (93953)
Rates: $280-$425;
Tel: (408) 624-3811

# PETALUMA

**QUALITY INN-PETALUMA**
5100 Montero Way (94954)
Rates: $54-$102;
Tel: (707) 664-115

# PETROLLA

**MATTOLE RIVER RESORT**
42354 Mattole Rd (95558)
Rates: N/A;
Tel: (800) 845-4607

# PHELAN

**ECONOMY INN**
8317 Hwy 138
(Cajon Pass 92371)
Rates: $48-$57;
Tel: (619) 249-6777

# PIERCY

**HARTSOOK INN**
900 Hwy 101 (95467)
Rates: N/A;
Tel: (707) 573-8553

## PINE VALLEY

**SUNRISE MOTEL**
P. O. Box 378 (91962)
Rates: $39-$49;
Tel: (619) 473-8777

## PISMO BEACH

**QUALITY SUITES**
651 Five Cities Dr (93449)
Rates: $79-$128;
Tel: (805) 773-3773

**SANDCASTLE INN**
100 Stimson Ave (93449)
Rates: $75-$145;
Tel: (805) 773-2422

**SPYGLASS INN**
2705 Spyglass Dr (93449)
Rates: $74-$125;
Tel: (805) 773-4855

## PLACENTIA

**RESIDENCE INN
BY MARRIOTT**
700 W Kimberly Ave (92670)
Rates: $65-$105;
Tel: (714) 996-0555

## PLACERVILLE

**BEST WESTERN
PLACERVILLE INN**
6850 Greenleaf Dr (95667)
Rates: $59-$135;
Tel: (916) 622-9100

**GOLD TRAIL
MOTOR LODGE**
1970 Broadway (95667)
Rates: $36-$51;
Tel: (916) 622-2906

**MOTHER LODE MOTEL**
1940 Broadway (95667)
Rates: $34-$51;
Tel: (916) 622-0895

**STAGECOACH MOTOR INN**
5940 Pony Express Trl
(Pollock Pines 95726)
Rates: $48-$95;
Tel: (800) 622-8802

## PLEASANT HILL

**RESIDENCE INN BY
MARRIOTT-PLEASANT HILL**
700 Ellinwood Way (94523)
Rates: $89-$119;
Tel: (510) 689-1010

## PLEASANTON

**DOUBLETREE CLUB**
5990 Stoneridge Mall Rd
(94588)
Rates: $59-$99;
Tel: (510) 463-3330

**HOLIDAY INN**
11950 Dublin Canyon Rd
(94588)
Rates: $61-$90;
Tel: (510) 847-6000

**PLEASANTON HILTON**
7050 Johnson Dr (94588)
Rates: $59-$129;
Tel: (510) 463-8000

**SUPER 8 LODGE**
5375 Owens Ct (94588)
Rates: $52-$58;
Tel: (510) 463-1300

## PLYMOUTH

**SHENANDOAH INN**
17674 Village Dr (95669)
Rates: $52-$65;
Tel: (209) 245-4491

## POMONA

**SHERATON SUITES
FAIRPLEX**
600 W McKinley Ave (91768)
Rates: N/A;
Tel: (909) 622-2220

**SHILO INN HOTEL-
DIAMOND BAR/POMONA**
3200 Temple Ave (91768)
Rates: $84-$104;
Tel: (909) 598-0073

## PORTOLA

**UPPER FEATHER
BED & BREAKFAST**
256 Commercial St (96122)
Rates: N/A;
Tel: (916) 832-0107

## QUINCY

**GOLD PAN MOTEL**
200 Cresent (95971)
Rates: N/A;
Tel: (916) 283-3686

## RANCHO BERNARDO

**CARMEL HIGHLAND
DOUBLETREE GOLF
& TENNIS RESORT**
14455 Penasquitos Dr
(San Diego 92129)
Rates: $99-$129;
Tel: (619) 672-9100

**HOLIDAY INN
RANCHO BERNARDO**
17065 W Bernardo Dr
(San Diego 92127)
Rates: $62-$68;
Tel: (619) 485-6530

**LA QUINTA INN**
10185 Paseo Montril
(San Diego 92129)
Rates: $45-$58;
Tel: (619) 484-8800

**RADISSON SUITE HOTEL**
11520 W Bernardo Ct
(San Diego 92127)
Rates: $79-$119;
Tel: (619) 451-6600

**RANCHO BERNARDO
TRAVELODGE**
16929 W Bernardo Dr
(San Diego 92127)
Rates: $55-$70;
Tel: (619) 487-0445

**RESIDENCE INN
BY MARRIOTT**
11002 Rancho Carmel Dr
(San Diego 92128)
Rates: $109-$139;
Tel: (619) 673-1900

## RANCHO CORDOVA

**COMFORT INN**
3240 Mather Field Rd (95670)
Rates: $49-$74;
Tel: (916) 363-3344

**ECONOMY INN'S
OF AMERICA**
12249 Folsom Blvd (95670)
Rates: $34-$42;
Tel: (916) 351-1213

## RANCHO MIRAGE

**MARRIOTT'S RANCHO
LAS PALMAS RESORT**
41000 Bob Hope Dr (92270)
Rates: $75-$175;
Tel: (800) 458-8786

**THE WESTIN
MISSION HILLS RESORT**
71-333 Dinah Shore Dr
(92270)
Rates: $115-$385;
Tel: (619) 328-5955

## RED BLUFF

**CINDERELLA RIVERVIEW
MOTEL**
600 Rio St (96080)
Rates: $32-$48;
Tel: (916) 527-5490

**NENDELS VALU INN**
30 Gilmore Rd (96080)
Rates: $39-$49;
Tel: (916) 529-2028

## REDDING

**BEST WESTERN
HOSPITALITY HOUSE**
532 N Market St (96003)
Rates: $42-$52;
Tel: (916) 241-6464

**BEST WESTERN
PONDEROSA INN**
2220 Pine St (96001)
Rates: $39-$53;
Tel: (916) 241-6300

**DAYS HOTEL-REDDING**
2180 Hilltop Dr (96002)
Rates: $54-$89;
Tel: (916) 221-8200

**HOLIDAY INN OF REDDING**
1900 Hilltop Dr (96002)
Rates: $66-$82;
Tel: (916) 221-7500

**RED LION INN**
1830 Hilltop Dr (96002)
Rates: $81-$118;
Tel: (916) 221-8700

**RIVER INN**
1835 Park Marina Dr (96001)
Rates: $42-$48;
Tel: (916) 241-9500

**SHASTA DAM
EL RANCHO MOTEL**
P. O. Box 1033
(Project City 96079)
Rates: $26-$36;
Tel: (916) 275-1065

**THE VAGABOND INN**
536 E Cypress Ave (96002)
Rates: $47-$75;
Tel: (800) 522-1555

## REDONDO BEACH

**PORTOFINO
HOTEL & YACHT CLUB**
260 Portofino Way (90277)
Rates: $129-$159;
Tel: (310) 379-8481

**THE VAGABOND INN**
6226 Pacific Coast Hwy
(90277)
Rates: N/A;
Tel: (800) 522-1555

## REDWOOD CITY

**HOWARD JOHNSON
MOTOR LODGE**
485 Veterans Blvd (94063)
Rates: $59-$94;
Tel: (415) 365-5500

## RIDGECREST

**HERITAGE INN**
P. O. Box 640 (93556)
Rates: $69-$93;
Tel: (619) 446-6543

**HERITAGE SUITES**
P. O. Box 640 (93556)
Rates: $89-$111;
Tel: (619) 446-7951

## RIVERSIDE

**DYNASTY SUITES**
3735 Iowa Ave (92507)
Rates: $39-$49;
Tel: (909) 369-8200

**HOLIDAY INN**
1200 University Ave (92507)
Rates: $64-$75;
Tel: (909) 682-8000

**SUPER 8 MOTEL**
1199 University Ave (92507)
Rates: $32-$39;
Tel: (909) 682-9011

## ROCKLIN

**FIRST CHOICE INNS**
4420 Rocklin Rd (95677)
Rates: $60-$90;
Tel: (916) 624-4500

## ROHNERT PARK

**RED LION HOTEL**
1 Red Lion Dr (94928)
Rates: $101-$140;
Tel: (707) 584-5466

## ROSAMOND

**DEVONSHIRE INN MOTEL**
P. O. Box 2080 (93560)
Rates: $49-$59;
Tel: (805) 256-3454

## ROSEMEAD

**THE VAGABOND INN**
3633 N Rosemead Blvd
(91770)
Rates: $44-$64;
Tel: (800) 522-1555

## ROSEVILLE

**BEST WESTERN
HERITAGE INN**
204 Harding Blvd (95678)
Rates: $51-$65;
Tel: (916) 782-4466

**BEST WESTERN
ROSEVILLE INN**
220 Harding Blvd (95678)
Rates: $48-$55;
Tel: (916) 782-4434

## SACRAMENTO
(and Vicinity)

**BEVERLY GARLAND HOTEL**
1780 Tribute Rd (95815)
Rates: $55-$95;
Tel: (916) 929-7900

**CANTERBURY INN**
1900 Canterbury Rd (95815)
Rates: $55-$65;
Tel: (916) 927-3492

**CLARION MOTOR HOTEL**
700 16th St (95814)
Rates: $99-$262,
Tel: (916) 444-8000

**CROSSROADS INN**
221 Jibboom St (95814)
Rates: $38-$60;
Tel: (916) 442-7777

**DAYS INN**
200 Jibboom St (95814)
Rates: $52-$68;
Tel: (916) 448-8100

**ECONO LODGE**
1319 30th St (95816)
Rates: $44-$50;
Tel: (916) 454-4400

**HILTON INN-SACRAMENTO**
2200 Harvard St (95815)
Rates: $99-$109;
Tel: (916) 922-4700

**HOLIDAY INN-
CAPITOL PLAZA**
300 J St (95814)
Rates: $82-$550;
Tel: (916) 446-0100

**HOLIDAY INN
NORTH EAST**
5321 Date Ave (95841)
Rates: $66;
Tel: (916) 338-5800

**HOWARD JOHNSON
HOTEL**
3343 Bradshaw Rd (95827)
Rates: $61-$66;
Tel: (916) 366-1266

**LA QUINTA INN**
4064 Madison Ave (95841)
Rates: $52-$65;
Tel: (916) 348-0900

**MANSION VIEW LODGE**
771 16th St (95814)
Rates: $36-$42;
Tel: (916) 443-6631

**MOTEL ORLEANS**
228 Jibboom St (95814)
Rates: N/A;
Tel: (916) 443-4811

**RADISSON HOTEL**
500 Leisure Ln (95815)
Rates: $72-$82;
Tel: (916) 922-2020

**RED LION INN**
2001 Point West Way (95815)
Rates: $82-$143;
Tel: (916) 929-8855

**RED LION'S
SACRAMENTO INN**
1401 Arden Way (95815)
Rates: $65-$117;
Tel: (916) 922-8041

**SIERRA INN**
2600 Auburn Blvd (95821)
Rates: N/A;
Tel: (916) 482-4770

**THE VAGABOND INN**
903 3rd St (95814)
Rates: $50-$74;
Tel: (800) 522-1555

## ST. HELENA

**EL BONITA MOTEL**
195 Main St (94574)
Rates: $46-$99;
Tel: (707) 963-3216

**HARVEST INN**
One Main St (94574)
Rates: $90-$325;
Tel: (707) 963-9463

## SALINAS

**BEST WESTERN
AIRPORT MOTOR INN**
555 Airport Blvd (93905)
Rates: $38-$95;
Tel: (408) 424-1741

**DAYS INN**
1226 de la Torre St (93905)
Rates: $35-$90;
Tel: (408) 759-9900

**EL DORADO MOTEL**
1351 N Main St (93906)
Rates: $28-$60;
Tel: (408) 449-2442

**THE VAGABOND INN**
131 Kern St (93905)
Rates: $35-$60;
Tel: (800) 522-1555

## SAN BERNARDINO

**BEST WESTERN
SANDS MOTEL**
606 North H St (92410)
Rates: $52-$60;
Tel: (909) 889-8391

**LA QUINTA INN**
205 E Hospitality Ln (92408)
Rates: $52-$67;
Tel: (909) 888-7571

# SAN CLEMENTE

## HOLIDAY INN-
## SAN CLEMENTE RESORT
111 S Avenida de Estrella
(92672)
Rates: $70-$95;
Tel: (714) 361-3000

# SAN DIEGO
(and Vicinity)

## BEACH HAVEN INN
4740 Mission Blvd (92109)
Rates: $60-$105;
Tel: (619) 272-3812

## BEST WESTERN
## SEVEN SEAS
411 Hotel Circle S (92108)
Rates: $49-$99;
Tel: (619) 291-1300

## CROWN POINT VIEW
## SUITE-HOTEL
4088 Crown Point Dr (92109)
Rates: $70-$150;
Tel: (619) 272-0676

## HOLIDAY INN
## MONTGOMERY FIELD
8110 Aero Dr (92123)
Rates: $76-$112;
Tel: (619) 277-8888

## HOLIDAY INN
## ON THE BAY
1355 N Harbor Dr (92101)
Rates: $68-$98;
Tel: (619) 232-3861

## HOTEL CIRCLE INN
## & SUITES
2201 Hotel Circle S (92108)
Rates: $49-$99;
Tel: (619) 291-2711

## HOWARD JOHNSON
## HOTEL
4545 Waring Rd (92120)
Rates: $50-$85;
Tel: (619) 286-7000

## LA QUINTA INN
10185 Paseo Montril (92129)
Rates: $53-$80;
Tel: (619) 484-8800

## LOEWS CORONADO
## BAY RESORT
4000 Coronado Bay Rd
(Coronado 92118)
Rates: $180-$240;
Tel: (619) 424-4000

## MARRIOTT
## SAN DIEGO MARINA
333 W Harbor Dr (92101)
Rates: $149-$179;
Tel: (619) 234-1500

## RADISSON HOTEL
## HARBOR VIEW
1646 Front St (92101)
Rates: $109-$129;
Tel: (619) 239-6800

## RADISSON HOTEL-
## SAN DIEGO
1433 Camino Del Rio S
(92108)
Rates: $79-$135;
Tel: (619) 260-0111

## RED LION INN
7450 Hazard Center Dr
(92108)
Rates: $130-$165;
Tel: (619) 297-5466

## RESIDENCE INN BY
## MARRIOTT KEARNY MESA
5400 Kearny Mesa Rd
(92111)
Rates: $75-$129;
Tel: (619) 278-2100

## SAN DIEGO HILTON
## BEACH & TENNIS RESORT
1775 E Mission Bay Dr
(92109)
Rates: $130-$235;
Tel: (619) 276-4010

## SAN DIEGO MARRIOTT
## MISSION VALLEY
8757 Rio San Diego Dr
(92108)
Rates: $149-$159;
Tel: (619) 692-3800

## SAN DIEGO MARRIOTT
## SUITES-DOWNTOWN
701 A St (92101)
Rates: $170-$180;
Tel: (619) 696-9800

## SAN DIEGO
## MISSION VALLEY HILTON
901 Camino Del Rio S (92108)
Rates: $79-$129;
Tel: (619) 543-9000

## SAN DIEGO
## PRINCESS RESORT
1404 W Vacation Rd (92109)
Rates: $120-$195;
Tel: (619) 274-4630

## SHERATON
## HARBOR ISLAND HOTEL
1380 Harbor Island Dr
(92101)
Rates: $150-$170;
Tel: (619) 291-2900

## TOWN HOUSE LODGE
810 Ash St (92101)
Rates: N/A;
Tel: (619) 233-8826

## THE VAGABOND INN
1325 Scott St (92106)
Rates: N/A;
Tel: (800) 522-1555

## THE VAGABOND INN-
## EL CAJON
6440 El Cajon Blvd (92115)
Rates: N/A;
Tel: (800) 522-1555

## THE VAGABOND INN-
## MISSION VALLEY
625 Hotel Circle South
(92108)
Rates: $41-$67;
Tel: (800) 522-1555

# SAN FRANCISCO
(and Vicinity)

## BERESFORD HOTEL
635 Sutter St (94102)
Rates: $79-$89;
Tel: (415) 673-9900

## BEST WESTERN
## CARRIAGE INN
140 7th St (94103)
Rates: $74-$109;
Tel: (415) 552-8600

**BEST WESTERN
EL RANCHO INN**
1100 El Camino Real
(Millbrae 94030)
Rates: $74-$150;
Tel: (415) 588-8500

**CAMPTON PLACE
HOTEL-KEMPINSKI
SAN FRANCISCO**
340 Stockton St (94108)
Rates: $185-$320;
Tel: (415) 781-5555

**CLARION-
SAN FRANCISCO AIRPORT**
401 E Millbrae Ave
(Millbrae 94030)
Rates: $99-$250;
Tel: (415) 692-6363

**DAYS INN-AIRPORT**
777 Airport Blvd
(Burlingame 94010)
Rates: $70-$100;
Tel: (415) 342-7772

**DOUBLETREE HOTEL-
SAN FRANCISCO AIRPORT**
835 Airport Blvd
(Burlingame 94010)
Rates: $69-$79;
Tel: (415) 344-5500

**FOUR SEASONS CLIFT**
495 Geary St (94102)
Rates: $205-$690;
Tel: (415) 775-4700

**HOLIDAY INN-AIRPORT**
245 S Airport Blvd
(S San Francisco 94080)
Rates: $70-$110;
Tel: (415) 589-7200

**HOLIDAY INN-
FISHERMAN'S WHARF**
1300 Columbus Ave (94133)
Rates: $125-$400;
Tel: (415) 771-900

**LAUREL MOTOR INN**
444 Presidio Ave (94115)
Rates: $70-$98;
Tel: (415) 567-8467

**THE MANSIONS HOTEL**
2220 Sacramento St (94115)
Rates: N/A;
Tel: (415) 929-9444

**MARRIOTT
FISHERMAN'S WHARF**
1250 Columbus Ave (94133)
Rates: $148-$450;
Tel: (415) 775-7555

**THE PAN PACIFIC HOTEL**
500 Post St (94102)
Rates: $185-$350;
Tel: (415) 771-8600

**PICKWICK HOTEL**
85 Fifth St (94103)
Rates: N/A;
Tel: (415) 673-2322

**RODEWAY INN**
1450 Lombard St (94123)
Rates: $55-$135;
Tel: (415) 673-0691

**SAN FRANCISCO
AIRPORT HILTON**
P. O. Box 9355 (94128)
Rates: $139-$175;
Tel: (415) 589-0770

**SAN FRANCISCO
AIRPORT MARRIOTT**
1800 Old Bayshore Hwy
(Burlingame 94010)
Rates: $133-$159;
Tel: (415) 692-9100

**SHERATON HOTEL**
1177 Airport Blvd
(Burlingame 94010)
Rates: $99-$190;
Tel: (415) 342-9200

**SHERATON
AT FISHERMAN'S WHARF**
2500 Mason St (94133)
Rates: $100-$230;
Tel: (415) 362-5500

**SIR FRANCIS DRAKE
HOTEL**
450 Powell St (94102)
Rates: $110-$180;
Tel: (415) 392-7755

**STOUFFER
STANFORD COURT**
Nob Hill (94108)
Rates: $195-$1750;
Tel: (415) 989-3500

**THE VAGABOND INN-
AIRPORT**
1640 Bayshore Hwy
(Burlingame 94010)
Rates: $60-$90;
Tel: (800) 522-1555

**THE WESTIN ST. FRANCIS**
335 Powell St (94102)
Rates: $160-$315;
Tel: (415) 397-7000

**THE WESTIN-
SAN FRANCISCO AIRPORT**
One Old Bayshore Hwy
(Millbrae 94030)
Rates: $119-$500;
Tel: (415) 692-3500

## SAN JACINTO

**CROWN MOTEL**
138 S Ramona Blvd (92583)
Rates: $36-$54;
Tel: (909) 654-7133

## SAN JOSE

**BEST WESTERN
SAN JOSE LODGE**
1440 N 1st St (95112)
Rates: $56-$68;
Tel: (408) 453-7750

**DAYS INN**
4170 Monterey Rd (95111)
Rates: $50-$75;
Tel: (408) 224-4122

**HOLIDAY INN-AIRPORT**
1355 N 4th St (95112)
Rates: $71-$88;
Tel: (408) 453-5340

**HOLIDAY INN
PARK CENTER PLAZA**
282 Almaden Blvd (95113)
Rates: $90 $285;
Tel: (408) 998-0400

**HOMEWOOD SUITES**
10 W Trimble Rd (95131)
Rates: $89-$159;
Tel: (408) 428-9900

**HYATT SAN JOSE**
1740 N 1st St (95112)
Rates: $69-$154;
Tel: (408) 993-1234

**RED LION HOTEL**
2050 Gateway Pl (95110)
Rates: $79-$600;
Tel: (408) 453-4000

**SUMMERFIELD SUITES**
1602 Crane Ct (95122)
Rates: $119-$149;
Tel: (408) 436-1600

**THE VAGABOND INN**
1488 N First St (95112)
Rates: N/A;
Tel: (800) 522-1555

## SAN JUAN BAUTISTA

**SAN JUAN INN**
P. O. Box 1080 (95045)
Rates: $42-$60;
Tel: (408) 623-4380

## SAN JUAN CAPISTRANO

**BEST WESTERN
CAPISTRANO INN**
27174 Ortega Hwy (92675)
Rates: $59-$75;
Tel: (714) 493-5661

## SAN LUIS OBISPO

**BEST WESTERN ROYAL
OAK MOTOR HOTEL**
214 Madonna Rd (93405)
Rates: $61-$89;
Tel: (805) 544-4410

**CAMPUS MOTEL**
404 Santa Rosa St (93405)
Rates: $44-$79;
Tel: (805) 544-0881

**HOWARD JOHNSON
HOTEL**
1585 Calle Joaquin (93405)
Rates: $49-$99;
Tel: (805) 544-5300

**SANDS MOTEL & SUITES**
1930 Monterey St (93401)
Rates: $49-$99;
Tel: (805) 544-0500

**THE VAGABOND INN**
210 Madonna Rd (93401)
Rates: $44-$73;
Tel: (800) 522-1555

## SAN MARCOS

**QUAILS INN AT LAKE
SAN MARCOS RESORT**
1025 La Bonita Dr (92069)
Rates: $90-$125;
Tel: (619) 744-0120

## SAN MATEO

**DUNFEY
SAN MATEO HOTEL**
1770 S Amphlett Blvd (94402)
Rates: $69;
Tel: (415) 573-7661

**QUALITY HOTEL
AIRPORT SOUTH**
4000 S El Camino Real
(94403)
Rates: $65-$84;
Tel: (415) 341-0966

**RESIDENCE INN
BY MARRIOTT**
2000 Winward Way (94404)
Rates: $124-$149;
Tel: (415) 574-4700

## SAN MIGUEL

**SAN MIGUEL MISSION INN**
P. O. Box 58 (93451)
Rates: $30-$45;
Tel: (805) 467-3674

## SAN PEDRO

**SHERATON
LOS ANGELES HARBOR**
601 S Palos Verdes St (90731)
Rates: $95-$695;
Tel: (310) 519-8200

**THE VAGABOND INN**
215 S Gaffey (90731)
Rates: $44-$67;
Tel: (800) 522-1555

## SAN RAFAEL

**EMBASSY SUITES HOTEL**
101 McInnis Pkwy (94903)
Rates: $99-$165;
Tel: (415) 499-9222

**HOLIDAY INN**
1010 Northgate Dr (94903)
Rates: $89-$122;
Tel: (415) 479-8800

**VILLA INN**
1600 Lincoln Ave (94901)
Rates: $58-$80;
Tel: (415) 456-4975

## SAN RAMON

**RESIDENCE INN
BY MARRIOTT**
1071 Market Pl (94583)
Rates: $79-$139;
Tel: (510) 277-9292

**SAN RAMON MARRIOTT
AT BISHOP RANCH**
2600 Bishop Dr (94583)
Rates: $85-$145;
Tel: (510) 867-9200

## SANTA ANA

**DAYS INN**
1600 E First St (92701)
Rates: $55-$75;
Tel: (714) 835-3051

**HOWARD JOHNSON
MOTOR LODGE**
939 E 17th St (92701)
Rates: $46-$71;
Tel: (714) 558-3700

**NENDELS INN-SANTA ANA**
1519 E First St (92701)
Rates: $38-$48;
Tel: (714) 547-9426

# SANTA BARBARA

**THE BAYBERRY INN
BED & BREAKFAST**
111 W Valerio St (93101)
Rates: N/A;
Tel: (805) 682-3199

**BEST WESTERN-
EL PATIO BEACHSIDE INN**
336 W Cabrillo Blvd (93101)
Rates: $85-$140;
Tel: (805) 965-6556

**FESS PARKER'S
RED LION RESORT**
633 E Cabrillo Blvd (93103)
Rates: $190-$290;
Tel: (805) 564-4333

**FOUR SEASONS BILTMORE**
1260 Channel Dr (93108)
Rates: $290-$360;
Tel: (805) 969-2261

**HOLIDAY INN-
SANTA BARBARA/GOLETA**
5650 Calle Real
(Goleta 93117)
Rates: $86-$135;
Tel: (805) 964-6241

**QUALITY SUITES**
5490 Hollister Ave (93111)
Rates: $135-$155;
Tel: (805) 683-6722

**THE VAGABOND INN-
MIDTOWN**
1920 State St (93101)
Rates: $50-$68;
Tel: (800) 522-1555

**THE VAGABOND INN-
STATE ST**
2819 State St (93105)
Rates: $46-$78;
Tel: (800) 522-1555

# SANTA CLARA

**BUDGET INN**
2499 El Camino Real (95051)
Rates: $44-$52;
Tel: (408) 244-9610

**DAYS INN**
4200 Great America Pkwy
(95054)
Rates: $59-$89;
Tel: (408) 980-1525

**ECONO LODGE**
P. O. Box 2841 (95051)
Rates: $50-$95;
Tel: (408) 241-3010

**HOWARD JOHNSON
LODGE**
5405 Stevens Creek Blvd
(95051)
Rates: $75-$90;
Tel: (408) 257-8600

**MARRIOTT HOTEL**
2700 Mission College Blvd
(95054)
Rates: $69-$400;
Tel: (408) 988-1500

**THE VAGABOND INN**
3580 El Camino Real (95051)
Rates: $40-$60;
Tel: (408) 241-0771

**THE WESTIN HOTEL-
SANTA CLARA**
5101 Great America Pkwy
(95054)
Rates: $89-$185;
Tel: (408) 986-0700

# SANTA CLARITA

**HAMPTON INN**
25259 The Old Rd (91381)
Rates: $59-$86;
Tel: (805) 253-2400

**HILTON GARDEN INN**
27710 The Old Rd (91355)
Rates: $79-$119;
Tel: (805) 254-8800

# SANTA CRUZ

**MOTEL CONTINENTAL**
414 Ocean St (95060)
Rates: $38-$98;
Tel: (408) 429-1221

**OCEAN PACIFIC INN**
120 Washington (95060)
Rates: $60-$125;
Tel: (408) 457-1234

**PACIFIC INN**
330 Ocean St (95060)
Rates: $38-$98;
Tel: (408) 425-3722

# SANTA FE SPRINGS

**BEST WESTERN
SANDMAN MOTEL**
13530 E Firestone Blvd
(90670)
Rates: $39-$52;
Tel: (310) 921-8571

# SANTA MARIA

**HOWARD JOHNSON
LODGE**
210 S Nicholson Ave (93454)
Rates: $39-$64;
Tel: (805) 922-5891

**HUNTER'S INN**
1514 S Broadway (93454)
Rates: $49-$75;
Tel: (805) 922-2123

**RAMADA SUITES**
2050 N Preisker Ln (93454)
Rates: $55-$150;
Tel: (805) 928-6000

**WESTERN HOST
MOTOR HOTEL**
1007 E Main St (93454)
Rates: $35-$69;
Tel: (805) 922-4505

# SANTA MONICA

**LOEWS SANTA MONICA
BEACH HOTEL**
1700 Ocean Ave (90401)
Rates: $195-$450;
Tel: (310) 458-6700

# SANTA NELLA

**BEST WESTERN
ANDERSEN'S INN**
Hwy 5 at 33 (95322)
Rates: N/A;
Tel: (800) 527-5534

**HOLIDAY INN
MISSION DE ORO**
13070 Hwy 33S (95322)
Rates: $39-$69;
Tel: (209) 826-4444

## SANTA ROSA

**BEST WESTERN
GARDEN INN**
1500 Santa Rosa Ave (95404)
Rates: $45-$70;
Tel: (707) 546-4031

**HERITAGE INN**
870 Hopper Ave (95403)
Rates: $47-$68;
Tel: (707) 545-9000

**LOS ROBLES LODGE**
925 Edwards Ave (95401)
Rates: $65-$90;
Tel: (707) 545-6330

**SANTA ROSA DOWN-
TOWN TRAVELODGE**
635 Healdsburg Ave (95401)
Rates: $45-$70;
Tel: (707) 544-4141

**TRAVELODGE**
1815 Santa Rosa Ave (95407)
Rates: N/A;
Tel: (707) 542-3472

## SAN YSIDRO

**ECONOMY INNS
OF AMERICA**
230 Via de San Ysidro
(92073)
Rates: $25-$40;
Tel: (619) 428-6191

## SEASIDE

**DAYS INN**
1400 Del Monte Blvd (93955)
Rates: $53-$115;
Tel: (408) 394-5335

**SEASIDE MOTEL 8**
1131 Fremont Blvd (93955)
Rates: $50-$95;
Tel: (408) 394-8881

## SHASTA LAKE

**BRIDGE BAY RESORT**
10300 Bridge Bay Rd
(Redding 96003)
Rates: $55-$69;
Tel: (916) 275-3021

## SIERRA CITY

**HERRINGTON'S
SIERRA PINES**
P. O. Box 235 (96125)
Rates: $55-$75;
Tel: (916) 862-1151

## SIMI VALLEY

**CLARION HOTEL**
1775 Madera Rd (93065)
Rates: $70-$100;
Tel: (805) 584-6300

**RADISSON-SIMI VALLEY**
999 Enchanted Way (93065)
Rates: $69-$92;
Tel: (805) 583-2000

## SOLVANG

**MEADOWLARK MOTEL**
2644 Mission Dr (93463)
Rates: N/A;
Tel: (805) 688-4631

**VIKING MOTEL**
1506 Mission Dr (93463)
Rates: $32-$85;
Tel: (805) 688-1337

## SONOMA

**BEST WESTERN
SONOMA VALLEY INN**
550 2nd St W (95476)
Rates: $75-$135;
Tel: (707) 938-9200

## SONORA

**ALADDIN MOTOR INN**
14260 Mono Way (95370)
Rates: $47-$65;
Tel: (209) 533-4971

**BEST WESTERN SONORA
OAKS MOTOR HOTEL**
19551 Hess Ave (95370)
Rates: $56-$80;
Tel: (209) 533-4400

**HISTORIC NATIONAL
HOTEL B & B**
P. O. Box 502
(Jamestown 95327)
Rates: $65-$80;
Tel: (209) 984-3446

## STOCKTON

**BEST WESTERN
CHARTER WAY INN**
550 W Charter Way (95206)
Rates: $45-$62;
Tel: (209) 948-0321

**HOLIDAY INN
PLUM TREE PLAZA**
111 E March Ln (95207)
Rates: $85-$93;
Tel: (209) 474-3301

**LA QUINTA INN**
2710 W March Ln (95219)
Rates: $51-$66;
Tel: (209) 952-7800

**VAGABOND INN**
33 N Center St (95202)
Rates: $36-$45;
Tel: (209) 948-6151

## SUNNYVALE

**CAPTAIN'S COVE MOTEL**
600 N Mathilda Ave (94086)
Rates: $59-$61;
Tel: (408) 735-7800

**RESIDENCE INN
BY MARRIOTT**
750 Lakeway Dr (94086)
Rates: $69-$149;
Tel: (408) 720-1000

**RESIDENCE INN
BY MARRIOTT**
1080 Stewart Dr (94086)
Rates: $128-$148;
Tel: (408) 720-8893

**SUMMERFIELD SUITES**
900 Hamlin Ct (94089)
Rates: $79-$159;
Tel: (408) 745-1515

**THE VAGABOND INN**
816 Ahwanee Ave (94086)
Rates: N/A;
Tel: (800) 522-1555

**WOODFIN SUITES
MOTOR HOTEL**
635 E El Camino Real (94087)
Rates: $109-$145;
Tel: (408) 738-1700

## SUSANVILLE

**RIVER INN MOTEL**
1710 Main St (96130)
Rates: $32-$45;
Tel: (916) 257-6051

## TAHOE VISTA

**HOLIDAY HOUSE**
7276 N Lake Blvd (96148)
Rates: N/A;
Tel: (916) 546-2369

## TEHACHAPI

**BEST WESTERN
MOUNTAIN INN**
416 W Tehachapi Blvd
(93561)
Rates $45-$51;
Tel: (805) 822-5591

**SKY MOUNTAIN RESORT**
Star Rt 1, Box 2931 (93561)
Rates: $65-$180;
Tel: (800) 244-0864

## TEMECULA

**RAMADA INN**
28980 Front St (92592)
Rates: $49-$59;
Tel: (909) 676-8770

## THOUSAND OAKS

**HOWARD JOHNSON
HOTEL**
75 W Thousand Oaks Blvd
(91360)
Rates: $47-$70;
Tel: (805) 497-3701

## THREE RIVERS

**BEST WESTERN
HOLIDAY LODGE**
P. O. Box 129 (93271)
Rates: $46-$76;
Tel: (209) 561-4119

**BUCKEYE TREE LODGE**
46000 Sierra Dr (93271)
Rates: $39-$61;
Tel: (209) 561-5900

**LAZY J RANCH MOTEL**
39625 Sierra Dr (93271)
Rates: $40-$80;
Tel: (209) 561-4449

**THE RIVER INN**
45176 Sierra Dr (93271)
Rates: $35-$59;
Tel: (209) 561-4367

**SIERRA LODGE**
43175 Sierra Dr (93271)
Rates: $45-$125;
Tel: (209) 561-3681

## TIBURON

**TIBURON LODGE**
1651 Tiburon Blvd (94920)
Rates: $85-$120;
Tel: (415) 435-3133

## TORRANCE

**DAYS INN**
4111 Pacific Coast Hwy
(90505)
Rates: $55-$70;
Tel: (310) 378-8511

**RESIDENCE INN
BY MARRIOTT**
3701 Torrance Blvd (90503)
Rates: $124-$162;
Tel: (310) 543-4566

**SUMMERFIELD SUITES
HOTEL**
19901 Prairie Ave (90503)
Rates: $89-$159;
Tel: (310) 371-8525

**TORRANCE HOLIDAY INN**
21333 Hawthorne Blvd
(90503)
Rates: $89-$119;
Tel: (310) 540-0500

## TRINIDAD

**BISHOP PINE LODGE**
1481 Patricks Point Dr
(95570)
Rates: $50-$75;
Tel: (707) 677-3314

## TULARE

**TULARE INN MOTEL**
1301 E Paige (93274)
Rates: N/A;
Tel: (209) 686-8571

## TURLOCK

**BEST WESTERN
ORCHARD INN**
5025 N Golden State Blvd
(95380)
Rates: $47-$63;
Tel: (209) 667-2827

## TWAIN HARTE

**ELDORADO MOTEL**
P. O. Box 368 (95383)
Rates: $45-$65;
Tel: (209) 586-4479

## UKIAH

**WESTERN TRAVELER MOTEL**
693 S Orchard Ave (95482)
Rates: $32-$56;
Tel: (707) 468-9167

## VACAVILLE

**VACAVILLE SUPER 8**
101 Allison Ct (95688)
Rates: $39-$46;
Tel: (707) 449-8884

## VALENCIA

**BEST WESTERN RANCH HOUSE INN**
27143 N Tourney Rd (91355)
Rates: $70-$100;
Tel: (805) 255-0555

**HILTON GARDEN INN**
27710 The Old Road (91355)
Rates: $79-$178;
Tel: (805) 254-8800

## VALLEJO

**ROYAL BAY INN**
44 Admiral Callaghan Ln (94590)
Rates: $35-$68;
Tel: (707) 643-1061

## VENTURA

**DOUBLETREE HOTEL AT VENTURA**
2055 Harbor Blvd (93001)
Rates: $89-$139;
Tel: (805) 643-6000

**LA QUINTA INN**
5818 Valentine Rd (93003)
Rates: $51-$63;
Tel: (805) 658-6200

## VICTORVILLE

**BUDGET INN**
14153 Kentwood Blvd (92392)
Rates: $30-$42;
Tel: (619) 241-8010

**HI DESERT TRAVELERS MOTEL**
13409 Mariposa Rd (92392)
Rates: $45-$51;
Tel: (619) 241-1577

**HOLIDAY INN MOTOR HOTEL**
15494 Palmdale Rd (92392)
Rates: $51-$89;
Tel: (619) 245-6565

**SCOTTISH INNS**
15499 Village Dr (92392)
Rates: $22-$36;
Tel: (619) 243-5858

**TRAVELODGE NORTH MOTEL**
16868 Stoddard Wells Rd (92392)
Rates: $27-$81;
Tel: (619) 243-7700

## VISALIA

**BEST WESTERN VISALIA INN MOTEL**
623 W Main St (93291)
Rates: $53-$62;
Tel: (209) 732-4561

**HOLIDAY INN PLAZA PARK**
9000 W Airport Dr (93277)
Rates: $66-$81;
Tel: (209) 651-5000

## VISTA

**LA QUINTA INN**
630 Sycamore Ave (92083)
Rates: $46-$61;
Tel: (619) 727-8180

## WALNUT CREEK

**WALNUT CREEK MOTOR LODGE**
1960 N Main St (94596)
Rates: $65-$90;
Tel: (510) 932-2811

## WATSONVILLE

**EL RANCHO MOTEL**
976 Salinas Rd (95076)
Rates: $30-$59;
Tel: (408) 722-2766

## WEAVERVILLE

**49ER MOTEL**
P. O. Box 1608 (96093)
Rates: $30-$40;
Tel: (916) 623-4937

## WEED

**SIS-Q-INN MOTEL**
1825 Shastina Dr (96094)
Rates: $29-$46;
Tel: (916) 938-4194

**TOWN HOUSE MOTEL**
157 S Weed Blvd (96094)
Rates: N/A;
Tel: (916) 938-4431

## WEST COVINA

**HAMPTON INN**
3145 E Garvey Ave N (91791)
Rates: $50-$63;
Tel: (818) 967-5800

## WESTMINSTER

**BEACH MOTOR INN**
15559 Beach Blvd (92683)
Rates: $38-$45;
Tel: (714) 895-5584

## WESTPORT

**HOWARD CREEK RANCH
BED & BREAKFAST**
40501 N Hwy One (95488)
Rates: N/A;
Tel: (707) 964-6725

## WHITTIER

**THE VAGABOND INN**
14125 E Whittier Blvd (90605)
Rates: $35-$59;
Tel: (800) 522-1555

**WHITTIER HILTON**
7320 Greenleaf Ave (90602)
Rates: N/A·
Tel: (213) 945-8511

## WILLIAMS

**COMFORT INN**
P. O. Box 729 (95987)
Rates: $43-$48;
Tel: (916) 473-2381

**STAGE STOP MOTEL**
330 7th St (95987)
Rates: $38-$50;
Tel: (916) 473 2281

## WILLOWS

**BEST WESTERN
GOLDEN PHEASANT IN**
249 N Humboldt Ave (9598
Rates: $45-$64;
Tel: (916) 934-4603

**BLUE GUM INN**
Rt 2, Box 171A (95988)
Rates: $26-$42;
Tel: (916) 934-5401

**CROSS ROADS WEST INN**
452 N Humboldt Ave (95988)
Rates: $26-$36;
Tel: (916) 934-7026

**GROVE MOTEL**
Rt 2, Box 172 Hwy 99 W
(95988)
Rates: N/A;
Tel: (916) 934-5067

**SUPER 8 MOTEL**
457 N Humboldt (95988)
Rates: N/A;
Tel: (916) 934-2871

## WOODLAND

**CINDERELLA MOTEL**
99 W Main St (95695)
Rates: $35-$42;
Tel: (916) 662-1091

**COMFORT INN**
1562 E Main St (95695)
Rates: $45-$65;
Tel: (916) 666-3050

## YOSEMITE
## NATIONAL PARK

**THE REDWOOD COTTAGES**
P. O. Box 2085
(Wawona Station 95389)
Rates: $71-$280;
Tel: (209) 375-6666

## YOUNTVILLE

**VINTAGE INN**
6541 Washington St (94599)
Rates: $124-$174;
Tel: (707) 944-1112

## YREKA

**BEST WESTERN MINER'S INN**
122 E Miner St (96097)
Rates: $44-$55;
Tel· (916) 842-4355

**THUNDERBIRD LODGE**
526 S Main St (96097)
Rates: $32-$40;
Tel: (916) 842-4404

**WAYSIDE INN**
1235 S Main St (96097)
Rates: $32-$44;
Tel: (916) 842-4412

81

# COLORADO

## ALAMOSA

**LAMPLIGHTER MOTEL**
425 Main St (81101)
Rates: N/A;
Tel: (800) 359-2138

**BEST WESTERN
ALAMOSA INN**
1919 Main St (81101)
Rates: $49-$69;
Tel: (719) 589-2567

## ARVADA

**ON GOLDEN POND**
7831 Eldridge (80005)
Rates: N/A;
Tel: (303) 424-2296

## ASPEN

**LIMELITE LODGE**
228 E Cooper St (81611)
Rates: $58-$188;
Tel: (303) 925-3025

**THE LITTLE NELL**
675 E Durant Ave (81611)
Rates: $160-$425;
Tel: (303) 920-4600

## BEAVER CREEK

**COMFORT INN-
VAIL/BEAVER CREEK**
P. O. Box 5510 (Avon 81620)
Rates: $69-$225;
Tel: (303) 949-5511

## BOULDER

**BOULDER
MOUNTAIN LODGE**
91 Four Mile Canyon Rd
(80302)
Rates: $35-$70;
Tel: (303) 444-0882

**THE BROKER INN**
555 30th St (80303)
Rates: $91-$101;
Tel: (303) 444-3330

**FOOT OF THE MOUNTAIN
MOTEL**
200 Arapahoe Ave (80302)
Rates: $35-$60;
Tel: (303) 442-5688

**HIGHLANDER INN MOTEL**
970 28th St (80303)
Rates: $45-$79;
Tel: (303) 443-7800

**HOLIDAY INN**
800 28th St (80303)
Rates: $74-$84;
Tel: (303) 443-3322

**HOMEWOOD SUITES**
4950 Baseline Rd (80303)
Rates: $95-$127;
Tel: (303) 499-9922

**PEARL STREET INN**
1820 Pearl St (80302)
Rates: $78-$103;
Tel: (800) 232-5949

**RESIDENCE INN
BY MARRIOTT**
3030 Center Green Dr
(80301)
Rates: $109-$129;
Tel: (303) 449-5545

**SANDY POINT INN**
6485 Twin Lakes Rd (80301)
Rates: $50-$74;
Tel: (303) 530-2939

## BUENA VISTA

**COTTONWOOD INN**
18999 County Rd 306
(81211)
Rates: N/A;
Tel: (719) 395-6434

## BURLINGTON

**CHAPPARAL
BUDGET HOST**
405 S Lincoln (80807)
Rates: $26-$38;
Tel: (719) 346-5361

**ECONO LODGE**
450 S Lincoln (80807)
Rates: $31-$45;
Tel: (719) 346-5555

**SLOAN'S MOTEL**
1901 Rose Ave (80807)
Rates: $20-$34;
Tel: (719) 346-5333

## CANON CITY

**BEST WESTERN
ROYAL GORGE MOTEL**
1925 Fremont Dr (81212)
Rates: N/A;
Tel: (719) 275-3377

**CANON INN**
3075 E Hwy 50 (81212)
Rates: $45-$90;
Tel: (719) 275-8676

**HOLIDAY MOTEL**
1502 Main St (81212)
Rates: $22-$40;
Tel: (719) 275-3317

## COLORADO CITY

**GREENHORN INN**
I-25 Exit 74 (81019)
Rates: N/A;
Tel: (719) 676-3315

## COLORADO SPRINGS

**THE ALIKAR GARDENS
RESORT**
1123 Verde Dr (80910)
Rates: $69-$149;
Tel: (719) 475-2564

**ANTLERS
DOUBLETREE HOTEL**
4 S Cascade (80903)
Rates: $95-$125;
Tel: (719) 473-5600

**THE BEST WESTERN
PALMER HOUSE**
3010 N Chestnut (80907)
Rates: $55-$77;
Tel: (719) 636-5201

**CHIEF MOTEL**
1624 S Nevada Ave (80906)
Rates: $23-$42;
Tel: (719) 473-5228

**COMFORT INN**
8280 Hwy 83 (80920)
Rates: $35-$65;
Tel: (719) 598-6700

**DRURY INN-PIKES PEAK**
8155 N Academy Blvd
(80920)
Rates: $47-$66;
Tel. (719) 598-2500

**HAMPTON INN-NORTH**
7245 Commerce Center Dr
(80919)
Rates: $42-$62.
Tel: (719) 593-9700

**HOLIDAY INN-NORTH**
3125 Sinton Rd (80907)
Rates: $35-$87;
Tel: (719) 633 5541

**LA QUINTA INN**
4385 Sinton Rd (80907)
Rates: $38-$74;
Tel: (719) 528-5060

**RADISSON INN COLORADO
SPRINGS AIRPORT**
1645 Newport Dr (80916)
Rates: $59-$77;
Tel: (719) 597-7000

**RADISSON INN NORTH**
8110 N Academy Blvd
(80920)
Rates: $60-$105;
Tel: (719) 598-5770

**RAINTREE INN-WEST**
2625 Ore Mill Rd (80904)
Rates: $28-$60;
Tel: (719) 632-4600

**RED LION HOTEL**
1775 E Cheyenne Blvd
(80906)
Rates: $70-$125;
Tel: (719) 576-8900

**RESIDENCE INN
BY MARRIOTT**
3880 N Academy Blvd
(80917)
Rates: $82-$135;
Tel: (719) 574-0370

**RODEWAY INN**
2409 E Pikes Peak Ave
(80909)
Rates: $34-$50;
Tel: (719) 471 0990

**STAGECOACH MOTEL**
1647 S Nevada Ave (80906)
Rates: $28-$42;
Tel: (719) 633-3894

**SWISS CHALET**
3410-3420 W Colorado Ave
(80904)
Rates: $24-$61;
Tel: (719) 471-2260

**TRAVELERS
UPTOWN MOTEL**
220 E Cimarron St (80903)
Rates: $25-$42;
Tel: (719) 473-2774

## CORTEZ

**ANASAZI MOTOR INN**
640 S Broadway (81321)
Rates: $40-$63;
Tel: (303) 565-3773

**ANETH LODGE**
645 E Main St (81321)
Rates: $29-$41;
Tel: (303) 565-3453

**ARROW NATIONAL 9 INN**
440 S Broadway (81321)
Rates: $28-$58;
Tel: (303) 565-7778

**BEL RAU LODGE**
2040 E Main St (81321)
Rates: $34-$70;
Tel: (303) 565-3738

**BEST WESTERN
SANDS MOTEL**
1120 E Main St (81321)
Rates: $48-$68;
Tel: (800) 528-1234

**BEST WESTERN
TURQUOISE MOTOR INN**
535 E Main St (81321)
Rates: $44-$73;
Tel: (303) 565-3778

**COMFORT INN**
2308 E Main St (81321)
Rates: $38-$88;
Tel: (303) 565-4228

**HOLIDAY INN EXPRESS**
2121 E Main St (81321)
Rates: $42-$88;
Tel: (303) 565-6000

**NORTH BROADWAY
MOTEL**
510 N Broadway (81321)
Rates: $23+;
Tel: (303) 565-2481

**RAMADA LTD**
2020 E Main (81321)
Rates: $40-$90;
Tel: (800) 672-6232

**SAND CANYON INN**
301 W Main St (81321)
Rates: $38+;
Tel. (800) 258-3699

**TOMAHAWK LODGE**
728 S Broadway (81321)
Rates: $27-$47;
Tel: (303) 565-8521

**UTE MOUNTAIN MOTEL**
531 S Broadway (81321)
Rates: $26-$40;
Tel: (303) 565-8507

## CRAIG

**BEST WESTERN
INN OF CRAIG**
755 E Victory Way (81625)
Rates: $25-$55;
Tel: (303) 824-8101

**BLACK NUGGET MOTEL**
2855 W Victory Way (81625)
Rates: $28-$32;
Tel: (303) 824-8161

**CRAIG MOTEL**
894 Yampa Ave (81625)
Rates: $22-$36;
Tel: (303) 824-4491

**HOLIDAY INN-CRAIG**
300 S Hwy 13 (81625)
Rates: $49-$57;
Tel: (303) 824-4000

## CREEDE

**BROADACRES RANCH**
P. O. Box 39 (81130)
Rates: N/A;
Tel: (719) 658-2291

## DELTA

**BEST WESTERN SUNDANCE**
903 Main St (81416)
Rates: $34-$48;
Tel: (303) 874-9781

## DENVER
(and Vicinity)

**BEST BUDGET
MOTOR BAR X**
5001 W Colfax Ave (80204)
Rates: $32-$37;
Tel: (303) 534-7191

**BEST WESTERN
COUNTRY VILLA INN**
4700 Kipling St
(Wheatridge 80033)
Rates: $34-$52;
Tel: (303) 423-4000

**BEST WESTERN
LANDMARK INN**
455 S Colorado Blvd (80222)
Rates: $39-$59;
Tel: (303) 388-5561

**BEST WESTERN
PINE COURT INN**
4411 Peoria St (80239)
Rates: $49-$54;
Tel: (303) 373-5730

**CHALET MOTEL**
6051 W Alameda Ave
(Lakewood 80226)
Rates: $31-$38;
Tel: (303) 237-7775

**THE CLARION HOTEL
DENVER SOUTHEAST**
7770 S Peoria St
(Englewood 80112)
Rates: $55-$75;
Tel: (303) 790-7770

**COMFORT INN AIRPORT**
7201 E 36th Ave (80207)
Rates: $48-$54;
Tel: (303) 393-7666

**CONCORDE
AIRPORT HOTEL**
6090 Smith Rd (80216)
Rates: N/A;
Tel: (303) 388-4051

**DAYS HOTEL-
DENVER AIRPORT**
4590 Quebec St (80216)
Rates: $44-$55;
Tel: (303) 320-0260

**DAYS INN MIDTOWN**
1680 S Colorado Blvd
(80222)
Rates: $52-$78;
Tel: (303) 691-2223

**DAYS INN-NORTH**
36 E 120th Ave
(Northglenn 80233)
Rates: $39-$65;
Tel: (303) 457-0688

**DAYS INN SUITES-
DENVER WEST**
15059 W Colfax Ave
(Golden 80401)
Rates: $39-$65;
Tel: (303) 277-0200

**DENVER HILTON SOUTH**
7801 E Orchard Rd
(Englewood 80111)
Rates: $76-$129;
Tel: (303) 779-6161

**DENVER LAKEWOOD INN**
7150 Colfax (80215)
Rates: $29-$39;
Tel: (303) 238-1251

**DENVER MARRIOTT
HOTEL CITY CENTER**
1701 California St at 17th St
(80202)
Rates: $74-$155;
Tel: (303) 297-1300

**DENVER MARRIOTT
HOTEL-SOUTHEAST**
6363 E Hampden Ave (80222)
Rates: $58-$86;
Tel: (303) 758-7000

**DENVER MARRIOTT WEST**
1717 Denver West Blvd
(Golden 80401)
Rates: $78-$114;
Tel: (303) 279-9100

**DENVER TRAVELODGE
HOTEL**
200 W 48th Ave (80216)
Rates: $52;
Tel: (303) 296-4000

**DOUBLETREE CLUB HOTEL**
137 Union Blvd (80228)
Rates: $49-$69;
Tel: (303) 969-9900

**DRURY INN-DENVER**
4400 Peoria St (80239)
Rates: $49-$61;
Tel: (303) 373-1983

**EMBASSY SUITES-
DENVER AIRPORT**
4444 N Havana (80239)
Rates: $84-$120;
Tel: (303) 375-0400

**EMBASSY SUITES-
DENVER TECH CENTER**
10250 E Costilla Ave
(Englewood 80112)
Rates: $89-$129;
Tel: (303) 792-0433

**EXECUTIVE TOWER INN**
1405 Curtis St (80202)
Rates: $59-$132;
Tel: (303) 571-0300

**HAMPTON INN-
DENVER SOUTHWEST**
3605 S Wadsworth Blvd
(Lakewood 80235)
Rates: $48-$62;
Tel: (303) 989-6900

**HOLIDAY CHALET
HOTEL APARTMENTS**
1820 E Colfax Ave (80218)
Rates: $49-$67;
Tel: (303) 321-9975

84

**HOLIDAY INN-AIRPORT**
4040 Quebec St (80216)
Rates: $49-$72;
Tel: (303) 321-6666

**HOLIDAY INN DENVER I-70
EAST & TRADE CENTER**
15500 40th Ave (80239)
Rates: $66-$78;
Tel: (303) 371-9494

**HOLIDAY INN-
DENVER NORTH**
4849 Bannock St (80216)
Rates: $60-$65;
Tel: (303) 292-9500

**HOLIDAY INN
DENVER-NORTHGLENN**
10 E 120th Ave (80233)
Rates: $66-$75;
Tel: (303) 452-4100

**HOLIDAY INN-
SPORTS CENTER**
1975 Bryant St (80204)
Rates: $58-$70;
Tel: (303) 433-8331

**HOTEL DENVER-
DOWNTOWN**
1450 Glenarm Pl (80202)
Rates: $69-$125;
Tel: (303) 573-1450

**LA QUINTA INN-AIRPORT**
3975 Peoria Way (80239)
Rates: $45-$58;
Tel: (303) 371-5640

**LA QUINTA INN-AURORA**
1011 S Abilene
(Aurora 80012)
Rates: $45-$58;
Tel: (303) 337-0206

**LA QUINTA INN-CENTRAL**
3500 Fox St (80216-5126)
Rates: $44-$54;
Tel: (303) 458-1222

**LA QUINTA INN-
DENVER NORTH**
345 W 120th Ave
(Westminster 80234)
Rates: $42-$54;
Tel: (303) 252-9800

**LA QUINTA INN-GOLDEN**
3301 Youngfield Service Rd
(Golden 80401)
Rates: $45-$58;
Tel: (303) 279-5565

**LA QUINTA INN-SOUTH**
1975 S Colorado Blvd
(80222)
Rates: $45-$58;
Tel: (303) 758-8886

**LA QUINTA INN-
WESTMINSTER MALL**
8701 Turnpike Dr (80030)
Rates: $45-$60;
Tel: (303) 425-9099

**LOEWS GIORGIO HOTEL**
4150 E Mississippi Ave
(80222)
Rates: $74-$124;
Tel: (303) 782-9300

**901 PENN HOUSE**
901 Pennsylvania St (80203)
Rates: $172-$335;
Tel: (303) 831-8060

**QUALITY INN SOUTH**
6300 E Hampden Ave (80222)
Rates: $52-$69;
Tel: (303) 758-2211

**QUEEN ANNE INN**
2147 Tremont Pl (80205)
Rates: N/A;
Tel: (303) 296-6666

**RADISSON
HOTEL DENVER**
1550 Court Pl (80202)
Rates: $59-$140;
Tel: (303) 893-3333

**RADISSON
HOTEL/DENVER SOUTH**
7007 S Clinton St
(Englewood 80112)
Rates: $55-$72;
Tel: (303) 799-6200

**RAMADA DENVER
MIDTOWN**
1475 S Colorado Blvd
(80222)
Rates: $68-$82;
Tel: (303) 757-8797

**RAMADA INN AIRPORT**
3737 Quebec St (80207)
Rates: $68-$92;
Tel: (303) 388-6161

**RAMADA INN DENVER
DOWNTOWN**
1150 E Colfax Ave (80218)
Rates: $55-$60;
Tel: (303) 831-7700

**RED LION HOTEL**
3203 Quebec St (80207)
Rates: $87-$118;
Tel: (303) 321-3333

**REGENCY INN**
3900 Elati St (80216)
Rates: $39;
Tel: (303) 458-0808

**RESIDENCE INN
BY MARRIOTT DENVER
DOWNTOWN**
2777 Zuni St (80211)
Rates: $99-$129;
Tel: (303) 458-5318

**RESIDENCE INN
BY MARRIOTT
DENVER SOUTH**
6565 S Yosemite St
(Englewood 80111)
Rates: $102-$130;
Tel: (303) 740-7177

**RODEWAY INN-
DENVER WEST**
11595 W 6th Ave
(Lakewood 80215)
Rates: $45-$57;
Tel: (303) 238-7751

**SHERATON
DENVER TECH CENTER**
4900 DTC Pkwy (80237)
Rates: $69-$159;
Tel: (303) 779-1100

**SHERATON-
DENVER WEST HOTEL
& CONFERENCE CTR**
360 Union Blvd
(Lakewood 80228)
Rates: $65-$139;
Tel: (303) 987-2000

**SHERATON GRAYSTONE
CASTLE-DENVER NORTH**
83 E 120th Ave
(Thornton 80233)
Rates: $69;
Tel: (303) 451-1002

**SHERATON INN
DENVER AIRPORT**
3535 Quebec St (80207)
Rates: $69-$84;
Tel: (303) 333-7711

**SUPER 8 MOTEL
DENVER NORTH**
12055 Melody Dr
(Westminster 80234)
Rates: $36-$46;
Tel: (303) 451-7200

**THE WARWICK HOTEL-
DENVER**
1776 Grant St at 18th Ave
(80203)
Rates: $135-$500;
Tel: (303) 861-2000

**THE WESTIN HOTEL**
1672 Lawrence St (80202)
Rates: $145-$190;
Tel: (303) 572-9100

## DILLON

**BEST WESTERN
PTARMIGAN LODGE**
P. O. Box 218 (80435)
Rates: $45-$130;
Tel: (303) 468-2341

## DOLORES

**DOLORES MOUNTAIN INN**
701 Hwy 145 (81323)
Rates: $37-$60;
Tel: (800) 842-8113

**LOST CANYON
LAKE LODGE**
P. O. Box 1289 (81323)
Rates: $75;
Tel: (303) 882-4913

**OUTPOST MOTEL**
1800 Hwy 145 (81323)
Rates: $32-$38;
Tel: (800) 382-4892

**PRIEST GULCH RANCH CAMP**
2670 Hwy 145 (81323)
Rates: $54-$59;
Tel: (303) 562-3810

**RAG O'MUFFIN RANCH**
26030 Hwy 145 (81323)
Rates: $75+;
Tel: (303) 562-3803

**RAMADA INN**
1121 Central Ave (81323)
Rates: $27+;
Tel: (303) 882-4633

## DURANGO

**ADOBE INN**
2178 Main Ave (81301)
Rates: $38-$102;
Tel: (303) 247-2743

**BEST WESTERN
LODGE AT PURGATORY**
49617 US 550N (81301)
Rates: $55-$230;
Tel: (303) 247-9669

**CABOOSE MOTEL**
3363 Main (81301)
Rates: N/A;
Tel: (303) 247-1191

**DAYS INN DURANGO**
CR 203 (81301)
Rates: $39-$82;
Tel: (303) 259-1430

**HOLIDAY INN**
800 Camino Del Rio (81301)
Rates: $49-$99;
Tel: (303) 247-5393

**IRON HORSE INN**
5800 N Main Ave (81301)
Rates: $65-$105;
Tel: (303) 259-1010

**NATIONAL 9 SUNSET**
2855 N Main Ave (81301)
Rates: $26-$68;
Tel: (303) 247-2653

**RED LION INN**
501 Camino Del Rio (81301)
Rates: $75-$130;
Tel: (303) 259-6580

**RODEWAY INN**
2701 N Main Ave (81301)
Rates: $42-$96;
Tel: (303) 259-2540

**SIESTA MOTEL**
3475 N Main Ave (81301)
Rates: $20-$64;
Tel: (303) 247-0741

## EADS

**COUNTRY MANOR MOTEL**
609 East 15th Hwy 287 & 96
(81036)
Rates: N/A;
Tel: (719) 438-5451

## ESTES PARK

**CASTLE MOUNTAIN
LODGE**
1520 Fall River Rd (80517)
Rates: $45-$239;
Tel: (303) 586-3664

**FOUR WINDS
MOTOR LODGE**
1120 Big Thompson Ave
(80517)
Rates: $25-$62;
Tel: (303) 586-3313

**MACHINS COTTAGE
IN THE PINES**
P. O. Box 2687 (80517)
Rates: N/A;
Tel: (303) 586-4276

**OLYMPUS LODGE**
P. O. Box 547 (80517)
Rates: $28-$125;
Tel: (303) 586-8141

**STEAMSIDE CABINS**
1260 Fall River Rd (80517)
Rates: N/A;
Tel: (303) 586-6464

## EVANS

**WINTERSET INN**
800 31 St (80620)
Rates: N/A;
Tel: (303) 339-2493

## EVERGREEN

**HIGHLAND HAVEN
RESORT MOTEL**
4395 Independence Tr (80439)
Rates: $45-$110;
Tel: (303) 674-3577

## FAIRPLAY

**THE WESTERN INN**
P. O. Box 187 (80440)
Rates: $35-$45;
Tel: (303) 836-2026

## FORT COLLINS

**COMFORT INN**
1638 E Mulberry St (80524)
Rates: $44-$74;
Tel: (303) 484-2444

**DAYS INN**
3625 E Mulberry St (80524)
Rates: $35-$45;
Tel: (303) 221-5490

**ECONO LODGE**
4333 E Mulberry St (80524)
Rates: $39-$55;
Tel: (303) 493-9000

**FORT COLLINS MARRIOTT**
350 E Horsetooth Rd (80525)
Rates: $66;
Tel: (303) 226-5200

**HOLIDAY INN I-25**
3836 E Mulberry St (80524)
Rates: $40-$64;
Tel: (303) 484-4660

**MONTCLAIR MOTEL**
1405 N College Ave (80524)
Rates: $24-$45;
Tel: (303) 482-5452

**RAMADA INN**
3709 E Mulberry St (85024)
Rates: $38-$54;
Tel: (303) 493-7800

**TOWN & COUNTRY MOTEL**
1513 North College Ave
(80524)
Rates: N/A;
Tel: (303) 484-0870

**UNIVERSITY PARK
HOLIDAY INN**
425 W Prospect Rd (80526)
Rates: $38-$54;
Tel: (303) 482-2626

## FORT MORGAN

**BEST WESTERN
PARK TERRACE MOTEL**
725 Main (80701)
Rates: N/A;
Tel: (303) 867-8256

**CENTRAL MOTEL**
201 W Platte Ave (80701)
Rates: $29-$42;
Tel: (303) 867-2401

**ECONO LODGE**
1409 Barlow Rd (80701)
Rates: $32-$46;
Tel: (303) 867-9481

## FRISCO

**BEST WESTERN
LAKE DILLON LODGE**
1202 Summit Blvd (80443)
Rates: $67-$184;
Tel: (303) 668-5094

**HOLIDAY INN
SUMMIT COUNTY**
1129 N Summit Blvd (80443)
Rates: $55-$135;
Tel: (303) 668-5000

## GLENWOOD SPRINGS

**AFFORDABLE INNS**
51823 Hwys 6 & 24 (81601)
Rates: $29-$79;
Tel: (303) 945-8888

**BEST WESTERN
CARAVAN INN**
1826 Grand Ave (81601)
Rates: $44-$82;
Tel: (303) 945-7451

**HOLIDAY INN**
51359 Hwys 6 & 24 (81601)
Rates: $43-$64;
Tel: (303) 945-8551

**RAMADA INN**
124 W 6th St (81601)
Rates: $39-$76;
Tel: (303) 945-2500

**SILVER SPRUCE MOTEL**
162 W 6th St (81601)
Rates: $39-$84;
Tel: (303) 945-5458

## GOLDEN

**GOLDEN MOTEL**
510 24th St (80401)
Rates: N/A;
Tel: (303) 279-5581

## GRAND JUNCTION

**BEST WESTERN
HORIZON INN**
754 Horizon Dr (81506)
Rates: $35-$57;
Tel: (303) 245-1410

**GRAND JUNCTION HILTON**
743 Horizon Dr (81506)
Rates: $49-$140;
Tel: (303) 241-8888

**PEACHTREE INN**
1600 North Avenue (81501)
Rates: N/A;
Tel: (303) 245-5770

**RAMADA INN
OF GRAND JUNCTION**
2790 Crossroads Blvd
(81506)
Rates: $49-$66;
Tel: (303) 241-8411

**VALUE LODGE**
104 White Ave (81501)
Rates: N/A;
Tel: (303) 242-0651

**WEST GATE INN**
2210 Hwys 6 & 50 (81505)
Rates: $33-$49;
Tel: (303) 241-3020

## GRAND LAKE

**RIVERSIDE GUESTHOUSES**
P. O. Box 1469 (80447)
Rates: N/A;
Tel: (303) 627-3619

## GREELEY

**BEST WESTERN-RAMKOTA
INN & CONFERENCE CTR**
701 8th St (80631)
Rates: $50-$58;
Tel: (303) 353-8444

**HOLIDAY INN OF GREELEY**
609 8th Ave (80631)
Rates: $50-$62;
Tel: (303) 356-3000

**WINTERSET INN
OF GREELEY**
800 31st St (Evans 80620)
Rates: $29-$45;
Tel: (303) 339-2492

## GUNNISON

**DAYS INN**
701 Hwy 50W (81230)
Rates: $29-$60;
Tel: (303) 641-0608

**HYLANDER INN**
412 E Tomichi Ave (81230)
Rates: $28-$58;
Tel: (303) 641-0700

## HESPERUS

**CANYON MOTEL**
Hwy 160 & CR 124 (81326)
Rates: N/A;
Tel: (303) 259-6277

## IDAHO SPRINGS

**ARGO MOTOR INN**
2622 Colorado Blvd (80452)
Rates: N/A;
Tel: (303) 567-4473

**H & H MOTOR LODGE**
2445 Colorado Blvd (80452)
Rates: $29-$73;
Tel: (303) 567-2838

**PEORIANA MOTEL**
2901 Colorado Blvd (80452)
Rates: $25-$35;
Tel: (303) 567-2021

**6 & 40 NATIONAL INN**
2920 Colorado Blvd (80452)
Rates: $27-$45;
Tel: (303) 567-2691

## JULESBURG

**PLATTE VALLEY INN**
P. O. Box 67 (80737)
Rates: $34-$61;
Tel: (303) 474-3336

## KIT CARSON

**STAGE STOP MOTEL**
P. O. Box 207 (80825)
Rates: $26-$34;
Tel: (719) 962-3277

## LA JUNTA

**QUALITY INN**
1325 E 3rd St (81050)
Rates: $35-$50;
Tel: (719) 384-2571

## LAKE CITY

**WESTERN BELLE LODGE**
1221 Hwy 149 N (81235)
Rates: N/A;
Tel: (303) 944-2415

## LAMAR

**BEST WESTERN
COW PALACE INN**
1301 N Main St (81052)
Rates: $50-$75;
Tel: (719) 336-7753

**BLUE SPRUCE MOTEL**
1801 S Main St (81052)
Rates: $27-$35;
Tel: (719) 336-7454

## LAS ANIMAS

**BEST WESTERN
BENTS FORT INN**
P. O. Box 108 (81054)
Rates: $36-$48;
Tel: (719) 456-0011

## LEADVILLE

**SILVER KING MOTOR INN**
2020 N Poplar (80461)
Rates: $42-$59;
Tel: (719) 486-2610

## LIMON

**ECONO LODGE OF LIMON**
985 Hwy 24 (80828)
Rates: $33-$62;
Tel: (719) 775-2867

**LIMON INN 4 LESS EAST**
250 E Main St (80828)
Rates: $32-$39;
Tel: (719) 775-2821

**SAFARI MOTEL**
637 Main St (80828)
Rates: $34-$40;
Tel: (719) 775-2363

## LONGMONT

**RAINTREE PLAZA HOTEL**
1900 Diagonal Hwy (80501)
Rates: $92;
Tel: (303) 776-2000

**TWIN PEAKS
SUPER 8 MOTEL**
2446 N Main St (80501)
Rates: $30-$47;
Tel: (303) 772-8106

## LONGMONT
## DEL CAMINO

**SUPER 8 MOTEL**
1080 Sturner Blvd & I-25
(80504)
Rates: N/A;
Tel: (303) 772-0888

## LOVELAND

**BEST WESTERN
COACH HOUSE RESORT**
5542 Hwy 34E (80537)
Rates: $29-$59;
Tel: (303) 667-7810

**BUDGET HOST
EXIT 254 INN**
2716 SE Frontage Rd (80537)
Rates: $30-$44;
Tel: (303) 667-5202

## MANCOS

**BLUE SPRUCE MOTEL**
40700 Hwy 160 West
(81328)
Rates: $27-$50;
Tel: (303) 533-7073

**PONDEROSA CABINS**
Cty Road 37 & Hwy 184
(81328)
Rates: $40+;
Tel: (303) 882-7396

## MESA

**WAGON WHEEL MOTEL**
1090 Hwy 65 (81643)
Rates: $40-$45;
Tel: (303) 268-5224

## MESA VERDE NATIONAL PARK

**FAR VIEW LODGE
IN MESA VERDE**
P. O. Box 277 (Mancos 81328)
Rates: $72-$84;
Tel: (303) 529-4421

## MONTE VISTA

**BEST WESTERN MOVIE
MANOR MOTOR INN**
2830 W Hwy 160 (81144)
Rates: $39-$70;
Tel: (719) 852-5921

**COMFORT INN**
1519 Grande Ave (81144)
Rates: $55-$75;
Tel: (719) 852-0612

## MONTROSE

**BLACK CANYON MOTEL**
1605 E Main (81401)
Rates: $30-$54;
Tel: (303) 249-3495

**COUNTRY LODGE**
1624 E Main (81401)
Rates: $38-$72;
Tel: (303) 249-4567

## NEDERLAND

**NEDERHAUS MOTEL**
686 Hwy 119 South (80466)
Rates: N/A;
Tel: (800) 422-4629

## OURAY

**OURAY VICTORIAN INN**
P. O. Box 1812 (81427-1812)
Rates: $44-$75;
Tel: (303) 325-7222

**TIMBER RIDGE MOTEL**
1515 North Main St (81427)
Rates: N/A;
Tel: (303) 325-4523

## PAGOSA SPRINGS

**BEST WESTERN
OAK RIDGE MOTOR INN**
P. O. Box 1200 (81147)
Rates: $40-$60;
Tel: (303) 264-4173

## PUEBLO

**BEST WESTERN
TOWN HOUSE MOTEL**
8th St & Santa Fe Ave (81103)
Rates: $43-$55;
Tel: (719) 543-6530

**HAMPTON INN**
4703 N Frwy (81108)
Rates: $54-$66;
Tel: (719) 544-4700

**HOLIDAY INN**
4001 N Elizabeth (81108)
Rates: $59-$79;
Tel: (719) 543-8050

## RED STONE

**AVALANCHE RANCH
BED & BREAKFAST**
12863 Hwy 133 (81623)
Rates: $75-$115;
Tel: (303) 963-2846

## ROCKY FORD

**MELON VALLEY INN**
1319 Elm Ave (81067)
Rates: $30-$45;
Tel: (719) 254-3306

## SALIDA

**ASPEN LEAF LODGE**
7350 Hwy 50W (81201)
Rates $26-$50;
Tel: (719) 539-6733

**CIRCLE R MOTEL**
304 E Rainbow Blvd (81201)
Rates: $24-$48;
Tel: (719) 539-6296

**MONARCH
MOUNTAIN LODGE**
Number One Powder Pt
(Monarch 81227)
Rates: $39-$110;
Tel: (719) 539-2581

**RAINBOW INN**
105 Hwy 50E (81201)
Rates: $28-$50;
Tel: (719) 539-4444

**WESTERN HOLIDAY MOTEL**
545 W Rainbow Blvd (81201)
Rates: $35-$60;
Tel: (719) 539-2553

**WOODLAND MOTEL
& RESIDENCE INN**
903 W 1st (81201)
Rates: $22-$63;
Tel: (719) 539-4980

## SILVER CREEK

**THE INN AT SILVER CREEK**
P. O. Box 4222 (80446)
Rates: N/A;
Tel: (800) 926-4386

## SILVERTHORNE

**I-70 INN**
361 Blueriver Pkwy (80498)
Rates: N/A;
Tel: (303) 468-5170

## SNOWMASS VILLAGE

**SILVERTREE HOTEL**
P. O. Box 5009 (81615)
Rates: $135-$375;
Tel: (303) 923-3520

## SOUTH FORK

**THE INN MOTEL**
30362 West Hwy 160
(81154)
Rates: N/A;
Tel: (719) 873-5514

**WOLF CREEK SKI LODGE**
P. O. Box 283 (81154)
Rates: $48-$55;
Tel: (719) 873-5547

## STEAMBOAT SPRINGS

**THE ALPINER LODGE**
424 Lincoln Ave (80477)
Rates: $48-$115;
Tel: (303) 879-1430

**HARBOR HOTEL &
HOTEL HARBOR CONDOS**
P. O. Box 774109 (80477)
Rates: $40-$180;
Tel: (303) 879-1522

**HOLIDAY INN
OF STEAMBOAT**
P. O. Box 5007 (80477)
Rates: $50-$149;
Tel: (303) 879-2600

**THE OVERLOOK LODGE**
P. O. Box 770388 (80477)
Rates: $65-$175;
Tel: (303) 879-2900

**RABBIT EARS MOTEL**
P. O. Box 770573 (80477)
Rates: $38-$120;
Tel: (303) 879-1150

**SKY VALLEY LODGE**
P. O. Box 773132 (80477)
Rates: $55-$195;
Tel: (303) 879-7749

## STERLING

**COLONIAL MOTEL**
915 S Division (80751)
Rates: $20-$32;
Tel: (303) 522-3382

**PARK INN INTERNATIONAL**
I-76 & Hwy 6E (80751)
Rates: $32-$67;
Tel: (303) 522-2625

## STRATTON

**BEST WESTERN
GOLDEN PRAIRIE INN**
700 Colorado Ave (80836)
Rates: $43-$59;
Tel: (719) 348-5311

## TRINIDAD

**BEST WESTERN
COUNTRY CLUB INN**
900 W Adams (81082)
Rates: $45-$69;
Tel: (719) 846-2215

**BUDGET HOST TRINIDAD**
10301 Santa Fe Trail Dr
(81082)
Rates: $24-$69;
Tel: (719) 846-3307

**BUDGET SUMMIT INN**
I-25 Exit 11 (81082)
Rates: N/A;
Tel: (719) 846-2251

**TRINIDAD MOTOR INN**
702 W Main St (81082)
Rates: $30-$51;
Tel: (719) 846-2271

## VAIL

**ANTLERS AT VAIL**
680 W Lionshead Pl (81657)
Rates: $85-$345;
Tel: (303) 476-2471

**L'OSTELLO**
704 W Lionshead Cir (81657)
Rates: $49-$245;
Tel: (303) 476-2050

## WALSENBURG

**ANCHOR MOTEL**
1001 Main St (81089)
Rates: $28-$55;
Tel: (719) 738-2800

**BEST WESTERN RAMBLER**
P. O. Box 48 (81089)
Rates: $55-$80;
Tel: (719) 738-1121

## WINTER PARK

**ALPENGLO
MOTOR LODGE**
US Hwy 40, Box 35 (80482)
Rates: N/A;
Tel: (303) 726-8301

# CONNECTICUT

## BRANFORD

**BRANFORD MOTOR INN**
P. O. Box 449 (06405)
Rates: $50-$74;
Tel: (203) 488-8314

## BRIDGEPORT

**MARRIOTT
TRUMBULL HOTEL**
180 Hawley Lane
(Trumbull 06611)
Rates: $129-$300;
Tel. (203) 378-1400

## CLINTON

**CLINTON MOTEL**
163 East Main St (06413)
Rates: N/A;
Tel: (203) 669-8850

## CORNWALL BRIDGE

**THE CORNWALL INN**
Route 7 (06754)
Rates: N/A;
Tel: (800) 786-6884

## CROMWELL

**COMFORT INN**
111 Berlin Rd (06416)
Rates: $46-$58;
Tel: (203) 635-4100

**RADISSON HOTEL
AND CONFERENCE CTR**
100 Berlin Rd (06416)
Rates: $84-$106;
Tel: (203) 635-2000

**SUPER 8 MOTEL**
1 Industrial Park Rd (06416)
Rates: $39-$45;
Tel: (203) 632-8888

## DANBURY

**DANBURY
HILTON & TOWERS**
18 Old Ridgebury Rd (06810)
Rates: $79-$159;
Tel: (203) 794-0600

**ETHAN ALLEN INN**
21 Lake Ave Extension (06811)
Rates: $67-$109;
Tel: (203) 744-1776

**HOLIDAY INN**
80 Newtown Rd (06810)
Rates: $59-$104;
Tel: (203) 792-4000

**RAMADA INN**
1 1/2 Mi NE at Exit 8 (06810)
Rates: $69-$150;
Tel: (203) 792-3800

## DARIEN

**COMFORT INN**
50 Ledge Rd (06820)
Rates: $66-$75;
Tel: (203) 655-8211

## EAST HARTFORD

**HOLIDAY INN**
363 Roberts St (06108)
Rates: $79;
Tel: (203) 528-9611

**RAMADA HOTEL**
100 E River Dr (06108)
Rates: $79-$114;
Tel: (203) 528-9703

**WELLESLY INN**
333 Roberts St (06108)
Rates: $45-$75;
Tel: (203) 289-4950

## EAST WINDSOR

**COMFORT INN**
260 Main St (06088)
Rates: $49-$59;
Tel: (203) 627-6585

**RAMADA INN**
161 Bridge St (06088)
Rates: $55-$72;
Tel: (203) 623-9411

## ENFIELD

**RED ROOF INN**
5 Hazard Ave (06802)
Rates: $32-$37;
Tel: (203) 741-2571

## FAIRFIELD

**FAIRFIELD MOTOR INN**
417 Post Rd (06430)
Rates: $63-$70;
Tel: (800) 257-0496

## FARMINGTON

**CENTENNIAL INN**
5 Spring Ln (06032)
Rates: $85-$160;
Tel: (203) 677-4647

**MARRIOTT HOTEL**
15 Farm Springs Rd (06032)
Rates: $99-$125;
Tel: (203) 678-1000

## HARTFORD
(and Vicinity)

**HOLIDAY INN-
DOWNTOWN**
50 Morgan St (06120)
Rates: $99-$135;
Tel: (203) 549-2400

91

**RAMADA INN-CAPITOL HILL**
440 Asylum St (06103)
Rates: $39-$55;
Tel: (203) 246-6591

**RAMADA INN DOWNTOWN**
100 East River Dr
(E Hartford 06108)
Rates: $75-$175;
Tel: (203) 528-9703

**SHERATON-HARTFORD HOTEL**
315 Trumbull St (06103)
Rates: $115-$130;
Tel: (203) 728-5151

**SUPER 8 MOTEL**
57 W Service Rd (06120)
Rates: $39-$45;
Tel: (203) 246-8888

## LAKEVILLE

**IRON MASTERS MOTOR INN**
P. O. Box 690 (06039)
Rates: $59-$120;
Tel: (203) 435-9844

## LITCHFIELD

**TOLLGATE HILL INN**
P. O. Box 1339 (06759)
Rates: $100-$175;
Tel: (203) 567-4545

## MANCHESTER

**MANCHESTER VILLAGE MOTOR INN**
100 E Center St (06040)
Rates: $49-$57;
Tel: (203) 646-2300

## MERIDEN

**HAMPTON INN**
10 Bee St (06450)
Rates: $48-$64;
Tel: (203) 235-5154

**RAMADA INN**
275 Research Pkwy (06450)
Rates: $69-$99;
Tel: (203) 238-2380

**RESIDENCE INN BY MARRIOTT**
390 Bee St (06450)
Rates: $99-$119;
Tel: (203) 634-7770

## MILFORD

**COMFORT INN-MILFORD**
278 Old Gate Ln (06460)
Rates: $54-$60;
Tel: (203) 877-9411

**HAMPTON INN**
129 Plains Rd (06460)
Rates: $54-$65;
Tel: (203) 874-4400

**HOLIDAY INN**
1212 Boston Post Rd (06460)
Rates: $65-$112;
Tel: (203) 879-6561

**RED ROOF INN**
10 Rowe Ave (06460)
Rates: $44-$55;
Tel: (203) 877-6060

## MYSTIC

**CHARLEY'S GUEST HOUSE**
Edgemont St (06355)
Rates: N/A;
Tel: (203) 572-9253

## MYSTIC-LEDYARD

**APPLEWOOD FARMS INN**
528 Col Ledyard Hwy (06339)
Rates: N/A;
Tel: (203) 536-2022

## NEW BRITAIN

**RAMADA INN**
65 Columbus Blvd (06051)
Rates: $50-$70;
Tel: (203) 224-9161

## NEW LONDON

**OAKDELL MOTEL**
983 Hartford Tpke
(Waterford 06385)
Rates: N/A;
Tel: (203) 442-9446

**RED ROOF INN**
707 Colman St (06320)
Rates: $29-$67;
Tel: (203) 444-0001

## NEW MILFORD

**THE HERITAGE INN OF LITCHFIELD COUNTY**
34 Bridge St (06776)
Rates: $59-$94;
Tel: (203) 354-8883

## NIANTIC

**HOWARD JOHNSON LODGE**
265 Flanders Rd (06333)
Rates: $32-$105;
Tel: (203) 739-6921

## NIANTIC/NEW LONDON

**CONNECTICUT YANKEE INN**
Exit 74 I-95 & 161 (06357)
Rates: N/A;
Tel: (800) 942-8466

## NORTH HAVEN

**HOLIDAY INN**
201 Washington Ave (06473)
Rates: $63;
Tel: (203) 239-4225

## NORWALK

**NORWALK HOLIDAY INN**
789 Connecticut Ave (06854)
Rates: $75-$81;
Tel: (203) 853-3477

## NORWICH

**SHERATON
MOTOR HOTEL**
10 Laura Blvd (06360)
Rates: $80-$150;
Tel: (203) 889-5201

## OLD LYME

**OLD LYME INN**
P. O. Box 787 (06371)
Rates: $85-$140;
Tel: (203) 434-2600

## PLAINFIELD

**PLAINFIELD MOTEL**
Box 101, RR 2
(Moosup 06354)
Rates: $37-$64;
Tel: (203) 564-2791

## PLAINVILLE

**INN AT PLAINVILLE**
400 New Britain Ave (06062)
Rates: $34;
Tel: (203) 747-6876

## PUTNAM

**KING'S INN**
5 Heritage Rd (06260)
Rates: $62-$78;
Tel: (203) 928-7961

## ROCKY HILL

**HOWARD JOHNSON
LODGE & CONFERENCE CTR**
1499 Silas Deane Hwy
(06067)
Rates: $39;
Tel: (203) 529-7446

## SHELTON

**RAMADA HOTEL**
780 Bridgeport Ave (06484)
Rates: $114-$164;
Tel: (203) 929-1500

**RESIDENCE INN
BY MARRIOTT**
1001 Bridgeport Ave (06484)
Rates: $117-$150;
Tel: (203) 926-9000

## SIMSBURY

**THE EXECUTIVE INN**
969 Hopmeadow St (06070)
Rates: $59-$75;
Tel: (203) 658-2216

**THE SIMSBURY
1820 HOUSE**
731 Hopmeadow St (06070)
Rates: $85-$135;
Tel: (203) 658-7658

## SOUTHINGTON

**COMFORT INN**
120 Laning St (06489)
Rates: $45-$57;
Tel: (203) 276-0736

**HOWARD JOHNSON
LODGE**
30 Laning St (06489)
Rates: $36-$69;
Tel: (203) 628-0921

## STAMFORD

**BUDGET HOST
HOSPITALITY INN**
19 Clarks Hill Ave (06902)
Rates: $52-$75;
Tel: (203) 327-4300

**DAYS INN**
135 Harvard Ave (06902)
Rates: $50-$65;
Tel: (203) 357-7100

**SUPER 8 MOTEL**
32 Grenhart Rd (06902)
Rates: N/A;
Tel: (203) 324-8887

## VERNON

**HOWARD JOHNSON
LODGE**
451 Hartford Tpk (06066)
Rates: $45-$65;
Tel: (203) 875-0781

## WATERBURY

**BEST WESTERN
RED BULL INN**
South of I-84 exit 25 to
Schrafft's Dr (06705)
Rates: $42-$81;
Tel: (203) 597-8000

**HOLIDAY INN WATERBURY
AT BUCKINGHAM SQ**
63 Grand St (06702)
Rates: $59-$65;
Tel: (203) 596-1000

**QUALITY INN
OF WATERBURY**
88 Union St (06702)
Rates: $49-$55;
Tel: (203) 575-1500

## WESTBROOK

**MAPLES MOTEL**
1935 Boston Post Rd (06498)
Rates: $36-$55;
Tel: (203) 399-9345

## WEST HAVEN

**DAYS HOTEL NEW
HAVEN/WEST HAVEN**
490 Sawmill Rd (06516)
Rates: $64-$87;
Tel: (203) 933-0344

## WETHERSFIELD

**RAMADA INN-
HARTFORD AREA**
1330 Silas Deane Hwy
(06109)
Rates: $49-$59;
Tel: (203) 563-2311

## WINDSOR

**THE RESIDENCE INN
HARTFORD-WINDSOR**
100 Dunfey Ln (06095)
Rates: $75-$145;
Tel: (203) 688-7474

## WINDSOR LOCKS

**BUDGETEL INN**
64 Ella T Grasso Tpk (06096)
Rates: $33-$49;
Tel: (203) 623-3336

**HOMEWOOD SUITES
HARTFORD-WINDSOR
LOCKS**
65 Ella T Grasso Tpk (06096)
Rates: $69-$99;
Tel: (203) 627-8463

**THE WINDSOR COURT HOTEL
& CONFERENCE CTR**
383 S Center St (06096)
Rates: $55-$78;
Tel: (203) 623-9811

## WOODSTOCK-PUTNAM

**INN AT WOODSTOCK HILL**
94 Plaine Hill Road (06267)
Rates: N/A;
Tel: (203) 928-0528

# DELAWARE

## DEWEY

**ATLANTIC OCEANSIDE**
1700 Hwy 1 (19939)
Rates: N/A;
Tel: (302) 227-8811

## DOVER

**HOLIDAY INN-DOVER**
348 N DuPont Hwy (19901)
Rates: $39-$60;
Tel: (302) 734-5701

**SHERATON INN-DOVER**
1570 N DuPont Hwy (19901)
Rates: $54-$60;
Tel: (302) 678-8500

## NEWARK

**COMFORT INN**
1120 S College Ave (19713)
Rates: $42-$54;
Tel: (302) 368-8715

**HAMPTON INN**
3 Concord Ln (19713)
Rates: $55-$70;
Tel: (302) 737-3900

**RED ROOF INN**
415 Stanton Christiana Rd
(19713)
Rates: $41-$50;
Tel: (302) 292-2870

**RESIDENCE INN
BY MARRIOTT**
240 Chapman Rd (19702)
Rates: $115-$135;
Tel: (302) 453-9200

**SHERATON INN**
260 Chapman Rd (19702)
Rates: $58-$79;
Tel: (302) 738-3400

## NEW CASTLE

**ECONO LODGE**
232 S DuPont Hwy (19720)
Rates: $34-$42;
Tel: (302) 322-4500

**HOWARD JOHNSON
MOTOR LODGE**
2162 New Castle Ave
(19720)
Rates: $50-$80;
Tel: (302) 656-7771

**NEW CASTLE TRAVELODGE**
1213 West Ave (19720)
Rates: $38-$42;
Tel: (302) 654-5544

**QUALITY INN SKYWAYS**
147 N DuPont Hwy (19720)
Rates: $50-$58;
Tel: (302) 328-6666

**RAMADA INN**
P. O. Box 647 (19720)
Rates: $67-$85;
Tel: (302) 658-8511

**RODEWAY INN**
111 S DuPont Hwy (19720)
Rates: $35-$54;
Tel: (302) 328-6246

## REHOBOTH BEACH

**ATLANTIC
OCEANSIDE MOTEL**
1700 Hwy 1
(Dewey Beach 19971)
Rates: $29-$95;
Tel: (302) 227-8811

**BELLBUOY MOTEL**
21 Van Dyke St
(Dewey Beach 19971)
Rates: $40-$98;
Tel: (302) 227-6000

## SEAFORD

**COMFORT INN**
1450 Beaver Dam Rd (19973)
Rates: $49-$65;
Tel: (302) 629-8385

## WILMINGTON

**BEST WESTERN
BRANDYWINE VALLEY INN**
1807 Concord Pike (19803)
Rates: $49-$79;
Tel: (302) 656-9436

**CHRISTINA HOUSE**
707 N King St (19801)
Rates: $75-$135;
Tel: (302) 656 9300

**DAYS INN**
1102 West St (19801)
Rates: $79-$119;
Tel: (302) 429-7600

**HOLIDAY INN
DOWNTOWN**
700 King St (19801)
Rates: $68-$99;
Tel: (302) 655 0400

**TALLY-HO MOTOR LODGE**
5209 Concord Pike (19803)
Rates: $38-$45;
Tel: (302) 478-0300

**WILMINGTON HILTON**
630 Naamans Rd
(Claymont 19703)
Rates: $59-$139;
Tel: (302) 792-2700

# DISTRICT OF COLUMBIA

## WASHINGTON
(Downtown)

**ANA HOTEL-
WASHINGTON D.C.**
2401 M St NW (20037)
Rates: $102-$305;
Tel: (202) 429-2400

**BEST WESTERN
CENTER CITY HOTEL**
1201 13th St NW (20005)
Rates: $73-$121;
Tel: (202) 682-5300

**CAPITAL HILTON**
16th & K Sts NW (20036)
Rates: $225-$295;
Tel: (202) 393-1000

**THE CARLTON-
ITT LUXURY HOTEL**
923 16th St at K St NW
(20006)
Rates: $139-$295;
Tel: (202) 879-6911

**CARLYLE SUITES HOTEL**
1731 New Hampshire Ave
(20009)
Rates: N/A;
Tel: (202) 234-3200

**COMFORT INN
DOWNTOWN**
500 H St NW (20001)
Rates: $69-$139;
Tel: (202) 289-5959

**FOUR SEASONS HOTEL**
2800 Pennsylvania Ave NW
(20007)
Rates: $195-$310;
Tel: (202) 342-0444

**GEORGETOWN
DUTCH INN**
1075 Thomas Jefferson NW
(20007)
Rates: N/A;
Tel: (202) 337-0900

**GEORGETOWN MEWS**
1111 20th St NW (20007)
Rates: N/A;
Tel: (202) 298-7731

**GUEST QUARTERS
SUITE HOTEL-NH**
801 New Hampshire Ave NW
(20037)
Rates: $180-$195;
Tel: (202) 785-2000

**HOLIDAY INN-CAPITOL**
550 C St SW (20024)
Rates: $99;
Tel: (202) 479-4000

**HOLIDAY INN-
GEORGETOWN**
2101 Wisconsin Ave NW
(20007)
Rates: $79;
Tel: (202) 338-4600

**HOLIDAY INN-
THOMAS CIRCLE**
1155 14th St NW (20005)
Rates: $89;
Tel: (202) 737-1200

**HOTEL WASHINGTON**
Pennsylvania Ave NW at 15th
St (20004)
Rates: $148-$200;
Tel: (202) 638-5900

**THE JEFFERSON HOTEL**
16th & M Sts NW (20036)
Rates: $145-$295;
Tel: (202) 347-2200

**LOEWS L'ENFANT
PLAZA HOTEL**
480 L'Enfant Plaza SW
(20024)
Rates: $185-$225;
Tel: (202) 484-1000

**THE MADISON HOTEL**
15th & M Sts NW (20005)
Rates: $225-$395;
Tel: (202) 862-1600

**MASTER HOSTS INN**
1917 Bladensburg Rd (20002)
Rates: N/A;
Tel: (202) 832-8600

**ONE WASHINGTON CIRCLE HOTEL**
One Washington Cir NW (20037)
Rates: $75-$290;
Tel: (202) 872-1680

**PARK HYATT WASHINGTON D.C.**
24th St at M St NW (20037)
Rates: $159-$310;
Tel: (202) 789-1234

**QUALITY HOTEL CAPITOL HILL**
415 New Jersey Ave NW (20001)
Rates: $59-$165;
Tel: (202) 638-1616

**THE SAVOY SUITES HOTEL**
2505 Wisconsin Ave NW (20007)
Rates: $69-$119;
Tel: (202) 337-9700

**SHERATON WASHINGTON HOTEL**
2660 Woodley Rd NW (20008)
Rates: $186-$266;
Tel: (202) 328-2000

**STOUFFER MAYFLOWER HOTEL**
1127 Connecticut Ave NW (20036)
Rates: $159-$320;
Tel: (202) 347-2000

**SWISS INN HOTEL NORTHWEST**
1204 Massachusetts Ave (20005)
Rates: N/A;
Tel: (202) 371-1816

**WASHINGTON HILTON & TOWERS**
1919 Connecticut Ave NW (20009)
Rates: $89-$255;
Tel: (202) 483-3000

**WASHINGTON HOTEL**
515 15th St NW (20004)
Rates: $149-$589:
Tel: (800) 424-9540

**WASHINGTON MARRIOTT HOTEL**
1221 22nd St at M St NW (20037)
Rates: $119-$200;
Tel: (202) 872-1500

**WASHINGTON PLAZA HOTEL**
10 Thomas Circle (20005)
Rates: N/A;
Tel: (202) 842-1300

**THE WATERGATE HOTEL**
2650 Virginia Ave NW (20037)
Rates: $235-$495;
Tel: (202) 965-2300

**THE WILLARD INTER-CONTINENTAL**
1401 Pennsylvania Ave NW (20004)
Rates: $179-$330;
Tel: (202) 628-9100

# WASHINGTON
(West and South)

**BEST WESTERN ARLINGTON INN & TOWER**
2480 S Glebe Rd (Arlington, VA 22206)
Rates: $59-$89;
Tel: (703) 979-4400

**BEST WESTERN-OLD COLONY INN**
625 First St (Alexandria, VA 22314)
Rates: $95-$140;
Tel: (703) 548-6300

**BEST WESTERN ROSSLYN WESTPARK HOTEL**
1900 N Fort Myer Dr (Arlington, VA 22209)
Rates: $67-$150;
Tel: (703) 527-4814

**BEST WESTERN SPRINGFIELD INN**
6550 Loisdale Ct (Springfield, VA 22150)
Rates: $45-$69;
Tel: (703) 922-9000

**BEST WESTERN TYSON'S WESTPARK HOTEL**
8401 Westpark Dr (McLean, VA 22102)
Rates: $59-$95;
Tel: (703) 734-2800

**COMFORT INN-DULLES INTL AIRPORT**
4050 Westfax Dr (Chantilly, VA 22021)
Rates: $49-$79;
Tel: (703) 818-8200

**COMFORT INN-MOUNT VERNON**
7212 Richmond Hwy (Alexandria, VA 22306)
Rates: $40-$75;
Tel: (703) 765-9000

**COMFORT INN-UNIVERISTY CENTER**
11180 Main St (Fairfax, VA 22030)
Rates: $49-$70;
Tel: (703) 591-5900

**COMFORT INN-VAN DORN**
5716 S Van Dorn St (Alexandria, VA 22310)
Rates: $55-$66;
Tel: (703) 922-9200

**DAYS INN-ALEXANDRIA**
110 S Bragg St (Alexandria, VA 22312)
Rates: $46-$61;
Tel: (703) 354-4950

**DAYS INN-RICHMOND HIGHWAY**
6100 Richmond Hwy (Alexandria, VA 22303)
Rates: $51-$67;
Tel: (703) 329-0500

**DOUBLETREE HOTEL-NATIONAL AIRPORT**
300 Army Navy Dr (Arlington, VA 22202)
Rates: $65-$155;
Tel: (703) 892-4100

**ECONO LODGE-MOUNT VERNON**
8849 Richmond Hwy (Alexandria, VA 22309)
Rates: $55-$60;
Tel: (703) 780-0300

**ECONO LODGE-PENTAGON**
5666 Columbia Pike (Baileys Crossroads, VA 22041)
Rates: $60-$65;
Tel: (703) 820-5600

**FAIRVIEW PARK MARRIOTT HOTEL**
3111 Fairview Park Dr
(Falls Church, VA 22042)
Rates: $75-$150;
Tel: (703) 849-9400

**GUEST QUARTERS SUITE HOTEL-ALEXANDRIA**
100 S Reynolds St
(Alexandria, VA 22304)
Rates: $89;
Tel: (703) 370-9600

**HAMPTON INN WASHINGTON-DULLES AIRPORT**
45440 Holiday Dr
(Sterling, VA 22170)
Rates: $57-$71;
Tel. (703) 471-8300

**HOLIDAY INN ARLINGTON AT BALLSTON**
4610 N Fairfax Dr
(Arlington, VA 22203)
Rates: $79-$132;
Tel. (703) 243-9800

**HOLIDAY INN EISENHOWER METRO**
2460 Eisenhower Ave
(Alexandria, VA 22314)
Rates: $72-$118;
Tel: (703) 960-3400

**HOLIDAY INN FAIRFAX CITY**
3535 Chain Bridge Rd
(Fairfax, VA 22030)
Rates: $65-$95;
Tel: (703) 591-5500

**HOLIDAY INN-KEY BRIDGE**
1850 N Fort Myer Dr
(Arlington, VA 22209)
Rates: $95-$115;
Tel: (703) 522-0400

**HOLIDAY INN-OLD TOWN**
480 King St
(Alexandria, VA 22314)
Rates: $114-$157;
Tel: (703) 549-6080

**HOLIDAY INN WASHINGTON-DULLES**
1000 Sully Rd
(Sterling, VA 22170)
Rates: $75-$115;
Tel: (703) 471-7411

**HOWARD JOHNSON HOTEL-ALEXANDRIA**
5821 Richmond Hwy
(Alexandria, VA 22303)
Rates: $59-$94;
Tel: (703) 329-1400

**HOWARD JOHNSON HOTEL-NATL AIRPORT**
2650 Jefferson Davis Hwy
(Arlington, VA 22202)
Rates: $80-$128;
Tel: (703) 684-7200

**HYATT ARLINGTON AT KEY BRIDGE**
1325 Wilson Blvd
(Arlington, VA 22209)
Rates: $69-$181;
Tel. (703) 525-1234

**HYATT FAIR LAKES**
12777 Fair Lakes Cir
(Fairfax, VA 22033)
Rates: $59-$170;
Tel: (703) 818-1234

**MCLEAN HILTON AT TYSONS CORNER**
7920 Jones Branch Dr
(McLean, VA 22102)
Rates: $95-$205;
Tel: (703) 847-5000

**QUALITY INN EXECUTIVE**
6111 Arlington Blvd
(Falls Church, VA 22044)
Rates: $60-$70;
Tel: (703) 534-9100

**RAMADA INN SEMINARY PLAZA**
4641 Kenmore Ave
(Alexandria, VA 22304)
Rates: $59-$104;
Tel: (703) 751-4510

**RAMADA RENAISSANCE ARLINGTON HOTEL**
950 N Stafford St
(Arlington, VA 22203)
Rates: $120-$180;
Tel: (703) 528-6000

**RAMADA RENAISSANCE HOTEL-WASHINGTON**
13869 Park Center Rd
(Herndon, VA 22071)
Rates: $109-$144;
Tel: (703) 478-2900

**RED ROOF INN-ALEXANDRIA**
5975 Richmond Hwy
(Alexandria, VA 22303)
Rates: $44-$63;
Tel: (703) 960-5200

**RESIDENCE INN BY MARRIOTT-HERNDON**
315 Elden St
(Herndon, VA 22070)
Rates: $110-$145;
Tel: (703) 435-0044

**RESIDENCE INN BY MARRIOTT-TYSONS CORNER**
8616 Westwood Center Dr
(Vienna, VA 22182)
Rates: $126-$166;
Tel: (703) 893-0120

**THE RITZ-CARLTON TYSONS CORNER**
1700 Tysons Blvd
(McLean, VA 22102)
Rates: $135-$210;
Tel: (703) 506-4300

**SHERATON SUITES ALEXANDRIA**
801 N St. Asaph St
(Alexandria, VA 22314)
Rates: $99-$164;
Tel: (703) 836-4700

**STOUFFER CONCOURSE HOTEL**
2399 Jefferson Davis Hwy
(Arlington, VA 22202)
Rates: $89-$240;
Tel: (703) 418-6800

**TYSONS CORNER MARRIOTT HOTEL**
8028 Leesburg Pike
(Vienna, VA 22182)
Rates: $79-$156;
Tel: (703) 734-3200

**WELLESLEY INN-HERNDON**
485 Elden St
(Herndon, VA 22070)
Rates: $52-$75;
Tel: (703) 478-9777

**WELLESLEY INN
OF FAIRFAX**
10327 Lee Hwy
(Fairfax, VA 22030)
Rates: $46-$70;
Tel: (703) 359-2888

# WASHINGTON
(West and North)

**COMFORT INN
GERMANTOWN**
20260 Goldenrod Ln
(Germantown, MD 20874)
Rates: $54-$63;
Tel: (301) 428-1300

**DAYS INN-
ROCKVILLE/GAITHERSBURG**
16001 Shady Grove Rd
(Rockville, MD 20850)
Rates: $50-$60;
Tel: (301) 948-4300

**EMBASSY SUITES
CHEVY CHASE PAVILLION**
4300 Military Rd NW (20015)
Rates: $119-$165;
Tel: (202) 362-9300

**HOLIDAY INN BETHESDA**
8120 Wisconsin Ave
(Bethesda, MD 20814)
Rates: $109-$134;
Tel: (301) 652-2000

**HOLIDAY INN
CHEVY CHASE**
5520 Wisconsin Ave
(Chevy Chase, MD 20815)
Rates: $95-$129;
Tel: (301) 656-1500

**HOLIDAY INN-
GAITHERSBURG**
2 Montgomery Village Ave
(Gaithersburg, MD 20879)
Rates: $69-$101;
Tel: (301) 948-8900

**HOLIDAY INN-
SILVER SPRING PLAZA**
8777 Georgia Ave
(Silver Spring, MD 20910)
Rates: $80-$115;
Tel: (301) 589-0800

**RAMADA INN ROCKVILLE**
1775 Rockville Pike
(Rockville, MD 20852)
Rates: $55-$115;
Tel: (301) 881-2300

**RED ROOF INN-
GAITHERSBURG**
497 Quince Orchard Rd
(Gaithersburg, MD 20878)
Rates: $29-$53;
Tel: (301) 977-3311

**RESIDENCE INN-BETHESDA**
7335 Wisconsin Ave
(Bethesda, MD 20814)
Rates: $145-$165;
Tel: (301) 718-0200

**WOODFIN SUITES HOTEL**
1380 Piccard Dr
(Rockville, MD 20850)
Rates: $69-$158;
Tel: (301) 590-9880

# WASHINGTON
(Eastern)

**THE GREENBELT
MARRIOTT**
6400 Ivy Ln
(Greenbelt, MD 20770)
Rates: $69-$119;
Tel: (301) 441-3700

**HOJO INN**
600 New York Ave NE
(20002)
Rates: $50-$62;
Tel: (202) 546-9200

**HOLIDAY INN
CAPITAL BELTWAY EAST**
5910 Princess Garden Pkwy
(Lanham, MD 20706)
Rates: $50-$69;
Tel: (301) 459-1000

**HOLIDAY INN-GREENBELT**
7200 Hanover Dr
(Greenbelt, MD 20770)
Rates: $63-$88;
Tel: (301) 982-7000

**HOWARD JOHNSON
LODGE-WASHINGTON NE**
5811 Annapolis Rd
(Cheverly, MD 20784)
Rates: $49-$69;
Tel: (301) 779-7700

**MASTER HOST INN**
1917 Bladensburg Rd NE
(20002)
Rates: $50-$66;
Tel: (202) 832-8600

**PARK VIEW INN-
COLLEGE PARK**
9020 Baltimore Blvd
(College Park, MD 20740)
Rates: $39-$54;
Tel: (301) 441-8110

**RED ROOF INN-LANHAM**
9050 Lanham Severn Rd
(Lanham, MD 20706)
Rates: $44-$54;
Tel: (301) 731-8830

**RED ROOF INN-
OXON HILL**
6170 Oxon Hill Rd
(Oxon Hill, MD 20745)
Rates: $34-$55;
Tel: (301) 567-8030

**SHERATON
GREENBELT HOTEL**
8500 Annapolis Rd
(New Carrollton, MD 20784)
Rates: $97-$137;
Tel: (301) 459-6700

**SUPER 8-
WASHINGTON D.C.**
501 New York Ave NE
(20002)
Rates: $52-$59;
Tel: (202) 543-7400

# FLORIDA

## ALACHUA

**HOJO INN**
Rt 1, Box 229A (32615)
Rates: $32-$35;
Tel: (904) 462-2244

## ALTAMONTE SPRINGS

**LA QUINTA INN**
150 S Westmonte Dr (32714)
Rates: $53-$70;
Tel: (407) 788-1411

**RESIDENDE INN
BY MARRIOTT**
270 Douglas Ave (32714)
Rates: $109-$159;
Tel: (407) 788-7991

## APALACHICOLA

**THE GIBSON INN**
P. O. Box 221 (32320)
Rates: $60-$110;
Tel: (904) 653-2191

**RANCHO INN**
Hwy 98 W (32320)
Rates: $32-$38;
Tel: (904) 653-9435

**SPORTSMAN'S LODGE
MOTEL AND MARINA**
P. O. Box 606
(Eastpoint 32328)
Rates: $32-$42;
Tel: (904) 670-8423

## APOLLO BEACH

**HOLIDAY INN-
TAMPA APOLLO BEACH**
6414 Surfside (33572)
Rates: $55-$90;
Tel: (813) 645-3271

## APOPKA

**CROSBY'S MOTOR INN**
1440 W Orange Blossom Tr
(32712)
Rates: $39-$69;
Tel: (407) 886-3220

## ARCADIA

**BEST WESTERN M & M MOTEL**
504 S Brevard Ave (33821)
Rates: $40-$50;
Tel: (813) 494-4884

## AVON PARK

**ECONO LODGE**
2511 US Hwy 27S (33825)
Rates: $36-$69;
Tel: (813) 452-2000

## BOCA RATON

**BOCA RATON MARRIOTT
CROCKER CENTER**
5150 Town Center Cir
(33486)
Rates: $129-$184;
Tel: (407) 392-4600

**BOCA RATON
RADISSON SUITE HOTEL**
7920 Glades Rd (33434)
Rates: $89-$169;
Tel: (407) 483-3600

**THE BRIDGE HOTEL**
999 E Camino Real (33432)
Rates: $65-$180;
Tel: (407) 368-9500

**CROWN STERLING SUITES
BOCA RATON**
701 NW 53rd St (33487)
Rates: $79-$139;
Tel: (407) 997-9500

**RESIDENCE INN BY
MARRIOTT-BOCA RATON**
525 NW 77th St (33487)
Rates: $104-$185;
Tel: (407) 994-3222

## BONIFAY

**BEST WESTERN-TIVOLI INN**
Rt 1, Box N (32425)
Rates: $35-$50;
Tel: (904) 547-4251

## BOYNTON BEACH

**RAMADA INN**
1935 S Federal Hwy (33435)
Rates: $59-$125;
Tel: (407) 736-5805

## BRADENTON

**DAYS INN**
3506 1st St W (34208)
Rates: $42-$67;
Tel: (813) 746-1141

**DAYSTOP**
644 67th St Circle E (34208)
Rates: $28-$65;
Tel: (813) 746-2505

**ECONO LODGE**
6727 14th St W (34207)
Rates: $60-$75;
Tel: (813) 758-7199

**HOJO INN**
6511 14th St W (34207)
Rates: $55-$70;
Tel: (813) 756-8399

**PARK INN CLUB
& BREAKFAST**
4450 47th St W (34210)
Rates: $50-$85;
Tel: (813) 795-4633

**PARK INN LIMITED**
688 67th St Circle E (34208)
Rates: $33-$70;
Tel: (813) 745-1876

## BROOKSVILLE

**HOLIDAY INN**
30307 Cortez Blvd (34602)
Rates: $54-$59;
Tel: (904) 796-9481

**HOLIDAY INN**
6172 Commercial Way
(Weeki Wachee 34606)
Rates: $54-$75;
Tel: (904) 596-2007

## BUSHNELL

**BEST WESTERN
GUEST HOUSE MOTEL**
P.O. Box 847 (33513)
Rates: $36-$53;
Tel: (904) 793-5010

## CALLAHAN

**FRIENDSHIP INN**
US I-301 & 23 North (32011)
Rates: N/A;
Tel: (904) 879-3451

## CAPE CORAL

**DEL PRADO INN**
1502 Miramar St (33904)
Rates: $60-$75;
Tel: (800) 231-6818

**QUALITY INN**
1538 Cape Coral Pkwy
(33904)
Rates: $45-$80;
Tel: (813) 542-2121

## CAPTIVA ISLAND

**TWEEN WATERS INN**
15951 Captiva Dr (33924)
Rates: N/A;
Tel: (813) 472-5161

## CARRABELLE

**THE MOORINGS
AT CARRABELLE**
1000 US 98 (32322)
Rates: $48-$55;
Tel: (904) 697-2800

## CEDAR KEY

**BEACHFRONT MOTEL**
G and 1st St (32625)
Rates: N/A;
Tel: (904) 543-5113

**PARK PLACE MOTEL**
P. O. Box 613 (32625)
Rates: $65-$80;
Tel: (904) 543-5737

## CLEARWATER

**HOLIDAY INN EXPRESS**
13625 Icot Blvd (34620)
Rates: $61-$81;
Tel: (813) 536-7275

**LA QUINTA MOTOR INN**
3301 Ulmerton Rd (34622)
Rates: $45-$70;
Tel: (813) 572-7222

**RAMADA INN
COUNTRYSIDE**
26508 US 19N (34621)
Rates: $54-$86;
Tel: (813) 796-1234

**RESIDENCE INN
BY MARRIOTT**
5050 Ulmerton Rd (34620)
Rates: $115-$165;
Tel: (813) 573-4444

**RODEWAY INN-CENTRAL**
20967 US 19N (34625)
Rates: $45-$75;
Tel: (813) 799-1181

**ST. PETERSBURG SUPER 8**
13260 34th St (34622)
Rates: $35-$56;
Tel: (813) 572-8881

## CLERMONT

**DAYSTOP**
20339 US 27 (34711)
Rates: $25-$60;
Tel: (904) 429-2151

## COCOA

**BEST WESTERN
COCOA INN**
4225 W King St (32926)
Rates: $37-$48;
Tel: (407) 632-1065

**DAYS INN**
5600 Hwy 524 (32926)
Rates: $42-$54;
Tel: (407) 636-6500

**ECONO LODGE**
3220 N Cocoa Blvd (32926)
Rates: $32-$45;
Tel: (407) 632-4561

**RAMADA INN COCOA-
KENNEDY SPACE CTR**
900 Friday Rd (32922)
Rates: $50-$75;
Tel: (407) 631-1210

## COCOA BEACH

**DAYS INN-OCEANFRONT**
5600 N Atlantic Ave (32931)
Rates: $49-$74;
Tel: (407) 783-7621

**ECONO LODGE OCEAN VIEW**
5500 N Atlantic Ave (32931)
Rates: $43-$63;
Tel: (407) 784-2550

**ROYAL MANSION RESORT**
8600 Ridgewood Ave
(Cape Canaveral 32920)
Rates: $90-$205;
Tel: (407) 784-8484

**SILVER SANDS MOTEL**
225 N Atlantic Ave (32931)
Rates: N/A;
Tel: (407) 783-2415

**SURF STUDIO
BEACH RESORT**
1801 S Atlantic Ave (32931)
Rates: $40-$110;
Tel: (407) 783-7100

## CORAL SPRINGS

**WELLESLEY INNS-
CORAL SPRINGS**
3100 N University Dr (33065)
Rates: $39-$69;
Tel: (305) 344-2200

## CRESTVIEW

**DAYS INN**
P. O. Box J (32536)
Rates: $34-$44;
Tel: (904) 682-8842

## CROSS CITY

**CARRIAGE INN**
P. O. Box 1360 (32628)
Rates: $38-$42;
Tel: (904) 498-3910

## CRYSTAL RIVER

**COMFORT INN**
4486 N Suncoast Blvd (32629)
Rates: $34-$55;
Tel: (904) 563 1500

**DAYS INN RESORT**
P. O. Box 785 (32629)
Rates: $39-$55;
Tel: (904) 795-2111

**ECONO LODGE
CRYSTAL RESORT**
P.O. Box 456 (32629)
Rates: $42-$58;
Tel: (904) 795-3171

## DAVENPORT

**DAYS INN-SOUTH
OF MAGIC KINGDOM**
2425 Frontage Rd (33837)
Rates: $45-$77;
Tel: (813) 424-2596

**HOLIDAY INN
SOUTH OF DISNEY**
P. O. Box 1536 (33845)
Rates: $46-$86;
Tel: (813) 424-2211

## DAYTONA BEACH

**CASA MARINA MOTEL**
828 N Atlantic Ave (32118)
Rates: N/A;
Tel: (800) 225-3891

**COMFORT INN BEACHSIDE**
507 S Atlantic Ave
(Ormond Beach 32176)
Rates: $56-$125;
Tel. (904) 677-8550

**DAYTONA BEACH HOLLY
HILL TRAVELODGE**
749 Ridgewood Ave
(Holly Hill 32117)
Rates: $38-$50;
Tel: (904) 255-6511

**HOLIDAY INN-SPEEDWAY**
1798 Volusia Ave (32114)
Rates: $50-$150;
Tel: (904) 255-2422

**HOWARD JOHNSON
LODGE-DAYTONA NORTH**
1633 N US 1
(Ormond Beach 32174)
Rates: $34-$115;
Tel: (904) 677 7310

**JAMAICAN BEACH MOTEL**
505 S Atlantic Ave
(Ormond Beach 32176)
Rates: N/A;
Tel: (904) 677-3353

**LA QUINTA INN**
2725 Volusia Ave (32114)
Rates: $47-$62;
Tel: (904) 255-7412

**OCEAN CREST MOTEL**
2040 Ocean Shore Blvd
(Ormond Beach 32176)
Rates: $40-$70;
Tel: (904) 441-0707

**QUALITY INN DAVIS BROS**
1567 N US 1
(Ormond Beach 32174)
Rates: $32-$88;
Tel: (904) 672-8621

**RAMADA RESORT**
2700 N Atlantic Ave (32118)
Rates: $69 $110;
Tel: (904) 672-3770

**SEA OATS BEACH MOTEL**
2539 S Atlantic Ave
(Daytona Beach Shores 32118)
Rates: $39-$119;
Tel: (904) 767-5684

**TRAVELODGE
BOARDWALK**
333 S Atlantic Ave (32118)
Rates: N/A;
Tel: (800) 544-8133

**WHITEHALL HOTEL**
640 N Atlantic Ave (32118)
Rates: N/A;
Tel. (800) 874-7016

## DEERFIELD BEACH

**COMFORT INN**
1050 E Newport Center Dr
(33442)
Rates: $79-$95;
Tel. (305) 570-8887

**DAYS INN OCEANSIDE**
50 SE 20th Ave (33441)
Rates: $39-$99;
Tel: (305) 428-0650

**LA QUINTA MOTOR INN**
351 W Hillsboro Blvd (33441)
Rates: $44-$78;
Tel: (305) 421 1004

**QUALITY SUITES**
1050 E Newport Center Dr
(33442)
Rates: $109-$134;
Tel: (305) 570-8888

**WELLESLEY INN**
100 SW 12th Ave (33442)
Rates: $39-$99;
Tel: (305) 428-0661

## DE FUNIAK SPRINGS

**BEST WESTERN
CROSSROADS INN**
P. O. Box 852 (32433)
Rates: $40-$44;
Tel: (904) 892-5111

# DELAND

**DELAND HOTEL**
350 Intl Speedway Blvd
(32724)
Rates: $65-$105;
Tel: (904) 738-5200

**QUALITY INN**
2801 E New York Ave
(32724)
Rates: $34-$150;
Tel: (904) 736-3440

**UNIVERSITY INN**
644 N Woodland Blvd (32720)
Rates: $44-$74;
Tel: (904) 734-5711

# DELRAY BEACH

**THE COLONY**
525 E Atlantic Ave (33483)
Rates: $60-$160;
Tel: (407) 276-4123

# DESTIN

**ADMIRAL BENBOW INN**
713 Hwy 98E (32541)
Rates: $34-$64;
Tel: (904) 837-5455

**DAYS INN**
1029 Hwy 98E (32541)
Rates: $36-$85;
Tel: (904) 837-2599

# ELLENTON

**BEST WESTERN INN-ELLENTON**
5218 17th St E (34222)
Rates: $40-$81;
Tel: (813) 729-8505

# ENGLEWOOD

**DAYS INN**
2540 S McCall Rd (34224)
Rates: $53-$95;
Tel: (813) 474-5544

**VERANDA INN**
2073 S McCall Rd (34224)
Rates: N/A;
Tel: (813) 475-6533

**WESTON'S RESORTS**
985 Gulf Blvd (34223)
Rates: N/A;
Tel: (813) 474-3431

# FERNANDINA BEACH

**OCEAN VIEW INN MOTEL**
2801 Atlantic Ave (32034)
Rates: N/A;
Tel: (904) 261-0193

# FLAGLER BEACH

**TOPAZ MOTEL**
1224 S Oceanshore Blvd
(32136)
Rates: $45-$90;
Tel: (904) 439-3301

# FLORIDA CITY

**FLORIA KEYS-KNIGHTS INN**
401 US Hwy 1 (33034)
Rates: $39-$54;
Tel: (305) 245-2800

**HAMPTON INN**
124 E Palm Dr (33034)
Rates: $42-$65;
Tel: (305) 247-8833

# FORT LAUDERDALE
(and Vicinity)

**ADMIRAL'S COURT**
21 Hendricks Isle (33301)
Rates: N/A;
Tel: (305) 462-5072

**BONAVENTURE RESORT & SPA**
250 Racquet Club Rd (33326)
Rates: $105-$250;
Tel: (305) 389-3300

**BUDGETEL INN-FORT LAUDERDALE**
3800 W Commercial Blvd
(Tamarac 33309)
Rates: $36-$65;
Tel: (305) 485-7900

**CROWN STERLING SUITES**
1100 SE 17th St (33316)
Rates: $139-$169;
Tel: (305) 527-2700

**DAYS INN FT LAUDERDALE-DOWNTOWN/AIRPORT NORTH**
1700 W Broward Blvd
(33312)
Rates: $49-$75;
Tel: (305) 463-2500

**FORT LAUDERDALE MARRIOTT NORTH**
6650 N Andrews Ave (33309)
Rates: $79-$169;
Tel: (305) 711-0440

**GUEST QUARTERS SUITE HOTEL**
2670 E Sunrise Blvd (33304)
Rates: $89-$189;
Tel: (305) 565-3800

**MARK 2100 RESORT HOTEL**
2100 N Atlantic Blvd (33305)
Rates: N/A;
Tel: (800) 334-6275

**SHERATON DESIGN CTR HOTEL-FT LAUDERDALE AIRPORT**
1825 Griffin Rd
(Dania 33004)
Rates: $85-$195;
Tel: (305) 920-3500

**THE TREVERS APARTMENT/MOTEL**
552 N Birch Rd (33304)
Rates: $35-$87;
Tel: (800) 533-4744

**WELLESLEY INNS-FT LAUDERDALE WEST**
5070 N SR 7 (33319)
Rates: $39-$99;
Tel: (305) 484-6909

**WELLESLEY INNS-FT LAUDERDALE EAST**
4800 NW 9th Ave (33309)
Rates: $39-$99;
Tel: (305) 776-6333

**WELLESLEY INNS-PLANTATION**
7901 SW 6th St
(Plantation 33324)
Rates: $44-$99;
Tel: (305) 473-8257

## THE WESTIN HOTEL-CYPRESS CREEK
400 Corporate Dr (33334)
Rates: $85-$210;
Tel: (305) 772-1331

## FORT MYERS

### BUDGETEL INN
2717 Colonial Blvd (33907)
Rates: $42-$72;
Tel: (813) 275-3500

### COMFORT SUITES
13651 Indian Paint Ln (33912)
Rates: $54-$105;
Tel. (813) 768-0005

### DAYS INN-NORTH FORT MYERS/CAPE CORAL
13353 N Cleveland Ave
(N Ft Myers 33903)
Rates: $35-$80;
Tel: (813) 995-0535

### DAYS INN SOUTH-FORT MYERS AIRPORT
11435 Cleveland Ave (33907)
Rates: $33-$71;
Tel: (813) 936-1311

### GOLF VIEW MOTEL
3523 Cleveland Ave (33901)
Rates: N/A;
Tel: (813) 936-1858

### LA QUINTA MOTOR INN
4850 Cleveland Ave (33907)
Rates: $42-$71;
Tel: (813) 275-3300

### MOTEL 6
3350 Marina Town Ln
(N Ft Myers 33903)
Rates: $32-$62;
Tel: (813) 656-5544

### RADISSON INN SANIBEL GATEWAY
20091 Summerlin Rd SW
(33908)
Rates: $59-$124;
Tel: (813) 466-1200

### SHERATON HARBOR PLACE
2500 Edwards Dr (33901)
Rates: $80-$170;
Tel: (813) 337-0300

### SLEEP INN
13651 Indian Paint Ln (33912)
Rates: $45-$85;
Tel: (813) 561-1117

### WELLESLEY INN
4400 Ford St Extension
(33916)
Rates: $39-$89;
Tel: (813) 278-3949

## FORT MYERS BEACH

### BEST WESTERN BEACH RESORT
684 Estero Blvd (33931)
Rates: $90-$170;
Tel: (813) 463-6000

## FORT PIERCE

### DAYS INN-FORT PIERCE
6651 Darter Ct (34945)
Rates: $45-$80;
Tel: (407) 466-4066

### HOLIDAY INN-SUNSHINE PARKWAY
7151 Okeechobee Rd (34945)
Rates: $46-$65;
Tel: (407) 464-5000

### HOLIDAY INN-SURFSIDE
2600 SR A1A N (34949)
Rates: $49-$105;
Tel: (407) 465-6000

### HOWARD JOHNSON LODGE
7150 Okeechobee Rd (34945)
Rates: $38-$71;
Tel: (407) 464-4500

## FORT WALTON BEACH

### DAYS INN
135 Miracle Strip Pkwy
(32548)
Rates: $32-$67;
Tel: (904) 244-6184

### ECONO LODGE
100 Miracle Strip Pkwy
(32548)
Rates: $36-$60;
Tel: (904) 244-0121

### EDGEWATER MOTEL
1284 Marler Dr (32548)
Rates: N/A;
Tel: (904) 243-7123

### MARINA MOTEL & EFFICIENCIES
1345 US 908 E Okaloosa Isl.
(32548)
Rates: $31-$66;
Tel: (904) 244-1129

## GAINESVILLE

### APARTMENT INN
4401 Southwest 13th St
(32608)
Rates: N/A;
Tel: (904) 371-3811

### HOJO INN
1900 SW 13th St (32608)
Rates: $30-$40;
Tel: (904) 372-1880

### KNIGHTS INN
4021 SW 40th Blvd (32608)
Rates: $29-$37;
Tel: (904) 373-0392

### LA QUINTA MOTOR INN
920 NW 69th Terr (32601)
Rates: $44-$61;
Tel: (904) 332-6466

### RESIDENCE IN BY MARRIOTT
4001 SW 13th St (32608)
Rates: $898-$105;
Tel: (904) 371-2101

## HAINES CITY

### BEST WESTERN ORANGE GROVE INN
1504 US 27S (33844)
Rates: $34-$75;
Tel: (813) 422-8621

### HOLIDAY INN
P. O. Box 1536
(Baseball City 33845)
Rates: $59-$76;
Tel: (813) 424-2211

# HOLIDAY

**BEST WESTERN-
TAHITIAN RESORT**
2337 US 19 (34691)
Rates: $41-$78;
Tel: (813) 937-4121

# HOLLYWOOD

**COMFORT INN-
FT LAUDERDALE/
HOLLYWOOD AIRPORT**
2520 Stirling Rd (33020)
Rates: $44-$85;
Tel: (305) 922-1600

**DAYS HOTEL-GULF
STREAM BEACH RESORT**
2711 S Ocean Dr (33019)
Rates: $55-$175;
Tel: (305) 922-8200

# HOMESTEAD

**HOWARD JOHNSON
LODGE**
1020 N Homestead Blvd
(33030)
Rates: $44-$68;
Tel: (305) 248-2121

# HOMOSASSA SPRINGS

**HOMOSASSA LODGE**
P. O. Box 8 (32647)
Rates: $45-$75;
Tel: (904) 628-4311

**RIVERSIDE INN**
P. O. Box 258
(Homosassa 32687)
Rates: $59-$79;
Tel: (904) 628-2474

# INDIALANTIC

**HOLIDAY INN MELBOURNE
OCEANFRONT**
2605 N FL A1A (32903)
Rates: $90-$169;
Tel: (407) 777-4100

**MELBOURNE OCEAN-
FRONT QUALITY SUITES**
1665 N SR A1A (32903)
Rates: $79-$99;
Tel: (407) 723-4222

# INVERNESS

**CENTRAL MOTEL**
721 US 41S (32651)
Rates: $49;
Tel: (904) 726-4515

# JACKSONVILLE
(and Vicinity)

**ADMIRAL BENBOW
INN-AIRPORT**
14691 Duval Rd (32218)
Rates: $36-$44;
Tel: (904) 741-4254

**BEST INNS OF AMERICA**
8220 Dix Ellis Tr (32256)
Rates: $34-$43;
Tel: (904) 739-3323

**BEST WESTERN
EXECUTIVE INN**
10888 Harts Rd (32218)
Rates: $38-$55;
Tel: (904) 751-5600

**BUDGETEL INN**
3199 Hartley Rd (32257)
Rates: $32-$48;
Tel: (904) 268-9999

**COMFORT SUITES HOTEL**
8444 Dix Ellis Tr (32256)
Rates: $56-$85;
Tel: (904) 739-1155

**COURTYARD
BY MARRIOTT**
4600 San Pablo Rd (32224)
Rates: $52-$110;
Tel: (904) 223-1700

**ECONO LODGE
JACKSONVILLE/
ORANGE PARK**
141 Park Ave
(Orange Park 32073)
Rates: $30-$47;
Tel: (904) 264-5107

**ECONOMY INNS
OF AMERICA**
4300 Salisbury Rd (32216)
Rates: $29;
Tel: (904) 281-0198

**HAMPTON INN**
1170 Airport Entrance Rd
(32218)
Rates: $40-$55;
Tel: (904) 741-4980

**HOLIDAY INN-AIRPORT**
P. O. Drawer 18409 (32229)
Rates: $59-$78;
Tel: (904) 741-4404

**HOLIDAY INN-
EAST CONFERENCE CTR**
5865 Arlington Expy (32211)
Rates: $48-$75;
Tel: (904) 724-3410

**HOLIDAY INN-
ORANGE PARK**
150 Park Ave
(Orange Park 32073)
Rates: $49-$62;
Tel: (904) 264-9513

**HOMEWOOD SUITES**
8737 Baymeadows Rd
(32256)
Rates: $99-$129;
Tel: (904) 733-9299

**HOSPITALITY INN
BED & BREAKFAST**
7071 103rd St (32210)
Rates: N/A;
Tel: (904) 777-5700

**LA QUINTA MOTOR INN-
BAYMEADOWS**
8255 Dix Ellis Tr (32256)
Rates: $43-$56;
Tel: (904) 731-9940

**LA QUINTA MOTOR INN
JACKSONVILLE/ORANGE
PARK**
8555 Blanding Blvd (32244)
Rates: $40-$53;
Tel: (904) 778-9539

**LA QUINTA
MOTOR INN-NORTH**
812 Dunn Ave (32218)
Rates: $42-$55;
Tel: (904) 751-6960

## QUALITY INN SOUTHSIDE
4660 Salisbury Rd (32256)
Rates: $39-$53;
Tel: (904) 281-0900

## RAMADA INN CONFERENCE CTR
3130 Hartley Rd (32257)
Rates: $39-$44;
Tel: (904) 268-8080

## RED ROOF INN-AIRPORT
14701 Airport Entrance Rd (32218)
Rates: $29;
Tel: (904) 741-4488

## RED ROOF INN-SOUTH
6099 Youngerman Cir (32244)
Rates: $28-$38;
Tel: (904) 777-1000

## RESIDENCE INN BY MARRIOTT
8365 Dix Ellis Rd (32256)
Rates: $125-$150;
Tel: (904) 733-8088

## RODEWAY INN-EMERSON STREET
3233 Emerson St (32207)
Rates: $35-$40;
Tel: (904) 398-3331

## WILSON INN
4580 Collins Rd
(Orange Park 32073)
Rates: $37-$53;
Tel: (904) 264-4466

## JASPER

## ECONO LODGE
Rt 3, Box 133 (32052)
Rates: $25-$45;
Tel: (904) 792-1987

## JENNINGS

## JENNINGS HOUSE INN
P. O. Box 179 (32053)
Rates: $19-$24;
Tel: (904) 938-3305

## JUPITER

## WELLESLEY INN-JUPITER
34 Fishermans Wharf (33477)
Rates: $39-$99;
Tel: (407) 575-7201

## KEY LARGO

## MARINA DEL MAR BAYSIDE
P. O. Box 1050 (33037)
Rates: $65-$150;
Tel: (305) 451-4450

## KEY WEST

## COURTNEY'S PLACE
720 Whitmarsh Ln (33040)
Rates: $65-$145;
Tel: (305) 294-3480

## CURRY MANSION INN
511 Caroline St (33040)
Rates: $110-$200;
Tel: (305) 294-5349

## HAMPTON INN
2801 N Roosevelt Blvd (33040)
Rates: $75-$162;
Tel: (305) 294-2917

## KEY LODGE
1004 Duval St (33040)
Rates: $130-$148;
Tel: (305) 296-9915

## RAMADA INN-KEY WEST
3420 N Roosevelt Blvd (33040)
Rates: $49-$239;
Tel: (305) 294-5541

## SUGAR LOAF LODGE RESORT
Box 148
(Sugar Loaf Key 33044)
Rates: $85-$100;
Tel: (305) 745-3211

## KISSIMMEE

## BEST WESTERN-EASTGATE
5565 W Irlo Bronson Mem. Hwy (34746)
Rates: $43-$75;
Tel: (407) 396-0707

## BEST WESTERN-KISSIMMEE
2261 E Irlo Bronson Mem. Hwy (34744)
Rates: $34-$60;
Tel: (407) 846-2221

## COMFORT INN-MAIN GATE
7571 W Irlo Bronson Mem. Hwy (34746)
Rates: $32-$94;
Tel: (407) 396-7500

## FORTUNE PLACE RESORT
1475 Astro Lake Dr N (34744)
Rates: $109-$189;
Tel: (407) 348-0330

## HOJO INN
9240 W US 192
(Clermont 34711)
Rates: $38-$55;
Tel: (800) 446-5669

## HOLIDAY INN-MAIN GATE EAST
5678 W Irlo Bronson Mem. Hwy (34746)
Rates: $75-$119;
Tel: (407) 396-4488

## HOMEWOOD SUITES MAIN GATE/PARKWAY
3100 Parkway Blvd (34746)
Rates: $94-$189;
Tel: (407) 396-2229

## HOWARD JOHNSON LODGE-KISSIMMEE
2323 E Irlo Bronson Mem. Hwy (34744)
Rates: $29-$69;
Tel: (407) 846-4900

## INNS OF AMERICA
2945 Entry Point Blvd (34746)
Rates: $39-$79;
Tel: (407) 396-7743

## KNIGHTS INN ORLANDO/ MAIN GATE
7475 W Irlo Bronson Mem. Hwy (34746)
Rates: $35-$56;
Tel: (407) 396-4200

## KNIGHTS INN ORLANDO/ MAIN GATE EAST
2880 Poinciana Blvd (34746)
Rates: $35-$56;
Tel: (407) 396-8186

**LARSON'S LODGE-KISSIMMEE**
2009 W Vine St (34742)
Rates: $35-$69;
Tel: (407) 846-2713

**OLYMPIC INN**
4669 W Irlo Bronson Mem.
Hwy (34746)
Rates: $28-$40;
Tel: (800) 523-8729

**RAMADA LIMITED**
5055 W Irlo Bronson Mem.
Hwy (34746)
Rates: $39-$59;
Tel: (407) 396-2212

**RED ROOF INN**
4970 Kyngs Heath Rd (34741)
Rates: $39-$54;
Tel: (407) 396-0065

## LAKE BUENA VISTA

**CASA ADOBE**
9107 South Rt 535 (32819)
Rates: N/A;
Tel: (407) 876-5432

**COMFORT INN
AT LAKE BUENA VISTA**
P. O. Box 22776 (32830)
Rates: $37-$57;
Tel: (407) 239-7300

**DAYS INN
LAKE BUENA VISTA VILLAGE**
12490 Apopka-Vineland Rd
(32830)
Rates: $55-$95;
Tel: (407) 239-4646

**RADISSON INN
LAKE BUENA VISTA**
8686 Palm Pkwy (32830)
Rates: $79-$119;
Tel: (407) 239-8400

## LAKE CITY

**CYPRESS INN**
Rt 13, Box 180A (32055)
Rates: $25-$39;
Tel: (904) 752-9369

**DAYS INN**
Rt 13, Box 1140 (32055)
Rates: $30-$39;
Tel: (904) 752-9350

**DRIFTWOOD MOTEL**
Rt 13, Box 1156 (32055)
Rates: $23-$28;
Tel: (904) 755-3545

**ECONO LODGE**
P. O.Box 430 (32055)
Rates: $25-$42;
Tel: (904) 752-7891

**FRIENDSHIP INN**
P. O. Box 2156 (32056)
Rates: $24-$38;
Tel: (904) 755-5203

**HOLIDAY INN**
Drawer 1239 (32055)
Rates: $44-$48;
Tel: (904) 752-3901

**QUALITY INN LAKE CITY**
Rt 13, Box 1075 (32055)
Rates: $25-$45;
Tel: (904) 752-7550

**SCOTTISH INN**
Rt 13, Box 1150 (32055)
Rates: $23-$32;
Tel: (904) 755-0230

## LAKELAND

**ECONO LODGE MOTEL**
1817 E Memorial Blvd
(33801)
Rates: $32-$53;
Tel: (813) 688-9221

**MARYLAND MOTEL**
1433 Lakeland Hills Blvd
(33805)
Rates: $28-$45;
Tel: (813) 683-6745

## LAKE WALES

**CHALET SUZANNE**
US Hwy 27 & 17A (33853)
Rates: N/A;
Tel: (800) 288-6011

**EMERALD MOTEL**
530 S Scenic Hwy (33853)
Rates: $24-$39;
Tel: (813) 676-3310

**KNIGHTS INN-LAKE WALES**
541 W Central Ave (33853)
Rates: $31-$55;
Tel: (813) 676-7925

**LANTERN MOTEL**
3949 Hwy 27 North (33853)
Rates: N/A;
Tel: (813) 676-4821

**RIDGE MOTOR INN**
513 S Scenic Hwy (33853)
Rates: $24-$39;
Tel: (813) 676-1249

## LAKE WORTH

**HOLIDAY INN WEST PALM BEACH TURNPIKE**
7859 Lake Worth Rd (33467)
Rates: $68-$80;
Tel: (407) 968-5000

**LAGO MOTOR INN**
714 S Dixie Hwy (33460)
Rates: $32-$66;
Tel: (407) 585-5246

**MARTINIQUE
MOTOR LODGE**
801 S Dixie Hwy (33460)
Rates: $28-$75;
Tel: (407) 585-2501

**WHITE MANOR MOTEL**
1618 S Federal Hwy (33460)
Rates: $32-$58;
Tel: (407) 582-7437

## LANTANA

**KNIGHT'S INN-W PALM BEACH SOUTH**
1255 Hypoluxo Rd (33462)
Rates: $42-$53;
Tel: (407) 585-3970

## LEESBURG

**BUDGET HOST INN**
1225 N 14th St (34748)
Rates: $36-$46;
Tel: (904) 787-3534

**DAYS INN OF LEESBURG**
1308 N 14th St (34748)
Rates: $32-$55;
Tel: (904) 787-1210

## LIVE OAK

**ECONO LODGE**
P.O. Box 820 (32060)
Rates: $37-$46;
Tel: (904) 362-7459

## LONGBOAT KEY

**HOLIDAY INN-
LONGBOAT KEY**
4949 Gulf of Mexico Dr
(34228)
Rates: $69-$181;
Tel: (813) 383-3771

**RIVIERA BEACH MOTEL**
5451 Gulf of Mexico Dr
(34228)
Rates: $400-$625;
Tel: (813) 383-2552

## MACCLENNY

**ECONO LODGE**
P. O. Box 425 (32063)
Rates: $28-$50;
Tel: (904) 259-3000

## MARATHON

**HOWARD JOHNSON
RESORT**
13351 Overseas Hwy (33050)
Rates: $50-$155;
Tel: (305) 743-8550

**RAINBOW BEND RESORT**
Rt 1, Box 159 (33050)
Rates: $120-$185;
Tel: (305) 289-1505

## MARIANNA

**BEST WESTERN
MARIANNA INN**
P. O. Box 980 (32446)
Rates: $38-$48;
Tel: (904) 526-5666

**COMFORT INN**
P. O. Box 1507 (32446)
Rates: $42-$50;
Tel: (904) 526-5600

**ECONO LODGE**
4113 Lafayette St (32446)
Rates: $31-$36;
Tel: (904) 526-3710

**HOLIDAY INN**
P. O. Box 979 (32446)
Rates: $44-$53;
Tel: (904) 526-3251

**TRAVELODGE**
4132 Lafayette St (32446)
Rates: $30-$45;
Tel: (904) 526-4311

## MELBOURNE

**ECONO LODGE-
RIVERFRONT**
420 S Harbor City Blvd
(32901)
Rates: $36-$41;
Tel: (407) 723-5320

**HOLIDAY INN-WEST I-95**
4500 W New Haven Ave
(32904)
Rates: $69-$85;
Tel: (407) 724-2050

**MELBOURNE HILTON
AT RIALTO PLACE**
200 Rialto Pl (32901)
Rates: $89-$109;
Tel: (407) 768-0200

**RIO VISTA MOTEL**
1046 S Harbor City Blvd
(32901)
Rates: N/A;
Tel: (407) 727-2818

## MIAMI
(and Vicinity)

**BUDGETEL INN-
MIAMI AIRPORT**
3501 NW Le Jeune Rd (33142)
Rates: $44-$61;
Tel: (305) 871-1777

**CROWN STERLING SUITES
MIAMI AIRPORT**
3974 NW South River Dr
(Miami Spgs 33142)
Rates: $119 $179;
Tel: (305) 634-5000

**HAMPTON INN-
DOWNTOWN**
2500 Brickell Ave (33129)
Rates: $60-$81;
Tel: (305) 854-2070

**HAMPTON INN-
MIAMI AIRPORT**
5125 NW 36th St
(Miami Spgs 33166)
Rates: $39-$66;
Tel: (305) 887-2153

**HILTON & MARINA HOTEL**
5101 Blue Lagoon Dr (33126)
Rates: $140-$500;
Tel: (305) 262-1000

**HOJO INN
BROAD CAUSEWAY**
12210 Biscayne Blvd
(No Miami 33181)
Rates: $50-$80;
Tel: (305) 891-7350

**HOLIDAY INN-
AIRPORT LAKES SOUTH**
1101 NW 57th Ave (33126)
Rates: $61-$85;
Tel: (305) 266 0000

**LA QUINTA MOTOR INN**
7401 NW 36th St (33166)
Rates: $52-$78;
Tel: (305) 599-9902

**MARDI GRAS MOTEL**
3400 Biscayne Blvd (33137)
Rates: N/A;
Tel: (800) 552-1251

**MIAMI AIRPORT HILTON
AND MARINA**
5101 Blue Lagoon Dr (33126)
Rates: $145-$195;
Tel: (305) 262-1000

**MIAMI AIRPORT
MARRIOTT HOTEL
& RACQUET CLUB**
1201 NW Le Jeune Rd (33126)
Rates: $99-$158;
Tel: (305) 649-5000

**QUALITY INN-SOUTH**
14501 S Dixie Hwy (33176)
Rates: $55-$84;
Tel: (305) 251-2000

**RADISSON MART
PLAZA MOTEL**
711 NW 72nd Ave (33126)
Rates: $115-$135;
Tel: (305) 261-3800

**RAMADA HOTEL
MIAMI INTL AIRPORT**
3941 NW 22nd St (33142)
Rates: $69-$159;
Tel: (305) 871-1700

**SOFITEL HOTEL**
5800 Blue Lagoon Dr (33126)
Rates: $125-$500;
Tel: (305) 264-4888

**WELLESLEY INNS
AT KENDALL**
11750 Mills Dr
(Kendall 33183)
Rates: $49-$99;
Tel: (305) 270-0359

**WELLESLEY INNS
MIAMI AIRPORT WEST**
8436 NW 36th St (33166)
Rates: $39-$99;
Tel: (305) 592-4799

**WELLESLEY INNS
MIAMI LAKES**
7925 NW 154th St
(Miami Lakes 33016)
Rates: $49-$99;
Tel: (305) 821-8274

## MIAMI BEACH
(and Vicinity)

**DAYS INN-OCEANSIDE**
4229 Collins Ave (33140)
Rates: $65-$90;
Tel: (305) 673-1513

**FONTAINEBLEAU HILTON
RESORT & SPA**
4441 Collins Ave (33140)
Rates: $130-$260;
Tel: (305) 538-2000

**HOLIDAY INN
NEWPORT PIER RESORT**
16701 Collins Ave
(Sunny Isles 33160)
Rates: $79-$209;
Tel: (305) 949-1300

**HOLIDAY INN-OCEANSIDE
CONVENTION CTR**
2201 Collins Ave (33139)
Rates: $108-$165;
Tel: (305) 534-1511

**HOWARD JOHNSON
HOTEL**
4000 Alton Rd (33140)
Rates: $70-$100;
Tel: (305) 532-4411

**SHERATON
BAL HARBOUR RESORT**
9701 Collins Ave
(Bal Harbour 33154)
Rates: $170-$340;
Tel: (305) 865-7511

**SUEZ OCEAN
FRONT RESORT**
18215 Collins Ave
(Sunny Isles 33160)
Rates: $39-$87;
Tel: (305) 932-0661

## MOUNT DORA

**THE LAKESIDE INN**
100 N Alexander St (32757)
Rates: $65-$135;
Tel: (904) 383-4101

## NAPLES

**SPINNAKER INN
OF NAPLES**
6600 Dudley Dr (33999)
Rates: $36-$70;
Tel: (813) 434-0444

**STONEY'S
COURTYARD INN**
2630 N Tamiami Tr (33940)
Rates: $75-$85;
Tel: (800) 432-3870

**WELLESLEY INNS**
1555 5th Ave S (33942)
Rates: $39-$99;
Tel: (813) 793-4646

**WORLD TENNIS
CENTER & RESORT**
4800 Airport Rd (33942)
Rates: $145;
Tel: (800) 292-6663

## NAVARRE

**COMFORT INN**
8680 Navarre Pkwy (32566)
Rates: $44-$78;
Tel: (904) 939-1761

## NEW PORT RICHEY

**ECONO LODGE**
7631 US Hwy 19 (34652)
Rates: $27-$49;
Tel: (813) 845-4990

**HOLIDAY INN BAYSIDE**
5015 US 19 (34652)
Rates: $49-$71;
Tel: (813) 849-8551

**SHERATON INN**
5316 US 19 (34652)
Rates: $40-$56;
Tel: (813) 847-9005

## NEW SMYRNA BEACH

**BUENA VISTA MOTEL
AND APARTMENTS**
500 N Causeway (32169)
Rates: $33-$55;
Tel: (904) 428-5565

## NICEVILLE

**COMFORT INN**
101 Hwy 85 N (32578)
Rates: $56-$61;
Tel: (904) 678-8077

## NORTH PALM BEACH

**ECONO LODGE**
757 US 1 (33408)
Rates: $39-$80;
Tel: (407) 848-1424

## OCALA

**BUDGET HOST-
WESTERN MOTEL**
4013 NW Blitchton Rd (32675)
Rates: $25-$35;
Tel: (904) 732-6940

**DAVIS BROS
MOTOR LODGE**
3924 W Silver Springs Blvd
(32675)
Rates: $29-$39;
Tel: (904) 629-8794

**DAYS INN PADDOCK PARK**
3434 SW College Rd (32674)
Rates: $40-$80;
Tel: (904) 854-3200

**DAYS INN-SILVER SPRINGS**
4040 W Silver Springs Blvd
(32675)
Rates: $45-$50;
Tel: (904) 629-8850

**HILTON OCALA/
SILVER SPRINGS**
3600 SW 36th Ave (32674)
Rates: $75-$100;
Tel: (904) 854-1400

**HOLIDAY INN-OCALA**
3621 W Silver Springs Blvd
(32675)
Rates: $45-$50;
Tel: (904) 629-0381

**HOWARD JOHNSON PARK
SQUARE INN**
3712 SW 38th Ave (32674)
Rates: $40-$61;
Tel: (904) 237-8000

**QUALITY INN I-75**
3767 NW Blitchton Rd (32675)
Rates: $26-$39;
Tel: (904) 732-2300

**RADISSON INN OF OCALA**
3620 W Silver Springs Blvd
(32675)
Rates: $39-$76;
Tel: (904) 629-0091

## OKEECHOBEE

**BUDGET INN MOTEL**
201 S Parrott Ave (34974)
Rates: $35-$65;
Tel: (813) 763-3185

**MOTEL PIER II**
2200 SE Hwy 441 (34974)
Rates: $30-$50;
Tel: (813) 763-8003

## OLD TOWN

**SUWANEE GABLES MOTEL**
Rt 3, Box 208 (32680)
Rates: $36-$48;
Tel: (904) 542-7752

## ORANGE CITY

**COMFORT INN**
445 S Volusia Ave (32763)
Rates: $40-$69;
Tel: (904) 775-7444

## ORLANDO
(and Vicinity)

**BUDGETEL INN**
2051 Consulate Dr (32837)
Rates: $34-$49;
Tel: (407) 240-0500

**THE COURTYARD
AT LAKE LUCERNE**
211 N Lucerne Cir E (32801)
Rates: $85;
Tel: (407) 648-5188

**DAVIS PARK MOTEL**
221 E Colonial Dr (32801)
Rates: $39-$53;
Tel: (407) 425-9065

**DAYS INN-
INTERNATIONAL DRIVE**
7200 International Dr (32819)
Rates: $36-$81;
Tel: (407) 351-1200

**DAYS INN
LODGE-FLORIDA MALL**
1851 W Landstreet Rd
(32809)
Rates: $33-$99;
Tel: (407) 859-7700

**DAYS INN
ORLANDO LAKESIDE**
7335 Sand Lake Rd (32819)
Rates: $44-$80;
Tel: (407) 351-1900

**DAYS INN
ORLANDO 33RD STREET**
2500 W 33rd St (32839)
Rates: $32-$75;
Tel: (407) 841-3731

**DELTA ORLANDO RESORT**
5715 Major Blvd (32819)
Rates: $120-$150;
Tel: (407) 351-3340

**HOLIDAY INN-CENTROPLEX/
ORLANDO ARENA**
929 W Colonial Dr (32804)
Rates: $39-$85;
Tel: (407) 843-1360

**HOLIDAY INN-
UNIVERSITY OF CENTRAL FL**
12125 High Tech Ave (32817)
Rates: $75-$135;
Tel: (407) 274-9000

**HOWARD JOHNSON
MIDTOWN**
2014 W Colonial Dr (32804)
Rates: $36-$56;
Tel: (407) 841-8600

**INNS OF AMERICA**
8222 Jamaican Ct (32819)
Rates: $39-$69;
Tel: (407) 345-1172

**LA QUINTA
MOTOR INN AIRPORT**
7931 Daetwyler Dr (32812)
Rates: $53-$70;
Tel: (407) 857-9215

**MOTEL 6**
5909 American Way (32819)
Rates: $35;
Tel: (407) 351-6500

**QUALITY INN AT
INTERNATIONAL DRIVE**
7600 International Dr (32819)
Rates: $29-$45;
Tel: (407) 351-1600

**QUALITY INN-PLAZA**
9000 International Dr (32819)
Rates: $29-$43;
Tel: (407) 345-8585

**RADISSON INN**
8686 Palm Pkwy (32836)
Rates: N/A;
Tel: (407) 239-8400

**RAMADA INN
PLAZA INTERNATIONAL**
8300 Jamaican Ct (32819)
Rates: $49-$100;
Tel: (407) 351-1660

**RED ROOF INN**
9922 Hawaiian Ct (32819)
Rates: $39-$54;
Tel: (407) 352-1507

**SHERATON
WORLD RESORT**
10100 International Dr
(32821)
Rates: $70-$135;
Tel: (407) 352-1100

## PALATKA

**HOLIDAY INN RIVERSIDE**
201 N First St (32177)
Rates: $45-$50;
Tel: (904) 328-3481

## PALM BAY

**HOLIDAY INN PALM BAY**
1881 Palm Bay Rd NE (32905)
Rates: $49-$69;
Tel: (407) 723-8181

**KNIGHTS INN**
1170 Malabar Rd (32907)
Rates: $29-$44;
Tel: (407) 951-8222

## PALM BEACH

**BRAZILIAN COURT**
301 Australian Ave (33480)
Rates: $75-$290;
Tel: (407) 655-7740

**THE CHESTERFIELD
HOTEL DELUXE**
363 Cocoanut Row (33480)
Rates: $75-$250;
Tel: (407) 659-5800

**HEART OF
PALM BEACH MOTEL**
160 Royal Palm Way (33480)
Rates: $99-$199;
Tel: (800) 523-5377

**PLAZA INN**
215 Brazilian Ave (33480)
Rates: $65-$155;
Tel: (407) 832-8666

## PALM BEACH GARDENS

**MACARTHUR'S
HOLIDAY INN**
4431 PGA Blvd (33410)
Rates: $39-$125;
Tel: (407) 622-2260

**PALM BEACH GARDENS
MARRIOTT**
4000 RCA Blvd (33410)
Rates: $109-$155;
Tel: (407) 622-8888

## PALM COAST

**SHERATON
PALM COAST RESORT**
300 Club House Dr (32137)
Rates: $90-$160;
Tel: (904) 445-3000

## PALM HARBOR

**ECONO LODGE**
32000 US 19N (34684)
Rates: $34-$59;
Tel: (813) 786-2529

**KNIGHTS INN**
34106 US 19N (34684)
Rates: $29-$50;
Tel: (813) 789-2002

## PANAMA CITY

**BEST WESTERN
BAYSIDE INN**
711 W Beach Dr (32401)
Rates: $40-$75;
Tel: (904) 763-4622

**DAYS INN-PANAMA CITY**
4111 W Hwy 98 (32401)
Rates: $30-$54;
Tel: (904) 784-1777

## PANAMA CITY BEACH

**BEST WESTERN
CASALOMA**
13615 Front Beach Rd (32417)
Rates: $50-$150;
Tel: (904) 234-1100

**SURF HIGH INN
ON THE GULF**
10611 Front Beach Rd (32407)
Rates: $35-$55;
Tel: (904) 234-2129

## PENSACOLA

**COMFORT INN**
6919 Pensacola Blvd (32505)
Rates: $30-$50;
Tel: (904) 478-4499

**DAYS INN**
710 N Palafox St (32501)
Rates: $35-$65;
Tel: (904) 438-4922

**DAYS INN NORTH**
7051 Pensacola Blvd (32505)
Rates: $39-$59;
Tel: (904) 476-9090

**ECONO LODGE**
7194 Pensacola Blvd (32505)
Rates: $38-$42;
Tel: (904) 479-8600

**HAMPTON INN**
7330 Plantation Rd (32504)
Rates: $43-$85;
Tel: (904) 477-3333

**HOLIDAY INN BAY BEACH**
51 Gulf Breeze Pkwy
(Gulf Breeze 32561)
Rates: $70-$90;
Tel: (904) 932-2214

**HOLIDAY INN EXPRESS**
6501 Pensacola Blvd (32505)
Rates: $45;
Tel: (904) 476-7200

**HOLIDAY INN-
UNIVERSITY MALL**
7200 Plantation Rd (32504)
Rates: $59-$125;
Tel: (904) 474-0100

**HOSPITALITY INN**
6900 Pensacola Blvd (32505)
Rates: $70-$80;
Tel: (904) 477-2333

**HOSPITALITY INN**
4910 Mobile Hwy (32506)
Rates: $53-$69;
Tel: (904) 453-3333

## KNIGHTS INN
1953 Northcross Ln (32514)
Rates: $33-$35;
Tel: (904) 477-2554

## LA QUINTA MOTOR INN
7750 N Davis Hwy (32514)
Rates: $43-$60;
Tel: (904) 474-0411

## PENSACOLA HILTON
200 E Gregory St (32501)
Rates: $80-$100;
Tel: (904) 433-3336

## QUALITY INN
6911 Pensacola Blvd (32505)
Rates: $39 $65;
Tel: (904) 479-3800

## RAMADA INN BAYVIEW
7601 Scenic Hwy (32504)
Rates: $49-$60;
Tel: (904) 477-7155

## RAMADA INN NORTH
6550 N Pensacola Blvd (32505)
Rates: $48-$54;
Tel: (904) 477-0711

## RED ROOF INN
7340 Plantation Rd (32504)
Rates: $36-$44;
Tel: (904) 476-7960

## PERRY

## BEST BUDGET INN
2220 Byron Butler Pkwy (32347)
Rates: $29;
Tel: (904) 584-6231

## DAYS INN
2277 US 19S (32347)
Rates: $38-$54;
Tel: (904) 584-5311

## SOUTHERN INN MOTEL
2238 S Byron Butler Pkwy (32347)
Rates: $30-$45;
Tel: (904) 584-4221

## PLANT CITY

## HOLIDAY INN-PLANT CITY
2011 N Wheeler St (33566)
Rates: $50-$75;
Tel: (813) 752-3141

## POMPANO BEACH

## SANTA ROSA MOTEL
308 S Ocean Blvd (33062)
Rates: N/A;
Tel. (305) 782-2500

## PONTE VEDRA BEACH

## MARRIOTT AT SAWGRASS
1000 TPC Blvd (32082)
Rates: $109 $500;
Tel: (904) 285-7777

## PORT CHARLOTTE

## RAMADA INN-DOWNTOWN
3400 Tamiami Tr (33952)
Rates: $45-$110;
Tel: (813) 625-4181

## PORT RICHEY

## DAYS INN
11736 US 19N (34668)
Rates: $36-$65;
Tel: (813) 863-1502

## PUNTA GORDA

## BEST WESTERN INN
26560 N Jones Loop Rd (33950)
Rates: $35-$73;
Tel: (813) 637-7200

## HOLIDAY INN
300 Retta Esplanade (33950)
Rates: $54-$129;
Tel: (813) 639-1165

## HOWARD JOHNSON RIVERSIDE LODGE
33 Tamiami Tr (33950)
Rates: $40-$95;
Tel: (813) 639-2167

## MOTEL 6
9300 Knights Dr (33950)
Rates: $21-$27;
Tel: (813) 639-9585

## RIVIERA BEACH

## BEST WESTERN SEASPRAY INN
P. O. Box 10418
(Palm Beach Shores 33404)
Rates: $45-$135;
Tel: (407) 844-0233

## ROCKLEDGE

## SPITZER'S SWISS MOTEL
3220 S Fiske Blvd (32955)
Rates: $40-$50;
Tel: (407) 631-9445

## ST. AUGUSTINE

## BEST WESTERN OCEAN INN
3955 A-1-A South (32084)
Rates: N/A;
Tel. (904) 471-8010

## DAYS INN HISTORIC
2800 Ponce de Leon Blvd (32084)
Rates: $34-$80;
Tel: (904) 829-6581

## DAYS INN INTERSTATE
25600 SR 16 (32092)
Rates: $26-$49;
Tel: (904) 824-4341

## ECONO LODGE OF ST. AUGUSTINE
2625 SR 207 (Elkton 32033)
Rates: $32-$49;
Tel: (904) 829-3435

## HOJO INN BY HOWARD JOHNSON LODGE
P. O. Box 365 (32085)
Rates: $30-$80;
Tel: (904) 829-5686

## HOWARD JOHNSON HISTORIC DOWNTOWN
137 San Marco Ave (32084)
Rates: $72-$88;
Tel: (904) 824-6181

**MONTEREY INN**
16 Avenida Menendez
(32084)
Rates: $32-$75;
Tel: (904) 824-4482

**QUALITY INN**
2445 SR 16 (32092)
Rates: $29-$49;
Tel: (904) 829-1999

## ST. AUGUSTINE BEACH

**BEST WESTERN
OCEAN INN**
3955 A1A S (32084)
Rates: $44-$75;
Tel: (904) 471-8010

**ENCORE ISLAND INN**
3400 A1A S (32084)
Rates: $39-$89;
Tel: (904) 471-1440

**HOLIDAY INN-
ST. AUGUSTINE BEACH**
3250 Hwy A1A S (32084)
Rates: $64-$130;
Tel: (904) 471-2555

**SURF VILLAGE MOTEL**
2201 South A1A (32084)
Rates: N/A;
Tel: (904) 471-3131

## ST. PETERSBURG
(and Vicinity)

**DAYS INN**
9359 US 19N
(Pinellas Park 34666)
Rates: $35-$85;
Tel: (813) 577-3838

**ECONO LODGE**
3000 34th St S (33711)
Rates: $34-$59;
Tel: (813) 867-1111

**HOLIDAY INN SOUTH**
4601 34th St S (33711)
Rates: $49-$94;
Tel: (813) 867-3131

**HOWARD JOHNSON
HOTEL**
3600 34th St S (33711)
Rates: $48-$60;
Tel: (813) 867-6070

**LA MARK CHARLES MOTEL**
6200 34th St N
(Pinellas Park 34665)
Rates: $45-$80;
Tel: (813) 527-7334

**LA QUINTA MOTOR INN**
7500 US 19N
(Pinellas Park 34665)
Rates: $45-$70;
Tel: (813) 545-5611

**LA QUINTA MOTOR INN**
4999 34th St N (33714)
Rates: $45-$70;
Tel: (813) 894-5000

**PENNSYLVANIA HOTEL**
300 4th North (33713)
Rates: N/A;
Tel: (813) 822-4045

**PINEGROVE COTTAGES**
5139 Tangerine Ave S (33707)
Rates: N/A;
Tel: (813) 321-7263

**TRAVELER'S INN**
2595 54th Ave N (33714)
Rates: $34-$60;
Tel: (813) 522-3191

**TRAVELODGE**
4600 34th St S (33711)
Rates: $35-$54;
Tel: (813) 866-0706

## SARASOTA

**COMFORT INN**
4800 N Tamiami Tr (34234)
Rates: $45-$75;
Tel: (813) 355-7091

**COQUINA ON THE BEACH**
1008 Ben Franklin Dr (34236)
Rates: $79-$275;
Tel: (813) 388-2141

**DAYS INN-
SARASOTA AIRPORT**
4900 N Tamiami Tr (34234)
Rates: $32-$70;
Tel: (813) 355-9721

**DAYS INN SARASOTA-
SIESTA KEY**
6600 S Tamiami Tr (34231)
Rates: $53-$99;
Tel: (813) 924-4900

**HOLIDAY INN-
LIDO BEACH**
233 Ben Franklin Dr (34236)
Rates: $79-$189;
Tel: (813) 388-3941

## SATELLITE BEACH

**DAYS INN**
180 SR A1A (32937)
Rates: $40-$70;
Tel: (407) 777-3552

## SEBRING

**MILLER MOTEL**
3751 US 27 S (33870)
Rates: N/A;
Tel: (813) 385-7049

## SIESTA KEY

**SURFRIDER BEACH
APARTMENTS**
6400 Midnight Pass Rd
(Sarasota 34242)
Rates: $58-$114;
Tel: (813) 349-2121

## SILVER SPRINGS

**DAYS INN OCALA EAST**
5001 E Silver Springs Blvd
(32688)
Rates: $36-$48;
Tel: (904) 236-2891

**HOLIDAY INN**
P. O. Box 156 (32688)
Rates: $49-$55;
Tel: (904) 236-2575

**HOWARD JOHNSON
MOTEL**
P. O. Box 475 (32688)
Rates: $35-$42;
Tel: (904) 236-2616

**SPRING SIDE MOTEL**
5440 E Silver Springs Blvd
(32688)
Rates: $18-$28;
Tel: (904) 236-2788

**SUN PLAZA MOTEL**
5461 E Silver Springs Blvd
(32688)
Rates: $26-$40;
Tel: (904) 236-2343

## SOUTH BAY

**OKEECHOBEE INN**
265 N US Hwy 27 (33493)
Rates: $40-$45;
Tel: (407) 996-7617

## STARKE

**DAYS INN**
P. O. Box 1090 (32091)
Rates: $47-$52;
Tel: (904) 964-7600

**SLEEPY HOLLOW MOTEL**
2317 N Temple Ave (32091)
Rates: $23-$27;
Tel. (904) 964-5006

## STUART

**INDIAN PIER PLANTATION
RESORT & MARINA**
555 NE Ocean Blvd (34996)
Rates: $110-$300;
Tel: (407) 225-3700

## SUN CITY CENTER

**SUN CITY CENTER HOTEL**
1335 Rickenbacker Dr (33573)
Rates: $45-$65;
Tel: (813) 634-33341

## TALLAHASSEE

**BEST INNS OF AMERICA**
2738 Graves Rd (32303)
Rates: $35-$46;
Tel: (904) 562-2378

**BEST WESTERN
PRIDE INN SUITES**
2016 Apalachee Pkwy
(32301)
Rates: $38-$66;
Tel: (904) 656-6312

**DAYS INN
AIRPORT SOUTH**
2100 Apalachee Pkwy
(32301)
Rates: $33-$37;
Tel; (904) 877-6121

**DAYS INN DOWNTOWN-
CAPITAL CENTER**
722 Apalachee Pkwy (32301)
Rates: $38-$65;
Tel: (904) 224-2181

**ECONO LODGE**
2681 N Monroe St (32303)
Rules. $28-$36;
Tel: (904) 385-6155

**KILLEARN COUNTRY
CLUB & INN**
100 Tyron Cir (32308)
Rates: $54-$80;
Tel: (904) 893-2186

**KNIGHTS INN**
2728 Graves Rd (32303)
Rates: $30-$37;
Tel: (904) 562-4700

**LA QUINTA
MOTOR INN-NORTH**
2905 N Monroe St (32303)
Rates: $44 57;
Tel: (904) 385-7172

**LA QUINTA MOTOR INN-
TALLAHASSEE SOUTH**
2050 Apalachee Pkwy
(32301)
Rates: $44-$57;
Tel: (904) 878-5099

**RED ROOF INN**
2930 Hospitality St (32303)
Rates: $32-$40;
Tel: (904) 385-7884

**SEMINOLE INN**
6737 Mahan Dr (32308)
Rates: $38-$50;
Tel: (904) 656-2938

**SHERATON
TALLAHASSEE HOTEL**
101 S Adams St (32301)
Rates: $69-$179;
Tel: (904) 224-5000

**SUPER I MOTEL**
2702 N Monroe St (32303)
Rates: $30-$42;
Tel: (904) 386-8818

**UNIVERSITY INN**
2121 W Tennessee (32304)
Rates: N/A;
Tel: (904) 576-6121

## TAMPA
(and Vicinity)

**BUDGETEL INN**
4811 US Hwy 301N (33610)
Rates: $31-$45;
Tel: (813) 626-0885

**BUDGETEL INN-
TAMPA SOUTHEAST**
602 S Falkenburg Rd (33619)
Rates: $31-$54;
Tel: (813) 684-4007

**CROWN STERLING SUITES
TAMPA AIRPORT**
4400 W Cypress St (33607)
Rates: $69-$139;
Tel: (813) 873-8675

**DAYS INN-
BUSCH GARDENS EAST**
2520 N 50th St (33619)
Rates: $42-$70;
Tel: (813) 247-3300

**DAYS INN-TAMPA
BUSCH GARDENS NORTH**
701 E Fletcher Ave (33612)
Rates: $27-$53;
Tel: (813) 977 1550

**ECONO LODGE MIDTOWN**
1020 S Dale Mabry (33629)
Rates: $32-$46;
Tel: (813) 254 3005

**ECONOMY INNS
OF AMERICA**
6606 E Buffalo Ave (33619)
Rates: N/A;
Tel: (813) 623-6667

**EMBASSY SUITES-TAMPA/
AIRPORT/WESTSHORE**
555 N Westshore Blvd (33609)
Rates: $99-$149;
Tel: (813) 875-1555

**HAMPTON INN
TAMPA INTL AIRPORT**
4817 W Laurel St (33607)
Rates: $49-$69;
Tel: (813) 287-0778

**HOLIDAY INN-
BUSCH GARDENS**
2701 E Fowler Ave (33612)
Rates: $65-$88;
Tel: (813) 971-4710

**LA QUINTA INN AIRPORT**
4730 Spruce St (33607)
Rates: $49-$70;
Tel: (813) 287-0440

**LA QUINTA
MOTOR INN EAST**
2904 Melbourne Blvd (33605)
Rates: $40-$61;
Tel: (813) 623-3591

**MARRIOTT
TAMPA WESTSHORE**
1001 N Westshore Blvd
(33607)
Rates: $129-$400;
Tel: (813) 287-2555

**MASTERS ECONOMY INN**
6010 SR 579 (Seffner 33584)
Rates: $23-$43;
Tel: (813) 621-4681

**RAMADA INN-
UNIVERSITY-U.S.F.**
400 E Bearss Ave (33613)
Rates: $38-$59;
Tel: (813) 961-1000

**RED ROOF INN-BRANDON**
10121 Horace Ave (33619)
Rates: $29-$49;
Tel: (813) 681-8484

**RED ROOF INN-
BUSCH GARDENS**
2307 E Busch Blvd (33612)
Rates: $29-$53;
Tel: (813) 932-0073

**RED ROOF INN-
FAIRGROUND**
5001 N US 301 (33610)
Rates: $28-$42;
Tel: (813) 623-5245

**RESIDENCE INN
BY MARRIOTT**
3075 N Rocky Point Dr
(33607)
Rates: $85-$135;
Tel: (813) 281-5677

**RODEWAY SAFARI RESORT**
4139 E Busch Blvd (33617)
Rates: $38-$86;
Tel: (813) 988-9191

**SHERATON TAMPA EAST**
7401 E Hillsborough Ave
(33610)
Rates: $59-$99;
Tel: (813) 626-0999

**TAHITIAN INN**
601 S Dale Mabry (33609)
Rates: $42-$56;
Tel: (813) 877-6721

**TRAVELODGE-
TAMPA/BUSCH GARDENS**
9202 30th St N (33612)
Rates: $40-$50;
Tel: (813) 935-7855

## TAVARES

**HOSPITALITY INN**
700 E Burleigh Blvd (32778)
Rates: $30-$65;
Tel: (904) 343-6373

**LAKESIDE INN
OF MT. DORA**
100 N Alexander St
(Mt. Dora 32757)
Rates: $80-$135;
Tel: (800) 556-5016

## TITUSVILLE

**BEST WESTERN
SPACE SHUTTLE INN**
3455 Cheney Hwy (32780)
Rates: $44-$65;
Tel: (407) 269-9100

**QUALITY INN-
KENNEDY SPACE CENTER**
3755 Cheney Hwy (32780)
Rates: $36-$60;
Tel: (407) 269-4480

## VENICE

**BEST WESTERN VENICE
RESORT & DINNER THEATRE**
455 US 41 Bypass N (34292)
Rates: $48-$92;
Tel: (813) 485-5411

**DAYS INN**
1710 Tamiami Tr (34293)
Rates: $42-$92;
Tel: (813) 493-4558

## VERO BEACH

**DAYS INN**
8800 20th St (32966)
Rates: $41-$65;
Tel: (407) 562-9991

**HOLIDAY INN-
COUNTRYSIDE WEST**
P. O. Box 1449 (32966)
Rates: $45-$70;
Tel: (407) 567-8321

**REXTON INN HOTEL**
1985 90th St (32966)
Rates: $35-$55;
Tel: (407) 778-1985

**VERO BEACH INN**
4700 N SR A1A (32963)
Rates: $65-$100;
Tel: (407) 231-1600

## WEST PALM BEACH

**DAYS INN-TURNPIKE**
6255 Okeechobee Blvd
(33417)
Rates: $48-$86;
Tel: (407) 686-6000

**DAYS INN-WEST PALM
BEACH/AIRPORT NORTH**
2300 45th St (33407)
Rates: $35-$65;
Tel: (407) 689-0450

**HAMPTON INN PALM
BEACH/INTL AIRPORT**
1505 Belvedere Rd (33406)
Rates: $49-$84;
Tel: (407) 471-8700

**KNIGHTS INN**
2200 45th St (33407)
Rates: N/A;
Tel: (800) 843-5644

**RADISSON SUITE INN**
1808 Australian Ave S
(33409)
Rates: $59-$149;
Tel: (407) 689-6888

## WHITE SPRINGS

**SCOTTISH INN**
Rt 1, Box 97A-1 (32096)
Rates: $22-$26;
Tel: (904) 963-2501

## WINTER HAVEN

**BUDGET HOST
DRIFTWOOD**
970 Cypress Gardens Blvd
(33880)
Rates: $28-$58;
Tel: (813) 294-4229

**CYPRESS MOTEL**
5651 Cypress Gardens Rd
(33884)
Rates: $27-$55;
Tel: (813) 324-5867

**HOWARD JOHNSON
LODGE**
1300 US 17 SW (33880)
Rates: $36-$95;
Tel: (813) 294-7321

## ZEPHYRHILLS

**BEST WESTERN
OF ZEPHYRHILLS**
5734 Gall Blvd (33541)
Rates: $40-$54;
Tel: (813) 782-5527

# GEORGIA

## ACWORTH

**BEST WESTERN
FRONTIER INN**
P. O. Box 600 (30101)
Rates: $35-$60;
Tel: (404) 974-0116

**DAYS INN**
5035 Cowan Rd (30101)
Rates: $35-$45;
Tel: (404) 974-1700

**QUALITY INN**
4980 Cowan Rd (30101)
Rates: $40-$45;
Tel: (404) 974 1922

## ADEL

**DAYS INN I-75**
1200 W 4th St (31620)
Rates: $28-$36;
Tel: (912) 896-4574

**HOJO INN I-75**
1103 W 4th St (31620)
Rates: $25-$50;
Tel: (912) 896-2244

## ALBANY

**DAYS INN**
422 W Oglethorpe Blvd
(31701)
Rates: $40-$44;
Tel: (912) 888-2632

**HERITAGE HOUSE**
732 W Oglethorpe (31701)
Rates: N/A;
Tel: (912) 888-1910

**HOLIDAY INN ALBANY**
2701 Dawson Rd (31707)
Rates: $56-$70;
Tel: (912) 883-8100

**KNIGHTS INN**
1201 Schley Ave (31707)
Rates: $34-$41;
Tel: (912) 888-9600

**RAMADA INN**
2505 N Slappey Blvd (31701)
Rates: $54-$65;
Tel: (912) 883-3211

## ALPHARETTA

**RESIDENCE INN
BY MARRIOTT**
5465 Windward Pkwy W
(30201)
Rates: $59-$130;
Tel: (404) 664-0664

## ASHBURN

**QUALITY INN**
P. O. Box 806 (31714)
Rates: $16-$32;
Tel: (912) 567-3334

## ATHENS

**BEST WESTERN-
COLONIAL INN**
170 N Milledge Ave (30601)
Rates: $36-$44;
Tel: (706) 546-7311

**DAYS INN**
2741 Atlanta Hwy (30606)
Rates: $33-$38;
Tel: (706) 546-9750

**DAYS INN-DOWNTOWN**
166 Finley St (30601)
Rates: $45-$54;
Tel: (706) 369-7000

**HOLIDAY INN**
P. O. Box 1666 (30603)
Rates: $54-$89;
Tel: (706) 549-4433

**RAMADA INN**
513 W Broad St (30601)
Rates: $51-$57;
Tel: (706) 546-8122

## ATLANTA
(and Vicinity)

**ATLANTA MARRIOTT
GWINNETT PLACE**
1775 Pleasant Hill Rd
(Duluth 30136)
Rates: $75;
Tel: (404) 923-1775

**ATLANTA MARRIOTT
NORCROSS**
475 Technology Pkwy
(Norcross 30092)
Rates: $48-$69;
Tel: (404) 263-8558

**ATLANTA MARRIOTT
NORTHWEST**
200 Interstate North Pkwy
(30339)
Rates: $69-$121;
Tel: (404) 952-7900

**ATLANTA MARRIOTT
SUITES MIDTOWN**
35 14th St (30309)
Rates: $79-$174;
Tel: (404) 876-8888

**BEST INNS OF AMERICA**
1255 Franklin Rd (Marietta
30067)
Rates: $37-$47;
Tel: (404) 955-0004

**BEST WESTERN
ATLANTA SOUTH**
3509 Hwy 138
(Stockbridge 30281)
Rates: $32-$52;
Tel: (404) 474-8771

**BEST WESTERN
BRADBURY SUITES**
4500 Circle 75 Pkwy (30339)
Rates: $39-$74;
Tel: (404) 956-9919

**BEST WESTERN
GRANADA SUITE HOTEL**
1302 W Peachtree St (30309)
Rates: $85-$150;
Tel: (404) 876-6100

**BEVERLY HILLS INN**
65 Sheridan Dr (30305)
Rates: $59-$120;
Tel: (800) 331-8520

**BUDGETEL INN**
575 Old Holcomb Bridge Rd
(Roswell 30076)
Rates: $37-$53;
Tel: (404) 552-0200

**BUDGETEL INN**
5395 Peachtree Ind Blvd
(Norcross 30092)
Rates: $27-$42;
Tel: (404) 446-2882

**BUDGETEL INN-
ATLANTA AIRPORT**
2480 Old National Pkwy
(College Park 30349)
Rates: $36-$40;
Tel: (404) 766-0000

**BUDGETEL INN
ATLANTA LENOX**
2535 Chantilly Dr NE (30324)
Rates: $35-$44;
Tel: (404) 321-0999

**CASTLEGATE HOTEL
& CONFERENCE CTR**
1750 Commerce Dr NW
(30318)
Rates: $45-$59;
Tel: (404) 351-6100

**DAYS INN-
GWINNETT PLACE**
1948 Day Dr (Duluth 30136)
Rates: $39-$69;
Tel: (404) 476-1211

**GUEST QUARTERS
SUITE HOTEL**
111 Perimeter Center W
(30346)
Rates: $59-$119;
Tel: (404) 396-6800

**HAMPTON INN**
9995 Old Dogwood Rd
(Roswell 30076)
Rates: $43-$58;
Tel: (404) 587-5161

**HAMPTON INN-
ATLANTA AIRPORT**
1888 Sullivan Rd
(College Park 30337)
Rates: $47-$62;
Tel: (404) 996-2220

**HAMPTON INN
ATLANTA BUCKHEAD**
3398 Piedmont Rd NE (30305)
Rates: $50-$67;
Tel: (404) 233-5656

**HAMPTON INN-
DRUID HILLS ROAD**
1974 N Druid Hills Rd (30329)
Rates: $45-$59;
Tel: (404) 320-6600

**HAMPTON INN HOTEL**
3400 Northlake Pkwy (30345)
Rates: $42-$56;
Tel: (404) 493-1966

**HAWTHORN SUITES-
ATLANTA NW**
1500 Parkwood Cir (30339)
Rates: $69-$108;
Tel: (404) 952-9595

**HILTON & TOWERS**
255 Courtland St NE (30303)
Rates: $160-$400;
Tel: (404) 659-2000

**HOLIDAY INN-BUCKHEAD**
3340 Peachtree Rd NE
(30026)
Rates: $69-$275;
Tel: (404) 231-1234

**HOLIDAY INN
EXPRESS I-20 EAST**
4300 Snapfinger Woods Dr
(Decatur 30035)
Rates: $39-$53;
Tel: (404) 981-5670

**HOLIDAY INN
EXPRESS I-85 NORTH**
4422 Northeast Expwy
(Doraville 30340)
Rates: $49-$62;
Tel: (404) 448-7220

**HOLIDAY INN MARIETTA**
2255 Delk Rd (30067)
Rates: $69-$82;
Tel: (404) 952-7581

**HOLIDAY INN MIDTOWN NORTH**
1810 Howell Mill Rd (30318)
Rates: $45-$60;
Tel: (404) 351-3831

**HOLIDAY INN- PEACHTREE CORNERS**
6050 Peachtree Ind Blvd
(Norcross 30071)
Rates: $59-$87;
Tel: (404) 448-4400

**HOLIDAY INN PERIMETER DUNWOODY**
4386 Chamblee-Dunwoody Rd
(30341)
Rates: $64-$74;
Tel: (404) 457-6363

**HOLIDAY INN ROSWELL/ATLANTA**
1075 Holcomb Bridge Rd
(Roswell 30076)
Rates: $49-$84;
Tel: (404) 992-9600

**HOLIDAY INN-SOUTH**
6288 Old Dixie Hwy
(Jonesboro 30236)
Rates: $46-$71;
Tel: (404) 968-4300

**HOMEWOOD SUITES- CUMBERLAND**
3200 Cobb Pkwy (30339)
Rates: $69-$99;
Tel: (404) 988-9449

**HOMEWOOD SUITES- NORCROSS**
450 Technology Pkwy
(Norcross 30092)
Rates: $89-$99;
Tel: (404) 448-4663

**HOWARD JOHNSON- ATLANTA AIRPORT**
1377 Virginia Ave
(East Point 30344)
Rates: $40-$77;
Tel: (404) 762-5111

**KNIGHTS INN ATLANTA EAST**
2942 Lawrenceville Hwy
(Tucker 30084)
Rates: N/A;
Tel: (800) 843-5644

**KNIGHTS INN ATLANTA NORTHWEST**
5230 S Cobb Dr
(Smyrna 30080)
Rates: $31-$37;
Tel: (404) 794-3000

**LA QUINTA ATLANTA STONE MOUNTAIN**
1819 Mountain Ind Blvd
(Tucker 30084)
Rates: $46-$59;
Tel: (404) 496-1317

**LA QUINTA ATLANTA WEST**
7377 N Service Rd
(Austell 30001)
Rates: $41-$81;
Tel: (404) 944-2110

**LA QUINTA MOTOR INN AIRPORT**
4874 Old National Hwy
(College Park 30337)
Rates: $47-$60;
Tel: (404) 768-1241

**LA QUINTA MOTOR INN MARIETTA**
2170 Delk Rd
(Marietta 30067)
Rates: $47-$60;
Tel: (404) 951-0026

**LA QUINTA-PEACHTREE**
5375 Peachtree Ind Blvd
(Norcross 30092)
Rates: $42-$55;
Tel: (404) 449-5144

**LA QUINTA-PIEDMONT**
2115 Piedmont Rd NE (30324)
Rates: $49-$62;
Tel: (404) 876-4365

**MARRIOTT ATLANTA AIRPORT**
4711 Best Rd
(College Park 30337)
Rates: $69-$155;
Tel: (404) 766-7900

**MASTERS ECONOMY INN SIX FLAGS**
4120 Fulton Ind Blvd (30336)
Rates: $24-$63;
Tel: (404) 696 4690

**MONROE DRIVE INN**
1944 Piedmont Cir NE (30324)
Rates: $39-$68;
Tel: (404) 875-3571

**PERIMETER NORTH INN**
2001 Clearview Ave (30340)
Rates: $29-$39;
Tel: (404) 455-1811

**QUALITY INN HABERSHAM**
330 Peachtree St NE (30308)
Rates: $59-$82;
Tel: (404) 577-1980

**RADISSON HOTEL ATLANTA**
165 Courtland St (30303)
Rates: $95-$189;
Tel: (404) 659-6500

**RAMADA HOTEL**
1850 Cotillion Dr (30338)
Rates: $49-$69;
Tel: (404) 394-5000

**RAMADA INN ATLANTA SIX FLAGS**
4225 Fulton Ind Blvd (30336)
Rates: $45-$55;
Tel: (404) 691-4100

**RAMADA RENAISSANCE HOTEL**
4736 Best Rd
(College Park 30337)
Rates: $105-$165;
Tel: (404) 762-7676

**RED ROOF INN-AIRPORT**
2471 Old National Pkwy
(College Park 30349)
Rates: $27-$36;
Tel: (404) 761-9701

**RED ROOF INN- ATLANTA (TUCKER)**
2810 Lawrenceville Hwy
(Tucker 30084)
Rates: $25-$41;
Tel: (404) 496-1311

**RED ROOF INN-
DRUID HILLS**
1960 N Druid Hills Rd (30329)
Rates: $29-$48;
Tel: (404) 321-1653

**RED ROOF INN-
INDIAN TRAIL**
5171 Indian Trail Ind Pkwy
(Norcross 30071)
Rates: $33-$38;
Tel: (404) 448-8944

**RED ROOF INN-NORTH**
2200 Corporate Plaza
(Smyrna 30080)
Rates: $28-$36;
Tel: (404) 952-6966

**RED ROOF INN-SIX FLAGS**
4265 Shirley Dr SW (30336)
Rates: $27-$50;
Tel: (404) 696-4391

**RED ROOF INN-SOUTH**
1348 South Lake Plaza Dr
(Monroe 30260)
Rates: $26-$38;
Tel: (404) 968-1483

**RESIDENCE INN
BY MARRIOTT**
6096 Barfield Rd (30328)
Rates: $125-$150;
Tel: (404) 252-5066

**RESIDENCE INN
BY MARRIOTT
ATLANTA AIRPORT**
3401 International Blvd
(Hapeville 30354)
Rates: $105-$145;
Tel: (404) 761-0511

**RESIDENCE INN
BY MARRIOTT-BUCKHEAD**
2960 Piedmont Rd NE (30305)
Rates: $109;
Tel: (404) 239-0677

**RESIDENCE INN
BY MARRIOTT MIDTOWN**
1041 W Peachtree St (30309)
Rates: $119-$149;
Tel: (404) 872-8885

**RESIDENCE INN BY MARRIOTT
PERIMETER EAST**
1901 Savoy Dr (30341)
Rates: $69-$124;
Tel: (404) 455-4446

**SHERATON ATLANTA
AIRPORT HOTEL**
1325 Virginia Ave
(East Point 30344)
Rates: $82-$110;
Tel: (404) 768-6660

**SHERATON COLONY
SQUARE HOTEL**
188 14th St (30361)
Rates: $129-$189;
Tel: (404) 892-6000

**SHERATON INN
HARTSVILLE-
W ATLANTA AIRPORT**
3601 N Desert Dr
(Atlanta 30344)
Rates: $69-$89;
Tel: (404) 762-5141

**SHONEY'S INN**
3900 Fulton Ind Blvd (30336)
Rates: $31-$49;
Tel: (404) 691-2444

**SHONEY'S INN-
ATLANTA NORTHEAST**
2050 Willow Trail Pkwy
(Norcross 30093)
Rates: $36-$49;
Tel: (404) 564-0492

**SHONEY'S INN-
ATLANTA/STOCKBRIDGE**
110 Hwy 138
(Stockbridge 30281)
Rates: $35-$45;
Tel: (404) 389-5179

**SUMMERFIELD SUITES
HOTEL**
760 Mt. Vernon Hwy NE
(30328)
Rates: $82-$145;
Tel: (404) 250-0110

**SUMMERFIELD SUITES
HOTEL BUCKHEAD**
505 Pharr Rd (30305)
Rates: $89-$159;
Tel: (404) 262-7880

**SWISSOTEL ATLANTA**
3391 Peachtree Rd (30326)
Rates: N/A;
Tel: (404) 365-0065

**UNIVERSITY INN
AT EMORY**
1767 N Decatur Rd (30307)
Rates: $58-$86;
Tel: (404) 634-7327

**VANTAGE HOTEL-
NORTHLAKE**
2180 Northlake Pkwy
(Tucker 30084)
Rates: $49-$69;
Tel: (404) 939-8120

**VILLAGER LODGE**
5122 Indian Tr
(Norcross 30071)
Rates: $26-$32;
Tel: (404) 446-5490

**THE WESTIN
PEACHTREE PLAZA**
210 Peachtree St (30343)
Rates: $135-$245;
Tel: (404) 659-1400

# AUGUSTA

**AUGUSTA DAYS INN**
555 Broad St (30901)
Rates: $29-$39;
Tel: (706) 724-8100

**DELUXE INN-WEST**
4324 Belair Frontage Rd
(30909)
Rates: $26-$35;
Tel: (706) 860-8840

**HAMPTON INN**
3030 Washington Rd (30907)
Rates: $40-$55;
Tel: (706) 737-1122

**HOLIDAY INN GORDON
HIWAY/BOBBY JONES**
2155 Gordon Hwy (30909)
Rates: $49-$175;
Tel: (706) 737-2300

**HOLIDAY INN I-20**
1075 Stevens Creek Rd
(30907)
Rates: $49-$200;
Tel: (706) 738-8811

**KNIGHTS INN**
210 Boy Scout Rd (30909)
Rates: $26-$33;
Tel: (706) 737-3166

**LA QUINTA MOTOR INN**
3020 Washington Rd (30907)
Rates: $37-$48;
Tel: (706) 733-2660

**THE PARTRIDGE INN
SUITES HOTEL**
2110 Walton Way (30904)
Rates: $65-$105;
Tel: (706) 737-8888

**PERRIN GUEST
HOUSE INN**
208 Lafayette Dr (30909)
Rates: $65-$150;
Tel: (706)736-3737

**RADISSON INN**
3038 Washington Rd (30907)
Rates: $39-$84;
Tel: (706) 868-1800

**RAMADA INN-AIRPORT**
1365 Gordon Hwy (30901)
Rates: $35-$39;
Tel: (706) 722-4344

## AUSTELL

**ATLANTA WEST
SIX FLAGS**
1595 Blair Bridge Rd (30001)
Rates: N/A;
Tel: (800) 843-5644

## BAINBRIDGE

**HOLIDAY INN EXPRESS**
751 W Shotwell St (31717)
Rates: $39-$65;
Tel: (912) 246-0015

## BAXLEY

**PINE LODGE MOTEL**
500 S Main St (31513)
Rates: $30-$36;
Tel: (912) 367-3622

## BREMEN

**BEST WESTERN
CARROLTON**
35 Price Creek Rd (30110)
Rates: $39-$43;
Tel: (404) 537-4646

**SHILO INN**
1077 Alabama Ave (30110)
Rates: $40-$50;
Tel: (404) 537-3833

## BLAIRSVILLE

**7 CREEKS
HOUSEKEEPING CABINS**
Rt 2, Box 2647 (30512)
Rates: N/A;
Tel: (404) 745-4753

## BLUE RIDGE

**BLUE RIDGE
MOUNTAIN CABINS**
P. O. Box 1182 (30513)
Rates: N/A;
Tel: (404) 632-8999

## BREMEN

**SHILO INN**
1077 Alabama Ave (30110)
Rates: N/A;
Tel: (404) 537-3833

## BRUNSWICK

**BEST WESTERN
BRUNSWICK INN**
US 25 & 341, Exit 7B (31520)
Rates: $36-$53;
Tel: (912) 264-0144

**BUDGETEL INN**
105 Tourist Dr (31520)
Rates: $32-$48;
Tel: (912) 265-7725

**COMFORT INN**
490 New Jessup Hwy (31520)
Rates: $49-$67;
Tel: (912) 264-6540

**DAYS INN**
2307 Gloucester St (31520)
Rates: $35-$55;
Tel: (912) 265-8830

**DAYS INN-
NEW JESSUP HWY**
409 New Jessup Hwy (31520)
Rates: $40-$48;
Tel: (912) 264-4330

**HOLIDAY INN**
3302 Glynn Ave (31520)
Rates: $48-$62;
Tel: (912) 264-9111

**HOLIDAY INN I-95**
US 341 at I-95 (31525)
Rates: $49-$74;
Tel: (912) 264-4033

**KNIGHTS INN**
US Hwy 341 (31520)
Rates: N/A;
Tel: (800) 843-5644

**RAMADA INN-EAST**
3241 Glynn Ave (31523)
Rates: $47-$57;
Tel: (912) 264-8611

**RAMADA INN-NORTH**
Jct I-95 & US 341, Exit 7A
(31520)
Rates: $45-$55;
Tel: (912) 264-3621

## CALHOUN

**BEST WESTERN
OF CALHOUN**
2261 US 41 NE (30701)
Rates: $30-$44;
Tel: (706) 629-4521

**BUDGET HOST
SHEPHERD MOTEL**
139 Fairmont Hwy SE (30703)
Rates: $21-$33;
Tel: (706) 629-8644

**DAYS INN**
742 Hwy 53 SE (30701)
Rates: $26-$44;
Tel: (706) 629-8271

**DUFFY'S MOTEL NORTH**
1441 US 41N (30701)
Rates: $14-$19;
Tel: (706) 629-4436

**HOLIDAY INN**
P. O. Box 252 (30703)
Rates: $40-$48;
Tel: (706) 629-9191

**RED CARPET INN-
CALHOUN**
915 Hwy 53E, SE (30701)
Rates: $21-$36;
Tel: (706) 629-9501

**SCOTTISH INNS**
1510 Red Bud Rd NE (30701)
Rates: N/A;
Tel: (706) 629-8261

## CARTERSVILLE

**BUDGET HOST INN**
851 Cass-White Rd (30120)
Rates: $21-$26;
Tel: (404) 386-0350

**COMFORT INN**
28 Hwy 294 SE (30120)
Rates: $28-$43;
Tel: (404) 387-1800

**CROWN INN**
1214 N Tennessee St (30120)
Rates: $22-$26;
Tel: (404) 382-7100

**ECONO LODGE MOTEL**
P.O. Box 600 (Acworth 30101)
Rates: $27-$49;
Tel: (404) 386-3303

**ECONO LODGE MOTOR INN**
P. O. Box 600
(Acworth 30101)
Rates: $28-$33;
Tel: (404) 386-0700

**HOLIDAY INN**
P. O. Box 200306 (30120)
Rates: $52-$67;
Tel: (404) 386-0830

**KNIGHTS INN**
420 E Church St (30120)
Rates: $30-$35;
Tel: (404) 386-7263

**QUALITY INN**
P. O. Box 158 (30120)
Rates: $32-$38;
Tel: (404) 386-0510

**RED CARPET INN-CARTERSVILLE**
851 Cass-White Rd (30120)
Rates: $19-$24;
Tel: (404) 382-8000

## CHATSWORTH

**BEST WESTERN COHUTTA LODGE**
5000 Cochise Tr (30705)
Rates: $59-$115;
Tel: (706) 695-9601

**KEY WEST INN**
501 GI Maddox Pkwy (30705)
Rates: $38-$41;
Tel: (706) 517-1155

## CHULA

**RED CARPET INN**
P. O. Box 40 (31733)
Rates: $23-$29;
Tel: (912) 382-2686

## CLARKESVILLE

**HABERSHAM HOLLOW COUNTRY INN & CABINS**
Rt 6, Box 6208 (30523)
Rates: N/A;
Tel: (404) 754-5147

## CLAYTON

**ENGLISH MANOR INNS**
Hwy 76 East (30525)
Rates: N/A;
Tel: (800) 782-5780

## COLLEGE PARK

**RED ROOF INN**
2471 Old National Pkwy (30349)
Rates: N/A;
Tel: (800) 843-8773

## COLUMBUS

**BUDGETEL**
2919 Warm Springs Rd (31909)
Rates: $34-$50;
Tel: (706) 323-4344

**COMFORT INN**
3443B Macon Rd (31907)
Rates: $40-$50;
Tel: (706) 568-3300

**DAYS INN**
3452 Macon Rd (31907)
Rates: $39-$57;
Tel: (706) 561-4400

**ECONO LODGE OF COLUMBUS/ FORT BENNING**
4483 Victory Dr (31903)
Rates: $35-$39;
Tel: (706) 682-3803

**LA QUINTA MOTOR INN-MIDTOWN**
3201 Macon Rd (31906)
Rates: $40-$52;
Tel: (706) 568-1740

**RAMADA CITY CENTER**
1325 4th Ave (31901)
Rates: $36-$40;
Tel: (706) 322-2522

**SHERATON AIRPORT**
5351 Simons Blvd (31904)
Rates: $55-$78;
Tel: (706) 327-6868

## COMMERCE

**BULLDOG INN-COMMERCE**
P. O. Box 209 (30529)
Rates: $26-$33;
Tel: (706) 335-5147

**HOJO INN**
Rt 1, Box 163-D (30529)
Rates: $30-$50;
Tel: (706) 335-5581

**HOLIDAY INN**
P. O. Box 247 (30529)
Rates: $45-$51;
Tel: (706) 335-5183

## CONYERS

**COMFORT INN**
1363 Klondike Rd (30207)
Rates: $49-$75;
Tel: (404) 760-0300

**VILLAGER LODGE-CONYERS**
1297 Dogwood Dr (30207)
Rates: $31-$36;
Tel: (404) 483-1332

# CORDELE

**COLONIAL INN**
2016 16th Ave E (31015)
Rates: $33-$42;
Tel: (912) 273-5420

**DAYS INN**
Jct I-75 & US 280, Exit 33
(31015)
Rates: $37-$49;
Tel: (912) 273-1123

**FRIENDSHIP INN**
1618 E 16th Ave (31015)
Rates: $30-$45;
Tel: (912) 273-2456

**HOLIDAY INN**
P. O. Box 916 (31015)
Rates: $48-$62;
Tel: (912) 273-4117

**RAMADA INN**
2016 16th Ave E (31015)
Rates: $42-$49;
Tel: (912) 273-5000

# COVINGTON

**BEST WESTERN
WHITE COLUMNS INN**
10130 Alcovy Rd (30209)
Rates: $36-$44;
Tel: (404) 786-5800

# DALTON

**BEST INNS OF AMERICA**
1529 W Walnut Ave (30720)
Rates: $37-$47;
Tel: (404) 226-1100

**BEST WESTERN INN
OF DALTON**
2106 Chattanooga Rd
(30720)
Rates: $29-$44;
Tel: (404) 226-5022

**DAYS INN**
1518 W Walnut Ave (30720)
Rates: $33-$55;
Tel: (404) 278-0850

**ECONO LODGE**
P. O.Box 1794 (30722)
Rates: $28-$45;
Tel: (404) 277-9323

**HOLIDAY INN**
515 Holiday Dr (30720)
Rates: $45-$59;
Tel: (404) 278-0500

# DILLARD

**THE DILLARD HOUSE**
P. O. Box 10 (30537)
Rates: $39-$75;
Tel: (706) 746-5348

# DORAVILLE

**ECONOMY INNS
OF AMERICA**
3092 Presidential Pkwy
(30340)
Rates: N/A;
Tel: (404) 454-8373

# DOUGLAS

**DAYS INN**
907 N Peterson Ave (31533)
Rates: $30-$34;
Tel: (912) 384-5190

**HOLIDAY INN**
P. O. Box 1170 (31533)
Rates: $40-$50;
Tel: (912) 384-9100

**SHONEY'S INN**
1009 N Peterson Ave (31533)
Rates: $33-$41;
Tel: (912) 384-2621

# DOUGLASVILLE

**DAYS INN**
5489 Westmoreland Plaza
(30134)
Rates: $35-$65;
Tel: (404) 949-1499

# DUBLIN

**HOLIDAY INN**
P. O. Box 768 (31040)
Rates: $40-$53;
Tel: (912) 272-7862

# EAST ELLIJAY

**STRATFORD MOTOR INN**
P. O. Box 130 (30539)
Rates: $36-$55;
Tel: (706) 276-1080

# EULONIA

**BEST WESTERN
VILLAGE INN**
P. O. Box 156
(Townsend 31331)
Rates: $29-$39;
Tel: (912) 832-4444

# FOLKSTON

**DAYSTOP TAHITI**
1201 S 2nd St (31537)
Rates: $28-$39;
Tel: (912) 496-2514

# FORSYTH

**BEST WESTERN
HILLTOP INN**
SR 42 & I-75 (31029)
Rates: $35-$45;
Tel: (912) 994-9260

**HAMPTON INN**
P. O. Box 126 (31029)
Rates: $35-$48;
Tel: (912) 994-9697

**HOLIDAY INN**
480 Holiday Cir (31029)
Rates: $43-$55;
Tel: (912) 994-5691

# FORT OGLETHORPE

**BEST WESTERN
BATTLEFIELD INN**
1715 Lafayette Rd (37042)
Rates: $39-$49;
Tel: (706) 866-0222

## GAINESVILLE

**HOLIDAY INN**
726 Jesse Jewell Pkwy
(30501)
Rates: $54-$58;
Tel: (404) 536-4451

## GLENNVILLE

**CHEERI-O MOTEL**
P. O. Box 393 (30427)
Rates: $28-$36;
Tel: (912) 654-2176

## HAZLEHURST

**THE VILLAGE INN**
312 Coffee St (31539)
Rates: $36-$52;
Tel: (912) 375-4527

## HELEN

**THE HELENDORF
RIVER INN**
P. O. Box 305 (30545)
Rates: $40-$79;
Tel: (706) 878-2271

**VALLEY HAUS MOTEL**
P.O. Box 319 (30545)
Rates: $50-$71;
Tel: (706) 877-2111

## HIAWASSEE

**SALALE LODGE**
Rt 1, Box 36 (30546)
Rates: $29-$74;
Tel: (706) 896-3943

## HOBOKEN

**BLUEBERRY HILL**
Rt 1, Box 253 (31542)
Rates: N/A;
Tel: (912) 458-2605

## JEKYLL ISLAND

**BEST WESTERN-
JEKYLL INN**
975 N Beachview Dr (31527)
Rates: $49-$82;
Tel: (912) 635-2531

**CLARION-BUCCANEER
MOTOR HOTEL**
85 S Beachview Dr (31520)
Rates: $95-$159;
Tel: (912) 635-2261

**COMFORT INN
ISLAND SUITES**
711 N Beachview Dr (31527)
Rates: $55-$149;
Tel: (912) 635-2211

**DAYS INN BEACH RESORT**
60 S Beachview Dr (31527)
Rates: $39-$89;
Tel: (912) 635-3319

## JESUP

**PRIDE INN**
US 301S (31545)
Rates: $30-$43;
Tel: (912) 427-3751

## KENNESAW

**BEST AMERICAN LODGE**
1460 Busbee Pkwy (30144)
Rates: $25-$39;
Tel: (404) 499-1700

**COMFORT INN**
775 George Busbee Pkwy
(30144)
Rates: $48-$55;
Tel: (404) 424-7666

**RED ROOF INN-
TOWN CENTER MALL**
520 Roberts Ct NW (30144)
Rates: $28-$36;
Tel: (404) 429-0323

## KINGSLAND

**COMFORT INN-
KINGSLAND**
I-95 & SR 40E (31548)
Rates: $41-$66;
Tel: (912) 729-6979

## LA GRANGE

**COMFORT INN**
1601 Lafayette Pkwy (30240)
Rates: $42-$47;
Tel: (404) 882-9540

**DAYS INN-LA GRANGE/
CALLAWAY GARDENS**
2606 Whitesville Rd (30240)
Rates: $35-$45;
Tel: (404) 882-8881

## LAKE PARK

**SHONEY'S INN**
621 Hwy 376 Ext. 2 (31636)
Rates: N/A;
Tel: (912) 559-5660

## LOCUST GROVE

**SCOTTISH INNS**
4679 Hampton Rd I-75 Ex. 68
(30248)
Rates: N/A;
Tel: (404) 957-9001

## MACON

**BEST WESTERN
REGENCY INN**
4630 Chambers Rd (31206)
Rates: $30-$50;
Tel: (912) 781-7131

**COMFORT INN-NORTH**
2690 Riverside Dr (31204)
Rates: $35-$57;
Tel: (912) 746-8855

**DAYS INN NORTH**
2737 Sheraton Dr (31204)
Rates: $35-$50;
Tel: (912) 745-8521

**HAMPTON INN**
3680 Riverside Dr (31210)
Rates: $39-$49;
Tel: (912) 471-0660

**HOWARD JOHNSON
LODGE**
2566 Riverside Dr (31204)
Rates: $38-$42;
Tel: (912) 746-7671

**KNIGHTS INN-MACON I-475**
4952 Romiser Rd (31206)
Rates: $29-$35;
Tel: (912) 471-1230

**MACON'S DOWNTOWN HOTEL**
108 1st St (31202)
Rates: $50-$68;
Tel: (912) 746-1461

**QUALITY INN-NORTH**
P. O. Box 7006 (31209)
Rates: $30-$38;
Tel: (912) 743-1482

**RAMADA INN**
5009 Harrison Rd (31206)
Rates: $46-$54;
Tel: (912) 474-0871

**RODEWAY INN**
4999 Eisenhower Pkwy
(31206)
Rates: $36-$40;
Tel: (912) 781-4343

## MADISON

**BRADY INN**
250 N Second St (30650)
Rates: $40-$70;
Tel: (706) 342-4400

**DAYS INN**
2001 Eatonton Hwy (30650)
Rates: $36-$48;
Tel: (706) 342-1839

**RAMADA INN ANTEBELLUM**
2020 Eatonton Hwy (30650)
Rates: $39-$65;
Tel: (706) 342-2121

## MARIETTA

**LA QUINTA MOTEL**
2170 Delk Rd (30067)
Rates: $48-$54;
Tel: (404) 951-0026

## MCDONOUGH

**THE BRITTANY MOTOR INN**
P. O. Box 477 (30253)
Rates: $24-$29;
Tel: (404) 957-5821

**FRIENDSHIP INN**
SR 155, NE of I-75, Exit 69
(30253)
Rates: $26-$39;
Tel: (404) 957-5261

**HOLIDAY INN MCDONOUGH**
930 Hwy 155 S (30253)
Rates: $42-$59;
Tel: (404) 957-5291

## MILLEDGEVILLE

**DAYS INN**
3001 Heritage Rd (31061)
Rates: $33-$39;
Tel. (912) 453-3551

**HOLIDAY INN**
Hwy 441N (31061)
Rates: $40-$45;
Tel: (912) 452-3502

## NEWNAN

**ADMIRAL BENBOW INN**
40 Parkway N (30265)
Rates: $39-$47;
Tel: (404) 251-4580

**DAYS INN**
P. O. Box 548 (30263)
Rates: $39-$49;
Tel: (404) 253-8550

**HOLIDAY INN EXPRESS**
6 Herring Rd (30265)
Rates: $42-$50;
Tel: (404) 251-2828

## PERRY

**BEL AIRE MOTEL**
1345 Sam Nunn Blvd (31069)
Rates: N/A;
Tel: (912) 987-2970

**COMFORT INN**
1602 Sam Nunn Blvd (31069)
Rates: $44-$52;
Tel: (912) 987-7710

**DAYS INN OF PERRY**
800 Valley Dr (31069)
Rates: $36-$46;
Tel: (912) 987-2142

**ECONO LODGE**
405 General Hodges Blvd
(31069)
Rates: $28-$34;
Tel: (912) 987-7747

**HOLIDAY INN**
700 Valley Dr (31069)
Rates: $45-$56;
Tel: (912) 987-3313

**NEW PERRY INN**
800 Main St (31069)
Rates: $26-$48;
Tel: (912) 987-1000

**QUALITY INN-PERRY**
P. O. Box 1012 (31069)
Rates: $35-$55;
Tel: (912) 987-1345

**SHONEY'S INN**
110 Perimeter Rd (31069)
Rates: $42-$47;
Tel: (912) 987-4454

**TRAVELODGE**
100 Westview Ln (31069)
Rates: $25-$29;
Tel: (912) 987-7355

## PINE MOUNTAIN

**WHITE COLUMNS MOTEL**
P. O. Box 531 (31822)
Rates: $33-$45;
Tel: (404) 663-2312

## POOLER

**SAVANNAH WEST KNIGHTS INN**
500 Hwy 80 E (31322)
Rates: N/A;
Tel: (800) 843-5644

## RICHMOND HILL

**ECONO LODGE**
P. O. Box 47 (31324)
Rates: $23-$29;
Tel: (912) 756-3312

## RINGGOLD

**SUPER 8 MOTEL**
401 S Hwy 151 (30736)
Rates: $32-$39;
Tel: (706) 965-7080

# ROME

**DAYS INN**
840 Turner McCall Blvd
(30161)
Rates: $41-$52;
Tel: (706) 295-0400

**HOLIDAY INN-
SKY TOP CENTER**
Hwy 411E (30161)
Rates: $50-$55;
Tel: (706) 295-1100

**RAMADA INN**
707 Turner McCall Blvd
(30161)
Rates: $48-$52;
Tel: (706) 291-0101

# ST. SIMONS ISLAND

**COUNTRY HEARTH INN**
301 Main St (31522)
Rates: $55-$80;
Tel: (912) 638-7805

# SAVANNAH
(and Vicinity)

**BALLASTONE INN**
14 E Oglethorpe Ave (31401)
Rates: $85-$175;
Tel: (912) 236-1484

**BEST WESTERN CENTRAL**
45 Eisenhower Dr (31406)
Rates: $38-$55;
Tel: (912) 355-1000

**BEST WESTERN
SAVANNAH**
1 Gateway Blvd (31419)
Rates: $44-$64;
Tel: (912) 925-2420

**BUDGETEL INN**
8484 Abercorn St (31406)
Rates: $34-$50;
Tel: (912) 927-7660

**DAYS INN ABERCORN**
11750 Abercorn St (31419)
Rates: $42-$57;
Tel: (912) 927-7720

**ECONO LODGE GATEWAY**
7 Gateway Blvd W (31419)
Rates: $34-$48;
Tel: (912) 925-2280

**HAMPTON INN**
201 Stephenson Ave (31405)
Rates: $42-$50;
Tel: (912) 355-4100

**HASLAM-FORT HOUSE**
417 E Charlton St (31401)
Rates: N/A;
Tel: (912) 233-6380

**HOLIDAY INN-DOWNTOWN**
121 W Boundary St (31401)
Rates: $47-$67;
Tel: (912) 236-1355

**HOLIDAY INN-MIDTOWN**
7100 Abercorn St (31406)
Rates: $48-$59;
Tel: (912) 352-7100

**HOLIDAY INN-SOUTH**
P. O. Box 441B (31419)
Rates: $43-$57;
Tel: (912) 925-2770

**HOMEWOOD SUITES**
5820 White Bluff Rd (31405)
Rates: $89-$119;
Tel: (912) 353-8500

**HOWARD JOHNSON
I-95 SAVANNAH**
Rt 4, Box 441C (31419)
Rates: $35-$59;
Tel: (912) 925-3680

**HYATT REGENCY-
SAVANNAH**
2 W Bay St (31401)
Rates: $95-$149;
Tel: (912) 238-1234

**LA QUINTA MOTOR INN**
6805 Abercorn St (31405)
Rates: $38-$55;
Tel: (912) 355-3004

**MASTER HOSTS INN**
1 Fort Argyle Rd (31419)
Rates: N/A;
Tel: (912) 925-2640

**QUALITY INN-AIRPORT**
Rt 5, Box 285 (31408)
Rates: $44-$49;
Tel: (912) 964-1421

**QUALITY INN
DOWNTOWN**
231 W Boundary St (31401)
Rates: $50-$55;
Tel: (912) 232-3200

**QUALITY INN
HEART OF SAVANNAH**
300 W Bay St (31401)
Rates: $42-$64;
Tel: (912) 236-6321

**RADISSON PLAZA HOTEL
SAVANNAH**
100 General McIntosh Blvd
(31401)
Rates: $99-$159;
Tel: (912) 233-7722

**SUPER 8 MOTEL**
15 Fort Argyle Rd (31419)
Rates: $33-$39;
Tel: (912) 927-8550

**TRAVELODGE
SAVANNAH I-95**
390 Canebrake Rd (31419)
Rates: $40-$50;
Tel: (912) 927-2999

# STATESBORO

**BRYANT'S
MASTER HOSTS INN**
461 S Main St (30458)
Rates: $29-$37;
Tel: (912) 764-5666

**HOLIDAY INN**
230 S Main St (30458)
Rates: $44-$49;
Tel: (912) 764-6121

# SUWANEE

**BEST WESTERN FALCON
INN & CONF CTR**
Suwanee Rd at I-85 (30174)
Rates: $39-$49;
Tel: (404) 945-6751

**COMFORT INN
SUWANEE I-85**
2945 Hwy 217 (30174)
Rates: $39-$44;
Tel: (404) 945-1608

**HOLIDAY INN**
2955 Hwy 217 (30174)
Rates: $45-$49;
Tel: (404) 945-4921

## TATE

**TATE HOUSE**
Hwy 52, Box 33 (30177)
Rates: N/A;
Tel: (404) 735-3122

## THOMASVILLE

**EVANS HOUSE
BED & BREAKFAST**
725 S Hansell St (31792)
Rates: $45-$70;
Tel: (912) 226-7111

**HOLIDAY INN
THOMASVILLE**
211 US Hwy 19S (31792)
Rates: $42-$53;
Tel: (912) 226-7111

**SHONEY'S INN**
305 US 19S (31792)
Rates: $39-$45;
Tel. (912) 228 5555

**SUSINA PLANTATION INN**
Rt 3, Box 1010 (31792)
Rates: $100-$150;
Tel: (912) 377-9644

## THOMSON

**ADMIRAL BENBOW INN**
P. O. Box 1387 (30824)
Rates: $29-$39;
Tel: (404) 595-2262

**BEST WESTERN
WHITE COLUMNS INN**
1890 Washington Rd (30824)
Rates: $40-$50;
Tel: (404) 595 8000

## TIFTON

**CARSON MOTEL**
309 W 7th St (31794)
Rates: N/A;
Tel: (912) 382-3111

**COMFORT INN**
1104 King Rd (31794)
Rates: $45-$50;
Tel: (912) 382-4410

**DAYS INN**
1008 W 8th St (31794)
Rates: $37-$49;
Tel: (912) 382-7210

**HAMPTON INN**
720 Hwy 319S (31794)
Rates: $37-$42;
Tel: (912) 382 8800

**HOLIDAY INN**
P. O. Box 1267 (31973)
Rates: $43-$48;
Tel: (912) 382-6687

**QUALITY INN**
1103 King Rd (31794)
Rates: $34-$42;
Tel: (912) 386-2100

**RED CARPET INN**
1025 W 2nd St (31794)
Rates: $25-$34;
Tel: (912) 382-0280

## UNADILLA

**DAYS INN OF UNADILLA**
P. O. Box 405 (31091)
Rates: $24-$36;
Tel: (912) 627-3211

**SCOTTISH INN**
Rt 2, Box 82 (31091)
Rates: $19-$23;
Tel: (912) 627-3228

## VALDOSTA

**BEST WESTERN
KING OF THE ROAD**
1403 N St. Augustine Rd
(31601)
Rates: $34-$39;
Tel: (912) 244-7600

**BEST WESTERN-
OUTPOST INN**
676 Hwy 376
(Lake Park 31636)
Rates: $35-$45;
Tel: (912) 559-5181

**COMFORT INN
CONFERENCE CENTER**
P.O. Box 1191 (31603)
Rates: $44-$52;
Tel: (912) 242-1212

**DAYS INN**
106 Timber Dr
(Lake Park 31636)
Rates: $34-$37;
Tel: (912) 559-0229

**HAMPTON INN**
1705 Gortno Rd (31601)
Rates: $39-$51·
Tel: (912) 244-8800

**HOJO INN I-75**
N Valdosta Rd (31602)
Rates: $25-$36;
Tel: (912) 244-4460

**HOLIDAY INN**
1309 St. Augustine Rd (31602)
Rates: $37-$45;
Tel: (912) 242-3881

**JOLLY INN MOTEL**
1701 Ellis Dr (31601)
Rates: $24-$32;
Tel: (912) 244 9500

**QUALITY INN SOUTH**
1902 W Hill Ave (31601)
Rates: $31-$37;
Tel: (912) 244-4520

**RAMADA INN**
P. O. Box 931 (31603)
Rates: $34-$45;
Tel: (912) 242-1225

**SHONEY'S INN
OF LAKE PARK**
621 Hwy 376
(Lake Park 31636)
Rates: $38-$48;
Tel: (912) 559-5660

**SHONEY'S INN VALDOSTA**
1828 W Hill Ave (31601)
Rates: $38-$48;
Tel: (912) 244-7711

**TRAVELODGE**
107 Timber Dr
(Lake Park 31636)
Rates: $29-$33;
Tel: (912) 559-0110

**TRAVELODGE**
1330 N St Augustine Rd
(31601)
Rates: $36-$48;
Tel: (912) 242-3464

## VIDALIA

**CAPTAIN'S INN**
P. O. Box 100 (30474)
Rates: $28-$35;
Tel: (912) 537-9251

## VILLA RICA

**COMFORT INN**
128 Hwy 61 (30180)
Rates: $32-$70;
Tel: (404) 459-8000

## WARNER ROBINS

**ADMIRAL BENBOW INN**
2079 Watson Blvd (31088)
Rates: $39-$44;
Tel: (912) 929-9526

**HOLIDAY INN
OF WARNER ROBINS**
2024 Watson Blvd (31093)
Rates: $38-$54;
Tel: (912) 923-8871

## WASHINGTON

**HOLLY RIDGE INN**
2221 Sandtown Rd (30673)
Rates: $49-$75;
Tel: (706) 285-2594

## WAYCROSS

**DAYS INN**
2016 Memorial Dr (31501)
Rates: $32-$38;
Tel: (912) 285-4700

**HOLIDAY INN**
P. O. Box 1357 (31502)
Rates: $42-$49;
Tel: (912) 283-4490

# HAWAII

**Special Note:** In the state of Hawaii, pets are not permitted in rooms. In addition, there is a quarantine on pets arriving from the mainland. If you intend to visit Hawaii with your pet, contact the Hawaii Visitors Bureau, 800-257-2999 for additional information.

# IDAHO

## ALBION

**MOUNTAIN MANOR
BED & BREAKFAST**
P. O. Box 128 (83311)
Rates: $35-$55;
Tel: (208) 673-6642

## AMERICAN FALLS

**HILLVIEW MOTEL**
2799 Lakeview Rd (83211)
Rates: N/A;
Tel: (208) 226-5151

## ARCO

**LOST RIVER MOTEL**
405 Hwy Dr (83213)
Rates: N/A;
Tel: (208) 527-3600

## BLISS

**AMBER INN**
HC 60, Box 1330 (83314)
Rates: $24-$34;
Tel: (208) 352-4441

## BOISE

**THE BOISEAN**
1300 S Capitol Blvd (83706)
Rates: $35-$59;
Tel: (208) 343-3645

**BOISE SUPER 8 LODGE**
2773 Elder St (83705)
Rates: $38-$46;
Tel: (208) 344-8871

**FLYING J INN**
8002 Overland Rd (83709)
Rates: $35-$45;
Tel: (208) 322-4404

**HOLIDAY INN**
3300 Vista Ave (83705)
Rates: $69-$89;
Tel: (208) 344-8365

**MACKAY BAR RANCH**
3190 Airport Way (83705)
Rates: $85-$150;
Tel: (800) 635-5336

**NENDELS INN**
2155 N Garden (83704)
Rates: $34-$36;
Tel: (208) 344-4030

**OWYHEE PLAZA HOTEL**
1109 Main St (83702)
Rates: $50-$80;
Tel: (208) 343-4611

**QUALITY INN
AIRPORT SUITES**
2717 Vista Ave (83705)
Rates: $48-$60;
Tel: (208) 343-7505

**SHILO INN
BOISE AIRPORT**
4111 Broadway Ave (83705)
Rates: $57-$67;
Tel: (208) 343-7662

**SHILO INN RIVERSIDE**
3031 Main (83702)
Rates: $51-$68;
Tel: (208) 344-3521

**THE STATEHOUSE INN**
981 Grove St (83702)
Rates: $49-$125;
Tel: (800) 243-4622

**UNIVERSITY INN**
2360 University Dr (83706)
Rates: $42-$56;
Tel: (208) 345-7170

## BURLEY

**BUDGET MOTEL
OF BURLEY**
900 N Overland Ave (83318)
Rates: $34-$46;
Tel: (208) 676-2200

**GREENWELL MOTEL**
904 E Main St (83318)
Rates: $24-$47;
Tel: (208) 678-5576

## CALDWELL

**COMFORT INN**
901 Specht (83605)
Rates: $50-$63;
Tel: (208) 454-2222

## CASCADE

**AURORA MOTEL
& RV PARK**
P. O. Box 799 (83611)
Rates: $26-$48;
Tel: (208) 382-4948

## CHALLIS

**NORTHGATE INN**
HC 63, Box 1665 (83226)
Rates: $26-$40;
Tel: (208) 879-2490

**THE VILLAGE INN**
Hwy 93 (83226)
Rates: N/A;
Tel: (208) 879-2239

## COEUR D'ALENE

**BEST WESTERN
TEMPLIN'S RESORT**
414 East First Ave (83814)
Rates: N/A;
Tel: (208) 773-1611

**COMFORT INN**
280 W Appleway (83814)
Rates: $47-$109;
Tel: (208) 765-5500

**DAYS INN-COEUR D'ALENE**
2200 NW Blvd (83814)
Rates: $50-$68;
Tel: (208) 667-8668

**EL RANCHO MOTEL**
1915 E Sherman Ave (83814)
Rates: $25-$69;
Tel: (208) 664-8794

**FLAMINGO MOTEL**
718 Sherman Ave (83814)
Rates: $24-$95;
Tel: (208) 664-2159

**HOLIDAY INN**
414 W Appleway (83814)
Rates: $67-$119;
Tel: (208) 765-3200

**PINES RESORT MOTEL**
1422 NW Blvd (83814)
Rates: $45-$90;
Tel: (208) 664-8244

**SHILO INN**
702 W Appleway (83814)
Rates: $73-$130;
Tel: (208) 664-2300

**SUPER 8 MOTEL**
505 W Appleway (83814)
Rates: $32-$66;
Tel: (208) 765-8880

## DONNELLY

**LONG VALLEY MOTEL**
Hwy 55 (83615)
Rates: N/A;
Tel: (208) 325-8545

## DRIGGS

**PINES MOTEL
BED & BREAKFAST**
105 South Main (83422)
Rates: N/A;
Tel: (208) 354-2774

## EDEN

**AMBER INN**
1132 E 1000 E (83325)
Rates: $24-$36;
Tel: (208) 825-5200

## ELK CITY

**CANTERBURY HOUSE INN
BED & BREAKFAST**
501 Elk Creek Rd (83525)
Rates: $40-$50;
Tel: (208) 842-2366

**SABLE TRAIL RANCH**
Box 21, Red River Rd (83525)
Rates: $20;
Tel: (208) 983-1418

**WHITEWATER OUTFITTERS GUEST RANCH**
P. O. Box 642 (Kamiah 83536)
Rates: $75;
Tel: (208) 926-4231

## FAIRFIELD

**COUNTRY INN**
P. O. Box 393 (83327)
Rates: $32-$38;
Tel: (208) 764-2247

## GARDEN CITY

**SEVEN K MOTEL**
3633 Chinden Blvd (83714)
Rates: N/A;
Tel: (208) 343-7723

## GRANGEVILLE

**MONTY'S MOTEL**
700 W Main (83530)
Rates: $30-$40;
Tel: (208) 983-2500

## HAILEY

**AIRPORT INN**
820 4th Ave (83333)
Rates: $50-$60;
Tel: (208) 788-2477

## HARRISON

**PEG'S BED 'N BREAKFAST PLACE**
P. O. Box 144 (83833)
Rates: $50-$95;
Tel: (208) 689-3525

## IDAHO CITY

**IDAHO CITY HOTEL**
215 Montgomery St (83631)
Rates: N/A;
Tel: (208) 392-4290

**PROSPECTOR MOTEL**
517 Main St (83631)
Rates: N/A;
Tel: (208) 392-4290

## IDAHO FALLS

**BEST WESTERN DRIFTWOOD MOTEL**
575 River Pkwy (83402)
Rates: $38-$60;
Tel: (208) 523-2242

**BONNEVILLE MOTEL**
2000 South Yellowstone (83402)
Rates: N/A;
Tel: (208) 522-7847

**HAVEN MOTEL**
2480 South Yellowstone (83402)
Rates: N/A;
Tel: (208) 523-0112

**LITTLETREE INN**
888 N Holmes (83401)
Rates: $49-$65;
Tel: (208) 523-5993

**SHILO INN**
780 Lindsay Blvd (83402)
Rates: N/A;
Tel: (208) 523-0088

**WESTON INN**
850 Lindsay Blvd (83402)
Rates: $42-$60;
Tel: (208) 523-6260

## ISLAND PARK

**ELK CREEK RANCH**
P. O. Box 2 (83429)
Rates: $65;
Tel: (208) 558-7404

## JEROME

**CREST MOTEL**
2983 S Lincoln (83338)
Rates: $29-$38;
Tel: (208) 324-2670

## KELLOGG

**SILVERHORN MOTOR INN**
699 W Cameron Ave (83837)
Rates: $47-$57;
Tel: (208) 783-1151

## KETCHUM

**BALD MOUNTAIN LODGE**
151 S Main (83340)
Rates: $40-$85;
Tel: (208) 726-9963

**BEST WESTERN CHRISTIANIA LODGE**
651 Sun Valley Rd (83340)
Rates: $53-$94;
Tel: (208) 726-3351

**BEST WESTERN TYROLEAN LODGE**
308 Cottonwood (83340)
Rates: $60-$115;
Tel: (208) 726-5336

**HEIDELBERG INN**
P. O. Box 304
(Sun Valley 83353)
Rates: $55-$100;
Tel: (208) 726-5361

## KOOSKIA

**BEAR HOLLOW BED & BREAKFAST**
HC 75, Box 16 (83539)
Rates: $55-$85;
Tel: (800) 831-3713

**THREE RIVERS RESORT**
HC 75, Box 61 (83539)
Rates: N/A;
Tel: (208) 926-4430

## LEWISTON

**CHURCHILL INN**
1021 Main St (83501)
Rates: N/A;
Tel: (800) 635-2225

**HOLLYWOOD INN**
3001 N & S Hwy (83501)
Rates: N/A;
Tel: (208) 743-9424

**PONY SOLDIER MOTOR INN**
1716 Main St (83501)
Rates: $49-$60;
Tel: (208) 743-9526

**RAMADA INN**
621 21st St (83501)
Rates: $61-$94;
Tel: (208) 799-1000

**SHEEP CREEK RANCH**
227 Snake River Ave (83501)
Rates: $85-$280;
Tel: (800) 262-8874

**TAPADERA MOTOR INN**
1325 Main St (83501)
Rates: $36-$58;
Tel: (208) 746-3311

## MACKAY

**WAGON WHEEL MOTEL**
809 W Custer (83251)
Rates: $26-$34;
Tel: (208) 588-3331

## McCALL

**NORTHWEST PASSAGE BED & BREAKFAST**
Box 4208 (83638)
Rates: $45-$125;
Tel: (208) 634 5349

**RIVERSIDE MOTEL AND CONDOMINIUMS**
P. O. Box 746 (83638)
Rates: $37-$45;
Tel: (208) 634-5610

## MONTPELIER

**MICHELLE MOTEL**
601 N 4th (83254)
Rates: $20-$33;
Tel: (208) 847-1772

**THE PARK MOTEL**
745 Washington (83254)
Rates: N/A;
Tel: (208) 847-1911

## MOSCOW

**BEST WESTERN UNIVERSITY INN**
1516 Pullman Rd (83843)
Rates: $64-$90;
Tel: (208) 882-0550

**MARK IV MOTOR INN**
414 N Main St (83843)
Rates: $32-$51;
Tel: (208) 882-7557

**ROYAL MOTOR INN**
120 West 6th St (83843)
Rates: N/A;
Tel: (208) 882-2581

## MOUNTAIN HOME

**BEST WESTERN FOOTHILLS MOTOR INN**
1080 Hwy 20 (83647)
Rates: $40-$62;
Tel: (208) 587-8477

**HILANDER MOTOR & STEAK HOUSE**
615 S 3rd W (83647)
Rates: $26-$35;
Tel: (208) 587-3311

**MOTEL THUNDERBIRD**
910 Sunset Strip (83647)
Rates: $20-$30;
Tel: (208) 587-7927

## NAMPA

**FIVE CROWNS INN**
908 3rd St South (83651)
Rates: N/A;
Tel: (208) 466-3594

**SHILO INN-NAMPA**
617 Nampa Blvd (83687)
Rates: $51-$63;
Tel: (208) 466-8993

**SHILO INN NAMPA SUITES**
1401 Shilo Dr (83687)
Rates: $55-$69;
Tel: (208) 465-3250

## NORTH FORK

**INDIAN CREEK GUEST RANCH**
HC 64, Box 105 (83466)
Rates: $40-$70;
Tel: (208) 394-2126

## OROFINO

**KONKOLVILLE MOTEL**
2000 Konkolville Rd (83544)
Rates: $28-$40;
Tel: (208) 476-5584

## PARMA

**COURT MOTEL**
721 Grove (83660)
Rates: N/A;
Tel: (208) 722-5579

## POCATELLO

**COMFORT INN**
1333 Bench Rd (83201)
Rates: $37-$47;
Tel: (208) 237-8155

**DAYS INN OF POCATELLO**
133 W Burnside Ave
(Chubbuck 83202)
Rates: $40-$45;
Tel: (208) 237-0020

**HOWARD JOHNSON**
1399 Bench Rd (83201)
Rates: $45-$65;
Tel: (208) 237-1400

**IMPERIAL 400 MOTEL**
1055 S 5th Ave (83201)
Rates: $23-$30;
Tel: (208) 233-5120

**NENDEL'S INN**
4333 Yellowstone Ave
(83202)
Rates: $29-$34;
Tel: (208) 237-3100

**POCATELLO QUALITY INN**
1555 Pocatello Creek Rd
(83201)
Rates: $47-$62;
Tel: (208) 233-2200

**SUPER 8 MOTEL**
1330 Bench Rd (83201)
Rates: $35-$41;
Tel: (208) 234-0888

**THUNDERBIRD MOTEL**
1415 S 5th Ave (83201)
Rate: $20-$32;
Tel: (208) 232-6330

## POST FALLS

**BEST WESTERN
TEMPLIN'S RESORT HOTEL**
414 E First Ave (83854)
Rates: $49-$99;
Tel: (208) 773-1611

**KAMPS MOTEL**
West 202 Seltice Way (83854)
Rates: N/A;
Tel; (208) 773-4215

**SUNTREE INN**
W 3705 5th Ave (83854)
Rates: $40-$55;
Tel: (208) 773-4541

## PRIEST LAKE

**HILL'S RESORT**
HCR 5, Box 162A (83856)
Rates: $525-$1500;
Tel: (208) 443-2551

## RIGGINS

**THE LODGE
BED & BREAKFAST**
P. O. Box 498 (83549)
Rates: $24-$50;
Tel: (208) 628-3863

**PINEHURST
RESORT COTTAGES**
5604 Hwy 95
(New Meadows 83654)
Rates: $25-$50;
Tel: (208) 628-3323

**SALMON RIVER MOTEL**
1203 South Hwy 95 (83549)
Rates: N/A;
Tel: (208) 628-3231

## ROGERSON

**MAGIC HOT SPRINGS
BED & BATH**
P. O. Box 368
(Jackpot, NV 89825)
Rates: $25-$45;
Tel: (702) 755-2371

## SALMON

**MOTEL DE LUXE-
DOWNTOWNER**
112 S Church St (83467)
Rates: $25-$36;
Tel: (208) 756-2231

**SUNCREST MOTEL**
705 Challis St (83467)
Rates: $25-$39;
Tel: (208) 756-2294

**WILLIAMS LAKE RESORT**
P. O. Box 1150 (83467)
Rates: $25-$95;
Tel: (208) 756-2007

## SANDPOINT

**BOTTLE BAY
RESORT & MARINA**
1360 Bottle Bay Rd (83864)
Rates: $535;
Tel: (208) 263-5916

**LAKESIDE INN**
106 Bridge St (83864)
Rates: $35-$72;
Tel: (208) 263-3717

**QUALITY INN SANDPOINT**
807 N 5th (83864)
Rates: $38-$72;
Tel: (208) 263-2111

**WHITAKER HOUSE
BED & BREAKFAST**
410 Railroad Ave #10
(83864)
Rates: $30-$46;
Tel: (208) 263-0816

## SHOUP

**SMITH HOUSE
BED & BREAKFAST**
49 Salmon River Rd (83469)
Rates: $35-$54;
Tel: (800) 238-5915

## SODA SPRINGS

**CARIBOU LODGE MOTEL**
110 West 2nd S (83276)
Rates: N/A;
Tel: (208) 547-3377

## STANLEY

**DIAMOND D RANCH**
Box 1 (Clayton 83227)
Rates: $400-$645;
Tel: (208) 336-9772

**JERRY'S COUNTRY STORE
& MOTEL**
HC 67, Box 300 (83278)
Rates: $38-$55;
Tel: (208) 774-3566

**MOUNTAIN VILLAGE
LODGE**
P. O. Box 150 (83278)
Rates: $38-$52;
Tel: (208) 774-3661

## TWIN FALLS

**BEST WESTERN
APOLLO MOTOR INN**
296 Addison Ave W (83301)
Rates: $36-$48;
Tel: (208) 733-2010

**ECONO LODGE**
320 Main Ave S (83301)
Rates: $32-$46;
Tel: (208) 733-8770

**MONTEREY MOTOR INN**
433 Addison Ave W (83301)
Rates: $24-$36;
Tel: (208) 733-5151

**WESTON PLAZA HOTEL**
1350 Blue Lakes Blvd N
(83301)
Rates: $44-$56;
Tel: (208) 733-0650

## WALLACE

**THE WALLACE INN-
BEST WESTERN**
100 Front St (83873)
Rates: $74-$96;
Tel: (208) 752-1252

## WEISER

**INDIANHEAD MOTEL**
US Hwy 95 (83672)
Rates: $25-$36;
Tel: (208) 549-0331

## YELLOW PINE

**YELLOW PINE LODGE**
P. O. Box 77 (83677)
Rates: N/A;
Tel: (208) 382-4336

# ILLINOIS

## ALTAMONT

**ALOHA INN**
Rt 2, Box 296 (62411)
Rates: $25-$31;
Tel: (618) 483-6300

**BEST WESTERN
CARRIAGE INN**
P. O. Box 303 (62411)
Rates: $31-$44;
Tel: (618) 483-6101

## ALTON

**HOLIDAY INN ALTON**
3800 Homer Adams Pkwy
(62002)
Rates: $63-$78,
Tel: (618) 462-1220

**RAMADA INN**
1900 Homer Adams Pkwy
(62002)
Rates: $56-$62;
Tel: (618) 463-0800

## ARCOLA

**ARCOLA INN
BUDGET HOST**
236 S Jacques St (61910)
Rates: $27-$37;
Tel: (217) 268-4971

**DAYS INN**
640 E Springfield Rd (61910)
Rates: $37-$48;
Tel: (217) 268-3031

## ARLINGTON HEIGHTS

**LA QUINTA INN-
ARLINGTON HEIGHTS**
1415 W Dundee Rd (60004)
Rates: $53-$67;
Tel: (708) 253-8777

**MOTEL 6**
441 W Algonquin Rd (60005)
Rates: $30-$36;
Tel: (708) 806-1230

**RADISSON HOTEL
ARLINGTON HEIGHTS**
75 W Algonquin Rd (60005)
Rates: $49-$89;
Tel: (708) 364-7600

**RED ROOF INN**
22 W Algonquin Rd (60005)
Rates: $36-$48;
Tel: (708) 228-6650

## BARRINGTON

**BARRINGTON
MOTOR LODGE**
405 W Northwest Hwy
(60010)
Rates: N/A;
Tel: (708) 381-2610

## BELLEVILLE

**IMPERIAL INN**
600 E Main St (62220)
Rates: $23-$35;
Tel: (618) 234-9670

**TOWN HOUSE MOTEL**
400 S Illinois (62220)
Rates: $35-$38;
Tel: (618) 233-7881

## BENTON

**DAYS INN**
711 W Main St (62812)
Rates: $28-$48;
Tel: (618) 439-3183

## BLOOMINGTON

**BEST INNS OF AMERICA**
1905 W Market St (61701)
Rates: $32-$41;
Tel: (309) 827-5333

**DAYS INN-EAST**
1803 E Empire St (61704)
Rates: $42-$47;
Tel: (309) 663-1361

**JUMER'S CHATEAU**
1601 Jumer Dr (61704)
Rates: $70-$149;
Tel: (309) 662-2020

**RAMADA INN**
1219 Holiday Lane (61701)
Rates: $58-$73;
Tel: (309) 662-5311

## BRIDGEVIEW

**EXEL INN**
9625 S 76th Ave (60455)
Rates: N/A;
Tel: (708) 430-1818

## CARBONDALE

**BEST INNS OF AMERICA**
1345 E Main St (62901)
Rates: $35-$43;
Tel: (618) 529-4801

**SUPER 8 MOTEL**
1180 E Main St (62901)
Rates: $34-$41;
Tel: (618) 457-8822

## CARLINVILLE

**CARLIN VILLA MOTEL**
Rt 3, Box 7 (62626)
Rates: $29-$51;
Tel: (217) 854-3201

**HOLIDAY INN-CARLINVILLE**
P.O. Box 377 (62626)
Rates: $44-$68;
Tel: (217) 324-2100

# CARTHAGE

**PRAIRIE WINDS MOTEL**
Hwy 136 West (62321)
Rates: N/A;
Tel: (217) 357-3101

# CASEYVILLE

**BEST INNS OF AMERICA**
2423 Old Country Inn Rd
(62232)
Rates: $35-$46;
Tel: (618) 397-3300

# CENTRALIA

**BELL TOWER INN**
200 E Noleman St (62801)
Rates: $37-$62;
Tel: (618) 533-1300

# CHAMPAIGN

**BEST WESTERN
PARADISE INN MOTEL**
1001 N Dunlap (Savoy 61874)
Rates: $38-$49;
Tel: (217) 356-1824

**BEST WESTERN
UNIVERSITY PLACE**
Box 605 (Urbana 61801)
Rates: $49-$95;
Tel: (217) 367-8331

**CHANCELLOR HOTEL**
1501 S Neil St (61820)
Rates: $59-$150;
Tel: (217) 352-7891

**COMFORT INN**
305 Marketview Dr (61821)
Rates: $39-$60;
Tel: (217) 352-4055

**DAYS INN-UNIVERSITY**
1701 S State St (61820)
Rates: $37-$45;
Tel: (217) 359-8888

**HOLIDAY INN**
1505 N Neil St (61820)
Rates: $47-$60;
Tel: (217) 359-1601

**LA QUINTA MOTOR INN**
1900 Center Dr (61820)
Rates: $46-$60;
Tel: (217) 356-4000

**RED ROOF INN**
212 W Anthony Dr (61820)
Rates: $29-$50;
Tel: (217) 352-0101

# CHICAGO
(and Vicinity)

**BEST WESTERN MIDWAY**
1600 Oakton St
(Elk Grove Village 60007)
Rates: $65-$100;
Tel: (708) 981-0010

**BISMARCK HOTEL**
171 W Randolph St (60601)
Rates: $85-$375;
Tel: (312) 236-0123

**BUDGETEL INN**
1625 Milwaukee Ave
(Glenview 60025)
Rates: $41-$56;
Tel: (708) 635-8300

**BUDGETEL INN**
17225 S Halsted St
(So Holland 60473)
Rates: $38-$54;
Tel: (708) 596-8700

**BUDGETEL-
WILLOWBROOK**
855 W 79th St
(Willowbrook 60521)
Rates: $39-$55;
Tel: (708) 654-0077

**CLARIDGE HOTEL**
1244 N Dearborn Pkwy
(60610)
Rates: $100-$300;
Tel: (800) 245-1258

**CLARION INTERNATIONAL
AT O'HARE**
6810 N Mannheim Rd
(Rosemont 60018)
Rates: $72-$102;
Tel: (708) 297-1234

**COMFORT INN-O'HARE**
2175 E Touhy Ave
(Des Plaines 60018)
Rates: $52-$85;
Tel: (708) 635-1300

**COMFORT INN
ORLAND PARK**
8800 W 159th St
(Orland Park 60462)
Rates: $63-$70;
Tel: (708) 403-1100

**COURTYARD
BY MARRIOTT**
30 E Hubbard St (60611)
Rates: $135-$190;
Tel: (312) 329-2500

**DAYS INN
OF CLARENDON HILLS**
407 Ogden Ave
(Clarendon Hills 60514)
Rates: $40-$55;
Tel: (708) 325-2500

**DAYS INN-O'HARE SOUTH**
2801 N Mannheim Rd
(Schiller Park 60176)
Rates: $47-$72;
Tel: (708) 678-0670

**EMBASSY SUITES
CHICAGO**
600 N State St (60610)
Rates: $159-$209;
Tel: (312) 943-3800

**ESSEX INN**
800 S Michigan Ave (60605)
Rates: $86-$112;
Tel: (312) 939-2800

**EXEL INN
OF ELK GROVE VILLAGE**
1000 W Devon Ave
(Elk Grove Village 60007)
Rates: $43-$57;
Tel: (708) 894-2085

**EXEL INN OF OAK LAWN**
9625 S 76th Ave
(Bridgeview 60455)
Rates: $43-$58;
Tel: (708) 430-1818

**EXEL INN OF O'HARE**
2881 Touhy Ave
(Elk Grove Village 60007)
Rates: $40-$58;
Tel: (708) 803-9400

**FOUR SEASONS HOTEL**
120 E Delaware (60611)
Rates: $200-$320;
Tel: (312) 280-8800

**HILTON-O'HARE**
P. O. Box 66414
(O'Hare Airport 60666)
Rates: $143;
Tel: (312) 686-8000

**HOLIDAY INN-ALSIP**
5000 W 127th St
(Alsip 60658)
Rates: $69-$79;
Tel: (708) 371-7300

**HOLIDAY INN-CHICAGO
SO HARVEY AT EXPO CTR**
17040 S Halsted St
(Harvey 60426)
Rates: $49-$98;
Tel: (708) 596-1500

**HOLIDAY INN
OF ELK GROVE**
1000 Busse Rd
(Elk Grove Village 60007)
Rates: $75-$100;
Tel: (708) 437-6010

**HOLIDAY INN-ELMHURST**
624 N York Rd
(Elmhurst 60126)
Rates: $75-$193;
Tel: (708) 279-1100

**HOLIDAY INN-HILLSIDE**
4400 Frontage Rd
(Hillside 60162)
Rates: $59-$73;
Tel: (708) 544-9300

**HOLIDAY INN-MART PLAZA**
350 N Orleans St (60654)
Rates: $124-$650;
Tel: (312) 836-5000

**HOLIDAY INN
NORTH SHORE**
5300 W Touhy Ave
(Skokie 60077)
Rates: $89-$104;
Tel: (708) 679-8900

**HOLIDAY INN
O'HARE INTERNATIONAL**
5440 N River Rd
(Rosemont 60018)
Rates: $95-$140;
Tel: (708) 671-6350

**HOLIDAY INN-
WILLOWBROOK**
7800 S Kingery Hwy
(Willowbrook 60521)
Rates: $74-$102;
Tel: (708) 325-6400

**HOTEL NIKKO CHICAGO**
320 N Dearborn St (60610)
Rates: $205-$260;
Tel: (312) 744-1900

**HOTEL SOFITEL CHICAGO
AT O'HARE**
5550 N River Rd
(Rosemont 60018)
Rates: $156-$280;
Tel: (708) 678-4488

**HOWARD JOHNSON
MOTEL**
9333 Skokie Blvd
(Skokie 60077)
Rates: $65-$106;
Tel: (708) 679-4200

**THE INN
AT UNIVERSITY VILLAGE**
625 S Ashland Ave (60607)
Rates: $70-$170;
Tel: (312) 243-7200

**LA QUINTA MOTOR INN-
OAKBROOK TERRACE**
1 S 666 Midwest Rd
(Oakbrook Terrace 60181)
Rates: $50-$64;
Tel: (708) 495-4600

**LA QUINTA MOTOR INN
O'HARE AIRPORT**
1900 Oakton St
(Elk Grove Village 60007)
Rates: $50-$64;
Tel: (708) 439-6767

**MARRIOTT HOTEL-
CHICAGO**
540 N Michigan Ave (60611)
Rates: $159-$1150;
Tel: (312) 836-0100

**MARRIOTT
OAK BROOK HOTEL**
1401 W 22nd St
(Oak Brook 60521)
Rates: $69-$143;
Tel: (708) 573-8555

**MARRIOTT O'HARE**
8535 W Higgins Rd (60631)
Rates: $74-$166;
Tel: (312) 693-4444

**MARRIOTT SUITES
CHICAGO O'HARE**
6155 N River Rd
(Rosemont 60018)
Rates: $89-$175;
Tel: (708) 696-4400

**MCCORMICK
CENTER HOTEL**
Lake Shore Dr & 23rd St
(60616)
Rates: $109-$179;
Tel: (312) 791-1900

**MIDWAY AIRPORT INN**
5400 S Cicero Ave (60638)
Rates: $55-$75;
Tel: (312) 581-0500

**NILES TRAVELODGE**
7247 N Waukegan Rd
(60648)
Rates: $44-$50;
Tel: (708) 647-9444

**NORTH SHORE HILTON**
9599 Skokie Blvd
(Skokie 60077)
Rates: $110-$145;
Tel: (708) 679-7000

**OAKBROOK TERRACE
HILTON SUITES**
10 Drury Ln
(Oak Brook Terrace 60181)
Rates: $89-$134;
Tel: (708) 941-0100

**OMNI AMBASSADOR EAST**
1301 N State Pkwy (60610)
Rates: N/A;
Tel: (312) 787-7200

**THE PALMER HOUSE
HILTON**
17 E Monroe St (60603)
Rates: $119-$224;
Tel: (312) 726-7500

**QUALITY INN
INTERNATIONAL
AT O'HARE**
6810 N Mannheim Rd
(Rosemont 60018)
Rates: $62-$88;
Tel: (708) 297-1234

**RAMADA HOTEL
OAKBROOK TERRACE**
17 W 350 22nd St
(Oakbrook Terrace 60181)
Rates: $62-$79;
Tel: (708) 833-3600

**RAMADA HOTEL-O'HARE**
6600 N Mannheim Rd
(Rosemont 60018)
Rates: $89-$125;
Tel: (708) 827-5131

133

**THE RAPHAEL HOTEL**
201 E Delaware Pl (60611)
Rates: $105-$165;
Tel: (312) 943-5000

**RED ROOF INN**
17301 S Halsted Rd
(So Holland 60473)
Rates: $42-$44;
Tel: (708) 331-1621

**RED ROOF INN**
7535 Robert Kingery Hwy
(Willowbrook 60521)
Rates: $33-$45;
Tel: (708) 323-8811

**RESIDENCE INN
BY MARRIOTT**
201 E Walton Pl (60611)
Rates: $189-$269;
Tel: (312) 943-9800

**RESIDENCE INN
BY MARRIOTT-LOMBARD**
2001 S Highland Ave
(Lombard 60148)
Rates: $109-$129;
Tel: (708) 629-7800

**RESIDENCE INN
BY MARRIOTT-O'HARE**
9450 W Lawrence Ave
(Schiller Park 60176)
Rates: $115-$145;
Tel: (708) 678-2210

**THE RITZ-CARLTON,
CHICAGO**
160 E Pearson St (60611)
Rates: $200-$280;
Tel: (312) 266-1000

**SHERATON CHICAGO
HOTEL & TOWERS**
301 E North Water St (60611)
Rates: $180-$800;
Tel: (312) 464-1000

**SHERATON PLAZA**
160 E Huron St (60611)
Rates: $145-$250;
Tel: (312) 787-2900

**SHERATON SUITES
ELK GROVE VILLAGE**
121 NW Point Blvd
(Elk Grove Village 60007)
Rates: $79-$150;
Tel: (708) 290-1600

**STOUFFER RIVIERE HOTEL**
1 W Wacker Dr (60601)
Rates: $205-$265;
Tel: (312) 372-7200

**THE WESTIN HOTEL,
CHICAGO**
909 N Michigan Ave (60611)
Rates: $140-$190;
Tel: (312) 943-7200

# CLINTON

**TOWN & COUNTRY MOTEL**
1151 Rt 54W (61727)
Rates: $25-$32;
Tel: (217) 935-2121

# COLLINSVILLE

**BEST WESTERN
BO-JON INN**
SR 159 (62234)
Rates: $28-$44;
Tel: (618) 345-5720

**DAYS INN-COLLINSVILLE**
1803 Ramada Blvd (62234)
Rates: $37-$49;
Tel: (618) 345-8100

**DRURY INN-COLLINSVILLE**
602 N Bluff Rd (62234)
Rates: $49-$63;
Tel: (618) 345-7700

**PEAR TREE INN BY DRURY**
552 Ramada Blvd (62234)
Rates: $37-$50;
Tel: (618) 345-9500

**QUALITY INN**
475 Bluff Rd (62234)
Rates: $29-$60;
Tel: (618) 344-7171

**SUPER 8 MOTEL**
2 Gateway Dr (62234)
Rates: $32-$54;
Tel: (618) 345-8008

# DALLAS CITY

**NEW ELMS MOTEL**
RR 1, Box 29 Hwy North 96
(62330)
Rates: N/A;
Tel: (217) 852-3829

# DANVILLE

**COMFORT INN**
383 Lynch Rd (61832)
Rates: $41-$54;
Tel: (217) 443-8004

**RAMADA INN**
388 Eastgate Dr (61832)
Rates: $48-$60;
Tel: (217) 446-2400

**REDWOOD MOTOR INN**
411 Lynch Rd (61832)
Rates: $35-$75;
Tel: (217) 443-3690

**SUPER 8**
377 Lynch Dr (61832)
Rates: $36-$44;
Tel: (217) 443-4499

# DECATUR

**BEST WESTERN SHELTON**
450 E Pershing Rd (62526)
Rates: $39-$49;
Tel: (217) 877-7255

**BUDGETEL INN**
5100 Hickory Pt Frontage Rd
(62526)
Rates: $33-$49;
Tel: (217) 875-5800

**COMFORT INN
OF FORSYTH**
134 Barnett Ave
(Forsyth 62535)
Rates: $41-$47;
Tel: (217) 875-1166

**DAYS INN DECATUR**
333 N Wyckles Rd (62522)
Rates: $33-$49;
Tel: (217) 422-5900

**FAIRFIELD INN**
1417 Hickory Point Dr
(Forsyth 62526)
Rates: $41-$60;
Tel: (217) 875-3337

**HOLIDAY INN
CONFERENCE HOTEL**
US 36W & Wyckles Rd (62522)
Rates: $65-$83;
Tel: (217) 422-8800

## DEERFIELD

**RESIDENCE INN
BY MARRIOTT**
530 Lake Cook Rd (60015)
Rates: $109-$135;
Tel: (708) 940-4644

## DE KALB

**DAYS INN-DE KALB**
1212 W Lincoln Hwy (60115)
Rates: $40-$47;
Tel: (815) 758-8661

## DOWNERS GROVE

**MARRIOTT SUITES
DOWNERS GROVE**
1500 Opus Pl (60515)
Rates: $69-$133;
Tel: (708) 852-1500

**RADISSON SUITE HOTEL**
2111 Butterfield Rd (60515)
Rates: $69-$115;
Tel: (708) 971-2000

**RED ROOF INN**
1113 Butterfield Rd (60515)
Rates: $31-$46;
Tel: (708) 963-4205

## DUQUOIN

**HUB MOTEL**
423 West Main St (62832)
Rates: N/A;
Tel: (618) 542-2108

## EAST PEORIA

**SUPER 8 MOTEL**
725 Taylor St (61611)
Rates: $34-$49;
Tel: (309) 698-8889

## EFFINGHAM

**BEST INNS OF AMERICA**
1209 N Keller Dr (62401)
Rates: $31-$42;
Tel: (217) 347-5141

**BEST WESTERN
RAINTREE INN**
P. O. Box 663 (62401)
Rates: $31-$49;
Tel: (217) 342-4121

**BUDGETEL**
1103 Ave of Mid-America
(62401)
Rates: $33-$51;
Tel: (217) 342-2525

**BUDGET HOST
LINCOLN LODGE**
N Rt 45 at I-57 & 70 (62401)
Rates: N/A;
Tel: (800) 283-4678

**DAYS INN**
P. O. Box 1168 (62401)
Rates: $31-$48;
Tel: (217) 342-9271

**HOLIDAY INN**
1600 W Fayette Ave (62401)
Rates: $46-$54;
Tel: (217) 342-4161

**HOWARD JOHNSON
LODGE**
1606 W Fayette Ave (62401)
Rates: $34-$49;
Tel: (217) 342-4667

**PARADISE INN MOTEL**
1000 W Fayette Ave (62401)
Rates: $25-$32;
Tel: (217) 342-2165

**RAMADA INN**
P. O. Box 747 (62401)
Rates: $49-$75;
Tel: (217) 342-2131

## ELGIN

**HOLIDAY INN**
345 W River Rd (60123)
Rates: $60-$72;
Tel: (708) 695-5000

## FAIRFIELD

**UPTOWN MOTEL**
201 South 1st St (62837)
Rates: N/A;
Tel: (618) 842-2191

## FAIRVIEW HEIGHTS

**DRURY INN**
12 Ludwig Dr (62208)
Rates: $51-$65;
Tel: (618) 398-8530

**SUPER 8 MOTEL**
45 Ludwig Dr (62208)
Rates: $36-$43;
Tel: (618) 398-8338

## FLORA

**RANCH MOTEL**
RR 1, Box 93 (62839)
Rates: $23-$28;
Tel: (618) 662-2181

## FREEPORT

**HOLIDAY INN**
1300 E South St (61032)
Rates: $55-$69;
Tel: (815) 235-3121

## GALENA

**BEST WESTERN
QUIET HOUSE SUITES**
9923 Hwy 20 (61036)
Rates: $79-$190;
Tel: (815) 777-2577

**PALACE MOTEL**
RFD 1 (61036)
Rates: $26-$185;
Tel: (815) 777-2043

**PINE HOLLOW INN**
4700 N Council Hill Rd
(61036)
Rates: $85-$90;
Tel: (815) 777-1071

## GALESBURG

**COMFORT INN**
907 W Carl Sandburg Dr
(61401)
Rates: $38-$56;
Tel: (309) 344-5445

**HOJO INN**
3282 N Henderson St (61401)
Rates: $43-$58;
Tel: (309) 344-1111

**JUMER'S
CONTINENTAL INN**
260 S Soangetaha Rd (61401)
Rates: $55-$71;
Tel: (309) 343-7151

**RAMADA INN**
29 Public Sq (61401)
Rates: $41-$51;
Tel: (309) 343-9161

**STARLITE MOTEL**
1966 N Henderson St (61401)
Rates: $24-$30;
Tel: (309) 344-1515

**THRIFTY MOTEL**
1777 Grand Ave (61401)
Rates: N/A;
Tel: (309) 343-2812

## GENESEO

**DECK PLAZA MOTEL**
I-80 & Rte 82 (61254)
Rates: N/A;
Tel: (309) 944-4651

**THE OAKWOOD MOTEL**
225 US Hwy 6E (61254)
Rates: $19-$25;
Tel: (309) 944-3696

## GILMAN

**DEL-MAR MOTEL**
P. O. Box 139C (60938)
Rates: $26-$31;
Tel: (815) 265-7283

## GLEN ELLYN

**HOLIDAY INN**
1250 Roosevelt Rd (60137)
Rates: $53-$69;
Tel: (708) 629-6000

## GRAYVILLE

**BEST WESTERN
WINDSOR OAKS INN**
2200 S Court St (62844)
Rates: $50-$74;
Tel: (618) 375-7930

## GREENVILLE

**BEST WESTERN
COUNTRY VIEW INN**
RR 4, Box 221 (62246)
Rates: $28-$48;
Tel: (618) 664-3030

**BUDGET HOST-
BEL AIR MOTEL**
Rt 4, Box 183 (62246)
Rates: $27-$43;
Tel: (618) 664-1950

## HAMEL

**INNKEEPER MOTEL**
I-55 & Rt 140 (62234)
Rates: N/A;
Tel: (618) 633-2551

## HARRISBURG

**DAYS INN**
Rt 45, Box 3 (Muddy 62965)
Rates: $34-$39;
Tel: (618) 252-6354

## HOFFMAN ESTATES

**BUDGETEL INN**
2075 Barrington Rd (60195)
Rates: $34-$51;
Tel: (708) 882-8848

**LA QUINTA MOTOR INN**
2280 Barrington Rd (60195)
Rates: $56-$70;
Tel: (708) 882-3312

**RED ROOF INN**
2500 Hassell Rd (60195)
Rates: $33-$45;
Tel: (708) 885-7877

## HOMEWOOD

**DAYS INN**
17220 S Halsted St
(E Hazelcrest 60429)
Rates: $38-$45;
Tel: (708) 957-5900

**RAMADA HOTEL**
17400 S Halsted St (60430)
Rates: $70-$100;
Tel: (708) 957-1600

## ITASCA

**NORDIC HILLS RESORT
& CONFERENCE CTR**
Nordic Rd (60143)
Rates: $90-$120;
Tel: (708) 773-2750

## JACKSONVILLE

**HOLIDAY INN**
1717 W Morton Ave (62650)
Rates: $47-$59;
Tel: (217) 245-9571

**STAR LITE MOTEL**
1910 W Morton Ave (62650)
Rates: $30-$45;
Tel: (217) 245-7184

## JOHNSTON CITY

**FARRIS MOTEL**
Rt 37 South, Box 6 (62951)
Rates: N/A;
Tel: (618) 983-8086

## JOLIET

**COMFORT INN-
JOLIET SOUTH**
135 S Larkin Ave (60436)
Rates: $45-$55;
Tel: (815) 744-1770

**COMFORT INN NORTH**
3235 Norman Ave (60435)
Rates: $47-$67;
Tel: (815) 436-5141

**FAIRFIELD INN
BY MARRIOTT-NORTH**
3239 Norman Ave (60435)
Rates: $47-$58;
Tel: (815) 436-6577

**MANOR MOTEL**
2821 E Eames Rd (60436)
Rates: $28-$38;
Tel: (815) 467-5385

**RED ROOF INN**
1750 McDonough St (60436)
Rates: $31-$47;
Tel: (815) 741-2304

## KANKAKEE

**DAYS INN**
1975 E Court St (60901)
Rates: $38-$46;
Tel: (815) 939-7171

**LEES INN**
1500 N SR 50
(Bourbonnais 60914)
Rates: $53-$74;
Tel: (815) 932-8080

## KEWANEE

**HERITAGE INN**
Rt 34 & 78 (61443)
Rates: N/A;
Tel: (309) 853-3357

## LANSING

**RED ROOF INN**
2450 E 173rd St (60438)
Rates: $34-$50;
Tel: (708) 895-9570

## LA SALLE

**DAYS INN**
P. O. Box 626 (Peru 61354)
Rates: $32-$46;
Tel: (815) 224-1060

## LIBERTYVILLE

**BEST INNS OF AMERICA**
1809 W Milwaukee Ave
(60048)
Rates: $41-$47;
Tel: (708) 816-8006

## LINCOLN

**COMFORT INN**
2811 Woodlawn Rd (62656)
Rates: $41-$48;
Tel: (217) 735-3960

## LINCOLNSHIRE

**HAWTHORN
SUITES HOTEL**
10 Westminster Way (60069)
Rates: $89 $135;
Tel: (708) 945-9300

## LISLE

**LISLE/NAPERVILLE
HILTON INN**
3003 Corporate West Dr
(60532)
Rates: $60-$94;
Tel: (708) 505-0900

## MACOMB

**HOLIDAY INN**
1400 N Lafayette St (61455)
Rates: $47-$57;
Tel: (309) 833-5511

## MARION

**BEST INNS OF AMERICA**
Rt 8, Box 70 (62959)
Rates: $33-$41;
Tel: (618) 997-9421

**BEST WESTERN
AIRPORT INN**
Rt 3, Box 348-1 (62959)
Rates: $34 $64;
Tel: (618) 993-3222

**SUPER 8 MOTEL**
2601 De Young St (62959)
Rates: $31-$46;
Tel: (618) 993-5577

## MARSHALL

**LINCOLN MOTEL**
RR 3, Box 14A (62441)
Rates: N/A;
Tel: (217) 826-2941

## MATTESON

**BUDGETEL**
5210 W Southwick Dr (60443)
Rates: $42-$59;
Tel: (708) 503-0999

**HAMPTON INN**
5200 W Lincoln Hwy (60443)
Rates: $55-$67;
Tel: (708) 481-3900

## MATTOON

**HOLIDAY INN**
300 Broadway Ave E (61938)
Rates: $51-$69;
Tel: (217) 235-0313

## MORRIS

**HOLIDAY INN**
200 Gore Rd (60450)
Rates: $42-$48;
Tel: (815) 942-6600

## MOUNT MORRIS

**MOUNT MORRIS MOTEL**
3691 W Route 64 (61054)
Rates: N/A;
Tel: (818) 734-4114

## MOUNT VERNON

**BEST INNS OF AMERICA**
222 S 44th (62864)
Rates: $31-$43;
Tel: (618) 244-4343

**DRURY INN**
P. O. Box 805 (62864)
Rates: $43-$49;
Tel: (618) 244-4550

**HOLIDAY INN**
P. O. Box 1328 (62864)
Rates: $48-$65;
Tel: (618) 244-3670

**RAMADA HOTEL**
222 Potomac Blvd (62864)
Rates: $45-$60;
Tel: (618) 244-7100

**SUPER 8 MOTEL**
401 S 44th St (62864)
Rates: $33-$41;
Tel: (618) 242-8800

**THRIFTY INN**
100 N 44th St (62864)
Rates: $27-$42;
Tel: (618) 244-7750

## MUNDELEIN

**HOLIDAY INN-MUNDELEIN**
510 Rt 83S (60060)
Rates: $57-$63;
Tel: (708) 949-5100

## MURPHYSBORO

**MOTEL MURPHYSBORO**
100 North 2nd St (62966)
Rates: N/A;
Tel: (800) 626-4356

## NAPERVILLE

**DAYS INN OF NAPERVILLE**
1350 E Ogden Ave (60566)
Rates: $34-$54;
Tel: (708) 369-3600

**EXEL INN OF NAPERVILLE**
1585 N Naperville/
Wheaton Rd (60563)
Rates: $38-$51;
Tel: (708) 357-0022

**RED ROOF INN**
1698 W Diehl Rd (60540)
Rates: $34-$48;
Tel: (708) 369-2500

## NASHVILLE

**U.S. INN**
P. O. Box 327 (62263)
Rates: $31-$40;
Tel: (618) 478-5341

## NAUVOO

**NAUVOO MOTEL**
P.O. Box 272 (62354)
Rates: $24-$57;
Tel: (217) 453-6527

**NAUVOO VILLAGE INN**
P. O. Box 191 (62354)
Rates: $20-$30;
Tel: (217) 453-6634

## NORMAL

**BEST WESTERN
UNIVERSITY INN**
6 Traders Cir (61761)
Rates: $39-$50;
Tel: (309) 454-4070

**HOLIDAY INN
BLOOMINGTON-NORMAL/
NORTH**
8 Traders Cir (61761)
Rates: $61-$74;
Tel: (309) 452-8300

## NORTHBROOK

**RED ROOF INN**
340 Waukegan Rd (60062)
Rates: $40-$59;
Tel: (708) 205-1755

## O'FALLON

**COMFORT INN**
1100 S Eastgate Dr (62269)
Rates: $42-$64;
Tel: (618) 624-6060

## OREGON

**VIP MOTEL**
1326 IL 2 N (61061)
Rates: $27-$32;
Tel: (815) 732-6195

## OTTAWA

**OTTAWA INN-
STARVED ROCK**
3000 Columbus St (61350)
Rates: $31-$65;
Tel: (815) 434-3400

## PALATINE

**QUALITY HOTEL
OF WOODFIELD**
920 E NW Hwy (60067)
Rates: $59-$69;
Tel: (708) 359-6900

## PARIS

**PINNELL MOTEL**
P. O. Box 313 (61944)
Rates: $29-$42;
Tel: (217) 465-6441

## PEKIN

**CLASSIC FRIENDSHIP INN**
2801 E Court St (61554)
Rates: $42-$47;
Tel: (309) 347-5533

## PEORIA

**BEST WESTERN
MARK TWAIN HOTEL**
225 NE Adams (61602)
Rates: $57-$75;
Tel: (309) 676-3600

**COMFORT SUITES**
4021 War Memorial Dr
(61614)
Rates: $46-$71;
Tel: (309) 688-3800

**HOLIDAY INN**
500 Hamilton Blvd (61602)
Rates: $64-$350;
Tel: (309) 674-2500

**JUMER'S CASTLE LODGE**
117 N Western Ave (61604)
Rates: $69-$134;
Tel: (309) 673-8040

**RAMADA INN**
401 N Main St
(East Peoria 61611)
Rates: $57-$77;
Tel: (309) 699-7231

**RED ROOF INN**
4031 N War Memorial Dr
(61614)
Rates: $42-$56;
Tel: (309) 685-3911

**TOWNE HOUSE MOTEL**
1519 N Knoxville Ave (61603)
Rates: $25-$169;
Tel: (309) 688-8646

## PONTIAC

**COMFORT INN**
1821 W Reynolds St (61764)
Rates: $47-$54;
Tel: (815) 842-2777

## PRINCETON

**LINCOLN INN**
P. O. Box 382 (61356)
Rates: $31-$40;
Tel: (815) 875-3371

**PRINCETON
MOTOR LODGE**
P. O. Box 382 (61356)
Rates: $25-$30;
Tel: (815) 875-1121

## PROSPECT HEIGHTS

**EXEL INN
OF PROSPECT HEIGHTS**
540 Milwaukee Ave (60070)
Rates: $31-$46;
Tel: (708) 459-0545

## QUAD CITIES

**BEST WESTERN
STEEPLEGATE INN**
100 W 76th St
(Davenport 52806)
Rates: $62-$85;
Tel: (319) 386-6900

**COMFORT INN**
2600 52nd Ave
(Moline 61265)
Rates: $39-$69;
Tel: (309) 762-7000

**COMFORT INN-
DAVENPORT**
7222 Northwest Blvd
(Davenport 52806)
Rates: $38-$47;
Tel: (319) 391-8222

**DAYS INN OF DAVENPORT**
3202 E Kimberly Rd
(Davenport 52807)
Rates: $38-$60;
Tel; (319) 355-1190

**EXEL INN OF DAVENPORT**
6310 N Brady St
(Davenport 52806)
Rates: $31-$45;
Tel: (319) 386-6350

**EXEL INN OF MOLINE**
2501 52nd Ave
(Moline 61265)
Rates: $28-$42;
Tel: (309) 797-5580

**FAIRFIELD INN**
2705 48th Ave
(Moline 61265)
Rates: $43-$55;
Tel: (309) 762-9083

**FAIRFIELD INN BY
MARRIOTT-DAVENPORT**
3206 E Kimberly Rd
(Davenport 52807)
Rates: $43-$69;
Tel: (319) 355-3364

**HAMPTON INN-AIRPORT**
6920 27th St (Moline 61265)
Rates: $47-$53;
Tel: (309) 762-1711

**HAMPTON INN-
DAVENPORT**
3330 E Kimberly Rd
(Davenport 52807)
Rates: $42-$53;
Tel: (319) 359-3921

**HOLIDAY INN-AIRPORT
CONVENTION CTR**
6902 27th St (Moline 61265)
Rates: $50-$88;
Tel: (309) 762-8811

**HOLIDAY INN-
BETTENDORF**
909 Middle Rd
(Bettendorf 52722)
Rates: $76-$96;
Tel: (319) 355-4761

**HOWARD JOHNSON
MOTEL**
Quad City Airport
(Moline 61265)
Rates: $42-$64;
Tel: (309) 797-1211

**JUMER'S CASTLE LODGE-
BETTENDORF**
900 Spruce Hills Dr
(Bettendorf 52722)
Rates: $76-$97;
Tel: (319) 359-7141

**LA QUINTA**
Airport Corners
(Moline 61265)
Rates: $44-$58;
Tel: (309) 762-9008

**RAMADA INN-
DAVENPORT**
6263 N Brady
(Davenport 52806)
Rates: $55-$63;
Tel: (319) 386-1940

**STARDUST MOTEL**
19th St & 12th Ave
(Moline 61265)
Rates: $50-$105;
Tel: (309) 764-9644

**TWIN BRIDGES MOTOR
INN-BETTENDORF**
221 15th St
(Bettendorf 52722)
Rates: $39-$48;
Tel: (319) 355-6451

## QUINCY

**BEL-AIRE MOTEL**
2314 North 12th St (62301)
Rates: N/A;
Tel: (217) 223-1356

**COMFORT INN**
4100 Broadway (62301)
Rates: $41-$66;
Tel: (217) 228-2700

**HOLIDAY INN-QUINCY**
201 S 3rd St (62301)
Rates: $57-$74;
Tel: (217) 222-2666

## RANTOUL

**BEST WESTERN
HERITAGE INN**
420 S Murray Rd (61866)
Rates: N/A;
Tel: (217) 892-9292

## ROBINSON

**DAYS INN**
1500 W Main St (62454)
Rates: $42-$51;
Tel: (618) 544-8448

## ROCKFORD

**ALPINE INN**
4404 E State St (61108)
Rates: $30-$54;
Tel: (815) 399-1890

**BEST WESTERN COLONIAL
INN MOTOR LODGE**
4850 E State St (61108)
Rates: $54-$72;
Tel: (815) 398-5050

**COMFORT INN**
7392 Argus Dr (61107)
Rates: $42-$63;
Tel: (815) 398-7061

**EXEL INN OF ROCKFORD**
220 S Lyford Rd (61108)
Rates: $34-$46;
Tel: (815) 332-4915

**MOTEL 6**
2851 11th St (61109)
Rates: $20-$26;
Tel: (815) 398-6080

**RAMADA INN**
P. O. Box 5686 (61125)
Rates: $54-$65;
Tel: (815) 398-2200

**RED ROOF INN**
7434 E State St (61108)
Rates: $31-$51;
Tel: (815) 398-9750

**SWEDEN HOUSE LODGE**
4605 E State St (61108)
Rates: $36-$59;
Tel: (815) 398-4130

## ROCK ISLAND

**PLAZA ONE HOTEL**
17th St at 3rd Ave (61201)
Rates: $80-$248;
Tel: (309) 794-1212

## ROLLING MEADOWS

**COMFORT INN**
2801 Algonquin Rd (60008)
Rates: $50-$56;
Tel: (708) 259-5900

**HOLIDAY INN**
3405 Algonquin Rd (60008)
Rates: $89-$99;
Tel: (708) 259-5000

## ST. CHARLES

**BEST WESTERN INN
OF ST CHARLES**
1635 E Main St (60174)
Rates: $40-$60;
Tel: (708) 584-4550

## SALEM

**CONTINENTAL MOTEL**
P.O. Box 370 (62881)
Rates: $18-$22;
Tel: (618) 548-3090

**DAYS INN**
1812 W Main St (62881)
Rates: $33-$43;
Tel: (618) 548-4212

**GRAND MOTEL**
1234 West Main St (62881)
Rates: N/A;
Tel: (618) 548-2040

**MOTEL LAKEWOOD**
1500 E Main St (62881)
Rates: $18-$23;
Tel: (618) 548-2785

## SCHAUMBURG

**HOMEWOOD SUITES
SCHAUMBURG**
815 E American Ln (60173)
Rates: $53-$89;
Tel: (708) 605-0400

**LA QUINTA INN**
1730 E Higgins Rd (60173)
Rates: $55-$69;
Tel: (708) 517-8484

**SCHAUMBURG
MARRIOTT HOTEL**
50 N Martingale Rd (60173)
Rates: $69-$145;
Tel: (708) 240-0100

## SOUTH HOLLAND

**RED ROOF INN**
17301 South Halsted (60473)
Rates: N/A;
Tel: (800) 843-7663

## SPRINGFIELD

**BEST INNS OF AMERICA**
500 N 1st St (62702)
Rates: $42-$49;
Tel: (217) 522-1100

**BEST WESTERN
LINCOLN PLAZA HOTEL**
101 E Adams St (62701)
Rates: $48-$70;
Tel: (217) 523-5661

**BEST WESTERN
SKY HARBOR INN**
1701 J David Jones Pkwy
(62702)
Rates: $46-$56;
Tel: (217) 753-3446

**BEST WESTERN
SPRINGFIELD EAST**
3090 Stevenson Dr (62703)
Rates: $43-$71;
Tel: (217) 529-6611

**COMFORT INN**
3442 Freedom Dr (62704)
Rates: $41-$53;
Tel: (217) 787-2250

**DAYS INN**
3000 Stevenson Dr (62703)
Rates: $39-$49;
Tel: (217) 529-0171

**FAIRFIELD INN**
3446 Freedom Dr (62704)
Rates: $41-$58;
Tel: (217) 793-9277

**HAMPTON INN**
3185 S Dirksen Pkwy (62703)
Rates: $50-$90;
Tel: (217) 529-1100

**HOLIDAY INN-EAST HOTEL & CONFERENCE CTR**
3100 S Dirksen Pkwy (62703)
Rates: $63-$85;
Tel: (217) 529-7171

**MANSION VIEW MOTEL**
529 S 4th St (62701)
Rates: $34-$52;
Tel: (217) 544 7411

**PEAR TREE INN BY DRURY**
3190 S Dirksen Pkwy (62703)
Rates: $37-$48;
Tel: (217) 529-9100

**QUALITY INN**
300 N 9th St (62702)
Rates: $46-$60;
Tel: (217) 522-7711

**RED ROOF INN**
3200 Singer Ave (62703)
Rates: $29-$45;
Tel: (217) 753-4302

**SKY HARBOR INN**
1701 J D Jones Pkwy (62702)
Rates: N/A;
Tel: (217) 753-3446

**SUPER 8 LODGE**
3675 S 6th St (62703)
Rates: $37-$47;
Tel: (217) 529-8898

## STREATOR

**TOWN & COUNTRY INN**
2110 N Bloomington St
(61364)
Rates: $34-$44;
Tel: (815) 672-3183

## TAYLORVILLE

**29 WEST MOTEL**
709 Springfield Rd (62568)
Rates: $27-$33;
Tel: (217) 824-2216

## ULLIN

**BEST WESTERN CHEEKWOOD**
P. O. Box 280 (62992)
Rates: $34-$47;
Tel: (618) 845-3700

## URBANA

**JUMER'S CASTLE LODGE**
209 S Broadway (61801)
Rates: $69-$83;
Tel: (217) 384-8800

## VANDALIA

**DAYS INN**
Rt 40W (62471)
Rates: $34-$59;
Tel: (618) 283-1400

**JAY'S MOTEL**
1 Mi N on US 40 (62471)
Rates: $23-$30;
Tel: (618) 283-1200

**TRAVELODGE**
1500 N 6th St (62471)
Rates: $31-$39;
Tel: (618) 283-2363

## WASHINGTON

**SUPER 8 MOTEL**
1884 Washington Rd (61571)
Rates: $33-$40;
Tel: (309) 444-8881

## WAUKEGAN

**BEST INNS OF AMERICA**
31 N Green Bay Rd (60085)
Rates: $35-$49;
Tel: (708) 336-9000

## WHEELING

**HAWTHORN SUITES**
10 Westminster Way Rd
(Lincolnshire 60069)
Rates: $109-$145;
Tel: (708) 945-9300

**MARRIOTT'S LINCOLNSHIRE**
10 Marriott Dr
(Lincolnshire 60069)
Rates: $99-$300
Tel: (708) 634-0100

## WILLOWBROOK

**RED ROOF INN**
7535 Kingery Hwy, Rt 83
(60521)
Rates: N/A;
Tel: (800) 843-7663

## WOOD RIVER

**BEL AIR MOTEL**
542 West Ferguson Ave
(62095)
Rates: N/A;
Tel: (618) 254-0683

# INDIANA

## ANDERSON

**BEST INNS**
5706 Scatterfield Rd (46013)
Rates: $36-$44;
Tel: (317) 644-2000

**BEST WESTERN
STERLING HOUSE**
5901 Scatterfield Rd (46013)
Rates: $49-$55;
Tel: (317) 649-0451

**COMFORT INN**
2205 E 59th St (46013)
Rates: $38-$60;
Tel: (317) 644-4422

**HOLIDAY INN**
5920 Scatterfield Rd (46013)
Rates: $57-$78;
Tel: (317) 644-2581

**LEES INN**
2114 E 59th St (46013)
Rates: $51-$72;
Tel: (317) 649-2500

**MARK MOTOR INN**
2400 State Rd 9 South
(46016)
Rates: N/A;
Tel: (317) 642-9966

**RISE MOTEL**
Rt 1 (Daleville 47334)
Rates: $33-$46;
Tel: (317) 378-1215

## ANGOLA

**E & L MOTEL**
35 W SR 120 (Fremont 46737)
Rates: $25-$38;
Tel: (219) 495-3300

## AUBURN

**AUBURN INN**
225 Touring Dr (46706)
Rates: $50-$62;
Tel: (800) 255-2541

## BEDFORD

**MARK III MOTEL**
1711 M Street (47421)
Rates: $28-$31;
Tel: (812) 275-5935

**ROSEMOUNT MOTEL**
1923 M St (47421)
Rates: $28-$31;
Tel: (812) 275-5953

## BLOOMINGTON

**ECONO LODGE**
4501 E 3rd St (47401)
Rates: $38-$52;
Tel: (812) 332-2141

**HAMPTON INN**
2100 N Walnut St (47408)
Rates: $49-$61;
Tel: (812) 334-2100

**INDIANA
MOTOR LODGE**
P. O. Box 2475 (47401)
Rates: $34-$57;
Tel: (812) 336-0905

**SAVE INN**
1800 N Walnut St (47404)
Rates: N/A;
Tel: (812) 332-0820

**UNIVERSITY INN**
2100 N Walnut (47401)
Rates: $30-$45;
Tel: (812) 332-9453

## CARLISLE

**COUNTRY LODGE
MOTEL**
P. O. Box 205 (47838)
Rates: $34-$39;
Tel: (812) 398-2500

## CLARKSVILLE

**BEST WESTERN
GREENTREE INN**
1425 Broadway (47129)
Rates: $39-$47;
Tel: (812) 288-9281

**ECONO LODGE**
460 Auburn Ave (47129)
Rates: $30-$60;
Tel: (812) 288-6661

**LAKEVIEW HOTEL
& RESORT**
505 Marriott Dr (47129)
Rates: $54-$60;
Tel: (812) 283-4411

## CLOVERDALE

**DAYS INN**
RR 1, Box 79BB (46120)
Rates: $35-$50;
Tel: (317) 795-6400

**HOLIDAY INN**
Rt 1, Box 79CC (46120)
Rates: $36-$65;
Tel: (317) 795-3500

## COLUMBIA CITY

**COLUMBIA CITY MOTEL**
500 Old US 30W (46725)
Rates: $21-$38;
Tel: (219) 244-5103

**LEES INN**
235 Frontage Rd (46725)
Rates: $49-$63;
Tel: (219) 244-5300

## COLUMBUS

**COMFORT INN**
P. O. Box 506
(Taylorsville 47280)
Rates: $41-$48;
Tel: (812) 526-9747

**DAYS INN**
Box 2157 (47202)
Rates: $47-$65;
Tel: (812) 376-9951

**HOLIDAY INN**
2480 Jonathan Moore Pike
(47201)
Rates: $58-$91;
Tel: (812) 372-1541

**KNIGHTS INN**
I-65 & SR 46 (47201)
Rates: N/A;
Tel: (812) 378-3100

## CORYDON

**BEST WESTERN
OLD CAPITOL INN**
SR 135 (47112)
Rates: $38-$51;
Tel: (812) 738-4192

**BUDGETEL INN**
2495 Landmark Ave (47112)
Rates: $29-$42;
Tel: (812) 738-1500

## CRAWFORDSVILLE

**GENERAL LEW
WALLACE INN**
309 W Pike St (47933)
Rates: $34-$39;
Tel: (317) 362-8400

**HOLIDAY INN**
2500 N Lafayette Rd (47933)
Rates: $48-$64;
Tel: (317) 362-8700

**SUPER 8 MOTEL**
1025 Carey Blvd (47933)
Rates: $35-$50;
Tel: (317) 364-9999

## ELKHART

**ECONO LODGE**
52078 SR 19N (46514)
Rates: $24-$50;
Tel: (219) 262-0540

**KNIGHTS INN**
52188 SR 19 (46514)
Rates: $38-$48;
Tel: (219) 264-4262

**QUALITY HOTEL
CITY CENTRE**
300 S Main St (46516)
Rates: $35-$62;
Tel: (219) 295-0280

**RED ROOF INN**
2902 Cassopolis St (46514)
Rates: $31-$47;
Tel: (219) 262-3691

**WESTON PLAZA MOTEL**
2723 Cassopolis St (46514)
Rates: $60-$75;
Tel: (219) 264-7502

## EVANSVILLE

**COMFORT INN**
5006 Morgan Ave (47715)
Rates: $42-$65;
Tel: (812) 477-2211

**DRURY INN-EVANSVILLE**
3901 US 41N (47711)
Rates: $46-$55;
Tel: (812) 423-5818

**LEES INN**
5538 E Indiana St (47715)
Rates: $49-$70;
Tel: (812) 477-6663

**SUPER 8 MOTEL**
4600 Morgan Ave (47715)
Rates: $36-$44;
Tel: (812) 476-4008

**TRAVELODGE**
701 1st Ave (47710)
Rates: $35-$45;
Tel: (812) 424-3886

## FORT WAYNE

**BEST INNS OF AMERICA**
3017 W Coliseum Blvd
(46808)
Rates: $33-$41;
Tel: (219) 483-0091

**BUDGETEL INN**
1005 W Washington Center Rd
(46825)
Rates: $32-$47;
Tel: (219) 489-2220

**DAYS INN
EAST DOWNTOWN**
3730 E Washington Blvd
(46803)
Rates: $30-$36;
Tel: (219) 424-1980

**FORT WAYNE MARRIOTT**
305 E Washington Center Rd
(46825)
Rates: $65-$109;
Tel: (219) 484-0411

**HOLIDAY INN
DOWNTOWN**
300 E Washington Blvd
(46802)
Rates: $70-$78;
Tel: (219) 422-5511

**HOMETOWN INN**
6910 US 30E (46803)
Rates: $31-$39;
Tel: (219) 749-5058

**KNIGHT'S INN-NORTH**
2901 Goshen Rd (46808)
Rates: $33-$41;
Tel: (219) 484-2669

**RAMADA INN**
1212 Maganvox Way (46804)
Rates: $44-$48;
Tel: (219) 432-0511

**RED ROOF INN**
2920 Goshen Rd (46808)
Rates: $29-$38;
Tel: (219) 484-8641

RESIDENCE INN
BY MARRIOTT
4919 Lima Rd (46808)
Rates: $98-$136;
Tel: (219) 484-4700

## FRANKLIN

DAYS INN
2180 E King St (46131)
Rates: $47-$75;
Tel: (317) 736-8000

## FRENCH LICK

LANE MOTEL
Box 224 (47432)
Rates: $30-$37;
Tel: (812) 936-9919

THE PINES AT
PATOKA LAKE VILLAGE
RR 2, Box 255E (47432)
Rates: $60-$75;
Tel: (812) 936-9854

## GOSHEN

BEST WESTERN INN
900 Lincolnway E (46526)
Rates: $38-$46;
Tel: (219) 533-9551

CARLTON LODGE
1930 Lincolnway E (46526)
Rates: $51-$99;
Tel: (219) 534-3133

## GREENCASTLE

COLLEGE CASTLE MOTEL
315 Bloomington St (46135)
Rates: $22-$33;
Tel: (317) 653-4167

## GREENFIELD

HOWARD HUGHES
MOTOR LODGE
1310 W Main St (46140)
Rates: $31-$38;
Tel: (317) 462-4493

LEES INN
2270 N State St (46140)
Rates: $49-$70;
Tel: (317) 462-7112

## GREENSBURG

BEST WESTERN PINES INN
Rt 1, Box 61E (47240)
Rates: $46-$52;
Tel: (812) 663-6055

LEES INN
2211 N State Rd 3 (47240)
Rates: $49-$63;
Tel: (812) 663-9998

## GREENWOOD

COMFORT INN
GREENWOOD
P. O. Box 901 (46143)
Rates: $41-$48;
Tel: (317) 887-1515

## HAMMOND

QUALITY INN
3830 179th St (46323)
Rates: $40-$51;
Tel: (219) 844-2140

## HUNTINGBURG

BEST WESTERN
DUTCHMAN INN
406 E 22nd St (47542)
Rates: $43-$58;
Tel: (812) 683-2334

## INDIANAPOLIS
(and Vicinity)

AMERISUITES
9104 Keystone Crossing
(46240)
Rates: $69-$79;
Tel: (317) 843-0064

BEST WESTERN
INDIANAPOLIS EAST
2141 N Post Rd (46219)
Rates: $48-$62;
Tel: (317) 897-2000

BUDGETEL INN
2650 Executive Dr (46241)
Rates: $36-$52;
Tel: (317) 244-8100

THE CANTERBURY HOTEL
123 S Illinois St (46225)
Rates: $118;
Tel: (317) 634-3000

COMFORT INN
5040 S East St (46227)
Rates: $44-$72;
Tel: (317) 783-6711

COMFORT INN-NORTH
3880 W 92nd St (46268)
Rates: $38-$54;
Tel: (317) 872-3100

COURTYARD BY
MARRIOTT-DOWNTOWN
501 W Washington St (46204)
Rates: $82-$92;
Tel: (317) 635-4443

DAYS INN EAST
7314 E 21st St (46219)
Rates: $33-$39;
Tel: (317) 359-5500

DAYS INN-PLAINFIELD
6111 Cambridge Way
(46231)
Rates: $47-$55;
Tel: (317) 839-5000

DAYS INN-SOUTH
450 Bixler Rd (46227)
Rates: $36-$40;
Tel: (317) 788-0811

DRURY INN
9320 N Michigan Rd (46268)
Rates: $50-$56;
Tel: (317) 876-9777

ECONO LODGE-EAST
4326 Sellers St (46226)
Rates: $29-$44;
Tel: (317) 542-1031

ECONO LODGE-SOUTH
4505 S Hardin St (46217)
Rates: $35-$50;
Tel: (317) 788-9361

**EMBASSY SUITES HOTEL-NORTH**
3912 W Vincennes Rd (46268)
Rates: $84-$159;
Tel: (317) 872-7700

**HAMPTON INN-CASTLETON**
6817 E 82nd St
(Castleton 46250)
Rates: $49-$72;
Tel: (317) 576-0220

**HAMPTON INN-EAST**
2311 N Shadeland Ave
(46219)
Rates: $50-$61;
Tel: (317) 359-9900

**HAMPTON INN-INDIANAPOLIS AIRPORT**
5601 W Fortune Cir (46241)
Rates: $52-$70;
Tel: (317) 244-1221

**HAMPTON INN-NORTHWEST**
7220 Woodland Dr (46278)
Rates: $50-$61;
Tel: (317) 290-1212

**HAMPTON INN-SOUTH**
7045 McFarland Blvd (46237)
Rates: $41-$54;
Tel: (317) 889-0722

**HILTON INN-AIRPORT**
2500 S High School Rd
(46241)
Rates: $79-$111;
Tel: (317) 244-3361

**HOJO INN SPEEDWAY**
2602 N High School Rd
(46224)
Rates: $35-$60;
Tel: (317) 291-8800

**HOLIDAY INN-AIRPORT**
2501 S High School Rd
(46241)
Rates: $96;
Tel: (317) 244-6861

**HOLIDAY INN-EAST**
6990 E 21st St (46219)
Rates: $61-$66;
Tel: (317) 359-5341

**HOLIDAY INN EXPRESS**
3514 S Keystone Ave (46227)
Rates: $48-$63;
Tel: (317) 788-3100

**HOLIDAY INN-SOUTH**
520 E Thompson St (46227)
Rates: $63-$84;
Tel: (317) 787-8341

**HOMEWOOD SUITES-AT THE CROSSING**
2501 E 86th St (46240)
Rates: $84-$99;
Tel: (317) 253-1919

**INDIANAPOLIS HILTON**
P. O. Box 1966 (46204)
Rates: $95-$110;
Tel: (317) 635-2000

**INDIANAPOLIS MOTOR SPEEDWAY MOTEL**
4400 W 16th St (46222)
Rates: $50-$60;
Tel: (317) 241-2500

**KNIGHTS INN-EAST**
7101 E 21st St (46219)
Rates: $29-$40;
Tel: (800) 843-5644

**KNIGHTS INN-NORTH**
9402 Haver Way (46240)
Rates: N/A;
Tel: (800) 843-5644

**KNIGHTS INN-SOUTH**
4909 Knights Way (46217)
Rates: $31-$37;
Tel: (800) 843-5644

**LA QUINTA MOTOR INN-AIRPORT**
5316 W Southern Ave (46241)
Rates: $48-$62;
Tel: (317) 247-4281

**LA QUINTA MOTOR INN-EAST**
7304 E 21st St (46219)
Rates: $42-$56;
Tel: (317) 359-1021

**LEES INN**
5011 N Lafayette Rd (46254)
Rates: $52-$73;
Tel: (317) 297-8880

**MARRIOTT HOTEL**
7202 E 21st St (46219)
Rates: $92;
Tel: (317) 352-1231

**OMNI INDIANAPOLIS NORTH HOTEL**
8181 N Shadeland Ave
(46250)
Rates: $59-$110;
Tel: (317) 849-6668

**OMNI SEVERIN HOTEL**
40 W Jackson Pl (46225)
Rates: $75-$160;
Tel: (317) 634-6664

**RADISSON PLAZA AND SUITE HOTEL-INDPLS**
8787 Keystone Crossing
(46240)
Rates: $94-$124;
Tel: (317) 846-2700

**RED ROOF INN-NORTH**
9520 Vaparaiso Ct (46268)
Rates: $30-$53;
Tel: (317) 872-3030

**RED ROOF INN-SOUTH**
5221 Victory Dr (46203)
Rates: $26-$48;
Tel: (317) 788-9551

**RED ROOF INN-SPEEDWAY**
6415 Debonair Ln (46224)
Rates: $30-$51;
Tel: (317) 293-6881

**RESIDENCE INN BY MARRIOTT**
3553 Founders Rd (46268)
Rates: $89-$109;
Tel: (317) 872-0462

**SUPER 8 MOTEL**
4502 S Harding (46217)
Rates: $31-$45;
Tel: (317) 788-4774

**UNIVERSITY PLACE CONFERENCE CTR & HOTEL**
P. O. Box 6044 (46206)
Rates: $105-$120;
Tel: (317) 269-9000

**THE WESTIN**
50 S Capitol (46204)
Rates: $140-$225;
Tel: (317) 262-8100

## JASPER

**DAYS INN JAPSER**
P. O. Box 762 (47547)
Rates: $42-$55;
Tel: (812) 482-6000

**HOLIDAY INN**
Box 6 (47546)
Rates: $52-$80;
Tel: (812) 482-5555

## JEFFERSONVILLE

**RAMADA HOTEL**
700 W Riverside Dr (47130)
Rates: $56-$88;
Tel: (812) 284-6711

## KENTLAND

**TRI-WAY INN**
611 E Dunlap St (47951)
Rates: $31-$42;
Tel: (219) 474-5141

## KOKOMO

**COMFORT INN**
522 Essex Dr (46901)
Rates: $40-$65;
Tel: (317) 452-5050

**KOKOMO FAIRFIELD INN**
1717 E Lincoln Rd (46902)
Rates: $42-$75;
Tel: (317) 453-8822

**WORLD INN**
268 US 31S (46902)
Rates: $28-$32;
Tel: (317) 453-7100

## LAFAYETTE

**DAYS INN OF LAFAYETTE**
400 S Sagamore Pkwy
(47905)
Rates: $40-$61;
Tel: (317) 447-4131

**HOLIDAY INN**
5600 SR 43N
(W Lafayette 47906)
Rates: $53-$68;
Tel: (317) 567-2131

**HOMEWOOD SUITES**
3939 SR 26E (47905)
Rates: $75-$139;
Tel: (317) 448-9700

**HOWARD JOHNSON-PLAZA HOTEL**
4343 SR 26E (47905)
Rates: $72-$84;
Tel: (317) 447-0575

**KNIGHTS INN**
4110 SR 26E (47905)
Rates: $30-$46;
Tel: (317) 447-5611

**RED ROOF INN**
4201 SR 26E (47905)
Rates: $27-$44;
Tel: (317) 448-4671

**UNIVERSITY INN**
3001 Northwestern Ave
(W Lafayette 47906)
Rates: $58-$200;
Tel: (800) 777-9808

## LA PORTE

**HOLIDAY INN LA PORTE**
444 Pine Lake Ave (46350)
Rates: $50-$74;
Tel: (219) 362-4585

**MIDWAY MOTEL**
1838 West US 20 (46350)
Rates: N/A;
Tel: (219) 362-7321

## LEBANON

**HOLIDAY INN**
P. O. Box 582 (46052)
Rates: $48-$75;
Tel: (317) 482-0500

## LOGANSPORT

**HOLIDAY INN**
P. O. Box 813 (46947)
Rates: $58-$75;
Tel: (219) 753-6351

**SUPER 8 MOTEL**
P. O. Box 813 (46947)
Rates: $44-$53;
Tel: (219) 722-1273

## MADISON

**PRESIDENT MADISON MOTEL**
906 E 1st St (47250)
Rates: $30-$36;
Tel: (812) 265-2361

## MARION

**SHERATON INN**
501 E 4th St (46952)
Rates: $45-$48;
Tel: (317) 668-8801

## MARTINSVILLE

**LEES INN**
50 Bill's Blvd (46151)
Rates: $49-$63;
Tel: (317) 342-1842

## MERRILLVILLE

**CARLTON LODGE**
7850 Rhode Island Ave
(46410)
Rates: $69-$130;
Tel: (219) 756-1600

**KNIGHTS INN**
8250 Louisiana St (46410)
Rates: $31-$44;
Tel: (219) 736-5100

**LA QUINTA MOTOR INN**
8210 Louisiana St (46410)
Rates: $46-$60;
Tel: (219) 738-2870

**LEES INN**
6201 Opportunity Ln (46410)
Rates: $52-$72;
Tel: (219) 942-8555

**RADISSON HOTEL
AT STAR PLAZA**
800 E 81st Ave (46410)
Rates: $82-$152;
Tel: (219) 769-6311

**RED ROOF INN**
8290 Georgia St (46410)
Rates: $33-$50;
Tel: (800) 843-7663

## MICHIGAN CITY

**RED ROOF INN**
110 W Kieffer Rd (46360)
Rates: $32-$46;
Tel: (800) 843-7663

## MISHAWAKA

**MISHAWAKA INN**
2754 Lincoln Way E (46544)
Rates: $37-$45;
Tel: (219) 256-2300

## MOUNT VERNON

**FOUR SEASONS MOTEL**
2400 W 4th St (41620)
Rates: $41-$66;
Tel: (812) 838-4821

## MUNCIE

**COMFORT INN**
4011 W Bethel Ave (47305)
Rates: $38-$51;
Tel: (317) 282-6666

**HOLIDAY INN**
P. O. Box 2605 (47302)
Rates: $42-$55;
Tel: (317) 288-1911

**HOTEL ROBERTS MUNCIE**
420 S High St (47305)
Rates: $54;
Tel: (317) 741-7777

**LEES INN**
3302 Everbrook Ln (47304)
Rates: $51-$65;
Tel: (317) 282-7557

**MUNCIE DAYS INN**
3509 N Everbrook Ln (47304)
Rates: $34-$47;
Tel: (317) 288-2311

**SUPER 8 MOTEL**
3601 W Fox Ridge Ln (47304)
Rates: $35-$46;
Tel: (317) 286-4333

## NEW ALBANY

**HOLIDAY INN-
NORTHWEST**
411 W Spring St (47150)
Rates: $57-$67;
Tel: (812) 945-2771

## NEW CASTLE

**L-K MOTEL**
5243 South State Rd 3
(47362)
Rates: N/A
Tel: (317) 987-8205

## PERU

**L-K MOTEL**
675 US 313 (46970)
Rates: $36-$50;
Tel: (317) 472-3971

## PLYMOUTH

**HOLIDAY INN**
2550 N Michigan St (46563)
Rates: $47-$65;
Tel: (219) 936-4013

## PORTAGE

**DAYS INN**
6161 Melton Rd (46368)
Rates: $34-$57;
Tel: (219) 762-2136

**HOLIDAY INN**
6200 Melton Rd (46368)
Rates: $66-$72;
Tel: (219) 762-5546

**LEES INN**
2300 Willow Creek (46368)
Rates: $49-$70;
Tel: (219) 763-7177

## PORTER

**SPRING HOUSE INN**
303 N Mineral Springs Rd
(46304)
Rates: $64-$84;
Tel: (219) 929-4600

## REMINGTON

**DAYS INN OF REMINGTON**
RR 2, Box 240B (47977)
Rates: $29-$33;
Tel: (219) 261-2178

**INTERSTATE MOTEL**
Rte 3, Box 78
(Rensselaer 47978)
Rates: $28-$33;
Tel: (219) 866 4164

## REYNOLDS

**PARK VIEW MOTEL**
RR 1, Box 4 (47980)
Rates: $25-$55;
Tel: (219) 984 5380

## RICHMOND

**BEST WESTERN
IMPERIAL MOTOR LODGE**
3020 E Main St (47374)
Rates: $29-$40;
Tel: (317) 966-1505

**COMFORT INN**
912 Mendelson Dr (47374)
Rates: $41-$66;
Tel: (317) 935-4766

**DAYS INN**
540 W Eaton Pike (47374)
Rates: $34-$44;
Tel: (317) 966-7591

**GOLDEN INN**
7701 E National Rd
(New Paris, OH 45347)
Rates: $23-$37;
Tel: (513) 437-0722

**HOLIDAY INN**
4700 E National Rd (47374)
Rates: $49-$59;
Tel: (317) 962-5551

**HOWARD JOHNSON LODGE**
2525 Chester Blvd (47374)
Rates: $32-$47;
Tel: (317) 962-7576

**KNIGHTS INN**
419 Commerce Dr (47374)
Rates: $33-$40;
Tel: (317) 966-6682

**LEES INN**
6030 E National Rd (47374)
Rates: $52-$73;
Tel: (317) 966-6559

**QUALITY INN**
5501 E National Rd (47374)
Rates: $44-$55;
Tel: (317) 966-7511

**VILLA MOTEL**
533 W Eaton Pike (47374)
Rates: $20-$27;
Tel: (317) 962-5202

## ROCHESTER

**ROSE DALE MOTEL**
RR 1, Box 280 (46975)
Rates: $21-$29;
Tel: (219) 223-3185

## SCOTTSBURG

**BEST WESTERN SCOTTSBURG INN**
P. O. Box 129 (47170)
Rates: $40-$52;
Tel: (812) 752-2212

**MARIANN TRAVEL INN**
P. O. Box 36 (47170)
Rates: $30-$46;
Tel: (812) 752-3396

## SELLERSBURG

**DAYS INN**
7618 Old SR 60W (47172)
Rates: $36-$65;
Tel: (812) 246-4451

## SEYMOUR

**ALLSTATE MOTEL**
2 Mi E on US 50 at I-65
(47274)
Rates: $20-$26;
Tel; (812) 522-2666

**BEST WESTERN MOTEL**
220 Commerce Dr (47274)
Rates: $30-$47;
Tel: (812) 522-8000

**HOLIDAY INN**
2025 E Tipton St (47274)
Rates: $48-$63;
Tel: (812) 522-6767

**KNIGHTS INN**
207 N Frontage Rd (47274)
Rates: $31-$47;
Tel: (800) 722-7220

**LEES INN**
2075 E Tipton St (47274)
Rates: $51-$72;
Tel: (812) 523-1850

## SHELBYVILLE

**HOLIDAY INN**
1810 N Riley Hwy (46176)
Rates: $55-$67;
Tel: (317) 392-3221

**LEES INN SHELBYVILLE**
2880 SR 44E (46176)
Rates: $57-$72;
Tel: (317) 392-2299

## SOUTH BEND

**BEST INNS OF AMERICA**
425 Dixie Hwy N (46637)
Rates: $35-$49;
Tel: (219) 277-7700

**BUDGET HOST HICKORY INN**
50520 US 33N (46637)
Rates: $21-$27;
Tel: (219) 272-7555

**BUDGETEER MOTOR INN**
52825 US 33N & US 31N
(46637)
Rates: $25-$39;
Tel: (219) 272-9000

**DAYS INN**
52757 US 31 & 33 (46637)
Rates: $33-$60;
Tel: 219) 277-0510

**ECONO LODGE**
3233 W Lincoln Way (46628)
Rates: $34-$39;
Tel: (219) 232-9019

**HOLIDAY INN-UNIVERSITY AREA**
515 Dixie Way N (46637)
Rates: $65-$85;
Tel: (219) 272-6600

**HOWARD JOHNSON MOTOR LODGE**
52939 US 31 & 33N (46637)
Rates: $24-$67;
Tel: (219) 272-1500

**KNIGHTS INN-SOUTH BEND**
236 Dixie Way N (46637)
Rates: $33-$40;
Tel: (219) 277-2960

**MARRIOTT HOTEL**
123 N St Joseph St (46601)
Rates: $84-$375;
Tel: (219) 234-2000

**THE MORRIS INN**
P. O. Box 1085
(Notre Dame 46556)
Rates: $64-$88;
Tel: (219) 234-0141

148

**RAMADA INN**
52890 US 31 & 33N (46637)
Rates: $54-$68;
Tel: (219) 272-5220

## SULLIVAN

**DAYS INN**
P. O. Box 97 (47882)
Rates: $34-$47;
Tel: (812) 268-6391

## TERRE HAUTE

**BEST WESTERN-LINDEN**
3325 Dixie Bee Rd (47802)
Rates: $48-$160;
Tel: (812) 234-7781

**DAYS INN**
2800 S Dixie Bee Rd (47802)
Rates: 37-$69;
Tel: (812) 234-4268

**HOLIDAY INN**
3300 Dixie Bee Rd (47802)
Rates: $64-$83;
Tel: (812) 232-6091

**KNIGHTS INN**
401 Margaret Ave (47802)
Rates: $37-$44;
Tel: (812) 234-9931

**MID TOWN MOTEL**
400 S 3rd St (47807)
Rates: $25-$32;
Tel: (812) 232-0383

**SUPER 8 LODGE**
3089 S 1st St (47802)
Rates: $38-$54;
Tel: (812) 232-4890

## VALPARAISO

**BRIDGE VIEW INN**
760 Morthland Dr (46383)
Rates: $44-$63;
Tel: (219) 464-8555

**CARLTON LODGE**
2301 E Morthland Dr (46383)
Rates: $55-$79;
Tel: (219) 465-1700

## VINCENNES

**HOLIDAY INN**
600 Wheatland Rd (47591)
Rates: $45-$54;
Tel: (812) 886-9900

**VINCENNES LODGE**
1411 Willow St (47591)
Rates: $28-$36;
Tel: (812) 882-1282

## WABASH

**DAYS INN**
1950 S Wabash St (46992)
Rates: $43-$79;
Tel: (219) 563-7451

## WARSAW

**COMFORT INN**
2605 E Center St (46580)
Rates: $55-$85;
Tel: (219) 267-7337

# IOWA

## AMANA COLONIES

**AMANA HOLIDAY INN**
P. O. Box 187 (52203)
Rates: $60-$85;
Tel: (319) 668-1175

**DIE HEIMAT COUNTRY INN**
Box 160 (Homestead 52236)
Rates: $35-$62;
Tel: (319) 622-3937

## AMES

**AMES BUDGETEL INN**
2500 Elwood Dr (50010)
Rates: $43-$47;
Tel: (515) 296-2500

**COMFORT INN-AMES**
1605 S Dayton Ave (50010)
Rates: $38-$68;
Tel: (515) 232-0689

**HEARTLAND INN-AMES**
Hwy 30 & I-35 (50010)
Rates: $38-$49;
Tel: (515) 233-6060

**HOLIDAY INN-
GATEWAY CENTER**
P. O. Box X (50010)
Rates: $63-$90;
Tel: (515) 292-8600

**NEW FRONTIER MOTEL**
5000 W Lincoln Way (50010)
Rates: $28-$40;
Tel: (515) 292-2056

**PARK INN OF AMES**
1206 S Duff (50010)
Rates: $42-$52;
Tel: (515) 232-3410

**UNIVERSITY INN**
316 S Duff (50010)
Rates: $36-$78;
Tel: (515) 232-0280

## ATLANTIC

**ECONO LODGE**
Rt 3, Box 199 (50022)
Rates: $27-$40;
Tel: (712) 243-4067

## AVOCA

**CAPRI MOTEL**
P. O. Box 699 (51521)
Rates: $28-$36;
Tel: (712) 343-6301

## BLOOMFIELD

**SOUTHFORK INN**
P. O. Box 155 (52537)
Rates: $28-$37;
Tel: (515) 664-1063

## BURLINGTON

**BEST WESTERN
PZAZZ MOTOR INN**
3001 Winegard Dr (52601)
Rates: $53-$65;
Tel: (319) 753-2223

**DAYS INN**
1601 N Roosevelt (52601)
Rates: $30-$50;
Tel: (319) 754-4681

**FRIENDSHIP INN**
2731 Mt Pleasant St (52601)
Rates: $27-$45;
Tel: (319) 754-7571

**THE HOLIDAY**
2759 Mt Pleasant St (52601)
Rates: $47-$58;
Tel: (319) 754-5781

## CARROLL

**71-30 MOTEL**
Jct US 30 & 71 (51401)
Rates: $28-$40;
Tel: (712) 792-1100

## CEDAR FALLS

**BLACKHAWK MOTOR INN**
122 Washington (50613)
Rates: $28-$34;
Tel: (319) 271-1161

**HOLIDAY INN**
5826 University Ave (50613)
Rates: $52-$69;
Tel: (319) 277-2230

**VAGABOND MOTEL**
4711 University Ave (50613)
Rates: $25-$41;
Tel: (319) 277-1412

## CEDAR RAPIDS

**BEST WESTERN
LONGBRANCH MOTOR INN**
90 Twist Town Rd (52402)
Rates: $40-$58;
Tel: (319) 377-6386

**COMFORT INN
OF CEDAR RAPIDS NORTH**
5055 Rockwell Dr (52402)
Rates: $42-$48;
Tel: (319) 393-8247

**DAYS INN
OF CEDAR RAPIDS**
3245 Southgate Pl SW
(52404)
Rates: $42-$51;
Tel: (319) 365-4339

**ECONO LODGE**
622 33rd Ave SW (52404)
Rates: $35-$52;
Tel: (319) 363-8888

**EXEL INN
OF CEDAR RAPIDS**
616 33rd Ave SW (52404)
Rates: $27-$41;
Tel: (319) 366-2475

**FIVE SEASONS HOTEL**
350 1st Ave NE (52401)
Rates: $59-$119;
Tel: (319) 363-8161

**HEARTLAND INN**
3315 Southgate Ct SW
(52404)
Rates: $40-$64;
Tel: (319) 362-9012

**HOLIDAY INN**
2501 Williams Blvd SW
(52404)
Rate: $52-$68;
Tel: (319) 365-9441

**RAMADA INN CITY CENTER**
4747 1st Ave SE (52403)
Rates: $45 $60;
Tel: (319) 393-8800

**RED ROOF INN**
3325 Southgate Ct SW
(52404)
Rates: $27-$56;
Tel. (319) 366-7523

**SHERATON INN**
525 33rd Ave SW (52404)
Rates: $59-$74;
Tel: (319) 366-8671

## CLEAR LAKE

**BLUE HORIZON INN**
467 N Shore Dr (50428)
Rates: $33-$80;
Tel: (515) 357-2161

**BUDGET INN MOTEL**
1306 N 25th St (50428)
Rates: $33-$39;
Tel: (515) 357 8700

## CLINTON

**BEST WESTERN-
FRONTIER MOTOR INN**
2300 Lincolnway (52732)
Rates: $42-$75;
Tel: (319) 242-7112

**CLINTON TRAVELODGE**
302 6th Ave S (52732)
Rates: $35-$45;
Tel: (319) 243-4730

**RAMADA INN**
1522 Lincolnway (52732)
Rates: $46-$60;
Tel: (319) 243-8841

**TIMBER MOTEL**
2225 Lincolnway (52732)
Rates: N/A;
Tel: (319) 243-6901

## COLUMBUS JUNCTION

**COLUMBUS MOTEL**
Hwy 92D (52738)
Rates: $29-$45;
Tel: (319) 728-8080

## CORALVILLE

**BEST WESTERN
WESTFIELD INN**
I-80 & 965 Exit 240 (52241)
Rates: N/A;
Tel: (319) 354-7770

## COUNCIL BLUFFS

**BEST WESTERN CROSS-
ROADS OF THE BLUFFS**
2216 27th Ave (51501)
Rates: $49-$69;
Tel: (712) 322-3150

**COMFORT INN-MANAWA**
3208 S 7th St (51501)
Rates: $33-$42;
Tel: (712) 366-9699

**DAYS INN**
3619 9th Ave (51501)
Rates: $33-$38;
Tel: (712) 323-2200

**HEARTLAND INN**
1000 Woodbury Ave (51503)
Rates: $39-$51;
Tel: (712) 322-8400

**HOWARD JOHNSON
LODGE & SUITES**
3537 W Broadway (51501)
Rates: $44-$64;
Tel: (712) 328-3171

## DENISON

**BEST WESTERN
DENISON'S INN**
RR 3, P. O. Box 42 (51442)
Rates: $30-$40;
Tel: (712) 263-5081

## DES MOINES
(and Vicinity)

**ARCHER MOTEL**
4965 Hubbell Ave (50317)
Rates: N/A;
Tel: (515) 265-0368

**BEST INNS OF AMERICA**
5050 Merle Hay Rd
(Johnston 50131)
Rates: $39 $50;
Tel: (515) 270-1111

**BEST WESTERN COLONIAL**
5020 NE 14th St (50313)
Rates: $34-$43;
Tel: (515) 265-7511

**BEST WESTERN
STARLITE VILLAGE**
929 3rd St (50309)
Rates: $48-$56;
Tel: (515) 282-5251

**BUDGET HOST**
7625 Hickman Rd (50322)
Rates: $28-$38;
Tel: (515) 276-5401

**COMFORT INN**
5231 Fleur Dr (50321)
Rates: $40-$75;
Tel: (515) 287-3434

**COMFORT INN
OF URBANDALE**
5900 Sutton Pl
(Urbandale 50322)
Rates: $35-$55;
Tel: (515) 270-1037

**DAYS INN CAPITOL CITY**
3501 E 14th St (50316)
Rates: $35-$75;
Tel: (515) 265-2541

**DAYS INN-WEST**
10841 Douglas Ave (50322)
Rates: $34-$58;
Tel: (515) 278-2811

## DES MOINES-
## WEST TRAVELODGE
11001 University Ave (50325)
Rates: $30-$55;
Tel: (515) 225-2222

## EMBASSY SUITES
## ON THE RIVER
101 E Locust St (50309)
Rates: $99-$124;
Tel: (515) 244-1700

## HICKMAN MOTOR LODGE
6500 Hickman Rd (50322)
Rates: $29-$36;
Tel: (515) 276-8591

## HOLIDAY INN-MERLE HAY
5000 Merle Hay Rd (50322)
Rates: $45-$75;
Tel: (515) 278-0271

## HOTEL FORT DES MOINES
10th & Walnut Sts (50309)
Rates: $55-$65;
Tel: (515) 243-1161

## THE INN & CONFERENCE
## CENTER AT MERLE HAY
5055 Merle Hay Rd
(Johnston 50131)
Rates: $35-$44;
Tel: (515) 276-5411

## SAVERY HOTEL AND SPA
401 Locust St (50309)
Rates: $35-$75;
Tel: (515) 244-2151

## SHERATON INN
11040 Hickman Rd (50325)
Rates: $64-$75;
Tel: (515) 278-5575

## SUPER 8 LODGE
4755 Merle Hay Rd (50322)
Rates: $39-$47;
Tel: (515) 278-8858

## DE SOTO

## EDGETOWNER MOTEL
P. O. Box 8 (50069)
Rates: $28-$35;
Tel: (515) 834-2641

## DUBUQUE

## BEST WESTERN
## MIDWAY HOTEL
3100 Dodge St (52003)
Rates: $55-$80;
Tel: (319) 557-8000

## COMFORT INN
## OF DUBUQUE
4055 Dodge St (52003)
Rates: $38-$71;
Tel: (319) 556-3006

## DAYS INN-DUBUQUE
1111 Dodge St (52001)
Rates: $42-$60;
Tel: (319) 583-3297

## FAIRFIELD INN
## BY MARRIOTT
3400 Dodge St (52001)
Rates: $39-$61;
Tel: (319) 588-2349

## EARLY

## EARLY MOTEL
403 Hwys 71 & 20 (50535)
Rates: N/A;
Tel: (712) 273-5599

## ELDORA

## VILLAGE MOTEL
2005 E Edgington Ave (50627)
Rates: $24-$35;
Tel: (515) 858-3441

## EMMETSBURG

## SUBURBAN MOTEL
1 1/2 Mi NW on US 18 & SR 4
(50536)
Rates: $26-$39;
Tel: (712) 852-2626

## FAIRFIELD

## BEST WESTERN
## FAIRFIELD INN
2200 W Burlington (52556)
Rates: $51-$68;
Tel: (515) 472-2200

## FORT DODGE

## BEST WESTERN
## STARLITE VILLAGE MOTEL
P. O. Box 1297 (50501)
Rates: $43-$60;
Tel: (515) 573-7177

## BUDGET HOST INN
At Jct US 20 & 169 (50501)
Rates: $28-$57;
Tel: (515) 955-8501

## FORT MADISON

## BEST WESTERN
## IOWAN MOTOR LODGE
P. O. Box 485 (52627)
Rates: $50-$62;
Tel: (319) 372-7510

## THE MADISON INN MOTEL
3440 Ave L (52627)
Rates: $30-$45;
Tel: (319) 372-7740

## MERICANA MOTEL
Hwy 61 & Hwy 2 West
(52627)
Rates: N/A;
Tel: (319) 372-5123

## GLENWOOD

## BLUFF VIEW MOTEL
RR 1 (Pacific Junction 51561)
Rates: $26-$30;
Tel: (800) 582-9366

## WESTERN INN
## OF GLENWOOD
707 S Locust (51534)
Rates: $28-$33;
Tel: (712) 527-3175

## GRINNELL

## BEST WESTERN GRINNELL
Rt 1, Box 21 (50112)
Rates: $36-$45;
Tel: (515) 236-6116

## INDIANOLA

**WOODS MOTEL**
906 South Jefferson (50125)
Rates: N/A;
Tel. (515) 961-5311

## IOWA CITY

**BEST WESTERN-
CANTERBURY INN**
704 1st Ave
(Coralville 52241)
Rates: $49-$65;
Tel: (319) 351-0400

**BEST WESTERN
WESTFIELD INN**
1895 27th Ave
(Coralville 52241)
Rates: $42 $76;
Tel: (319) 354-7770

**BLUE TOP MOTEL**
1015 5th St (Coralville 52241)
Rates: $25-$42;
Tel: (319) 351-0900

**COMFORT INN
OF CORVALVILLE**
209 W 9th St
(Coralville 52241)
Rates: $38-$65;
Tel: (319) 351-8144

**DAYS INN IRONMEN**
1200 1st Ave
(Coralville 52241)
Rates: $33-$63;
Tel: (319) 351-6600

**FAIRFIELD INN
BY MARRIOTT**
214 W 9th St
(Coralville 52241)
Rates: $42-$63;
Tel: (319) 337-8382

**HOLIDAY INN IOWA CITY**
210 S Dubuque St (52240)
Rates: $66-$98;
Tel: (319) 337-4058

**HOWARD JOHNSON
MOTOR LODGE**
2216 N Dodge St (52240)
Rates: $44-$56;
Tel: (319) 351-1010

## KNOXVILLE

**RED CARPET INN**
1702 N Lincoln (50138)
Rates: $23-$32;
Tel: (515) 842-3191

## LE MARS

**AMBER INN MOTEL**
635 Eighth Ave SW (51031)
Rates: $28-$34;
Tel: (712) 546-7066

## MAPLETON

**MAPLE MOTEL**
Rt 1, Box 1 (51034)
Rates: $29-$38;
Tel: (712) 882-1271

## MAQUOKETA

**KEY MOTEL**
Hwy 61 & 64 (52060)
Rates: N/A;
Tel. (319) 652-5131

## MARQUETTE

**THE FRONTIER MOTEL**
101 S 1st St (52158)
Rates: $30-$65;
Tel: (319) 873-3497

## MARSHALLTOWN

**BEST WESTERN
REGENCY INN**
3303 S Center St (50158)
Rates: $51-$68;
Tel: (515) 752-6321

**BEST WESTERN
THUNDERBIRD MOTEL**
2009 S Center St (50158)
Rates: $33-$52;
Tel: (515) 752-3631

## MASON CITY

**TRAVELODGE**
24 5th St SW (50401)
Rates: $39-$48;
Tel: (515) 424-2910

## MOUNT PLEASANT

**HEARTLAND INN**
Hwy 218N (52641)
Rates: $37-$51;
Tel: (319) 385-2102

## MUSCATINE

**HOLIDAY INN**
2915 N Hwy 61 (52761)
Rates: $49-$60;
Tel: (319) 264-5550

## NEW HAMPTON

**FERKIN'S MOTEL**
2199 McCloud Ave (50659)
Rates: $23-$40;
Tel: (515) 394-4145

## NEWTON

**BEST WESTERN
NEWTON INN**
P. O. Box 8 (50208)
Rates: $39-$67;
Tel: (515) 792-4200

## OKOBOJI

**FILLENWARTH NEW BEACH
COTTAGES**
W Lake Okoboji
(Arnolds Park 51331)
Rates: $240-$960;
Tel: (712) 332-5646

## ONAWA

**MIDWAY MOTEL**
P. O. Box 45 (51040)
Rates: $28-$38;
Tel: (712) 423-2101

## OSCEOLA

**BEST WESTERN REGAL INN**
P. O. Box 238 (50213)
Rates: $34-$49;
Tel: (515) 342-2123

**BLUE HAVEN MOTEL**
325 S Main St (50213)
Rates: $30-$53;
Tel: (515) 342-2115

## OSKALOOSA

**TRAVELER BUDGET INN**
1210 A Ave East (52577)
Rates: $28-$34;
Tel: (515) 673-8333

## OTTUMWA

**COLONIAL MOTOR INN**
1534 Albia Rd (52501)
Rates: $21-$31;
Tel: (515) 683-1661

**DAYS INN OF OTTUMWA**
206 Church St (52501)
Rates: $36-$58;
Tel: (515) 682-8131

**HEARTLAND INN**
125 W Joseph Ave (52501)
Rates: $37-$50;
Tel: (515) 682-8526

## QUAD CITIES

**BEST WESTERN
AIRPORT INN**
2550 52nd Ave
(Moline 61265)
Rates: $44-$60;
Tel: (309) 762-9191

**BEST WESTERN
STEEPLEGATE INN**
100 W 76th St
(Davenport 52806)
Rates: $62-$85;
Tel: (319) 386-6900

**COMFORT INN**
2600 52nd Ave
(Moline 61265)
Rates: $39-$69;
Tel: (309) 762-7000

**COMFORT INN-
DAVENPORT**
7222 Northwest Blvd
(Davenport 52806)
Rates: $38-$47;
Tel: (319) 391-8222

**DAYS INN OF DAVENPORT**
3202 E Kimberly Rd
(Davenport 52807)
Rates: $38-$60:
Tel: (319) 355-1190

**EXEL INN OF DAVENPORT**
6310 N Brady St
(Davenport 52806)
Rates: $31-$45;
Tel: (319) 386-6350

**EXEL INN OF MOLINE**
2501 52nd Ave
(Moline 61265)
Rates: $28-$42;
Tel: (309) 797-5580

**FAIRFIELD INN**
2705 48th Ave
(Moline 61265)
Rates: $43-$55;
Tel: (309) 762-9083

**FAIRFIELD INN BY
MARRIOTT-DAVENPORT**
3206 E Kimberly Rd
(Davenport 52807)
Rates: $43-$69;
Tel: (319) 355-2264

**HAMPTON INN-AIRPORT**
6920 27th St (Moline 61265)
Rates: $47-$53;
Tel: (309) 762-1711

**HAMPTON INN-
DAVENPORT**
3330 E Kimberly Rd
(Davenport 52807)
Rates: $42-$53;
Tel: (319) 359-3921

**HOLIDAY INN-AIRPORT
CONVENTION CENTER**
6902 27th St (Moline 61265)
Rates: $50-$88;
Tel: (309) 762-8811

**HOLIDAY INN-
BETTENDORF**
909 Middle Rd
(Bettendorf 52722)
Rates: $76-$96;
Tel: (319) 355-4761

**JUMER'S CASTLE LODGE-
BETTENDORF**
900 Spruce Hills Dr
(Bettendorf 52722)
Rates: $76-$97;
Tel: (319) 359-7141

**LA QUINTA**
Airport Corners
(Moline 61265)
Rates: $44-$58;
Tel: (309) 762-9008

**RAMADA INN-DAVENPORT**
6263 N Brady
(Davenport 52806)
Rates: $55-$63;
Tel: (319) 386-1940

**TWIN BRIDGES MOTOR
INN-BETTENDORF**
221 15th St
(Bettendorf 52722)
Rates: $39-$48;
Tel: (319) 355-6451

## SIOUX CENTER

**COLONIAL MOTEL**
1367 South Main (51250)
Rates: N/A;
Tel: (800) 762-9149

**ECONO LODGE**
86 9th St Circle NE (51250)
Rate: $31-$35;
Tel: (712) 722-4000

## SIOUX CITY

**BEST WESTERN
REGENCY EXECUTIVE**
130 Nebraska St (51101)
Rates: $59-$65;
Tel: (712) 277-1550

**ECONOMY INN**
2921 E Gordon Dr (51105)
Rates: $22-$32;
Tel: (712) 277-4242

**FAIRFIELD INN
BY MARRIOTT**
4716 Southern Hills Dr
(51106)
Rates: $39-$52;
Tel: (712) 276-5600

**PALMER HOUSE MOTEL**
3440 E Gordon Dr (51106)
Rates: $32-$45;
Tel: (712) 276-4221

**RIVERBOAT INN**
701 Gordon Dr (51101)
Rates: $37-$45;
Tel: (712) 277-9400

## STORM LAKE

**CROSS ROADS MOTEL**
Jct Hwys 3 & 71 (50588)
Rates: N/A;
Tel: (800) 383-1456

## STORY CITY

**VIKING MOTOR INN**
Just West of I-35, exit 124
(50248)
Rates: $34-$42;
Tel: (515) 733-4306

## WATERLOO

**COMFORT INN
OF WATERLOO**
1945 La Porte Rd (50702)
Rates: $41-$50;
Tel: (319) 234-7411

**CONWAY INNE**
226 W Fifth St (50701)
Rates: $28-$33;
Tel: (319) 235-0301

**EXEL INN OF WATERLOO**
3350 University Ave (50701)
Rates: $27-$41;
Tel: (319) 235-2165

**FAIRFIELD INN**
2011 La Porte Rd (50702)
Rates: $43-$61;
Tel: (319) 234-5452

**HEARTLAND INN-
CROSSROADS**
1809 La Porte Rd (50702)
Rates: $42-$56;
Tel: (319) 235-4461

**HEARTLAND INN-
GREYHOUND**
3052 Marnie Ave (50701)
Rates: $42-$56;
Tel: (319) 232-7467

**RAMADA HOTEL**
214 Washington St (50701)
Rates: $52-$59;
Tel: (319) 235-0321

**SUPER 8 MOTEL-
WATERLOO**
1825 La Porte Rd (50702)
Rates: $35-$65;
Tel: (319) 233-1800

## WAVERLY

**BEST WESTERN
RED FOX INN**
1900 Heritage Way (50677)
Rates: $50-$68;
Tel: (319) 352-5330

## WEBSTER CITY

**THE EXECUTIVE INN**
1700 Superior St (50595)
Rates: $29-$39;
Tel: (515) 832-3631

## WEST LIBERTY

**LIBERTY INN**
Box 200 (52776)
Rates: N/A;
Tel: (319) 627-2171

## WEST UNION

**ELMS MOTEL**
Hwy 150 South (52175)
Rates: N/A;
Tel: (800) 422-3843

## WILLIAMSBURG

**CREST MOTEL**
Rt 1, Box 181 (52361)
Rate: $25-$40;
Tel: (319) 668-1522

## WYOMING

**SUNSET MOTEL**
RR #1 (52362)
Rates: N/A;
Tel: (319) 488-2240

# KANSAS

## ABILENE

**BEST WESTERN INN**
2210 N Buckeye (67410)
Rates: $30-$50;
Tel: (913) 263-2050

**DIAMOND MOTEL**
1407 NW 3rd St (67410)
Rates: $18-$40;
Tel: (913) 263-2360

**SUPER 8 MOTEL**
2207 N Buckeye (67410)
Rates: $32-$54;
Tel: (913) 263-4545

## ARKANSAS CITY

**BEST WESTERN
HALLMARK MOTOR INN**
1617 N Summit St (67005)
Rates: $34-$40;
Tel: (316) 442-1400

**HERITAGE REGENCY
COURT INN**
3232 N Summit St (67005)
Rates: $36-$42;
Tel: (316) 442-7700

## ATCHISON

**ATCHISON MOTOR INN**
401 S 10th (66002)
Rates: $30-$45;
Tel: (913) 367-7000

## BELLEVILLE

**BEST WESTERN
BEL VILLA MOTEL**
Jct US 36 & 81 (66935)
Rates: $34-$40;
Tel: (913) 527-2231

## CHANUTE

**GUEST HOUSE
MOTOR INN**
1814 S Santa Fe (66720)
Rates: $25-$32;
Tel: (316) 431-0600

**HOLIDAY PARK MOTEL**
3030 S Santa Fe (66720)
Rates: $30;
Tel: (316) 431-0850

**SAFARI INN MOTEL**
P. O.Box 841 (66720)
Rates: $31-$38;
Tel: (800) 432-9460

## CLAY CENTER

**CEDAR COURT MOTEL**
905 Crawford (67432)
Rates: $24-$40;
Tel: (913) 632-2148

## COFFEYVILLE

**APPLETREE INN**
820 E 11th (67337)
Rates: $40-$46;
Tel: (316) 251-0002

**FOUNTAIN PLAZA INN**
104 W 11th St (67337)
Rates: $39-$55;
Tel: (316) 251-2250

## COLBY

**BEST WESTERN
CROWN MOTEL**
2320 S Range (67701)
Rates: $33-$54;
Tel: (913) 462-3943

**BUDGET HOST INN**
1745 W 4th St (67701)
Rates: $26-$46;
Tel: (913) 462-3338

**DAYS INN**
1925 S Range (67701)
Rates: $41-$50;
Tel: (913) 462-8691

**RAMADA INN**
1950 S Range (67701)
Rates: $39-$51;
Tel: (913) 462-3933

## CONCORDIA

**BEST WESTERN
THUNDERBIRD MOTOR INN**
P. O. Box 673 (66901)
Rates: $35-$42;
Tel: (913) 243-4545

## COUNCIL GROVE

**THE COTTAGE HOUSE
HOTEL & MOTEL**
25 N Neosho (66846)
Rates: $25-$80;
Tel: (316) 767-6828

## DODGE CITY

**ASTRO MOTEL**
2200 W Wyatt Earp Blvd
(67801)
Rates: $26-$44;
Tel: (316) 227-8146

**BEST WESTERN
SILVER SPUR LODGE**
P. O. Box 119 (67801)
Rates: $41-$67;
Tel: (316) 227-2125

**DODGE HOUSE MOTEL**
2408 W Wyatt Earp Blvd
(67801)
Rates: $21-$120;
Tel: (800) 553-9901

**ECONO LODGE
OF DODGE CITY**
1610 W Wyatt Earp Blvd
(67801)
Rates: $30-$50;
Tel: (316) 225-0231

**SUPER 8 MOTEL**
1708 W Wyatt Earp Blvd
(67801)
Rates: $39-$49;
Tel: (316) 225-3924

## EL DORADO

**BEST WESTERN
RED COACH INN**
2525 W Central Ave (67042)
Rates: $36-$65;
Tel: (316) 321-6900

**HERITAGE INN**
2515 W Central Ave (67042)
Rates: $26-$40;
Tel: (316) 321-6800

## ELLSWORTH

**BUDGET HOST
GARDEN MOTEL**
P. O. Box 44 (67439)
Rates: $31-$49;
Tel: (913) 472-3116

## EMPORIA

**BEST WESTERN
HOSPITALITY HOUSE MOTEL**
3181 Hwy 50W (66801)
Rates: $34-$60;
Tel: (316) 342-7587

**DAYS INN**
3032 Hwy 50W (66801)
Rates: $40-$54;
Tel: (316) 342-1787

**ECONO LODGE
OF EMPORIA**
2630 W 18th (66801)
Rates: $29-$35;
Tel: (316) 343-1240

**HOLIDAY INN HOLIDOME**
2700 W 18th (66801)
Rates: $42-$55;
Tel: (316) 343-2200

**QUALITY INN**
3021 Hwy 50W (66801)
Rates: $36-$58;
Tel: (316) 342-3770

**RAMADA INN**
1839 Merchant St (66801)
Rates: $38-$42;
Tel: (316) 342-8850

## EUREKA

**BLUE STEM LODGE**
1314 E River St (67045)
Rates: $28-$38;
Tel: (316) 583-5531

## FORT SCOTT

**BEST WESTERN
FORT SCOTT INN**
101 State St (66701)
Rates: $36-$45;
Tel: (316) 223-0100

**FRONTIER INN 4 LESS**
2222 S Main (66701)
Rates: $29-$35;
Tel: (316) 223-5330

**RANCH HOUSE MOTEL**
Hwy 54 West (66701)
Rates: N/A;
Tel: (316) 223-9734

**RED RAM MOTEL**
Hwy 54 WEst (66704)
Rates: N/A;
Tel: (316) 223-2400

## GARDEN CITY

**BEST WESTERN
RED BARON MOTOR INN**
Jct US 50 & US 83 Spur
(67846)
Rates: $31-$45;
Tel: (316) 275-4164

**BEST WESTERN
WHEAT LANDS MOTOR INN**
1311 E Fulton (67846)
Rates: $35-$51;
Tel: (316) 276-2387

**BUDGET HOST**
123 Honey Bee Ct (67846)
Rates: $30-$44;
Tel: (316) 275-0677

**CONTINENTAL INN**
1408 Jones Ave (67846)
Rates: $27-$35;
Tel: (316) 276-7691

**HILTON INN GARDEN CITY**
1911 E Kansas (67846)
Rates: $48-$64;
Tel: (316) 275-7471

**NATIONAL 9 INN**
1502 E Fulton (67846)
Rates: $31-$42;
Tel: (316) 276-2304

**WINCHESTER INN**
1818 Commanche Dr (67846)
Rates: $26-$42;
Tel: (316) 275-5095

## GOODLAND

**BEST WESTERN
BUFFALO INN**
830 W Hwy 24 (67735)
Rates: $33-$55;
Tel: (913) 899-3621

**HOLIDAY INN**
Rt 1, Box 95 (67735)
Rates: $39-$62;
Tel: (913) 899-3644

**WINCHESTER INNS**
2520 Commerce Rd (67735)
Rates: N/A;
Tel: (913) 899-7566

## GREAT BEND

**BEST WESTERN
ANGUS INN**
2920 10th St (67530)
Rates: $30-$67;
Tel: (316) 792-3541

**INN 4 LESS**
4701 10th St (67530)
Rates: $29-$39;
Tel: (316) 792-8235

**HOLIDAY INN**
3017 W 10th St (67530)
Rates: $38-$80;
Tel: (316) 792-2431

**TRAVELERS BUDGET INN**
4200 W 10th St (67530)
Rates: $23-$31;
Tel: (316) 793-5448

## GREENSBURG

**BEST WESTERN
J-HAWK MOTEL**
515 W Kansas Ave (67054)
Rates: $34-$44;
Tel: (316) 723-2121

**KANSAN INN**
800 E Kansas Ave (67054)
Rates: $26-$41;
Tel: (316) 723-2141

## HAYS

**BEST WESTERN
VAGABOND MOTEL**
2524 Vine St (67601)
Rates: $38-$60;
Tel: (913) 625-2511

**BUDGET HOST VILLA**
810 E 8th (67601)
Rates: $21-$39;
Tel: (913) 625-2563

**DAYS INN**
3205 N Vine St (67601)
Rates: $35-$65;
Tel: (913) 628-8261

**HAMPTON INN**
3801 Vine St (67601)
Rates: $31-$75;
Tel: (913) 625-8103

**HOLIDAY INN**
3603 Vine St (67601)
Rates: $45-$100;
Tel: (913) 625-7371

## HIAWATHA

**HIAWATHA HEARTLAND
RESTAURANT & INN**
1100 S 1st (66434)
Rates: $35-$43;
Tel: (913) 742-7401

## HUTCHINSON

**BEST WESTERN
SUN DOME HOTEL**
11 Des Moines (67505)
Rates: $50-$55;
Tel: (316) 663-4444

**COMFORT INN**
1621 Super Plaza (67501)
Rates: $42-$53;
Tel: (316) 663-7822

**HOLIDAY INN**
1400 N Lorraine St (67501)
Rates: $55-$82;
Tel: (316) 669-9311

**QUALITY INN CITY CENTER**
15 W 4th St (67501)
Rates: $36-$55;
Tel: (316) 663-1211

## INDEPENDENCE

**APPLETREE INN**
201 N 8th St (67301)
Rates: $43-$53;
Tel: (316) 331-5500

**BEST WESTERN
PRAIRIE INN**
P.O. Box 26 (67301)
Rates: $36-$44;
Tel: (316) 331-7300

## JUNCTION CITY

**BEST WESTERN
JAYHAWK THIRD MOTEL**
110 E Flint Hills Blvd (66441)
Rates: $32-$42;
Tel: (913) 238-5188

**BUDGET HOST-
GOLDEN WHEAT INN**
820 S Washington St (66441)
Rates: $25-$40;
Tel: (913) 238-5106

**DAYS INN**
1024 S Washington St (66441)
Rates: $48-$55;
Tel: (913) 762-2727

**DREAMLAND MOTEL**
520 E Flint Hills Blvd (66441)
Rates: $24-$36;
Tel: (913) 238-1108

**ECONO LODGE**
211 E Flint Hills Blvd (66441)
Rates: $28-$39;
Tel: (913) 238-8181

**HARVEST INN**
1001 E 6th St (66441)
Rates: $40-$85;
Tel: (800) 762-0270

## KANSAS CITY

**BEST WESTERN INN**
501 Southwest Blvd (66103)
Rates: $44-$69;
Tel: (913) 677-3060

**CIVIC CENTRE HOTEL**
424 Minnesota Ave (66101)
Rates: $49-$125;
Tel: (800) 542-2983

## LARNED

**BEST WESTERN
TOWNSMAN MOTEL**
123 E 14th St (67550)
Rates: $35-$50;
Tel: (316) 285-3114

## LAWRENCE

**BEST WESTERN
HALLMARK INN**
730 Iowa St (66044)
Rates: $37-$47;
Tel: (913) 841-6500

**DAYS INN**
2309 Iowa St (66046)
Rates: $32-$60;
Tel: (913) 843-9100

**HOLIDAY INN**
200 McDonald Dr (66044)
Rates: $56-$86;
Tel: (913) 841-7077

**TRAVELODGE**
801 Iowa St (66044)
Rates: $30-$45;
Tel: (913) 842-5100

**WESTMINSTER INN**
2525 W 6th St (66049)
Rates: $30-$46;
Tel: (913) 841-8410

## LEAVENWORTH

**BEST WESTERN
HALLMARK INN**
3211 S 4th St (66048)
Rates: $35-$45;
Tel: (913) 651-6000

**COMMANDER'S INN**
6th and Metropolitan (66048)
Rates: $31-$75;
Tel: (913) 651-5800

**THE LANSING INN 4 LESS**
504 N Main (Lansing 66043)
Rates: $27-$39;
Tel: (913) 727-2777

**RAMADA INN
LEAVENWORTH**
101 S 3rd St (66048)
Rates: $37-$51;
Tel: (913) 651-5500

## LENEXA

**LA QUINTA INN**
9461 Lenexa Dr (66215)
Rates: $44-$67;
Tel: (913) 394-5500

## LIBERAL

**BEST WESTERN LAFONDA
MOTEL & RESTAURANT**
229 W Pancake Blvd (67901)
Rates: $34-$52;
Tel: (316) 624-5601

**GATEWAY INN**
720 E Pancake Blvd (67901)
Rates: $34-$42;
Tel: (316) 624-0242

**KANSAN MOTEL**
310 E Pancake Blvd (67901)
Rates: N/A;
Tel: (316) 624-7215

**LIBERAL INN**
603 E Pancake Blvd (67901)
Rates: $34-$48;
Tel: (316) 624-7254

**THUNDERBIRD INN**
2100 N Hwy 83 (67901)
Rates: $24-$29;
Tel: (316) 624-7271

**TRAVELERS LODGE**
564 E Pancake Blvd (67901)
Rates: $25-$35;
Tel: (316) 624-6203

## LINDSBORG

**CORONADO MOTEL**
305 N Harrison (67456)
Rates: N/A;
Tel: (913) 227-3943

## LYONS

**LYONS INN**
817 W Main (67554)
Rates: $27-$39;
Tel: (316) 257-3185

## MANHATTAN

**BEST WESTERN
CONTINENTAL INN**
100 Bluemont (66502)
Rates: $42-$58;
Tel: (913) 776-4771

**DAYS INN**
1501 Tuttle Creek Blvd
(66502)
Rates: $36-$52;
Tel: (913) 539-5391

**HOLIDAY INN/HOLIDOME**
530 Richards Dr (66502)
Rates: $67-$80;
Tel: (913) 539-5311

## MANKATO

**CREST-VUE MOTEL**
1/2 Mi East on US 36 (66956)
Rates: $25-$31;
Tel: (913) 378-3515

**DREAMLINER MOTEL**
RR 2, Box 8 (66956)
Rates: $26-$32;
Tel: (913) 378-3107

## MARYSVILLE

**BEST WESTERN
SURF MOTEL**
2105 Center Rd (66508)
Rates: $30-$48;
Tel: (913) 562-2354

**THUNDERBIRD MOTEL**
Hwy 36W (66508)
Rates: $28-$39;
Tel: (913) 562-2373

## MCPHERSON

**BEST WESTERN
HOLIDAY MANOR MOTEL**
2211 E Kansas Ave (67460)
Rates: $34-$44;
Tel: (316) 241-5343

**RED COACH INN**
2111 E Kansas Ave (67460)
Rates: $30-$48;
Tel: (316) 241-6960

## MEADE

**DALTON'S
BEDPOST MOTEL**
E Hwy 54 (67864)
Rates: $22-$32;
Tel: (316) 873-2131

## MEDICINE LODGE

**BEST WESTERN
COPA MOTEL**
401 W Fowler (67104)
Rates: $31-$39;
Tel: (316) 886-5673

## NEWTON

**BEST WESTERN
RED COACH INN**
P. O. Box 872 (67114)
Rates: $40-$70;
Tel: (316) 283-9120

**DAYS INN NEWTON**
105 Manchester (67114)
Rates: $36-$40;
Tel: (316) 283-3330

## NORTON

**BEST WESTERN
BROOKS MOTEL**
900 N State St (67654)
Rates: $33-$40;
Tel: (913) 877-3381

## OAKLEY

**BEST WESTERN
GOLDEN PLAINS MOTEL**
I-70 Exit 76 (67748)
Rates: $44-$54;
Tel: (913) 672-3254

**FIRST INTERSTATE INN
MOTEL**
P. O. Box 426 (67748)
Rates: $20-$39;
Tel: (913) 672-3204

**I-70 INN**
I-70 & Hwy 40 (67748)
Rates: N/A;
Tel: (913) 672-3203

**PRICE RIGHT MOTEL**
708 Center Ave (67748)
Rates: $28-$42;
Tel: (913) 672-3226

## OBERLIN

**FRONTIER MOTEL**
207 E Frontier Pkwy (67749)
Rates: $24-$40;
Tel: (913) 475-2203

## OLATHE

**BEST WESTERN
HALLMARK INN**
211 W Rawhide Dr (66061)
Rates: $38-$48;
Tel: (913) 782-4343

**ECONO LODGE**
209 Flaming Rd (66061)
Rates: $34-$42;
Tel: (913) 829-1312

**HOLIDAY INN**
101 W 151st St (66061)
Rates: $69-$87;
Tel: (913) 829-4000

## OTTAWA

**BEST WESTERN
HALLMARK INN**
2209 S Princeton St (66067)
Rates: $34-$52;
Tel: (913) 242-7000

**ECONO LODGE**
2331 S Cedar Rd (66067)
Rates: $34-$44;
Tel: (913) 242-3400

## OVERLAND PARK

**BEST WESTERN HALLMARK
INN EXECUTIVE CTR**
7000 W 108th St (66211)
Rates: $60-$95;
Tel: (913) 383-2550

**COMFORT INN**
6401 E Frontage Rd
(Merriam 66202)
Rates: $38-$56;
Tel: (913) 262-2622

**DOUBLETREE HOTEL**
10100 College Blvd (66210)
Rates: N/A;
Tel: (913) 451-6100

**DRURY INN**
10951 Metcalf (66210)
Rates: N/A;
Tel: (913) 345-1500

**HOLIDAY INN**
7240 Shawnee Mission Pkwy
(66202)
Rates: $71-$85;
Tel: (913) 262-3010

**MARRIOTT-
OVERLAND PARK**
10800 Metcalf (66212)
Rates: $122-$350;
Tel: (913) 451-8000

**RESIDENCE INN
BY MARRIOTT**
6300 W 110th St (66211)
Rates: $97-$140;
Tel: (913) 491-3333

**WHITE HAVEN MOTEL**
8039 Metcalf Ave (66204)
Rates: $33-$50;
Tel: (800) 752-2892

## PARSONS

**TOWNSMAN MOTEL**
P. O. Box 813 (67357)
Rates: $28-$41;
Tel: (800) 552-4008

## PITTSBURG

**SUNSET MOTEL**
RR 3, Box 737 (66762)
Rates: $21-$26;
Tel: (316) 231-3950

## PRATT

**BEST WESTERN
HILLCREST MOTEL**
1336 E 1st St (67124)
Rates: $32-$45;
Tel: (316) 672-6407

**BUDGET INN**
1631 E 1st St (67124)
Rates: $27-$37;
Tel: (316) 672-6468

**EVERGREEN INN**
Hwy 54W (67124)
Rates: $27-$36;
Tel: (800) 456-6424

**PRATT BUDGET INN**
1631 E 1st St (67124)
Rates: $26-$31;
Tel: (316) 672-6468

## SALINA

**BEST WESTERN
HEART OF AMERICA**
632 Westport Blvd (67401)
Rates: $38-$48;
Tel: (913) 827-9315

**BEST WESTERN
MID-AMERICA INN**
1846 N 9th St (67401)
Rates: $38-$48;
Tel: (913) 827-0356

## BUDGET INN VAGABOND MOTEL
217 S Broadway (67401)
Rates: $24-$38;
Tel: (913) 825-7265

## BUDGET KING MOTEL
809 N Broadway (67401)
Rates: $19-$27;
Tel: (913) 827-4477

## HOLIDAY INN
P. O. Box 796 (67401)
Rates: $42-$105;
Tel: (913) 823-1739

## HOWARD JOHNSON MOTEL
2403 S 9th St (67401)
Rates: $29-$39;
Tel: (913) 827-5511

## RAMADA INN
1949 N 9th St (67401)
Rates: $42-$52;
Tel: (913) 825-8211

## RED COACH INN
2020 W Crawford (67401)
Rates: $34-$54;
Tel: (913) 825-2111

## SENECA

## STARLITE MOTEL
410 North St (66538)
Rates: $21-$32;
Tel: (913) 336-2191

## SHARON SPRINGS

## HEYL'S TRAVELER MOTEL
Jct US 40 & KS27 (67758)
Rates: N/A;
Tel: (913) 852-4293

## SHAWNEE MISSION

## RED ROOF INN
6800 W 108th St (66211)
Rates: N/A;
Tel: (800) 843-7663

## SMITH CENTER

## MODERN AIRE MOTEL
117 W US 36 (66967)
Rates: $23-$40;
Tel: (800) 727-7332

## TOPEKA

## BEST WESTERN MEADOW ACRES MOTEL
2950 S Topeka Blvd (66611)
Rates: $34-$56;
Tel: (913) 267-1681

## COMFORT INN
1518 SW Wanamaker Rd (66604)
Rates: $39-$48;
Tel: (913) 273-5365

## DAYS INN
1510 SW Wanamaker Rd (66604)
Rates: $37-$48;
Tel: (913) 272-8538

## FAIRFIELD INN BY MARRIOTT
1530 SW Westport Dr (66604)
Rates: $41-$60;
Tel: (913) 273-6800

## HOLIDAY INN-CITY CENTRE
914 Madison Ave (66607)
Rates: $50-$56;
Tel: (913) 232-7721

## HOLIDAY INN-WEST
605 Fairlawn Rd (66606)
Rates: $50-$62;
Tel: (913) 272-8040

## HOWARD JOHNSON MOTEL
3839 S Topeka Blvd (66609)
Rates: $37-$95;
Tel: (913) 266-4700

## MOTEL 6
1224 SW Wanamaker Rd (66604)
Rates: $24-$30;
Tel: (913) 273-9888

## PLAZA INN MOTEL
3802 S Topeka Blvd (66609)
Rates: $42-$54;
Tel: (913) 266-8880

## RAMADA INN I-70
P. O. Box 1598 (66601)
Rates: $42-$250;
Tel: (913) 234-5400

## WAMEGO

## LINTON MOTEL
1215 W 24 Hwy (66547)
Rates: N/A;
Tel: (913) 456-2303

## WICHITA

## AIR CAP MOTEL
6075 Air Cap Dr (67219)
Rates: N/A;
Tel: (316) 744-2071

## BEST WESTERN RED COACH INN
915 E 53rd St N (67219)
Rates: $35-$52;
Tel: (316) 832-9387

## BEST WESTERN RIDGE PLAZA INN
600 S Holland (67209)
Rates: $45-$55;
Tel: (316) 722-8730

## BUDGET INN
1631 East First (67124)
Rates: N/A;
Tel: (316) 672-6468

## COMFORT INN
4849 S Laura (67216)
Rates: $46-$56;
Tel: (316) 522-1800

## COMFORT SUITES AIRPORT
658 Westdale (67209)
Rates: $64-$69;
Tel: (316) 945-2600

## ECONO LODGE
6245 W Kellogg (67209)
Rates: $34-$42;
Tel: (316) 945-5261

**HOLIDAY INN-EAST**
7335 E Kellogg (67207)
Rates: $54-$79;
Tel: (316) 685-1281

**HOLIDAY INN
WICHITA/AIRPORT**
5500 W Kellogg (67209)
Rates: $67-$83;
Tel: (316) 943-2181

**LA QUINTA MOTOR INN**
7700 E Kellogg (67207)
Rates: $46-$61;
Tel: (316) 681-2881

**MARRIOTT
WICHITA HOTEL**
9100 Corporate Hills Dr
(67207)
Rates: $99-$275;
Tel: (316) 651-0333

**RESIDENCE INN
BY MARRIOTT**
411 S Webb Rd (67207)
Rates: $89-$109;
Tel: (316) 686-7331

**RESIDENCE INN
BY MARRIOTT**
120 W Orme St (67213)
Rates: $79-$109;
Tel: (316) 263-1061

**SANDS MOTEL**
8401 Hwy 54W (67209)
Rates: $23-$32;
Tel: (316) 722-4221

**WICHITA ROYALE HOTEL**
125 N Market St (67202)
Rates: $74-$250;
Tel: (800) 876-0240

# KENTUCKY

## ASHLAND

**DAYS INN**
12700 SR 180 (41101)
Rates: $34-$50;
Tel: (606) 928-3600

**KNIGHTS INN**
7216 US 60 (41102)
Rates: $37-$42;
Tel: (606) 928-9501

**WESTERN HILLS
MOTOR LODGE**
3466 13th St (41102)
Rates: N/A;
Tel: (606) 325-2375

## AUBURN

**AUBURN GUEST HOUSE**
421 W Main St (42206)
Rates: N/A;
Tel: (502) 542-6019

## AURORA

**CEDAR LANE RESORT**
Hwy 68, Rt 1, Box 520
(42048)
Rates: N/A;
Tel: (502) 474-8042

**EARLY AMERICAN MOTEL**
Hwy 68, Rt 1 (42048)
Rates: $26-$49;
Tel: (502) 474-2241

**FIN 'N' FEATHER**
Rt 1, Hwy 68 (42048)
Rates: N/A;
Tel: (502) 474-2351

## BARDSTOWN

**BARDSTOWN-
PARKVIEW MOTEL**
418 E Stephen Foster Ave
(40004)
Rates: $32-$48;
Tel: (502) 348-5983

**HOLIDAY INN
CONVENTION CENTER**
P. O. Box 520 (40004)
Rates: $58-$70;
Tel: (502) 348-9253

**OLD KENTUCKY
HOME MOTEL**
414 W Stephen Foster Ave
(40004)
Rates: $31-$45;
Tel: (502) 348-5979

## BENTON

**COZY COVE RESORT**
Rt 5, Box 534 (42025)
Rates: $199-$898;
Tel: (502) 354-8168

**SOUTHERN KOMFORT**
Rt 4, Box 348 (42025)
Rates: N/A;
Tel: (502) 354-6422

## BEREA

**BOONE TAVERN HOTEL-
BEREA COLLEGE**
CPO Box 2345 (40404)
Rates: $52-$79;
Tel: (606) 986-9358

**DAYS INN/EXIT 77**
1202 Walnut Meadow Rd
(40403)
Rates: $35-$49;
Tel: (606) 986-7373

**ECONO LODGE**
P. O. Box 183 (40403)
Rates: $27-$45;
Tel: (606) 986-9323

**RED CARPET INN**
Rt 3 (40403)
Rates: $27-$38;
Tel: (606) 986-8426

## BOWLING GREEN

**BUDGETEL INN**
165 Three Springs Rd (42104)
Rates: $34-$49;
Tel: (502) 843-3200

**HOLIDAY INN I-65**
3240 Scottsville Rd (42104)
Rates: $49-$90;
Tel: (502) 781-1500

**HOWARD JOHNSON HOTEL**
523 US 31 W Bypass (42101)
Rates: $44-$58;
Tel: (502) 842-9453

**NEW'S INN OF BOWLING GREEN**
3160 Scottsville Rd (42104)
Rates: $32-$36;
Tel. (502) 781-3460

**RAMADA INN**
4767 Scottsville Rd (42104)
Rates: $34-$70;
Tel: (502) 781-3000

## CADIZ

**COUNTRY INN BY CARLSTON**
5909 Hopkinsville Rd (42211)
Rates: $39-$49;
Tel: (502) 522-7007

## CARROLLTON

**BLUE GABLES COURT**
1501 Highland Ave (41008)
Rates: $26-$30;
Tel: (502) 732-4248

**DAYS INN**
RR 3, Box 108 (41008)
Rates: $42-$48;
Tel: (502) 732-9301

**HOLIDAY INN CARROLLTON**
RR 3, Box 108 (41008)
Rates: $36-$52;
Tel: (502) 732-6661

## CAVE CITY

**CAVE LAND MOTEL**
451 Dixie Hwy (42127)
Rates: $18-$36;
Tel: (502) 773-2321

**DAYS INN CAVE CITY**
822 Mammoth Cave St (42127)
Rates: $26-$56;
Tel. (502) 773-2151

**HERITAGE INN**
Box 2048 (42127)
Rates: $25-$62;
Tel: (800) 264-1514

**JOLLY'S MOTEL**
P. O. Box 327 (42127)
Rates: $15-$27;
Tel: (502) 773-3118

**QUALITY INN**
P. O. Box 547 (42127)
Rates: $26-$62;
Tel: (502) 773-2181

## CORBIN

**BEST WESTERN-CORBIN INN**
2630 Cumberland Falls Rd (40701)
Rates: $32-$49;
Tel: (606) 528-2100

**DAYS INN**
1860 Falls Hwy (40701)
Rates: $27-$36;
Tel: (606) 528-8150

**HOLIDAY INN**
2615 Cumberland Falls Hwy (40701)
Rates: $48-$62;
Tel: (606) 528-6301

**KNIGHTS INN**
Rte 11, Box 256 (40701)
Rates: $32-$50;
Tel: (606) 523-1500

**SUBURBAN MOTEL**
1320 Cumberland Falls Hwy (40701)
Rates: N/A;
Tel: (606) 528-1370

**SUPER 8 MOTEL**
P. O. Box 256-A1 (40701)
Rates: $31-$38;
Tel: (606) 528-8888

## CORINTH

**K & T MOTEL**
Hwy 330 & I-75 Exit 144 (41010)
Rates: N/A;
Tel: (506) 824-4371

## COVINGTON

**EMBASSY SUITES AT RIVERCENTER**
10 E Rivercenter Blvd (41011)
Rates: $119-$139;
Tel: (606) 261-8400

**ENVOY INN**
8075 Stellen Dr (Florence 41042)
Rates: $27-$35;
Tel: (606) 283-2030

**HOLIDAY INN-SOUTH**
2100 Dixie Hwy (Ft. Mitchell 41011)
Rates: $65-$85;
Tel: (606) 331-1500

**KNIGHTS INN**
8049 Dream St (Florence 41042)
Rates: $32-$42;
Tel: (606) 371-9711

## DANVILLE

**HOLIDAY INN**
Danville Bypass (40422)
Rates: $46-$52;
Tel: (606) 236-8600

## EDDYVILLE

**HOLIDAY HILLS TOWNHOUSES**
Rt 1, Box 406 (42038)
Rates: $100;
Tel: (502) 388-7236

## ELIZABETHTOWN

**BEST WESTERN CARDINAL INN**
642 E Dixie Hwy (42701)
Rates: $26-$50;
Tel: (502) 765-6139

**COMFORT INN**
1043 Executive Dr (42701)
Rates: $39-$64;
Tel: (502) 769-3030

**HOWARD JOHNSON COMMONWEALTH LODGE**
708 E Dixie Hwy (42701)
Rates: $34-$38;
Tel: (502) 765-2185

**LINCOLN TRAIL MOTEL**
905 N Mulberry St (42701)
Rates: $19-$25;
Tel: (502) 769-1301

**THE OLDE BETHLEHEM ACADEMY INN**
7051 St John Rd (42701)
Rates: $65;
Tel: (502) 862-9003

**TOWNE INN**
2009 N Mulberry (42701)
Rates: $26-$31;
Tel: (502) 765-4166

## FRANKFORT

**ANCHOR INN**
790 E Main (40601)
Rates: N/A;
Tel: (502) 227-7404

**BLUEGRASS INN**
635 Versailles Rd (40601)
Rates: $32-$40;
Tel: (502) 695-1800

## GEORGETOWN

**DAYS INN**
Jct Delaplain Rd & I-75, Exit 129 (40324)
Rates: $28-$45;
Tel: (502) 863-5000

**RAMADA LIMITED-GEORGETOWN**
P. O. Box 926 (40324)
Rates: $31-$36;
Tel: (502) 863-1166

**SHONEY'S INN-GEORGETOWN**
200 Shoney Dr (40324)
Rates: $39-$44;
Tel: (502) 868-9800

## GIBERTSVILLE

**MOORS RESORT**
Hwy 963 (42044)
Rates: N/A;
Tel: (800) 626-5472

**RAMADA INN RESORT AT KY DAM/CALVERT CITY**
P. O. Box 158 (42044)
Rates: $42-$77;
Tel: (502) 362-4278

## GLASGOW

**GLASGOW INN**
P. O. Box 353 (42142)
Rates: $40-$68;
Tel: (502) 651-5191

## GRAND RIVERS

**BEST WESTERN KENTUCKY-BARKLEY LAKES INN**
P. O. Box 280 (42045)
Rates: $31-$50;
Tel: (502) 928-2700

## HENDERSON

**DAYS INN**
2044 US 41N (42420)
Rates: $39-$60;
Tel: (502) 826-6600

**SCOTTISH INNS**
2820 US 41N (42420)
Rates: $25-$35;
Tel: (502) 827-1806

## HOPKINSVILLE

**HOLIDAY INN**
2910 Fort Campbell Blvd (42240)
Rates: $43-$67;
Tel: (502) 886-4413

**HOPKINSVILLE BEST WESTERN**
4101 Fort Campbell Blvd (42240)
Rates: $39-$43;
Tel: (502) 886-9000

## HORSE CAVE

**BUDGET HOST INN**
P. O. Box 332 (42749)
Rates: $18-$36;
Tel: (502) 786-2165

## KENLAKE STATE RESORT PARK

**EARLY AMERICAN MOTEL**
Rt 1 (Hardin 42048)
Rates: $30-$58;
Tel: (502) 474-2241

## LEBANON

**HOLLYHILL MOTEL**
459 Main St (40033)
Rates: N/A;
Tel: (502) 692-2175

## LEITCHFIELD

**COUNTRY SIDE INN**
Commerce Dr & W KY Pkwy (42754)
Rates: $29-$41;
Tel: (502) 259-4021

## LEXINGTON

**DAYS INN-SOUTH**
5575 Athens-Boonesboro Rd
(40509)
Rates: $32-$43;
Tel: (606) 263-3100

**ECONO LODGE**
5527 Athens-Boonesboro Rd
(40509)
Rates: $30-$40;
Tel: (606) 263-4101

**GREENLEAF MOTEL**
2280 Nicholasville Rd (40503)
Rates: $39-$48;
Tel. (606) 277-1191

**HOLIDAY INN
LEXINGTON SOUTH**
5532 Athens-Boonesboro Rd
(40509)
Rates: $57-$67;
Tel: (606) 263-5241

**HOLIDAY INN-NORTH**
1950 Newtown Pike (40511)
Rates: $84-$89;
Tel: (606) 233-0512

**THE KENTUCKY INN**
525 Waller Ave (40504)
Rates: $46-$52;
Tel: (606) 254-1177

**KNIGHTS INN**
1935 Stanton Way (40511)
Rates: $33-$44;
Tel: (800) 843-5644

**LA QUINTA MOTOR INN**
1919 Stanton Way (40511)
Rates: $38-$58;
Tel: (606) 231-7551

**MARRIOTT'S
GRIFFIN GATE RESORT**
1800 Newtown Pike (40511)
Rates: $125-$150;
Tel: (606) 231-5100

**QUALITY INN NORTHWEST**
1050 Newtown Pike (40511)
Rates: $35-$48;
Tel: (606) 233-0561

**RED ROOF INN-NORTH**
483 Haggard Ln (40505)
Rates: $28-$38;
Tel: (606) 293-2626

**RED ROOF INN-SOUTH**
2651 Wilhite Dr (40503)
Rates: $34-$44;
Tel. (606) 277-9400

**RESIDENCE INN
BY MARRIOTT**
1080 Newtown Pike (40511)
Rates: $112-$150;
Tel: (606) 231-6191

**SAVE INN LEXINGTON**
2250 Elkhorn Rd (40505)
Rates: $32-$38;
Tel. (606) 299-8481

**SPRINGS INN**
2020 Harrodsburg Rd (40503)
Rates: $38-$48;
Tel: (606) 277-5751

**TRAVELODGE**
1987 N Broadway (40505)
Rates: $32-$49;
Tel: (606) 299-1202

**WILSON INN**
2400 Buena Vista Dr (40505)
Rates: $37-$53;
Tel: (606) 293-6113

## LONDON

**BEST WESTERN
HARVEST INN**
West 80, Box 207 (40741)
Rates: $46-$55;
Tel: (606) 864-2222

**DAYS INN**
285 W Hwy 80 (40741)
Rates: $32-$52;
Tel: (606) 878-9800

**WESTGATE INN MOTEL**
254 W Daniel Boone Pkwy
(40741)
Rates: $29-$33;
Tel: (606) 878-7330

## LOUISVILLE
(and Vicinity)

**BRECKINRIDGE INN**
2800 Breckinridge Ln (40220)
Rates: $52-$55;
Tel: (502) 456-5050

**DAYS INN CENTRAL**
1620 Arthur St (40217)
Rates: $35-$65;
Tel: (502) 626-3781

**DAYS INN EAST**
4621 Shelbyville Rd (40207)
Rates: $38-$56;
Tel: (502) 896-8871

**EXECUTIVE INN**
978 Phillips Ln (40213)
Rates: $58-$68;
Tel: (502) 367-6161

**EXECUTIVE WEST**
830 Phillips Ln (40209)
Rates: $64-$74;
Tel: (502) 367-2251

**HOLIDAY INN
I-264 AIRPORT EAST**
1465 Gardiner Ln (40213)
Rates: $60-$72;
Tel: (502) 452-6361

**HOLIDAY INN-
LOUISVILLE/DOWNTOWN**
120 W Broadway (40202)
Rates: $55-$91;
Tel: (502) 582-2241

**HOLIDAY INN
SOUTH-AIRPORT**
3317 Fern Valley Rd (40213)
Rates: $67-$83;
Tel: (502) 964-3311

**HURSTBOURNE HOTEL
& CONFERENCE CTR**
9700 Bluegrass Pkwy (40299)
Rates: $70-$80;
Tel: (502) 491-4830

**KNIGHTS INN EAST**
1850 Embassy Sq Blvd
(40299)
Rates: N/A;
Tel: (800) 843-5644

**MELROSE INN & MOTEL**
13306 US 42 (Prospect
40059)
Rates: $20-$42;
Tel: (502) 228-1136

**QUALITY HOTEL**
100 E Jefferson St (40202)
Rates: $52-$57;
Tel: (502) 582-2481

**THE RADISSON HOTEL
LOUISVILLE EAST**
1903 Embassy Sq Blvd
(40299)
Rates: $82-$108;
Tel: (502) 499-6220

**RAMADA INN**
4805 Brownsboro Rd (40207)
Rates: $49-$77;
Tel: (502) 893-2551

**RED ROOF INN-AIRPORT**
4704 Preston Hwy (40213)
Rates: $28-$48;
Tel: (502) 968-0151

**RED ROOF INN-EAST**
9330 Blairwood Rd (40222)
Rates: $28-$49;
Tel: (502) 426-7621

**RED ROOF INN-
SOUTHEAST**
3322 Newburg Rd (40218)
Rates: $28-$45;
Tel: (502) 456-2993

**RESIDENCE INN
BY MARRIOTT**
120 Hurstbourne Pkwy
(40222)
Rates: $107-$135;
Tel: (502) 425-1821

**SEELBACH HOTEL**
500 Fourth Ave (40202)
Rates: $119-$495;
Tel: (800) 333-3399

**SUPER 8 MOTEL**
4800 Preston Hwy (40213)
Rates: $37-$47;
Tel: (502) 968-0088

**THRIFTY DUTCHMAN
MOTEL**
3357 Fern Valley Rd (40213)
Rates: $30-$42;
Tel: (502) 968-8124

**WILSON INN
LOUISVILLE AIRPORT**
3209 Kemmons Dr (40218)
Rates: $37-$53;
Tel: (502) 473-0000

**WILSON INN
LOUISVILLE EAST**
9802 Bunsen Way (40299)
Rates: $37-$53;
Tel: (502) 499-0000

## MADISONVILLE

**BEST WESTERN
PENNYRILE INN**
P. O. Box 612
(Mortons Gap 42440)
Rates: $30-$38;
Tel: (502) 258-5201

**DAYS INN**
1900 Lantaff Blvd (42431)
Rates: $39-$100;
Tel: (502) 821-8620

## MAMMOTH CAVE NATIONAL PARK

**MAMMOTH CAVE HOTEL**
11 Mi W of Jct I-65 & SR 70
(42259)
Rates: $35-$70;
Tel: (502) 758-2225

## MIDDLESBORO

**BEST WESTERN INN**
1623 E Cumberland Ave
(40965)
Rates: $31-$39;
Tel: (606) 248-5630

## MOUNT VERNON

**BEST WESTERN
KASTLE INN MOTEL**
P. O. Box 637 (40456)
Rates: $32-$38;
Tel: (606) 256-5156

**ECONO LODGE**
P. O. Box 1106 (40456)
Rates: $30-$46;
Tel: (606) 256-4621

## MULDRAUGH

**GOLDEN MANOR MOTEL**
346 Dixie Hwy (40155)
Rates: $33-$42;
Tel: (606) 942-2800

## MURRAY

**HOLIDAY INN**
Rt 4, Box 3 (42071)
Rates: $38-$49;
Tel: (502) 753-5986

**MURRAY PLAZA COURT**
P. O. Box 385 (42071)
Rates: $25-$31;
Tel: (502) 753-2682

**PARADISE RESORT**
Rt 6, Box 239 (42071)
Rates: N/A;
Tel: (502) 436-2767

**SHONEY'S INN**
1503 N 12th St (42071)
Rates: $40-$44;
Tel: (502) 753-5353

## NEW CONCORD

**MISSING HILL RESORT**
HC Box 215-A (42076)
Rates: N/A;
Tel: (502) 436-5519

## OWENSBORO

**DAYS INN**
3720 New Hartford Rd
(42301)
Rates: $35-$39;
Tel: (502) 684-9621

**HOLIDAY INN**
P. O. Box 1401 (42301)
Rates: $51-$55;
Tel: (502) 685-3941

**OWENSBORO
SUPER 8 MOTEL**
1027 Goetz Dr (42301)
Rates: $36-$44;
Tel: (502) 685-3388

## PADUCAH

**BEST INNS OF AMERICA**
P. O. Box 9586 (42002)
Rates: $36-$44;
Tel: (502) 442-3334

**DAYS INN**
3901 Hinkleville Rd (42001)
Rates: $38-$46;
Tel: (502) 442-7501

**DAYS INN**
P. O. Box 9246 (42002)
Rates: $36-$64;
Tel: (502) 443-3313

**FARLEY PLACE
BED & BREAKFAST**
166 Farley Pl (42003)
Rates: N/A;
Tel: (502) 442-2488

**HICKORY HOUSE MOTEL**
2504 Bridge St (42003)
Rates: N/A;
Tel: (502) 442-1601

**QUALITY INN**
1380 Irvin Cobb Dr (42001)
Rates: $32-$40;
Tel: (502) 443-8751

**ROYAL INN**
2160 S Beltline (42003)
Rates: N/A;
Tel: (502) 442-6171

**THRIFTY INN**
I-24 & US 60 (42001)
Rates: $36-$45;
Tel: (502) 442-4500

## PAINTSVILLE

**HEART O'HIGHLANDS
MOTEL**
1/2 Mi S on US 23 (41240)
Rates: $32-$38;
Tel. (606) 789-3551

## PARKERS LAKE

**HOLIDAY MOTOR LODGE**
Hwy 90, Box 300 (42634)
Rates: N/A;
Tel: (606) 376-2732

## PROSPECT

**MELROSE MOTEL**
13306 US Hwy 42 (40059)
Rates: N/A;
Tel: (502) 228-1136

## RADCLIFF

**ECONO LODGE**
261 N Dixie Hwy (40160)
Rates: $33-$41;
Tel: (502) 351-4488

**FORT KNOX INN**
1400 N Dixie Hwy (40160)
Rates: N/A;
Tel: (502) 351-3199

**QUALITY INN**
438 S Dixie Blvd (40160)
Rates: $40-$50;
Tel: (502) 351-8211

**SUPER 8 MOTEL**
395 Redmar Blvd (40160)
Rates: $34-$39;
Tel: (502) 352-1888

## RICHMOND

**DAYS INN**
2109 Belmont Dr (40475)
Rates: $34-$41;
Tel: (606) 624-5769

**HOLIDAY INN**
100 Eastern Bypass (40475)
Rates: $45-$57;
Tel: (606) 623-9220

**SAVE INN**
1688 Northgate Dr (40475)
Rates: $29-$36;
Tel: (606) 624-2612

**THRIFTY DUTCHMAN MOTEL**
230 Eastern Bypass (40475)
Rates: $28;
Tel: (606) 623-8813

**WISE MOTEL**
105 N Killarney Ln (40475)
Rates: $31-$32;
Tel: (606) 623-8126

## RICHWOOD

**DAYS INN**
11177 Frontage Rd
(Walton 41094)
Rates: $30-$40;
Tel: (606) 485-4151

**RED CARPET-
FOUNTAIN INN**
11165 Frontage Rd
(Walton 41094)
Rates: $32-$40;
Tel: (606) 485-4123

**RICHWOOD MOTEL**
10805 Dixie Hwy (41094)
Rates: N/A;
Tel: (606) 525-9525

## SHELBYVILLE

**DAYS INN**
101 Howard Dr (40065)
Rates: $39-$45;
Tel: (502) 633-4005

**SHELBYVILLE MOTEL**
Box 378 Hwy US 60 (40065)
Rates: N/A;
Tel: (502) 533-3350

## SHEPHERDSVILLE

**BEST WESTERN SOUTH**
P. O. Box 98 (40165)
Rates: $36-$45;
Tel: (502) 543-7097

**TRAVELODGE**
P. O. Box 248 (40165)
Rates: $39-$45;
Tel: (502) 543-4400

## SOMERSET

**CUMBERLAND MOTEL**
6050 S Hwy 27 (42501)
Rates: N/A;
Tel: (606) 561-5131

## SPRINGFIELD

**GLENMAR PLANTATION
BED & BREAKFAST**
Rt 1, Box 682 (40069)
Rates: $75;
Tel: (606) 284-7791

## TAYLORSVILLE

**BOWLING'S VILLA
BED & BREAKFAST**
Rt 4, Box 140, Hwy 44
(40071)
Rates: N/A;
Tel: (502) 477-2636

## WALTON

**DAYS INN**
Rt 2, Box 85 (41094)
Rates: $32-$48;
Tel: (606) 485-4151

## WEST SOMERSET

**BECKETT MOTEL**
2001 Lees Ford Dock (42564)
Rates: N/A;
Tel: (606) 636-6411

## WILLIAMSBURG

**BEST WESTERN
CONVENIENT MOTOR
LODGE**
P. O. Box 204 (40769)
Rates: $29-$37;
Tel: (606) 549-1500

**HOLIDAY INN**
Rt 4, Box 712 (40769)
Rates: $36;
Tel: (606) 549-3450

## WILLIAMSTOWN

**DAYS INN**
211 SR 36W (41097)
Rates: $29-$42;
Tel: (606) 824-5025

**HOJO INN**
10 Skyway Dr (41097)
Rates: $27-$38;
Tel: (606) 824-7177

## WINCHESTER

**HOLIDAY INN**
1100 Holiday Dr (40391)
Rates: $44-$50;
Tel: (606) 744-9111

# LOUISIANA

## ALEXANDRIA

**BEST WESTERN
OF ALEXANDRIA**
2720 W MacArthur Dr
(71303)
Rates: $45-$51;
Tel: (318) 445-5530

**DAYS INN**
2300 N MacArthur Dr (71303)
Rates: $35-$49;
Tel: (318) 443-7331

**HOLIDAY INN**
2716 N MacArthur Dr (71303)
Rates: $50-$55;
Tel: (318) 487-4261

**RODEWAY INN**
742 MacArthur Dr (71303)
Rates: $37-$55;
Tel: (318) 448-1611

**TRAVELODGE**
1146 MacArthur Dr (71303)
Rates: $37-$43;
Tel: (318) 443-1841

## BASTROP

**COMFORT INN**
1815 E Madison (71220)
Rates: $32-$36;
Tel: (318) 281-8100

## BATON ROUGE

**BEST WESTERN CHATEAU
LOUISIANNE SUITE**
710 N Lobdell Ave (70806)
Rates: $64-$74;
Tel: (504) 927-6700

**BUDGETEL INN**
10555 Rieger Rd (70809)
Rates: $33-$49;
Tel: (504) 291-6600

**HOLIDAY INN-SOUTH**
9940 Airline Hwy (70816)
Rates: $58-$83;
Tel: (504) 924-7021

**LA QUINTA MOTEL**
2333 S Acadian Thruway
(70808)
Rates: $49-$59;
Tel: (504) 924-9600

**QUALITY INN
SHERWOOD FOREST**
10920 Mead Rd (70816)
Rates: $44-$55;
Tel: (504) 293-9370

**RAMADA HOTEL**
1480 Nicholson Dr (70820)
Rates: $49-$89;
Tel: (504) 387-1111

**RED ROOF INN**
11314 Boardwalk Dr (70816)
Rates: $30-$43;
Tel: (504) 275-6600

## BOSSIER CITY

**SHERATON-BOSSIER INN**
2015 Old Minden Rd (71111)
Rates: $42-$145;
Tel: (318) 742-9700

# DE RIDDER

**BEST WESTERN
DE RIDDER INN**
1311 N Pine (70634)
Rates: $36-$40;
Tel: (318) 462-3665

**PARK MOTEL**
806 N Pine (70634)
Rates: $26-$43;
Tel: (318) 463-8605

# FRANKLIN

**BEST WESTERN
FOREST MOTEL**
P. O. Box 1069 (70538)
Rates: $42-$56;
Tel: (318) 828-1810

# HOUMA

**HOLIDAY INN-HOLIDOME**
210 S Hollywood Rd (70360)
Rates: $42-$60;
Tel: (504) 868-5851

**PLANTATION INN
OF HOUMA**
1381 W Tunnel Blvd (70360)
Rates: $29-$39;
Tel: (504) 868-0500

# JACKSON

**ASPHODEL INN**
Rt 2, Box 89A (70748)
Rates: $55 $130;
Tel: (504) 654-6868

# LAFAYETTE

**BOIS DES CHENES INN
BED & BREAKFAST**
338 N Sterling (70501)
Rates: $75-$105;
Tel: (318) 233-7816

**LA QUINTA MOTOR INN**
2100 NE Evangeline Thruway
(70501)
Rates: $47-$64;
Tel: (318) 233-5610 •

**RAMADA INN AIRPORT**
2501 SE Evangeline Thruway
(70508)
Rates: $43-$51;
Tel: (318) 234-8521

**RED ROOF INN**
1718 N University Ave
(70507)
Rates: $28-$36;
Tel: (318) 233-3339

**SUPER 8 MOTEL**
2224 NE Evangeline Thruway
(70501)
Rates: $26-$33;
Tel: (318) 232-8826

# LAKE CHARLES

**CHATEAU CHARLES MOTEL**
P. O.Box 1381 (70601)
Rates: $46-$76;
Tel: (318) 433 5213

**DAYS INN**
1010 Hwy 171N (70601)
Rates: $35-$41;
Tel: (318) 433-1711

# MANSFIELD

**BEST WESTERN-THE INN**
1055 Washington Ave (71052)
Rates: $33-$41;
Tel: (318) 872-5034

# MINDEN

**EXACTA INN**
Box 882 (71055)
Rates: $30-$63;
Tel: (318) 377-3200

# MONROE

**BEST WESTERN
MONROE MOTOR LODGE**
610 Lea Joyner, Civic Ctr Expy
(71201)
Rates: $35-$50;
Tel: (318) 323-4451

**COMFORT INN**
5650 Frontage Rd (71202)
Rates: $36-$44;
Tel: (318) 345-2220

**DAYS INN**
2102 Louisville Ave (71201)
Rates: $36-$50;
Tel: (318) 325-5851

**ECONO LODGE**
1311 State Farm Dr (71201)
Rates: $35-$48;
Tel: (318) 387-7333

**HOLIDAY INN-CIVIC CENTER**
P. O. Box 7860 (71203)
Rates: $56-$62;
Tel: (318) 387-5100

**HOLIDAY INN I-20 WEST**
P. O.Box 1766
(West Monroe 71294)
Rates: $39-$51;
Tel: (318) 388-3810

**HOLIDAY INN-
PROFESSIONAL CENTRE/
ATRIUM**
2001 Louisville Ave (71201)
Rates: $64-$77;
Tel: (318) 325-0641

**LA QUINTA MOTOR INN**
1035 US 165S Bypass
(71203)
Rates: $47-$64;
Tel: (318) 322-3900

**RED ROOF INN**
P. O. Box 1803
(West Monroe 71292)
Rates: $28-$35;
Tel: (318) 388-2420

# NATCHITOCHES

**HOLIDAY INN**
P. O.Box 2249 (71457)
Rates: $40-$85;
Tel: (318) 357-8281

**SUPER 8 MOTEL**
801 Hwy 1 & Bypass 3110
(71457)
Rates: $28-$34;
Tel: (318) 352-1700

# NEW IBERIA

**BEST WESTERN
OF NEW IBERIA**
2700 Center St (70560)
Rates: $48-$80;
Tel: (318) 364-3030

# NEW ORLEANS
(and Vicintiy)

**BEST WESTERN PATIO
DOWNTOWN MOTEL**
2820 Tulane Ave (70119)
Rates: $39-$75;
Tel: (504) 822-0200

**BEST WESTERN
WESTBANK HOTEL**
1700 Lapalco Blvd
(Harvey 70058)
Rates: $46-$55;
Tel: (504) 366-5369

**CLARION HOTEL**
1500 Canal St (70112)
Rates: N/A;
Tel: (504) 522-4500

**DAUPHINE
ORLEANS HOTEL**
415 Dauphine St (70112)
Rates: $74-$160;
Tel: (504) 586-1800

**DAYS INN
NEW ORLEANS AIRPORT**
1300 Veterans Blvd
(Kenner 70062)
Rates: $35-$45;
Tel: (504) 469-2531

**FRENCH QUARTER
MAISONNETTES**
1130 Chartres St (70116)
Rates: $45-$60;
Tel: (504) 524-9918

**HOLIDAY INN-EAST HIGHRISE**
6324 Chef Menteur Hwy
(70126)
Rates: $58-$95;
Tel: (504) 241-2900

**LA QUINTA INN
WEST BANK**
50 Terry Pkwy (Gretna 70056)
Rates: $52-$69;
Tel: (504) 368-5600

**NEW ORLEANS AIRPORT
HILTON & CONV CTR**
P. O. Box 340 (70063)
Rates: $104-$140;
Tel: (504) 469-5000

**NEW ORLEANS HILTON
RIVERSIDE & TOWERS**
Poydras St/Mississippi River
(70140)
Rates: $185-$255;
Tel: (504) 561-0500

**QUALITY INN MARINA**
5353 Paris Rd, LA 47
(Chalmette 70043)
Rates: $39-$95;
Tel: (504) 277-5353

**QUALITY INN MIDTOWN**
3900 Tulane Ave (70119)
Rates: $45-$225;
Tel: (504) 486-5541

# RAYVILLE

**COTTONLAND INN**
P. O. Box 29 (71269)
Rates: $24-$33;
Tel: (318) 728-5985

# RUSTON

**HOLIDAY INN**
P. O. Box 1189 (71270)
Rates: $43-$108;
Tel: (318) 255-5901

# ST. FRANCISVILLE

**RAMADA INN-ST. FRANCIS**
P. O. Box 440 (70775)
Rates: $50-$60;
Tel: (504) 635-3821

# SHREVEPORT

**DAYS INN**
4935 W Monkhouse Dr
(71109)
Rates: $23-$40;
Tel: (318) 636-0080

**DAYS INN-BOSSIER**
200 John Wesley Blvd
(Bossier City 71112)
Rates: $23-$40;
Tel: (318) 742-9200

**ECONO LODGE**
4911 Monkhouse Dr (71109)
Rates: $26-$42;
Tel: (318) 636-0771

**LA QUINTA MOTOR INN**
309 Preston Blvd
(Bossier City 71111)
Rates: $47-$64;
Tel: (318) 747-4400

**RAMADA INN**
150 Hamilton Rd (71111)
Rates: $44-$58;
Tel: (318) 746-8410

**RAMADA INN AIRPORT**
5116 Monkhouse Dr (71109)
Rates: $48-$67;
Tel: (318) 635-7531

**RED ROOF INN**
7296 Greenwood Rd (71119)
Rates: $26-$34;
Tel: (318) 938-5342

**THE RESIDENCE INN
BY MARRIOTT**
1001 Gould Dr
(Bossier City 71111)
Rates: $75-$95;
Tel: (318) 747-6220

# SLIDELL

**BUDGET HOST SLIDELL**
1662 Gause Blvd (70458)
Rates: $30-$45;
Tel: (504) 641-8800

**RAMADA INN OF SLIDELL**
798 E I-10 Service Rd (70461)
Rates: $36-$55;
Tel: (504) 653-9960

# SULPHUR

**LA QUINTA MOTOR INN**
2600 S Ruth St (70663)
Rates: $47-$64;
Tel: (318) 527-8303

# THIBODAUX

**HOWARD JOHNSON
MOTEL**
P. O. Box 1144 (70302)
Rates: $38-$75;
Tel: (504) 447-9071

# MAINE

## AUGUSTA

**BEST WESTERN
SENATOR INN**
284 Western Ave (04330)
Rates: $58-$88;
Tel: (207) 622-5804

## BANGOR

**AIRPORT HILTON INN**
308 Godfrey Blvd (04401)
Rates: $72-$127;
Tel: (207) 947-6721

**BEST WESTERN
WHITE HOUSE**
155 Littlefield Ave (04401)
Rates: $44-$74;
Tel: (207) 862-3737

**BREWER MOTOR INN**
359 Wilson St (Brewer 04412)
Rates: $35-$65;
Tel: (207) 989-4476

**COMFORT INN**
750 Hogan Rd (04401)
Rates: $45-$79;
Tel: (207) 942-7899

**DAYS INN**
250 Odlin Rd (04401)
Rates: $48-$70;
Tel: (207) 942-8272

**ECONO LODGE**
482 Odlin Rd (04401)
Rates: $38-$79;
Tel: (207) 942-6301

**ECONO LODGE**
448 Wilson St (Brewer 04412)
Rates: $38-$79;
Tel: (207) 989-3200

**HILTON-
BANGOR AIRPORT**
308 Godfrey Blvd (04401)
Rates: $85-$119;
Tel: (207) 947-6721

**HOLIDAY INN-
MAIN STREET**
500 Main St (04401)
Rates: $66-$150;
Tel: (207) 947-8651

**HOLIDAY INN-
ODLIN ROAD**
404 Odlin Rd (04401)
Rates: $66-$130;
Tel: (207) 947-0101

**MOTEL 6**
1100 Hammond St (04401)
Rates: $39-$45;
Tel: (207) 947-6921

**THE QUALITY INN-PHENIX**
20 Westmarket Sq (04401)
Rates: $35-$80;
Tel: (207) 947-3850

**PENOBSCOT INN**
570 Main St (04401)
Rates: $48-$68;
Tel: (207) 947-0566

**PHENIX INN**
20 Broad St (04401)
Rates: N/A;
Tel: (207) 947-3850

**RAMADA INN**
357 Odlin Rd (04401)
Rates: $86-$140;
Tel: (207) 947-6961

**RED CARPET INN**
480 Main St (04401)
Rates: $39-$67;
Tel: (207) 942-5282

## BAR HARBOR

**ATLANTIC OAKES
BY-THE-SEA**
P. O. Box 3 (04609)
Rates: $59-$146;
Tel: (207) 288-5801

**BALANCE ROCK INN**
21 Albert Meadow (04609)
Rates: $125-$395;
Tel: (207) 288-9900

**EDEN VILLAGE**
Rt 3, RFD 1, Box 1930 (04609)
Rates: N/A;
Tel: (207) 288-4670

**HANSCOMS**
RFD 1, Box 1070 (04609)
Rates: N/A;
Tel: (207) 288-3744

**HIGH SEAS MOTEL**
Rt 3 (04609)
Rates: N/A;
Tel: (207) 288-5836

## BATH

**FAIRHAVEN**
North Bath Rd (04530)
Rates: N/A;
Tel: (207) 443-4391

**NEW MEADOWS INN**
Bath Rd (West Bath 04530)
Rates: $30-$58;
Tel: (207) 443-3921

## BELFAST

**ADMIRAL'S OCEAN INN**
RR 1, Box 99A (04915)
Rates: $29-$64;
Tel: (207) 338-4260

**BAYSHORE MOTOR
VILLAGE**
RFD 1, Box 129 (04915)
Rates: N/A;
Tel: (207) 338-2103

**BELFAST MOTOR INN**
RR 2, Box 21 (04915)
Rates: $85-$95;
Tel: (207) 338-2740

**PENOSBSCOT MEADOWS
COUNTRY INN**
Route 1 (04915)
Rates: $39-$99;
Tel: (207) 338-5320

## BETHEL

**BETHEL INN
& COUNTRY CLUB**
P. O. Box 49 (04217)
Rates: $83-$222;
Tel: (207) 824-2175

**THE CAMERON HOUSE**
Maston St Box 468 (04217)
Rates: N/A;
Tel: (207) 824-3219

## BINGHAM

**BINGHAM MOTOR INN**
Route 201 (04920)
Rates: N/A;
Tel: (207) 672-4135

## BOOTHBAY HARBOR

**HILLSIDE ACRES MOTEL**
P. O. Box 300
(Boothbay 04537)
Rates: $40-$65;
Tel: (207) 633-3411

**THE PINES MOTEL**
P. O. Box 693 (04538)
Rates: $35-$70;
Tel: (207) 633-4555

**SMUGGLER'S COVE
MOTOR INN**
Dept A (East Boothbay 04544)
Rates: $48-$120;
Tel: (207) 633-2800

## BROWNFIELD

**FOOTHILLS FARM
BED & BREAKFAST**
RR 1, Box 598 (04010)
Rates: N/A;
Tel: (207) 935-3799

## BRUNSWICK

**THE ATRIUM MOTEL-
BRUNSWICK**
Cooks Corner exit (04011)
Rates: $45-$97;
Tel: (207) 729-5555

**COMFORT INN**
199 Pleasant St (04011)
Rates: $49-$79;
Tel: (207) 729-1129

**VIKING MOTOR INN**
287 Bath Rd (04011)
Rates: $35-$79;
Tel: (207) 729-6661

## BUCKSPORT

**SPRING FOUNTAIN MOTEL**
RFD 2, Box 710 (04416)
Rates: $29-$59;
Tel: (207) 469-3139

## CAMDEN

**BELOIN'S MOTEL**
HCR 60, Box 3105 US 1
(04843)
Rates: N/A;
Tel: (207) 236-3262

## CASTINE

**THE HOLIDAY HOUSE**
Box 215, Perkins St (04421)
Rates: N/A;
Tel: (207) 326-4335

**THE MANOR**
P. O. Box 276 (04421)
Rates: $65-$150;
Tel: (207) 326-4861

## DAMARISCOTTA

**COUNTY FAIR MOTEL**
RFD 1, Box 36 (04543)
Rates: $32-$55;
Tel: (207) 563-3769

**OYSTER SHELL RESORT**
Box 267 (04543)
Rates: $85-$99;
Tel: (207) 563-3747

## EAST HOLDEN

**THE LUCERNE INN**
Bar Harbor Rd (04429)
Rates: N/A;
Tel: (207) 843-5123

## EASTPORT

**TODD HOUSE**
Todd's Head (04631)
Rates: N/A;
Tel: (207) 853-2328

## EDGECOMB

**EDGECOMB INN**
Rt 1, Box 51 (04556)
Rates: $49-$99;
Tel: (207) 882-6343

## ELLSWORTH

**ACADIA GATEWAY MOTEL**
Rt 3, Bar Harbor Rd (04605)
Rates: N/A;
Tel: (207) 667-9458

**BROOKSIDE MOTEL**
High St (04605)
Rates: N/A;
Tel: (207) 667-2543

**HOLIDAY INN**
3 High St (04650)
Rates: $57-$119;
Tel: (207) 667-9341

**JASPER'S MOTEL**
200 High St (04605)
Rates: $38-$62;
Tel: (207) 667-5318

**THE WHITE BIRCHES**
P.O. Box 743 (04605)
Rates: $29-$64;
Tel: (207) 667-3621

# FARMINGTON

**MOUNT BLUE MOTEL**
RFD 4, Box 5260 (04938)
Rates: $34-$54;
Tel: (207) 778-6004

# FREEPORT

**CASCO BAY MOTEL**
317 US 1S (04032)
Rates: $59-$74;
Tel: (207) 865-4925

**EAGLE MOTEL**
RR 2, Box 292 (04032)
Rates: $39-$79;
Tel: (207) 865-3106

**FREEPORT INN**
335 US 1S (04032)
Rates: $39-$99;
Tel: (800) 242-8838

**ISAAC RANDALL
BED & BREAKFAST**
5 Independence Dr (04032)
Rates: N/A;
Tel: (207) 865-9295

**MAINE IDYLL MOTOR CT**
325 US Rt 1 North (04032)
Rates: N/A;
Tel: (207) 865-4201

# GRAND LAKE STREAM

**WEATHERBY'S COTTAGE**
Box 69 (04637)
Rates: $70-$140;
Tel: (207) 796-5558

# GREENVILLE

**SPENCER POND CAMPS**
Star Rt 76, Box 580 (04441)
Rates: N/A;
Tel: (207) 695-2821

# HOULTON

**AMERICAN MOTEL**
Rt 2A Bangor Rd (04730)
Rates: $24-$48;
Tel: (207) 532-2236

**SHIRETOWN MOTEL**
Rt 3, Box 30 (04730)
Rates: $48-$72;
Tel: (207) 532-9421

# JACKMAN

**TUCKAWAY SHORES**
Forest St (05945)
Rates: N/A;
Tel: (207) 668-3351

# JONESBORO

**BLUEBERRY PATCH MOTEL**
Rt 1 (04648)
Rates: N/A;
Tel: (207) 434-5411

# KENNEBUNK

**FRIENDSHIP COUNTRY
MOTOR INN**
P. O. Box 575
(West Kennebunk 04094)
Rates: $40-$70;
Tel: (207) 985-6525

**KENNEBUNK INN 1799**
45 Main St (04043)
Rates: $85-$135;
Tel: (800) 743-1799

# KENNEBUNKPORT

**CAPTAIN JEFFERDS INN**
P. O. Box 691 (04046)
Rates: $85-$145;
Tel: (207) 976-2311

**THE COLONY**
P. O. Box 511 (04046)
Rates: $105-$260;
Tel: (207) 967-3331

**COVESIDE COTTAGES**
South Maine St, Box 631
(04046)
Rates: N/A;
Tel: (207) 967-5424

**SEASIDE HOUSE
COTTAGES**
Beach St, Gooch's Beach
(04046)
Rates: N/A;
Tel: (207) 967-4461

# KINGFIELD

**THE HERBERT INN**
Box 67 (04947)
Rates: $38-$125;
Tel: (800) 843-4372

**INN ON WINTER'S HILL**
Winter Hill (04947)
Rates: N/A;
Tel: (207) 265-5421

# KITTERY

**KITTERY MOTOR INN**
Rt 1 Bypass (03904)
Rates: $40-$75;
Tel: (207) 439-2000

# LEWISTON

**CHALET MOTEL**
1243 Lisbon St (04240)
Rates: $32-$54;
Tel: (207) 784-0600

**HOLIDAY MOTEL**
1905 Lisbon Rd (04240)
Rates: $19-$41;
Tel: (207) 783-2277

**MOTEL 6**
516 Pleasant St (04240)
Rates: $32-$36;
Tel: (207) 782-6558

# LINCOLN

**LINCOLN HOUSE MOTEL**
85 Main St (04457)
Rates: $32-$42;
Tel: (207) 794-3096

# LUBEC

**EASTLAND MOTEL**
Box 220 (04652)
Rates: $36-$56;
Tel: (207) 733-5501

## MACHIAS

**THE BLUEBIRD MOTEL**
US 1, Box 45 (04654)
Rates: $42-$56;
Tel: (207) 255-3332

**MACHIAS MOTOR INN**
26 E Main St (04654)
Rates: $44-$58;
Tel: (207) 255-4861

**MAINELAND MOTEL**
RR 2 (East Machias 04630)
Rates: $30-$48;
Tel: (207) 255-3334

## MANSET

**SEAWALL MOTEL**
Rt 102A (04656)
Rates: N/A;
Tel: (207) 244-9250

## MATINICUS

**TUCKANUCK LODGE**
Shag Hollow Rd (04851)
Rates: N/A;
Tel: (207) 366-3830

## MILLINOCKET

**THE ATRIUM INN
& HEALTH CLUB**
740 Central St (04462)
Rates: $40-$75;
Tel: (207) 723-4555

**BEST WESTERN
HERITAGE MOTOR INN**
935 Central St (04462)
Rates: $39-$74;
Tel: (207) 723-9777

## MOODY

**NE'R BEACH MOTEL**
US 1, Box 389 (04054)
Rates: $29-$94;
Tel: (207) 646-2636

## NAPLES

**AUGUSTUS BOVE HOUSE**
RR 1, Box 501 (04055)
Rates: $49-$75;
Tel: (207) 693-6365

## NEWPORT

**LOVLEY'S MOTEL**
P. O. Box 147 (04953)
Rates: $29-$89;
Tel: (207) 368-4311

## NORWAY

**LEDGEWOOD MOTEL**
RFD 2, Box 30 (04268)
Rates: $38-$60;
Tel: (207) 743-6347

## OLD ORCHARD BEACH

**GRAND BEACH INN**
198 E Grand Ave (04064)
Rates: $75-$155;
Tel: (800) 926-3242

**OLD COLONIAL MOTEL**
61 W Grand Ave (04064)
Rates: N/A;
Tel: (207) 934-9862

**WAVES MOTOR INN**
87 W Grand Ave (04064)
Rates: $50-$150;
Tel: (207) 934-4949

## ORONO

**BEST WESTERN BLACK
BEAR INN & CONF CTR**
4 Godfrey Dr (04473)
Rates: $54-$84;
Tel: (207) 866-7120

**UNIVERSITY MOTOR INN**
5 College Ave (04473)
Rates: $36-$72;
Tel: (207) 866-4921

## PATTEN

**MT CHASE LODGE**
Shin Pond Rd, Box 281 (04765)
Rates: N/A;
Tel: (207) 528-2183

## PORTLAND

**BEST WESTERN
MERRY MANOR INN**
700 Main St
(So Portland 04106)
Rates: $44-$84;
Tel: (207) 774-6151

**BUDGET TRAVELER
MOTOR LODGE**
1 Riverside St (04102)
Rates: $42-$45;
Tel: (207) 775-0111

**COMFORT INN**
90 Maine Mall Rd
(So Portland 04106)
Rates: $49-$89;
Tel: (207) 775-0409

**HOWARD JOHNSON
HOTEL**
675 Main St
(So Portland 04106)
Rates: $50-$115;
Tel: (207) 775-5343

**HOWARD JOHNSON
LODGE**
155 Riverside (04103)
Rates: $63-$120;
Tel: (207) 774-5861

**PORTLAND MARRIOTT HOTEL**
200 Sable Oakes Dr
(So Portland 04106)
Rates: $115-$165;
Tel: (207) 871-8000

**RAMADA INN**
1230 Congress St (04102)
Rates: $65-$105;
Tel: (207) 774-5611

**SHERATON TARA HOTEL**
363 Maine Mall Rd
(So Portland 04106)
Rates: $109-$165;
Tel: (207) 775-6161

SONESTA HOTEL
157 High St (04101)
Rates: N/A;
Tel: (800) 777-6246

## PRESQUE ISLE

KEDDY'S MOTOR INN
P. O. Box 270 (04769)
Rates: $48-$53;
Tel: (207) 764-3321

NORTHERN LIGHTS MOTEL
692 Main St (04769)
Rates: $24-$39;
Tel: (207) 764-4441

## RANGELEY

COUNTRY CLUB INN
P. O. Box 680 (04970)
Rates: $94-$152;
Tel: (207) 864-3831

TOWN & LAKE MOTEL
Box 47 (04970)
Rates: $40-$500;
Tel: (207) 864-3755

## RAYMOND

SEBAGO INN
1262 Roosevelt Tr (04071)
Rates: $42-$74;
Tel: (207) 655-3345

## ROCKLAND

NAVIGATOR MOTOR INN
520 Main St (04841)
Rates: $62-$90;
Tel: (800) 545-8026

OAKLAND SEASHORE
RFD 1, Box 1449 (04841)
Rates: N/A;
Tel: (207) 594-8104

SEA VIEW MOTEL
P. O. Box 101
(Glen Cove 04846)
Rates: $59-$65;
Tel: (207) 594-8479

TRADE WINDS
MOTOR INN
2 Park View Dr (04841)
Rates: $36-$99;
Tel: (207) 596-6661

## ROCKWOOD

ABNAKI COTTAGES
Abnki Rd, P. O. Box 6 (04478)
Rates: N/A;
Tel: (207) 534-7318

MAYNARDS IN MAINE
P. O. Box 228 (04478)
Rates: N/A;
Tel: (207) 534-7702

## RUMFORD

LINNELL MOTEL
& REST INN CONF CTR
2 Mi W on US 2 (04276)
Rates: $42-$58;
Tel: (207) 364-4511

## SANFORD

BAR-H MOTEL
3 Mi S on SR 109 (04073)
Rates: $32-$52;
Tel: 9207) 324-4662

## SEARSPORT

LIGHT'S MOTEL
AND RESTAURANT
RFD Box 349 (04974)
Rates: $29-$46;
Tel: (207) 548-2405

## SEBAGO LAKE

SUBURBAN PINES MOTEL
322 Roosevelt Trail
(Windham 04062)
Rates: $52-$89;
Tel: (207) 892-4834

## SKOWHEGAN

BELMONT MOTEL
P. O. Box 160 (04976)
Rates: $45-$125;
Tel: (207) 474-8315

SOMERSET MOTOR LODGE
422 Madison Ave (04976)
Rates: $40-$44;
Tel: (207) 474-2227

## SOUTH HARPSWELL

SENTER BED & BREAKFAST
Fire Road 858 (04079)
Rates: N/A;
Tel: (207) 833-2874

## SOUTHPORT

OCEAN GATE MOTOR INN
Route 27 (04576)
Rates: N/A;
Tel: (207) 633-3321

## SPRUCE HEAD

CRAIGNAIR INN
Clark Island Rd (04859)
Rates: N/A;
Tel: (207) 594-7644

## STRATTON

SPILLOVER MOTEL
P. O. Box 427 (04982)
Rates: $40-$65;
Tel: (207) 246-6571

## SUNSET

GOOSE COVE LODGE
Goose Cove Rd (04683)
Rates: N/A;
Tel: (207) 348-2508

## WATERVILLE

THE ATRIUM MOTEL
332 Main St (04901)
Rates: $40-$70;
Tel: (207) 873-2777

**ECONO LODGE**
455 Kennedy Memorial Dr
(04901)
Rates: $39-$72;
Tel: (207) 872-5577

**HOLIDAY INN**
375 Upper Main St (04901)
Rates: $61-$150;
Tel: (207) 873-0111

**HOWARD JOHNSON LODGE**
Main St (04901)
Rates: $55-$89;
Tel: (207) 873-3335

## WELLS

**WATER CREST COTTAGES**
Rt 1, P. O. Box 37 (04090)
Rates: N/A;
Tel: (207) 646-2202

## WELP

**KAWANHEE INN LAKESIDE LODGE**
Route 142 (04285)
Rates: N/A;
Tel: (207) 585-2243

## WEST PARIS

**MOLLYOCKETT MOTEL**
Hwy Rte 26 (04289)
Rates: N/A;
Tel: (207) 674-2345

## WILTON

**WHISPERING PINES MOTEL**
P. O. Box 649 (04294)
Rates: $34-$68;
Tel: (207) 645-3721

## WINDHAM

**SEBAGO LAKE LODGE**
Box 110 Whites Bridge Rd
(04062)
Rates: N/A;
Tel: (207) 892-2698

## WINTERPORT

**THE COLONIAL WINTERPORT INN**
P. O. Box 525 (04496)
Rates: $50-$65;
Tel: (207) 223-5307

## WISCASSET

**BAY VIEW INN**
P. O. Box 117
(Edgecomb 04556)
Rates: $65-$99;
Tel: (207) 882-6911

# MARYLAND

## ABERDEEN

**DAYS INN**
783 W Bel Air Ave (21001)
Rates: $38-$46;
Tel: (410) 272-8500

**HOLIDAY INN CHESAPEAKE HOUSE**
1007 Beards Hill Rd (21001)
Rates: $74-$98;
Tel: (410) 272-8100

**HOWARD JOHNSON LODGE**
793 W Bel Air Ave (21001)
Rates: $46-$58;
Tel: (410) 272-6000

**RED ROOF INN**
988 Beards Hill Rd (21001)
Rates: $37-$47;
Tel: (410) 273-7800

**SHERATON ABERDEEN**
P. O. Box V (21001)
Rates: $59-$109;
Tel: (410) 273-6300

## ANNAPOLIS

**DAYS INN-ANNAPOLIS**
1542 Whitehall Rd (21401)
Rates: $43-$58;
Tel: (410) 974-4440

**HOLIDAY INN ANNAPOLIS HOTEL & CONF CTR**
210 Holiday Ct (21401)
Rates: $59;
Tel: (410) 224-3150

**LOEWS ANNAPOLIS HOTEL**
126 West St (21401)
Rates: $115-$175;
Tel: (410) 263-7777

**RESIDENCE INN BY MARRIOTT**
170 Admiral Cochrane Dr
(21401)
Rates: $109-$145;
Tel: (410) 573-0300

**THR-RIFT INN MOTEL**
2542 Riva Rd (21401)
Rates: $50-$75;
Tel: (410) 224-2800

## BALTIMORE
(and Vicinity)

**BEST WESTERN BALTIMORE EAST**
5625 O'Donnell St (21224)
Rates: $64-$99;
Tel: (410) 633-9500

**BWI AIRPORT MARRIOTT HOTEL**
1743 W Nursery Rd (21240)
Rates: $69-$155;
Tel: (410) 859-8300

**COMFORT INN AIRPORT**
6921 Baltimore Annapolis Blvd
(21225)
Rates: $68-$80;
Tel: (410) 789-9100

**DAYS INN-
BALTIMORE EAST**
8801 Loch Raven Blvd (21204)
Rates: $48-$56;
Tel: (410) 882-0900

**DOUBLETREE INN
AT THE COLONNADE**
4 W University Pkwy (21218)
Rates: $69;
Tel: (800) 456-3396

**ECONO LODGE MOTEL**
5801 Baltimore Natl Pike
(21228)
Rates: $42-$55;
Tel: (410) 744-5000

**EMBASSY SUITES HOTEL**
213 International Circle
(Hunt Valley 21030)
Rates: $109;
Tel: (410) 584-1400

**HAMPTON INN**
829 Elkridge Landing Rd
(Linthicum 21090)
Rates: $62-$66;
Tel: (410) 850-0600

**HOLIDAY INN-BELMONT**
1800 Belmont Ave (21244)
Rates: $65-74;
Tel: (410) 265-1400

**HOLIDAY INN-
BWI AIRPORT**
890 Elkridge Landing Rd
(Linthicum 21090)
Rates: $87-$97;
Tel: (410) 859-8400

**HOLIDAY INN-
CROMWELL BRIDGE**
1100 Cromwell Bridge Rd
(Towson 21204)
Rates: $59-$79;
Tel: (410) 823-4410

**HOLIDAY INN-
MORAVIA ROAD**
6510 Frankford Ave (21206)
Rates: $69-$79;
Tel: (410) 485-7900

**HOLIDAY INN-PIKESVILLE**
1721 Reisterstown Rd
(Pikesville 21208)
Rates: $69-$75;
Tel: (410) 486 5600

**HOLIDAY INN
SECURITY/BELMONT**
1800 Belmont Ave (21244)
Rates: $59-$83;
Tel: (410) 265-1400

**HOWARD JOHNSON
MOTEL**
5701 Baltimore Natl Pike
(21228)
Rates: $40-$60;
Tel: (410) 747-8900

**MARRIOTT INNER
HARBOR HOTEL**
110 S Eutaw St (21201)
Rates: $135-$195;
Tel: (410) 962-0202

**QUALITY INN-TOWSON
CONFERENCE CENTER**
1015 York Rd (Towson 21204)
Rates: $52-$74;
Tel; (410) 825-9190

**RADISSON PLAZA
LORD BALTIMORE**
20 W Baltimore St (21201)
Rates: $85-$154;
Tel: (410) 539-8400

**RAMADA HOTEL
BALTIMORE**
1701 Belmont Ave (21207)
Rates: $60-$68;
Tel: (410) 265-1100

**RED ROOF INN-
BWI AIRPORT**
827 Elkridge Landing Rd
(Linthicum 21090)
Rates: $41-$51;
Tel: (410) 850-7600

**RED ROOF INN-
BWI PARKWAY**
7306 Parkway Dr
(Hanover 21076)
Rates: $41-$50;
Tel: (410) 712-4070

**RED ROOF INN-TIMONIUM**
111 W Timonium Rd
(Timonium 21093)
Rates: $34-$50;
Tel: (410) 666-0380

**SHERATON INNER
HARBOR HOTEL**
300 S Charles St (21201)
Rates: $109-$170;
Tel: (410) 962-8300

**SHERATON INTL HOTEL
ON BWI AIRPORT**
P. O. Box 8741 (21240)
Rates: $65-$150;
Tel: (410) 859-3300

**THE TREMONT HOTEL**
8 E Pleasant St (21202)
Rates: $89-$170;
Tel: (410) 576-1200

**TREMONT PLAZA HOTEL**
222 St. Paul Pl (21202)
Rates: $89-$155;
Tel: (410) 727-2222

# BETHESDA

**HOLIDAY INN**
8120 Wisconsin Ave (20814)
Rates: $109 250;
Tel: (301) 652-2000

**HOLIDAY INN CHEVY CHASE**
5520 Wisconsin Ave
(Chevy Chase 20815)
Rates: $70-$149;
Tel: (301) 656-1500

**MARRIOTT HOTEL**
5151 Pooks Hill Rd (20814)
Rates: $95-$700;
Tel: (301) 897 9400

# CAMBRIDGE

**ECONO LODGE**
P. O. Box 1107 (21613)
Rates: $41-$59;
Tel: (410) 221-0800

**QUALITY INN MOTEL**
P.O. Box 311 (21613)
Rates: $38-$43;
Tel: (410) 228-6900

## CHESAPEAKE BAY BRIDGE AREA

**CHESAPEAKE MOTEL**
Rt 1, Box 145
(Grasonville 21638)
Rates: $31-$43;
Tel: (800) 562-8196

## COLLEGE PARK

**MARRIOTT GREENBELT HOTEL**
6400 Ivy Ln
(Greenbelt 20770)
Rates: $80-$144;
Tel: (301) 441-3700

## COLUMBIA

**THE COLUMBIA INN**
10207 Wincopin Cir (21044)
Rates: $105-$120;
Tel: (800) 638-2817

## CUMBERLAND

**DIPLOMAT MOTEL**
Rt 6, Box 216 (21502)
Rates: $29-$37;
Tel: (301) 729-2311

**HOLIDAY INN**
100 S George St (21502)
Rates: $58-$76;
Tel: (301) 724-8800

**SUPER 8 MOTEL**
1301 National Hwy
(La Vale 21502)
Rates: $33-$54;
Tel: (301) 729-6265

## EASTON

**ECONO LODGE**
8175 Ocean Gateway
(21601)
Rates: $36-$52;
Tel: (410) 820-5555

## ELLICOTT CITY

**FOREST MOTEL**
10021 Baltimore Natl Pike
(21042)
Rates: $41-$50;
Tel: (410) 465-2090

## FREDERICK

**COMFORT INN**
420 Prospect Blvd (21701)
Rates: $49-$64;
Tel: (301) 695-6200

**DAYS INN**
5646 Buckeyestown Pike
(21701)
Rates: $49-$61;
Tel: (301) 694-6600

**FREDERICK SUPER 8 MOTEL**
5579 Spectrum Dr (21701)
Rates: $43-$51;
Tel: (301) 695-2881

**HOLIDAY INN FREDERICK/FT. DETRICK**
999 W Patrick St (21702)
Rates: $75;
Tel: (301) 662-5141

**KNIGHTS INN**
6005 Urbana Pike (21701)
Rates: $37-$46;
Tel: (301) 698-0555

## FROSTBURG

**COMFORT INN**
Rt 36 (21532)
Rates: $45-$50;
Tel: (301) 689-2050

## GAITHERSBURG

**HOLIDAY INN**
2 Montgomeryey Village Ave
(20879)
Rates: $87-$105;
Tel: (301) 948-8900

**MARRIOTT HOTEL**
620 Perry Pkwy (20877)
Rates: $56-$250;
Tel: (301) 977-8900

**RED ROOF INN**
497 Quince Orchard Rd
(20878)
Rates: N/A;
Tel: (800) 843-7663

## GERMANTOWN

**COMFORT INN**
20260 Goldenrod Ln (20876)
Rates: $48-$85;
Tel: (301) 428-1300

## GRANTSVILLE

**HOLIDAY INN**
I-68 & US 219 N (21536)
Rates: $39-$66;
Tel: (301) 895-5993

## HAGERSTOWN

**BEST WESTERN-HAGERSTOWN**
18221 Mason Dixon Rd
(21740)
Rates: $35-$42;
Tel: (301) 791-3560

**HOLIDAY INN**
900 Dual Hwy (21740)
Rates: $49-$54;
Tel: (301) 739-9050

**RAMADA INN CONVENTION CENTER**
901 Dual Hwy (21740)
Rates: $59-$69;
Tel: (301) 733-5100

**SHERATON INN CONFERENCE CENTER**
1910 Dual Hwy (21740)
Rates: $56-$69;
Tel: (301) 790-3010

**STATE LINE MOTEL**
Rt 6, Box 195C (21740)
Rates: $24-$31;
Tel: (301) 733-8262

**TRAVELODGE**
101 Massey Blvd (21740)
Rates: $33-$40;
Tel: (301) 582-4445

**VENICE**
**BEST WESTERN INN**
431 Dual Hwy (21740)
Rates: N/A;
Tel: (301) 733-0830

**WELLSLEY INN**
**BY HOWARD JOHNSON**
1101 Dual Hwy (21740)
Rates: $37-$60;
Tel: (301) 733-2700

## HUNT VALLEY

**EMBASSY SUITES HOTEL**
213 International Cir (21030)
Rates: $89-$119;
Tel: (410) 584-1400

**HAMPTON INN**
**HUNT VALLEY**
11200 York Rd (21031)
Rates: $50-$63;
Tel: (410) 527-1500

**MARRIOTT'S**
**HUNT VALLEY INN**
245 Shawan Rd (21031)
Rates: $89-$128;
Tel: (410) 785-7000

**RESIDENCE INN**
**BY MARRIOTT**
10710 Beaver Dam Rd
(21030)
Rates: $94-$124;
Tel: (410) 584-7370

## JESSUP

**RED ROOF INN-**
**COLUMBIA/JESSUP**
8000 Washington Blvd
(20794)
Rates: $43-$51;
Tel: (410) 796-0380

## JOPPA

**LAKESIDE MOTEL**
1015 Pulaski Hwy (21085)
Rates: N/A;
Tel: (410) 676-2700

## KENT ISLAND

**COMFORT INN**
**KENT NARROWS**
P. O. Box 541
(Grasonville 21638)
Rates: $54-$98;
Tel: (410) 827-6767

## LANHAM

**RED ROOF INN**
9050 Lanham Severn Rd
(20706)
Rates: N/A;
Tel: (800) 843-7663

## LA PLATA

**BEST WESTERN**
**LA PLATA INN**
400 US 301S (20646)
Rates: $48-$57;
Tel: (301) 934-4900

## LAUREL

**COMFORT SUITES HOTEL**
**AT LAUREL LAKE**
14402 Laurel Pl (20707)
Rates: $49-$90;
Tel: (301) 206-2600

**KNIGHTS INN**
3380 Fort Meade Rd (20724)
Rates: $39-$49;
Tel: (301) 498-5553

**RED ROOF INN-LAUREL**
12525 Laurel Bowie Rd
(20708)
Rates: $29-$37;
Tel: (301) 498-8811

## LEXINGTON PARK

**BELVEDERE MOTOR INN**
60 Main St (20653)
Rates: $37-$48;
Tel: (301) 863-6666

## MCHENRY

**INNLET MOTOR LODGE**
Deep Creek Rd (21541)
Rates: N/A;
Tel: (301) 387-5596

## OCEAN CITY

**FENWICK INN**
13801 Coastal Hwy (21842)
Rates: $40-$129;
Tel: (410) 250-1100

**SHERATON OCEAN CITY**
**RESORT & CONF CTR**
10100 Ocean Hwy (21842)
Rates: $55-$190;
Tel: (410) 524-3535

**TAKA-A-MITSIA**
401 11th St (21842)
Rates: N/A;
Tel: (410) 289-3200

## ODENTON

**RED CARPET INN**
1630 Annapolis Rd (21113)
Rates: N/A;
Tel: (301) 674-8900

## OXON HILL

**RED ROOF INN**
6170 Oxon Hill Rd (20745)
Rates: N/A;
Tel: (800) 843-7663

## POCOMOKE CITY

**DAYS INN**
1540 Ocean Hwy (21851)
Rates: $35-$75;
Tel: (410) 957-3000

**QUALITY INN**
**OF POCOMOKE**
825 Ocean Hwy (21851)
Rates: $44-$75;
Tel: (410) 957-1300

## PRINCESS ANNE

**ECONO LODGE**
Rt 2, Box 253A (21853)
Rates: $39-$70;
Tel: (410) 651-9400

## ROCKVILLE

**DAYS INN**
16001 Shady Grove Rd
(20850)
Rates: $45-$70;
Tel: (301) 948-4300

**SHERATON
POTOMAC HOTEL**
3 Research Court (20850)
Rates: $80-$111;
Tel: (301) 840-0200

## ST. MARY'S CITY

**BELVEDERE MOTOR INN**
60 Main St
(Lexington Park 20653)
Rates: $37-$46;
Tel: (800) 428-2871

## ST. MICHAELS

**ST. MICHAELS MOTOR INN**
1228 S Talbot St (21663)
Rates: $49-$79;
Tel: (410) 745-3333

## SALISBURY

**BEST WESTERN
STATESMAN MOTEL**
712 N Salisbury Blvd (21801)
Rates: $44-$61;
Tel: (410) 749-7155

**COMFORT INN**
Rt 11, Box 235 (21801)
Rates: $36-$59;
Tel: (410) 543-4666

**DAYS INN**
US 13N, RR 6, Box 978
(21801)
Rates: $41-$64;
Tel: (410) 749-6200

**HAMPTON INN SALISBURY**
P. O. Box 4035 (21801)
Rates: $39-$69;
Tel: (410) 546-1300

**HOJO INN
BY HOWARD JOHNSON**
Rt 6, Box 984 (21801)
Rates: $33-$69;
Tel: (410) 742-5195

**HOLIDAY INN SALISBURY**
Rt 11, Box 226 (21801)
Rates: $39-$88;
Tel: (410) 742-7194

**LORD SALISBURY MOTEL**
Rt 11, Box 232 (21801)
Rates: $39-$75;
Tel: (410) 742-3251

**SHERATON SALISBURY**
300 S Salisbury Blvd (21801)
Rates: $65-$116;
Tel: (410) 546-4400

## SILVER SPRING

**HOLIDAY INN-
SILVER SPRING PLAZA**
8777 Georgia Ave (20910)
Rates: $85-$135;
Tel: (301) 589-0800

## SOLOMONS

**HOLIDAY INN HOTEL
CONF CTR & MARINA**
P. O. Box 1099 (20688)
Rates: $68-$140;
Tel: (410) 326-6311

## TOWSON

**DAYS INN
BALTIMORE-EAST**
8801 Loch Raven Blvd (21204)
Rates: $48-$56;
Tel: (410) 882-0900

## WALDORF

**ECONO LODGE
OF WALDORF**
No. 4 Business Park Dr (20601)
Rates: $41-$49;
Tel: (310) 645-0022

**HOJO INN
BY HOWARD JOHNSON**
P. O. Box 99 (20603)
Rates: $41-$46;
Tel: (310) 932-5090

**HOLIDAY INN**
1 St. Patrick's Dr (20603)
Rates: $55-$63;
Tel: (310) 645-8200

**SUPER 8 MOTEL**
5050 US 301 (20603)
Rates: $35-$60;
Tel: (310) 932-8957

## WESTMINSTER

**DAYS INN-WESTMINSTER**
25 S Cranberry Rd (21157)
Rates: $44-$60;
Tel: (410) 857-0500

## WILLIAMSPORT

**DAYS INN**
310 E Potomac St (21795)
Rates: $49-$53;
Tel: (301) 582-3500

# MASSACHUSETTS

## AMHERST

**HOWARD JOHNSON LODGE**
401 Russell St (Hadley 01035)
Rates: $49-$97;
Tel: (413) 586-0114

**LORD JEFFREY INN**
30 Boltwood Ave (01002)
Rates: $80-$120;
Tel· (413) 253 2576

**UNIVERSITY MOTOR LODGE**
345 N Pleasant St (01002)
Rates: $42-$87;
Tel: (413) 256-8111

## ANDOVER

**ANDOVER INN**
Chapel Ave (01810)
Rates: $79-$89;
Tel: (508) 475-5903

**BOSTON MARRIOTT ANDOVER**
123 Old River Rd (01810)
Rates: $92;
Tel· (508) 975-3600

## ASHFIELD

**THE ASHFIELD INN**
P. O. Box 129 (01330)
Rates: $65-$105;
Tel: (413) 628-4571

## BOSTON
(and Vicinity)

**BATTLE GREEN INN**
1720 Massachusetts Ave
(Lexington 02173)
Rates: $48-$52;
Tel: (617) 862-6100

**BOSTON BACK BAY HILTON**
40 Dalton St (02115)
Rates: $165-$215;
Tel: (617) 236-1100

**BOSTON HARBOR HOTEL**
70 Rowes Wharf (02110)
Rates: $195-$375;
Tel: (617) 439-7000

**BOSTON MARRIOTT HOTEL COPLEY PLACE**
110 Huntington Ave (02116)
Rates: $165-$189;
Tel: (617) 236-5800

**BOSTON/NEWTON MARRIOTT HOTEL**
2345 Commonwealth Ave
(Newton 02166)
Rates: $92-$149;
Tel: (617) 969-1000

**COLONIAL TRAVELER MOTOR COURT**
1753 Broadway
(Saugus 01906)
Rates: $40-$60;
Tel: (617) 233-6700

**COPLEY PLAZA HOTEL**
138 St James Ave (02116)
Rates: $95-$280;
Tel: (617) 267-5300

**DAYS INN-BURLINGTON**
30 Wheeler Rd
(Burlington 01803)
Rates: $69-$89;
Tel: (617) 272-8800

**DAYS INN-NEWTON**
399 Grove St (Newton 02162)
Rates: $79-$119;
Tel. (617) 969-5300

**DAYS INN-SAUGUS**
999 Broadway
(Saugus 01906)
Rates: $49-$89;
Tel: (617) 233-1800

**DAYS INN-WOBURN**
19 Commerce Way
(Woburn 01801)
Rates: $69-$104;
Tel: (617) 935-7110

**57 PARK PLAZA HOTEL-HOWARD JOHNSON**
200 Stuart St (02116)
Rates: $110-$160;
Tel: (617) 482-1800

**FOUR SEASONS HOTEL**
200 Boylston St (02116)
Rates: $230-$420;
Tel: (617) 338 4400

**HOTEL LE MERIDIEN**
250 Franklin St (02110)
Rates: $210-$255;
Tel: (617) 451-1900

**HOWARD JOHNSON HOTEL CAMBRIDGE**
777 Memorial Dr
(Cambridge 02139)
Rates: $85-$140;
Tel: (617) 492-7777

**HOWARD JOHNSON HOTEL-KENMORE**
575 Commonwealth Ave
(02215)
Rates: $85-$140;
Tel: (617) 267-3100

**HOWARD JOHNSON LODGE-BURLINGTON**
98 Middlesex Tpk
(Burlington 01803)
Rates: $78-$95;
Tel: (617) 272-6550

**HOWARD JOHNSON LODGE-FENWAY**
1271 Boylston St (02215)
Rates: $75-$125;
Tel: (617) 267-8300

**HOWARD JOHNSON-57 PARK PLAZA**
200 Stuart St (02116)
Rates: $90-$350;
Tel: (617) 482-1800

**HOWARD JOHNSON LODGE-REVERE**
407 Squire Rd (Revere 02151)
Rates: $70-$100;
Tel: (617) 284-7200

**LOGAN AIRPORT HILTON**
Logan Intl Airport
(East Boston 02128)
Rates: $105-$200;
Tel: (617) 569-9300

**NEW ENGLANDER MOTOR COURT**
551 Broadway
(Malden 02148)
Rates: $40-$60;
Tel: (617) 321-0505

**THE RITZ CARLTON-BOSTON**
15 Arlington St (02117)
Rates: $215-$360;
Tel: (617) 536-5700

**SHERATON NEEDHAM HOTEL**
100 Cabot St
(Needham 02194)
Rates: $90-$145;
Tel: (617) 444-1110

**SWISSOTEL BOSTON**
One Ave de Lafayette (02111)
Rates: $205-$265;
Tel: (617) 451-2600

**TRAVELODGE-BEDFORD**
285 Great Rd
(Bedford 01730)
Rates: $54-$65;
Tel: (617) 275-6120

**THE WESTIN HOTEL-COPLEY PLACE BOSTON**
10 Huntington Ave (02116)
Rates: $175-$240;
Tel: (617) 262-9600

# BOXBOROUGH

**BOXBOROUGH HOST HOTEL**
1 Adams Pl (01719)
Rates: $94-$104;
Tel: (508) 263-8701

# BRAINTREE

**DAYS INN**
190 Wood Rd (02184)
Rates: $50-$85;
Tel: (617) 848-1260

**HOLIDAY INN-BOSTON/RANDOLPH**
1374 N Main St
(Randolph 02368)
Rates: $82-$98;
Tel: (617) 961-1000

**SHERATON-TARA**
37 Forbes Rd (02184)
Rates: $119-$341;
Tel: (617) 848-0600

# BUZZARDS BAY

**BAY MOTOR INN**
223 Main St (02532)
Rates: N/A;
Tel: (508) 759-3989

# CAPE COD

**ALL SEASONS MOTOR INN**
1199 Main St, Rt 28
(South Yarmouth 02664)
Rates: $40-$95;
Tel: (508) 394-7600

**ANCHOR-IN MOTEL**
1 South St (Hyannis 02601)
Rates: $40-$99;
Tel: (508) 775-0357

**BLUE DOLPHIN INN**
P. O. Box 122
(North Eastham 02651)
Rates: $39-$84;
Tel: (508) 255-1159

**CAPE COD PLAZA HOTEL**
P. O. Box 936 (Hyannis 02601)
Rates: $47-$142;
Tel: (508) 771-3000

**CENTERVILLE CORNERS MOTOR LODGE**
P. O. Box 507
(Centerville 02632)
Rates: $42-$91;
Tel: (508) 775-7223

**DAYS INN**
867 Iyanough Rd, Rt 132
(Hyannis 02601)
Rates: $50-$105;
Tel: (508) 771-6100

**DENNIS WEST MOTOR LODGE**
691 Main St
(West Dennis 02670)
Rates: $35-$69;
Tel: (508) 394-7434

**THE EARL OF SANDWICH MOTOR MANOR**
378 Rt 6A
(East Sandwich 02537)
Rates: $35-$85;
Tel: (508) 888-1415

**HANDKERCHIEF SHOALS MOTEL**
MA 28 (S Harwich 02661)
Rates: $63-$70;
Tel: (508) 432-2200

**HARBOR VILLAGE**
P. O. Box 635
(Hyannis Port 02647)
Rates: $90-1150;
Tel: (508) 775-7581

**HARGOOD HOUSE APTS**
493 Commercial St
(Provincetown 02657)
Rates: N/A;
Tel: (508) 487-9133

**HIGH BREWSTER INN**
964 Satucket Rd
(Brewster 02631)
Rates: $80-$220;
Tel: (508) 896-3636

**HOLIDAY INN**
P. O. Box 392
(Provincetown 02657)
Rates: $59-$125;
Tel: (508) 487-1711

**LAMB & LION INN**
P. O. Box 511
(Barnstable 02630)
Rates: $80-$105;
Tel: (508) 362-6823

**QUALITY INN**
Jones & Gillford St
(Falmouth 02540)
Rates: $58-$109;
Tel: (508) 540-2000

**SANDWICH
MOTOR LODGE**
P. O. Box 557
(Sandwich 02563)
Rates: $45-$105;
Tel: (508) 888-2275

**SEA BREEZE COTTAGES
BY THE BEACH**
P. O. Box 553
(Hyannis Port 02647)
Rates: $450-$850;
Tel: (508) 775-4269

**SKAKET BEACH MOTEL**
203 Cranberry Hwy
(Orleans 02653)
Rates: $43-$96;
Tel· (508) 255 1020

**TOWN CRIER MOTEL**
P. O. Box 457
(Eastham 02642)
Rates: $44-$75;
Tel: (508) 255-4000

**WINDJAMMER MOTOR INN**
192 South Shore Dr
(South Yarmouth 02664)
Rates: $39-$99;
Tel· (508) 398-2370

## CHICOPEE

**BEST WESTERN**
463 Memorial Dr (01020)
Rates: N/A;
Tel: (413) 592-6171

## CONCORD

**HOWARD JOHNSON
LODGE**
740 Elm St (01742)
Rates: $67-$90;
Tel: (508) 369-6100

## DANVERS

**HAWTHORNE MOTOR INN**
225 Newbury St (01923)
Rates: $55-$95;
Tel: (508) 774-6500

**MOTEL 6**
65 Newbury St (01923)
Rates: $38-$44;
Tel: (508) 774-8045

**RESIDENCE INN
BY MARRIOTT**
51 Newbury St (01923)
Rates: $120-$140;
Tel: (508) 777-7171

## FALL RIVER

**DAYS INN**
332 Millken Blvd (02725)
Rates: $53-$92;
Tel: (508) 676 1991

## FITCHBURG

**ROYAL PLAZA HOTEL
& TRADE CENTER**
150 Royal Plaza Dr (01420)
Rates: $65-$78;
Tel: (508) 342-7100

## FOXBORO

**QUALITY INN**
60 Forbes Blvd
(Mansfield 02048)
Rates: $49-$67;
Tel. (508) 339-2323

## FRAMINGHAM CENTER

**RED ROOF INN**
650 Cochituate Rd
(Framingham 01701)
Rates: $34-$65;
Tel: (508) 872-4499

## GLOUCESTER

**SPRUCE MANOR MOTEL
AND GUEST HOUSE**
141 Essex Ave (01930)
Rates: $30-$90;
Tel: (508) 283-0614

## GREENFIELD

**CANDLELIGHT
MOTOR INN**
208 Mohawk Tr (01301)
Rates: $38-$84;
Tel: (413) 772-0101

## HAVERHILL

**BEST WESTERN
MERRIMACK VALLEY LODGE**
401 Lowell Ave (01832)
Rates: $39-$70;
Tel: (508) 373-1511

**COMFORT SUITES**
106 Bank Rd (01832)
Rates: $60-$67;
Tel: (508) 374-7755

## HOLYOKE

**HOLIDAY INN HOLYOKE
HOLIDOME & CONF CTR**
245 Whiting Farms Rd (01040)
Rates: $76-$90;
Tel: (413) 534-3311

## LAWRENCE

**HAMPTON INN NORTH
ANDOVER/LAWRENCE**
224 Winthrop Ave (01843)
Rates: $49-$65;
Tel: (508) 975-4050

## LEE

**MORGAN HOUSE INN**
33 Main St (01238)
Rates: $42-$160;
Tel: (413) 243-0181

## LENOX

**WALKER HOUSE INN**
74 Walker St (01240)
Rates: $70-$160;
Tel: (800) 235-3098

## LEOMINSTER

**WESTMINSTER
VILLAGE INN**
9 Village Inn Rd
(Westminster 01473)
Rates: $68-$135;
Tel: (800) 342-1905

## LOWELL

**SHERATON INN-LOWELL**
50 Warren St (01852)
Rates: $49;
Tel: (508) 452-1200

**THE SHERMAN-
BARRY HOUSE B & B**
163 Dartmouth St (01851)
Rates: N/A;
FAX: (508) 459-4760

## MARLBOROUGH

**BEST WESTERN ROYAL
PLAZA HOTEL**
181 Boston Post Rd W (01752)
Rates: $92-$108;
Tel: (508) 460-0700

**SUPER 8-MARLBORO**
880 Donald J Lynch Blvd
(01752)
Rates: $45-$49;
Tel: (508) 460-1000

## MIDDLEBORO

**DAYS INN-
PLYMOUTH/MIDDLEBORO**
Clark St East (02346)
Rates: $53-$65;
Tel: (508) 946-4400

## NANTUCKET ISLAND

**NANTUCKET INN
& CONFERENCE CENTER**
27 Macy's Ln
(Nantucket 02554)
Rates: $50-$195;
Tel: (508) 228-6900

## NATICK

**HOLIDAY INN
CROWNE PLAZA**
1360 Worcester Rd (01760)
Rates: $117-$160;
Tel: (508) 653-8800

**NATICK INN**
Route 9 & Speen St (01760)
Rates: N/A;
Tel: (508) 653-5000

## NEW BEDFORD

**DAYS INN-NEW BEDFORD**
500 Hathaway Rd (02740)
Rates: $54-$85;
Tel: (508) 997-1231

## NEWBURYPORT

**MORRILL PLACE INN**
209 High St (01950)
Rates: $55-$70;
Tel: (508) 462-2808

## NORTHAMPTON

**QUALITY HOTEL**
1 Atwood Dr (01060)
Rates: $65-$120;
Tel: (413) 586-1211

## NORTHBOROUGH

**FRIENDSHIP INN**
At Jct SR 9 & 20 (01532)
Rates: $39-$44;
Tel: (508) 842-8941

## PITTSFIELD

**BERKSHIRE HILTON INN**
Berkshire Common (01201)
Rates: $95-$185;
Tel: (413) 499-2000

**THE WEATHERVANE
MOTEL**
475 S Main St
(Lanesboro 01237)
Rates: $32-$98;
Tel: (413) 443-3230

## PLYMOUTH

**HOWARD JOHNSON
LODGE & CONFERENCE CTR**
Rt 3 at exit 9 (Kingston 02364)
Rates: $59-$99;
Tel: (617) 585-3831

## RAYNHAM

**DAYS INN-
TAUNTON/RAYNHAM**
Rt 44 (02767)
Rates: $42-$50;
Tel: (508) 824-8647

## SALEM

**HAWTHORNE HOTEL**
On The Common (01970)
Rates: $80-$127;
Tel: (508) 744-4080

**THE SALEM INN**
7 Summer St (01970)
Rates: $85-$135;
Tel: (508) 741-0680

## SCITUATE

**CLIPPER SHIP LODGE**
7 Beaver Dam Rd (02066)
Rates: N/A;
Tel: (800) 368-3818

## SHREWSBURY

**DAYS INN
WORCESTER/SHREWSBURY**
889 Boston Tpk (01545)
Rates: $48-$59;
Tel: (508) 842-8500

## SOUTHBOROUGH

**RED ROOF INN**
367 Turnpike Rd (01772)
Rates: $35-$48;
Tel: (508) 481-3904

## SPRINGFIELD

**BEST WESTERN-CHICOPEE
MOTOR LODGE**
463 Memorial Dr
(Chicopee 01020)
Rates: $40-$70;
Tel: (413) 592-6171

**BLACK HORSE MOTEL**
500 Riverdale St
(West Springfield 01089)
Rates: $39-$69;
Tel: (413) 733-2161

**GOODLIFE INN**
21 Baldwin St
(West Springfield 01089)
Rates: $69-$82;
Tel: (413) 781-2300

**HAMPTON INN**
1011 Riverdale St
(West Springfield 01089)
Rates: $60-$66;
Tel: (413) 732-1300

**HOLIDAY INN**
711 Dwight St (01104)
Rates: $82-$125;
Tel: (413) 781-0900

**HOLIDAY INN-HOLIDOME & CONVENTION CTR**
245 Whiting Farms Rd
(Holyoke 01041)
Rates: $76-$106;
Tel: (413) 534-3311

**RAMADA HOTEL**
1080 Riverdale St
(West Springfield 01089)
Rates: $77-$250;
Tel: (413) 781-8750

**RED ROOF INN**
1254 Riverdale St
(West Springfield 01089)
Rates: $29-$56;
Tel: (413) 731-1010

**SPRINGFIELD-MARRIOTT HOTEL**
Boland Way & Columbus Ave
(01115)
Rates: $125-$135;
Tel: (413) 781-7111

## STURBRIDGE

**AMERICAN MOTOR LODGE-BEST WESTERN**
US 20 (01566)
Rates: $55-$83;
Tel: (508) 347-9121

**BETHANY BED & BREAKFAST**
5 McGregory Rd (01566)
Rates: $55-$75;
Tel: (508) 347-5993

**ECONO LODGE**
682 Main St (01518)
Rates: $50-$80;
Tel: (508) 347-2324

**STURBRIDGE HOST HOTEL & CONFERENCE CTR**
366 Main ST (01566)
Rates: $99-$135;
Tel: (508) 347-7393

**STURBRIDGE MOTOR INN**
P. O. Box 185 (01566)
Rates: $45-$70;
Tel: (508) 347-3391

## TEWKSBURY

**RESIDENCE INN BY MARRIOTT-BOSTON/TEWKSBURY**
1775 Andover St (01876)
Rates: $105-$130;
Tel: (508) 640-1003

## WESTBOROUGH

**RAMADA INN**
399 Turnpike Rd (01581)
Rates: $50 $65,
Tel: (508) 366-0202

**RESIDENCE INN BY MARRIOTT BOSTON/WEST BOROUGH**
25 Connector Rd
(01581)
Rates: $69-$135;
Tel: (508) 366-7700

## WESTMINSTER

**TOWN CRIER MOTEL**
Rt 2A & 140 (04173)
Rates: $29-$45;
Tel: (508) 874-5951

## WESTPORT

**HAMPTON INN-FALL RIVER-WESTPORT**
53 Old Bedford Rd (02790)
Rates: $66-$77;
Tel: (508) 675-8500

## WEST STOCKBRIDGE

**PLEASANT VALLEY MOTEL**
SR 102 (01266)
Rates: $35-$125;
Tel: (413) 232-8511

## WILLIAMSTOWN

**COZY CORNER MOTEL**
284 Sand Springs Rd & US 7
(01267)
Rates: $35-$75;
Tel: (413) 458-8006

**JERICHO VALLEY INN**
P.O. Box 239 (01267)
Rates: $58-$98;
Tel: (413) 458-9511

**WILLIAMS INN**
On The Green (01267)
Rates: $85-$145;
Tel: (413) 458-9371

## WORCESTER
(and Vicinity)

**BUDGETEL INN**
444 Southbridge St
(Auburn 01501)
Rates: $44-$60;
Tel: (508) 832-7000

**HAMPTON INN**
110 Summer St (01608)
Rates: $59;
Tel: (508) 757-0400

**HOLIDAY INN**
500 Lincoln St (01605)
Rates: $79-$109;
Tel: (508) 852-4000

**WORCESTER MARRIOTT**
10 Lincoln Sq (01608)
Rates: $135-$155;
Tel: (508) 791-1600

## YARMOUTHPORT

**COLONIAL HOUSE INN**
277 Main St, Rt 6A (02675)
Rates: N/A;
Tel: (508) 362-4348

# MICHIGAN

## ACME

**SUN 'N SAND MOTEL**
P. O. Box 307 (49610)
Rates: N/A;
Tel: (616) 938-2190

## ADRIAN

**ADRIAN INN**
1575 W Maumee St (49221)
Rates: $36-$75;
Tel: (517) 263-5741

**CARLTON LODGE**
1629 W Maumee St (49221)
Rates: $53-$73;
Tel: (517) 263-7000

## ALBION

**BEST WESTERN
ADAMS ARMS MOTEL**
400 B Dr N (49224)
Rates: $40-$70;
Tel: (517) 629-3966

**DAYS INN**
P. O. Box 865 (49224)
Rates: $39-$49;
Tel: (517) 629-9411

## ALLEGAN

**BUDGET HOST
SUNSET MOTEL**
1580 Lincoln Rd (49010)
Rates: N/A;
Tel: (616) 673-6622

## ALPENA

**FIRESIDE INN**
18730 Fireside Hwy (49707)
Rates: N/A;
Tel: (517) 595-6369

**FLETCHER MOTEL**
1001 Hwy 23N (49707)
Rates: $55-$61;
Tel: (517) 354-4191

**HOLIDAY INN**
1000 Hwy 23N (49707)
Rates: $59-$79;
Tel: (517) 356-2151

## ANN ARBOR

**BEST WESTERN DOMINO'S
FARMS HOTEL & CONF CTR**
3600 Plymouth Rd (48105)
Rates: $95;
Tel: (313) 769-9800

**BEST WESTERN
WOLVERINE INN**
3505 S State St (48108)
Rates: $44-$48;
Tel: (313) 665-3500

**COMFORT INN**
2455 Carpenter Rd (48108)
Rates: $60-$65;
Tel: (313) 973-6100

**HO JO INN**
2424 E Stadium Blvd (48104)
Rates: $39-$46;
Tel: (313) 971-8000

**HOWARD JOHNSON
MOTEL**
2380 Carpenter Rd (48108)
Rates: $50-$70;
Tel: (313) 971-0700

**KNIGHTS INN**
3764 S State St (48108)
Rates: $40-$47;
Tel: (313) 665-9900

**RED ROOF INN**
3621 Plymouth Rd (48105)
Rates: $38-$61;
Tel: (313) 996-5800

**REGENCY CAMPUS INN**
615 E Huron St (48104)
Rates: $87-$155;
Tel: (800) 666-8693

**SHERATON INN**
3200 Boardwalk (48108)
Rates: $75-$250;
Tel: (313) 996-0600

## AUBURN HILLS

**MOTEL 6**
1471 Opdyke Rd (48057)
Rates: $25-$31;
Tel: (313) 373-8440

## AUGRES

**POINT AUGRES HOTEL**
3279 South Point Ln (48703)
Rates: N/A;
Tel: (517) 876-7217

## BAD AXE

**THE FRANKLIN INN**
1070 E Huron Ave (48413)
Rates: $44-$52;
Tel: (517) 269-9951

## BARAGA

**CARLA'S LAKE SHORE MOTEL**
Rt 1, Box 233 (49908)
Rates: $32-$49;
Tel: (906) 353-6256

**SUPER 8 MOTEL**
790 Michigan Ave (49908)
Rates: $34-$44;
Tel: (906) 353-6680

## BATTLE CREEK

**APPLETREE INN**
4786 Beckley Rd (49017)
Rates: $36-$42;
Tel: (616) 979-3561

**BATTLE CREEK INN**
5050 Beckley Rd (49015)
Rates: $45-$73;
Tel: (616) 979-1100

**HOWARD JOHNSON LODGE**
2590 Capital Ave SW (49015)
Rates: $45-$65;
Tel: (616) 965-3201

**KNIGHTS INN**
2595 Capital Ave SW (49015)
Rates: $30-$41;
Tel: (616) 964-2600

**MICHIGAN MOTEL**
20475 Capital Ave NE (49017)
Rates: $30-$39;
Tel: (616) 963-1565

## BAY CITY

**BAY VALLEY HOTEL & RESORT**
2470 Old Bridge Rd (48706)
Rates: $65-$108;
Tel: (517) 686-3500

**DELTA MOTEL**
1000 S Euclid Ave (48706)
Rates: $27-$40;
Tel: (517) 684-4490

**HOLIDAY INN**
501 Saginaw St (48708)
Rates: $70-$80;
Tel: (517) 892-3501

## BAYPORT

**WOODLAND MOTEL**
9551 Pt. Austin Rd (48720)
Rates: N/A;
Tel: (517) 656-9955

## BEAR LAKE

**BELLA VISTA MOTOR LODGE**
US #31 in Village (49614)
Rates: N/A;
Tel: (616) 864 3000

## BELLAIRE

**WINDWARD SHORE MOTEL**
5812 E Torch Lake Dr (49615)
Rates: N/A;
Tel: (616) 377-6321

## BELLEVILLE

**RED ROOF INN METRO AIRPORT**
45501 I-94 N Expwy (48111)
Rates: $29-$47;
Tel: (313) 697-2244

**SUPER 8 MOTEL**
45707 I-94 S (48111)
Rates: $32-$47;
Tel: (313) 699-1888

## BENTON HARBOR

**BENTON HARBOR COMFORT INN**
1598 Mall Dr (49022)
Rates: $42-$60;
Tel: (616) 925-1880

**CARLTON LODGE**
1592 Mall Dr (49022)
Rates: $55-$72;
Tel: (616) 925-3000

**DAYS INN**
2699 Michigan Hwy M-139 (49022)
Rates: $41-$65;
Tel: (616) 925-7021

**RED ROOF INN**
1630 Mall Dr (49022)
Rates: $29-$45;
Tel: (616) 927-2484

**SUPER 8 MOTEL**
1950 E Napier Ave (49022)
Rates: $35-$42;
Tel: (616) 926-1371

## BEULAH

**PINE KNOT MOTEL**
171 N Center St (49617)
Rates: $30-$65;
Tel: (616) 882-7751

## BLISSFIELD

**H D ELLIS INN BED & BREAKFAST**
415 West Adrian St (49228)
Rates: $50-$70;
Tel: (517) 486-3155

## BLOOMFIELD HILLS

**HOLIDAY INN BLOOMFIELD HILLS-PONTIAC**
1801 S Telegraph Rd (48302)
Rates: $62-$78;
Tel: (313) 334-2444

**KINGSLEY INN**
1475 N Woodward Ave (48304)
Rates: $89;
Tel: (313) 644-1400

## BRANCH

**LAZY DAYS MOTEL**
P. O. Box 104 (49402)
Rates: N/A;
Tel: (616) 898-2252

## BREVORT

**CHAPEL HILL MOTEL**
4422 W US 2 (49760)
Rates: $28-$43;
Tel: (906) 292-5521

**NOR-STAR MOTEL**
4345 W US 2 (49760)
Rates: N/A;
Tel: (906) 292-5542

## BRIDGEPORT

**GARTEN HAUS INN**
6361 Dixie Hwy (48722)
Rates: $43-$50;
Tel: (517) 777-2582

## CADILLAC

**CADILLAC SANDS MOTOR INN**
6319 E M115 (49601)
Rates: $39-$89;
Tel: (616) 775-2407

**DAYS INN**
6001 E M115 (49601)
Rates: $64-$110;
Tel: (616) 775-4414

**MAPLE HILL MOTEL**
US 131S (49601)
Rates: $30-$48;
Tel: (616) 775-0164

**PILGRIM'S VILLAGE**
181 S Lake Mitchell (49601)
Rates: N/A;
Tel: (616) 774-5412

**PINE KNOLL MOTEL**
8072 Mackinaw Tr (49601)
Rates: $35-$45;
Tel: (616) 775-9471

**SOUTH SHORE MOTEL & RESORT**
1246 Sunnyside Dr (49601)
Rates: $30-$50;
Tel: (616) 775-7641

**SUN'N SNOW MOTEL**
301 S Lake Mitchell Dr (49601)
Rates: $34-$65;
Tel: (616) 775-7641

## CALUMET

**WHISPERING PINES MOTEL**
Rt 1, Box 85 US 41 (49913)
Rates: N/A;
Tel: (906) 482-5887

## CEDARVILLE

**COMFORT INN**
P. O. Box 189 (49719)
Rates: $49-$89;
Tel: (906) 484-2266

## CHARLEVOIX

**CAPRI MOTEL**
1455 S Bridge St (49720)
Rates: $60-$120;
Tel: (616) 547-2545

## CHEBOYGAN

**BIRCH HAUS MOTEL**
1301 Mackinaw Ave (49721)
Rates: $25-$42;
Tel: (616) 627-5862

**CHEBOYGAN MOTOR LODGE**
1355 Mackinaw Ave (49721)
Rates: $27-$46;
Tel: (616) 627-3129

**CONTINENTAL INN**
613 N Main St (49721)
Rates: $36-$72;
Tel: (616) 627-7164

**FLEETWOOD INN**
889 S Main St (49721)
Rates: $36-$88;
Tel: (616) 627-3126

**MONARCH MOTEL**
1257 Mackinaw Ave (49721)
Rates: N/A;
Tel: (616) 627-2143

**PINE RIVER MOTEL**
102 Lafayette (49721)
Rates: $25-$40;
Tel: (616) 627-5119

## CHRISTMAS

**YULE LOG RESORT**
R R 1 (49862)
Rates: N/A;
Tel: (906) 387-3184

## CLARE

**BUDGET HOST CLARE MOTEL**
1110 N McEwan St (48617)
Rates: $35-$52;
Tel: (517) 386-7201

**DOHERTY MOTEL**
604 McEwan St (48617)
Rates: $34-$120;
Tel: (517) 386-3441

**LONE PINE MOTEL**
1508 McEwan St (48617)
Rates: N/A;
Tel: (517) 386-7787

## COLDWATER

**LITTLE KING MOTEL**
847 E Chicago Rd (49036)
Rates: $27-$52;
Tel: (517) 278-6660

**QUALITY INN**
1000 Orleans Blvd (49036)
Rates: $54-$75;
Tel: (517) 278-2017

## COPPER HARBOR

**ASTOR HOUSE-
MINNETONKA RESORT**
P. O. Box 13 (49918)
Rates: $40-$400;
Tel: (906) 289-4449

**NORLAND MOTEL**
2 Mi E on US 41 (49918)
Rates: $28-$40;
Tel: (906) 289-4815

## CURTIS

**SEASONS MOTEL**
Main St (49820)
Rates: N/A;
Tel: (906) 586 3078

## DETOUR VILLAGE

**DETOUR PASSAGE MOTEL**
P O Box 152 (49725)
Rates: N/A;
Tel: (906) 297-2411

## DETROIT
(and Vicinity)

**BUDGETEL-CANTON**
41211 Ford Rd (48187)
Rates: $31-$49;
Tel: (313) 981-1808

**BUDGETEL-
METRO AIRPORT**
9000 Wickham Rd
(Romulus 48174)
Rates: $33-$42;
Tel: (313) 722-6000

**BUDGETEL-ROSEVILLE**
20675 13 Mile Road
(Roseville 48066)
Rates: $32-$48;
Tel: (313) 296-6910

**BUDGETEL-SOUTHGATE**
12888 Reeck Rd
(Southgate 48195)
Rates: $33-$49;
Tel: (313) 374-3000

**BUDGETEL-WARREN**
30900 N Van Dyke
(Warren 48093)
Rates: $30-$46;
Tel: (313) 574-0550

**COACH & LANTERN
MOTOR INN**
25255 Grand River Ave
(Redford 48240)
Rates: $29-$40;
Tel: (313) 533 4020

**COMFORT INN**
11301 Hall Rd (48317)
Rates: $41-$83;
Tel: (313) 739-7111

**COMFORT INN-LIVONIA**
29235 Buckingham Ave
(Livonia 48154)
Rates: $44-$89;
Tel: (313) 458-7111

**COMFORT INN-
METRO AIRPORT**
9501 Middlebelt Rd
(Romulus 48174)
Rates: $46-$64;
Tel: (313) 946-4300

**DAYS INN SOUTHFIELD
CONVENTION CTR**
17017 W 9 Mile Rd
(Southfield 48075)
Rates: $55-$85;
Tel: (313) 557-4800

**DEARBORN INN
& MARRIOTT HOTEL**
20301 Oakwood Blvd
(Dearborn 48124)
Rates: $85-$145;
Tel: (313) 271-2700

**ECONO LODGE**
23300 Telegraph Rd
(Southfield 48034)
Rates: $38-$92;
Tel: (313) 358-1800

**THE EMBASSY SUITES
HOTEL**
19525 Victor Pkwy
(Livonia 48152)
Rates: $109-$119;
Tel: (313) 462-6000

**GEORGIAN INN**
31327 Gratiot Ave
(Roseville 48066)
Rates: $49-$53;
Tel: (313) 294-0400

**HAMPTON INN-
MADISON HEIGHTS**
32420 Stephenson Hwy
(48071)
Rates: $46-$66;
Tel: (313) 585-8881

**HAMPTON INN-
NORTHVILLE**
20600 Haggerty Rd
(Northville 48167)
Rates: $45-$68;
Tel: (313) 462-1119

**HAMPTON INN-
SOUTHFIELD**
27500 Northwestern Hwy
(Southfield 48034)
Rates: $54-$68;
Tel: (313) 356-5500

**HILTON NOVI**
21111 Haggerty Rd
(Novi 48375)
Rates: $65-$124;
Tel: (313) 349-4000

**HOLIDAY INN-DEARBORN**
22900 Michigan Ave
(Dearborn 48124)
Rates: $67-$90;
Tel: (313) 278-4800

**HOLIDAY INN
FAIRLANE & CONF CTR**
5801 Southfield Service Dr
(48228)
Rates: $59-$69;
Tel: (313) 336-3340

**HOLIDAY INN-
LIVONIA WEST**
17123 Laurel Park Dr N
(Livonia 48152)
Rates: $68-$95;
Tel: (313) 464-1300

**HOLIDAY INN-
METRO AIRPORT**
31200 Detroit Industrial Expwy
(Romulus 48174)
Rates: $75-$95;
Tel: (313) 728-2800

**HOLIDAY INN-SOUTHFIELD**
26555 Telegraph Rd
(Southfield 48034)
Rates: $54-$82;
Tel: (313) 353-7700

**HOLIDAY INN-WARREN**
32035 Van Dyke Ave
(Warren 48093)
Rates: $65-$72;
Tel: (313) 264-0100

**HOMEWOOD SUITES**
30180 N Civic Center Blvd
(48093)
Rates: $65-$95;
Tel: (313) 558-7870

**HOTEL ST. REGIS**
3071 W Grand Blvd (48202)
Rates: $75;
Tel: (313) 873-3000

**HOWARD JOHNSON HOTEL-DETROIT AIRPORT**
8600 Merriman Rd
(Romulus 48174)
Rates: $29-$58;
Tel: (313) 728-7900

**KNIGHTS INN**
21880 West Rd
(Woodhaven 48183)
Rates: $28-$36;
Tel: (313) 676-8550

**KNIGHTS INN-FARMINGTON HILLS**
37527 Grand River Ave
(Farmington Hills 48024)
Rates: $29-$39;
Tel: (313) 477-3200

**KNIGHTS INN-MADISON HEIGHTS**
32703 Stephenson Hwy
(Madison Hgts 48071)
Rates: $29-$44;
Tel: (313) 583-7700

**KNIGHTS INN-MADISON HEIGHTS**
26091 Dequindre Rd
(Madison Hgts 48071)
Rates: $32-$39;
Tel: (313) 545-9930

**KNIGHTS INN-ROMULUS**
8500 Wickham Rd
(Romulus 48174)
Rates: $32-$57;
Tel: (313) 722-8500

**KNIGHTS INN-ROSEVILLE**
31811 Little Mack Rd
(Roseville 48066)
Rates: $29-$38;
Tel: (313) 294-6140

**KNIGHTS INN-WARREN**
7500 Miller Dr (48092)
Rates: N/A;
Tel: (313) 978-7500

**MARRIOTT HOTEL-LIVONIA**
17100 Laurel Park Dr N
(48152)
Rates: $62-$119;
Tel: (313) 462-3100

**MARRIOTT HOTEL METRO AIRPORT**
Detroit Metro Airport (48242)
Rates: $119-$128;
Tel: (313) 941-9400

**MERRIMAN EXECUTIVE INN**
7600 Merriman Rd
(Romulus 48174)
Rates: $49-$79;
Tel: (313) 728-2430

**MOTEL 6**
41216 Ford Rd
(Canton 48187)
Rates: $25-$31;
Tel: (313) 981-5000

**PARKCREST INN**
20000 Harper Ave
(Harper Woods 48225)
Rates: $53-$66;
Tel: (313) 884-8800

**QUALITY INN**
1 W 9 Mile Rd
(Hazel Park 48030)
Rates: $44-$60;
Tel: (313) 399-5800

**RADISSON HOTEL PONTCHARTRAIN**
2 Washignton Blvd (48226)
Rates: $69-$150;
Tel: (313) 965-0200

**RAMADA HERITAGE CENTER**
17201 Northline Rd
(Southgate 48195)
Rates: $65-$74;
Tel: (313) 283-4400

**RAMADA INN-LIVONIA**
30375 Plymouth Rd
(Livonia 48150)
Rates: $45-$50;
Tel: (313) 261-6800

**RAMADA INN METRO AIRPORT**
8270 Wickham Rd
(Romulus 48174)
Rates: $49-$93;
Tel: (313) 729-6300

**RED ROOF INN**
21230 Eureka Rd
(Taylor 48180)
Rates: $29-$40;
Tel: (313) 374-1150

**RED ROOF INN-DEARBORN**
24130 Michigan Ave
(Dearborn 48124)
Rates: $35-$46;
Tel: (313) 278-9732

**RED ROOF INN-FARMINGTON HILLS**
24300 Sinacola Ct
(Farmington Hills 48335)
Rates: $26-$42;
Tel: (313) 478-8640

**RED ROOF INN-MADISON HEIGHTS**
32511 Concord Dr
(Madison Hgts 48071)
Rates: $26-$39;
Tel: (313) 583-4700

**RED ROOF INN-PLYMOUTH**
39700 Ann Arbor Rd
(Plymouth 48170)
Rates: $26-$40;
Tel: (313) 459-3300

**RED ROOF INN-ROSEVILLE**
31800 Little Mack Rd
(Roseville 48066)
Rates: $34-$45;
Tel: (313) 296-0310

**RED ROOF INN-SOUTHFIELD**
27660 Northwestern Hwy
(48034)
Rates: $39-53;
Tel: (313) 353-7200

**RED ROOF INN-WARREN**
26300 Dequindre Rd
(Warren 48091)
Rates: $29-$40;
Tel: (313) 573-4300

190

**RESIDENCE INN
BY MARRIOTT-DEARBORN**
5777 Southfield Service Dr
(Dearborn 48228)
Rates: $110-$150;
Tel: (313) 441-1700

**RESIDENCE INN
BY MARRIOTT-
MADISON HEIGHTS**
32650 Stephenson Hwy
(Madison Hgts 48071)
Rates: $104-$130;
Tel: (313) 583-4322

**RESIDENCE INN
BY MARRIOTT-SOUTHFIELD**
26700 Central Park Blvd
(48076)
Rates: $89-$139;
Tel: (313) 352-8900

**RESIDENCE INN
BY MARRIOTT-WARREN**
30120 Civic Center Blvd
(Warren 48093)
Rates: $104-$119;
Tel: (313) 558-8050

**ROMULUS MARRIOTT**
30559 Flynn Dr
(Romulus 10174)
Rates: $79-$109;
Tel: (313) 729-7555

**SAGAMORE
MOTOR LODGE**
3220 N Woodward Ave
(Royal Oak 48073)
Rates: $25-$40;
Tel: (313) 549-1600

**SOUTHFIELD HILTON
GARDEN INN**
26000 American Dr
(Southfield 48034)
Rates: $49-$79;
Tel: (313) 357-1100

**SOUTHFIELD
MARRIOTT HOTEL**
27033 Northwestern Hwy
(Southfield 48034)
Rates: $69-$99;
Tel: (313) 356-7400

**SUPER 8 MOTEL-CANTON**
3933 Lotz Rd (48188)
Rates: $33-$40;
Tel: (313) 722-8880

**SUPER 8 MOTEL-
METRO AIRPORT**
9863 Middlebelt Rd
(Romulus 48174)
Rates: $32-$38;
Tel: (313) 946-8808

**SUPER 8 MOTEL-TAYLOR**
15101 Huron St (48180)
Rates: $29-$41;
Tel: (313) 283-8830

**TRAVELODGE-
DETROIT/NOVI**
21100 Haggerty Rd
(Northville 48167)
Rates: $43;
Tel: (313) 349-7400

**TRAVELODGE-SOUTHFIELD**
27650 Northwestern Hwy
(48034)
Rates: $41-$47;
Tel: (313) 353-6777

**VAN DYKE PARK
HOTEL & CONF CTR**
31800 Van Dyke Ave
(Warren 48093)
Rates: $59-$500;
Tel: (800) 321-1008

**THE VILLAGER LODGE**
34858 Van Dyke Rd
(Sterling Hgts 48077)
Rates: $29-$36;
Tel: (313) 939-5300

**WESTIN HOTEL-
RENAISSANCE CENTER**
Renaissance Center (48243)
Rates: $135-$170;
Tel: (313) 568-8000

# DRUMMOND ISLAND

**VECHELL'S CEDAR
VIEW RESORT**
P. O. Box 175 (49726)
Rates: $225-$255;
Tel: (906) 493-5381

# DUNDEE

**COMFORT INN**
621 Tecumseh Rd (48131)
Rates: $42-$72;
Tel: (313) 529-5505

# EAGLE HARBOR

**SHORELINE RESORT**
HYC 1, Box 262 (49950)
Rates: $40-$46;
Tel: (906) 289-4441

# EAST JORDAN

**WESTBROOK MOTEL**
218 Elizabeth St (49727)
Rates: N/A;
Tel: (616) 536-2674

# EAST TAWAS

**NORTHLAND
BEACH COTTAGES**
808 East Bay St (48730)
Rates: N/A;
Tel: (517) 362-2601

# ELK RAPIDS

**CAMELOT INN**
P. O. Box 910 (49629)
Rates: $30-$75;
Tel: (616) 264-8473

# EPOUFETTE

**WONDERLAND MOTEL**
80 West US 2 (49762)
Rates: N/A;
Tel: (906) 292-5574

# ESCANABA

**HIAWATHA MOTEL**
2400 Ludington St (49829)
Rates: $36-$44;
Tel: (906) 786-1341

**SUNSET MOTEL**
P. O. Box 343 (49829)
Rates: $25-$40;
Tel: (906) 786-1213

# FLINT

**DAYS INN**
2207 W Bristol Rd (48507)
Rates: $42-$57;
Tel: (313) 239-4681

**KNIGHTS INN**
G-3277 Miller Rd (48507)
Rates: N/A;
Tel: (800) 843-5644

**MISTER GIBBY'S INN**
G-3129 Miller Rd (48507)
Rates: $35-$105;
Tel: (313) 235-4500

**RED ROOF INN**
G-3219 Miller Rd (48507)
Rates: $33-$44;
Tel: (313) 733-1660

# FRANKENMUTH

**BED & BREAKFAST
AT THE PINES**
327 Ardussi St (48734)
Rates: N/A;
Tel: (517) 652-9019

# FRANKFORT

**BAY VALLEY INN**
1561 Scenic Hwy (49635)
Rates: $45-$75;
Tel: (616) 352-7113

**CHIMNEY CORNERS RESORT**
1602 Crystal Dr (49635)
Rates: $37-$1100;
Tel: (616) 352-7522

# GAYLORD

**BUDGET HOST
ROYAL CREST**
803 S Otsego Ave (49735)
Rates: $45-$60;
Tel: (517) 732-6451

**THE CEDARS MOTEL**
701 North Center (49735)
Rates: N/A;
Tel: (517) 732-4525

**DOWNTOWN MOTEL**
208 S Otsego Ave (49735)
Rates: $32-$52;
Tel: (517) 732-5010

**HOLIDAY INN**
P. O. Box 544 (49735)
Rates: $59-$89;
Tel: (517) 732-2431

**NORTHLAND INN
AND MOTEL**
P. O. Box 188 (Waters 49797)
Rates: $28-$56;
Tel: (517) 732-4470

**TIMBERLY MOTEL**
881 S Otsego Ave (49735)
Rates: $36-$54;
Tel: (517) 732-5166

# GRAND BLANC

**SCENIC INN**
G8308 S Saginaw Rd (48439)
Rates: N/A;
Tel: (313) 694-6611

# GRAND HAVEN

**FOUNTAIN INN**
1010 S Beacon Blvd (49417)
Rates: $35-$50;
Tel: (616) 846-1800

# GRAND MARAIS

**ALVERSON'S MOTEL**
P. O. Box 188 (49839)
Rates: $28-$33;
Tel: (906) 494-2681

**BUDGET HOST-
WELKER'S RESORT**
P. O. Box 277 (49839)
Rates: $34-$350;
Tel: (906) 494-2361

**HILLTOP CABINS**
P. O. Box 377 (49839)
Rates: N/A;
Tel: (906) 494-2331

# GRAND RAPIDS

**BUDGETEL INN**
2873 Kraft Ave SE (49512)
Rates: $33-$44;
Tel: (616) 956-3300

**DAYS INN-DOWNTOWN**
310 Pearl St NW (49504)
Rates: $59-$75;
Tel: (616) 235-7611

**DAYS INN**
4855 28th St SE (49512)
Rates: $31-$41;
Tel: (616) 957-3000

**ECONO LODGE**
250 28th St SW (49508)
Rates: $34-$48;
Tel: (616) 452-2131

**EXEL INN**
4855 28th St SE
(Kentwood 49512)
Rates: $31-$40;
Tel: (616) 957-3000

**HAMPTON INN**
2981 28th St SE (49512)
Rates: $47-$61;
Tel: (616) 956-9304

**HOLIDAY INN-NORTH**
270 Ann St NW (49504)
Rates: $65-$84;
Tel: (616) 363-9001

**HOLIDAY INN-SOUTH**
255 28th St SW (49548)
Rates: $54-68;
Tel: (616) 241-6444

**MAIN STREET INNS**
5175 28th St SE (49512)
Rates: $34-$41;
Tel: (616) 956-6601

**NEW ENGLAND SUITES
HOTEL**
2985 Kraft Ave SE (49512)
Rates: $47-$65;
Tel: (616) 940-1777

**PRESIDENT INN**
3221 Plainfield NE (49505)
Rates: N/A;
Tel: (616) 363-0800

**RED ROOF INN**
5131 29th St SE (49512)
Rates: $35-$43;
Tel: (616) 942-0800

**RESIDENCE INN
BY MARRIOTT**
2701 E Beltline (49546)
Rates: $102-$135;
Tel: (616) 957-8111

**RIVIERA MOTEL**
4350 Rememberance Rd
(49504)
Rates: $28-$42;
Tel: (616) 453-2404

## GRAYLING

**HOLIDAY INN**
P. O. Box 473 (49738)
Rates: $48-$92;
Tel: (517) 348-7611

**NORTH COUNTRY LODGE**
P. O. Box 290 (49738)
Rates: $40-$150;
Tel: (517) 348-8471

## HAGAR SHORE

**SWEET CHERRY RESORT**
3313 Chestnut (49038)
Rates: N/A;
Tel: (616) 849-1233

## HARBOR BEACH

**THE TRAIN STATION
MOTEL**
2044 N Lakeshore Dr (48441)
Rates: $35-$55;
Tel: (517) 479-3215

## HARBOR SPRINGS

**HARBOR SPRINGS
COTTAGE INN**
145 Zoll St (49740)
Rates: $38-$88;
Tel: (616) 526-5431

## HARRISON

**LAKESIDE MOTEL**
South Business #27 (48625)
Rates: N/A;
Tel: (517) 539-3796

**WAGON WHEEL MOTEL**
4294 North Clare Ave
(48625)
Rates: N/A;
Tel: (517) 539-1841

## HESSEL

**LAKEVIEW MOTEL**
P. O. Box 277 (49745)
Rates: N/A;
Tel: (906) 484-2474

## HOLLAND

**BEST WESTERN
HOLLAND INN**
482 E 32nd St (49423)
Rates: $43-$64;
Tel: (616) 396-1424

**BLUE MILL INN**
409 US 31S (49423)
Rates: $39-$51;
Tel: (616) 392-7073

**DAYS INN**
717 Hastings (49423)
Rates: $43-$59;
Tel: (616) 392-7001

## HONOR

**SUNNY WOODS RESORT**
14065 Honor Hwy
(Beulah 49617)
Rates: $28-$37;
Tel: (616) 325-3952

## HOUGHTON LAKE

**HILLSIDE MOTEL**
3419 W Houghton Lake Dr
(48629)
Rates: $36-$42;
Tel: (517) 366-5711

**HOLIDAY INN**
9285 W Houghton Lake Dr
(48629)
Rates: $65-$81;
Tel: (517) 422-5175

**HOLIDAY ON THE LAKE**
100 Clearview Rd (48629)
Rates: $23-$48;
Tel: (517) 422-5195

**POPULARS RESORT**
10360 West Shore Dr (48629)
Rates: N/A;
Tel: (517) 422-5132

**SWISS INN ON THE LAKE**
472 W Houghton Lake Dr
(Prudenville 48651)
Rates: $28-$65;
Tel: (517) 366-7881

**VAL HALLA MOTEL**
9869 West Shore Dr (48629)
Rates: $40-$48;
Tel: (517) 422-5137

**VENTURE INN**
8939 W Houghton Lake Dr
(48629)
Rates: $33-$48;
Tel: (517) 422-5591

**WAY NORTH MOTEL**
9052 N Old US 27 (48629)
Rates: $34-$58;
Tel: (517) 422-5523

## HOWELL

**PARK INN
INTERNATIONAL**
125 Holiday Ln (48843)
Rates: $35-$53;
Tel: (517) 546-6800

## HULBERT

**THE LEEJA MOTEL**
2000 M28 (49748)
Rates: N/A;
Tel: (906) 876-2323

# IMLAY CITY

**SUPER 8 MOTEL-IMLAY CITY**
6951 Newark Rd (48444)
Rates: $38-$48;
Tel: (313) 724-5501

# INDIAN RIVER

**CARAVAN MOTEL COTTAGES**
4904 S Straits Hwy (49749)
Rates: N/A;
Tel: (616) 238-7481

**REIDS MOTOR COURT**
3977 S Straits Hwy (49749)
Rates: N/A;
Tel: (616) 238-9353

**STAR GATE MOTEL**
4646 S Straits Hwy (49749)
Rates: $28-$48;
Tel: (616) 238-7371

# IONIA

**EVERGREEN MOTEL**
2030 N State Rd (48846)
Rates: N/A;
Tel: (616) 527-0930

# IRON MOUNTAIN

**BEST WESTERN EXECUTIVE INN**
1518 S Stephenson Ave (49801)
Rates: $54-$60;
Tel: (906) 774-2040

**WOODLANDS MOTEL**
N 3957 North US 2 (49801)
Rates: N/A;
Tel: (906) 774-6106

# IRON RIVER

**IRON RIVER MOTEL**
3073 East US 2 (49935)
Rates: N/A;
Tel: (906) 265-4212

# IRONWOOD

**ARMATA MOTEL**
124 W Cloverland Dr (49938)
Rates: $24-$34;
Tel: (906) 932-4421

**BLUE CLOUD MOTEL**
105 W Cloverland Dr (49938)
Rates: N/A;
Tel: (906) 932-0920

# JACKSON

**BUDGETEL INN**
2035 N Service Dr (49202)
Rates: $34-$50;
Tel: (517) 789-6000

**HOLIDAY INN**
2000 Holiday Inn Dr (49202)
Rates: $58-$79;
Tel: (517) 783-2681

**MOTEL 6**
830 Royal Dr (49202)
Rates: $26-$32;
Tel: (517) 789-7186

# JONESVILLE

**PINECREST MOTEL**
516 W Chicago St (49250)
Rates: N/A;
Tel: (517) 849-2137

# KALAMAZOO

**BUDGETEL INN**
2203 S 11th St (49009)
Rates: $33-$49;
Tel: (616) 372-7999

**DAYS INN**
1912 E Kilgore (49002)
Rates: $35-$59;
Tel: (616) 382-2303

**HOLIDAY INN-EXPRESSWAY**
3522 Sprinkle Rd (49002)
Rates: $70-$86;
Tel: (616) 381-7070

**HOLIDAY INN-WEST**
2747 S 11th St (49009)
Rates: $75-$95;
Tel: (616) 375-6000

**KNIGHTS INN**
3704 Van Rick Rd (49002)
Rates: N/A;
Tel: (800) 843-5644

**LA QUINTA MOTOR INN**
3750 Easy St (49002)
Rates: $45-$59;
Tel: (616) 388-3551

**LEE'S INN**
2615 Fairfield Rd (49002)
Rates: $52-$73;
Tel: (616) 382-6100

**MOTEL 6**
3704 Van Rick Rd (49002)
Rates: $25-$31;
Tel: (616) 344-9255

**QUALITY INN**
5300 S Westnedge Ave (49008)
Rates: $46-$54;
Tel: (616) 382-1000

**THE RAMADA HOTEL KALAMAZOO**
3600 E Cork St (49001)
Rates: $59-$67;
Tel: (616) 385-3922

**RED ROOF INN-EAST**
3701 E Cork St (49001)
Rates: $35-$43;
Tel: (616) 382-6350

**RED ROOF INN-WEST**
5425 W Michigan Ave (49009)
Rates: $40-$43;
Tel: (616) 375-7400

**RESIDENCE INN BY MARRIOTT**
1500 E Kilgore (49001)
Rates: $98-$125;
Tel: (616) 349-0855

**UNIVERSITY INN**
1211 S Westnedge Ave (49008)
Rates: N/A;
Tel: (616) 381-5000

## LAKE CITY

**LAKE CITY MOTEL**
704 N Morey Rd (49651)
Rates: N/A;
Tel: (616) 839-4857

**NORTHCREST MOTEL**
1341 S Lakeshore (49651)
Rates: $38-$48;
Tel: (616) 839-2075

## LANSING

**BEST WESTERN
GOVERNOR'S INN CONF CTR**
6133 S Pennsylvania Ave
(48911)
Rates: $48-$58;
Tel: (517) 393-5500

**BEST WESTERN
MIDWAY HOTEL**
7711 W Saginaw Hwy
(48917)
Rates: $60-$75;
Tel: (517) 627-8471

**COMFORT INN
OF EAST LANSING**
2209 University Park
(Okemos 48864)
Rates: $52-$58;
Tel: (517) 349-8700

**DAYS INN-
CAPITAL CENTRE**
500 S Capitol Ave (48933)
Rates: $44-$55;
Tel: (517) 482-1000

**DAYS INN
LANSING-SOUTH**
6501 S Pennsylvania Ave
(48911)
Rates: $44-$59;
Tel: (517) 393-1650

**HAMPTON INN
OF LANSING**
525 N Canal Rd (48917)
Rates: $39-$58;
Tel: (517) 627-8381

**KNIGHTS INN-SOUTH**
1100 Ramada Dr (48911)
Rates: $33-$42;
Tel: (517) 394-7200

**PARK INN
INTERNATIONAL**
1100 Trowbridge Rd
(E Lansing 48823)
Rates: $42-$44;
Tel: (517) 351-5500

**QUALITY SUITES**
901 Delta Commerce (48917)
Rates: $67-$77;
Tel: (517) 886-0600

**RED ROOF INN-EAST**
3615 Dunckel Rd (48910)
Rates: $34-$47;
Tel: (517) 332-2575

**RED ROOF INN-WEST**
7412 W Saginaw Hwy
(48917)
Rates: $35-$43;
Tel: (517) 321-7246

**REGAL 8 INN**
6501 S Cedar St (48911)
Rates: N/A;
Tel: (517) 393-2030

**RESIDENCE INN
BY MARRIOTT**
1600 E Grand River Ave
(48823)
Rates: $99-$129;
Tel: (517) 332-7711

**SAVE INN**
7326 W Saginaw Hwy
(48917)
Rates: $44-$48;
Tel: (517) 321-1444

**SHERATON
LANSING HOTEL**
925 S Creyts Rd (48917)
Rates: $95-$105;
Tel: (517) 323-7100

## LEWISTON

**FAIRWAY INN**
County Rd 489 (49756)
Rates: N/A;
Tel: (517) 786-2217

## LUDINGTON

**FOUR SEASONS MOTEL**
717 E Ludington Ave (49431)
Rates: $38-$92;
Tel: (616) 843-3448

**NADER'S LAKE SHORE
MOTOR LODGE**
612 N Lakeshore Dr (49431)
Rates: $50-$58;
Tel: (616) 843-8757

**NOVA MOTEL**
472 S Pere Marquette Hwy
(49431)
Rates: $28-$69;
Tel: (616) 843-3454

**RAMADA INN**
4079 W US 10 (49431)
Rates: $84-$110;
Tel: (616) 843-8551

**VENTURA MOTEL**
604 W Ludington Ave (49431)
Rates: $30-$89;
Tel: (616) 845-5124

## MACKINAW CITY

**AFFORDABLE INNS
OF AMERICA**
206 Nicolet St (49701)
Rates: $38-$74;
Tel: (616) 436-8961

**AMERICAN MOTEL**
14351 S US 31 (49701)
Rates: N/A;
Tel: (616) 436-5231

**BEACHCOMBER MOTEL
ON THE WATER**
P. O. Box 159 (49701)
Rates: $29-$78;
Tel: (616) 436-8451

**THE BEACH HOUSE**
P. O. Box 141 (49701)
Rates: $26-$96;
Tel: (616) 436-5353

**BELL'S MELODY MOTEL**
P. O. Box 896 (49701)
Rates: $28-$73;
Tel: (616) 436-5463

**BUDGET HOST
MACKINAW CITY**
P. O. Box 672 (49701)
Rates: $28-$82;
Tel: (616) 436-5543

**CAPRI MOTEL**
P.O. Box 718 (49701)
Rates: $20-$52;
Tel: (616) 436-5498

**ECONO LODGE
AT THE BRIDGE**
P.O. Box 812 (49701)
Rates: $28-$86;
Tel: (616) 436-5026

**HOLIDAY INN
EXPRESS HOTEL**
364 Louvingney (49701)
Rates: $36-$135;
Tel: (616) 436-7100

**KNIGHTS INN**
P. O. Box 302 (49701)
Rates: $26-$75;
Tel: (616) 436-5527

**LAMPLIGHTER MOTEL**
303 Jamet St (49701)
Rates: $24-$49;
Tel: (616) 436-5350

**LOVELAND'S LA MIRAGE**
699 N Huron Ave (49701)
Rates: $60-$150;
Tel: (616) 436-5304

**NORTHWINDS MOTEL**
P. O. Box 896 (49701)
Rates: $28-$73;
Tel: (616) 436-5463

**OTTAWA MOTEL**
P. O. Box 908 (49701)
Rates: $24-$65;
Tel: (616) 436-8041

**PARKSIDE INN-
BRIDGESIDE**
P. O. Box 788 (49701)
Rates: $28-$82;
Tel: (616) 436-8301

**QUALITY INN**
P. O. Box 519 (49701)
Rates: $36-$92;
Tel: (616) 436-5051

**RAMADA INN**
314 S Nicolet St (49701)
Rates: $60-$92;
Tel: (616) 436-5535

**RODEWAY INN**
619 S Nicolet St (49701)
Rates: $54-$74;
Tel: (616) 436-5332

**STARLITE THRIFTY INNS**
P. O. Box 758 (49701)
Rates: $26-$58;
Tel: (616) 436-5959

**SURF MOTEL**
P. O. Box 58 (49701)
Rates: $24-$89;
Tel: (616) 436-8831

**VAL-RU MOTEL**
P. O. Box 521 (49701)
Rates: $18-$36;
Tel: (616) 436-7691

**VIN-DEL MOTEL**
223 W Central Ave (49701)
Rates: $26-$55;
Tel: (616) 436-5273

## MANISTEE

**CARRIAGE INN**
200 Arthur St (49660)
Rates: $39-$69;
Tel: (616) 723-9949

## MANISTIQUE

**BUDGET HOST-
MANISTIQUE MOTOR INN**
Rte 1 (49854)
Rates: $40-$100;
Tel: (906) 341-2552

**HOJO INN**
726 E Lakeshore Dr (49854)
Rates: $38-$80;
Tel: (906) 341-6981

**HOLIDAY MOTEL**
Rt 1, Box 1514 (49854)
Rates: $26-$44;
Tel: (906) 341-2710

**MAPLE LEAF MOTEL**
P. O. Box 184 (49854)
Rates: $28-$44;
Tel: (906) 341-6014

**RAMADA INN**
P. O. Box 485 (49854)
Rates: $45-$78;
Tel: (906) 341-6911

## MANTON

**IRISH INN MOTEL**
415 N Michigan Ave (49663)
Rates: N/A;
Tel: (616) 824-6988

## MARINE CITY

**PORT SEAWAY INN**
7623 S River Rd (48039)
Rates: $32-$46;
Tel: (313) 765-4033

## MARQUETTE

**BIRCHMONT MOTEL**
2090 US 41S (49855)
Rates: $32-$40;
Tel: (906) 228-7538

**EDGEWATER MOTEL
& GARDEN ROOM REST.**
2050 US 41S (49855)
Rates: $31-$47;
Tel: (906) 225-1305

**HOLIDAY INN**
P. O. Box 368 (49855)
Rates: $58-$67;
Tel: (906) 225-1351

**RAMADA INN**
P. O. Box 464 (49855)
Rates: $65-$90;
Tel: (906) 228-6000

## MARSHALL

**ARBOR INN-
HISTORIC MARSHALL**
15435 W Michigan Ave
(49068)
Rates: $42-$49;
Tel: (616) 781-7772

**HOWARD'S MOTEL**
14884 W Michigan Ave
(49068)
Rates: $30-$44;
Tel: (616) 781-4201

## MCBAIN

**TOWNE MOTEL**
P. O. Box 164 (49657)
Rates: $32-$35;
Tel: (616) 825-2346

## MENOMINEE

**HOJO INN**
2516 10th St (49858)
Rates: $35-$60;
Tel: (906) 863-4431

## MIDLAND

**FAIRVIEW INN**
2200 W Wackerly St (48640)
Rates: $50-$54;
Tel: (517) 631-0070

**HOLIDAY INN**
1500 W Wackerly (48640)
Rates: $70-$100;
Tel: (517) 631-4220

## MIO

**MIO MOTEL**
415 N Morenci St (48647)
Rates: $35-$45;
Tel: (517) 826-3248

## MONROE

**ARBORGATE INN**
1885 Welcome Way (48161)
Rates: $27-$34;
Tel: (313) 289-1080

**DAYS INN**
1440 N Dixie Hwy (48161)
Rates: $39-$62;
Tel: (313) 289-4000

**HOLIDAY INN MONROE**
1225 N Dixie Hwy (48161)
Rates: $54-$69;
Tel: (313) 242-6000

**KNIGHTS INN**
1250 N Dixie Hwy (48161)
Rates: $28-$35;
Tel: (313) 243-0597

## MOUNT PLEASANT

**COMFORT INN-
UNIVERSITY PARK**
2424 S Mission St (48858)
Rates: $43-$99;
Tel: (517) 772-4000

**HOLIDAY INN**
5665 E Pickard Ave (48858)
Rates: $52-$125;
Tel: (517) 772-2905

## MUNISING

**ALGER FALLS MOTEL**
Rte 1, Box 967 (49862)
Rates: $40-$65;
Tel: (906) 387-3536

**BEST WESTERN MOTEL**
P. O. Box 310 (49862)
Rates: $35-$65;
Tel: (906) 387-4864

**COMFORT INN**
P. O. Box 276 (49862)
Rates: $39-$75;
Tel: (906) 387-5292

**STAR-LITE MOTEL**
500 M-28E (49862)
Rates: $32-$38;
Tel: (906) 387-2291

**SUNSET RESORT**
P. O. Box 521 (49862)
Rates: $32-$43;
Tel: (906) 387-4574

**TERRACE MOTEL**
420 Prospect (49862)
Rates: $32-$42;
Tel: (906) 387-2735

## MUSKEGON

**BEL-AIRE MOTEL**
4240 Airline Rd (49444)
Rates: $38-$55;
Tel: (616) 733-2196

**BEST WESTERN
PARK PLAZA HOTEL**
2967 Henry St (49441)
Rates: $45-$74;
Tel: (616) 733-2651

**ECONO LODGE**
3450 Hoyt St (49444)
Rates: $45-$49;
Tel: (616) 733-2601

## NEW BALTIMORE

**TRAVELODGE**
29101 23 Mile Rd (48047)
Rates: $39-$62;
Tel: (313) 949-4520

## NEWBERRY

**BEST WESTERN
VILLAGE INN**
P. O. Box 152 (49868)
Rates: $40-$60;
Tel: (906) 293-5114

**MANOR MOTEL**
Rte 1, Box 979 (49868)
Rates: $38-$64;
Tel: (906) 293-5000

**RAINBOW LODGE**
County Rd 423, P. O. Box 386
(49868)
Rates: N/A;
Tel: (906) 658-3357

## NEW BUFFALO

**COMFORT INN**
11539 O'Brien Ct (49117)
Rates: $43-$97;
Tel: (616) 469-4440

**GRAND BEACH MOTEL**
19189 US 12 (49117)
Rates: $25-$45;
Tel: (616) 469-1555

## NILES

**HOLIDAY INN**
930 S 11th St (49120)
Rates: $52-$67;
Tel: (616) 684-3000

## OKEMOS

**COMFORT INN
& EXECUTIVE SUITES**
2209 University Park Dr
(48864)
Rates: $52-$99;
Tel: (517) 349-8700

## ONAWAY

**LAKESIDE MOTEL**
County Rd 489, Rt 1 (49765)
Rates: N/A;
Tel: (517) 733-4298

## OSCODA

**ASPEN MOTOR INN**
115 N Lake St (48750)
Rates: N/A;
Tel: (800) 892-7736

**NORTHERN TRAVELER**
5493 N US 23 (48750)
Rates: N/A;
Tel: (517) 739-9261

**SHENANDOAH
ON THE LAKE**
3312 N US 23 (48750)
Rates: N/A;
Tel: (517) 739-3997

## PARADISE

**CURLEY'S
PARADISE MOTEL**
P. O. Box 57, M-123 (49768)
Rates: N/A;
Tel: (906) 492-3445

## PAW PAW

**GREEN ACRES MOTEL**
38245 W Red Arrow (49079)
Rates: N/A;
Tel: (616) 657-4037

**MROCZEK INN**
139 Ampey Rd (49079)
Rates: $31-$40;
Tel: (616) 657-2578

## PERRY

**HEB'S INN MOTEL**
2811 Temp I-69 (48872)
Rates: $28-$32;
Tel: (517) 625-7500

## PETOSKEY

**COACH HOUSE MOTEL**
2445 Charlevoix Ave (49770)
Rates: $45-$60;
Tel: (616) 347-2593

**COMFORT INN**
1314 US 31N (49770)
Rates: $60-$125;
Tel: (616) 347-3220

**DAYS INN**
630 W Mitchell St (49770)
Rates: $41-$96;
Tel: (616) 347-8717

**ECONO LODGE**
1858 US 131S (49770)
Rates: $54-$64;
Tel: (616) 348-3324

## PLAINWELL

**COMFORT INN**
622 Allegan St (49080)
Rates: $45-$150;
Tel: (616) 685-9891

## PLYMOUTH

**RED ROOF INN**
39700 Ann Arbor Rd (48170)
Rates: N/A;
Tel: (800) 843-7663

## PONTIAC

**COMFORT INN-AIRPORT**
7076 Highland Rd
(Waterford 48327)
Rates: $45-$99;
Tel: (313) 852-0750

**MCGUIRE'S MOTOR INN**
120 S Telegraph Rd (48328)
Rates: $29-$39;
Tel: (313) 682-5100

## PORT HURON

**COLONIAL MOTOR INN**
2908 Pine Grove Ave (48060)
Rates: $48-$59;
Tel: (313) 984-1522

**ECONOMY LODGE**
1720 Hancock St (48060)
Rates: $49-$55;
Tel: (313) 984-2661

**KNIGHTS INN**
2160 Water St (48060)
Rates: $42-$53;
Tel: (313) 982-1022

## PRUDENVILLE

**SWISS INN ON THE LAKE**
472 W Houghton Lake Dr
(48651)
Rates: N/A;
Tel: (517) 366-7881

## ROCHESTER HILLS

**RED ROOF INN**
2580 Crooks Rd (48309)
Rates: $29-$41;
Tel: (313) 853-6400

**ROCHESTER
MOTOR LODGE**
2070 S Rochester Rd (48307)
Rates: $33-$40;
Tel: (313) 651-8591

## ROGERS CITY

**DRIFTWOOD MOTEL**
540 W Third St (49779)
Rates: $39-$65;
Tel: (517) 734-4777

## SAGINAW

**BEST WESTERN**
3325 Davenport Ave (48602)
Rates: $30-$50;
Tel: (517) 793-2080

**HAMPTON INN**
2222 Tittabawassee Rd
(48604)
Rates: $49-$61;
Tel: (517) 792-7666

**HOLIDAY INN SAGINAW
I-75/FRANKENMUTH**
1408 S Outer Dr (48601)
Rates: $58-$80;
Tel: (517) 755-0461

**KNIGHTS INN-NORTH**
2225 Tittabawassee Rd
(48604)
Rates: $35-$41;
Tel: (517) 791-1411

**KNIGHTS INN
SAGINAW SOUTH**
1415 S Outer Dr (48601)
Rates: $31-$49;
Tel: (517) 754-9200

**QUALITY INN**
3425 Holland Rd (48601)
Rates: $36-$55;
Tel: (517) 753-2461

**RED ROOF INN**
966 S Outer Dr (48601)
Rates: $33-$41;
Tel: (517) 754-8414

**SHERATON INN-
FASHION SQUARE**
4960 Towne Center Rd
(48604)
Rates: $70-$108;
Tel: (517) 790-5050

## ST. IGNACE

**BAY VIEW
BEACH FRONT MOTEL**
1133 N State St (49781)
Rates: $25-$52;
Tel: (906) 643-9444

**BLUE BAY MOTEL**
1071 N State St (49781)
Rates: $26-$48;
Tel: (906) 643-7414

**BUDGET HOST INN**
700 N State St (49781)
Rates: $36-$68;
Tel: (906) 643-9666

**CEDAR'S MOTEL**
2040 N Business Loop I-75
(49781)
Rates: N/A;
Tel: (906) 643-9578

**CHALET NORTH MOTEL**
1140 N State St (49781)
Rates: $28-$59;
Tel: (906) 643-9141

**THE DRIFTWOOD MOTEL**
590 N State St (49781)
Rates: $30-$52;
Tel: (906) 643-7744

**HOWARD JOHNSON
LODGE**
913 Boulevard Dr (49781)
Rates: $37-$76;
Tel: (906) 653-9700

**NORTHERNAIRE MOTEL**
2020 Business Loop I-75N
(49781)
Rates: $20-$42;
Tel: (906) 643-8704

**PINES MOTEL**
1919 State St (49781)
Rates: $35-$45;
Tel: (906) 643-9250

**ROCKVIEW MOTEL**
2055 N Business Loop I-75
(49781)
Rates: N/A;
Tel: (906) 643-8839

**VITEK'S MOTEL**
980 N State St (49781)
Rates: N/A;
Tel: (906) 643-7922

**WAYSIDE MOTEL**
751 N State St (49781)
Rates: $22-$42;
Tel: (906) 643-8944

## ST. JOSEPH

**BEST WESTERN
GOLDEN LINK MOTEL**
2723 Niles Ave (49085)
Rates: $29-$55;
Tel: (616) 983-6321

## SAND LAKE

**SHADY LAWN MOTEL**
16390 Northland Dr (49343)
Rates: N/A;
Tel: (616) 696-0386

## SAUGATUCK

**THE KIRBY HOUSE**
294 W Center St (49453)
Rates: $65-$100;
Tel: (616) 857-2904

## SAULT STE. MARIE

**BAVARIAN LODGE
BUDGET HOST**
2006 Ashmun St (49783)
Rates: $29-$58;
Tel: (906) 632-6864

**BEST WESTERN
COLONIAL INNS**
P. O. Box 659 (49783)
Rates: $45-$87;
Tel: (906) 632-2170

**BILTMORE MOTEL**
331 E Portage Ave (49783)
Rates: N/A;
Tel: (800) 528-0612

**CRESTVIEW THRIFTY INNS**
1200 Ashmun St (49783)
Rates: $46-$56;
Tel: (906) 635-5213

**GRAND MOTEL**
1100 E Portage Ave (49783)
Rates: $26-$48;
Tel: (906) 632-2141

**LAKER INN**
1712 Ashmun St (49783)
Rates: $36-$40;
Tel: (906) 632-3581

**LONG SHIPS MOTEL**
427 W Portage (49783)
Rates: N/A;
Tel: (800) 626-3107

**MID-CITY MOTEL**
304 E Portage Ave (49783)
Rates: $33-$48;
Tel: (906) 632-6832

**ROYAL MOTEL**
1707 Ashmun St (49783)
Rates: $34-$48;
Tel: (906) 632-6323

**SEAWAY MOTEL**
1800 Ashmun St (49783)
Rates: $34-$48;
Tel: (906) 632-8201

**SUNSET MOTEL**
Rt 2, Box 226A (49783)
Rates: $29-$32;
Tel: (906) 632-3906

## SHELBY

**SHELBY MANOR**
115 E Fourth St (49455)
Rates: N/A;
Tel: (616) 861-9903

## SILVER CITY

**BEST WESTERN PORCUPINE
MOUNTAIN LODGE**
120 Lincoln St (49953)
Rates: $53-$63;
Tel: (906) 885-5311

**RAINBOW MOTEL
& CHALETS**
P. O. Box 2900
(Ontonagon 49953)
Rates: $30-$43;
Tel: (906) 885-5348

## SOUTH HAVEN

**FRIENDSHIP INN**
09817 M-140 Hwy (49090)
Rates: $57-$100;
Tel: (616) 637-5141

## STEPHENSON

**STEPHENSON MOTEL**
R 2, Box 20, Hwy 41 (49887)
Rates: N/A;
Tel: (906) 753-2552

## STURGIS

**HOLIDAY INN**
1300 S Centerville Rd (49091)
Rates: $48-$61;
Tel: (616) 651-7881

## TAWAS CITY

**NORTH STAR MOTEL**
1119 S US 23 (48763)
Rates: N/A;
Tel: (517) 362-2255

**TAWAS MOTEL**
1124 US 23 (48763)
Rates: $49-$73;
Tel: (517) 367-3822

## THREE RIVERS

**THREE RIVERS INN**
P. O. Box 349 (49093)
Rates: $60-$65;
Tel: (616) 273-9521

## TRAVERSE CITY

**BRIAR HILL MOTEL**
461 Munson Ave (49684)
Rates: $60-$75;
Tel: (616) 947-5525

**FOX HAUS MOTOR LODGE**
704 Munson Ave (49684)
Rates: $45-$185;
Tel; (616) 947-4450

**HOLIDAY INN**
615 E Front St (49684)
Rates: $70-$130;
Tel: (616) 947-3700

**MAIN STREET INNS**
618 E Front St (49684)
Rates: $29-$69;
Tel: (800) 255-7180

**OLD MISSION INN**
18599 Old Mission Rd
(49684)
Rates: N/A;
Tel: (616) 223-7770

**WENTWORTH INN**
1492 US 31N (49684)
Rates: $49-$79;
Tel: (616) 929-4423

## TROUT LAKE

**MCGOWAN FAMILY
MOTEL & RESTAURANT**
SR 123 (49793)
Rates: $33-$41;
Tel: (906) 569-3366

## TROY

**DRURY INN**
575 W Big Beaver Rd (48084)
Rates: $59-$65;
Tel: (313) 528-3330

**HOLIDAY INN**
2537 Rochester Ct (48083)
Rates: $78-$95;
Tel: (313) 689-7500

**NORTHFIELD HILTON**
5500 Crooks Rd (48098)
Rates: $59-$109;
Tel: (313) 879-2100

**RED ROOF INN**
2350 Rochester Rd (48083)
Rates: $26-$39;
Tel: (800) 843-7663

**RESIDENCE INN
BY MARRIOTT**
2600 Livernois Rd (48083)
Rates: $75-$130;
Tel: (313) 689-6856

**TROY MARRIOTT**
200 W Big Beaver Rd (48084)
Rates: $69-$144;
Tel: (313) 680-9797

## WATERS

**WATERS MOTEL**
10565 Old US 27 S (49797)
Rates: N/A;
Tel: (517) 732-3489

## WEST BRANCH

**LA HACIENDA MOTEL**
969 West Houghton Ave
(48661)
Rates: N/A;
Tel: (517) 345-2345

**RED ROSE MOTEL**
836 S M-33 (48661)
Rates: N/A;
Tel: (517) 345-2136

## WHITEHALL

**TODD'S MOTEL**
8215 Whitehall Rd (49461)
Rates: N/A;
Tel: (616) 894-9097

## WHITE PIGEON

**PLAZA MOTEL**
71410 US 131S (49099)
Rates: $21-$45;
Tel: (616) 483-7285

## WYOMING

**JIM WILLIAMS MOTEL**
3821 S Division (49548)
Rates: N/A;
Tel: (616) 241-5461

# MINNESOTA

## AITKIN

**BILL'S RESORT**
Rt 2. Box 521 (56431)
Rates: N/A;
Tel. (210) 927-3841

**40 CLUB INN**
950 2nd St NW (56431)
Rates: $35-$46;
Tel: (218) 927-2903

**RIPPLE RIVER MOTEL**
701 Minnesota Ave (56431)
Rates: $35-$55;
Tel: (218) 927-3734

## ALBERT LEA

**ALBERT LEA
SUPER 8 LODGE**
2019 E Main St (56007)
Rates: $35-$43;
Tel: (507) 377-0591

**BEL AIRE MOTOR INN**
700 US Hwy 69 S (56007)
Rates: N/A;
Tel: (507) 373-3983

**BEST WESTERN
ALBERT LEA INN**
2301 E Main St (56007)
Rates: $48-$65;
Tel: (507) 373-8291

**DAYS INN**
2306 E Main St (56007)
Rates: $43-$59;
Tel: (507) 373-6471

## ALEXANDRIA

**COMFORT INN**
507 50th Ave W (56308)
Rates: $37-$52;
Tel: (612) 762-5161

**DAYS INN**
4810 Hwy 29S (56308)
Rates: $35-$50;
Tel: (612) 762-1171

**PARK INN
INTERNATIONAL**
P. O. Box 459 (56308)
Rates: $47-$85;
Tel: (612) 763-6577

**SUPER 8 MOTEL**
4620 MN 29S (56308)
Rates: $30-$49;
Tel: (612) 763-6552

## AUSTIN

**AUSTIN SUPER 8 MOTEL**
1401 NW 14th St (55912)
Rates: $35-$43;
Tel: (507) 433-1801

**BEST WESTERN
COUNTRYSIDE INN**
3303 Oakland Ave W (55912)
Rates: $39-$49;
Tel: (507) 437-7774

**HOLIDAY INN
HOLIDOME & AUSTIN
CONFERENCE CENTER**
1701 4th St NW (55912)
Rates: $55-$80;
Tel: (507) 433-1000

## AVON

**AMERICINN MOTEL**
304 Blattner Dr (56310)
Rates: $31-$46;
Tel: (612) 356-2211

## BABBITT

**RED CARPET MOTEL**
11 Babbitt Rd (55706)
Rates: N/A;
Tel: (218) 827-3152

## BECKER

**JOHNSON'S
STRAWBERRY MOTEL**
13804 First St (55308)
Rates: $26-$35;
Tel: (612) 261-4440

## BEMIDJI

**COMFORT INN**
P. O. Box 698 (56601)
Rates: $38-$58;
Tel: (218) 751-7700

**EDGEWATER MOTEL**
1015 Paul Bunyan Dr NE
(56601)
Rates: $29-$68;
Tel: (218) 751-3600

**HOLIDAY INN-BEMIDJI**
P. O. Box 307 (56601)
Rates: $49-$70;
Tel: (218) 751-9500

**RUTTER'S
BIRCHMONT LODGE**
530 Birchmont Beach Rd NE
(56601)
Rates: $66-$142;
Tel: (800) 726-3866

## BENSON

**MOTEL 1**
RR 3, Box 229 (56215)
Rates: $25-$34;
Tel: (612) 843-4434

## BLACKDUCK

**AMERICINN MOTEL**
P. O. Box 358 (56630)
Rates: $49-$59;
Tel: (218) 835-4500

## BRAINERD

**BRAINERD SUPER 8 MOTEL**
P. O. Box 2505 (Baxter 56425)
Rates: $36-$51;
Tel: (218) 828-4288

**DAYS INN**
1630 Fairview Dr N (56401)
Rates: $39-$49;
Tel: (218) 829-0391

**DELLWOOD MOTEL**
1302 S 6th St (56401)
Rates: $23-$35;
Tel: (218) 828-8756

**ECONO LODGE**
26655 SR 371S (56401)
Rates: $30-$49;
Tel: (218) 828-0027

**HOLIDAY INN**
2115 S 6th St (56401)
Rates: $53-$72;
Tel: (218) 829-1441

**SUPER 8 MOTEL**
P. O. Box 2505 (Baxter 56425)
Rates: $39-$49;
Tel: (218) 828-4288

## BURNSVILLE

**RED ROOF INN**
12920 Aldrich Ave S (55337)
Rates: N/A;
Tel: (800) 843-7663

## CHANHASSEN

**CHANHASSEN INN MOTEL**
531 W 79th St (55317)
Rates: $37-$44;
Tel: (612) 934-7373

**COUNTRY SUITES
BY CARLSON**
591 W 78th St (55317)
Rates: $64-$141;
Tel: (612) 937-2424

## CHISAGO CITY

**SUPER 8 MOTEL-
CHISAGO CITY/LINDSTROM**
11650 Lake Blvd (55013)
Rates: $30-$40;
Tel: (612) 257-8088

## CLEARWATER

**BUDGET INN**
945 SR 24 (55320)
Rates: $27-$36;
Tel: (612) 558-2221

## CLOQUET

**AMERICINN MOTEL**
MN 33 & Big Lake Rd (55720)
Rates: $34-$61;
Tel: (800) 634-3444

## COLD SPRING

**AMERICINN MOTEL**
118 3rd St S (56320)
Rates: $36-$56;
Tel: (612) 685-4539

## COOK

**VERMILLION DAM LODGE**
3276 Randa Rd (55723)
Rates: $625-$990;
Tel: (218) 666-5418

## COON RAPIDS

**COUNTRY SUITES
BY CARLSON**
155 Coon Rapids Blvd (55433)
Rates: $61-$77;
Tel: (612) 780-3797

## CRANE LAKE

**OLSON'S BORDERLAND**
7488 Crane Lake Rd (55725)
Rates: N/A;
Tel: (218) 993-2233

# CROOKSTON

## NORTHLAND INN OF CROOKSTON
2200 University Ave (56716)
Rates: $39-$53;
Tel: (218) 281-5210

# DEER RIVER

## BAHR'S MOTEL
P. O. Box 614 (56636)
Rates: N/A;
Tel: (218) 246-8271

# DEERWOOD

## COUNTRY INN BY CARLSON
115 Front St E (56444)
Rates: $49-$65;
Tel: (218) 534-3101

# DETROIT LAKES

## BUDGET HOST OAK MANOR MOTEL
893 Hwy 10E (56501)
Rates: $24-$57;
Tel: (218) 847-4454

## INN ON THE LAKE-HOLIDAY INN
Hwy 10E (56501)
Rates: $49-$77;
Tel: (218) 847-2121

# DULUTH

## BEST WESTERN DOWNTOWN MOTEL
131 W 2nd St (55802)
Rates: $37-$80;
Tel: (218) 727-6851

## BEST WESTERN EDGEWATER EAST MOTEL
2400 London Rd (55812)
Rates: $44-$115;
Tel: (218) 728-3601

## DAYS INN
909 Cottonwood Ave (55811)
Rates: $54-$60;
Tel: (218) 727-3110

## FITGER'S INN
600 E Superior St (55802)
Rates: $54-$104;
Tel: (218) 722-8826

## HOLIDAY INN
200 W 1st St (55802)
Rates: $76-$195;
Tel: (218) 722-1202

## PARK INN INTERNATIONAL-DULUTH LAKESHORE
250 Canal Park Dr (55802)
Rates: $59-$88;
Tel: (218) 727-8821

## RADISSON DULUTH
505 W Superior St (55802)
Rates: $64-$102;
Tel: (218) 727-8981

## SELECT INN
200 S 27th Ave W (55806)
Rates: $29-$48;
Tel: (218) 723-1123

## VOYAGEUR MOTEL
333 E Superior St (55802)
Rates: $35-$55;
Tel: (218) 722-3911

# ELK RIVER

## AMERICINN MOTEL
17432 Hwy 10 (55330)
Rates: $39-$52;
Tel: (612) 441-8554

## RED CARPET INN
17291 Hwy 10 (55330)
Rates: $26-$42;
Tel: (612) 441-2424

# ELY

## BEAR ISLAND RESORT
P. O. Box 179 (55731)
Rates: $85-$195;
Tel: (218) 827-3396

## OLSON BAY RESORT COTTAGES
2279 Grant McMahan Blvd (55731)
Rates: $320-$465;
Tel: (800) 777-4419

## SILVER RAPIDS LODGE RESORT
HC 1, Box 2992 (55731)
Rates: $50-$60;
Tel: (218) 365-4877

## TIMBER BAY LODGE & HOUSEBOATS
P. O. Box 248 (Babbitt 55706)
Rates: $450-$550;
Tel: (218) 827-3682

# EVELETH

## HOLIDAY INN-EVELETH/VIRGINIA
701 Hat Trick Ave (55734)
Rates: $50-$74;
Tel: (218) 744-2703

## KOKE'S DOWNTOWN MOTEL
714 Fayal Rd (55734)
Rates: $25-$32;
Tel: (218) 744-4500

# FAIRMONT

## HIGHLAND COURT MOTEL
1345 Lake Ave (56031)
Rates: N/A;
Tel: (507) 235-6686

## HOLIDAY INN
P. O. Box 922 (56031)
Rates: $53-$70;
Tel: (507) 238-4771

## SUPER 8 MOTEL
MN 15 & I-90 Exit 102 (56031)
Rates: $38-$46;
Tel: (507) 238-4771

# FARIBAULT

## ECONO LODGE
4040 Hwy 60W (55021)
Rates: $35-$49;
Tel: (507) 334-2051

## FARIBAULT SUPER 8 MOTEL
2509 N Lyndale Ave (55021)
Rates: $27-$38;
Tel: (507) 334-1634

## FERGUS FALLS

**MOTEL 7**
P. O. Box 364 (56537)
Rates: $32-$39;
Tel: (218) 736-2554

**PARK INN
INTERNATIONAL**
P. O. Box 103 (56538)
Rates: $55-$70;
Tel: (218) 739-2211

**TRAVEL HOST MOTEL**
610 Western Ave (56537)
Rates: $28-$44;
Tel: (218) 739-3311

## FOREST LAKE

**AMERICINN MOTEL**
1291 W Broadway (55025)
Rates: $45-$55;
Tel: (612) 464-1930

**FOREST MOTEL**
7 NE 6th Ave (55025)
Rates: $28-$44;
Tel: (612) 464-4077

## FRIDLEY

**SUNLINER MOTEL**
6881 Hwy 65 NE (55432)
Rates: N/A;
Tel: (612) 571-0420

## GLENCOE

**SUPER 8 MOTEL**
717 Morningside Dr (55336)
Rates: $33-$40;
Tel: (612) 864-6191

## GLENWOOD

**HI-VIEW MOTEL**
P. O. Box 181 (56334)
Rates: $32-$40;
Tel: (612) 634-4541

## GRAND MARAIS

**BEST WESTERN
SUPERIOR INN**
P. O. Box 456 (55604)
Rates: $71-$98;
Tel: (218) 387-2240

**BORDERLAND LODGE**
855 Gunflint Trail (55604)
Rates: $440-$660;
Tel: (800) 451-1667

**CLEARWATER LODGE**
355 Gunflint Trail (55604)
Rates: $585-$765;
Tel: (800) 527-0554

**ECONO LODGE
GRAND MARAIS**
P. O. Box 667 (55604)
Rates: $36-$69;
Tel: (218) 387-2547

**GRAND MARAIS
SUPER 8 MOTEL**
Box 667 (55604)
Rates: $36-$64;
Tel: (218) 387-2448

**GUNFLINT LODGE**
750 Gunflint Trail (55604)
Rates: $99-$270;
Tel: (218) 388-2294

**GUNFLINT PINES RESORT**
755 Gunflint Trail (55604)
Rates: N/A;
Tel: (800) 533-5814

**HARBOR INN**
207 Wisconsin St (55604)
Rates: N/A;
Tel: (218) 387-1191

**MOTEL WEDGEWOOD**
HC 1, Box 100 (55604)
Rates: $30-$35;
Tel: (218) 387-2944

**NOR' WESTER LODGE**
550 Gunflint Trail (55604)
Rates: $550-$800;
Tel: (218) 388-2252

**SANDGREN MOTEL**
P. O. Box 1056 (55604)
Rates: $30-$45;
Tel: (218) 387-2975

**SEAWALL MOTEL**
Hwy 61 (55604)
Rates: N/A;
Tel: (218) 387-2095

**TOMTEBODA MOTEL**
P. O. Box 247 (55604)
Rates: $35-$50;
Tel: (218) 387-1585

## GRAND RAPIDS

**BEST WESTERN
RAINBOW INN**
1300 US 169E (55744)
Rates: $45-$65;
Tel: (218) 326-9655

**DAYS INN GRAND RAPIDS**
311 US 2E (55744)
Rates: $36-$68;
Tel: (218) 326-3457

**FOREST LAKE MOTEL**
1215 NW 4th St (55744)
Rates: $28-$46;
Tel: (218) 326-6609

**SAWMILL INN**
2301 S Pokegama Ave
(55744)
Rates: $50-$68;
Tel: (218) 326-8501

## HASTINGS

**AMERICINN MOTEL**
2400 Vermillion St (55033)
Rates: $34-$42;
Tel: (800) 634-3444

**HASTINGS INN**
1520 Vermillion St (55033)
Rates: $31-$40;
Tel: (612) 437-3155

## HIBBING

**DAYS INN OF HIBBING**
P. O. Box 662 (55746)
Rates: $42-$54;
Tel: (218) 263-8306

# HINCKLEY

**DAYSTOP**
104 Grindstone Ct (55037)
Rates: (612) 384-7751
Tel: (612) 384-7751

# HUTCHINSON

**KING MOTEL**
1255 Hwy 7 W (55350)
Rates: N/A;
Tel: (612) 587-4737

# INTERNATIONAL FALLS

**DAYS INN**
2331 Hwy 53 South (56649)
Rates: $43-$51;
Tel: (218) 283-9441

**HOLIDAY INN**
1810 Hwy 11 & 71 W
(56649)
Rates: $51-$65;
Tel: (218) 283-4451

**ISLAND VIEW**
**LODGE & MOTEL**
HCR8, Box 411 (56649)
Rates: N/A;
Tel: (218) 266-3511

**NORTHERNAIRE**
**FLOATING LODGES**
P. O.Box 510 (56649)
Rates: $750-$1750;
Tel: (218) 286-5221

**THUNDERBIRD LODGE**
Rt 8, Box 407 (56649)
Rates: $32-$66;
Tel: (218) 286-3151

# KELLIHER

**ROYAL SHOOKS MOTEL**
Corner of 1 & 72 (56661)
Rates: N/A;
Tel: (218) 647-8379

# LAKE CITY

**AMERICINN MOTEL**
1615 N Lakeshore Dr (55041)
Rates: $47-$79;
Tel: (612) 345-5611

**SUNSET MOTEL**
1515 N Lakeshore Dr (55041)
Rates: N/A;
Tel: (612) 345-5331

# LAKEVILLE

**DAYSTOP MOTEL**
11274 210th St (55044)
Rates: $26-$41;
Tel: (612) 469-1900

**SUPER 8-LAKEVILLE**
20800 Kenrick Ave (55044)
Rates: $44-$74;
Tel: (612) 469-1134

# LITTLE FALLS

**PINE EDGE MOTEL**
308 1st St SE (56345)
Rates: $27-$56;
Tel: (612) 632-6681

# LONG PRAIRIE

**FLAMINGO MOTEL**
417 Lake St (56347)
Rates: $31-$44;
Tel: (612) 732-6118

# LUTSEN

**BEST WESTERN CLIFF**
**DWELLER MOTEL**
HCR 3, Box 140 (Tofte 55615)
Rates: $39-$89;
Tel: (218) 663-7273

**BLUEFIN BAY MOTEL**
P. O. Box 2125 (Tofte 55615)
Rates: $69-$295;
Tel: (800) 258-3346

**SOLBAKKEN RESORT**
HCR Box 170 (55612)
Rates: $30-$90;
Tel: (218) 663-7566

**THOMSONITE BEACH**
R3, Box 470 (55612)
Rates: $33-$127;
Tel: (218) 387-1532

# LUVERNE

**SUNRISE MOTEL**
West Hwy 4 (56156)
Rates: N/A;
Tel: (507) 283-2347

# MANKATO

**BUDGETEL INN**
111 West Lind Ct (56001)
Rates: $30-$40;
Tel: (507) 345-8800

**CLIFF KYES MOTEL**
1727 N Riverfront Dr (56001)
Rates: $27-$59;
Tel: (507) 388-1638

**DAYS INN**
1285 Range St (56001)
Rates: $40-$53;
Tel: (507) 387-3332

**HOLIDAY INN-DOWNTOWN**
101 E Main St (56001)
Rates: $50-$72;
Tel: (507) 345-1234

# MARSHALL

**BEST WESTERN MARSHALL INN**
1500 E College Dr (56258)
Rates: $43-$61;
Tel: (507) 532-3221

**COMFORT INN**
1511 E College Dr (56258)
Rates: $36-$46;
Tel: (507) 532-3070

**TRAVELER'S LODGE**
1425 East College Dr (56258)
Rates: N/A;
Tel: (507) 532-5721

# McGREGOR

### HILLCREST RESORT
HCR 3, Box 754 (55760)
Rates: N/A;
Tel: (218) 426-3323

### TOWN & COUNTRY MOTEL
Hwy 65 & 210 (55760)
Rates: N/A;
Tel: (218) 768-3271

# MINNEAPOLIS
(and Vicinity)

### AQUA CITY MOTEL
5739 Lyndale Ave S (55419)
Rates: $24-$44;
Tel: (612) 861-6061

### BEST WESTERN GOLDEN VALLEY HOUSE
4820 Olson Memorial Hwy
(Golden Valley 55422)
Rates: $45-$55;
Tel: (612) 588-0511

### BEST WESTERN HOTEL SEVILLE
8151 Bridge Rd
(Bloomington 55437)
Rates: $58-$66;
Tel: (612) 830-1300

### BEST WESTERN KELLY INN-PLYMOUTH
2705 Annapolis Ln
(Plymouth 55441)
Rates: $56-$62;
Tel: (612) 553-1600

### BEST WESTERN NORMANDY HOTEL
405 S 8th St (55404)
Rates: $64-$85;
Tel: (612) 370-1400

### BEST WESTERN NORTHWEST INN
Jct I-94 exit 31-CR 81
(Brooklyn Park 55428)
Rates: $64-$114;
Tel: (612) 566-8855

### BEST WESTERN THUNDERBIRD
2201 E 78th St
(Bloomington 55425)
Rates: $68-$330;
Tel: (612) 854-3411

### BOULEVARD MOTEL
5637 Lyndale Ave S (55419)
Rates: N/A;
Tel: (612) 861-6011

### BUDGETEL INN (AIRPORT)
7815 Nicollet Ave S
(Bloomington 55420)
Rates: $38-$54;
Tel: (612) 881-7311

### BUDGETEL INN-BROOKLYN CENTER
6415 James Cir N
(Brooklyn Center 55430)
Rates: $33-$47;
Tel: (612) 561-8400

### CROWN STERLING SUITES-MINNEAPOLIS AIRPORT
7901 34th Ave
(Bloomington 55425)
Rates: $99-$110;
Tel: (612) 854-1000

### CROWN STERLING SUITES-CENTRE VILLAGE
425 S 7th St (55415)
Rates: $106-$129;
Tel: (612) 333-3111

### DAYS INN-BURNSVILLE
13080 Aldrich Ave S
(Burnsville 55337)
Rates: $30-$49;
Tel: (612) 894-8280

### DAYS INN-MINNEAPOLIS NORTH
1501 Freeway Blvd
(Brooklyn Center 55403)
Rates: $43-$78;
Tel: (612) 566-4140

### EXEL INN OF MINNEAPOLIS
2701 E 78th St
(Bloomington 55425)
Rates: $34-$48;
Tel: (612) 854-7200

### HOLIDAY INN METRODOME
1500 Washington Ave (55454)
Rates: $97-$117;
Tel: (612) 332-6800

### HOLIDAY INN-NORTH
2200 Freeway Blvd
(Brooklyn Center 55430)
Rates: $78-$81;
Tel: (612) 566-8000

### HOLIDAY INN-PLYMOUTH NW
3000 Harbor Ln
(Plymouth 55447)
Rates: $53-$57;
Tel: (612) 559-1222

### MEDINA RED CARPET INN
400 SR 55 (Hamel 55340)
Rates: $31-$48;
Tel: (612) 478-9770

### MINNEAPOLIS AIRPORT MARRIOTT BLOOMINGTON
2020 E 79th St
(Bloomington 55425)
Rates: $65-$129;
Tel: (612) 854-7441

### MINNEAPOLIS HILTON AND TOWERS
1001 Marquette Ave (55403)
Rates: $99-$210;
Tel: (612) 376-1000

### MINNEAPOLIS METRODOME HILTON
1330 Industrial Blvd (55413)
Rates: $83-$103;
Tel: (612) 331-1900

### MINNEAPOLIS-ST. PAUL AIRPORT HILTON
3800 E 80th St
(Bloomington 55425)
Rates: $69-$123;
Tel: (612) 854-2100

### PARK INN INTERNATIONAL-NICOLLET MALL
1313 Nicollet Mall (55403)
Rates: $110-$120;
Tel: (612) 332-0371

### RADISSON HOTEL & CONFERENCE CENTER
3131 Campus Dr
(Plymouth 55441)
Rates: $99-$119;
Tel: (612) 559-6600

### RADISSON HOTEL METRODOME-UNIVERSITY OF MINNESOTA
615 Washington Ave SE
(55414)
Rates: $89-$114;
Tel: (612) 379-8888

**RADISSON HOTEL SOUTH
& PLAZA TOWER**
7800 Normandale Blvd
(Bloomington 55439)
Rates: $65-$75;
Tel: (612) 835-7800

**RADISSON PLAZA HOTEL**
35 S 7th St (55402)
Rates: $91;
Tel: (612) 339-4900

**RED ROOF INN-BURNSVILLE**
12920 Aldrich Ave S
(Burnsville 55337)
Rates: $32-$52;
Tel: (612) 890-1420

**THE RESIDENCE INN BY
MARRIOTT-MINNEAPOLIS SW**
7780 Flying Cloud Dr
(Eden Prairie 55344)
Rates: $99-$129;
Tel: (612) 829-0033

**SELECT INN**
7851 Normandale Blvd
(Bloomington 55435)
Rates: $34-$44;
Tel: (612) 835-7400

**THE THUNDERBIRD HOTEL
& CONVENTION CENTER**
2201 E 78th St
(Bloomington 55425)
Rates: $68-$85;
Tel: (612) 854-3411

## MONTEVIDEO

**BEST WESTERN
ROYALE INN**
207 N 1st St (56265)
Rates: $39-$61;
Tel: (612) 269-5554

## MONTICELLO

**COMFORT INN**
200 E Oakwood Dr (55362)
Rates: $39-$50;
Tel: (612) 295-1111

## MOORHEAD

**GUEST HOUSE MOTEL**
2107 SE Main (56560)
Rates: $22-$30;
Tel: (218) 233-2471

**THE MADISON HOTEL
& CONFERENCE CENTER**
600 30 Ave S (56560)
Rates: $49-$78;
Tel: (218) 233-6171

**MOTEL 75**
810 Belsly Blvd (56560)
Rates: $29-$36,
Tel: (218) 233-7501

## NEW ULM

**COLONIAL INN MOTEL**
1315 N Broadway (56073)
Rates: $20-$45;
Tel: (507) 354-3128

**SUPER 8 MOTEL-NEW ULM**
1901 S Broadway (56073)
Rates: $40-$54;
Tel: (507) 359-2400

## NEW YORK MILLS

**MILLS MOTEL**
P. O. Box B (56567)
Rates: $25-$35;
Tel: (218) 385-3600

## NISSWA

**DAYSTOP**
45 N Smiley Rd (56466)
Rates: $36-$56;
Tel: (218) 963-3500

**NISSWA MOTEL**
P. O. Box 45 (56466)
Rates: $39-$48;
Tel: (218) 963-7611

## NORTH BRANCH

**CROSSROADS MOTEL**
1118 Main St (55056)
Rates: $32-$41;
Tel: (612) 674-7074

## OWATONNA

**COUNTRY HEARTH MOTEL**
745 State Ave (55060)
Rates: $27-$32;
Tel: (507) 451-8712

**OWATONNA INN**
Vine & Oak Sts (55060)
Rates: $32-$55;
Tel: (507) 451-4620

**WESTERN INN**
P. O. Box 609 (55060)
Rates: $37-$50;
Tel: (507) 455-0606

## PIPESTONE

**KINGS KOURT**
821 Southeast 7th St (56164)
Rates: N/A;
Tel: (507) 825-3314

**SUPER 8 MOTEL**
605 8th Ave SE (56164)
Rates: $33-$45;
Tel: (507) 825-4217

## PLYMOUTH

**DAYS INN**
2955 Empire Ln (55447)
Rates: $40-$46;
Tel: (612) 559-2400

**PLYMOUTH PLACE HOTEL**
2705 Annapolis Lane (55441)
Rates: N/A;
Tel: (612) 553-1600

**RED ROOF INN**
2600 Annapolis Ln N (55441)
Rates: N/A;
Tel: (800) 843-7663

## RED WING

**BEST WESTERN
QUIET HOUSE SUITES**
752 Withers Harbor Dr
(55066)
Rates: $74-$170;
Tel: (612) 388-1547

# REDWOOD FALLS

## REDWOOD INN MOTEL
1303 E Bridge St (56283)
Rates: $39-$49;
Tel: (507) 637-2507

# ROCHESTER

## BEST WESTERN
## APACHE MALL
1517 16th St SW (55902)
Rates: $58-$76;
Tel: (507) 289-8866

## BEST WESTERN FIFTH AVE
## MOTEL & MINI SUITES
20 NW 5th Ave (55901)
Rates: $47-$59;
Tel: (507) 289-3987

## BLONDELL'S CROWN
## SQUARE MOTEL
1406 2nd St SW (55902)
Rates: $35-$51;
Tel: (507) 282-9444

## COMFORT INN
111 28th St SE (55904)
Rates: $42-$59;
Tel: (507) 286-1001

## DAYS INN-DOWNTOWN
6 1st Ave NW (55901)
Rates: $45-$65;
Tel: (507) 282-3801

## DAYS INN-SOUTH
106 21st St SE (55904)
Rates: $37-$49;
Tel: (507) 282-1756

## DAYSTOP
11 17th Ave SW (55902)
Rates: $32-$46;
Tel: (507) 282-2733

## ECONO LODGE
519 3rd Ave SW (55902)
Rates: $35-$47;
Tel: (507) 288-1855

## FRIENDSHIP INN
## CENTER TOWNE
116 5th St SW (55902)
Rates: $37-$49;
Tel: (507) 289-1628

## HOLIDAY INN DOWNTOWN
220 S Broadway (55904)
Rate: $57-$85;
Tel: (507) 288-3231

## HOLIDAY INN SOUTH
1630 S Broadway (55904)
Rates: $49-$65;
Tel: (507) 288-1844

## HOWARD JOHNSON
## LODGE
435 16th Ave NW (55901)
Rates: $59-$79;
Tel: (507) 288-9090

## THE KAHLER HOTEL
20 2nd Ave SW (55903)
Rates: $39-$135;
Tel: (507) 282-2581

## KAHLER PLAZA HOTEL
101 1st Ave W (55902)
Rates: $120-$150;
Tel: (507) 280-6000

## RADISSON HOTEL
## CENTERPLACE
150 S Broadway (55904)
Rates: $59-$105;
Tel: (507) 281-8000

## RAMADA INN-ROCHESTER
1625 S Broadway (55904)
Rates: $48-$64;
Tel: (507) 281-2211

## ROYALTY SUITES
1620 1st Ave SE (55904)
Rates: $69-$74;
Tel: (507) 282-8091

## SUPER 8 MOTEL-SOUTH #1
1230 S Broadway (55904)
Rates: $38-$46;
Tel: (507) 288-8288

## SUPER 8 MOTEL-SOUTH #2
1850 S Broadway (55904)
Rates: $38-$46;
Tel: (507) 282-9905

## SUPER 8 MOTEL-WEST
1608 2nd St SW (55902)
Rates: $38-$52;
Tel: (507) 281-5100

## TRAVELODGE DOWNTOWN
426 2nd St SW (55902)
Rates: $39-$75;
Tel: (507) 289-4095

## TRAVELODGE-SOUTH
1837 S Broadway (55904)
Rates: $28-$40;
Tel: (507) 288-2031

# ROGERS

## AMERICINN MOTEL
21800 Industrial Blvd (55374)
Rates: $32-$45;
Tel: (612) 428-4346

# ROSEAU

## AMERICINN MOTEL
1090 3rd St NW (56751)
Rates: $34-$46;
Tel: (218) 463-1045

# ST. CLOUD

## BEST WESTERN AMERICANNA
## INN & CONFERENCE CTR
520 S Hwy 10 (56304)
Rates: $42-$99;
Tel: (612) 252-8700

## BUDGETEL INN
70 37th Ave S (56301)
Rates: $28-$44;
Tel: (612) 253-4444

## COMFORT INN
4040 S 2nd St (56302)
Rates: $45-$65;
Tel: (612) 251-1500

## ECONOLODGE
420 SE Hwy 10 (56304)
Rates: $30-$38;
Tel: (612) 263-0500

## FAIRFIELD INN
## BY MARRIOTT
4120 South 2nd St (56301)
Rates: $35-$56;
Tel: (612) 654-1881

## GATEWAY MOTEL
310 Lincoln Ave SE (56304)
Rates: $24-$42;
Tel: (612) 252-4050

## HOLIDAY INN
75 37th Ave S (56302)
Rates: $53-$73;
Tel: (612) 253-9000

**SUNWOOD INN
& CONVENTION CENTER**
1 Sunwood Plaza (56302)
Rates: $50-$75;
Tel: (612) 253-0606

**THRIFTY MOTEL**
130 14th Ave NE (56304)
Rates: $24-$32;
Tel: (612) 253-6320

## ST. JOSEPH

**SUPER 8 MOTEL-
ST. JOSEPH**
8864 Lancer Rd (56374)
Rates: $35-$45;
Tel: (612) 363-7711

## ST. PAUL
(and Vicinity)

**THE BANDANA INN**
1010 Bandana Blvd W
(55108)
Rates: N/A;
Tel: (612) 647-1637

**BEST WESTERN KELLY INN-
STATE CAPITOL**
161 St Anthony Ave (55103)
Rates: $60-$73;
Tel: (612) 227-8711

**BEST WESTERN WHITE
BEAR COUNTRY INN**
4940 Hwy 61
(White Bear Lake 55110)
Rates: $52-$59;
Tel: (612) 429-5393

**CIVIC CENTER INN**
175 W 7th St (55102)
Rates: $58-$125;
Tel: (800) 635-4766

**CROWN STERLING SUITES
ST. PAUL**
175 E 10th St (55101)
Rates: $89-$96;
Tel: (612) 224-5400

**DAYS INN CIVIC CENTER**
175 W 7th St (55102)
Rates: $58-$79;
Tel: (612) 292-8929

**EXEL INN OF ST. PAUL**
1739 Old Hudson Rd (55106)
Rates: $33-$47;
Tel: (612) 771-5566

**HOLIDAY INN ST. PAUL
EAST-3M AREA**
2201 Burns Ave (55119)
Rates: $75-$96;
Tel: (612) 731-2220

**HOLIDAY INN SHOREVIEW**
1000 Gramsie Rd
(Shoreview 55126)
Rates: $60-$74;
Tel: (612) 482-0402

**MAPLEWOOD INN**
1780 E CR D
(Maplewood 55109)
Rates: $54-$58;
Tel: (612) 770-2811

**RADISSON HOTEL
ST. PAUL**
11 E Kellogg Blvd (55101)
Rates: $95-$145;
Tel: (612) 292-1900

**RAMADA HOTEL
& CONFERENCE CENTER**
1201 W Country Rd E
(Arden Hills 55112)
Rates: $58-$75;
Tel: (612) 636-4123

**RAMADA HOTEL-ST. PAUL**
1870 Old Hudson Rd (55119)
Rates: $49-$83;
Tel: (612) 735-2330

**RED ROOF INN-WOODBURY**
1806 Wooddale Dr
(Woodbury 55125)
Rates: $34-$45;
Tel: (612) 737-7160

**RESIDENCE INN
BY MARRIOTT-MPLS/
ST. PAUL AIRPORT**
3040 Eagandale Pl
(Eagan 55121)
Rates: $117-$147;
Tel: (612) 688-0363

**ROAD STAR INN**
6003 Hudson Rd (55125)
Rates: N/A;
Tel: (612) 739-7300

**SHERATON MIDWAY,
ST. PAUL**
400 Hamline Ave N (55104)
Rates: $75-$95;
Tel: (612) 642-1234

**SUNWOOD INN-
BANDANA SQUARE**
1010 Bandana Blvd W
(55108)
Rates: $57-$69;
Tel: (612) 647-1637

## ST. PETER

**VIKING JR MOTEL**
169 & 90 West (56082)
Rates: N/A;
Tel: (507) 931-3081

## SAUK CENTRE

**ECONO LODGE MOTEL**
P. O. Box 46 (56378)
Rates: $32-$41;
Tel: (612) 352-6581

**GOPHER PRAIRIE MOTEL**
I-94 & US 71 (56378)
Rates: N/A;
Tel: (612) 352-2275

**HILLCREST MOTEL**
965 S Main St (56378)
Rates: $23-$32;
Tel: (612) 352-2215

**PALMER HOUSE INN**
500 Sinclair Lewis Ave
(56378)
Rates: $17-$38;
Tel: (612) 352-3431

## SAUK RAPID

**RED CARPET INN**
1420 Second St N (56379)
Rates: N/A;
Tel: (612) 251-9333

## SAVAGE

**DAN PATCH INN**
4601 Hwy 13W (55378)
Rates: $39-$50;
Tel: (612) 894-6124

## SCHROEDER

**LAMB'S RESORT**
North Shore Dr Hwy 61
(55613)
Rates: N/A;
Tel: (218) 663-7292

## SEBEKA

**K'S MOTEL**
Hwy 71 (56477)
Rates: N/A;
Tel: (218) 837-5162

## SHAKOPEE

**BEST WESTERN
CANTERBURY INN**
1244 Canterbury Rd (55379)
Rates: $44-$89;
Tel: (612) 445-3644

**SHAKOPEE VALLEY MOTEL**
1251 E 1st Ave (55379)
Rates: $35-$53;
Tel: (612) 445-5074

## SILVER BAY

**MARINER MOTEL**
46 Outer Dr (55614)
Rates: $32-$46;
Tel: (218) 226-4488

## SPRING VALLEY

**66 MOTEL**
612 North Huron Ave (55975)
Rates: N/A;
Tel: (507) 346-9993

## STEWARTVILLE

**AMERICINN MOTEL**
1700 NW 2nd Ave (55976)
Rates: $41-$50;
Tel: (507) 533-4747

## STILLWATER

**BEST WESTERN
STILLWATER INN**
1750 Frontage Rd W (55082)
Rates: $46-$56;
Tel: (612) 430-1300

## STURGEON LAKE

**STURGEON LAKE MOTEL**
I-35 & County Rd 46 (55783)
Rates: N/A;
Tel: (218) 372-3194

## TAYLORS FALLS

**SPRINGS INN**
90 Government St (55084)
Rates: N/A;
Tel: (612) 465-6565

## THIEF RIVER FALLS

**BEST WESTERN INN OF
THIEF RIVER FALLS**
P. O. Box 573 (56701)
Rates: $40-$54;
Tel: (218) 681-7555

**C'MON INN**
1586 Hwy 59 SE (56701)
Rates: $39-$61;
Tel: (218) 681-3000

**HARTWOOD MOTEL**
1010 N Main Ave (56701)
Rates: $21-$33;
Tel: (218) 681-2640

**SUPER 8 MOTEL**
1915 Hwy 59 SE (56701)
Rates: $33-$42;
Tel: (218) 681-6205

## TOFTE

**ASPENWOOD
RESORT MOTEL**
130 Aspenwood (55615)
Rates: N/A;
Tel: (218) 663-7978

## TWO HARBORS

**SUPERIOR SHORES LODGE
& LAKE HOMES**
10 Superior Shores (55616)
Rates: $49-$89;
Tel: (218) 834-5671

## VIRGINIA

**COATES PLAZA HOTEL**
502 Chestnut St (55792)
Rates: N/A;
Tel: (218) 749-1000

**GOPHER MOTEL**
906 15th St N (55792)
Rates: N/A;
Tel: (218) 741-2790

**LAKESHOR MOTOR INN
DOWNTOWN**
404 N 6th Ave (55792)
Rates: $28-$39;
Tel: (218) 741-3360

**SKI-VIEW MOTEL**
903 N 17th St (55792)
Rates: $26-$38;
Tel: (218) 741-8918

## WACONIA

**PRAIRIE HOUSE MOTEL**
301 E Frontage Rd (55387)
Rates: $27-$38;
Tel: (612) 442-5147

## WADENA

**BEST WESTERN
FOUR SEASONS MOTEL**
500 Ash Ave NW (56482)
Rates: $35-$60;
Tel: (218) 631-3725

## WALKER

**MERIT LODGE**
HCR 84, Box 464 (56484)
Rates: $220-$410;
Tel: (218) 836-2321

## WARROAD

**THE PATCH MOTEL**
P. O. Box N (56763)
Rates: $31-$42;
Tel: (218) 386-2723

## WILLMAR

**COLONIAL INN MOTEL**
1102 S 1st St (56201)
Rates: $21-$34;
Tel: (612) 235-4444

**DAYS INN-WILLMAR**
P. O. Box 1157 (56201)
Rates: $35-$40;
Tel: (612) 231-1275

**HOLIDAY INN & WILLMAR CONFERENCE CENTER**
P. O. Box 1157 (56201)
Rates: $58-$85;
Tel: (612) 235 6060

**SUPER 8 MOTEL**
US 71S (56201)
Rates: $29-$45;
Tel: (612) 235-7260

## WINONA

**HOLIDAY INN**
956 Mankato Ave (55987)
Rates: $39-$65;
Tel: (507) 454-4390

**SUGAR LOAF MOTEL**
1066 Homer Rd (55987)
Rates: N/A;
Tel: (507) 452-1491

## WOODBURY

**RED ROOF INN**
1806 Wooddale Dr (55125)
Rates: N/A;
Tel: (800) 843-7663

**ROAD STAR INN**
6003 Hudson Rd (55125)
Rates: N/A;
Tel: (612) 739-7300

## WORTHINGTON

**BEST WESTERN WORTHINGTON MOTEL**
1923 Dover St (56187)
Rates: $33-$44;
Tel: (507) 376-4146

**BUDGET HOST INN**
207 Oxford St (56187)
Rates: $29-$43;
Tel: (507) 376-6155

**HOLIDAY INN**
2015 Humiston Ave (56187)
Rates: $47-$55;
Tel: (507) 372-2991

**SUPER 8 MOTEL**
P. O.Box 98 (56187)
Rates: $38-$48;
Tel: (507) 372-7755

# MISSISSIPPI

## BATESVILLE

**BATESVILLE SKYLINE MOTEL**
311 Hwy 51S (38606)
Rates: $26-$35;
Tel: (601) 563-7651

## BILOXI

**BREAKERS INN**
2506 Beach Blvd (39531)
Rates: N/A;
Tel: (601) 386-6320

**EDGEWATER INN**
1936 Beach Blvd (39531)
Rates: $45-$95;
Tel: (601) 388-1100

**HOLIDAY INN-BEACH-FRONT (COLISEUM)**
2400 Beach Blvd (39531)
Rates: $42-$92;
Tel: (601) 388-3551

**HOLIDAY INN-EXPRESS**
2416 Beach Blvd (39531)
Rates: $35-$57;
Tel: (601) 388-1000

**SEAVIEW RESORT**
1870 Beach Blvd (39531)
Rates: $35-$75;
Tel: (601) 388-5512

## BROOKHAVEN

**BEST WESTERN-BROOKHAVEN**
P. O. Box 1276 (39601)
Rates: $38-$43;
Tel: (601) 835-1053

**HOLIDAY INN**
1210 Brookway Blvd (39601)
Rates: $38-$55;
Tel: (601) 833-1341

## CLARKSDALE

**COMFORT INN**
710 S State St (38614)
Rates: $44-$50;
Tel: (601) 627-9292

## COLUMBUS

**HOLIDAY INN**
506 Hwy 45N (39701)
Rates: $39-$56;
Tel: (601) 328-5202

## CORINTH

**HOLIDAY INN**
P. O. Box 2400 (38834)
Rates: $33-$48;
Tel: (601) 286-6071

## FOREST

**BEST WESTERN
FOREST INN**
P. O. Box 402 (39074)
Rates: $40-$50;
Tel: (601) 469-2640

## GREENVILLE

**DAYS INN**
P. O. Box 1139 (38701)
Rates: $29-$40;
Tel: (601) 335-1999

**RAMADA INN**
P. O. Box 4486 (38701)
Rates: $39-$47;
Tel: (601) 332-4411

## GREENWOOD

**DAYS INN**
621 Hwy 82W (38930)
Rates: $28-$38;
Tel: (601) 453-0030

**RAMADA INN**
900 W Park Ave (38930)
Rates: $37-$48;
Tel: (601) 455-2321

## GRENADA

**BEST WESTERN
MOTOR INN**
1660A Frontage Rd (38901)
Rates: $35-$47;
Tel: (601) 226-7816

**HOLIDAY INN**
1660 Frontage Rd (38901)
Rates: $46;
Tel: (601) 226-2851

## GULFPORT

**BEST WESTERN
SEAWAY INN**
US 49 I1-10 (39503)
Rates: $34-$54;
Tel: (601) 864-0050

**HOLIDAY INN
I-10/AIRPORT**
9415 Hwy 49N (39503)
Rates: $46-$69;
Tel: (601) 868-8200

**SHONEY'S INN
OF GULFPORT**
9375 Hwy 49 (39503)
Rates: $38-$59;
Tel: (601) 868-8500

## HATTIESBURG

**DAYS INN**
6518 US Hwy 49 (39401)
Rates: $28-$37;
Tel: (601) 544-6300

**HOWARD JOHNSON
HOTEL**
6553 US Hwy 49 (39401)
Rates: $31-$34;
Tel: (601) 268-2251

**PEDDLER'S MOTOR INN**
900 Broadway Dr (39401)
Rates: $30-$39;
Tel: (601) 582-7101

**QUALITY INN**
6528 Hwy 49N (39401)
Rates: $36-$43;
Tel: (601) 544-4530

**RAMADA INN**
6595 Hwy 49N (39401)
Rates: $46-$58;
Tel: (601) 268-2170

## HOLLY SPRINGS

**HERITAGE INN**
P. O. Box 476 (38635)
Rates: $38-$53;
Tel: (601) 252-1120

## IUKA

**KEY WEST INN**
P. O. Box 659 (38852)
Rates: $42-$60;
Tel: (601) 423-9221

## JACKSON

**BEST WESTERN
METRO INN**
1520 Ellis Ave (39204)
Rates: $41-$50;
Tel: (601) 355-7483

**COLISEUM RAMADA INN**
400 Greymont Ave (39202)
Rates: $53-$68;
Tel: (601) 969-2141

**DAYS INN EAST**
716 Hwy 80E (39208)
Rates: $30-$45;
Tel: (601) 939-8200

**DAYS INN NORTH**
616 Briarwood Rd (39211)
Rates: $29-$47;
Tel: (601) 957-1741

**EDISON WALTHALL HOTEL**
225 E Capitol St (39201)
Rates: $50-$185;
Tel: (601) 948-6161

**HOLIDAY INN-DOWNTOWN
CONVENTION CTR**
200 E Amite St (39201)
Rates: $50-$72;
Tel: (601) 969-5100

**HOLIDAY INN-
MEDICAL CENTER**
2375 N State St (39202)
Rates: $49-$64;
Tel; (601) 948 8650

**HOLIDAY INN-NORTH**
P. O. Box 16083 (39206)
Rates: $46-$62;
Tel: (601) 366-9411

**HOLIDAY INN-SOUTHWEST**
2649 Hwy 80W (39204)
Rates: $46-$62;
Tel: (601) 355-3472

**HOWARD JOHNSON
LODGE**
5925 I-55N (39213)
Rates: $40 $49;
Tel (601) 956-8000

**LA QUINTA MOTOR INN**
150 Angle St (39204)
Rates: $45-$62;
Tel: (601) 373-6110

**MARRIOTT RESIDENCE INN**
881 E River Pl (39202)
Rates: $89-$109;
Tel: (601) 355-3599

**PASSPORT INN**
P. O. Box 16275 (39236)
Rates: $39-$45;
Tel: (601) 982-1011

**RAMADA
RENAISSANCE HOTEL**
P. O. Box 12710 (39211)
Rates: $78-$98;
Tel: (601) 957-2800

**RED ROOF INN COLISEUM**
700 Larson St (39202)
Rates: $30-$40;
Tel: (601) 969-5006

**WILSON INN**
310 Greymont Ave (39202)
Rates: $37-$53;
Tel: (601) 948-4466

## KOSCIUSKO

**BEST WESTERN
PARKWAY INN**
1052 Hwy 35 Bypass (39090)
Rates: $36-$42;
Tel: (601) 289-6252

**DAYS INN**
1000 Hwy 35S (39090)
Rates: $30-$38;
Tel: (601) 289-2271

## LAUREL

**DAYS INN**
P. O. Box 2517 (39442)
Rates: $33-$40;
Tel: (601) 428-8421

**RAMADA INN SAWMILL**
1105 Sawmill Rd (39440)
Rates: $40-$60;
Tel: (601) 649-9100

**TOWN HOUSE**
P. O. Box 2606 (39442)
Rates: $25-$42;
Tel: (601) 428-1527

## MCCOMB

**HOLIDAY INN**
1900 Delaware Ave (39648)
Rates: $42-$52;
Tel: (601) 684-6211

**RAMADA INN**
P. O. Box 1460 (39648)
Rates: $39 $200;
Tel: (601) 684-5566

## MERIDIAN

**BEST WESTERN
OF MERIDIAN**
P. O. Box 5537 (39302)
Rates: $34-$39;
Tel: (601) 693-3210

**BUDGETEL INN**
1400 Roebuck Dr (39301)
Rates: $32-$48;
Tel: (601) 693-2300

**COMFORT INN**
2901 St. Paul St (39301)
Rates: $28-$35;
Tel: (601) 485-2722

**DAYS INN**
1521 Tom Bailey Dr (39301)
Rates: $36-$59;
Tel: (601) 483-3812

**ECONO LODGE**
2405 S Frontage Rd (39301)
Rates: $29-$35;
Tel: (601) 693-9393

**HOLIDAY INN-SOUTH**
P. O. Box 5513 (39302)
Rates: $41-$56;
Tel: (601) 693-4521

## NATCHEZ

**BEST WESTERN
RIVER PARK HOTEL**
645 S Canal St (39120)
Rates: $54-$79;
Tel: (601) 446-6688

**HOLIDAY INN**
271 D'Evereaux Dr (39120)
Rates: $45-$83;
Tel: (601) 442-3686

**HOWARD JOHNSON
LODGE**
P. O. Box 1347 (39120)
Rates: $41-$53;
Tel: (601) 442-1691

**NATCHEZ EOLA HOTEL**
110 N Pearl St (39120)
Rates: $50-$85;
Tel: (601) 445-6000

**SCOTTISH INNS**
40 Sgt Prentis Dr (39120)
Rates: N/A;
Tel: (601) 442-9141

## NEWTON

**DAYS INN**
P. O. Box 433 (39345)
Rates: $30-$34;
Tel: (601) 683-3361

## OXFORD

**BEST WESTERN
OXFORD INN**
1101 Frontage Rd (38655)
Rates: $40-$49;
Tel: (601) 234-9500

HOLIDAY INN
400 N Lamar Ave (38655)
Rates: $44-$52;
Tel: (601) 234-3031

## PASCAGOULA

LA FONT INN
P. O. Box 1028 (39568)
Rates: $50-$71;
Tel: (601) 762-7111

## RIDGELAND

RED ROOF INN
828 Hwy 51 N (39157)
Rates: N/A;
Tel: (800) 843-7663

## STARKVILLE

HOLIDAY INN
P. O. Box 751 (39759)
Rates: $42-$60;
Tel: (601) 323-6161

THE IVY GUEST HOUSE
P. O. Box 2002 (39759)
Rates: $45-$70;
Tel: (601) 323-2000

## VICKSBURG

ANCHUCA
1010 First East St (39180)
Rates: $70-$135;
Tel: (601) 636-4931

THE CORNERS
601 Klein St (39180)
Rates: $75-$95;
Tel: (601) 636-7421

DELUXE INN
2751 N I-20, Exit 3 (39180)
Rates: $28-$40;
Tel: (601) 636-5121

DUFF GREEN
MANSION INN
1114 First East St (39180)
Rates: $75-$150;
Tel: (800) 992-0037

HOWARD JOHNSON
LODGE
4155 Washington St (39180)
Rates: $28-$65;
Tel: (601) 636-5145

PARK INN INTERNATIONAL
NE Frontage Rd (39180)
Rates: $29-$75;
Tel: (601) 638-5811

# MISSOURI

## ALBANY

EASTWOOD MOTEL
US 136E (64402)
Rates: $22-$33;
Tel: (816) 726-5208

## ARNOLD

DRURY INN
1201 Drury Ln (63010)
Rates: $45-$55;
Tel: (314) 296-9600

## AURORA

AURORA INN MOTEL
Rt 3, Box 200 (65605)
Rates: $36-$42;
Tel: (417) 678-5035

## BETHANEY

BEST WESTERN I-35 INN
Rt 1, Box 2498 (64424)
Rates: N/A;
Tel: (816) 425-7915

## BIRCH TREE

HICKORY HOUSE
MOTOR INN
P. O. Box 306 (65438)
Rates: $20-$32;
Tel: (314) 292-3232

## BLUE SPRINGS

RAMADA LTD
1110 N 7 Hwy (64014)
Rates: $39-$51;
Tel: (816) 229-6363

## BOONVILLE

COMFORT INN
Star Rt, Box 2A (65233)
Rates: $38-$53;
Tel: (816) 882-5317

## BRANSON

BEST WESTERN
RUSTIC OAK
403 W Main St (65616)
Rates: $$36-$62;
Tel: (417) 334-6464

COLONIAL
MOUNTAIN INN
P. O. Box 2068
(Lakeview 65737)
Rates: $30-$50;
Tel: (417) 272-8414

**DAYS INN OF BRANSON**
3524 Keeter St (65616)
Rates: $48-$80;
Tel: (417) 334-5544

**ROCK VIEW RESORT**
HCR 2, Box 870
(Hollister 65672)
Rates: $38-$45;
Tel: (417) 334-4678

**TANEY MOTEL**
311 Hwy 65N Business
(65616)
Rates: $22-$69;
Tel: (417) 334-3143

**TRAVELERS MOTEL**
402 North Bus. 65 (65616)
Rates: N/A;
Tel: (417) 334-3868

## BRANSON WEST

**RUSTIC GATE MOTOR INN**
P. O. Box 1088
(Lakeview 65737)
Rates: $32-$42;
Tel: (417) 272-3326

## BRIDGETON

**RED ROOF INN**
3470 Hollenberg Dr (63044)
Rates: N/A;
Tel: (800) 843-7663

## BUTLER

**BUTLER INN**
Rt 3, Box 74 (64730)
Rates: $28-$35;
Tel: (816) 679-6183

## CAMDENTON

**LAN-O-LAK MOTEL**
P. O. Box 619 (65020)
Rates: $38-$55;
Tel: (314) 346-2256

## CAMERON

**BEST WESTERN
ACORN INN**
P. O. Box 436 (64429)
Rates: $33-$42;
Tel: (816) 632-2187

**BEST WESTERN
RAMBLER MOTEL**
P. O. Box 375 (64429)
Rates: $33-$45;
Tel: (816) 632-6571

**COUNTRY SQUIRE INN**
501 Northland Dr (64429)
Rates: $27-$37;
Tel: (816) 632-6623

## CAPE GIRARDEAU

**CAPE BUDGET INN**
I-55 & Route K (63701)
Rates: $29-$39;
Tel: (314) 334-0501

**DRURY LODGE**
I-55 & Route K (63701)
Rates: $55-$62;
Tel: (314) 334-7151

**HOLIDAY INN
OF CAPE GIRARDEAU**
P. O. Box 1570 (63701)
Rates: $70-$80;
Tel: (314) 334-4491

**THRIFTY INN**
3248 William St (63701)
Rates: $36-$49;
Tel: (314) 334-3000

**VICTORIAN INN
OF CAPE GIRARDEAU**
3249 William St (63701)
Rates: $39-$61;
Tel: (314) 651-4486

## CARTHAGE

**ECONO LODGE**
1441 W Central (64836)
Rates: $37-$45;
Tel: (417) 358-3900

## CASSVILLE

**HOLIDAY MOTEL**
85 S Main (65625)
Rates: $32-$36;
Tel: (417) 847-3163

**TOWNHOUSE MOTEL**
HCR 81, Box 9570 (65625)
Rates: $35-$43;
Tel: (417) 847-4196

## CHILLICOTHE

**BEST WESTERN
SHAMROCK MOTEL**
1020 S Washington St (64601)
Rates: $38-$49;
Tel: (816) 646-0572

**GRAND RIVER INN**
606 W Business 36 (64601)
Rates: $44-$55;
Tel: (816) 646 6590

**TRAVEL INN**
901 Hwy 36W (64601)
Rates: $28-$38;
Tel: (816) 646-0784

## CLARKSVILLE

**CLARKSVILLE INN**
2nd & Lewis Sts (63336)
Rates: $29-$41;
Tel: (314) 242 3324

## CLINTON

**BEST WESTERN COLONIAL**
On MO 13 Bypass (64735)
Rates: $26-$43;
Tel: (816) 885-2206

## COLUMBIA

**BEST WESTERN
COLUMBIA INN**
3100 I-70 Dr SE (65201)
Rates: $39-$54;
Tel: (313) 474-6161

**BUDGETEL INN-COLUMBIA**
2500 I-70 Dr SW (65203)
Rates: $32-$48;
Tel: (314) 445-1899

**BUDGET HOST
CROSSWAYS INN**
900 Vandiver Dr (65202)
Rates: $22-$44;
Tel: (314) 449-1065

**DAYS INN
UNIVERSITY CENTER**
1900 I-70 Dr SW (65203)
Rates: $36-$65;
Tel: (314) 445-8511

**DRURY INN**
1000 Knipp St (65203)
Rates: $54-$61;
Tel: (314) 445-1800

**GUESTHOUSE INN**
801 Keene St (65201)
Rates: $39-$49;
Tel: (314) 474-1408

**HOLIDAY INN
EAST-HOLIDOME**
1612 N Providence Rd (65202)
Rates: $49-$69;
Tel: (314) 449-2491

**HOLIDAY INN
EXECUTIVE CENTER**
2200 I-70 Dr SW (65203)
Rates: $62-$94;
Tel: (314) 445-8531

**RAMADA INN**
1100 Vandiver Dr (65202)
Rates: $52-$70;
Tel: (314) 449-0051

**RED ROOF INN**
201 E Texas Ave (65202)
Rates: N/A;
Tel: (800) 843-7663

**SCOTTISH INN**
2112 Business Loop 70 E
(65201)
Rates: N/A;
Tel: (314) 449-3771

## CONCORDIA

**BEST WESTERN
HEIDELBERG INN**
406 Williams St (64020)
Rates: $32-$47;
Tel: (816) 463-2114

**CONCORDIA INN**
200 N West St (64020)
Rates: $31-$39;
Tel: (816) 463-7987

## CUBA

**BEST WESTERN CUBA INN**
Rt 2, Box 2983 (65453)
Rates: $34-$44;
Tel: (314) 885-7707

## DONIPHAN

**TIN LIZZIE MOTEL**
Hwy 160 (63935)
Rates: N/A;
Tel: (314) 996-2101

## EL DORADO SPRINGS

**EL DORADO MOTEL**
102 Hwy 54 East (64744)
Rates: N/A;
Tel: (417) 876-6888

## ELLINGTON

**SCENIC RIVERS MOTEL**
231 N 2nd St (63638)
Rates: $29-$37;
Tel: (314) 663-7722

## EUREKA

**BEST REST MOTEL**
1725 W 5th St (63025)
Rates: $25-$56;
Tel: (314) 938-5348

**OAK GROVE INN EUREKA**
1733 W 5th St (63025)
Rates: $22-$50;
Tel: (314) 938-4368

**RAMADA INN
AT SIX FLAGS**
P. O. Box 999 (63025)
Rates: $57-$123;
Tel: (314) 938-6661

## FARMINGTON

**BEST WESTERN
TRADITION INN**
1627 W Columbia (63640)
Rates: $45-$48;
Tel: (314) 756-8031

**DAYS INN**
1400 W Liberty St (63640)
Rates: $38-$42;
Tel: (314) 756-8951

## FESTUS

**BUDGETEL INN**
1303 Veterans Blvd (63028)
Rates: $34-$44;
Tel: (314) 937-2888

**DRURY INN**
1001 Veterans Blvd (63028)
Rates: $44-$51;
Tel: (314) 933-2400

## FLAT RIVER

**ROSENER'S INN**
Hwy 67N (63601)
Rates: $29-$45;
Tel: (314) 431-4241

## FLORISSANT

**RED ROOF INN**
307 Dunn Rd (63031)
Rates: N/A;
Tel: (800) 843-7663

## FORISTELL

**BEST WESTERN
WEST 70 INN**
Rt W, Box 10 (63348)
Rates: $37-$41;
Tel: (314) 673-2900

## FREDERICKTOWN

**LONGHORN MOTEL**
P. O. Box 721 (63645)
Rates: $19-$34;
Tel: (314) 783-3363

## FULTON

**BUDGET HOST
WESTWOODS MOTEL**
422 Gaylord Dr (65251)
Rates: $28-$36;
Tel: (314) 642-5991

## GRAIN VALLEY

**SCOTTISH INN**
105 Sunny Lane Dr (64029)
Rates: $25-$41;
Tel: (816) 224-3420

## GRAY SUMMIT

**BEST WESTERN
DIAMOND INN MOTEL**
581 Hwy 100E
(Villa Ridge 63089)
Rates: $49-$69;
Tel: (314) 742-3501

## HANNIBAL

**BEST WESTERN
HOTEL CLEMENS**
401 N 3rd St (63401)
Rates: $45-$80;
Tel: (314) 248-1150

**ECONO LODGE**
612 Mark Twain Ave (63401)
Rates: $25-$79;
Tel: (314) 221-1490

**HANNIBAL TRAVELODGE**
502 Mark Twain Ave (63401)
Rates: $30-$60;
Tel: (314) 221-4100

**HOLIDAY INN**
4141 Market St (63401)
Rates: $35-$125;
Tel: (314) 221-6610

## HARRISONVILLE

**CARAVAN MOTEL**
1705 Hwy 291N (64701)
Rates: $27-$36;
Tel: (816) 884-4100

**HARRISONVILLE
BEST WESTERN**
P. O. Box 363 (64701)
Rates: $35-$50;
Tel: (816) 884 3200

## HAYTI

**DRURY INN**
P. O. Box 9 (63851)
Rates: $42-$48;
Tel: (314) 359 2702

## HIGGINSVILLE

**SUPER 8 MOTEL-
HIGGINSVILLE**
P. O. Box 306 (64037)
Rates: $32-$39;
Tel: (816) 584-7781

## INDEPENDENCE

**HOWARD JOHNSON
EAST MOTEL**
4200 S Noland Rd (64055)
Rates: $45-$65;
Tel: (816) 373-8856

**RED ROOF INN**
13712 E 42nd Ter (64055)
Rates: N/A;
Tel: (800) 843-7663

## ISABELLA

**LAKEPOINT RESORT**
HCR 1, Box 1152 (65676)
Rates: $42-$47;
Tel: (417) 273-4343

## JACKSON

**DAYS INN**
517 Hwy 61E (63755)
Rates: $32-$50;
Tel: (314) 243-3577

## JEFFERSON CITY

**BEST WESTERN INN**
1937 Christy Dr (65101)
Rates: $41-$48;
Tel: (314) 635-4175

**CAPITOL PLAZA HOTEL
& CONVENTION CENTER**
415 W McCarty St (65101)
Rates: $78-$117;
Tel; (314) 635-1234

**DAYS HOTEL**
422 Monroe St (65101)
Rates: $49-$59;
Tel: (314) 636-5101

**PARK INN INTERNATIONAL**
319 W Miller St (65101)
Rates: $49-$56;
Tel: (314) 636-5231

**RAMADA INN**
1510 Jefferson St (65110)
Rates: $50-$59;
Tel: (314) 635-7171

## JOPLIN

**BEST INNS OF AMERICA**
3508 S Range Line Rd (64804)
Rates: $29-$37;
Tel: (417) 781-6776

**CAPRI MOTEL**
3401 South Main (64804)
Rates: N/A;
Tel: (417) 623-0391

**DAYS INN**
3500 Range Line Rd (64804)
Rates: $35-$55;
Tel: (417) 623-0100

**DRURY INN**
3001 Range Line Rd (64804)
Rates: $52-$58;
Tel: (417) 781-8000

**HOLIDAY INN-HOTEL AND
CONVENTION CENTER**
3615 Range Line Rd (64804)
Rates: $61-$79;
Tel: (417) 782-1000

**RAMADA INN**
3320 Range Line Rd (64804)
Rates: $50-$68;
Tel: (417) 781-0500

**THRIFTY INN-JOPLIN**
3510 Range Line Rd (64804)
Rates: $31-$44;
Tel: (417) 623-0000

**THUNDERBIRD MOTEL**
2121 Range Line Rd (64804)
Rates: $30-$42;
Tel: (417) 624-7600

**TROPICANA MOTEL**
2417 Range Line Rd (64804)
Rates: $26-$32;
Tel: (417) 624-8200

# KANSAS CITY
(and Vicinity)

**ALLIS PLAZA HOTEL**
200 W 12th St (64105)
Rates: $85-$150;
Tel: (816) 421-6800

**AMERICAN INN MOTEL**
1211 Armour Rd (64118)
Rates: $30-$45;
Tel: (816) 471-3451

**AMERICANA HOTEL ON
CONVENTION SQUARE**
1301 Wyandotte St (64105)
Rates: $59-$77;
Tel: (816) 221-8800

**BEST WESTERN
AIRPORT INN**
P. O. Box 319
(Platte City 64079)
Rates: $39-$50;
Tel: (816) 464-2300

**BEST WESTERN
HALLMARK INN EXECUTIVE**
7000 W 108th St
(Overland Park KS 66211)
Rates: $65-$75;
Tel: (913) 383-2550

**BEST WESTERN
HALLMARK INN-NORTH**
209 N 291 Hwy
(Liberty 64068)
Rates: $40-$55;
Tel: (816) 781-8770

**BEST WESTERN INN**
501 Southwest Blvd
(Kansas City, KS 66103)
Rates: $48-$66;
Tel: (913) 677-3060

**BEST WESTERN
SUMMIT INN**
625 N Murray Rd
(Lee's Summit 64081)
Rates: $44-$60;
Tel: (816) 525-1400

**BUDGETEL INN-NORTH**
2214 Taney St (64116)
Rates: $33-$49;
Tel: (816) 221-1200

**COMFORT INN**
1200 Hwy 92 (64079)
Rates: $47-$56;
Tel: (816) 431-5430

**COMFORT INN-MERRIAM**
6401 E Frontage Rd
(Merriam, KS 66202)
Rates: $39-$55;
Tel: (913) 262-2622

**COMFORT INN
OF LEE'S SUMMIT**
607 SE Oldham Pkwy
(Lee's Summit 64063)
Rates: $39-$58;
Tel: (816) 542-8181

**COMFORT INN
WESTPORT PLAZA**
801 Westport Rd (64111)
Rates: $54-$62;
Tel: (816) 931-1000

**DAYS INN-NORTH**
2232 Taney St (64116)
Rates: $36-$42;
Tel: (816) 421-6000

**DOUBLETREE HOTEL**
10100 College Blvd
(Overland Park KS 66210)
Rates: $59-$79;
Tel: (913) 451-6100

**DRURY INN MERRIAM**
9009 Shawnee Mission Pkwy
(Merriam, KS 66202)
Rates: $47-$54;
Tel: (913) 236-9200

**DRURY INN-
OVERLAND PARK**
10951 Metcalf Ave
(Overland Park, KS 66210)
Rates: $56-$63;
Tel: (913) 345-1500

**DRURY INN-STADIUM**
3830 Blue Ridge Cutoff
(64133)
Rates: $55-$66;
Tel: (816) 923-3000

**ECONO LODGE
KCI AIRPORT**
11300 NW Prairie View Rd
(64153)
Rates: $31-$49;
Tel: (816) 464-5082

**THE EMBASSY
ON THE PARK**
1215 Wyandotte St (64105)
Rates: $49-$64;
Tel: (816) 471-1333

**HALLMARK INN
MIDTOWN/MED CENTER**
3930 Rainbow Blvd (66103)
Rates: $34-$47;
Tel: (913) 236-6880

**HOLIDAY INN
CROWNE PLAZA**
4445 Main St (64111)
Rates: $95-$119;
Tel: (816) 531-3000

**HOLIDAY INN EXPRESS**
7200 W 107th St
(Overland Park, KS 66212)
Rates: $56-$62;
Tel: (913) 648-7858

**HOLIDAY INN KCI**
11832 Plaza Circle NW
(64153)
Rates: $50;
Tel: (816) 464-2345

**HOLIDAY INN-NORTHEAST**
7333 Parvin Rd (64117)
Rates: $69-$95;
Tel: (816) 455-1060

**HOLIDAY INN OF
MISSION-OVERLAND PARK**
7240 Shawnee Mission Pkwy
(Overland Park, KS 66202)
Rates: $71-$85;
Tel: (913) 262-3010

**HOWARD JOHNSON-
CENTRAL**
610 Washington St (64105)
Rates: $25-$45;
Tel: (816) 421-1800

**HOWARD JOHNSON
LODGE-EAST**
4200 S Noland Rd
(Independence 64055)
Rates: $45-$65;
Tel: (816) 373-8856

**HOWARD JOHNSON
LODGE-SOUTHWEST**
12381 W 95th St
(Lenexa, KS 66215)
Rates: $51-$65;
Tel: (913) 888-9400

**LA QUINTA MOTOR INN**
9461 Lenexa Dr
(Lenexa, KS 66215)
Rates: $43-$55;
Tel: (913) 492-5500

**MARRIOTT-
KANSAS CITY AIRPORT**
775 Brasilia Ave (64153)
Rates: $54-$143;
Tel: (816) 464-2200

**MOTEL 6**
6400 E 87th St (64138)
Rates: $27-$33;
Tel: (816) 333-4468

**OVERLAND PARK
MARRIOTT HOTEL**
10800 Metcalf Ave
(Overland Park KS 66210)
Rates: $79-$135;
Tel: (913) 451-8000

**PARK PLACE HOTEL**
1601 N Universal Ave (64120)
Rates: $59-$89;
Tel: (816) 483-9900

**QUALITY INN**
1600 NE Parvin Rd (64116)
Rates: $65-$68;
Tel: (816) 453-5210

**RADISSON SUITE HOTEL-
KANSAS CITY**
106 W 12th St (64105)
Rates: $89-$109;
Tel: (816) 221-7000

**RAMADA HOTEL-AIRPORT**
7301 NW Tiffany Spgs Rd
(64153)
Rates: $39-$69;
Tel: (816) 741-9500

**RAMADA INN & SUITES
OF OVERLAND PARK**
8787 Reeder
(Overland Park, KS 66214)
Rates: $62-$90;
Tel: (913) 888-8440

**RAMADA INN SOUTH**
5701 Longview Rd (64137)
Rates: $41-$46;
Tel: (816) 765-4100

**RAMADA INN SOUTHEAST**
6101 E 87th St (64138)
Rates: $54-$60;
Tel: (816) 765-4331

**RED ROOF INN-
INDEPENDENCE**
13712 E 42nd Terr
(Independence 64055)
Rates: $31-$41;
Tel: (816) 373-2800

**RED ROOF INN-NORTH**
3636 NE Randolph Rd (64161)
Rates: $26-$47;
Tel: (800) 843-7663

**RED ROOF INN-
OVERLAND PARK**
6800 W 108th St
(Oveland Park, KS 66211)
Rates: $30-$48;
Tel: (913) 341-0100

**RESIDENCE INN
BY MARRIOTT**
6300 W 110th
(Overland Park KS 66211)
Rates: $75-$130;
Tel: (913) 491-3333

**THE RESIDENCE
BY MARRIOTT KCI**
9900 NW Prairie View Rd
(64153)
Rates: $59-$115;
Tel: (816) 891-9009

**RESIDENCE INN BY
MARRIOTT UNION HILL**
2975 Main St (64108)
Rates: $98-$125;
Tel: (816) 561-3000

**THE RITZ-CARLTON
KANSAS CITY**
401 Ward Pkwy (64112)
Rates: $109-$199;
Tel: (816) 756-1500

**SAVOY HOTEL**
219 W 9th St (64105)
Rates: $79-$120;
Tel: (816) 842-3575

**THE WESTIN CROWN CENTER**
1 Pershing Rd (64108)
Rates: $139-$179;
Tel: (816) 474-4400

## KIMBERLING CITY

**KIMBERLING ARMS
BEST WESTERN**
P. O. Box 429 (65686)
Rates: $44-$79;
Tel: (417) 739-2461

**KIMBERLING HEIGHTS
RESORT MOTEL**
Rt 3, Box 980 (65686)
Rates: $29-$59;
Tel: (417) 779-4158

**KING'S KOVE RESORT**
Rt 5, Box 498A
(Reeds Spring 65737)
Rates: $51;
Tel: (417) 739-4513

## KIRKSVILLE

**BEST WESTERN
SHAMROCK INN**
P. O. Box 1005 (63501)
Rates: $35-$41;
Tel: (816) 665-8352

**BUDGET HOST
VILLAGE INN**
P. O. Box 673 (63501)
Rates: $29-$37;
Tel: (816) 665-3722

**DAYS INN**
P. O. Box M (63501)
Rates: $43-$62;
Tel: (816) 665-8244

**TRAVELERS HOTEL**
301 West Washington (63501)
Rates: $32-$39;
Tel: (816) 665-5191

## KNOB NOSTER

**WHITEMAN INN**
2340 W Irish Ln (65336)
Rates: $32-$35;
Tel: (816) 563-3000

## LAKE OF THE OZARKS

**MILLSTONE
LODGE RESORT**
Rt 1, Box 515
(Gravois Mills 65037)
Rates: $60-$299;
Tel: (314) 372-5111

## LAKE OZARK

**HOWARD JOHNSON
MOTEL**
P. O.Box 8 (65049)
Rates: $65-$81;
Tel: (314) 365-5353

## LAKE ST. LOUIS

**DAYS INN AT THE LAKE**
2560 S Outer Rd (63367)
Rates: $39-$49;
Tel: (314) 625-1711

## LEBANON

**BRENTWOOD MOTEL**
1320 S Jefferson (65536)
Rates: $29-$36;
Tel: (417) 532-6131

**ECONO LODGE**
P. O. Box 972 (65536)
Rates: $26-$36;
Tel: (417) 588-3226

**HOLIDAY INN
OF LEBANON**
P. O. Box 972 (65536)
Rates: $39-$50;
Tel: (417) 532-7111

**SHEPHERD HILLS MOTEL**
P. O. Box 1100 (65536)
Rates: $28-$38;
Tel: (417) 532-3133

## LEXINGTON

**LEXINGTON INN**
Jct US 24 & SR 13 (64067)
Rates: $32-$37;
Tel: (816) 259-4641

## MACON

**BEST WESTERN
SKY-VUE INN MOTEL**
Hwy 36 W, RR 4 (63552)
Rates: $31-$41;
Tel: (816) 385-2125

## MARYVILLE

**SUPER 8 MOTEL-
MARYVILLE**
Hwy 71S (64468)
Rates: $35-$41;
Tel: (816) 582-8088

## MEXICO

**COMFORT INN**
P.O. Box 113 (65265)
Rates: $23-$30;
Tel: (314) 581-8350

## MOBERLY

**KNOLL MOTEL**
P. O. Box 146 (65270)
Rates: $26-$32;
Tel: (816) 263-5000

**RAMADA INN
OF MOBERLY**
Jct US 24 & 63 (65270)
Rates: $45-$54;
Tel: (816) 263-6540

## MONETT

**HARTLAND LODGE**
929 Hwy 60E (65708)
Rates: $37-$43;
Tel: (417) 235-4000

## MONROE CITY

**MONROE CITY INN**
3 Gateway Sq (63456)
Rates: $38-$45;
Tel: (314) 735-4200

## MOUND CITY

**AUDREY'S MOTEL**
RR 2, Box 231 (64470)
Rates: $24-$33;
Tel: (816) 442-3191

## MOUNT VERNON

**BUDGET HOST
RANCH MOTEL**
Rt 1, Box 68 (65712)
Rates: $30-$44;
Tel: (417) 466-2125

## NEOSHO

**NEOSHO INN**
2500 S 71 Hwy (64850)
Rates: $42-$48;
Tel: (417) 451-6500

## NEVADA

**RAMSEY'S NEVADA MOTEL**
1514 E Austin St (64772)
Rates: $28-$36;
Tel: (417) 667-5273

## OAK GROVE

**ECONO LODGE**
410 SE 1st St (64075)
Rates: $29-$39;
Tel: (816) 625-3681

## OSAGE BEACH

**BEST WESTERN
DOGWOOD HILLS RESORT
AND GOLF CLUB**
Rt 4, Box 1300 (65065)
Rates: $47-$84;
Tel: (314) 348-1735

**SCOTTISH INNS**
Rt 2, Box 3630 (65065)
Rates: $24-$48;
Tel: (314) 348-3123

## PERRYVILLE

**BUDGET HOST PARK-ET**
221 S Kings Hwy (63775)
Rates: $24-$38;
Tel: (314) 547-4516

## POPLAR BLUFF

**DRURY INN**
2220 N Westwood Blvd
(63901)
Rates: $45-$51;
Tel: (314) 686-2451

**HOLIDAY INN**
2115 N Westwood Blvd
(63901)
Rates: $40-$60;
Tel: (314) 785-7711

**THRIFTY INN**
2218 N Westwood Blvd
(63901)
Rates: $31-$41;
Tel: (314) 785-7100

## RICH HILL

**APACHE MOTEL**
Rt 3, Box 309A (64779)
Rates: $21-$27;
Tel: (417) 395-2161

## ROCKAWAY BEACH

**EDEN ROC RESORT**
607 Beach Blvd (65740)
Rates: $25-$35;
Tel: (417) 561-4163

**KENNY'S COURT**
P. O. Box 87 (65740)
Rates: $29-$45;
Tel: (417) 561-4131

## ROCK PORT

**ROCK PORT INN**
Rt 4, Box 218 (64482)
Rates: $32-$41;
Tel: (816) 744-6282

## ROLLA

**BESTWAY INN**
1631 Martin Springs Dr
(65401)
Rates: $18-$29;
Tel: (314) 341-2158

**BEST WESTERN
COACHLIGHT MOTEL**
P. O. Box 826 (65401)
Rates: $45-$55;
Tel: (314) 341-2511

**DRURY INN**
2006 N Bishop (65401)
Rates: $49-$56;
Tel: (314) 364-4000

**ECONO LODGE**
1417 Martin Springs Dr
(65401)
Rates: $26-$36;
Tel: (314) 341-3130

**HOWARD JOHNSON
LODGE**
127 H J Dr (65401)
Rates: $36-$58;
Tel: (314) 364-7111

## ST. CHARLES

**ECONO LODGE**
3040 W Clay St (63301)
Rates: $23-$45;
Tel: (314) 946-9992

**HOLIDAY INN-ST PETERS**
P. O. Box 310
(St. Peters 63376)
Rates: $59-$150;
Tel: (314) 928-1500

**KNIGHTS INN**
3800 Harry S Truman Blvd
(63301)
Rates: $33-$50;
Tel: (314) 925-2020

**RED ROOF INNS**
2010 Zumbehl Rd (63303)
Rates: $36-$49;
Tel: (800) 843-7663

## ST. CLAIR

**BUDGET LODGING**
866 Service Rd (63077)
Rates: $33-$47;
Tel: (314) 629-1000

## ST. GENEVIEVE

**ECONO LODGE**
P. O. Box 429 (63670)
Rates: $32-$49;
Tel: (314) 543-2272

## ST. JOSEPH

**DRURY INN**
4213 Frederick Blvd (64506)
Rates: $40-$50;
Tel: (816) 364-4700

**HOLIDAY INN-DOWNTOWN**
102 S Third St (64501)
Rates: $51-$64;
Tel: (816) 279-8000

**RAMADA INN**
4016 Frederick Ave (64506)
Rates: $48-$54;
Tel: (816) 233-6192

## ST. LOUIS
(and Vicinity)

**ADAM'S MARKET-
ST. LOUIS**
4th & Chestnut Sts (63102)
Rates: $85-$109;
Tel: (314) 241-7400

**AIRPORT
MARRIOTT HOTEL**
I-70 exit 236 (63134)
Rates: $69-$140;
Tel: (314) 423-9700

**BEST INNS OF AMERICA**
2423 Old Country Inn Rd
(Caseyville, IL 62232)
Rates: $36-$44;
Tel: (618) 397-3300

**BEST WESTERN
BO-JON INN**
SR 159, exit 15B
(Collinsville, IL 62234)
Rates: $28-$44;
Tel: (618) 345-5720

**BEST WESTERN
WESTPORT PARK**
2434 Old Dorsett Rd
(Maryland Hgts 63043)
Rates: $55-$76;
Tel: (314) 291-8700

**BRIDGEPORT INN**
4199 N Lindbergh (63044)
Rates: $26-$33;
Tel: (314) 739-4600

**BUDGETEL-HAZELWOOD**
318 Taylor D
(Hazelwood 63042)
Rates: $32-$43;
Tel: (314) 731-4200

**BUDGETEL INN-WESTPORT**
12330 Dorsett Rd
(Maryland Hgts 63043)
Rates: $35-$49;
Tel: (314) 878-1212

**COMFORT INN
SOUTHWEST**
3730 S Lindbergh Blvd
(Sunset Hills 63127)
Rates: $44-$55;
Tel: (314) 842-1200

**THE DANIELE**
216 N Meramec Ave
(Clayton 63105)
Rates: $75-$129;
Tel: (314) 721-0101

**DAYS INN-AIRPORT**
4545 Woodson Rd
(Woodson Terrace 63134)
Rates: $43-$53;
Tel: (314) 423-6770

**DAYS INN-COLLINSVILLE**
1803 Ramada Blvd
(Collinsville, IL 62234)
Rates: $37-$49;
Tel: (618) 345-8100

**DOUBLETREE HOTEL
& CONFERENCE CENTER**
16625 Swingley Ridge Rd
(Chesterfield 63017)
Rates: $135-$335;
Tel: (314) 532-5000

**DRURY INN**
12 Ludwig Dr
(Fairview Hgts, IL 62208)
Rates: $52-$62;
Tel: (618) 398-8530

**DRURY INN-AIRPORT**
10800 Pear Tree Ln
(St. Ann 63074)
Rates: $60-$67;
Tel: (314) 423-7700

**DRURY INN COLLINSVILLE**
602 N Bluff Rd
(Collinsville, IL 62234)
Rates: $49-$62;
Tel: (618) 345-7700

**DRURY INN-
SOUTHWEST (FENTON)**
1088 S Hwy Dr
(Fenton 63026)
Rates: $49-$63;
Tel: (314) 343-7822

**DRURY INN
UNION STATION**
201 S 20th St (63103)
Rates: $74-$84;
Tel: (314) 231-3900

**DRURY INN-WESTPORT**
12220 Dorsett Rd
(Maryland Hgts 63043)
Rates: $56-$62;
Tel: (314) 576-9966

**ECONO LODGE-
ST. LOUIS-BRIDGETON**
4575 N Lindbergh Blvd
(Bridgeton 63044)
Rates: $31-$91;
Tel: (314) 731-3000

**THE FRONTENAC GRAND**
1335 S Lindbergh Blvd
(63131)
Rates: $70-$95;
Tel: (314) 993-1100

**HAMPTON INN
UNION STATION**
2211 Market St (63103)
Rates: $64-$84;
Tel: (314) 241-3200

**HOLIDAY INN-
AIRPORT NORTH**
4545 N Lindbergh Blvd
(Bridgeton 63044)
Rates: $73-$83;
Tel: (314) 731-2100

**HOLIDAY INN DOWNTOWN
CONVENTION CENTER**
811 N 9th St (63101)
Rates: $59;
Tel: (314) 421-4000

**HOLIDAY INN
DOWNTOWN/RIVERFRONT**
200 N 4th St (63102)
Rates: $49-$99;
Tel: (314) 621-8200

**HOLIDAY INN-SOUTH I-55**
4234 Butler Hill Rd (63129)
Rates: $73-$89;
Tel: (314) 894-0700

**HOWARD JOHNSON
HOSTEL SOUTHWEST**
1200 S Kirkwood
(Kirkwood 63122)
Rates: $57-$87;
Tel: (314) 821-3950

**HOWARD JOHNSON-
HAMPTON AVE MIDTOWN**
5915 Wilson Ave (63110)
Rates: $58-$86;
Tel: (314) 645-0700

**IMPERIAL INN**
600 E Main St
(Belleville, IL 62221)
Rates: $25-$35;
Tel: (618) 234-9670

**KNIGHTS INN-
ST. LOUIS-BRIDGETON**
12433 St Charles Rock Rd
(Bridgeton 63044)
Rates: $31-$47;
Tel: (314) 291-8545

**LA QUINTA-AIRPORT**
5781 Campus St
(Hazelwood 63042)
Rates: $38-$59;
Tel: (314) 731-3881

222

**MARRIOTT HOTEL**
I-70 at Lambert St Louis
Airport (63134)
Rates: $125-$375;
Tel: (314) 423-9700

**OAK GROVE INN-
ST. LOUIS SOUTH**
6602 S Lindbergh Blvd
(Affton 63123)
Rates: $30-$42;
Tel: (314) 894-9449

**PEAR TREE INN**
552 Ramada Blvd
(Collinsville, IL 62234)
Rates: $38-$50;
Tel: (618) 345-9500

**QUALITY HOTEL-
ST. LOUIS AIRPORT**
9600 Natural Bridge Rd
(Berkley 63134)
Rates: $55-$90;
Tel: (314) 427-7600)

**QUALITY INN**
475 Bluff Rd
(Collinsville, IL 62234)
Rates: $29-$60;
Tel: (618) 344-7171

**RADISSON HOTEL**
7750 Carondelet Ave
(Clayton 63105)
Rates: $70-$150;
Tel: (314) 726-5400

**RADISSON
ST. LOUIS AIRPORT**
11228 Lone Eagle Dr
(Bridgeton 63044)
Rates: $109-$379;
Tel: (314) 291-6700

**RAMADA INN WESTPORT**
12031 Lackland Rd
(Maryland Hgts 63146)
Rates: $49;
Tel: (314) 878-1400

**RED ROOF INN-
BRIDGETON**
3470 Hollenberg Dr
(Bridgeton 63044)
Rates: $28-$40;
Tel: (314) 291-3350

**RED ROOF INN-
FLORISSANT**
307 Dunn Rd
(Florissant 63031)
Rates: $43-$50;
Tel: (314) 831-7900

**RED ROOF INN-HAMPTON**
5823 Wilson Ave (63110)
Rates: $43-$67;
Tel: (314) 645-0101

**RED ROOF INN-WESTPORT**
11837 Lackland Rd
(Maryland Hgts 63146)
Rates: $32-$47;
Tel: (314) 991-4900

**THE REGAL
RIVERFRONT HOTEL**
200 S 4th St (63102)
Rates: $65-$160;
Tel: (314) 241-9500

**RESIDENCE INN
BY MARRIOTT-WESTPORT**
1881 Craigshire Rd (63146)
Rates: $89-$139;
Tel: (314) 469-0060

**SEVEN GABLES INN**
26 N Meramec St
(Clayton 63105)
Rates: $85-$130;
Tel: (314) 863-8400

**SHERATON-
WEST PORT INN**
191 West Port Plaza (63146)
Rates: $68-$129;
Tel: (314) 878-1500

**SUMMERFIELD SUITES
HOTEL**
1855 Craigshire Rd (63146)
Rates: $108-$158;
Tel: (314) 878-1555

**SUPER 8 MOTEL**
45 Ludwig Dr
(Fairview Hgts, IL 62208)
Rates: $33-$54;
Tel: (618) 398-8338

**SUPER 8 MOTEL-NORTH**
2790 Target Dr (63136)
Rates: $35-$43;
Tel: (314) 355-7808

**THRIFTY INN-
SOUTHWEST (FENTON)**
1100 S Hwy Dr
(Fenton 63026)
Rates: $29-$59;
Tel: (314) 343-8820

## SEDALIA

**BEST WESTERN
STATE FAIR MOTOR INN**
32nd & Hwy 65S (65301)
Rates: $40-$45;
Tel: (816) 826-6100

**KNIGHTS COURT**
3501 W Broadway (65301)
Rates: $39-$42;
Tel: (816) 826-8400

## SIKESTON

**DRURY INN**
2602 Rear East Malone
(63801)
Rates: $40-$47;
Tel: (314) 471-8660

## SPRINGFIELD

**BEST INNS OF AMERICA**
2355 N Glenstone Ave
(65803)
Rates: $31-$39;
Tel: (417) 866-6776

**BEST WESTERN
CHRISMAN INN**
2745 N Glenstone Ave
(65803)
Rates: $40-$45;
Tel: (417) 869-2505

**BEST WESTERN
COACH HOUSE INN**
2535 N Glenstone Ave
(65803)
Rates: $39-$58;
Tel: (417) 862-0701

**HAMPTON INN**
222 N Ingram Mill Rd (65802)
Rates: $50-$70;
Tel: (417) 863-1440

**HOLIDAY INN**
2720 N Glenstone (65803)
Rates: $68-$200;
Tel: (417) 765-8600

**HOLIDAY INN
UNIVERSITY PLAZA HOTEL**
333 John Q Hammons Pkwy
(65806)
Rates: $71-$84;
Tel: (417) 864-7333

**HOWARD JOHNSON
HOTEL**
2610 N Glenstone Ave
(65803)
Rates: $48-$85;
Tel: (417) 866-6671

**MARKHAM INN
OF THE OZARKS**
2820 N Glenstone Ave
(65803)
Rates: $45-$49;
Tel: (417) 866-3581

**MOUNT VERNON
MOTOR LODGE**
2006 S Glenstone (65804)
Rates: N/A;
Tel: (417) 881-2833

**QUALITY INN NORTH**
3050 N Kentwood (65803)
Rates: $49-$59;
Tel: (417) 833-3108

**RED ROOF INN**
2655 N Glenstone Ave
(65803)
Rates: $31-$43;
Tel: (417) 831-2100

**RESIDENCE INN
BY MARRIOTT**
1550 E Raynell Pl (65804)
Rates: $89-$115;
Tel: (417) 883-7300

**SKYLINE MOTEL**
2120 N Glenstone Ave
(65803)
Rates: $28-$38;
Tel: (417) 866-4356

## SULLIVAN

**FAMILY MOTOR INN**
209 N Service Rd (63080)
Rates: $23-$38;
Tel: (314) 468-4119

**HOLIDAY INN**
309 N Service Rd (63080)
Rates: $43-$52;
Tel: (314) 468-4172

**SULLILVAN
SUPER 8 MOTEL**
601 N Service Rd (63080)
Raters: $34-$43;
Tel: (314) 468-8076

## TIPTON

**TWIN PINE MOTEL**
P. O. Box 208 (65081)
Rates: $21-$30;
Tel: (816) 433-5525

## VAN BUREN

**HAWTHORNE MOTEL**
P. O. Box 615 (63965)
Rates: $22-$38;
Tel: (314) 323-4275

## VERSAILLES

**WESTERN HILLS MOTEL**
Rt 3, Box 86 (65084)
Rates: $23-$31;
Tel: (314) 378-4663

## WAPPAPELLO

**MILLERS MOTORLODGE**
Rt 2, Box 63 (3966)
Rates: $34-$46;
Tel: (314) 222-8579

## WARRENSBURG

**SUPER 8 MOTEL-
WARRENSBURG**
440 Russell Ave (64039)
Rates: $30-$43;
Tel: (816) 429-2183

## WARRENTON

**COLLIER HOSPITALITY INN**
2532 W Old Hwy 40 (63383)
Rates: $22-$34;
Tel: (314) 456-7272

**DAYS INN**
220 Arlington Way (63383)
Rates: $32-$39;
Tel: (314) 456-4301

## WENTZVILLE

**BUDGET HOST INN**
1500 Continental Dr (63385)
Rates: $19-$39;
Tel: (314) 327-5212

**COMFORT INN**
1400 Continental Dr (63385)
Rates: $24-$59;
Tel: (314) 327-5515

**HOLIDAY INN-
WEST I-70 & 40/61**
900 Corporate Pkwy (63385)
Rates: $59-$63;
Tel: (314) 327-7001

**SUPER 8 MOTEL-
WENTZVILLE**
4 Pantera Dr (63385)
Rates: $32-$39;
Tel: (314) 327-5300

## WEST PLAINS

**BUDGET HOST-
WAY STATION MOTEL**
P. O. Box 278 (65775)
Rates: $31-$41;
Tel: (417) 256-4135

**RAMADA INN**
1301 Preacher Row (65775)
Rates: $38-$56;
Tel: (417) 256-8191

# MONTANA

## ALBERTON

**RIVER EDGE MOTEL**
P. O. Box 64 (59820)
Rates: $24-$48;
Tel: (406) 722-4418

## BIG FORK

**COUNTRY LANE'S
BED & BREAKFAST**
Rainbow Dr (59911)
Rates: N/A;
Tel: (406) 837-4608

**O'DAUCH'AIN
COUNTRY INN**
675 Ferndale Dr (59911)
Rates: $50-$95;
Tel: (406) 837-6851

**TIMBERS MOTEL**
P. O. Box 757 (59911)
Rates: $30-$52,
Tel: (406) 837-6200

## BIG SKY

**BEST WESTERN
BUCK'S T-4 LODGE**
46625 Gallatin Rd (59716)
Rates: $46-$78;
Tel: (406) 995-4111

## BILLINGS

**AIRPORT METRA INN**
403 Main (59105)
Rates: $29-$36;
Tel: (406) 245-6611

**BEST WESTERN
PONDEROSA INN**
P. O. Box 1791 (59103)
Rates: $50-$70;
Tel: (406) 259-5511

**THE BILLINGS INN**
880 N 29th St (59101)
Rates: $33-$41;
Tel: (406) 252-5800

**BILLINGS SUPER 8 LODGE**
400 Southgate Dr (59102)
Rates: $35-$43;
Tel: (406) 248-8842

**CHERRY TREE INN**
823 N Broadway (59101)
Rates: $30-$38,
Tel: (406) 252-5603

**DAYSTOP MOTEL**
843 Parkway Ln (59101)
Rates: $36-$39;
Tel: (406) 252-4007

**DUDE RANCHER LODGE**
415 N 29th St (59101)
Rates: $36-$58;
Tel: (406) 259-5561

**ELLIOTT INN**
1345 Mullowney Ln (59101)
Rates: $40-$49;
Tel: (406) 252-2584

**HOLLIDAY INN
BILLINGS PLAZA**
5500 Midland Rd (59101)
Rates: $58-$99;
Tel: (406) 248-7701

**JUNIPER MOTEL**
1315 N 27th St (59101)
Rates: $41-$43;
Tel: (406) 245-4128

**KELLY INN**
5425 Midland Rd (59101)
Rates: $30-$50;
Tel: (406) 252-2700

**LAZY KT MOTEL**
1403 1st Ave N (59101)
Rates: N/A;
Tel: (406) 252-6606

**PICTURE COURT MOTEL**
5146 Laurel Rd (59101)
Rates: N/A;
Tel: (406) 252-8478

**QUALITY INN HOMESTEAD**
2035 Overland Ave (59102)
Rates: $43-$62;
Tel: (406) 652-1320

**RADISSON
NORTHERN HOTEL**
1st Ave N & Broadway
(59101)
Rates: $79-$89;
Tel: (406) 245-5121

**RAMADA INN**
1223 Mullowney Ln (59101)
Rates: $45-$57;
Tel: (406) 248-7151

**RIMROCK INN**
1203 North 27th St (59101)
Rates: N/A;
Tel: (406) 252-7107

## BOZEMAN

**THE BOZEMAN INN**
1235 N 7th Ave (59715)
Rates: $35-$57;
Tel: (406) 587-3176

**COMFORT INN**
1370 N 7th Ave (59715)
Rates: $40-$92;
Tel: (406) 587-2322

**FAIRFIELD INN
BY MARRIOTT**
828 Wheat Dr (59715)
Rates: $49-$63;
Tel: (406) 597-2222

**HOLIDAY INN**
5 Baxter Ln (59715)
Rates: $54-$71;
Tel: (406) 587-4561

**ROYAL "7" MOTEL**
310 N 7th Ave (59715)
Rates: $31-$45;
Tel: (406) 587-3103

**WESTERN HERITAGE INN**
1200 E Main St (59715)
Rates: $39-$56;
Tel: (406) 586-8534

## BUTTE

**BEST WESTERN COPPER
KING INN/CONF CTR**
4655 Harrison Ave S (59701)
Rates: $54-$69;
Tel: (406) 494-6666

**EDDY'S MOTEL**
1205 S Montana St (59701)
Rates: N/A;
Tel: (406) 723-4364

**ROCKER INN**
122001 W Brown's Gulch Rd
(59701)
Rates: $30-$40;
Tel: (406) 723-5464

**TOWNHOUSE INNS
OF BUTTE**
2777 Harrison Ave (59701)
Rates: $44-$59;
Tel: (406) 494-8850

## CHOTEAU

**WESTERN STAR MOTEL**
426 Main Ave S (59422)
Rates: N/A;
Tel: (406) 466-5737

## COLUMBUS

**COLUMBUS SUPER 8-
TOWNHOUSE INNS**
602 8th Ave N (59019)
Rates: $34-$45;
Tel: (800) 442-4667

## CONDON

**HOLLAND LAKE LODGE**
SR Box 2083 (59826)
Rates: N/A;
Tel: (800) 648-8859

## CONRAD

**CONRAD SUPER 8-
TOWNHOUSE INNS**
215 N Main (59425)
Rates: $32-$46;
Tel: (800) 442-4667

## COOKE CITY

**ALL SEASONS MINE CO.
HOTEL & CASINO**
P. O. Box 1130 (59020)
Rates: $50-$75;
Tel: (406) 838-2251

**HIGH COUNTRY MOTEL**
P. O. Box 1146 (59020)
Rates: $32-$58;
Tel: (406) 838-2272

## DEER LODGE

**SCHARF'S MOTOR INN**
819 Main St (59722)
Rates: $21-$38;
Tel: (406) 846-2810

**SUPER 8 MOTEL**
1150 N Main St (59722)
Rates: $34-$46;
Tel: (406) 846-2370

**WESTERN BIG SKY INN**
210 N Main St (59722)
Rates: $40-$52;
Tel: (406) 846-2590

## DILLON

**BEST WESTERN
PARADISE INN**
650 N Montana St (59725)
Rates: $40-$50;
Tel: (406) 683-4214

**CRESTON MOTEL**
335 S Atlantic (59725)
Rates: $24-$33;
Tel: (406) 683-2341

**SUNDOWNER MOTEL**
500 N Montana St (59725)
Rates: $26-$36;
Tel: (406) 683-2375

**SUPER 8 MOTEL**
550 N Montana St (59725)
Rates: $36-$47;
Tel: (406) 683-4288

**TOWNHOUSE INNS
OF DILLON**
450 N Interchange (59725)
Rates: $33-$45;
Tel: (800) 442-4667

## EAST GLACIER PARK

**JACOBSON'S
SCENIC VIEW COTTAGES**
1204 Hwy 49, Box 101
(59434)
Rates: $30-$47;
Tel: (406) 226-4422

**MANY GLACIER HOTEL**
12 Mi W of Babb off US 89
(59434)
Rates: $67-$135;
Tel: (406) 732-4411

**MOUNTAIN PINE MOTEL**
P. O. Box 260 (59434)
Rates: $35-$52;
Tel: (406) 226-4403

**PORTER'S ALPINE MOTEL**
P. O. Box 149 (59434)
Rates: $32-$52;
Tel: (406) 226-4402

**SEARS MOTEL**
1023 Hwy 49 N (59434)
Rates: N/A;
Tel: (406) 226-4432

## ELLISTON

**LAST CHANCE MOTEL**
Hwy 12 (59728)
Rates: N/A;
Tel: (406) 492-7250

## ENNIS

**THE EL WESTERN MOTEL**
P. O. Box 487 (59729)
Rates: $50-$80;
Tel: (406) 682-4127

**HICKEY'S FOUR SEASONS**
P. O. Box 687 (59729)
Rates: N/A;
Tel: (406) 682-4378

## FORSYTH

**BEST WESTERN
SUNDOWNER INN**
P. O. Box 1080 (59327)
Rates: $49-$58;
Tel: (406) 356-2115

**RESTWEL MOTEL**
P. O. Box 287 (59327)
Rates: $25-$32;
Tel: (406) 356-2771

**WESTWIND MOTOR INN**
P. O. Box 5025 (59327)
Rates: $33-$38;
Tel: (406) 356-2038

## FORT BENTON

**FORT MOTEL**
1809 St Charles (59442)
Rates: N/A;
Tel: (406) 622-3312

## GALLATIN GATEWAY

**CASTLE ROCK INN**
65840 Gallatin Gateway
(59730)
Rates: N/A;
Tel: (406) 763-4243

## GARDINER

**BEST WESTERN BY
MAMMOTH HOT SPRINGS**
P. O. Box 646 (59030)
Rates: $40-$89;
Tel: (406) 848-7311

**HILLCREST MOTEL**
Hwy 89 (59030)
Rates: N/A;
Tel: (406) 848-7353

**SUPER 8 MOTEL**
P. O. Box 755 (59030)
Rates: $54-$69;
Tel: (406) 848-7401

**WILSON'S YELLOWSTONE
RIVER MOTEL**
P. O. Box 223 (59030)
Rates: $35-$49;
Tel: (406) 848-7303

## GLASGOW

**CAMPBELL LODGE**
534 3rd Ave S (59230)
Rates: $29-$38;
Tel: (406) 228-9328

**COTTONWOOD INN**
P. O. Box 1240 (59230)
Rates: $40-$58;
Tel: (406) 228-8213

## GLENDIVE

**BEST WESTERN
HOLIDAY LODGE**
222 N Kendrick Ave (59330)
Rates: $49-$59;
Tel: (406) 365-5655

**BUDGET MOTEL**
1610 N Merrill Ave (59330)
Rates: N/A;
Tel: (406) 365-0004

**DAYS INN MOTEL**
P. O. Box 698 (59330)
Rates: $32-$42;
Tel: (406) 365-6011

**EL CENTRO MOTEL**
112 S Kendrick Ave (59330)
Rates: $23-$31;
Tel: (406) 365-5211

**JORDON MOTOR INN**
223 N Merrill Ave (59330)
Rates: $39-$49;
Tel: (406) 365-3371

**RUSTIC INN**
1902 N Merrill Ave (59330)
Rates: $15-$39;
Tel: (406) 365-5636

**SUPER 8 MOTEL**
P. O. Box 198 (59330)
Rates: $34-$42;
Tel: (406) 365-5671

## GREAT FALLS

**BEST WESTERN
HERITAGE INN**
1700 Fox Farm Rd (59404)
Rates: $54-$105;
Tel: (406) 761-1900

**BEST WESTERN
PONDEROSA INN**
220 Central Ave (59401)
Rates: $45-$63;
Tel: (406) 761-3410

**BUDGET INN MOTEL**
2 Treasure State Dr (59404)
Rates: $35-$41;
Tel: (406) 453-1602

**SHERATON GREAT FALLS**
400 10th Ave S (59405)
Rates: $52-$84;
Tel: (406) 727-7200

**TOWNHOUSE INNS
OF GREAT FALLS**
1410 Harrison Ave (59405)
Rates: $47-$62;
Tel: (406) 761-4600

**TRIPLE CROWN
MOTOR INN**
621 Central Ave (59401)
Rates: $34-$43;
Tel: (406) 727-8300

**VILLAGE MOTOR INN**
726 10th Ave S (59405)
Rates: N/A;
Tel: (406) 727-7666

## HAMILTON

**TOWNHOUSE INNS-
HAMILTON**
1115 N First St (59840)
Rates: $40-$56;
Tel: (406) 363-6600

## HARDIN

**LARIAT MOTEL**
709 North Center Ave (59034)
Rates: N/A;
Tel: (406) 665-2683

**WESTERN MOTEL**
831 W 3rd St (59034)
Rates: $32-$58;
Tel: (406) 665-2296

## HARLOWTON

**CORRAL MOTEL**
P. O. Box 721 (59036)
Rates: $29-$34;
Tel: (406) 632-4331

## HAVRE

**EL TORO INN**
521 1st St (59501)
Rates: $36-$46;
Tel: (406) 265-5414

**SUPER 8 MOTEL**
166 19th Ave W (59501)
Rates: $31-$65;
Tel: (406) 265-1411

**TOWNHOUSE INNS
OF HAVRE**
629 W 1st St (59501)
Rates: $39-$53;
Tel: (406) 265-6711

## HELENA

**ALADDIN MOTOR INN**
2101 11th Ave (59601)
Rates: $44-$52;
Tel: (406) 443-2300

**COMFORT INN OF HELENA**
750 Fee St (59623)
Rates: $39-$73;
Tel: (406) 443-1000

**DAYS INN HELENA**
2001 Prospect Ave (59601)
Rates: $35-$42;
Tel: (406) 442-3280

**JORGENSON'S
HOLIDAY MOTEL**
P. O. Box 857 (59624)
Rates: $32-$70;
Tel: (406) 442-1770

**PARK PLAZA HOTEL**
22 N Last Chance Gulch
(59601)
Rates: $55-$61;
Tel: (406) 443-2200

**SHILO INN**
2020 Prospect Ave (59601)
Rates: N/A;
Tel: (406) 442-0320

## KALISPELL

**BEST WESTERN
OUTLAW INN**
1701 Hwy 93S (59901)
Rates: $62-$120;
Tel: (406) 755-6100

**CAVANAUGH'S
AT KALIPSELL CENTER**
20 N Main (59901)
Rates: $65-$100;
Tel: (406) 752-6660

**DIAMOND LIL'S
INN MOTEL**
1680 US 93S (59901)
Rates: $58-$62;
Tel: (800) 843-7301

**FOUR SEASONS
MOTOR INN**
350 N Main St (59901)
Rates: $45-$53;
Tel: (406) 755-6123

**RED LION MOTEL**
1330 Hwy 2W (59901)
Rates: $45-$93;
Tel: (406) 755-6700

**WHITE BIRCH MOTEL**
17 Shady Ln (59901)
Rates: $25-$39;
Tel: (406) 752-4008

## LEWISTOWN

**B & B MOTEL**
520 E Main St (59457)
Rates: $31-$39;
Tel: (406) 538-5496

**MOUNTAIN VIEW MOTEL**
1422 West Main St (59457)
Rates: N/A;
Tel: (406) 538-3457

**PARK INN MOTOR HOTEL**
P. O. Box 939 (59457)
Rates: $47-$57;
Tel: (406) 538-8721

## LIBBY

**CABOOSE MOTEL**
P. O. Box 792 (59923)
Rates: $30-$40;
Tel: (406) 293-6201

**MOUNTAIN MAGIC MOTEL**
919 Mineral Ave (59923)
Rates: N/A;
Tel: (406) 293-7795

**SUPER 8 MOTEL**
448 US Hwy 2W (59923)
Rates: $33-$49;
Tel: (406) 293-2771

**VENTURE MOTOR INN**
443 US Hwy 2W (59923)
Rates: $36-$52;
Tel: (406) 293-7711

## LINCOLN

**LEEPER'S MOTEL**
P. O. Box 611 (59639)
Rates: $27-$40;
Tel: (406) 362-4333

## LIVINGSTON

**BUDGET HOST
PARKWAY MOTEL**
1124 W Park (59047)
Rates: $26-$56;
Tel: (406) 222-3840

**CHICO
HOT SPRINGS LODGE**
P. O. Drawer D (Pray 59065)
Rates: $36-$275;
Tel: (406) 333-4933

**DEL MAR MOTEL**
P. O. Box 636 (59047)
Rates: $25-$58;
Tel: (406) 222-3120

**PARADISE INN**
P. O. Box 684 (59047)
Rates: $35-$49;
Tel: (406) 222-6320

**THE TALCOTT HOUSE**
405 W Lewis (59047)
Rates: $40-$65;
Tel: (406) 222-7699

**YELLOWSTONE
MOTOR INN**
1515 West Park (59047)
Rates: N/A;
Tel: (406) 222-6110

## MILES CITY

**BEST WESTERN
WAR BONNET INN**
1015 S haynes (59301)
Rates: $51-$85;
Tel: (406) 232-4560

**BUCKBOARD INN MOTEL**
1006 S Haynes Ave (59301)
Rates: $28-$34;
Tel: (406) 232-3550

**BUDGET HOST
CUSTER'S INN**
1209 S Haynes Ave (59301)
Rates: $29-$35;
Tel: (406) 232-5170

**FRIENDSHIP INN &
HISTORIC OLIVE HOTEL**
501 Main St (59301)
Rates: N/A;
Tel: (406) 232-2450

**SUPER 8 MOTEL**
RR 2, Hwy 59S (59301)
Rates: $25-$39;
Tel: (406) 232-5772

## MISSOULA

**BEL AIRE MOTEL**
300 E Broadway (59802)
Rates: $38-$55;
Tel: (406) 543-3183

**BEST WESTERN
EXECUTIVE MOTOR INN**
201 E Main St (59802)
Rates: $44-$54;
Tel: (406) 543-7221

**CAMPUS INN**
744 E Broadway (59802)
Rates: $30-$46;
Tel: (406) 549-5134

**DAYS INN/WESTGATE**
RR 2, US 93 & I-90 (59802)
Rates: $35-$56;
Tel: (406) 721-9776

**DOWNTOWN MOTEL**
502 E Broadway (59802)
Rates: $28-$34;
Tel: (406) 549-5191

**ECONO LODGE**
1609 W Broadway (59802)
Rates: $29-$52;
Tel: (406) 543-7231

**4 B'S INN NORTH**
4953 N Reserve St (59802)
Rates: $31-$52;
Tel: (406) 251-2665

**4 B'S INN SOUTH**
3803 Brooks St (59801)
Rates: $35-$49;
Tel: (406) 251-2665

**HOLIDAY INN-
MISSOULA PARKSIDE**
200 S Pattee St (59802)
Rates: $57-$73;
Tel: (406) 721-8550

**ORANGE STREET
BUDGET MOTOR INN**
801 N Orange St (59802)
Rates: $39-$44;
Tel: (406) 721-3610

**RED LION INN**
700 W Broadway (59802)
Rates: $51-$71;
Tel: (406) 728-3300

**RED LION VILLAGE
MOTOR INN**
100 Madison (59802)
Rates: $63-$84;
Tel: (406) 728-3100

**REDWOOD LODGE**
8060 Hwy 93 (59802)
Rates: $39-$54;
Tel: (406) 721-2110

**RESERVE STREET INN**
4825 N Reserve St (59802)
Rates: $49-$64;
Tel: (406) 721-0990

**SOUTHGATE INN MOTEL**
3530 Brooks St (59801)
Rates: $43-$56;
Tel. (406) 251-2250

**THUNDERBIRD MOTEL**
1009 E Broadway (59802)
Rates: $33-$50;
Tel: (406) 543-7251

**TRAVELERS INN MOTEL**
4850 N Reserve St (59802)
Rates: $25-$38;
Tel: (406) 728-8330

## POLSON

**PORT POLSON INN**
P. O. Box 1411 (59860)
Rates. $36-$64;
Tel: (406) 883-5385

**SLEEPY TIGER INN**
914 Hwy 93 (59860)
Rates: $29-$52;
Tel: (406) 883-3120

## RED LODGE

**BEST WESTERN
LU PINE INN**
P. O. Box 30 (59068)
Rates: $34-$59;
Tel: (406) 446-1321

**SUPER 8 MOTEL**
1223 S Broadway (59068)
Rates: $35-$59;
Tel: (406) 446-2288

**VALLI HI MOTOR LODGE**
320 S Broadway (59068)
Rates: $28-$60;
Tel: (406) 446-1414

**YODELER MOTEL**
601 S Broadway (59068)
Rates: $27-$48;
Tel: (406) 446-1435

## ST. IGNATIUS

**SUNSET MOTEL**
Main Hwy Access (59865)
Rates: N/A;
Tel: (406) 745-3900

## ST. REGIS

**ST. REGIS SUPER 8**
P. O. Drawer L (59866)
Rates: $31-$42;
Tel: (406) 649-2422

## SEELEY LAKE

**LEISURE LODGE**
Boy Scout Rd (59868)
Rates: N/A;
Tel: (406) 677-2376

**WAPITI RESORT**
Hwy 83, Box 565 (59868)
Rates: N/A;
Tel: (406) 677-2775

**WILDERNESS
GATEWAY INN**
P. O. Box 661 (59868)
Rates: $32-$43;
Tel: (406) 677-2095

## SHELBY

**CROSSROADS INN MOTEL**
1200 Hwy 2 (59474)
Rates: N/A;
Tel: (406) 434-5134

**O'HAIRE MANOR MOTEL**
204 2nd St. (59474)
Rates: $26-$40;
Tel: (406) 434-5555

## SHERIDAN

**ZAK INN**
2905 Hwy 287 (59749)
Rates: N/A;
Tel: (406) 842-5540

## SIDNEY

**RICHLAND MOTOR INN**
1200 S Central (59270)
Rates: $40-$47;
Tel: (406) 482-6400

## SILVER GATE

**PARK VIEW CABINS**
Hwy 212 (59081)
Rates: N/A;
Tel: (406) 838-2371

## SUPERIOR

**BUDGET HOST
BIG SKY MOTEL**
P. O. Box 458 (59872)
Rates: $30-$40;
Tel: (406) 822-4831

## THREE FORKS

**BROKEN SPUR MOTEL**
P. O. Box 1009 (59752)
Rates: $30-$40;
Tel: (406) 285-3237

**SACAJAWEA INN**
P. O. Box 648 (59752)
Rates: $35-$85;
Tel: (406) 285-6515

## TOWNSEND

**MUSTANGE MOTEL**
412 North Front St (59644)
Rates: N/A;
Tel: (406) 266-3491

## VIRGINIA CITY

**NEVADA CITY
HOTEL & CABINS**
P. O. Box 338 (59755)
Rates: $40-$50;
Tel: (406) 843-5377

## WEST YELLOWSTONE

**AMBASSADOR
QUALITY INN**
P. O. Box 459 (59758)
Rates: $32-$70;
Tel: (406) 646-7365

**BEST WESTERN
CROSSWINDS MOTOR INN**
P. O. Box 340 (59758)
Rates: $32-$85;
Tel: (406) 646-9557

**BEST WESTERN
DESERT INN**
P. O. Box 340 (59758)
Rates: $30-$83;
Tel: (406) 646-7376

**BEST WESTERN
EXECUTIVE INN**
P.O. Box 1280 (59758)
Rates: $30-$75;
Tel: (406) 646-7681

**BEST WESTERN
WESTON INN**
103 Gibbon (59758)
Rates: $30-$75;
Tel: (406) 646-7373

**BIG WESTERN PINE MOTEL**
P. O. Box 67 (59758)
Rates: $32-$80;
Tel: (406) 646-7622

**CIRCLE R MOTEL**
P. O. Box 364 (59758)
Rates: $26-$85;
Tel: (406) 646-7641

**EVERGREEN MOTEL**
229 Firehold (59758)
Rates: N/A;
Tel: (406) 646-7655

**MID TOWN MOTEL**
P.O. Box 519 (59758)
Rates: $29-$61;
Tel: (406) 646-7301

**TEPEE MOTOR LODGE**
P. O. Box 519 (59758)
Rates: $29-$61;
Tel: (406) 646-7391

**THREE BEAR MOTOR
LODGE**
P. O. Box 519 (59758)
Rates: $31-$73;
Tel: (406) 646-7353

**THUNDERBIRD WEST**
216 Dunraven (59758)
Rates: N/A;
Tel: (406) 646-7677

## WHITEFISH

**CHALET MOTEL**
6430 US 93 S (59937)
Rates: $50-$55;
Tel: (800) 462-3266

**COMFORT INN
GLACIER PARK**
6390 US 93S (59937)
Rates: $69-$199;
Tel: (406) 862-4020

**MOUNTAIN
HOLIDAY MOTEL**
P. O. Box 302 (59937)
Rates: $40-$55;
Tel: (406) 862-2548

**QUALITY INN PINE LODGE**
920 Spokane Ave (59937)
Rates: $50-$90;
Tel: (406) 862-7600

**SUPER 8 MOTEL**
800 Spokane Ave (59937)
Rates: $41-$54;
Tel: (406) 862-8255

## WHITE HALL

**RICE MOTEL**
Box 8147 North A St (59759)
Rates: N/A;
Tel: (406) 287-3895

## WIBAUX

**WIBAUX MOTEL**
P. O. Box 275 (59353)
Rates: $20-$38;
Tel: (406) 795-2666

## WOLF POINT

**HOMESTEAD INN MOTEL**
101 US 2E (59201)
Rates: $25-$37;
Tel: (800) 232-0986

**SHERMAN MOTOR INN**
P. O. Box 879 (59201)
Rates: $26-$35;
Tel: (406) 653-1100

# NEBRASKA

## AINSWORTH

**LAZY A MOTEL**
1120 East 4th St (69210)
Rates: N/A;
Tel: (402) 387-2600

**REMINGTON ARMS MOTEL**
1000 E 4th (69210)
Rates: $26-$34;
Tel: (402) 387-2220

## ALBION

**DUNES MOTEL**
300 South 1st St (68620)
Rates: N/A;
Tel: (402) 395-2105

## ALLIANCE

**SUNSET MOTEL**
1210 E Hwy 2 (69301)
Rates: $35-$55;
Tel: (308) 762-8660

**WEST WAY MOTEL**
P. O. Box O (69301)
Rates: $31-$67;
Tel: (308) 762-4040

## AURORA

**HAMILTON MOTOR INN**
Rt 3, Box 41A (68818)
Rates: $35-$40;
Tel: (402) 694-6961

**KEN'S MOTEL
BEST WESTERN**
1515 11th St (68818)
Rates: $26-$32;
Tel: (402) 694-3141

## BASSETT

**SANDHILL MOTEL**
East Hwy 20 (68714)
Rates: N/A;
Tel: (402) 684-3791

## BEATRICE

**BEATRICE INN MOTEL**
3500 N 6th St (68310)
Rates: $35-$48;
Tel: (800) 232-8742

## BEAVER CITY

**FURNAS COUNTY INN**
Hwy 89 & 10th St (68926)
Rates: $25-$32;
Tel: (308) 268-7705

## BELLEVUE

**AMERICAN FAMILY INN**
1110 Fort Crook Rd S (68005)
Rates: $32-$43;
Tel: (402) 291-0804

## BRIDGEPORT

**BELL MOTOR INN**
P. O. Box 854 (69336)
Rates: $29-$38;
Tel: (308) 262-0557

## BROKEN BOW

**GATEWAY MOTEL**
P. O. Box 206 (68822)
Rates: $25-$30;
Tel: (308) 872-2478

**WM PENN LODGE**
Rt 2, Box 70 (68822)
Rates: $21-$28;
Tel: (308) 872-2412

## CENTRAL CITY

**CRAWFORD MOTEL**
RR 1, Box 270 (68826)
Rates: $18-$25;
Tel: (308) 946-3051

## CHADRON

**BEST WESTERN
WEST HILLS INN**
Jct US 385 & 10th St (69337)
Rates: $45-$100;
Tel: (308) 432-3305

**ECONOMY 9 MOTEL**
1201 W US 20 (69337)
Rates: $45-$62;
Tel: (308) 432-3119

## COLUMBUS

**NEW WORLD INN**
265 33rd Ave (68601)
Rates: $40-$58;
Tel: (402) 564-1492

## COZAD

**BUDGET HOST
CIRCLE S MOTEL**
P. O. Box 85 (69130)
Rates: $26-$34;
Tel: (308) 784-2290

## CRETE

**VILLA MADRID MOTEL**
Hwy 33W (68333)
Rates: $27-$35;
Tel: (402) 826-4341

## FREMONT

**COMFORT INN**
1649 E 23rd Ave (68025)
Rates: $36-$50;
Tel: (402) 721-1109

**HOLIDAY LODGE**
1220 E 23rd St (68025)
Rates: $38-$45;
Tel: (402) 727-1110

## GORDON

**HILLS MOTEL**
107 West Hwy 20 (69343)
Rates: N/A;
Tel: (308) 282-1795

## GRAND ISLAND

**BUDGET HOST ISLAND INN**
2311 S Locust St (68801)
Rates: $26-$32;
Tel: (308) 382-1815

**CONOCO MOTEL**
2107 W 2nd St (68803)
Rates: $32-$36;
Tel: (308) 384-2700

**ECONO LODGE**
3205 S Locust St (68801)
Rates: $25-$33;
Tel: (308) 384-1333

**HOLIDAY INN-
INTERSTATE 80**
P. O. Box 1501 (68802)
Rates: $39-$49;
Tel: (308) 384-7770

**HOLIDAY INN-MIDTOWN**
2503 S Locust St (68801)
Rates: $54-$61;
Tel: (308) 384-1330

**LAZY V MOTEL**
2703 E Hwy 30 (68801)
Rates: $21-$28;
Tel: (308) 384-0700

**RELAX INN**
507 W 2nd (68801)
Rates: $25-$35;
Tel: (308) 384-1000

**RIVERSIDE INN**
3333 Ramada Rd (68801)
Rates: $39-$44;
Tel: (308) 384-5150

**SUPER 8 MOTEL**
2603 S Locust (68801)
Rates: $31-$38;
Tel: (308) 384-4380

**USA INNS**
Rt 2, Box 190 E
(Doniphan 68832)
Rates: $31-$40;
Tel: (308) 381-0111

## HASTINGS

**HOLIDAY INN**
P. O. Box 896 (68901)
Rates: $59-$66;
Tel: (402) 463-6721

**MIDLANDS LODGE**
910 West J St (68901)
Rates: $26-$32;
Tel: (402) 463-2428

**RAINBOW MOTEL**
1000 West J St (68901)
Rates: $26-$35;
Tel: (402) 463-2989

**WAYFAIR MOTEL**
101 East J St (68901)
Rates: N/A;
Tel: (402) 463-2434

**X-L MOTEL**
1400 West J St (68901)
Rates: $27-$36;
Tel: (402) 463-3148

## HOLDREGE

**TOWER MOTEL**
413 West 4th Ave (68949)
Rates: N/A;
Tel: (308) 995-4488

## KEARNEY

**BEST WESTERN
TEL-STAR MOTOR INN**
P. O. Box 967 (68848)
Rates: $45-$56;
Tel: (308) 237-5185

**DAYS INN**
619 2nd Ave E (68847)
Rates: $31-$46;
Tel: (308) 234-5699

**FORT KEARNY INN**
Box 16881, I-80 Exit 272
(68848)
Rates: N/A;
Tel: (308) 234-2541

**HOLIDAY INN-HOLIDOME**
P. O. Box 1118 (68848)
Rates: $58-$73;
Tel: (308) 237-3141

**KEARNEY INN 4 LESS**
709 2nd Ave E (68847)
Rates: $29-$41;
Tel: (308) 237-2671

**RAMADA INN**
P. O. Box 1925 (68847)
Rates: $32-$95;
Tel: (308) 237-5971

## KIMBALL

**1ST INTERSTATE INN**
Rt 1, Box 136 (69145)
Rates: $26-$41;
Tel: (308) 235-4601

**WESTERN MOTEL**
914 West Hwy 30 (69145)
Rates: N/A;
Tel: (308) 235-4621

## LEXINGTON

**ECONO LODGE**
P. O. Box 775 (68850)
Rates: $28-$37;
Tel: (308) 324-5601

**TODDLE INN MOTEL**
P. O. Box 504 (68850)
Rates: $28-$45;
Tel: (308) 324-5595

## LINCOLN

**BEST WESTERN
VILLAGER MOTOR INN**
5200 O St (68510)
Rates: $43-$57;
Tel: (402) 464-9111

**COMFORT INN
OF LINCOLN**
2940 NW 12th St (68521)
Rates: $35-$46;
Tel: (402) 475-2200

**CONGRESS INN**
2001 West O St (68528)
Rates: $30-$59;
Tel: (402) 477-4488

**HOLIDAY INN AIRPORT**
1101 W Bond St (68521)
Rates: $49-$61;
Tel: (402) 475-4971

**HOLIDAY INN
NORTH EAST**
5250 Cornhusker Hwy
(68504)
Rates: $47-$69;
Tel: (402) 464-3171

**KING'S INN MOTEL**
3510 Cornhusker Hwy
(68504)
Rates: N/A;
Tel: (402) 466-2324

**RESIDENCE INN
BY MARRIOTT**
200 S 68th Pl (68510)
Rates: $94;
Tel: (402) 483-4900

**SENATE INN MOTEL**
2801 West O St (68528)
Rates: $24-$32;
Tel: (402) 475-4921

**SLEEPY HOLLOW MOTEL**
4848 O St (68510)
Rates: $25-$51;
Tel: (402) 464-3166

**STOP 'N' SLEEP**
1140 Calvert St (68502)
Rates: $32-$46;
Tel: (402) 423-7111

**TOWN HOUSE MOTEL**
1744 M St (68508)
Rates: $36-$43;
Tel: (402) 475-3000

## McCOOK

**BEST WESTERN
CHIEF MOTEL**
P. O. Box 650 (69001)
Rates: $46-$56;
Tel: (308) 345-3700

**SUPER 8 MOTEL**
1103 East B St (69001)
Rates: $26-$38;
Tel: (308) 345-1141

## NELIGH

**WEST HILLVIEW MOTEL**
RR 2, Box 43 (68756)
Rates: N/A;
Tel: (402) 887-4186

## NORFOLK

**NORFOLK COUNTRY INN**
P. O. Box 181 (68701)
Rates: $39-$45;
Tel: (402) 371-4430

## NORTH PLATTE

**BEST WESTERN
CHALET LODGE**
920 N Jeffers St (69101)
Rates: $34-$54;
Tel: (308) 532-2313

**FAR WEST MOTEL**
321 S Dewey St (69101)
Rates: $27-$32;
Tel: (308) 532-8130

**FIRST INTERSTATE INN**
P. O. Box 1201 (69101)
Rates: $31-$38;
Tel: (308) 532-6980

**HOLIDAY INN**
P. O. Box 430 (69101)
Rates: $50-$60;
Tel: (308) 532-9090

**RAMBLER INN**
1420 Rodeo Rd (69101)
Rates: $20-$26;
Tel: (308) 532-9290

**STANFORD MOTEL**
1400 E 4th St (69101)
Rates: $30-$38;
Tel: (308) 532-9380

**THE STOCKMAN INN**
P. O. Box 2003 (69103)
Rates: $41-$53;
Tel: (308) 534-3630

**SUPER 8 MOTEL**
Rt 4, Box 8 (69101)
Rates: $34-$41;
Tel: (308) 532-4224

## OGALLALA

**BEST WESTERN
STAGECOACH INN**
201 Statecoach Tr (69153)
Rates: $26-$60;
Tel: (308) 284-3656

**FIRST INTERSTATE INN**
108 Prospector Dr (69153)
Rates: $23-$40;
Tel: (308) 285-2056

**HOLIDAY INN**
201 Chuckwagon Rd (69153)
Rates: $41-$62;
Tel: (308) 284-3623

## OMAHA
(and Vicinity)

**BEN FRANKLIN MOTEL**
10308 Frontage Rd (68138)
Rates: $30-$43;
Tel: (402) 895-2200

**BEST WESTERN CENTRAL**
3650 S 72nd St (68124)
Rates: $48-$70;
Tel: (402) 397-3700

**BUDGETEL INN**
10760 M St (68127)
Rates: $40-$47;
Tel: (402) 592-5200

**CARLISLE HOTEL**
10909 M St (68137)
Rates: $69-$125;
Tel: (800) 526-6242

**COMFORT INN**
10919 J St (68137)
Rates: $36-$46;
Tel: (402) 592-2882

**EMBASSY SUITES HOTEL**
7270 Cedar St (68124)
Rates: $92-$125;
Tel: (402) 397-5141

**HAMPTON INN-
SOUTHWEST**
10728 L St (68127)
Rates: $48-$60;
Tel: (402) 593-2380

**HOMEWOOD SUITES**
7010 Hascall St (68106)
Rates: $85-$99;
Tel: (402) 397-7500

**LA QUINTA MOTOR INN**
3330 N 104th Ave (68134)
Rates: $38-$51;
Tel: (402) 493-1900

**OMAHA MARRIOTT HOTEL**
10220 Regency Cir (68114)
Rates: $124;
Tel: (402) 399-9000

**OMAHA WAYSIDE INN**
7833 Dodge St (68114)
Rates: $28-$40;
Tel: (402) 391-7100

**PARK INN INTERNATIONAL**
9305 S 145th St (68138)
Rates: $35-$47;
Tel: (402) 895-2555

**RAMADA CENTRAL HOTEL**
7007 Grover St (68106)
Rates: $53-$62;
Tel: (402) 397-7030

**RED LION HOTEL**
1616 Dodge St (68102)
Rates: $92-$102;
Tel: (402) 346-7600

**RESIDENCE INN
BY MARRIOTT**
6990 Dodge St (68132)
Rates: $99-$130;
Tel: (402) 553-8898

**SHERATON INN-OMAHA**
4888 S 118th St (68137)
Rates: $75-$86;
Tel: (402) 895-1000

## O'NEILL

**CAPRI MOTEL**
P. O. Box 306 (68763)
Rates: $25-$50;
Tel: (402) 336-2762

**ELMS MOTEL**
P. O. Box 228 (68763)
Rates: $25-$38;
Tel: (402) 336-3800

**GOLDEN HOTEL**
406 E Douglas (68763)
Rates: $19-$32;
Tel: (402) 336-4436

**TOWN HOUSE INN**
725 E Douglas (68763)
Rates: $30-$41;
Tel: (402) 336-1640

## OSHKOSH

**SHADY REST MOTEL**
Rt 1, Box 75 (69154)
Rates: $24-$30;
Tel: (308) 772-4115

## RANDOLPH

**CEDAR MOTEL**
107 East Hwy 20 (68771)
Rates: N/A;
Tel: (402) 337-0500

## RED CLOUD

**MCFARLAND HOTEL**
137 West 4th Ave (68970)
Rates: N/A;
Tel: (402) 746-3591

## RUSHVILLE

**ANTLERS MOTEL**
607 East 2nd St (69360)
Rates: N/A;
Tel: (308) 327-2444

**NEBRASKALAND MOTEL**
508 East 2nd, Box 377
(69360)
Rates: N/A;
Tel: (308) 327-2277

## SCHUYLER

**JOHNNIE'S MOTEL**
222 W 16th (68661)
Rates: $26-$32;
Tel: (402) 352-5454

## SCOTTSBLUFF

**CANDLELIGHT INN MOTEL**
1822 E 20th Pl (69361)
Rates: $46-$48;
Tel: (800) 424-2305

**CAPRI MOTEL**
2424 Ave I (69361)
Rates: $28-$40;
Tel: (308) 635 2057

**LAMPLIGHTER MOTEL**
606 E 27th St (69361)
Rates: $30-$38;
Tel: (308) 632-7108

**SANDS MOTEL**
814 W 27th St (69361)
Rates: $24-$32;
Tel: (308) 632-6191

**SCOTTSBLUFF INN**
1901 21st Ave (69361)
Rates: $38-$60;
Tel: (308) 635-3111

## SIDNEY

**DELUXE MOTEL**
2201 Illinois St (69162)
Rates: N/A;
Tel: (308) 254-4666

**FORT SIDNEY
MOTOR HOTEL**
935 9th Ave (69162)
Rates: $30-$40;
Tel: (308) 254 5863

**SIDNEY MOTOR LODGE**
2031 Illinois St (69162)
Rates: $25-$50;
Tel: (308) 254-4581

## SOUTH SIOUX CITY

**THE MARINA INN**
P. O. Box 218 (68776)
Rates: $54-$74;
Tel: (402) 494-4000

## SUTTON

**SUTTON MOTEL**
208 North French (68979)
Rates: N/A;
Tel: (402) 773-4803

## VALENTINE

**MOTEL RAINE**
P. O. Box 231 (69201)
Rates: $24-$37;
Tel: (402) 376-2030

**TRADE WINDS LODGE**
HC 37, Box 2 (69201)
Rates: $22-$45;
Tel: (402) 376-1600

## WAYNE

**K-D INN MOTEL**
311 East 7th St (68787)
Rates: N/A;
Tel: (402) 375-1770

## YORK

**BEST WESTERN
PALMER INN**
2426 S Lincoln Ave (68467)
Rates: $33-$49;
Tel: (402) 362-5585

# NEVADA

## AUSTIN

**LINCOLN MOTEL**
28 Main St (89310)
Rates: N/A;
Tel: (702) 964-2698

## BAKER

**BORDER INN**
Hwys 50 & 6 (89311)
Rates: N/A;
Tel: (702) 234-7300

## BATTLE MOUNTAIN

**BEST WESTERN
BIG CHIEF MOTEL**
434 W Front St (89820)
Rates: $45-$55;
Tel: (702) 635-2416

**HOLIDAY INN EXPRESS**
521 E Front St (89820)
Rates: $44-$49;
Tel: (702) 635-5880

## BEATTY

**BURRO INN**
P. O. Box 7 (89003)
Rates: $29-$36;
Tel: (702) 553-2225

**EL PORTAL MOTEL**
301 Main St (89003)
Rates: N/A;
Tel: (702) 553-2912

**PHOENIX INN**
Hwy 95 & 1st St (89003)
Rates: N/A;
Tel: (800) 845-7401

## BOULDER CITY

**NEVADA INN**
1009 Nevada Hwy (89005)
Rates: N/A;
Tel: (702) 293-2044

## CARSON CITY

**DESERT HILLS MOTEL**
1010 S Carson St (89701)
Rates: N/A;
Tel: (702) 882-1932

**NUGGET MOTEL**
651 N Stewart St (89701)
Rates: N/A;
Tel: (702) 882-7711

**ROYAL CREST INN**
1930 N Carson (89701)
Rates: N/A;
Tel: (702) 882-1785

## ECHO BAY

**ECHO BAY RESORT**
On Lake Mead
(Overton 89040)
Rates: $69-$84;
Tel: (702) 394-4000

## ELKO

**BEST WESTERN
RED LION MOTOR INN**
2050 Idaho St (89801)
Rates: $55-$73;
Tel: (702) 738-8421

**HOLIDAY INN**
3015 Idaho St (89801)
Rates: $53-$75;
Tel: (702) 738-8425

**RED LION INN & CASINO**
2065 Idaho St (89801)
Rates: $65-$83;
Tel: (702) 738-2111

**RODEWAY INN**
1300 Idaho St (89801)
Rates: $35-$54;
Tel: (702) 738-7000

**SHILO INN**
2401 Mountain City Hwy
(89801)
Rates: $62-$83;
Tel: (702) 738-5522

**THUNDERBIRD MOTEL**
345 Idaho St (89801)
Rates: $39-$57;
Tel: (702) 738-7115

## FALLON

**UPTOWN MOTEL**
180 W Williams Ave (89406)
Rates: N/A;
Tel: (702) 423-5151

**WESTERN MOTEL**
125 S Carson St (89406)
Rates: $32-$38;
Tel: (702) 423-5118

## FERNLEY

**REST RANCHO MOTEL**
350 Main (89408)
Rates: N/A;
Tel: (702) 575-4452

## HAWTHORNE

**SAND N SAGE MOTEL**
P. O. Box 2325 (89415)
Rates: $28-$40;
Tel: (702) 945-3352

## JARBIDGE

**OUTDOOR INN**
Main St (89826)
Rates: N/A;
Tel: (702) 488-2311

## LAKE TAHOE
(SEE CALIFORNIA)

## LAS VEGAS

**BARCELONA MOTEL**
5011 E Craig Rd (89115)
Rates: $35-$50;
Tel: (702) 644-6300

**BEST WESTERN
MAIN STREET INN**
1000 N Main St (89101)
Rates: $39-$60;
Tel: (702) 382-3455

**BEST WESTERN
MARIANA INN**
1322 E Fremont (89101)
Rates: N/A;
Tel: (800) 356-5329

**BEST WESTERN
NELLIS MOTOR INN**
5330 E Craig Rd (89115)
Rates: $38-$54;
Tel: (702) 643-611

**BESTERN WESTERN
PARKVIEW INN**
905 Las Vegas Blvd N
(89101)
Rates: $38-$58;
Tel: (702) 385-1213

**BOARDWALK
HOTEL-CASINO**
3750 Las Vegas Blvd S
(89109)
Rates: $34-$90;
Tel: (702) 735-1167

**CAPRI MOTEL**
3245 E Fremont (89104)
Rates: N/A;
Tel: (702) 457-1429

**DESERT ROSE MOTEL**
3774 Las Vegas Blvd S
(89109)
Rates: N/A;
Tel: (702) 739-6739

**EXCALIBUR
HOTEL & CASINO**
P. O. Box 96778 (89193)
Rates: $39-$70;
Tel: (702) 597-7777

**GLASS POOL INN**
4613 Las Vegas Blvd S
(89119)
Rates: N/A;
Tel: (800) 527-7118

**GOLDEN INN**
120 Las Vegas Blvd N (89101)
Rates: N/A;
Tel: (702) 384-8204

**KING ALBERT MOTEL**
185 Albert Ave (89109)
Rates: N/A;
Tel: (702) 735-1741

**LA QUINTA MOTOR INN**
3782 Las Vegas Blvd S
(89109)
Rates: $49-$67;
Tel: (702) 739-7457

**LUCKY LADY MOTEL**
1308 E Fremont St (89101)
Rates: N/A;
Tel: (702) 385-1098

**MOTEL REGENCY**
700 N Main St (89101)
Rates: N/A;
Tel: (702) 382-2332

**PLAZA SUITE HOTEL BY
HOWARD JOHNSON**
4255 S Paradise Rd (89109)
Rates: $55-$125;
Tel: (702) 369-400

**RESIDENCE INN
BY MARRIOTT**
3225 S Paradise Rd (89109)
Rates: $90-$165;
Tel: (702) 796-9300

**RODEWAY INN**
3786 Las Vegas Blvd S
(89109)
Rates: $45-$65;
Tel: (702) 736-1434

**TRAVEL INN**
217 Las Vegas Blvd N (89101)
Rates: N/A;
Tel: (702) 384-3040

## LAUGHLIN

**EDGEWATER
HOTEL & CASINO**
P. O. Box 30707 (89029)
Rates: $29-$125;
Tel: (800) 677-4837

## LOVELOCK

**SUNSET MOTEL**
1145 Cornell Ave (89419)
Rates: N/A;
Tel: (702) 273-7366

## MCDERMITT

**MCDERMITT MOTEL**
US Hwy 95 S (89421)
Rates: N/A;
Tel: (702) 532-8588

## MESQUITE

**VIRGIN RIVER
HOTEL & CASINO**
P. O. Box 1620 (89014)
Rates: $19-$45;
Tel: (702) 346-7777

## MOUNTAIN CITY

**MOUNTAIN CITY MOTEL**
Hwy 225 (89831)
Rates: N/A;
Tel: (702) 763-6622

## NORTH LAS VEGAS

**BARKER MOTEL**
26001 Las Vegas Blvd N
(89030)
Rates: N/A;
Tel: (702) 642-1138

## OLD NEVADA

**BONNIE SPRINGS MOTEL**
1 Bonnie Springs Rd (89004)
Rates: N/A;
Tel: (702) 875-4191

## OVERTON

**ECHO BAY RESORT**
North Shore Rd (89040)
Rates: $69-$84;
Tel: (702) 394-4000

# RENO

**BONANZA INN**
215 W Fourth St (89501)
Rates: N/A;
Tel: (702) 322-8632

**DAYS INN**
701 E 7th St (89512)
Rates: $30-$75;
Tel: (702) 786-4070

**GATEWAY INN**
1275 Stardust St (89503)
Rates: N/A;
Tel: (702) 747-4220

**HARRAH'S HOTEL**
Box 10 (89520)
Rates: $75-$375;
Tel: (702) 786-3232

**HOLIDAY INN-CONVENTION CENTER**
5851 S Virginia St (89502)
Rates: $30-$60;
Tel: (702) 825-2940

**HOLIDAY INN-DOWNTOWN**
1000 E 6th St (89512)
Rates: $65-$88;
Tel: (702) 786-5151

**LA QUINTA INN**
4001 Market St (89502-3110)
Rates: $46-$66;
Tel: (702) 348-6100

**RIVER HOUSE MOTOR HOTEL**
P. O. Box 2425 (89505)
Rates: $30-$60;
Tel: (702) 329-0036

**RODEWAY INN**
2050 Market St (89502)
Rates: $37-$77;
Tel: (702) 786-2500

**SEASONS INN**
495 West St (89503)
Rates: $34-$75;
Tel: (702) 322-6000

**TRUCKEE RIVER LODGE**
501 W 1st St (89503)
Rates: $55-$80;
Tel: (800) 635-8950

**VAGABOND INN**
3131 S Virginia St (89502)
Rates: $36-$64;
Tel: (800) 522-1555

# SEARCHLIGHT

**EL REY MOTEL**
430 S Hobson Box 1235 (89046)
Rates: N/A;
Tel: (702) 297-1144

# SPARKS

**BLUE FOUNTAIN INN**
1590 B St (89431)
Rates: N/A;
Tel: (702) 359-0359

# STATELINE

**HARRAH'S HOTEL CASINO**
Box 8 (89449)
Rates: $135-$850;
Tel: (800) 648-3773

# TONOPAH

**GOLDEN HILLS MOTEL**
826 E Main St (89049)
Rates: N/A;
Tel: (702) 482-6238

**JIM BUTLER MOTEL**
100 S Main St (89049)
Rates: N/A;
Tel: (800) 635-9455

**SILVER QUEEN MOTEL**
P. O. Box 311 (89049)
Rates: $28-$38;
Tel: (702) 482-6291

# UNIONVILLE

**OLD PIONEER GARDEN**
Main 79 (89418)
Rates: N/A;
Tel: (702) 538-7585

# VIRGINIA CITY

**VIRGINIA CITY MOTEL**
675 South C St (89440)
Rates: N/A;
Tel: (702) 847-0277

# WELLS

**LONE STAR MOTEL**
676 6th St (89835)
Rates: N/A;
Tel: (702) 752-3632

**SHELLCREST MOTEL**
575 6th St (89835)
Rates: N/A;
Tel: (702) 752-3755

**SNOR HAVEN MOTEL**
134 6th St (89835)
Rates: N/A;
Tel: (702) 752-3345

# WENDOVER, UTAH

**WESTERN RIDGE MOTEL**
P. O. Box 400 (84083)
Rates: $26-$68;
Tel: (801) 665-2211

# WINNEMUCCA

**BEST WESTERN HOLIDAY MOTEL**
670 W Winnemucca Blvd (89445)
Rates: $65-$85;
Tel: (702) 623-3684

**BEST WESTERN RED LION INN & CASINO**
741 W Winnemucca Blvd (89445)
Rates: $68-$150;
Tel: (702) 623-2565

**GOLD COUNTRY INN**
921 W Winnemucca Blvd (89445)
Rates: $70-$80;
Tel: (800) 436-5306

**LA VILLA MOTEL**
390 Lay St (89445)
Rates: $38-$65;
Tel: (702) 623-2334

**PYRENEES MOTEL**
714 W Winnemucca Blvd
(89445)
Rates: $35-$48;
Tel: (702) 623-1116

**THUNDERBIRD MOTEL**
511 W Winnemucca Blvd
(89445)
Rates: $60-$75;
Tel: (702) 623-3661

**VAL-U INN**
125 E Winnemucca Blvd
(89445)
Rates: $39-$55;
Tel: (702) 623-5248

## ZEPHYR COVE

**ZEPHYR COVE RESORT**
760 Hwy 50 (89448)
Rates: N/A;
Tel: (702) 588-6644

# NEW HAMPSHIRE

## ALTON

**EYE JOY COTTAGES**
Roberts Cove Rd (03809)
Rates: N/A;
Tel: (603) 569-4973

## ALTON BAY

**HORSE &
BUGGY COTTAGES**
Bay Hill Rd, P. O. Box 283
(03810)
Rates: N/A;
Tel: (603) 875-6771

**LEMAY'S BY THE BAY**
Rt 28A, Box 127 (03810)
Rates: N/A;
Tel: (603) 875-3629

## ANTRIM

**ANTRIM INN**
P. O. Box 155 (03440)
Rates: $60-$90;
Tel: (603) 588-8000

## ASHLAND

**BLACK HORSE
MOTOR COURT**
RFD 1, Box 46, Rt 3 (03217)
Rates: N/A;
Tel: (603) 968-7116

## BARTLETT

**THE VILLAGER MOTEL**
P. O. Box 427 (03812)
Rates: $25-$69;
Tel: (603) 374-2742

## BERLIN

**TRAVELER MOTEL**
25 Pleasant St (03570)
Rates: $32-$68;
Tel: (603) 752-2500

## BRADFORD

**BRADFORD INN**
RFD 1, Box 40, Main St
(03221)
Rates: N/A;
Tel: (603) 938-5309

## CENTER HARBOR

**LAKE SHORE
MOTEL & COTTAGES**
RR 2, Box 16T (03226)
Rates: N/A;
Tel: (603) 253-6244

**THE MEADOWS
LAKESIDE LODGING**
P. O. Box 204 (03226)
Rates: $44-$88;
Tel: (603) 253-4347

## CLAREMONT

**DEL-E-MOTEL**
24 Sullivan St (03743)
Rates: $28-$52;
Tel: (603) 542-9567

## CONCORD

**BRICK TOWER MOTOR INN**
414 S Main St (03301)
Rates: $39-$64;
Tel: (603) 224-9565

**COMFORT INN**
71 Hall St (03301)
Rates: $65-$180;
Tel: (603) 226-4100

**CONCORD COMFORT INN**
71 Hall St (03301)
Rates: $59-$78;
Tel: (603) 226-4100

**ECONO LODGE**
Gulf St exit off I-93 (03301)
Rates: $43-$75;
Tel: (603) 224-4011

**LAKE SHORE
FARM RESORT**
Jenness Pond Rd
(Northwood 03261)
Rates: $285-$305;
Tel: (603) 942-5921

**RAMADA INN**
172 N Main St (03301)
Rates: $69-$109;
Tel: (603) 224-9534

## CONWAY

**SUNNY BROOK PLACE COTTAGES**
Rt 16, P. O. Box 1429 (03818)
Rates: N/A;
Tel: (603) 447-3922

**TANGLEWOOD MOTEL**
Rt 16, Box 108 (03818)
Rates: N/A;
Tel: (603) 447-5932

## EAST SWANZEY

**COACH AND FOUR MOTOR INN**
755 Monadnock Hwy (03446)
Rates: N/A;
Tel: (603) 357-3705

## EXETER

**BEST WESTERN HEARTHSIDE MOTOR INN**
137 Portsmouth Ave (03833)
Rates: $60-$105;
Tel: (603) 772-3794

**EXETER INN**
P. O. Box 508 (03833)
Rates: $65-$125;
Tel: (603) 772-5901

## FRANCESTOWN

**THE INN AT CROTCHED MOUNTAIN**
Mountain Rd (03043)
Rates: $45-$120;
Tel: (603) 588-6840

## FRANCONIA

**THE HILLTOP INN**
Main St (Sugar Hill 03585)
Rates: $50-$110;
Tel: (603) 823-5695

**THE HORSE AND HOUND INN**
205 Wells Rd (03580)
Rates: $45-$85;
Tel: (603) 823-5501

## GLEN

**THE RED APPLE INN**
P.O. Box 103 (03838)
Rates: $39-$89;
Tel: (603) 383-9680

## GORHAM

**ARIES MOTOR INN**
265 Main St (03581)
Rates: $36-$72;
Tel: (603) 466-5496

**GORHAM MOTOR INN**
324 Main St (03581)
Rates: $42-$64;
Tel: (603) 466-3381

**NORTHERN PEAKS MOTEL**
289 Main St (03581)
Rates: $32-$62;
Tel: (603) 466-3374

**ROYALTY INN**
130 Main St (03581)
Rates: $46-$74;
Tel: (603) 466-3312

**TOWN & COUNTRY MOTOR INN**
P. O. Box 220 (03581)
Rates: $48-$84;
Tel: (603) 466-3315

## HAMPTON

**HAMPTON MOTOR INN**
815 Lafayette Rd (03842)
Rates: $75-$104;
Tel: (603) 926-6771

**HAMPTON VILLAGE RESORT**
660 Lafayette Rd (03842)
Rates: $59-$79;
Tel: (603) 926-6775

**THE VILLAGER MOTOR INN**
308 Lafayette Rd (03842)
Rates: $29-$69;
Tel: (603) 926-3964

## HANOVER

**HANOVER INN-DARTMOUTH COLLEGE ON THE GREEN**
Center on Dartmouth College Campus (03755)
Rates: $174;
Tel: (603) 643-4300

**LOCH LYME LODGE**
NH 10, RFD 278 (Lyme 03768)
Rates: $26-$625;
Tel: (800) 423-2141

## HENNIKER

**HENNIKER MOTEL**
P. O. Box 622 (03242)
Rates: $44-$72;
Tel: (603) 428-3536

## INTERVALE

**RIVERSIDE INN**
Rt 16A (03845)
Rates: $45-$95;
Tel: (603) 356-9060

**SWISS CHALETS MOTEL**
Rt 16A (03845)
Rates: N/A;
Tel: (800) 831-2727

## JACKSON

**DANA PLACE INN**
P. O. Box L (03846)
Rates: $75-$105;
Tel: (603) 383-6822

## JAFFREY

**WOODBOUND INN**
Woodbound Rd (03452)
Rates: $65-$190;
Tel: (603) 532-8341

## JEFFERSON

**EVERGREEN MOTEL**
P. O. Box 33 (03583)
Rates: $30-$55;
Tel: (603) 586-4449

## KEENE

**DAYS INN**
175 Key Rd (03431)
Rates: $56-$75;
Tel: (603) 352-7616

**THE MOTOR INN MOTEL**
921 Main St, Rt 12 S (03431)
Rates: N/A;
Tel: (603) 352-4138

**RAMADA INN**
401 Winchester St (03431)
Rates: $49-$85;
Tel: (603) 357-3038

**WINDING BROOK LODGE**
Box 372 (03431)
Rates: $34-$50;
Tel: (603) 352-3111

## LACONIA

**TIN WHISTLE INN**
1047 Union Ave (03246)
Rates: N/A;
Tel: (603) 528-4185

## LANCASTER

**LANCASTER MOTOR INN**
P. O. Box 543 (03584)
Rates: $33-$49;
Tel: (603) 788-4921

**PINETREE MOTEL**
RFD 2, Box 281 (03584)
Rates: $28-$40;
Tel: (603) 636-2479

## LEBANON

**AIRPORT ECONOMY INN**
7 Airport Rd (03784)
Rates: $40-$65;
Tel: (603) 298-8888

**SHERATON NORTH COUNTRY INN**
Airport Rd
(West Lebanon 03784)
Rates: $79-$140;
Tel: (603) 298-5906

## LITTLETON

**EASTGATE MOTOR INN**
RFD 1 (03561)
Rates: $39-$45;
Tel: (603) 444-3971

**MAPLE LEAF MOTEL**
297 W Main St (03561)
Rates: $37-$45;
Tel: (603) 444-5105

## MANCHESTER

**CENTER OF NEW HAMPSHIRE-HOLIDAY INN**
700 Elm St (03101)
Rates: $78-$102;
Tel: (603) 625-1000

**DAYS HOTEL MANCHESTER**
55 John E Devine Dr (03103)
Rates: $63-$80;
Tel: (603) 668-6110

**HOLIDAY INN-WEST**
21 Front St (03102)
Rates: $57-$81;
Tel: (603) 669-2660

**HOWARD JOHNSON HOTEL & CONF CTR**
298 Queen City Ave (03102)
Rates: $60-$110;
Tel: (603) 668-2600

## MERRIMACK

**RESIDENCE INN BY MARRIOTT**
246 Daniel Webster Hwy
(03054)
Rates: $55-$65;
Tel: (603) 424-8100

## MOULTONBORO

**ROB ROY MOTOR LODGE**
P. O. Box 420 (03254)
Rates: $49-$75;
Tel: (603) 476-5571

## NASHUA

**HOLIDAY INN**
9 Northeastern Blvd (03062)
Rates: $45-$120;
Tel: (603) 888-1551

**NASHUA MARRIOTT HOTEL**
2200 Southwood Dr (03063)
Rates: $69-$119;
Tel: (603) 880-9100

**RED ROOF INN**
77 Spitbrook Rd (03063)
Rates: $25-$55;
Tel: (603) 888-1893

**SHERATON-TARA HOTEL**
Tara Blvd (03062)
Rates: $80-$125;
Tel: (603) 888-9970

## NEWPORT

**NEWPORT MOTEL**
2 Mi E on NH 11-103 (03773)
Rates: $50-$65;
Tel: (603) 863-1440

## NORTH CONWAY

**MAPLE LEAF MOTEL**
Box 917, Rt 16 (03860)
Rates: N/A;
Tel: (603) 356-5388

**SACO RIVER MOTOR LODGE**
5 Mi E on US 302
(Center Conway 03813)
Rates: $42-$104;
Tel: (603) 447-3720

## NORTHWOOD STOCK

**PITRE'S CABINS**
Rt 112 West (03262)
Rates: N/A;
Tel: (603) 745-8646

## PITTSBURG

**THE GLEN**
Box 777, First Connecticut Lake
(03592)
Rates: $60-$148;
Tel: (603) 538-6500

## PLYMOUTH

**DAYS INN-
WHITE MOUNTAINS**
RR 1, Box 355 (03264)
Rates: $56-$78;
Tel: (603) 536-3520

**KNOLL MOTEL**
RFD 1 (03264)
Rates: $45-$47;
Tel: (603) 536-1245

**SUSSE CHALET**
RFD 1, Box 4 (03264)
Rates: $40-$60;
Tel: (603) 536-2330

## PORTSMOUTH

**ANCHORAGE INN**
417 Woodbury Ave (03801)
Rates: $49-$79;
Tel: (603) 431-8111

**COMFORT INN
AT YOKEN'S**
1390 Lafayette Rd (03801)
Rates: $45-100;
Tel: (603) 433-3338

**THE PORT MOTOR INN**
Portsmouth Circle (03801)
Rates: $32-$98;
Tel: (603) 436-4378

**WREN'S NEST MOTEL**
3548 Lafayette Rd (03801)
Rates: $36-$75;
Tel: (603) 436-2481

## ROCHESTER

**ANCHORAGE MOTOR INN**
P. O. Box 7325 (03839)
Rates: $39-$60;
Tel: (603) 332-3350

## SALEM

**RED ROOF INN**
15 Red Roof Ln (03079)
Rates: $30-$54;
Tel: (603) 898-6422

**SALEM HOTEL**
1 Keewaydin Dr (03079)
Rates: $35-$56;
Tel: (603) 893-5511

## SUGAR HILL

**THE HOMESTEAD INN**
NH 117 & Sunset Hill Rd
(03585)
Rates: N/A;
Tel: (603) 823-5564

## SUNAPEE

**BURKEHAVEN
RESORT MOTEL**
173 Burkehaven Hill Rd
(03782)
Rates: $50-$75;
Tel: (603) 763-2788

**DEXTER'S INN**
P. O. Box 703A (03782)
Rates: $90-$188;
Tel: (603) 763-5571

**THE OLD GOVERNORS
HOUSE**
Lower Main St (03782)
Rates: N/A;
Tel: (603) 763-9918

## TAMWORTH

**THE TAMWORTH INN**
Main St (03886)
Rates: $80-$130;
Tel: (603) 323-7721

## TROY

**THE INN
AT EAST HILL FARM**
Mountain Rd (03465)
Rates: N/A;
Tel: (603) 242-6495

## TUFTONBORO

**19 MILE BAY LODGES**
HC 69, Box 110 (03853)
Rates: N/A;
Tel: (603) 569-3507

## TWIN MOUNTAIN

**CHARLMONT MOTOR INN**
Rt 3, Box G (03595)
Rates: $35-$60;
Tel: (603) 846-5549

## WEST LEBANON

**AIRPORT ECONOMY INN**
7 Airport Rd (03784)
Rates: N/A;
Tel: (800) 433-3466

## WILTON CENTER

**STEPPING STONES**
Bennington Trail (03086)
Rates: N/A;
Tel: (603) 654-9048

## WOODSTOCK

**WHEELOCK
MOTOR COURT**
Rt 3 (03293)
Rates: N/A;
Tel: (603) 745-8771

## WOODSVILLE

**ALL SEASONS MOTEL**
36 Smith St (03785)
Rates: $34-$54;
Tel: (603) 747-2157

# NEW JERSEY

## BEACH HAVEN

**ENGLESIDE INN**
30 Engleside Ave (08008)
Rates: $64-$242;
Tel: (609) 492-1251

## BERNARDSVILLE

**OLD MILL INN**
US 202, Jct I-287
(Basking Ridge 07924)
Rates: $65-$95;
Tel: (609) 221-1100

## BORDENTOWN

**BEST WESTERN INN**
US 206S & Dunnsmill Rd
(08505)
Rates: $55-$70;
Tel: (609) 298-8000

**DAYS INN**
1073 US 206 (08505)
Rates: $49-$93;
Tel: (609) 298-6100

## CAPE MAY

**INN OF CAPE MAY**
Ocean & Beach Dr (08204)
Rates: N/A;
Tel: (609) 884-3500

**MARQUIS DE LAFAYETTE**
501 Beach Dr (08204)
Rates: N/A;
Tel: (609) 884-3500

## CARTERET

**HOLIDAY INN**
1000 Roosevelt Ave (07008)
Rates: $80-$110;
Tel: (908) 541-9500

## CHERRY HILL

**HAMPTON INN**
121 Laurel Oak Rd
(Voorhees 08043)
Rates: $56-$69;
Tel: (609) 346-4500

**HOLIDAY INN-CHERRY HILL**
Rt 70 & Sayer Ave (08002)
Rates: $68-$78; Tel: (609) 663-5300

## CLIFTON

**HOWARD JOHNSON MOTOR LODGE**
680 SR 3W at Passaic Ave
(07014)
Rates: $59-$69;
Tel: (201) 471-3800

**RAMADA HOTEL**
285 Rt 3E (07014)
Rates: $59-$139;
Tel: (201) 778-6500

## CLINTON

**HOLIDAY INN**
111 Rt 173 (08809)
Rates: $79-$107;
Tel: (908) 735-5111

## CRANFORD

**DAYS INN**
10 Jackson Dr (07016)
Rates: $49-$85;
Tel: (908) 272-4700

## DAYTON

**DAYS INN OF SOUTH BRUNSWICK**
2316 US 130 (08810)
Rates: $50-$55;
Tel: (908) 329-3000

## DEEPWATER

**HOWARD JOHNSON LODGE & SUITES**
US 40 & NJ Tpk Exit 1
(Penns Grove 08069)
Rates: $46-$51;
Tel: (609) 299-3800

## EAST BRUNSWICK

**SHERATON INN**
195 SR 18 (08816)
Rates: $59-$112;
Tel: (908) 828-6900

## EAST HANOVER

**RAMADA HOTEL**
130 Rt 10 (07936)
Rates: $49-$115;
Tel: (201) 386-5622

## EAST ORANGE

**THE ROYAL INN**
120 Evergreen Place (07018)
Rates: $55-$70;
Tel: (201) 677-3100

## EAST RUTHERFORD

**DAYS INN-MEADOWLANDS**
850 SR 120 (07073)
Rates: $52-$96;
Tel: (201) 507-5222

**SHERATON MEADOWLANDS**
2 Meadowlands Plaza
(07073)
Rates: $79-$129;
Tel: (201) 896-0500

## EATONTOWN

**CRYSTAL MOTOR LODGE**
170-174 Hwy 35 (07724)
Rates: $34-66;
Tel: (908) 542-4900

## EDISON

**RAMADA INN**
3050 Woodbridge Ave
(08837)
Rates: $78;
Tel: (908) 494-2000

**RED ROOF INN**
860 New Durham Rd (08817)
Rates: $35-$49;
Tel: (908) 248-9300

**WELLESLEY INN**
831 US 1S (08817)
Rates: $45-$70;
Tel: (908) 287-0171

## ENGLEWOOD

**RADISSON
HOTEL ENGLEWOOD**
401 S Van Brunt St (07631)
Rates: $79-$155;
Tel: (201) 871-2020

## FAIRFIELD

**RAMADA INN**
38 Two Bridges Rd (07004)
Rates: $49-$109;
Tel: (201) 575-1742

## FOLSOM

**PINECREST MOTEL**
Rt 322, RD 6 (08037)
Rates: N/A;
Tel: (609) 561-3098

## FORT LEE

**HOLIDAY INN**
2117 Rt 4E (07024)
Rates: $90-$110;
Tel: (201) 461-3100

## HASBROUCK HEIGHTS

**SHERATON HASBROUCK
HEIGHTS HOTEL**
650 Terrace Ave (07604)
Rates: $70-$139;
Tel: (201) 288-6100

## HIGHTSTOWN

**TOWN HOUSE MOTEL**
SR 33 W (08520)
Rates: $55-$115;
Tel: (609) 448-2400

## KENILWORTH

**HOLIDAY INN**
S 31st St & Garden State
Pkwy (07033)
Rates: $64-$78;
Tel: (908) 241-4100

## LYNDHURST

**NOVOTEL MEADOWLANDS**
1 Polito Ave (07071)
Rates: $60;
Tel: (201) 896-6666

**QUALITY INN-
SPORTS COMPLEX**
10 Polito Ave (07071)
Rates: $62-$65;
Tel: (201) 933-9800

## MAHWAH

**RAMADA INN MAHWAH**
180 NJ 17S (07430)
Rates: $69-$150;
Tel: (201) 529-5880

## MATAWAN

**WELLESLEY INN**
3215 NJ 35 (Hazlet 07730)
Rates: $43 $69;
Tel: (908) 888-2800

## MIDDLETOWN

**HOWARD JOHNSON
LODGE**
750 Hwy 35S (07748)
Rates: $60-$90;
Tel: (908) 671-3400

## MILLVILLE

**COUNTRY INN
BY CARLSON**
1125 Village Dr (08332)
Rates: $61-$95;
Tel: (800) 456-4000

**MILLVILLE MOTOR INN**
Rt 47, Delseas Dr (08332)
Rates: N/A;
Tel: (609) 327-3300

## MORRISTOWN

**THE MADISON HOTEL**
1 Convent Rd & Rt 24 (07960)
Rates: $79-$89;
Tel: (201) 285-1800

## MOUNT HOLLY

**BEST WESTERN
MOTOR INN**
RD 1 (08060)
Rates: $49-$65;
Tel: (609) 261-3800

**HOWARD JOHNSON
MOTOR LODGE**
P. O. Box 73 (08060)
Rates: $56-$90;
Tel: (609) 267-6550

## MOUNT LAUREL

**RED ROOF INN**
603 Fellowship Rd (08054)
Rates: $34-$39;
Tel: (609) 234-5589

**TRAVELODGE HOTEL &
CONFERENCE CENTER**
1111 SR 73 (08054)
Rates: $57;
Tel: (609) 234-7000

# NEWARK
(and Vicinity)

**HILTON GATEWAY**
Gateway Center-Raymond
Blvd (07102)
Rates: $69-$180,
Tel: (201) 622-5000

**HOLIDAY INN-JETPORT**
1000 Spring St
(Elizabeth 07201)
Rates: $69-$140;
Tel: (908) 355-1700

**HOLIDAY INN-NORTH**
160 Holiday Plaza (07114)
Rates: $58-$104;
Tel: (201) 589-1000

**NEWARK AIRPORT VISTA**
1170 Spring St
(Elizabeth 07201)
Rates: $75-$119;
Tel: (908) 351-3900

**RAMADA HOTEL**
US 1 & 9, off NJ Tpk (07114)
Rates: $70-$100;
Tel: (201) 824-4000

## NEW BRUNSWICK

**BRUNSWICK HOTEL**
10 Livingston Ave (08901)
Rates: $49-$85;
Tel: (908) 214-1717

**ECONO LODGE**
26 US 1 N (08901)
Rates: $45-$87;
Tel: (908) 828-8000

## PARAMUS

**HOWARD JOHNSON
LODGE**
393 SR 17 (07652)
Rates: $50-$73;
Tel: (201) 265-4200

**RADISSON INN PARAMUS**
601 From Rd (07652)
Rates: $105-$140;
Tel: (201) 262-6900

# PARK RIDGE

**MARRIOTT HOTEL**
300 Brae Blvd (07656)
Rates: $79-$147;
Tel: (201) 307-0800

## PARSIPPANY

**CONCORD PLACE**
3535 Rt 46 (07054)
Rates: $56-$108;
Tel: (201) 263-0095

**DAYS INN**
3159 Rt 46 (07054)
Rates: $56-$61;
Tel: (201) 335-0200

**HOJO INN
BY HOWARD JOHNSON**
625 Rt 46E (07054)
Rates: $39-$55;
Tel: (201) 882-8600

**HOLIDAY INN**
707 Rt 46E (07054)
Rates: $49-$106;
Tel: (201) 263-2000

**PARSIPPANY HILTON**
1 Hilton Court
(Parsippany-Troy Hills 07054)
Rates: $75-$139;
Tel: (201) 267-7373

**RED ROOF INN**
855 US 46E (07054)
Rates: $34-$56;
Tel: (201) 334-3737

## PHILLIPSBURG

**HOWARD JOHNSON
LODGE**
US 22 (08865)
Rates: $55-$65;
Tel. (908) 454-6461

## PISCATAWAY

**EMBASSY SUITES HOTEL**
121 Centennial Ave (08854)
Rates: $99-$175;
Tel: (908) 980-0500

# PRINCETON

**RAMADA HOTEL**
4355 US 1 at Ridge Rd
(08540)
Rates: $63 $140;
Tel: (609) 452-2400

**RED ROOF INN**
3203 Brunswick Pike
(Lawrenceville 08648)
Rates: $39-$54;
Tel: (609) 896-3388

**RED ROOF INN/
NORTH PRINCETON**
208 New Rd
(Monmouth Jct 08852)
Rates: $33-$57;
Tel: (908) 821-8800

**RESIDENCE INNS
BY MARRIOTT**
4225 Rt 1 (08540)
Rates: $109-$124;
Tel: (908) 329-9600

## RAMSEY

**HOWARD JOHNSON
MOTOR LODGE**
1255 Rt 17S (07446)
Rates: $45-$90;
Tel: (201) 327-4500

**WELLESLEY INN**
946 Rt 17N (07446)
Rates: $50-$75;
Tel: (201) 934-9250

## ROCHELLE PARK

**RAMADA HOTEL**
375 W Passaic St (07662)
Rates: $49-$137;
Tel: (201) 845-3400

## RUHNNEMEDE

**COMFORT INN**
101 9th Ave (08078)
Rates: $45-$95;
Tel: (609) 939-6700

**HOLIDAY INN-RUNNEMEDE**
109 9th Ave (08078)
Rates: $54-$59;
Tel: (609) 939-4200

## SADDLE BROOK

**HOLIDAY INN
& CONFERENCE CENTER**
50 Kenney Pl (07662)
Rates: $59-$99;
Tel: (201) 843-0600

**HOWARD JOHNSON
PLAZA HOTEL**
129 Pehle Ave (07662)
Rates: $59-$89;
Tel: (201) 845-7800

**MARRIOTT HOTEL**
Midland Ave & Garden State
Pkwy (07662)
Rates: $79-$164;
Tel: (201) 843-9500

## SECAUCUS

**HILTON MEADOWLANDS**
2 Harmon Plaza (07094)
Rates: $79-$145;
Tel: (201) 348-6900

**RED ROOF INN**
15 Meadowlands Pkwy
(07094)
Rates: $48-$63;
Tel: (201) 319-1000

## SOMERSET

**HOLIDAY INN**
195 Davidson Ave (08873)
Rates: $59-$85;
Tel: (908) 356-1700

**RAMADA INN**
Weston Canal Rd & Rt 287
(08873)
Rates: $49-$109;
Tel: (908) 560-9880

## SOMERS POINT

**RESIDENCE INN/MARRIOTT-
GREATE BAY RESORT**
900 Mays Landing Rd (08244)
Rates: $89-$180;
Tel: (609) 927-6400

## SOUTH PLAINFIELD

**HOLIDAY INN**
4701 Stelton Rd (07080)
Rates: $56-$106;
Tel: (908) 753-5500

**HOWARD JOHNSON
LODGE**
Stelton Rd & I-287 (07080)
Rates: $39-$95;
Tel: (908) 561-4488

## SPRINGFIELD

**HOLIDAY INN**
304 Rt 22W (07081)
Rates: $57-$63;
Tel: (201) 376-9400

## TINTON FALLS

**DAYS INN**
11 Center Plaza (07724)
Rates: $55-$64;
Tel: (908) 389-4646

**RESIDENCE INN
BY MARRIOTT**
90 Park Rd (07724)
Rates: $109-$139;
Tel: (908) 389-8100

## TOMS RIVER

**HOLIDAY INN**
290 Hwy 37E (08753)
Rates: $69-$118;
Tel: (908) 244-4000

**HOWARD JOHNSON
MOTOR LODGE**
955 Hooper Ave (08753)
Rates: $60-$98;
Tel: (908) 244-1000

**RAMADA HOTEL**
2373 Rt 9 (08755)
Rates: $59-$89;
Tel: (908) 905-2626

## TRENTON

**HOWARD JOHNSON
MOTOR LODGE**
2991 Brunswick Pike
(Lawrenceville 08648)
Rates: $65-$95;
Tel: (609) 896-1100

## WAYNE

**HOWARD JOHNSON
MOTOR LODGE**
1850 Rt 23 & Ratzer Rd
(07470)
Rates: $52-$67;
Tel: (201) 696-8050

## WILDWOOD CREST

**BISCAYNE MOTEL**
7807 Atlantic Ave (08260)
Rates: N/A;
Tel: (609) 522-4444

## WOODCLIFF LAKE

**WOODCLIFF LAKE HILTON**
200 Tice Blvd (07675)
Rates: $79-$105;
Tel: (201) 391-3600

# NEW MEXICO

## ALAMOGORDO

**ALL AMERICAN INN**
508 S White Sands Blvd
(88310)
Rates: $26-$32;
Tel: (505) 437-1850

**HOLIDAY INN**
1401 S White Sands Blvd
(88310)
Rates: $47-$60;
Tel: (505) 437-7100

**SATELLITE INN**
2224 N White Sands Blvd
(88310)
Rates: $30-$40;
Tel: (505) 437-8454

## ALBUQUERQUE

**THE ALBUQUERQUE
MARRIOTT HOTEL**
2101 Louisiana Blvd (87110)
Rates: $69-$119;
Tel: (505) 881-6800

**AMBERLEY SUITE HOTEL**
7620 Pan American Frwy NE
(87109)
Rates: $56-$105;
Tel: (505) 823-1300

**THE AMERICAN INN**
4501 Central Northeast
(87108)
Rates: N/A;
Tel: (505) 262-1681

**BEST WESTERN AMERICAN
MOTOR INN & RV PARK**
12999 Central Ave NE
(87123)
Rates: $41-$69;
Tel: (505) 298-7426

**BEST WESTERN
INN AT RIO RANCHO**
1465 Rio Rancho Dr (87124)
Rates: $42-$53;
Tel: (505) 892-1700

**BEST WESTERN
WINROCK INN**
Station D, Box 3220 (87110)
Rates: $52-$64;
Tel: (505) 883-5252

**BUDGETEL INN**
7439 Pan American Frwy NE
(87109)
Rates: $55-$89;
Tel: (505) 345-0010

**CASITA CHAMISA
BED & BREAKFAST**
850 Chamisal Rd NW (87107)
Rates: N/A;
Tel: (505) 897-4644

**COMFORT INN**
13031 Central Ave NE
(87123)
Rates: $37-$60;
Tel: (505) 294-1800

**COMFORT INN-AIRPORT**
2300 Yale Blvd SE (87106)
Rates: $50-$72;
Tel: (505) 243-2244

**COMFORT INN MID-TOWN**
2015 Menaul Blvd NE (87107)
Rates: $49-$59;
Tel: (505) 881-3210

**DAYS INN**
13317 Central Ave NE
(87123)
Rates: $32-$58;
Tel: (505) 294-3297

**DAYS INN EUBANK**
1032 Hotel Cir NE (87123)
Rates: $34-$58;
Tel: (505) 275-0599

**DE ANZA MOTOR LODGE**
4302 Central Ave NE (87108)
Rates: $22-$29;
Tel: (505) 255-1654

**HAMPTON INN**
7433 Pan American Frwy NE
(87109)
Rates: $41-$55;
Tel: (505) 344-1555

**HOLIDAY INN-MIDTOWN**
2020 Menaul Blvd NE (07107)
Rates: $74-$110;
Tel: (505) 884-2511

**HOLIDAY INN PYRAMID
HOTEL/JOURNAL CTR**
5151 San Francisco Rd NE
(87109)
Rates: $90-$140;
Tel: (505) 821-3333

**HOWARD JOHNSON
PLAZA MOTOR HOTEL**
6000 Pan American Frwy NE
(87109)
Rates: $61-$130;
Tel: (505) 821-9451

**LA QUINTA
MOTOR INN-AIRPORT**
2116 Yale Blvd SE (87106)
Rates: $46-$61;
Tel: (505) 243-5500

**LA QUINTA
MOTOR INN NORTH**
5241 San Antonio Dr NE
(87109)
Rates: $47-$60;
Tel: (505) 821-9000

**LA QUINTA
MOTOR INN SAN MATEO**
2424 San Mateo Blvd NE
(87110)
Rates: $47-$62;
Tel: (505) 884-3591

**PLAZA INN
ALBUQUERQUE**
900 Medical Arts NE (87120)
Rates: $55-$60;
Tel: (505) 243-5693

**QUALITY HOTEL
FOUR SEASONS**
2500 Carlisle Blvd NE (87110)
Rates: $74-$105;
Tel: (505) 888-3311

**RADISSON INN
ALBUQUERQUE**
1901 University Blvd SE
(87106)
Rates: $59-$85;
Tel: (505) 247-0512

**RAMADA HOTEL CLASSIC**
6815 Menaul Blvd NE (87110)
Rates: $85-$109;
Tel: (505) 881-0000

**RESIDENCE INN
BY MARRIOTT**
3300 Prospect NE (87107)
Rates: $109-$135;
Tel: (505) 881-2661

**RITEWAY INN**
5201 Central Ave NE (87108)
Rates: $34-$38;
Tel: (505) 265-8413

**ROYAL HOTEL
OF ALBUQUERQUE**
4119 Central Ave NE (87108)
Rates: N/A;
Tel: (505) 265-3585

**SUPER 8 MOTEL
OF ALBUQUERQUE**
2500 University Blvd NE
(87107)
Rates: $35-$43;
Tel: (505) 888-4884

**TRAVELODGE**
13139 Central Ave NE
(87123)
Rates: $36-$54;
Tel: (505) 292-4878

**THE W. E. MAUGER
ESTATE HOTEL**
701 Roma Ave NE (87102)
Rates: N/A;
Tel: (505) 242-8755

## CARLSBAD

**BEST WESTERN
MOTEL STEVENS**
1829 S Canal St (88220)
Rates: $45-$65;
Tel: (505) 887-2851

**CONTINENTAL INN**
3820 National Parks Hwy
(88220)
Rates: $32-$42;
Tel: (505) 887-0341

**LORLODGE**
2019 S Canal St (88220)
Rates: $24-$42;
Tel: (505) 887-1171

**PARK INN INTERNATIONAL**
3706 National Parks Hwy
(88220)
Rates: $46-$51;
Tel: (505) 887-2861

**PARKVIEW MOTEL**
401 E Greene St (88220)
Rates: $28-$39;
Tel: (505) 885-3117

**TRAVELODGE
CARLSBAD SOUTH**
3817 National Parks Hwy
(88220)
Rates: $35-$44;
Tel: (505) 887-8888

## CHAMA

**ELK HORN LODGE MOTEL**
Rte 1, Box 45 (87520)
Rates: $31-$75;
Tel: (800) 532-8874

## CIMARRON

**KIT CARSON INN**
P. O. Box 623 (87714)
Rates: $34-$48;
Tel: (505) 376-2288

## CLAYTON

**SUNSET MOTEL**
702 S 1st St (88415)
Rates: $25-$39;
Tel: (505) 374-2589

## CLOUDCROFT

**SUMMIT INN MOTEL**
P. O. Box 627 (88317)
Rates: $38-$93;
Tel: (505) 682-2814

## CLOVIS

**CLOVIS INN**
2912 Mabry Dr (88101)
Rates: $30-$38;
Tel: (505) 762-5600

**COMFORT INN**
1616 E Mabry Dr (88101)
Rates: $31-$41;
Tel: (505) 762-4591

**DAYS INN**
1720 Mabry Dr (88101)
Rates: $24-$48;
Tel: (505) 762-2971

**HOLIDAY INN**
P. O. Box 973 (88101)
Rates: $48-$60;
Tel: (505) 762-4491

## DEMING

**BEST WESTERN
CHILTON INN**
1709 E Spruce St (88030)
Rates: $41-$47;
Tel: (505) 546-8813

**DEMING MOTEL**
500 W Pine St (88030)
Rates: $22-$32;
Tel: (505) 546-2737

**GRAND MOTOR INN**
1721 E Spruce St (88030)
Rates: $38-$46;
Tel: (505) 546-2632

**HOLIDAY INN**
P. O. Box 1138 (88031)
Rates: $44-$50;
Tel: (505) 546-2661

**WAGON WHEEL MOTEL**
1109 W Pine St (88030)
Rates: $22-$29;
Tel: (505) 546-2681

## DULCE

**BEST WESTERN
JICARILLA INN**
US 64 & Hawks Dr (87528)
Rates: $45-$55;
Tel: (505) 759-3663

## ESPA•OLA

**PARK INN**
920 N Riverside Dr (87532)
Rates: $53-$63;
Tel: (505) 753-7291

## FARMINGTON

**THE BASIN LODGE**
701 Airport Dr (87401)
Rates: $25-$33;
Tel: (505) 325-5061

**BEST WESTERN THE INN**
700 Scott Ave (87401)
Rates: $57-$77;
Tel: (505) 327-5221

**COMFORT INN**
555 Scott Ave (87401)
Rates: $49-$64;
Tel: (505) 325-2626

**HOLIDAY INN
OF FARMINGTON**
600 E Broadway (87401)
Rates: $54-$64;
Tel: (505) 327-9811

**LA QUINTA MOTOR INN**
675 Scott Ave (87401)
Rates: $47-$55;
Tel: (505) 327-4706

## GALLUP

**BEST WESTERN-THE INN**
3009 W US 66 (87301)
Rates: $55-$130;
Tel: (505) 722-2221

**BLUE SPRUCE LODGE**
1119 US 66E (87301)
Rates: $18-$29;
Tel: (505) 863-5211

**COLONIAL MOTEL**
1007 W Coal Ave (87301)
Rates: $18-$30;
Tel: (505) 863-6821

**DAYS INN CENTRAL**
1603 W Hwy 66 (87301)
Rates: $30-$55;
Tel: (505) 863-3891

**DAYS INN WEST**
3201 W Hwy 66 (87301)
Rates: $30-$55;
Tel: (505) 863-6889

**ECONO LODGE
GALLUP INN**
3101 US 66W (87301)
Rates: $32-$51;
Tel: (505) 722-3800

**EL RANCHO
HOTEL & MOTEL**
1000 US 66E (87301)
Rates: $34-$49;
Tel: (505) 863-9311

**HOLIDAY INN HOLIDOME**
2915 US 66W (87301)
Rates: $52-$67;
Tel: (505) 722-2201

**RODEWAY INN**
2003 Hwy 66W (87301)
Rates: $34-$44;
Tel: (505) 863-9385

**TRAVELODGE**
1709 US 66W (87301)
Rates: $30-$45;
Tel: (505) 863-9301

## GRANTS

**BEST WESTERN THE INN**
1501 E Santa Fe Ave (87020)
Rates: $54-$74;
Tel: (505) 287-7901

**LEISURE LODGE**
1204 E Santa Fe Ave (87020)
Rates: $29-$38;
Tel: (505) 287-2991

**SANDS MOTEL**
112 McArthur St (87020)
Rates: $27-$43;
Tel: (505) 287-2996

## HOBBS

**BEST WESTERN
LEAWOOD MOTEL**
1301 E Broadway (88240)
Rates: $41-$49;
Tel: (505) 393-4101

**HOBBS MOTOR INN**
501 N Marland Blvd (88240)
Rates: $38-$44;
Tel: (505) 397-3251

**ZIA MOTEL**
619 N Marland Blvd (88240)
Rates: $23-$39;
Tel: (505) 397-3591

## LAS CRUCES

**BEST WESTERN
MESILLA VALLEY INN**
P. O. Drawer 849 (88005)
Rates: $42-$49;
Tel: (505) 524-8603

**BEST WESTERN
MISSION INN**
1765 S Main St (88001)
Rates: $41-$48;
Tel: (505) 524-8591

**DESERT LODGE MOTEL**
1900 W Picacho St (88005)
Rates: $19-$27;
Tel: (505) 524-1925

**HAMPTON INN**
755 Avenida de Mesilla
(88005)
Rates: $45-$53;
Tel: (505) 526-8311

**HOLIDAY INN
DE LAS CRUCES**
201 E University Ave (88004)
Rates: $61-$69;
Tel: (505) 526-5511

**LA QUINTA
MOTOR INN-LAS CRUCES**
790 Avenida de Mesilla
(88005)
Rates: $45-$59;
Tel: (505) 524-0331

**LAS CRUCES HILTON INN**
705 S Telshor (88001)
Rates: $65-$85;
Tel: (505) 522-4300

**LUNDEEN INN
OF THE ARTS**
618 S Alameda Blvd (88005)
Rates: N/A;
Tel: (505) 526-3327)

**MISSION INN**
1765 S Main (88001)
Rates: N/A;
Tel: (505) 524-8591

**PLAZA SUITES**
301 E University (88001)
Rates: N/A;
Tel: (505) 526-4411

## LAS VEGAS

**EL CAMNIO MOTEL**
1152 N Grand Ave (87701)
Rates: $26-$40;
Tel: (505) 425-5994

**INN ON THE
SANTA FE TRAIL**
1133 N Grand Ave (87701)
Rates: $34-$49;
Tel: (505) 425-6791

**PLAZA HOTEL**
230 Old Town Plaza (87701)
Rates: $49-$80;
Tel: (505) 425-3591

**TOWN HOUSE MOTEL**
1215 N Grand Ave (87701)
Rates: $26-$37;
Tel: (505) 425-6717

## LORDSBURG

**BEST WESTERN
AMERICAN MOTOR INN**
994 E Motel Dr (88045)
Rates: $39-$54;
Tel: (505) 542-3591

**BEST WESTERN
WESTERN SKIES**
1303 S Main (88045)
Rates: $41-$46;
Tel: (505) 542-8807

## LOS ALAMOS

**HILLTOP HOUSE MOTEL**
Trinity Dr at Central (87544)
Rates: $59-$73;
Tel: (505) 662-2441

## MORIARTY

**SUNSET MOTEL**
P. O. Box 36 (87035)
Rates: $27-$32;
Tel: (505) 832-4234

## PORTALES

**DUNES MOTEL**
1613 West 2nd St (88130)
Rates: N/A;
Tel: (505) 356-6668

**PORTALES INN**
218 West 3rd St (88130)
Rates: N/A;
Tel: (505) 359-1208

## RATON

**HARMONY MOTOR MOTEL**
351 Clayton Rd (87740)
Rates: $36-$58;
Tel: (505) 445-2763

**HOLIDAY CLASSIC MOTEL**
P. O. Box 640 (87740)
Rates: $48-$106;
Tel: (800) 255-8879

**MELODY LANE MOTEL**
136 Canyon Dr (87740)
Rates: $29-$55;
Tel: (505) 445-3655

## RED RIVER

**GOLDEN EAGLE LODGE**
P. O. Box 869 (87558)
Rates: $29-$75;
Tel: (505) 754-2227

**RIO COLORADO LODGE**
East Main St, Box 186 (87558)
Rates; N/A;
Tel: (505) 754-2212

**TALL PINE RESORT**
P. O. Box 567 (87558)
Rates: $55-$90;
Tel: (505) 754-2241

**TERRACE TOWERS LODGE**
P. O. Box 149 (87558)
Rates: $33-$90;
Tel: (505) 754-2962

## ROAD FORKS

**DESERT WEST MOTEL**
P. O. Box 2005 (88045)
Rates: $30-$35;
Tel: (505) 542-8801

## ROSWELL

**BEST WESTERN
EL RANCHO PALACIO
MOTOR LODGE**
2205 N Main St (88201)
Rates: $33-$48;
Tel: (505) 622-2721

**BEST WESTERN
SALLY PORT INN**
2000 N Main St (88201)
Rates: $52-$66;
Tel: (505) 622-6430

**BUDGET INN**
2101 N Main St (88201)
Rates: $28-$35;
Tel: (505) 623-6050

**COMFORT INN**
2803 W 2nd (88201)
Rates: $39-$42;
Tel: (505) 623-9440

**DAYS INN**
1310 N Main St (88201)
Rates: $33-$50;
Tel: (505) 623-4021

**FRONTIER MOTEL**
3010 N Main St (88201)
Rates: $26-$39;
Tel: (505) 622-1400

**LEISURE INNS OF AMERICA**
2700 W 2nd St (88201)
Rates: $25-$29;
Tel: (505) 622-2575

**ROSWELL INN**
1815 N Main St (88202)
Rates: $52-$58;
Tel: (505) 623-4920

**ROYAL MOTEL**
2001 N Main St (88201)
Rates: $28-$39;
Tel: (505) 622-0110

## RUIDOSO

**BEST WESTERN
SWISS CHALET**
1451 Mechem (88345)
Rates: $48-$80;
Tel: (505) 258-3333

**HIGH COUNTRY LODGE**
P. O. Box 137 (88312)
Rates: $59-$75;
Tel: (505) 336-4321

**RUIDOSO LODGE CABINS**
300 Main (88345)
Rates: N/A;
Tel: (800) 950-2510

**VILLAGE LODGE
AT INNSBROOK RESORT**
101 Innsbrook Dr (88345)
Rates: $59-$89;
Tel: (505) 258-5442

**VILLA INN**
P. O. Box 3329 (88345)
Rates: $29-$42;
Tel: (505) 378-4471

## SANTA FE

**ALEXANDER'S INN**
529 E Palace Ave (87501)
Rates: $65-$140;
Tel: (505) 986-1431

**CACTUS LODGE MOTEL**
2864 Cerrillos Rd (87501)
Rates: N/A;
Tel: (505) 471-7699

**ELDORADO HOTEL**
309 W San Francisco (87501)
Rates: $125-$210;
Tel: (505) 988-4455

**EL PARADERO INN**
220 W Manhattan (87501)
Rates: $45-$125;
Tel: (505) 988-1177

**HILTON OF SANTA FE**
100 Sandoval (87501)
Rates: $90-$245;
Tel: (505) 988-2811

**HOLIDAY INN**
4048 Cerrillos Rd (87501)
Rates: $105-$275;
Tel: (505) 473-4646

**INN ON THE ALAMEDA**
303 E Alameda St (87501)
Rates: $125-$155;
Tel: (505) 984-2121

**INN OF THE ANASAZI**
113 Washington Ave (87501)
Rates: $195-$395;
Tel: (800) 688-8100

**LA QUINTA MOTOR INN**
4296 Cerrillos Rd (87505)
Rates: $50-$74;
Tel: (505) 471-1142

**PARK INN LIMITED**
2900 Cerrillos Rd (87501)
Rates: N/A;
Tel: (505) 473-4281

**PRESTON HOUSE**
106 Faithway St (87501)
Rates: $58-$135;
Tel: (505) 982-3465

**QUALITY INN**
3011 Cerrillos Rd (87501)
Rates: $60-$80;
Tel: (505) 471-1211

**RESIDENCE INN
BY MARRIOTT**
1698 Gallisteo (87501)
Rates: $89-$167;
Tel: (505) 988-7300

## SANTA ROSA

**HOLIDAY SANTA ROSA**
P. O. Box E (88435)
Rates: $21-$39;
Tel: (505) 472-5411

## SILVER CITY

**BEAR MT GUEST RANCH**
2251 Bear Mt Rd (88061)
Rates: N/A;
Tel: (505) 538-2538

**HOLIDAY MOTOR HOTEL**
3420 Hwy 180E (88061)
Rates: $42-$46;
Tel: (505) 538-3711

**SUPER 8 MOTEL**
1040 Hwy 180E (88061)
Rates: $34-$47;
Tel: (505) 388-1983

## SOCORRO

**BEST WESTERN
GOLDEN MANOR MOTEL**
507 California Ave NW
(87801)
Rates: $42-$50;
Tel: (505) 835-0230

## TAOS

**AUSTING HAUS INN**
P. O. Box 8 (Ski Valley 87525)
Rates: $88-$110;
Tel: (800) 748-2932

**BEST WESTERN
KACHINA LODGE DE TAOS**
415 Paseo del Pueblo Norte
(87571)
Rates: $65-$110;
Tel: (505) 758-2275

**EL MONTE LODGE**
317 E Kit Carson Rd (87571)
Rates: $44-$89;
Tel: (505) 758-3171

**EL PUEBLO LODGE**
412 Paseo del Pueblo Norte
(87571)
Rates: $40-$60;
Tel: (505) 758-8700

**EL RINCON INN**
114 E Kit Carson (87571)
Rates: $45-$125;
Tel: (505) 758-4784

**HOLIDAY INN
DON FERNANDO DE TAOS**
1005 Paseo del Pueblo Sur
(87571)
Rates: $69-$165;
Tel: (505) 758-4444

**QUALITY INN**
1043 Paseo del Pueblo Sur
(87571)
Rates: $55-$80;
Tel: (505) 758-2200

**SAGEBRUSH INN**
P. O. Box 557 (87571)
Rates: $40-$102;
Tel: (505) 758-2254

**SUN GOD LODGE**
919 Paseo del Pueblo Sur
(87571)
Rates: $38-$57;
Tel: (505) 758-3162

## TRUTH OR CONSEQUENCES

**ACE LODGE MOTEL**
1302 Date St (87901)
Rates: $29-$60;
Tel: (505) 894-2151

**BEST WESTERN
HOT SPRING MOTOR INN**
2270 N Date St (87901)
Rates: $43-$48;
Tel: (505) 894-6665

**ELEPHANT BUTTE
RESORT INN**
P. O. Box E
(Elephant Butte 87935)
Rates: $50-$60;
Tel: (505) 744-5431

**SUPER 8 MOTEL**
2701 N Date St (87901)
Rates: $35-$44;
Tel: (505) 894-7888

## TUCUMCARI

**APACHE MOTEL**
1106 E Tucumcari Blvd
(88401)
Rates: N/A;
Tel: (505) 461-3367

**BEST WESTERN
ARUBA MOTEL**
1700 E Tucumcari Blvd
(88401)
Rates: $40-$50;
Tel: (505) 461-3335

**BEST WESTERN
DISCOVERY MOTOR INN**
200 E Estrella (88401)
Rates: $40-$52;
Tel: (505) 461-4884

**BEST WESTERN
POW WOW INN**
801 W Tucumcari Blvd (88401)
Rates: $40-$54;
Tel: (505) 461-0500

**BUCKAROO MOTEL**
1315 W Tucumcari Blvd
(88401)
Rates: $18-$22;
Tel: (505) 461-1650

**ECONO LODGE**
3400 E Tucumcari Blvd
(88401)
Rates: $21-$30;
Tel: (505) 461-4194

**FRIENDSHIP INN**
315 E Tucumcari Blvd (88401)
Rates: $20-$31;
Tel: (505) 461-0330

**HOLIDAY INN**
P. O. Box 808 (88401)
Rates: $49-$82;
Tel: (505) 461-3780

**RODEWAY INN**
1302 W Tucumcari Blvd
(88401)
Rates: $37-$65;
Tel: (505) 461-3140

**ROYAL PALACIO MOTEL**
1620 E Tucumcari Blvd
(88401)
Rates: $27-$35;
Tel: (505) 461-1212

**SAFARI MOTEL**
722 E Tucumcari Blvd (88401)
Rates: $23-$30;
Tel: (505) 461-3642

**TUCUMCARI TRAVELODGE**
1214 E Tucumcari Blvd
(88401)
Rates: $28-$37;
Tel: (505) 461-1401

## WHITE ROCK

**BANDELLER INN**
Center SR 4 (87544)
Rates: $46-$69;
Tel: (505) 672-3838

## WHITE'S CITY

**BEST WESTERN
CAVERN INN**
12 Carlsbad Caverns Hwy
(88268)
Rates: $50-$80;
Tel: (505) 785-2291

# NEW YORK

## ALBANY

**ALBANY MARRIOTT**
189 Wolf Rd (12205)
Rates: $99-$157;
Tel: (518) 458-8444

**ALBANY QUALITY INN**
1-3 Watervliet Ave (12206)
Rates: $63-$92;
Tel: (518) 438 8431

**AMBASSADOR
MOTOR INN**
1600 Central Ave (12205)
Rates: N/A;
Tel: (518) 456-8982

**COMFORT INN-AIRPORT**
866 Albany Shaker Rd
(12110)
Rates: $54-$63;
Tel: (518) 783-1216

**ECONO LODGE**
1632 Central Ave (12205)
Rates: $38-$74;
Tel: (518) 456-8811

**HAMPTON INN**
10 Ulenski Dr (12205)
Rates: $60-$70;
Tel: (518) 438-2822

**HAMPTON INN-LATHAN**
981 New Loudon Rd
(Cohoes 12047)
Rates: $58-$80;
Tel: (518) 785-0000

**HOWARD JOHNSON
LODGE**
SR 9W, off Jct I-87 (12209)
Rates: $60-$77;
Tel: (518) 462-6555

**INN AT THE CENTURY &
CONFERENCE CTR**
997 New Loudon Rd
(Cohoes 12047)
Rates: $71-$99;
Tel: (518) 785-0931

**QUALITY INN AIRPORT**
622 Watervliet-Shaker Rd
(Latham 12110)
Rates: $49-$90;
Tel: (518) 785-1414

**RAMADA INN**
1228 Western Ave (12203)
Rates: $59-$195;
Tel: (518) 489-2981

**RED ROOF INN**
188 Wolf Rd (12205)
Rates: N/A;
Tel: (800) 843-7663

**RESIDENCE INN
BY MARRIOTT-
ALBANY AIRPORT**
1 Residence Inn Dr (12110)
Rates: $130 $160;
Tel: (518) 783-0600

## AMHERST

**RED ROOF INN**
42 Flint Rd (14226)
Rates: N/A;
Tel: (800) 843-7663

## AMSTERDAM

**HOLIDAY INN**
10 Market St (12010)
Rates: $52-$65;
Tel: (518) 843-5760

**VALLEY VIEW MOTOR INN**
Rts 5S & 30 (12010)
Rates: $31-$58;
Tel: (518) 842-5637

## AUBURN

**DAYS INN-AUBURN**
37 William St (13021)
Rates: $46-$76
Tel: (315) 252-7567

**HOLIDAY INN**
75 North St (13021)
Rates: $64-$101;
Tel: (315) 253-4531

## AVOCA

**GOODRICH
CENTER MOTEL**
8620 State Rt 415 (14809)
Rates: $30-$43;
Tel: (607) 566-2216

## BAINBRIDGE

**ALGONKIN MOTEL**
RDS Box 45, Rt 7 (13733)
Rates: N/A;
Tel: (607) 967-5911

## BATAVIA

**CROWN INN/
FRIENDSHIP INN**
8212 Park Rd (14020)
Rates: $42-$78;
Tel: (716) 343-2311

**SHERATON INN BATAVIA**
8250 Park Rd (14020)
Rates: $55-$110;
Tel: (716) 344-2100

**TREADWAY BATAVIA INN**
8204 Park Rd (14020)
Rates: $50-$80;
Tel: (716) 343-1000

## BATH

**DAYS INN**
330 W Morris (14810)
Rates: $45-$65;
Tel: (607) 776-7655

**OLD NATIONAL HOTEL**
13 E Steuben St (14810)
Rates: $44-$50;
Tel: (607) 776-4104

253

## BERLIN

**THE SEDGWICK INN**
P. O. Box 250 (12022)
Rates: $55-$85;
Tel: (518) 658-2334

## BINGHAMTON

**BEST WESTERN
OF JOHNSON CITY**
569 Harry L Dr
(Johnson City 13790)
Rates: $41-$58;
Tel: (607) 729-9194

**COMFORT INN**
1156 Front St (13905)
Rates: $42-$84;
Tel: (607) 722-5353

**ECONO LODGE**
P. O. Box 196, E Side Sta
(13904)
Rates: $47-$89;
Tel: (607) 775-3443

**HOJO INN-BINGHAMTON**
700 Front St (13905)
Rates: $39-$79;
Tel: (607) 724-1341

**HOJO INN S.U.N.Y.**
3601 Vestal Pkwy E (13850)
Rates: $39-$79;
Tel: (607) 729-6181

**HOLIDAY INN ARENA**
2-8 Hawley St (13901)
Rates: $65-$79;
Tel: (607) 722-1212

**HOLIDAY INN
AT THE UNIVERSITY**
4105 Vestal Pkwy (13903)
Rates: $55-$66;
Tel: (607) 729-6371

**HOTEL DE VILLE**
80 State St (13901)
Rates: $85-$200;
Tel: (607) 722-0000

**MOTEL 6 BINGHAMTON**
1012 Front St (13905)
Rates: $29-$35;
Tel: (607) 771-0400

## BOONVILLE

**HEADWATERS
MOTOR LODGE**
P. O. Box 404 (13309)
Rates: $43-$55;
Tel: (315) 952-4493

## BOWMANSVILLE

**RED ROOF INN**
146 Maple Dr (14026)
Rates: N/A;
Tel: (800) 843-7663

## BUFFALO

**BUFFALO HILTON**
120 Church St (14202)
Rates: $102-$158;
Tel: (716) 845-5100

**BUFFALO SOUTH
MOTOR INN**
4344 Mile Strip Rd
(Blasdell 14219)
Rates: $29-$55;
Tel: (716) 825-7530

**HOLIDAY INN-
BUFFALO AIRPORT**
4600 Genesee St (14225)
Rates: $83-$94;
Tel: (716) 634-6969

**HOLIDAY INN-DOWNTOWN**
620 Delaware Ave (14202)
Rates: $71-$93;
Tel: (716) 886-2121

**JOURNEY'S END SUITES**
601 Main St (14203)
Rates: $84-$96;
Tel: (716) 854-5500

**LORD AMHERST
MOTOR HOTEL**
5000 Main St (14226)
Rates: $49-$79;
Tel: (716) 839-2200

**MICROTEL**
50 Freemand Rd
(Williamsville 14221)
Rates: $34-$37;
Tel: (716) 633-6200

**MICROTEL-TONAWANDA**
1 Hospitality Centre Way
(Tonawanda 14150)
Rates: $34-$37;
Tel: (716) 693-8100

**MOTEL 6**
4400 Maple Rd
(Amherst 14226)
Rates: $46-$60;
Tel: (716) 834-2231

**RESIDENCE INN BY MARRIOTT
BUFFALO/AMHERST**
100 Maple Rd
(Williamsville 14221)
Rates: $120-$160;
Tel: (716) 632-6622

**WELLESLEY INN
BUFFALO AIRPORT**
4630 Genesee St (14225)
Rates: $48-$68;
Tel: (716) 631-8966

## CAMBRIDGE

**BLUE WILLOW MOTEL**
51 S Park St (12816)
Rates: $28-$49;
Tel: (518) 677-3552

**TOWN HOUSE
MOTOR INN**
RR 2, Box 140 (12816)
Rates: $35-$45;
Tel: (518) 677-5524

## CANANDAIGUA

**ECONO LODGE
MUAR LAKE**
170 Eastern Blvd (14424)
Rates: $38-$53;
Tel: (716) 394-9000

## CANASTOTA

**DAYS INN-DAYSTOP**
P. O. Box 655 (13032)
Rates: $45-$55;
Tel: (315) 697-3309

# CANTON

**BEST WESTERN
UNIVERSITY INN**
US 11 adj to St. Lawrence Univ
(13617)
Rates: $55-$75;
Tel: (315) 386-8522

# CASTLETON

**BELAIR MOTEL**
1036 Rt 9 (12033)
Rates: N/A;
Tel: (518) 732-7744

# CAZENOVIA

**LINCKLAEN HOUSE**
79 Albany St (13035)
Rates: $65-$130;
Tel: (315) 655-3461

# CHAFFEE

**JOSIE'S BROOKSIDE MOTEL**
SR 16 & 39 (14030)
Rates: $29-$45;
Tel: (716) 496-5057

# CHAUTAUQUA

**ATHENAEUM HOTEL**
On W shore of Chautauqua
Lake (14722)
Rates: $118-$378;
Tel: (800) 821-1881

# CLAYTON
# (THOUSAND ISLANDS)

**WEST WINDS MOTEL**
Box 56 RD 2 (13624)
Rates: $37-$650;
Tel: (315) 686-3352

# CLIFTON PARK

**COMFORT INN**
41 Fire Rd, Old SR 146
(12065)
Rates: $49-$129;
Tel: (518) 373-0222

# COBLESKILL

**BEST WESTERN
INN OF COBLESKILL**
P. O. Box 189 (12043)
Rates: $51-$94;
Tel: (518) 234-4321

# COMMACK

**HOWARD JOHNSON
BED & BREAKFAST**
450 Moreland Rd (11725)
Rates: $59-$95;
Tel: (516) 864-8820

# COOPERSTOWN

**AALSMEER MOTEL**
Box 790, RD 2 (13326)
Rates: $75-$515;
Tel: (607) 547-8819

# CORNING

**BEST WESTERN
LODGE ON THE GREEN**
Box 150 (Painted Post 14870)
Rates: $65-$82;
Tel: (607) 962-2456

**CORNING HILTON**
125 Denison Pkwy E (14830)
Rates: $59-$158;
Tel: (607) 962-5000

**ECONO LODGE**
200 Robert Dann Dr
(Painted Post 14870)
Rates: $32-$60;
Tel: (607) 962-4444

**HOLIDAY INN**
304 S Hamilton St
(Painted Post 14870)
Rates: $54-$75;
Tel: (607) 962-5021

**LAMPLITER MOTEL**
543 Victory Hwy
(Painted Post 14870)
Rates: $73-$115;
Tel: (607) 962-3253

**STILES MOTEL**
9239 Victory Hwy
(Painted Post 14870)
Rates: $27-$42;
Tel: (607) 962-5221

# CORTLAND

**ECONO LODGE
OF CORTLAND**
P. O. Box 628
(McGraw 13101)
Rates: $41-$47;
Tel: (607) 753-7594

# DANSVILLE

**DAYSTOP**
Rt 390, Exit 5 (14437)
Rates: $33-$38;
Tel: (716) 335-6023

# DELHI

**BUENA VISTA MOTEL**
Box 212, Andes Rd (13753)
Rates: N/A;
Tel: (607) 746-2135

# DELMAR

**AMERICAN COLLECTION
OF BED & BREAKFASTS**
4 Greenwood Lane (12054)
Rates: N/A;
Tel: (518) 439-7001

# DIAMOND POINT

**DIAMOND COVE COTTAGES**
P. O. Box 2436 (12845)
Rates: $50-$110;
Tel: (518) 668-5787

# DOVER PLAINS

**OLD DROVERS INN**
Old Rt 22 (12522)
Rates: $80-$180;
Tel: (914) 832-9311

## DUNKIRK

**DAYS INN**
10455 Bennett Rd
(Fredonia 14063)
Rates: $39-$65;
Tel: (716) 673-1351

**DRAKES MOTOR INN**
5361 West Lake Rd (14048)
Rates: N/A;
Tel: (716) 672-4867

**ECONO LODGE**
310 Lake Shore Dr (14048)
Rates: $38-$53;
Tel: (716) 366-2200

**QUALITY INN VINEYARD**
Vineyard Dr (14048)
Rates: $46-$60;
Tel: (716) 366-4400

**SHERATON
HARBORFRONT INN**
30 Lake Shore Dr E (14048)
Rates: $60-$95;
Tel: (716) 366-8350

**SOUTH SHORE
MOTOR LODGE**
5040 West Lake Rd (14048)
Rates: $38-$79;
Tel: (716) 366-2822

## EAST GREENBUSH

**MOUNT VERNON MOTEL**
576 Columbia Tpke (12061)
Rates: N/A;
Tel: (518) 477-9352

## EAST HAMPTON

**DUTCH MOTEL**
488 Montauk Hwy (11937)
Rates: $55-$145;
Tel: (516) 324-4550

## EAST HERKIMER

**GLEN RIDGE MOTEL**
Rt 5 (13350)
Rates: N/A;
Tel: (315) 866-4149

## EAST WINDHAM

**POINT LOOKOUT INN**
Rt 23, Box 33 (12439)
Rates: N/A;
Tel: (518) 734-3381

## ELBRIDGE

**COZY COTTAGE**
4987 Kingston Rd (13060)
Rates: N/A;
Tel: (315) 689-2082

## ELMIRA

**COACHMAN
MOTOR LODGE**
908 Pennsylvania Ave (14904)
Rates: $48-$63;
Tel: (607) 733-5526

**BEST WESTERN
MARSHALL MANOR**
P. O. Box 238
(Horseheads 14845)
Rates: $32-$65;
Tel: (607) 739-3891

**HOLIDAY INN**
602 Corning Rd
(Horseheads 14845)
Rates: $59-$95;
Tel: (607) 739-3681

**HOLIDAY INN-DOWNTOWN**
1 Holiday Plaza (14901)
Rates: $65-$90;
Tel: (607) 734-4211

**HOWARD JOHNSON
LODGE**
Rts 17 & 14
(Horseheads 14845)
Rates: $42-$64;
Tel: (607) 739-5636

**HUCK FINN MOTEL**
101 Westinghouse Rd
(Horseheads 14845)
Rates: $33-$44;
Tel: (607) 739-3807

**MOTEL 6**
151 Rt 17 (Horseheads 14845)
Rates: $45-$55;
Tel: (607) 739-2525

**RED JACKET MOTOR INN**
P. O. Box 489 (14902)
Rates: $29-$65;
Tel: (607) 734-1616

## ELMSFORD

**DAYS INN**
200 Tarrytown Rd (10523)
Rates: $59-$105;
Tel: (914) 592-5680

**RAMADA INN**
540 Sawmill River Rd (10523)
Rates: $49-$129;
Tel: (914) 592-3300

## ENDICOTT

**BEST WESTERN
HOMESTEAD INN**
749 W Main St (13760)
Rates: $50-$65;
Tel: (607) 754-1533

## FARMINGTON

**BEST WESTERN
SUNRISE HILL INN**
P. O. Box 25237 (14425)
Rates: $47-$67;
Tel: (716) 924-2131

## FISHKILL

**RESIDENCE INN
BY MARRIOTT**
Rt 9 & I-84 (12524)
Rates: $99-$130;
Tel: (914) 896-5210

**WELLESLEY INN**
2477 Rt 9 (12524)
Rates: $50-$80;
Tel: (914) 896-4995

## FULTON

**FULTON MOTOR LODGE**
163 S 1st St (13069)
Rates: $48-$62;
Tel: (315) 598-6100

**QUALITY INN-RIVERSIDE**
930 S 1st St (13069)
Rates: $69-$87;
Tel: (315) 593-2444

## GARDEN CITY

**THE GARDEN CITY HOTEL**
45 Seventh St (11530)
Rates: $160-$340;
Tel: (516) 747-3000

**MARRIOTT-LONG ISLAND**
101 James Doolittle Blvd
(Uniondale 11553)
Rates: $155-$900;
Tel: (516) 794 5936

## GENEVA

**MOTEL 6**
485 Hamilton St (14456)
Rates: $47-$67;
Tel: (315) 789-4050

## GLENS FALLS

**RAMADA HOTEL**
Aviation Rd (12801)
Rates: $110-$200;
Tel: (518) 793-7701

**SUSSE CHALET**
Big Boom Rd (12804)
Rates: $39-$49;
Tel: (518) 793 8001

**TOWN & COUNTRY MOTEL**
Box 1411, Saratoga Rd
(So Glens Falls 12803)
Rates: N/A;
Tel: (518) 793-3471

## GRAND GORGE

**GOLDEN ACRES
FARM RANCH**
Windy Ridge Rd (12076)
Rates: $80-$330;
Tel: (607) 588-7329

## GRAND ISLAND

**CHATEAU MOTOR LODGE**
1810 Grand Island Blvd
(14072)
Rates: $31-$69;
Tel: (716) 773 2868

## GREENPORT

**SILVER SANDS MOTEL**
P. O. Box 285 (11944)
Rates: $70-$100;
Tel: (516) 477-0011

## HAGUE

**TROUT HOUSE VILLAGE**
Lake Shore Dr. Rt 9N (12836)
Rates: N/A;
Tel: (518) 543-6088

## HAMBURG

**RED ROOF INN**
5370 Camp Rd (14075)
Rates: $32-$59;
Tel: (716) 648-7222

**SAVE INN**
5245 Camp Rd (14075)
Rates: $38-$75;
Tel: (716) 648-2000

## HAMMONDSPORT

**ANOTHER TYME
BED & BREAKFAST**
11 William St (14840)
Rates: $55-$85;
Tel: (607) 569-3402

**VINEHURST MOTEL**
Box 203, Rt 54 (14840)
Rates: N/A;
Tel: (607) 569-2300

## HARRIMAN

**AMERICAN BUDGET INNS**
Rt 17 & 32 (10926)
Rates: $40-$54;
Tel: (914) 783-3211

## HAUPPAUGE

**RADISSON
HOTEL ISLANDIA**
3635 Express Dr N (11788)
Rates: $105-$129;
Tel: (516) 232 3000

**SHERATON SMITHTOWN**
110 Vanderbilt Motor Pkwy
(Smithtown 11788)
Rates: $119-$129;
Tel: (516) 231-1100

## HEMPSTEAD

**BEST WESTERN HOTEL
& CONFERENCE CTR**
80 Clinton St (11550)
Rates: $80-$95;
Tel: (516) 486-4100

## HENRIETTA

**RED ROOF INN**
4820 W Henrietta Rd (14467)
Rates: N/A;
Tel: (800) 843 7660

## HERKIMER

**HERKIMER MOTEL**
100 Marginal Rd (13350)
Rates: $38-$66;
Tel: (315) 866-0490

## HICKSVILLE

**ECONO LODGE**
429 Duffy Ave (11801)
Rates: $70-$80;
Tel: (516) 433-3900

## HILLSDALE

**SWISS HUTTE MOTEL**
3 Mi E on NY 23 (12529)
Rates: $90-$180;
Tel: (518) 325-3333

## HYDE PARK

**DUTCH PATROON MOTEL**
1 Mi S on US 9 (12538)
Rates: $40-$55;
Tel: (914) 229-7141

## ILION

**WHIFFLETREE MOTEL**
345 E Main St (13357)
Rates: $40-$75;
Tel: (315) 895-7777

## ITHACA

**COLLEGETOWN
MOTOR LODGE**
312 College Ave (14850)
Rates: $57-$91;
Tel: (607) 273-3542

**ITHACA RAMADA
INN/EXECUTIVE TOWER**
222 S Cayuga St (14850)
Rates: $65-$105;
Tel: (607) 272-1000

**JOURNEY'S END MOTELS**
356 Elmira Rd (14850)
Rates: $45-$56;
Tel: (607) 272-0100

**LA TOURELLE
COUNTRY INN**
1150 Danby Rd (14850)
Rates: $75-$150;
Tel: (607) 273-2734

**MEADOW COURT INN**
529 S Meadow St (14850)
Rates: $35-$135;
Tel: (607) 273-3885

## JAMESTOWN

**COMFORT INN**
2800 N Main St Extension
(14701)
Rates: $46-$79;
Tel: (716) 664-5920

**HOLIDAY INN**
150 W 4th St (14701)
Rates: $68-$78;
Tel: (716) 664-3400

## JOHNSON CITY

**RED ROOF INN**
590 Fairview St (13790)
Rates: N/A;
Tel: (800) 843-7663

## KINGSTON

**HOLIDAY INN**
503 Washington Ave (12401)
Rates: $63-$129;
Tel: (914) 338-0400

**RAMADA INN**
NY 28 Exit 19 (12401)
Rates: $49-$105;
Tel: (914) 339-3900

**SUPER 8 MOTEL**
487 Washington Ave (12401)
Rates: $48-$56;
Tel: (914) 338-3078

## LAKE GEORGE

**BEST WESTERN
OF LAKE GEORGE**
Luzerne Rd (12845)
Rates: $45-$125;
Tel: (518) 668-5701

**ECONO LODGE
LAKE GEORGE MOTEL**
431 Canada St (12845)
Rates: $40-$98;
Tel: (800) 477-3529

**FORT WILLIAM HENRY
MOTOR INN**
Canada St (12845)
Rates: $55-$150;
Tel: (518) 668-3081

**LAKE CREST MOTEL**
366 Canada St (12845)
Rates: N/A;
Tel: (518) 668-3374

**LYN AIRE MOTEL**
RR 3, Box 3362 (12845)
Rates: $36-$125;
Tel: (518) 668-4612

## LAKE PLACID

**ART DEVLIN'S OLYMPIC
MOTOR INN**
350 Main St (12946)
Rates: $38-$86;
Tel: (518) 523-3700

**BEST WESTERN-
GOLDEN ARROW HOTEL**
150 Main St (12946)
Rates: $60-$138;
Tel: (518) 523-3353

**HOLIDAY INN
GRANDVIEW HOTEL**
One Olympic Dr (12946)
Rates: $76-$195;
Tel: (518) 523-2556

**HOWARD JOHNSON
RESORT LODGE**
90 Saranac Ave (12946)
Rates: $45-$115;
Tel: (518) 523-9555

**LAKESHORE MOTEL**
54 Saranac Ave (12946)
Rates: N/A;
Tel: (518) 523-2261

**THUNDERBIRD
MOTOR INN**
Main St (12946)
Rates: N/A;
Tel: (518) 523-2439

**WILDWOOD MOTEL**
88 Saranac Ave (12946)
Rates: $68-$840;
Tel: (518) 523-2624

## LIBERTY

**HOLIDAY INN EXPRESS**
Rt 17 & 52 (12754)
Rates: $50-$75;
Tel: (800) 465-4329

**LANZA'S INN**
Rd 2, Box 446
(Livingston Manor 12758)
Rates: $54-$84;
Tel: (914) 439-5070

## LITTLE FALLS

BEST WESTERN
LITTLE FALLS MOTOR INN
20 Albany St (13365)
Rates: $54-$60;
Tel: (315) 823-4954

## MALONE

ECONO LODGE
227 W Main St (12953)
Rates: $42-$51;
Tel: (518) 483-0500

FLANAGAN HOTEL
One Elm St (12953)
Rates: $30-$60;
Tel: (518) 483-1400

FOUR SEASONS MOTEL
236 W Main St (12953)
Rates: $38-$48;
Tel: (518) 483-3490

## MARATHON

THREE BEAR INN
P.O. Box 507 (13803)
Rates: $28-$35;
Tel: (607) 849-3258

## MASONVILLE

MASON INN
& MOTOR LODGE
Rt 206, Box 81 (13804)
Rates: $38-$45;
Tel: (607) 265-3287

## MELVILLE

RADISSON PLAZA
1350 Old Walt Whitman Rd
(11747)
Rates: $109-$199;
Tel: (516) 423-1600

## MIDDLETOWN

DAYS INN
P. O.Box 279, Rt 17M
(New Hampton 10958)
Rates: $45-$85;
Tel: (914) 374-2411

SUPER 8 LODGE
563 Rt 211E (10940)
Rates: $53-$67;
Tel: (914) 692-5828

## MOUNT KISCO

HOLIDAY INN
1 Holiday Dr (10549)
Rates: $72-$132;
Tel: (914) 241-2600

## NANUET

SHERATON INN/NANUET
415 E US 59 (10954)
Rates: $75-$85;
Tel: (914) 623-6000

## NEWBURGH

HOLIDAY INN
90 Rt 17K (12550)
Rates: $59-$98;
Tel: (914) 564-9020

HOWARD JOHNSON
MOTOR LODGE
95 Rt 17K (12550)
Rates: $55-$70;
Tel: (914) 564-4000

## NEW WINDSOR

ECONOLODGE-
WEST POINT
310 Windsor Hwy (12553)
Rates: $46-$70;
Tel: (914) 561-6620

## NEW YORK CITY
(and Vicinity)

BARBIZON HOTEL
140 E 63rd St (10021)
Rates: $99-$650;
Tel: (212) 838-5700

BEDFORD HOTEL
118 E 40th St (10016)
Rates: $140-$170;
Tel: (212) 697-4800

THE BOX TREE INN
250 E 49th St (10017)
Rates: $250-$360;
Tel: (212) 758-8320

THE CARLYLE
35 E 76th St & Madison Ave
(10021)
Rates: $250-$375;
Tel: (212) 744-1600

DAYS INN NEW YORK CITY
440 W 57th St (10019)
Rates: $89-$174;
Tel: (212) 581-8100

DORSET HOTEL
30 W 54th St (10019)
Rates: $175-$475;
Tel: (212) 247-7300

DRAKE SWISSOTEL
440 Park Ave (10022)
Rates: $215-$410;
Tel: (212) 421-0900

ELYSEE HOTEL
60 E 54th St (10022)
Rates: $150-$600;
Tel: (212) 753-1066

THE ESSEX HOUSE
160 Central Park S (10019)
Rates: $170-$340;
Tel: (212) 247-0300

FORTE TRAVELODGE AT JFK
Belt Pkwy & Van Wyck Expwy
(Jamaica 11430)
Rates: $99-$119;
Tel: (718) 995-9000

FOUR SEASONS HOTEL
57 E 57th St (10022)
Rates: $295-$1250;
Tel: (212) 758-5700

**HILTON & TOWERS AT ROCKEFELLER CENTER**
1335 Avenue of the Americas (10019)
Rates: $199-$475;
Tel: (212) 586-7000

**HOLIDAY INN- CROWNE PLAZA**
1605 Broadway (10019)
Rates: $159-$240;
Tel: (212) 977-4000

**HOTEL MARIA**
138 Lafayette St (10013)
Rates: $125-$245;
Tel: (212) 966-8898

**HOTEL PIERRE- A FOUR SEASONS HOTEL**
2 E 61st St (10021)
Rates: $290-$1500;
Tel: (212) 838-8000

**HOTEL PLAZA ATHENEE**
37 E 64th St (10021)
Rates: $240-$390;
Tel: (212) 734-9100

**JFK AIRPORT HILTON**
138-10 135th Ave
(Jamaica 11436)
Rates: $149-$189;
Tel: (718) 322-8700

**JFK PLAZA HOTEL**
135-30 140th St
(Jamaica 11436)
Rates: N/A;
Tel: (718) 659-6003

**JOURNEY'S END HOTELS**
3 E 40th St (10016)
Rates: $131-$141;
Tel: (212) 447-1500

**LA GUARDIA MARRIOTT HOTEL**
102-05 Ditmars Blvd
(East Elmhurst 11369)
Rates: $155-$175;
Tel: (718) 565-8900

**THE LOWELL**
28 E 63rd St (10021)
Rates: $260-$520;
Tel: (212) 838-1400

**LOEWS NEW YORK**
569 Lexington Ave (10022)
Rates: $185-$375;
Tel: (212) 752-7000

**THE MARK**
25 E 77th St (10022)
Rates: $275-$2000;
Tel: (800) 843-6275

**MARRIOTT EAST SIDE**
525 Lexington Ave (10017)
Rates: $129-$300;
Tel: (212) 755-4000

**MARRIOTT MARQUIS**
1535 Broadway (10036)
Rates: $199-$229;
Tel: (212) 398-1900

**MAYFAIR HOTEL BAGLIONI**
610 Park Ave (10021)
Rates: $275-$1700;
Tel: (212) 288-0800

**THE MAYFLOWER HOTEL ON THE PARK**
15 Central Park W (10023)
Rates: $138-$180;
Tel: (212) 265-0060

**THE NEW YORK HILTON & TOWERS**
1335 Ave of the Americas (10019)
Rates: $179-$254;
Tel: (212) 586-7000

**NOVOTEL NEW YORK**
226 W 52nd St (10019)
Rates: $109-$159;
Tel: (212) 315-0100

**THE PLAZA HOTEL**
5th Ave at 59th St Central Park S (10019)
Rates: $235-$495;
Tel: (212) 759-3000

**QUALITY HOTEL AT LA GUARDIA AIRPORT**
9500 Ditmars Blvd (11369)
Rates: $99-$135;
Tel: (718) 335-1200

**RAMADA HOTEL PENNSYLVANIA**
401 Seventh Ave (10001)
Rates: $89-$450;
Tel: (212) 736-5000

**THE REGENCY HOTEL**
540 Park Ave (10021)
Rates: $245-$850;
Tel: (212) 759-4100

**ROGER SMITH HOTEL**
501 Lexington Ave (10017)
Rates: $160-$295;
Tel: (212) 755-1400

**THE ROOSEVELT HOTEL**
45 E 45th St (10017)
Rates: $119-$950;
Tel: (212) 661-9600

**THE ROYALTON HOTEL**
44 W 44th (10036)
Rates: $180-$325;
Tel: (212) 869-4400

**SHERATON MANHATTAN**
790 Seventh Ave (10019)
Rates: $195-$600;
Tel: (212) 581-3300

**SHERATON PARK AVENUE**
45 Park Ave (10016)
Rates: $135-$245;
Tel: (212) 685-7676

**THE STANHOPE HOTEL**
995 Fifth Ave (10028)
Rates: $275-$2500;
Tel: (212) 288-5800

**SURREY HOTEL**
20 E 76th St (10021)
Rates: $205-$580;
Tel: (212) 288-3700

**TRAVELODGE**
Van Wycke Expy near JKF Airport (11430)
Rates: $99-$410;
Tel: (718) 995-9000

**WALDORF- ASTORIA HOTEL**
301 Park Ave (10022)
Rates: $215-$750;
Tel: (212) 355-3000

**WESTBURY HOTEL**
15 E 69th St (10021)
Rates: $195-$295;
Tel: (212) 535-2000

# NIAGARA FALLS

**HOLIDAY INN DOWNTOWN AT THE FALLS**
114 Buffalo Ave (14303)
Rates: $59-$134;
Tel: (716) 285-2521

**HOWARD JOHNSON-EAST**
6505 Niagara Falls Blvd
(14303)
Rates: $39-$95;
Tel: (716) 283-8791

**THE RADISSON HOTEL NIAGARA FALLS**
Third St & Old Falls (14303)
Rates: $62-$140;
Tel: (716) 285-3361

**RAMADA INN-NIAGARA FALLS**
401 Buffalo Ave (14303)
Rates: $65-$129;
Tel: (716) 285-2541

**TRAVELERS BUDGET INN**
9001 Niagara Falls Blvd
(14304)
Rates: $28-$79;
Tel: (716) 297-3228

# NIAGARA FALLS
(Ontario, Canada)

**AURORA MOTEL**
5630 Dunn St (L2G 2N7)
Rates: $25-$70;
Tel: (416) 356-4490

**BEST WESTERN FALLVIEW MOTOR HOTEL**
5551 Murray St (L2G 2J4)
Rates: $59-$169;
Tel: (416) 356-0551

**COMFORT INN ON THE RIVER**
4009 River Rd (L2E 3E9)
Rates: $35-$118;
Tel: (416) 356-0131

**FLAMINGO MOTOR INN**
7701 Lundy's Ln (L2H 1H3)
Rates: $32-$84;
Tel: (416) 356-4646

**GLENGATE MOTEL**
5534 Stanley Ave (L2G 3X2)
Rates: $36-$69;
Tel: (416) 357-1333

**HOLIDAY INN-BY THE FALLS**
5339 Murray Hill (L2G 2J3)
Rates: $45-$144;
Tel: (416) 356-1333

**OAKES INN**
6546 Buchanan Ave
(L2G 3W2)
Rates: $46-$180;
Tel: (416) 356-4514

**RAMADA CORAL INN**
7429 Lundy's Ln (L2H 1G9)
Rates: $41-$114;
Tel: (416) 356-6116

**THE SKYLINE BROCK AT MAPLELEAF VILLAGE**
5685 Falls Ave (L2E 6W7)
Rates: $49-$169;
Tel: (416) 374-4445

**THE SKYLINE FOXHEAD AT MAPLELEAF VILLAGE**
5685 Falls Ave (L2E 6W7)
Rates: $69-$190;
Tel: (416) 374-4444

**UNIVERSAL MOTOR LODGE**
6000 Stanley Ave (L2G 3Y1)
Rates: $24-$69;
Tel: (416) 358-6243

# NORWICH

**HOWARD JOHNSON LODGE**
75 N Broad St (13815)
Rates: $50-$104; Tel: (607)
334-2200

# NYACK

**NYACK MOTOR LODGE**
NY 303 & NY 59
(West Nyack 10994)
Rates: $41-$68;
Tel: (914) 359-4100

# OGDENSBURG

**FRIENDSHIP INN-WINDJAMMER**
Rt 4, Box 84 (13669)
Rates: $29-$49;
Tel: (315) 393-3730

**QUALITY INN GRAN-VIEW**
Rt 4, Box 84 (13669)
Rates: $51-$85;
Tel: (315) 393-4550

**THE STONEFENCE HOTEL-MOTEL**
Rt 4, Box 29 (13669)
Rates: $49-$95;
Tel: (315) 393-1545

# OLD FORGE

**FORGE MOTEL**
Box 522 (13420)
Rates: $58-$74;
Tel: (315) 369-3313

**SUNSET MOTEL**
Rt 28, Box 261 (13420)
Rates: $60-$72;
Tel: (315) 369-6836

# ONEONTA

**CELTIC MOTEL**
112 Oneida St (13820)
Rates: N/A;
Tel: (607) 432-0860

**HOLIDAY INN**
Box 634 (13820)
Rates: $54-$92;
Tel: (607) 433-2250

# OWEGO

**SUNRISE MOTEL**
RD 2, Box 249 (13827)
Rates: $29-$37;
Tel: (607) 687-5666

## PARISH

**MONTCLAIR MOTEL**
Rt 69 (13131)
Rates: $35-$40;
Tel: (315) 625-7100

## PEEKSKILL

**PEEKSKILL MOTOR INN**
634 Main St (10566)
Rates: $59-$80;
Tel: (914) 739-1500

## PEMBROKE

**DARIEN LAKES
ECONOLODGE**
8493 Rt 77 (Corfu 14036)
Rates: $44-$75;
Tel: (716) 599-4681

## PLAINVIEW

**RESIDENCE INN
BY MARRIOTT**
9 Gerhard Rd (11803)
Rates: $130-$170;
Tel: (516) 433-6200

## PLATTSBURGH

**ECONO LODGE**
610 Upper Cornelia St
(12901)
Rates: $44-$68;
Tel: (518) 561-1500

**HOLIDAY INN**
Jct I-87 & NY 3 (12901)
Rates: $68-$83;
Tel: (518) 561-5000

**HOWARD JOHNSON
LODGE**
P. O. Box 1278 (12901)
Rates: $47-$89;
Tel: (518) 561-7750

**SUPER 8 MOTEL
PLATTSBURGH**
601 N Margaret St (12901)
Rates: $48-$68;
Tel: (518) 562-8888

## PORT JERVIS

**HOLIDAY INN EXPRESS**
Box 3158 (12771)
Rates: $62-$98;
Tel: (914) 856-6611

## POUGHKEEPSIE

**ECONO LODGE**
418 South Rd (12601)
Rates: $55-$62;
Tel: (914) 452-6600

**RAMADA INN**
679 South Rd (12601)
Rates: $58;
Tel: (914) 462-4600

## RENSSELAER

**FORT CRAILO MOTEL**
110 Columbia Tpke (12144)
Rates: N/A;
Tel: (518) 472-1360

## RIPLEY

**BUDGET HOST
COLONIAL SQUIRE**
P. O. Box 235 (14775)
Rates: $32-$46;
Tel: (716) 736-8000

## ROCHESTER

**COMFORT INN AIRPORT**
395 Buell Rd (14624)
Rates: $49-$60;
Tel: (716) 436-4400

**COMFORT INN-WEST**
1501 W Ridge Rd (14615)
Rates: $48-$60;
Tel: (716) 621-5700

**DAYS INN-
DOWNTOWN ROCHESTER**
384 East Ave (14607)
Rates: $63-$74;
Tel: (716) 325-5010

**ECONO LODGE-
ROCHESTER SOUTH**
940 Jefferson Rd (14623)
Rates: $40-$85;
Tel: (716) 427-2700

**HAMPTON INN**
717 E Henrietta Rd (14623)
Rates: $54-$66;
Tel: (716) 272-7800

**HOLIDAY INN-AIRPORT**
911 Brooks Ave (14624)
Rates: $90-$110;
Tel: (716) 328-6000

**HOLIDAY INN-
GENESEE PLAZA**
120 E Main St (14604)
Rates: $93-$109;
Tel: (716) 546-6400

**HOWARD JOHNSON
AIRPORT HOTEL**
1100 Brooks Ave (14624)
Rates: $85-$107;
Tel: (716) 235-6030

**KING JAMES MOTEL**
2835 Monroe Ave (14618)
Rates: N/A;
Tel: (716) 442-9220

**MARKETPLACE INN**
800 Jefferson Rd (14623)
Rates: $60-$65;
Tel: (716) 475-9190

**MARRIOTT AIRPORT**
1890 W Ridge Rd (14615)
Rates: $79-$310;
Tel: (716) 225-6880

**MICROTEL**
905 Lehigh Station Rd
(Henrietta 14467)
Rates: $32-$35;
Tel: (716) 334-3400

**RADISSON INN
ROCHESTER**
175 Jefferson Rd (14623)
Rates: $69-$109;
Tel: (716) 475-1910

**RED ROOF INN**
4820 W Henrietta Rd
(Henrietta 14467)
Rates: $26-$59;
Tel: (716) 359-1100

## RESIDENCE INN BY MARRIOTT
1300 Jefferson Rd (14623)
Rates: $89-$138;
Tel: (716) 272-8850

## STOUFFER ROCHESTER PLAZA HOTEL
70 State St (14614)
Rates: $79-$143;
Tel: (716) 546-3450

## TRAIL BREAK MOTOR INN
7340 Pittsford-Palmyra Rd (14450)
Rates: $36-$45;
Tel: (716) 223-1710

## WELLESLEY INN BRIGHTON
797 E Henrietta Rd (14623)
Rates: $39-$62;
Tel: (716) 427-0130

## WELLESLEY INN-GREECE
1635 W Ridge Rd (14615)
Rates: $39-$85;
Tel. (716) 621-2060

# ROCKVILLE CENTRE

## HOLIDAY INN
173 Sunrise Hwy (11570)
Rates: $88-$135;
Tel: (516) 678-1300

# ROME

## ADIRONDACK THIRTEEN PINES MOTEL
7353 River Rd (13440)
Rates: $25-$50;
Tel: (315) 337-4930

## ESQUIRE MOTOR LODGE
1801 Black River Blvd (13440)
Rates: N/A;
Tel: (800) 336-1801

## QUALITY INN
200 S James St (13440)
Rates: $55-$63;
Tel: (315) 336-4300

# ROSCOE

## ROSCOE MOTEL
Box 608 (12776)
Rates: $37-$50;
Tel: (607) 498-5220

# SALAMANCA

## DUDLEY HOTEL
132 Main St (14779)
Rates: $40-$50;
Tel: (716) 945-3200

# SARANAC LAKE

## ADIRONDACK MOTEL
23 Lake Flower Ave (12983)
Rates: $30-$60;
Tel: (518) 891-2116

## SARA-PLACID MOTOR INN
120 Lake Flower Ave (12983)
Rates: $35-$60;
Tel: (518) 891-2729

# SARATOGA SPRINGS

## ADELPHI HOTEL
365 Broadway (12866)
Rates: $70-$290;
Tel: (518) 587-4688

## GRAND UNION MOTEL
92 S Broadway (12866)
Rates: $42-$65;
Tel: (518) 584-9000

## HOLIDAY INN
Broadway at Circular St (12866)
Rates: $56-$189;
Tel: (518) 584-4550

## INN AT SARATOGA-CLARION CARRIAGE HOUSE
231 Broadway (12866)
Rates: $75-$245;
Tel: (518) 583-1890

## RAMADA RENAISSANCE HOTEL
534 Broadway (12866)
Rates: $74-$160;
Tel: (518) 584-4000

# SAUGERTIES

## HOJO INN
2764 Rt 32 (12477)
Rates: $50-$80;
Tel: (914) 246-9511

# SCHENECTADY

## HOLIDAY INN-DOWNTOWN SCHENECTADY
100 Nott Ter (12308)
Rates: $69-$120;
Tel: (518) 393-4141

# SCHROON LAKE

## BLUE RIDGE MOTEL
RR 1, Box 321 (12870)
Rates: $36-$60;
Tel: (518) 532-7521

## DUN ROAMIN CABINS
Rt 9, P. O. Box 535 (12870)
Rates: N/A;
Tel: (518) 532-7277

# SIDNEY

## COUNTRY MOTEL
Rt 7, 2 Mi E of Rt 8 (13838)
Rates: N/A;
Tel. (607) 563-1035

# SKANEATELES

## HI-WAY HOST MOTEL
834 W Genesee St (13152)
Rates: $45-$52;
Tel: (315) 685-7633

# SMITHTOWN

## SHERATON HOTEL
110 Vanderbilt Motor Pkwy (11787)
Rates: $109-$300;
Tel: (516) 231-1100

## SOUTHAMPTON

**COLD SPRING BAY RESORT**
Country Rd 39 (11968)
Rates: $90-$395;
Tel: (516) 283-7600

## SPRING VALLEY

**ECONO LODGE**
Rt 59 (10977)
Rates: $54-$59;
Tel: (914) 623-3838

## STAMFORD

**RED CARPET MOTOR INN**
At Jct NY 10 & NY 23 (12167)
Rates: $48-$85;
Tel: (607) 652-7394

## SUFFERN

**WELLESLEY INN**
17 N Airmont Rd (10901)
Rates: $48-$60;
Tel: (914) 368-1900

## SYRACUSE

**ARBORGATE INN**
430 Electronics Pkwy
(Liverpool 13088)
Rates: $41-$58;
Tel: (315) 453-6330

**BEST WESTERN
SYRACUSE AIRPORT INN**
Hancock Airport
(No Syracuse 13212)
Rates: $69-$91;
Tel: (315) 455-7362

**DAYS INN AT THE DINKLER**
1100 James & Sidgwick Sts
(13203)
Rates: $50-$70;
Tel: (315) 472-6961

**DAYS INN-NORTH**
400 7th North St
(Liverpool 13088)
Rates: $62-$93;
Tel: (315) 451-1511

**DAYS INN SYRACUSE EAST**
6609 Thompson Rd (13206)
Rates: $43-$58;
Tel: (315) 437-5998

**ECONO LODGE
SYRACUSE NORTH**
401-407 7th North St
(Liverpool 13088)
Rates: $54-$55;
Tel: (315) 451-6000

**EMBASSY SUITES**
6646 Old Collamer Rd
(E Syracuse 13057)
Rates: $99;
Tel: (315) 446-3200

**GENESEE INN
EXECUTIVE QUARTERS**
1060 E Genesee St (13210)
Rates: $79-$99;
Tel: (315) 476-4212

**HAMPTON INN**
6605 Old Collamer Rd
(E Syracuse 13057)
Rates: $53-$60;
Tel: (315) 463-6443

**HOLIDAY INN EAST-EXIT
35-CARRIER CIRCLE**
College Dr & Court St (13057)
Rates: $80-$85;
Tel: (315) 437-2761

**HOLIDAY INN-EXIT 39-
FAIRGROUNDS AREA**
State Fair Blvd & Farrell Rd
(13209)
Rates: $52-$73;
Tel: (315) 457-8700

**HOLIDAY INN
NORTH-EXIT 36**
6701 Buckley Rd
(N Syracuse 13212)
Rates: $80-$85;
Tel: (315) 457-4000

**HOLIDAY INN-
UNIVERSITY AREA**
701 E Genesee (13210)
Rates: $73-$175;
Tel: (315) 474-7251

**HOWARD JOHNSON
LODGE**
Thompson Rd & Carrier Cir
(13206)
Rates: $52-$85;
Tel: (315) 437-2711

**JOHN MILTON INN**
Exit 35 Carrier Cir (13206)
Rates: $35-$60;
Tel: (315) 463-8555

**MARRIOTT HOTEL**
6302 Carrier Pkwy
(East Syracuse 13057)
Rates: $122-$275;
Tel: (315) 432-0200

**MOTEL 6**
6577 Court St Rd
(E Syracuse 13057)
Rates: $45-$55;
Tel: (315) 433-1300

**RED CARPET INN**
6590 Thompson Rd (13206)
Rates: $36-$65;
Tel: (315) 463-0202

**RED ROOF INN**
6614 N Thompson Rd (13206)
Rates: $29-$55;
Tel: (800) 843-7663

**RESIDENCE INN
BY MARRIOTT**
6420 Yorktown Cir
(E Syracuse 13057)
Rates: $74-$140;
Tel: (315) 432-4488

**SHERATON INN SYRACUSE**
441 Electronics Pkwy
(Liverpool 13088)
Rates: $83-$130;
Tel: (315) 457-1122

**SYRACUSE
MARRIOTT HOTEL**
6302 Carrier Pkwy (13057)
Rates: $79-$124;
Tel: (315) 432-0200

## TICONDEROGA

**CIRCLE COURT MOTEL**
440 Montcalm St (12883)
Rates: $36-$59;
Tel: (518) 585-7660

**RANCH HOUSE
AT BALDWIN**
RR 1, 79 Baldwin Rd (12883)
Rates: $69;
Tel: (518) 585-6596

## TULLY

**BEST WESTERN
MARSHALL MANOR**
P.O. Box 156 (13159)
Rates: $44-$70;
Tel: (315) 696-6061

## TUPPER LAKE

**PINE TERRACE
MOTEL & TENNIS CLUB**
Moody Rd (12986)
Rates: $42-$450;
Tel: (518) 359-9258

**SUNSET PARK MOTEL**
De Mars Blvd (12986)
Rates: $44-56;
Tel: (518) 359-3995

## UTICA

**BEST WESTERN GATEWAY
ADIRONDACK MOTOR INN**
175 N Genesee St (13502)
Rates: $56-$88;
Tel: (315) 732-4121

**HAPPY JOURNEY MOTEL**
300 N Genesee St (13502)
Rates: $27-$41;
Tel: (315) 738-1959

**HOLIDAY INN UTICA**
1777 Burrstone Rd
(New Hartford 13413)
Rates: $85-$99;
Tel: (315) 797-2131

**HOWARD JOHNSON
LODGE**
302 N Genesee St (13502)
Rates: $39-$95;
Tel: (315) 724-4141

**MOTEL 6**
150 N Genesee St (13502)
Rates: $31-$37;
Tel: (315) 797-8743

**RADISSON HOTEL-
UTICA CENTRE**
200 Genesee St (13502)
Rates: $86-$109
Tel: (315) 797-8010

**RED ROOF INN**
20 Weaver St (13502)
Rates: $36-$60;
Tel: (800) 843-7663

**UTICA TRAVELODGE**
1700 Genesee St (13502)
Rates: $47-$59;
Tel: (315) 724-2101

## VICTOR

**CRAWSHAW'S MOTEL**
6001 Rt 96
(Farmington 14425)
Rates: $30-$40;
Tel: (716) 924-5020

## WADDINGTON

**RIVERVIEW OF
WADDINGTON
MOTEL & COTTAGES**
RR 1, Box 14 (13694)
Rates: $38-$45;
Tel: (315) 388-5912

## WARSAW

**MINI MART MOTEL**
3490 Rt 20A (14569)
Rates: N/A;
Tel: (716) 786-2685

## WATERLOO

**HOLIDAY INN
WATERLOO-SENECA FALLS**
P. O. Box 149 (13165)
Rates: $59-$85;
Tel: (315) 539-5011

## WATERTOWN

**ECONO LODGE**
1030 Arsenal St (13601)
Rates: $45-$69;
Tel: (315) 782-5500

**MICROTEL**
8000 Virginia Smith Dr
(Calcium 13616)
Rates: $32-$36;
Tel: (315) 629-5000

**NEW PARROT MOTEL**
5791 Outer Washington St
(13601)
Rates: $30-$52;
Tel: (315) 788-5080

**QUALITY INN**
1190 Arsenal St (13601)
Rates: $48-$72;
Tel: (315) 788-6800

**RAINBOW MOTEL**
RD 6 Bradley St, Box 20
(13601)
Rates: N/A;
Tel: (315) 788-2830

## WATKINS GLEN

**CHIEFTIAN MOTEL**
3815 State Rt 14 (14891)
Rates: N/A;
Tel: (607) 535-4759

**FALLS MOTEL**
P. O. Box 681
(Montour Falls 14865)
Rates: $30-$49;
Tel: (607) 535-7262

**QUEEN CATHERINE MOTEL**
436 S Franklin St (14891)
Rates: N/A;
Tel: (607) 535-2517

## WAVERLY

**O'BRIENS INN**
P. O. Box 108 (14892)
Rates: $38-$58;
Tel: (607) 565-2817

## WEEDSPORT

**BEST WESTERN
WEEDSPORT**
2709 Erie Dr (13166)
Rates: $39-$75;
Tel: (315) 834-6623

**PORT 40 MOTEL**
9050 Rt 24 (13166)
Rates: $30-$66;
Tel: (315) 834-6198

## WESTBURY

**HOLIDAY INN**
369 Old Country Rd
(Carle Place 11514)
Rates: $109-$125;
Tel: (516) 997-5000

**ISLAND INN**
Old Country Rd (11590)
Rates: $99-$400;
Tel: (516) 228-9500

## WESTMORELAND

**CARRIAGE MOTOR INN**
P. O. Box 379 (13490)
Rates: $29-$42;
Tel: (315) 853-3561

## WEST POINT

**BEST WESTERN
PALISADE MOTEL**
SR 218 (Highland Falls 10928)
Rates: $60-$75;
Tel: (914) 446-9400

## WHITE PLAINS

**LA RESERVE SUITES**
5 Barker Ave (10601)
Rates: $90-$200;
Tel: (914) 761-7700

## WILMINGTON

**HIGH VALLEY MOTEL**
HCR 2, Box 13 (12997)
Rates: $40-$61;
Tel: (518) 946-2355

**HOLIDAY LODGE**
P. O. Box 38 (12997)
Rates: $39-$89;
Tel: (518) 946-2251

**HUNGRY TROUT
MOTOR INN**
2 Mi W on Rt 86 (12997)
Rates: $49-$79;
Tel: (518) 946-2217

**LEDGE ROCK MOTEL**
HCR 2, Box 34 (12997)
Rates: $39-$93;
Tel: (518) 946-2302

**WINKELMAN MOTEL**
E of Jct NY 86 (12997)
Rates: $48-$56;
Tel: (518) 946-7761

## WOODBURY

**QUALITY INN**
7758 Jericho Tpk (11797)
Rates: $65-$100;
Tel: (516) 921-6900

# NORTH CAROLINA

## ABERDEEN

**BEST WESTERN
PINEHURST MOTOR INN**
1500 Sandhills Blvd (28315)
Rates: $33-$44;
Tel: (919) 944-2367

**SUPER 8 MOTEL**
1408 N Sandhills Blvd (28315)
Rates: $32-$44;
Tel: (919) 944-5633

## ASHEVILLE

**DAYS INN DOWNTOWN**
120 Patton Ave (28801)
Rates: $35-$65;
Tel: (704) 254-9661

**DAYS INN-EAST**
1500 Tunnel Rd (28805)
Rates: $31-$58;
Tel: (704) 298-5140

**ECONO LODGE BILTMORE**
190 Tunnel Rd (28805)
Rates: $30-$60;
Tel: (704) 254-9521

**RED ROOF INN-WEST**
16 Crowell Rd (28806)
Rates: $28-$52;
Tel: (704) 667-9803

## ATLANTIC BEACH

**ATLANTIS LODGE**
P. O. Box 310 (28512)
Rates: $45-$110;
Tel: (919) 726-5168

## BANNER ELK

**HOLIDAY INN/
ELK-BEECH MTN**
P. O. Box 1478 (28604)
Rates: $49-$95;
Tel: (704) 898-4571

## BURLINGTON

**TRAVELODGE**
2155 Hanford Rd (27215)
Rates: $34-$38;
Tel: (919) 226-1325

# CASHIERS

**LAURELWOOD
MOUNTAIN INN**
P. O. Box 188 (28717)
Rates: $37 $59;
Tel: (704) 743-9939

# CHAPEL HILL

**HAMPTON INN**
1740 US 15-501 (27514)
Rates: $39-$53;
Tel: (919) 968-3000

**HOLIDAY INN**
1301 N Fordham Blvd (27514)
Rates: $50 $80;
Tel: (919) 929 2171

**RED ROOF INN**
5623 Chapel Hill Blvd
(Durham 27707)
Rates: $30-$46;
Tel: (919) 489-9421

# CHARLOTTE
(and Vicinity)

**BEST WESTERN
MOTOR LODGE**
P. O Box 397
(Fort Mill, SC 28217)
Rates: $39-$49;
Tel: (803) 548-8000

**BRADLEY MOTEL**
4200 I-85S (28214)
Rates: $27-$36;
Tel: (704) 392-3206

**CHARLOTTE HILTON
AT UNIVERSITY PLACE**
8629 J M Keynes Dr (28262)
Rates: $69-$95;
Tel: (704) 547-7444

**CRICKET INN COLISEUM**
219 Archdale Dr (28217)
Rates: $32-$38;
Tel: (704) 527-8500

**HOLIDAY INN CENTER CITY**
230 N College St (28202)
Rates: $75-$125;
Tel: (704) 335-5400

**HOLIDAY INN I-85 NORTH**
5301 I-85N (28213)
Rates: $55-$68;
Tel: (704) 596-9390

**HOMEWOOD SUITES
CHARLOTTE-
AIRPORT/COLISEUM**
4920 S Tryon St (28217)
Rates: $90;
Tel: (704) 525-2600

**HOMEWOOD SUITES-
UNIVERSITY RESEARCH PARK**
8340 N Tryon St (28262)
Rates: $59-$139;
Tel: (704) 549-8800

**HOWARD JOHNSON
MOTOR LODGE COLISEUM**
118 E Woodlawn Rd (28217)
Rates: $39-$44;
Tel. (704) 525-6220

**HYATT CHARLOTTE
AT SOUTH PARK**
5501 Carnegie Blvd (28209)
Rates: $125-$150;
Tel: (704) 554-1234

**LA QUINTA
MOTOR INN-AIRPORT**
3100 I085S Service Rd
(28208)
Rates: $38 $52,
Tel: (704) 393-5306

**LA QUINTA SOUTH**
7900 Nations Ford Rd (20217)
Rates: $40-$57;
Tel: (704) 522-7110

**THE PARK HOTEL**
2200 Rexford Rd (28211)
Rates: $69-$135;
Tel: (704) 364-8220

**RED ROOF INN-AIRPORT**
3300 I-85S Service Rd
(28208)
Rates: $33-$43;
Tel: (704) 392-2316

**RED ROOF INN
AT UNIVERSITY**
5116 I-85N (28206)
Rates: $28;
Tel: (704) 596-8222

**RED ROOF INN COLISEUM**
131 Greenwood Dr (28217)
Rates: $30-$39;
Tel: (704) 529-1020

**THE REGISTRY HOTEL**
321 W Woodlawn Rd (28217)
Rates: $59-$95;
Tel: (704) 525-4441

**RESIDENCE INN/
MARRIOTT-TYVOLA
EXEC PARK**
5800 W Park Dr (28217)
Rates: $78-$95;
Tel: (704) 527-8110

**SHERATON
AIRPORT PLAZA HOTEL**
3315 I 85S at Billy Graham
Pkwy (28208)
Rates: $75-$109;
Tel: (704) 392-1200

**VILLAGER LODGE**
7901 Nations Ford Rd (28217)
Rates: $28-$38;
Tel: (704) 522-0364

**WINDHAM GARDEN
HOTEL**
4200 Wilmount Rd (28208)
Rates: $39-$104;
Tel: (704) 357 9100

**YORKSHIRE INN**
9900 York Rd (28273)
Rates: $31-$40;
Tel: (704) 588-3949

# CORNELIUS

**HOLIDAY INN
LAKE NORMAN**
P. O. Box 1278 (28031)
Rates: $54-$58;
Tel: (704) 892-9120

# DUNN

**ECONO LODGE**
I-95 & Pope Rd (28334)
Rates: $29-$49;
Tel: (919) 892-6181

**RAMADA INN**
P. O. Box 729 (28334)
Rates: $54-$65;
Tel: (919) 892-8101

# DURHAM

**BEST WESTERN
SKYLAND INN**
Rt 2, Box 560 (27705)
Rates: $35-$49;
Tel: (919) 383-2508

**CAROLINA DUKE
MOTOR INN**
2517 Guess Rd (27705)
Rates: $26-$34;
Tel: (919) 286-0771

**DAYS INN**
I-85 & Redwood Rd (27704)
Rates: $27-$39;
Tel: (919) 688-4338

**HAMPTON INN**
1816 Hillandale Rd (27705)
Rates: $40-$50;
Tel: (919) 471-6100

**HOLIDAY INN RALEIGH-
DURHAM AIRPORT**
P. O. Box 13816
(Research Triangle Park 27709)
Rates: $59-$109;
Tel: (919) 941-6000

**RED ROOF INN**
5623 Chapel Hill Blvd (27707)
Rates: N/A;
Tel: (919) 489-9421

**RED ROOF INN**
2000 I-85 Service Rd (27705)
Rates: N/A;
Tel: (919) 471-9882

**RED ROOF INN
RESEARCH TRIANGLE PARK**
4405 Hwy 55E (27713)
Rates: $29-$38;
Tel: (919) 361-1950

**SHERATON INN
UNIVERSITY CENTER**
2800 Middleton Ave (27705)
Rates: $39;
Tel: (919) 383-8575

**TRAVEL TIME INN**
4516 Chapel Hill Blvd (27707)
Rates: $26-$32;
Tel: (919) 489-9146

# FAYETTEVILLE

**COMFORT INN
CROSS CREEK**
1922 Skibo Rd (28314)
Rates: $44-$54;
Tel: (919) 867-1777

**COMFORT INN I-95**
Rt 9, Box 499C (28302)
Rates: $38-$42;
Tel: (919) 323-8333

**DAYS INN
FAYETTEVILLE-NORTH**
Rt 1, Box 216BB
(Wade 28395)
Rates: $29-$44;
Tel: (919) 323-1255

# GASTONIA

**DAYS INN
GASTONIA-CHARLOTTE**
1700 N Chester St (28052)
Rates: $29-$36;
Tel: (704) 864-9981

**KNIGHTS INN**
1721 Broadcast St (28052)
Rates: $32-$39;
Tel: (704) 868-4900

# GLENDALE SPRINGS

**MOUNTAIN VIEW
LODGE AND CABINS**
P. O. Box 90 (28629)
Rates: $44;
Tel: (919) 982-2233

# GOLD ROCK

**DAYS INN ROCKY MOUNT**
Rt 1, Box 166
(Battleboro 27809)
Rates: $28-$50;
Tel: (919) 446-0621

**ECONO LODGE**
Rt 1, Box 161B
(Battleboro 27809)
Rates: $36-$43;
Tel: (919) 446-2411

# GREENSBORO

**RAMADA INN-AIRPORT**
7067 Albert Pick Rd (27409)
Rates: $49-$55;
Tel: (919) 668-3900

**RED ROOF INN-COLISEUM**
2101 W Meadowview Rd
(27403)
Rates: $29-$55;
Tel: (919) 852-6560

**RED ROOF INN
GREENSBORO-
HIGH POINT**
615 Regional Rd S (27409)
Rates: $29-$41;
Tel: (919) 271-2636

# HENDERSONVILLE

**COMFORT INN**
206 Mitchell Dr (28739)
Rates: $39-$89;
Tel: (704) 693-8800

# HICKORY

**HOWARD JOHNSON
LODGE**
P. O. Box 129 (28601)
Rates: $38-$56;
Tel: (704) 322-1600

**RED ROOF INN**
1184 Lenoir Rhyne Blvd
(28602)
Rates: $26-$39;
Tel: (704) 323-1500

# HIGH POINT

**HOLIDAY INN
MARKET SQUARE**
236 S Main St (27260)
Rates: $53-$135;
Tel: (919) 886-7011

# JACKSONVILLE

**ONSLOW INN**
201 Marine Blvd (28540)
Rates: $37-$41;
Tel: (919) 347-3151

## JONESVILLE

**COUNTRY INN**
Rt 1, Box 266 (28642)
Rates: $21-$28;
Tel: (919) 835-2261

**SCOTTISH INN**
Exit 79 Off I-77 (28642)
Rates: N/A;
Tel: (919) 835-1461

## MARION

**ECONO LODGE**
Rt 1, Box 68A (28752)
Rates: $33-$39;
Tel: (704) 659-7940

## MOCKSVILLE

**COMFORT INN**
1500 Yadkinville Rd (27028)
Rates: $40-$51;
Tel: (704) 634-7310

## MORGANTON

**HOLIDAY INN**
2400 S Sterling St (28655)
Rates: $44-$54;
Tel: (704) 437-0171

## NAGS HEAD

**RAMADA INN
AT NAGS HEAD BEACH**
P. O. Box 2716
(Kill Devil Hills 27948)
Rates: $43-$135;
Tel: (919) 441-2151

## NEW BERN

**DAYS INN**
925 Broad St (28560)
Rates: $49-$56;
Tel: (919) 636-0150

## RALEIGH

**BEST WESTERN
HOSPITALITY INN**
2800 Brentwood Rd (27604)
Rates: $34-$49;
Tel: (919) 872-8600

**BUDGETEL INN**
1001 Aerial Center Pkwy
(Morrisville 27560)
Rates: $34-$50;
Tel: (919) 481-3600

**HAMPTON INN-
NORTH RALEIGH**
1001 Wake Towne Dr (27609)
Rates: $39-$59;
Tel: (919) 828-1813

**HOWARD JOHNSON-
CRABTREE PLAZA**
4100 Glenwood Ave (27612)
Rates: $49-$64;
Tel: (919) 782-8600

**THE PLANTATION INN
RESORT**
6401 Capital Blvd (27604)
Rates: $39-$44;
Tel: (919) 876-1411

**RED ROOF INN**
3520 Maitland Dr (27610)
Rates: N/A;
Tel: (919) 231-0200

**RESIDENCE INN
BY MARRIOTT**
1000 Navaho Dr (27609)
Rates: $69-$125;
Tel: (919) 878-6100

**VELVET CLOAK INN**
1505 Hillsborough St (27605)
Rates: $59-$99;
Tel: (919) 828-0333

## ROANOKE RAPIDS

**COMFORT INN**
1911 Weldon Rd (27870)
Rates: $32-$47;
Tel: (919) 537-5252

**ECONO LODGE**
1615 Roanoke Rapids Rd
(Weldon 27890)
Rates: $35-$40;
Tel: (919) 536-2131

**HOLIDAY INN**
100 Holiday Dr (27870)
Rates: $53-$62;
Tel: (919) 537-1031

## ROCKY MOUNT

**COMFORT INN
GATEWAY CENTER**
P. O. Box 8093 (27804)
Rates: $46-$62;
Tel: (919) 937-7765

## SALISBURY

**DAYS INN**
1810 Lutheran Synod Dr
(28144)
Rates: $33-$50;
Tel: (704) 633-4211

## SMITHFIELD

**LOG CABIN MOTEL**
Rt 2, Box 447 (27577)
Rates: $37-$47;
Tel: (919) 934-1534

## SOUTHERN PINES

**DAYS INN**
1420 US 1 S (28387)
Rates: $44-$48;
Tel: (919) 692-7581

## STATESVILLE

**COMFORT INN**
1214 Monroe St (28677)
Rates: $37-$47;
Tel: (704) 873-2044

**ECONO LODGE**
725 Sullivan Rd (28677)
Rates: $29-$36;
Tel: (704) 873-5236

**HOWARD JOHNSON
LODGE**
1209 Monroe St (28677)
Rates: $48-$53;
Tel: (704) 878-9691

**RED ROOF INN**
1508 E Broad St (28677)
Rates: $31-$41;
Tel: (704) 878-2051

## WILLIAMSTON

**HOLIDAY INN**
Jct Hwys 64 & 17 (27892)
Rates: $38-$52;
Tel: (919) 792-3184

## WILMINGTON

**HOLIDAY INN
OF WILMINGTON**
4903 Market St (28405)
Rates: $35-$60;
Tel: (919) 799-1440

**WATERWAY LODGE**
7246 Wrightsville Ave
(28403)
Rates: $55-$90;
Tel: (800) 677-3771

## WILSON

**QUALITY INN SOUTH**
Hwy 301S (27893)
Rates: $36-$46;
Tel: (919) 243-5165

## WINSTON-SALEM

**BEST WESTERN
REGENCY INN**
128 N Cherry St (27101)
Rates: $49-$88;
Tel: (919) 723-8861

**RESIDENCE INN
BY MARRIOTT**
7835 N Point Blvd (27106)
Rates: $86-$106;
Tel: (919) 759-0777

# NORTH DAKOTA

## BEACH

**BUCKBOARD INN**
HC2 Box 109A (58621)
Rates: $27-$31;
Tel: (701) 872-4794

## BISMARCK

**BEST WESTERN
DOUBLEWOOD INN**
1400 E Interchange Ave
(58501)
Rates: $54-$60;
Tel: (701) 258-7000

**BEST WESTERN
FLECK HOUSE MOTEL**
P. O. Box 2617 (58502)
Rates: $34-$48;
Tel: (701) 255-1450

**BEST WESTERN
SEVEN SEAS INN**
P. O. Box 1316
(Mandan 58554)
Rates: $46-$56;
Tel: (701) 663-7401

**BISMARCK MOTOR HOTEL**
P. O. Box 1724 (58502)
Rates: $20-$32;
Tel: (701) 223-2474

**EXPRESSWAY INN**
200 Bismarck Expwy (58504)
Rates: $27-$39;
Tel: (701) 222-2900

**HOLIDAY INN
HOTEL BISMARCK**
605 E Broadway (58502)
Rates: $49-$64;
Tel: (701) 255-6000

**KELLY INN**
1800 N 12th St (58501)
Rates: $42-$53;
Tel: (701) 233-8001

**RADISSON INN BISMARCK**
800 S 3rd St (58504)
Rates: $58-$88;
Tel: (701) 258-7700

**SELECT INN**
1505 Interchange Ave (58501)
Rates: $25-$33;
Tel: (701) 223-8060

**SUPER 8 MOTEL**
1124 E Capitol Ave (58501)
Rates: $35-$48;
Tel: (701) 255-1314

## BOTTINEAU

**TURTLE MOUNTAIN LODGE**
P. O. Box 165 (58318)
Rates: $29-$58;
Tel: (800) 998-2375

## BOWMAN

**BUDGET HOST 4U MOTEL**
P. O. Box 590 (58623)
Rates: $23-$41;
Tel. (701) 523-3243

**EL VU MOTEL**
Hwy 12 & 85 (58623)
Rates: N/A;
Tel: (800) 521-0379

**NORTH WINDS LODGE**
P. O. Box 346 (58623)
Rates: $23-$36;
Tel: (701) 523-5641

**SUPER 8 MOTEL**
P. O. Box 675 (58623)
Rates: $28-$43;
Tel: (701) 523-5613

## CARRINGTON

**CHIEFTAIN MOTOR LODGE**
Hwy 281 (58421)
Rates: $26-$38;
Tel: (701) 652-3131

## DEVILS LAKE

**COMFORT INN**
215 Hwy 2 E (58301)
Rates: $29-$34;
Tel: (701) 662-6760

**DAYS INN DEVILS LAKE**
Rt 5, Box 8 (58301)
Rates: $32-$39;
Tel: (701) 662-5381

**SUPER 8 MOTEL**
US 2 Just E of town (58301)
Rates: $27-$35;
Tel: (701) 662-8656

**TRAILS WEST MOTEL**
P. O. Box 1113 (58301)
Rates: $24-$30;
Tel: (701) 662-5011

## DICKINSON

**BUDGET INN**
529 12th St W (58601)
Rates: $19-$32;
Tel: (701) 225-9123

**COMFORT INN**
493 Elk Dr (58601)
Rates: $22-$39;
Tel: (701) 264-7300

**FRIENDSHIP INN**
1000 W Villard St (58601)
Rates: $24-$40;
Tel: (701) 225-6703

**HOSPITALITY INN
& CONVENTION CENTER**
P. O. Box 1778 (58602)
Rates: $38-$80;
Tel: (701) 227-1853

**SELECT INN**
642 12 St W (58601)
Rates: $21-$34;
Tel: (701) 227 1891

**SUPER 8 MOTEL**
637 12 St W (58601)
Rates: $20-$40;
Tel: (800) 800-8000

## FARGO

**AMERICINN MOTEL**
1421 35th St SW (58103)
Rates: $37-$53;
Tel: (701) 234-9946

**COMFORT INN EAST**
1407 35th St S (58103)
Rates: $36-$49;
Tel: (701) 280-9666

**COMFORT INN WEST**
3825 9th Ave SW (58103)
Rates: $41-$61;
Tel: (701) 282-9596

**COMFORT SUITES**
1415 35th St S (58103)
Rates: $45-$60;
Tel: (701) 237-5911

**COUNTRY SUITES
BY CARLSON**
3316 13th Ave S (58103)
Rates: $62-$135;
Tel: (701) 234-0565

**DAYS INN**
901 38th St SW (58103)
Rates: $39-$60;
Tel: (701) 282-9100

**ECONO LODGE OF FARGO**
1401 35th St S (58103)
Rates: $30-$34;
Tel: (701) 232-3412

**FAIRFIELD INN**
3902 9th Ave (58103)
Rates: $37-$63;
Tel: (701) 281-0494

**HOLIDAY INN**
P. O. Box 9555 (58106)
Rates: $63-$125;
Tel: (701) 282-2700

**KELLY INN**
3800 Main Ave (58103)
Rates: $44-$64;
Tel. (701) 282-2143

**MOTEL 75**
3402 14th Ave S (58103)
Rates: $28-$38;
Tel: (701) 232-1321

**RADISSON HOTEL FARGO**
201 5th St N (58102)
Rates: $84-$104;
Tel: (701) 232-7363

**SELECT INN**
1025 38th St SW (58103)
Rates: $27-$35;
Tel: (701) 282-6300

**SUPER 8 MOTEL**
3518 Interstate Blvd (58103)
Rates: $27-$45;
Tel: (701) 232-9202

## GARRISON

**GARRISON MOTEL**
P. O. Box 999 (58540)
Rates: $23-$29;
Tel: (701) 463-2858

## GRAFTON

**LEONARD MOTEL**
Hwy 17 West (58237)
Rates: N/A;
Tel: (701) 352-1730

## GRAND FORKS

**BEST WESTERN FABULOUS
WESTWARD HO MOTEL**
Hwy 2 West (58206)
Rates: N/A;
Tel: (701) 775-5341

**BEST WESTERN
TOWN HOUSE**
P. O. Box 309 (58203)
Rates: $53-$70;
Tel: (701) 746-5411

**COMFORT INN**
3251 30th Ave S (58201)
Rates: $39-$65;
Tel: (701) 775-7503

**DAYS INN**
3101 34th St S (58201)
Rates: $35-$69;
Tel: (701) 775-0060

**FAIRFIELD INN
BY MARRIOTT**
3051 S 34th St (58201)
Rates: $39-$60;
Tel: (701) 775-7910

**RAMADA INN**
P. O. Box 1757 (58203)
Rates: $54-$78;
Tel: (701) 775-3951

**ROADKING INN**
1015 N 43rd St (58203)
Rates: $32-$44;
Tel: (701) 775-0691

**ROADKING INN-
COLUMBIA MALL**
3300 30th Ave S (58201)
Rates: $35-$51;
Tel: (701) 746-1391

**SELECT INN**
1000 N 42nd St (58203)
Rates: $25-$39;
Tel: (701) 775-0555

## JAMESTOWN

**COMFORT INN**
811 20 St SW (58401)
Rates: $36-$49;
Tel: (701) 252-7125

**DAKOTA INN**
P. O. Box 1865 (58401)
Rates: $38-$50;
Tel: (701) 252-3611

**GLADSTONE
SELECT HOTEL**
P. O. Box 989 (58402)
Rates: $31-$55;
Tel: (701) 252-0700

**RANCH HOUSE MOTEL**
408 Business Loop W (58401)
Rates: $26-$36;
Tel: (701) 252-0222

**STAR LITE MOTEL**
1610 Business Loop E (58401)
Rates: N/A;
Tel: (701) 252-5111

## LAKOTA

**SUNLAC INN**
P. O. Box 648 (58344)
Rates: $23-$29;
Tel: (701) 247-2487

## LANGDON

**LANGDON MOTOR INN**
210 Ninth Ave (58249)
Rates: $26-$34;
Tel: (701) 256-3600

## MINOT

**BEST WESTERN
INTERNATIONAL INN**
1505 N Broadway (58701)
Rates: $40-$69;
Tel: (701) 852-3161

**BEST WESTERN
SAFARI INN**
1510 26th Ave SW (58701)
Rates: $39-$75;
Tel: (701) 852-4300

**CASA MOTEL**
1900 US 2 & 52 bypass
(58701)
Rates: $21-$32;
Tel: (701) 852-2352

**COMFORT INN**
1515 22nd Ave SW (58701)
Rates: $34-$64;
Tel: (701) 852-2201

**DAYS INN**
2100 4th ST SW (58701)
Rates: $34-$55;
Tel: (701) 852-3646

**FAIRFIELD INN BY
MARRIOTT**
900 24 Ave SW (58701)
Rates: $37-$68;
Tel: (701) 838-2424

**HOLIDAY INN**
P. O. Box 1236 (58702)
Rates: $61-$71;
Tel: (701) 852-4161

**SELECT INN**
P. O. Box 460 (58702)
Rates: $26-$36;
Tel: (701) 852-3411

## PARSHALL

**PARSHALL MOTOR INN**
North Main St Box 38 (58770)
Rates: N/A;
Tel: (701) 862-3127

## ROLLA

**NORTHERN LIGHTS**
Hwy 5 East (58367)
Rates: N/A;
Tel: (701) 477-6164

**T & M HOTEL**
223 Main Ave E (58367)
Rates: N/A;
Tel: (701) 477-3101

## RUGBY

**ECONO LODGE**
P. O. Box 346 (58368)
Rates: $36-$54;
Tel: (701) 776-5776

## STEELE

**LONE STEER MOTEL**
I-94 Hwy #3 (58482)
Rates: N/A;
Tel: (701) 475-2221

**O K MOTEL**
301 3rd Ave Northeast
(58482)
Rates: N/A;
Tel: (701) 475-2440

## VALLEY CITY

**WAGON WHEEL INN**
930 4th Ave SW (58072)
Rates: $21-$35;
Tel: (701) 845-5333

## WAHPETON

**COMFORT INN**
209 13th St S (58075)
Rates: $34-$43;
Tel: (701) 642-1115

**WAHPETON SUPER 8**
995 21st Ave N (58075)
Rates: $33-$43;
Tel: (701) 642-8731

## WESTHOPE

**GATEWAY INN**
P. O. Box 385 (58793)
Rates: $32-$37;
Tel: (701) 245-6441

## WILLISTON

**AIRPORT
INTERNATIONAL INN**
P. O. Box 1800 (58802)
Rates: $38-$70;
Tel: (701) 774-0241

**EL RANCHO
MOTOR HOTEL**
P. O. Box 4277 (58802)
Rates: $31-$36;
Tel: (701) 572-6321

**SELECT INN**
213 35th St W & Hwy 2N
(58801)
Rates: $29-$37;
Tel: (701) 572-4242

**SUPER 8 LODGE**
P. O. Box 907 (58801)
Rates: $21-$37;
Tel: (701) 572-8371

**TRAVEL HOST MOTEL**
3801 2nd Ave West (58801)
Rates: N/A;
Tel: (701) 774-0041

# OHIO

## AKRON

**CASCADE PLAZA HOTEL**
5 Cascade Plaza (44308)
Rates: $66-$84;
Tel: (216) 762-0661

**KNIGHTS INN-
AKRON SOUTH**
3237 S Arlington Rd (44312)
Rates: $36-$44;
Tel: (216) 644-1204

**RED ROOF INN**
2939 S Arlington Rd (44312)
Rates: $32-$48;
Tel: (216) 644-7748

**RED ROOF INN**
99 Rothrock Rd (44321)
Rates: $32-$42;
Tel: (216) 666-0566

**THE RESIDENCE INN
BY MARRIOTT**
120 W Montrose Ave (44321)
Rates: $95-$125;
Tel: (216) 666-4811

## ALLIANCE

**COMFORT INN**
2500 W State St (44601)
Rates: $47-$59;
Tel: (216) 821-5555

## AMHERST

**TRAVELODGE**
934 N Leavitt Rd (44001)
Rates: $35-$57;
Tel: (216) 985-1428

## ASHTABULA

**CEDARS MOTEL**
2015 W Prospect Rd (44004)
Rates: $35-$45;
Tel: (216) 992-5406

**HO HUM MOTEL**
3801 N Ridge West (44004)
Rates: $35-$45;
Tel: (216) 969-1136

**TRAVELODGE**
8 Mi SW/jct OH 45
(Austinburg 44010)
Rates: $45-$64;
Tel: (216) 275-2011

## ATHENS

**BUDGET HOST-
COACH INN**
1000 Albany Rd (45701)
Rates: $28-$50;
Tel: (614) 594-2294

**THE OHIO
UNIVERSITY INN**
331 Richland Ave (45701)
Rates: $57-$76;
Tel: (614) 593-6661

## AURORA

**THE AURORA INN**
P. O. Box 197 (44202)
Rates: $74-$135;
Tel: (216) 562-6121

## BELLEFONTAINE

**COMFORT INN**
260 Northview (43311)
Rates: $48-$62;
Tel: (513) 599-6666

**HOLIDAY INN**
1134 N Main St (43311)
Rates: $51-$62;
Tel: (513) 593-8515

**L-K MOTEL**
308 North Main St (43311)
Rates: N/A;
Tel: (513) 593-1015

## BOWLING GREEN

**BUCKEYE BUDGET
MOTOR INN**
1740 E Wooster St (43402)
Rates: $36-$41;
Tel: (419) 352-1520

**DAYS INN**
1550 E Wooster St (43402)
Rates: $47-$68;
Tel: (419) 352-5211

**HOLLY LODGE**
1630 E Wooster St (43042)
Rates: $40-$59;
Tel: (419) 352-2521

## BURBANK

**MOTEL PLAZA**
Rt 1, Box 8 (44214)
Rates: $27-$32;
Tel: (216) 624-3012

## CAMBRIDGE

**BEST WESTERN
CAMBRIDGE**
1945 Southgate Pkwy (43725)
Rates: $29-$57;
Tel: (614) 439-3581

**DAYS INN-CAMBRIDGE**
2328 Southgate Pkwy (43725)
Rates: $37-$59;
Tel: (614) 432-5691

**DEER CREEK INN**
SR 209, exit 178 (43725)
Rates: $29-$35;
Tel: (614) 432-6391

**EL RANCHO MOTEL**
I-70 Exit 176 (43725)
Rates: N/A;
Tel: (614) 432-2373

**HOLIDAY INN**
P. O. Box 1270 (43725)
Rates: $53-$74;
Tel: (614) 432-7313

## CANTON

**BEST SUITES OF AMERICA**
4914 Everhard Rd (44718)
Rates: $53-$63;
Tel: (216) 499-1011

**HAMPTON INN**
5335 Broadmoor Circle
(44709)
Rates: $45-$53;
Tel: (216) 492-0151

**HILTON HOTEL**
320 Market Ave S (44702)
Rates: $73-$325;
Tel: (216) 454-5000

**HOLIDAY INN-
BELDEN VILLAGE**
4520 Everhard Rd NW
(44718)
Rates: $63-$83;
Tel: (216) 494-2770

**KNIGHTS INN-
CANTON NORTH**
3950 Convenience Cir NW
(44718)
Rates: $33-$42;
Tel: (216) 492-5030

**MOTEL 6**
6880 Sunset Strip Ave NW
(44720)
Rates: $26-$32;
Tel: (216) 494-7611

**RED ROOF INN**
5353 Inn Circle Ct NW
(44720)
Rates: $34-$47;
Tel: (216) 499-1970

**SHERATON INN
CANTON/BELDEN VILLAGE**
4375 Metro Cir NW (44720)
Rates: $69-$90;
Tel: (216) 494-6494

## CELINA

**COMFORT INN**
1421 SR East 703 (45822)
Rates: $39-$75;
Tel: (419) 586-4656

## CHILLICOTHE

**COMFORT INN**
20 N Plaza (45601)
Rates: $55-$60;
Tel: (614) 775-3500

**HOLIDAY INN**
1250 N Bridge St (45601)
Rates: $50-$70;
Tel: (614) 775-7000

**TRAVELODGE**
1135 E Main St (45601)
Rates: $36-$55;
Tel: (614) 775-2500

# CINCINNATI
(and Vicinity)

**BEST WESTERN
KINGS ISLAND**
9815 Mason-Montgomery Rd
(Mason 45040)
Rates: $26-$110;
Tel: (513) 398-3633

**BUDGETEL INN**
12150 Springfield Pike
(Springdale 45246)
Rates: $36-$52;
Tel: (513) 671-2300

**CAROUSEL INN**
8001 Reading Rd (45237)
Rates: N/A;
Tel: (513) 821 5110

**CINCINNATI MARRIOTT**
11320 Chester Rd (45246)
Rates: $69-$150;
Tel: (513) 772-1720

**CINCINNATI TERRACE
HILTON**
15 W 6th St (45202)
Rates: $99-$119;
Tel: (513) 381-4000

**THE CLARION HOTEL
CINCINNATI**
141 W 6th St (45202)
Rates: $91-$145;
Tel: (513) 352-2100

**DAYS INN CINCINNATI**
US 42, Exit 46 (45241)
Rates: $36-$99;
Tel: (513) 554-1400

**DAYS INN-
CINCINNATI EAST**
4056 Mt Carmel-Tobasco Rd
(45255)
Rates: $28-$69;
Tel: (513) 528-3800

**DAYS INN-
CINCINNATI/FT WRIGHT**
1945 Dixiey Hwy
(Ft Wright, KY 41011)
Rates: $32-$38;
Tel: (603) 341-8801

**DAYS INN KINGS ISLAND**
9735 Mason-Montgomery Rd
(Mason 45040)
Rates: $25-$110;
Tel: (513) 398-3297

**DAYS INN OF ERLANGER**
599 Donaldson Rd
(Erlanger, KY 41018)
Rates: $29-$36;
Tel: (606) 342-7111

**EMBASSY SUITES HOTEL-
CINCINNATI NE**
4554 Lake Forest Dr (45242)
Rates: $99-$119;
Tel: (513) 733-8900

**ENVOY INN-FLORENCE**
8076 Stellen Dr
(Florence, KY 41042)
Rates: $32-$40;
Tel: (606) 371-0277

**HAMPTON INN**
10900 Crowne Point Dr
(45241)
Rates: $59-$65;
Tel: (513) 771-6888

**HOLIDAY INN-
CINCINNATI EASTGATE**
4501 Eastgate Blvd (45245)
Rates: $65-$75;
Tel: (513) 752-4400

**HOLIDAY INN FLORENCE**
8050 US 42
(Florence, KY 41042)
Rates: $47-$74;
Tel: (606) 371-2700

**HOLIDAY INN
I-275 NORTH**
3855 Hauck Rd
(Sharonville 45241)
Rates: $85-$135;
Tel: (513) 563-8330

**HOLIDAY INN-NORTH**
2235 Sharon Rd (45241)
Rates: $79-$89;
Tel: (513) 771-0700

**HOLIDAY INN-NORTHEAST
KINGS ISLAND**
10561 Mason-Montgomery Rd
(Mason 45040)
Rates: $42-$89;
Tel: (513) 398-8015

**HOLIDAY INN-QUEENSGATE**
800 W 8th St (45203)
Rates: $79-$175;
Tel: (513) 241-8660

**HOLIDAY INN-RIVERFRONT**
600 W 3rd St
(Covington, KY 41011)
Rates: $65-$75;
Tel: (606) 291-4300

**HOLIDAY INN-SOUTH**
2100 Dixie Hwy
(Ft Mitchell, KY 41017)
Rates: $72-$82;
Tel: (606) 331-1500

**HOMEWOOD SUITES-
CINCINNATI NORTH**
2670 E Kemper Rd
(Sharonville 45241)
Rates: $80-$105;
Tel: (513) 772-8888

**KNIGHTS INN-
CINCINNATI SOUTH**
8049 Dream St
(Florence, KY 41042)
Rates: $39-$41;
Tel: (606) 371-9711

**LA QUINTA MOTOR INN**
11335 Chester Rd (45246)
Rates: $33-$58;
Tel: (513) 772-3140

**QUALITY HOTEL CENTRAL**
4747 Montgomery Rd
(Norwood 45212)
Rates: $59-$64;
Tel: (513) 351-6000

**QUALITY INN KINGS
ISLAND CONFERENCE CTR**
P. O. Box 425
(Kings Island 45034)
Rates: $35-$89;
Tel: (513) 398-8075

**RAMADA HOTEL BLUE ASH**
5901 Pfeiffer Rd (45242)
Rates: $67-$73;
Tel: (513) 793-4500

**RAMADA INN SHARONVILLE**
11029 Dowlin Dr (45241)
Rates: $72-$89;
Tel: (513) 771-0300

**RED CARPET INN**
8590 Colerain Ave (45251)
Rates: $25-$65;
Tel: (513) 385-1444

**RED ROOF INN
CENTRAL (NORWOOD)**
5300 Kennedy Dr (45213)
Rates: $25-$63;
Tel: (513) 531-6589

**RED ROOF INN CHESTER RD**
11345 Chester Rd
(Sharonville 45246)
Rates: $25-$51;
Tel: (513) 771-5141

**RED ROOF INN EAST
(BEECHMONT)**
4035 Mt Carmel-Tobasco Rd
(45255)
Rates: $30-$40;
Tel: (513) 528-2741

**RED ROOF INN
NORTHEAST (BLUE ASH)**
5900 Pfeiffer Rd (45242)
Rates: $25-65;
Tel: (513) 793-8811

**RED ROOF INN-
SHARON ROAD**
2301 E Sharon Rd (45241)
Rates: $25-$59;
Tel: (513) 771-5552

**RESIDENCE INN
BY MARRIOTT-BLUE ASH**
11401 Reed-Hartman Hwy
(45241)
Rates: $109-$140;
Tel: (513) 530-5060

**RESIDENCE INN
BY MARRIOTT**
11689 Chester Rd (45246)
Rates: $94-$129;
Tel: (513) 771-2525

**RODEWAY INN-
CINCINNATI NORTH**
400 Glensprings Dr (45246)
Rates: $34-$64;
Tel: (513) 825-3129

**SHERATON-SPRINGDALE**
11911 Sheraton Ln
(Springdale 45246)
Rates: $87-$150;
Tel: (513) 671-6600

**VILLAGER LODGE**
10110 Princeton-Glendale Rd
(45246)
Rates: $29-$46;
Tel: (513) 874-3345

**WESTIN HOTEL
CINCINNATI**
At Fountain Square (45202)
Rates: $99-$240;
Tel: (513) 621-7700

## CIRCLEVILLE

**HOMETOWN INN**
23897 US 23S (43113)
Rates: $33-$41;
Tel: (614) 474-6006

## CLEVELAND
(and Vicinity)

**BUDGETEL INN**
6161 Quarry Ln
(Independence 44131)
Rates: $39-$48;
Tel: (216) 447-1133

**BUDGETEL INN**
1421 Golden Gate Blvd
(Mayfield Hgts 44124)
Rates: $38-$47;
Tel: (216) 442-8400

**CLARION EAST**
3500 Curtis Blvd (44095)
Rates: $86-$150;
Tel: (216) 953-8000

**CLEVELAND
AIRPORT MARRIOTT**
4277 W 150th St (44135)
Rates: $118-$128;
Tel: (216) 252-5333

**CLEVELAND
MARRIOTT EAST**
3663 E Park Dr
(Beachwood 44122)
Rates: $80-$119;
Tel: (216) 464-5950

**CLEVELAND SOUTH
HILTON INN**
6200 Quarry Ln (44131)
Rates: $102-$125;
Tel: (216) 447-1300

**EMBASSY SUITES**
3775 Park East Dr
(Beachwood 44122)
Rates: $130-$145;
Tel: (216) 765-8066

**HAMPTON INN**
29690 Detroit Rd (44145)
Rates: $49-$64;
Tel: (216) 892-0333

**HAMPTON INN**
28611 Euclid Ave
(Wickliffe 44092)
Rates: $51-$59;
Tel: (216) 944-4030

**HOLIDAY INN-
INDEPENDENCE/
ROCKSIDE I-77**
6001 Rockside Rd
(Independence 44131)
Rates: $69-$109;
Tel: (216) 524-8050

**HOLIDAY INN-RICHFIELD**
4742 Brecksville Rd
(Richfield 44286)
Rates: $53-$79;
Tel: (216) 659-6151

**HOLIDAY INN-WICKLIFFE**
28500 Euclid Ave
(Wickliffe 44092)
Rates: $67-$75;
Tel: (216) 585-2750

**KNIGHTS INN**
240 E Highland Rd
(Macedonia 44056)
Rates: $33-$45;
Tel: (216) 467-1981

**MARRIOTT SOCIETY CENTER**
127 Public Sq (44114)
Rates: $140-$900;
Tel: (216) 696-9200

**RADISSON PLAZA HOTEL
CLEVELAND**
1701 E 12th St (44114)
Rates: $89;
Tel: (216) 523-8000

**RED ROOF INN**
6020 Quarry Ln
(Independence 44131)
Rates: $44-$51;
Tel: (216) 447-0030

## RED ROOF INN-EAST
4166 SR 306
(Willoughby 44094)
Rates: $36-$56;
Tel: (216) 946-9872

## RED ROOF INN-MIDDLEBURG HEIGHTS
17555 Bagley Rd
(Middleburg Hgts 44130)
Rates: $39-$49;
Tel: (216) 243-2441

## RED ROOF INN-STRONGSVILLE
15385 Royalton Rd
(Strongsville 44136)
Rates: $38-$49;
Tel. (216) 238-0170

## RED ROOF INN-WESTLAKE
29595 Clements Rd
(Westlake 44145)
Rates: $33-$52;
Tel: (216) 892-7920

## RESIDENCE INN BY MARRIOTT
17525 Rosbough Dr
(Middleburg Hgts 44130)
Rates: $99-$131;
Tel: (216) 234-6688

## RESIDENCE INN BY MARRIOTT
30100 Clements St
(Westlake 44145)
Rates: $103-$129;
Tel: (216) 892-2254

## SAVE INN
4501 E Royalton Rd
(Broadview Hgts 44147)
Rates: $35-$39;
Tel: (216) 526-0640

# CLYDE

## PLAZA MOTEL
500 E McPherson Hwy (43410)
Rates: $24-$47;
Tel: (419) 547-6514

# COLUMBUS
(and Vicinity)

## BEST WESTERN EXECUTIVE INN
4026 Jackpot Rd
(Grove City 43123)
Rates: $34-$44;
Tel: (614) 875-7770

## DAYS INN-NORTH
1212 E Dublin-Granville Rd
(43229)
Rates: $36-$41;
Tel: (614) 885-9696

## DAYS INN-UNIVERSITY
3160 Olentangy River Rd
(43202)
Rates: $36-$45;
Tel: (614) 261-0523

## ECONO LODGE
920 Wilson Rd (43204)
Rates: $30-$45;
Tel: (614) 274-8581

## ENVOY INN-EAST
6201 Oak Tree Ln
(Reynoldsburg 43068)
Rates: $30-$46;
Tel: (614) 866-8000

## HOJO INN
5950 Scarborough Blvd
(43232)
Rates: $29-$53;
Tel: (614) 864-4670

## HOLIDAY INN-COLUMBUS AIRPORT
750 Stelzer Rd (43219)
Rates: $84-$92;
Tel: (614) 237-6360

## HOLIDAY INN-COLUMBUS/WORTHINGTON
175 Hutchinson Ave (43235)
Rates: $85;
Tel: (614) 885-3334

## HOLIDAY INN EAST I-70
4560 Hilton Corporate Dr
(43232)
Rates: $65-$86;
Tel: (614) 868-1380

## HOLIDAY INN ON THE LANE
328 W Lane Ave (43201)
Rates: $69-$86;
Tel: (614) 294-4848

## HOMEWOOD SUITES
115 Hutchinson Ave (43235)
Rates: $90-$150;
Tel: (614) 785-0001

## KNIGHTS INN
5950 Scarborough Blvd
(43232)
Rates: N/A·
Tel: (800) 843-5644

## KNIGHTS INN COLUMBUS WEST
1559 W Broad St (43222)
Rates: $32-$48;
Tel: (614) 275-0388

## KNIGHTS INN COLUMBUS/WESTERVILLE
32 Heatherdown Dr
(Westerville 43081)
Rates: $27-$69;
Tel: (614) 890-0426

## KNIGHTS INN I-71 NORTH
1300 E Dublin-Granville Rd
(43229)
Rates: $38-$46;
Tel: (614) 846-7635

## LA QUINTA MOTOR INN
2447 Brice Rd
(Reynoldsburg 43068)
Rates: $42-$56;
Tel: (614) 866-6456

## LENOX INN
P. O. Box 346
(Reynoldsburg 43068)
Rates: $46-$66;
Tel: (614) 861-7800

## L-K INN
50 E Wilson Bridge Rd
(Worthington 43085)
Rates: $37-$56;
Tel: (614) 846-8830

## MARRIOTT NORTH
6500 Doubletree Ave (43229)
Rates: $120-$250;
Tel: (614) 885-1885

**PARKE UNIVERSITY HOTEL**
3025 Olentangy River Rd
(43202)
Rates: $60-$66;
Tel: (614) 267-1111

**QUALITY HOTEL CITY CENTRE**
175 E Town St (43215)
Rates: $72-$86;
Tel: (614) 221-3281

**RADISSON NORTH**
4900 Sinclair Rd (43229)
Rates: $74-$175;
Tel: (614) 846-0300

**RAMADA INN-EAST AIRPORT**
2100 Brice Rd (43068)
Rates: $58-$74;
Tel: (614) 864-1280

**RAMADA UNIVERSITY
HOTEL & CONF CTR**
3110 Olentangy River Rd
(43202)
Rates: $69-$71;
Tel: (614) 267-7461

**RED ROOF INN-DUBLIN**
5125 Post Rd (Dublin 43017)
Rates: $31-$49;
Tel: (614) 764-3993

**RED ROOF INN-EAST**
2449 Brice Rd
(Reynoldsburg 43068)
Rates: $33-$40;
Tel: (614) 864-3683

**RED ROOF INN-MORSE ROAD**
750 Morse Rd (43229)
Rates: $30-$48;
Tel: (614) 846-8520

**RED ROOF INN-OSU**
441 Ackerman Rd (43202)
Rates: $34-$49;
Tel: (614) 267-9941

**RED ROOF INN-SOUTH**
1900 Stringtown Rd
(Grove City 43123)
Rates: $34-$43;
Tel: (614) 875-8543

**RED ROOF INN-WEST**
5001 Renner Rd (43228)
Rates: $31-$51;
Tel: (614) 878-9245

**RED ROOF INN-
WORTHINGTON**
7474 N High St (43235)
Rates: $36-$46;
Tel: (614) 846-3001

**RESIDENCE INN
BY MARRIOTT-
COLUMBUS EAST**
2084 S Hamilton Rd (43232)
Rates: $119-$149;
Tel: (614) 864-8844

**RESIDENCE INN
BY MARRIOTT-
COLUMBUS NORTH**
6191 W Zumstein Dr (43229)
Rates: $109-$139;
Tel: (614) 431-1819

**STOUFFER DUBLIN HOTEL**
600 Metro Place N
(Dublin 43017)
Rates: $74-$149;
Tel: (614) 764-2200

**THE TRUEMAN CLUB**
900 E Dubline-Granville Rd
(43229)
Rates: N/A;
Tel: (800) 477-7888

**VICTORIAN
BED & BREAKFAST**
78 Smith Pl (43201)
Rates: N/A;
Tel: (614) 299-1656

## COSHOCTON

**TRAVELODGE**
275 S Whitewoman St (43812)
Rates: $40-$62;
Tel: (614) 622-9823

## CURTICE

**ECONO LODGE**
10530 Corduroy Rd (42413)
Rates: $49-$53;
Tel: (419) 836-2822

## DAYTON
(and Vicinity)

**COMFORT INN-DAYTON**
2140 Edwin C Moses Blvd
(45408)
Rates: $35-$40;
Tel: (513) 223-0166

**COUNTRY HEARTH INN**
1944 Miamisburg/
Centerville Rd (45449)
Rates: $41-$52;
Tel: (513) 435-1550

**DAYS INN BROOKVILLE**
100 Parkview Dr
(Brookville 45309)
Rates: $39-$49;
Tel: (513) 833-4003

**DAYS INN-DAYTON SOUTH**
3555 Miamisburg/
Centerville Rd (45449)
Rates: $39-$81;
Tel: (513) 847-8422

**DAYTON HILTON**
11 S Ludlow St (45402)
Rates: $84-$109;
Tel: (513) 461-4700

**DAYTON
MARRIOTT HOTEL**
1414 S Patterson Blvd (45409)
Rates: $89-$120;
Tel: (513) 223-1000

**ECONO LODGE
OF DAYTON**
2221 Wagoner-Ford Rd
(45414)
Rates: $29-$38;
Tel: (513) 278-1500

**HOLIDAY INN-
DAYTON NORTHWEST**
10 Rockridge Rd
(Englewood 45322)
Rates: $67-$98;
Tel: (513) 832-1234

**HOLIDAY INN-SOUTH**
2455 Dryden Rd (45439)
Rates: $59-$69;
Tel: (513) 294-1471

KNIGHTS INN
185 Byers Rd
(Miamisburg 45342)
Rates: $32-$44;
Tel: (800) 843-5644

KNIGHTS INN-NORTH
3663 Maxton Rd (45414)
Rates: $33-$41;
Tel: (513) 898-1212

RADISSON INN-DAYTON
2401 Needmore Rd (45414)
Rates: $59-$76;
Tel: (513) 278-5711

RAMADA INN-NORTH
4079 Little York Rd (45414)
Rates: $52-$64;
Tel: (513) 890-9500

RED ROOF INN-NORTH
7370 Miller Ln (45414)
Rates: $30-$47;
Tel: (513) 898-1054

RED ROOF INN-SOUTH
222 Byers Rd
(Miamisburg 45342)
Rates: $31-$42;
Tel: (513) 866-0705

RESIDENCE INN
BY MARRIOTT-
DAYTON NORTH
7070 Poe Ave (45414)
Rates: $109-$140;
Tel: (513) 898-7764

RODEWAY INN NORTH
7575 Poe Rd (45414)
Rates: $33-$49;
Tel: (513) 454-0550

TRAVELODGE
7911 Brandt Pike (45424)
Rates: $38-$57;
Tel: (513) 236-9361

## DELAWARE

TRAVELODGE
1001 US 23 N (43015)
Rates: $36-$42;
Tel: (614) 369-4421

## DOVER

KNIGHTS INN
889 Commercial Pkwy
(44622)
Rates: $36-$44;
Tel: (216) 364-7724

## DUBLIN

RED ROOF INN
5125 Post Rd (43017)
Rates: N/A;
Tel: (800) 843-7663

## EATON

ECONO LODGE
RR 1 (45320)
Rates: $34-$42;
Tel: (513) 456-5959

## ELYRIA

COMFORT INN
739 Leona St (44035)
Rates: $38-$74;
Tel: (216) 324-7676

HOLIDAY INN
1825 Lorain Blvd (44035)
Rates: $70-$94;
Tel: (216) 324-5411

KNIGHTS INN
523 Griswold Rd (44035)
Rates: $35-$42;
Tel: (216) 324-3911

## FAIRBORN

HOLIDAY INN CONFERENCE
CENTER/I-675
2800 Presidential Dr (45324)
Rates: $85-$115;
Tel: (513) 426-7800

HOMEWOOD SUITES
2750 Presidential Dr (45324)
Rates: $69-$106;
Tel: (513) 429-0600

RAMADA INN
800 N Broad St (45324)
Rates: $51-$58;
Tel: (513) 879-3920

RED ROOF INN
2580 Colonel Glenn Hwy
(45324)
Rates: $35-$47;
Tel: (513) 426-6116

## FINDLAY

ECONO LODGE
316 Emma St (45840)
Rates: $26-$34;
Tel: (419) 422-0154

HOLIDAY INN
820 Trenton Ave (45840)
Rates: $50-$61;
Tel: (419) 423-8212

KNIGHTS INN
1901 Broad Ave (45840)
Rates: $39-$41;
Tel: (419) 424-1133

## FOSTORIA

DAYS INN
601 Findlay St (44830)
Rates: $40-$52;
Tel: (419) 435-6511

## FREMONT

FREMONT TURNPIKE MOTEL
520 CR 89E (43420)
Rates: $30-$65;
Tel: (419) 332-6489

HOLIDAY INN-
FREMONT/PORT CLINTON
3422 Port Clinton Rd (43420)
Rates: $58-$102;
Tel: (419) 334-2682

TRAVELODGE
1750 Cedar St (43420)
Rates: $37-$60;
Tel: (419) 334-9517

## GALION

**HOMETOWN INN**
172 N Portland Way (44833)
Rates: $35-$50;
Tel: (419) 468-9909

## GALLIPOLIS

**BEST WESTERN
WILLIAM ANN**
918 2nd Ave (45631)
Rates: $30-$40;
Tel: (419) 446-3373

## GROVE CITY

**RED ROOF INN**
1900 Stringtown Rd (43123)
Rates: N/A;
Tel: (800) 843-7663

## HAMILTON

**THE HAMILTON HOTEL**
1 Riverfront Plaza (45011)
Rates: $63-$89;
Tel: (513) 896-6200

## HOLLAND

**RED ROOF INN**
1214 Corporate Dr (43528)
Rates: N/A;
Tel: (800) 843-7663

## HUDSON

**REGENCY INN**
344 E Hines Hill Rd (44236)
Rates: N/A;
Tel: (216) 650-1100

**VIRGINIA MOTEL**
5374 Akron-Cleveland Rd
(Peninsula 44264)
Rates: $29-$44;
Tel: (216) 650-0449

## HURON

**PLANTATION MOTEL**
2815 E Cleveland Rd (44839)
Rates: $25-$70;
Tel: (419) 433-4790

## INDEPENDENCE

**RED ROOF INN**
6020 Quarry Ln (44131)
Rates: N/A;
Tel: (800) 843-7663

## IRONTON

**BEST WESTERN-SOUTHERN
HILLS MOTOR INN**
P. O. Box 397
(South Point 45680)
Rates: $36-$42;
Tel: (614) 894-3391

## JACKSON

**COMFORT INN**
605 E Main St (45640)
Rates: $48-$63;
Tel: (614) 286-7581

## KENT

**DAYS INN-AKRON KENT**
4422 Edsen Rd
(Brimfield 44240)
Rates: $30-$65;
Tel: (216) 677-9400

**HOLIDAY INN**
4363 SR 43 (44240)
Rates: $60-$68;
Tel: (216) 678-0101

**THE INN OF KENT**
303 E Main St (44240)
Rates: $38-$70;
Tel: (216) 673-3411

**KNIGHTS INN-
AKRON EAST**
4423 SR 43 (44240)
Rates: $38-$44;
Tel: (216) 678-5250

## LANCASTER

**ARBORGATE INN**
1327 River Valley Blvd
(43130)
Rates: $37-$45;
Tel: (614) 687-4823

## LEBANON

**BEST WESTERN
HERITAGE INN**
P. O. Box 303 (45036)
Rates: $27-$59;
Tel: (513) 932-4111

**DOWNTOWN MOTEL**
115 N Broadway (45036)
Rates: $24-$48;
Tel: (513) 932-1966

## LIMA

**ECONO LODGE**
1210 Neubrecht Rd (45801)
Rates: $30-$34;
Tel: (419) 228-4251

**HOLIDAY INN**
1816 Harding Hwy (45804)
Rates: $68-$86;
Tel: (419) 222-2176

**KNIGHTS COURT**
1430 Bellefontaine Rd (45804)
Rates: $29-$45;
Tel: (419) 227-2221

**MOTEL 6**
1800 Harding Hwy (45804)
Rates: $25-$31;
Tel: (419) 228-0456

**QUALITY INN**
1201 Neubrecht Rd (45801)
Rates: $41-$50;
Tel: (419) 222-0596

## MANSFIELD

**BEST WESTERN
MANSFIELD INN**
880 Laver Rd (44905)
Rates: $51-$69;
Tel: (419) 589-2200

**COMFORT INN**
500 N Trimble Rd (44906)
Rates: $52-$90;
Tel: (419) 529-1000

**42 MOTEL**
2444 Lexington Ave (44907)
Rates: N/A;
Tel: (419) 884-1315

**HOLIDAY INN-
CONFERENCE CENTER**
116 W Park Ave (44902)
Rates: $62-$110;
Tel: (419) 525-6000

**KNIGHTS INN**
555 N Trimble Rd (44906)
Rates: $36-$59;
Tel: (419) 529-2100

**MERIT INN**
137 W Park Ave (44902)
Rates: $48-$53;
Tel: (419) 522-5142

**TRAVELODGE-
MANSFIELD NORTHEAST**
Rt 11, Box 195 (44903)
Rates: $33-$55;
Tel: (419) 589-3938

**TRAVELODGE-
MANSFIELD SOUTH**
90 Hanley Rd (44903)
Rates: $35-$58;
Tel: (419) 756-7600

## MARIETTA

**ECONO LODGE**
702 Pike St (45750)
Rates: $37-$40;
Tel: (614) 374-8481

**KNIGHTS INN**
506 Pike St (45750)
Rates: $34-$41;
Tel: (614) 373-7373

**THE LAFAYETTE HOTEL**
101 Front St (45750)
Rates: $50-$95;
Tel: (614) 373-5522

## MARION

**FAIRFIELD INN BY MARRIOTT**
227 Jamesway (43302)
Rates: $42-$58;
Tel: (614) 389-6636

**L-K MOTEL**
1838 Marion-Mt Gilead Rd
(43302)
Rates: $29-$48;
Tel: (614) 389-4651

**RAMADA INN**
1065 Delaware Ave (43302)
Rates: $47-$59;
Tel: (614) 383-6771

**TRAVELODGE**
1952 Marion-Mt Gilead Rd
(43302)
Rates: $37-$58;
Tel: (614) 389-4671

## MAUMEE

**KNIGHTS INN**
1520 S Holland-Sylvania Rd
(43537)
Rates: N/A;
Tel: (419) 865 1380

**RED ROOF INN**
1570 S Reynolds Rd (43537)
Rates: N/A;
Tel: (800) 843-7663

## MEDINA

**LOTUS INN**
2860 Medina Rd (44256)
Rates: N/A;
Tel: (216) 725-0561

**KNIGHTS INN**
5200 Montville Dr (44256)
Rates: $29-$49;
Tel: (216) 722-4335

## MENTOR

**ARBORGATE INN**
7677 Reynolds Rd (44060)
Rates: $34-$42;
Tel: (216) 946-0749

**CLEVELAND EAST
KNIGHTS INN**
8370 Broadmore (44060)
Rates: N/A;
Tel: (800) 843-5644

**TERRACE INN**
9260 Mentor Ave (44060)
Rates: $35-$49;
Tel: (216) 255-3456

## MIDDLETOWN

**KNIGHTS INN-FRANKLIN**
8500 Claude Thomas Rd
(Franklin 45005)
Rates: $32-$40;
Tel: (513) 746-2841

**SUPER 8 MOTEL**
3553 Commerce Dr
(Franklin 45005)
Rates: $37-$42;
Tel: (513) 422-4888

## MONTPELIER

**HOLIDAY INN**
RR 3 (43543)
Rates: $40-$128;
Tel: (419) 485-5555

## MOUNT GILEAD

**DERRICK MOTEL**
5898 SR 95 (43338)
Rates: $29-$38;
Tel: (419) 946-6010

## MOUNT VERNON

**CURTIS MOTEL**
12 Public Sq (43050)
Rates: $40-$57;
Tel: (800) 934-6835

## NAPOLEON

**HOLIDAY INN**
P. O. Box 68 (43545)
Rates: $45;
Tel: (419) 592-5010

## NELSONVILLE

QUALITY INN
HOCKING VALLEY
P. O. Box 397 (45764)
Rates: $45-$52;
Tel: (614) 753-3531

## NEWARK

BEST WESTERN
NEWARK INN
50 N 2nd St (43055)
Rates: $51-$66;
Tel: (614) 349-8411

HOLIDAY INN
733 Hebron Rd (43056)
Rates: $47-$53;
Tel: (614) 522-1165

HOWARD JOHNSON
MOTEL
775 Hebron Rd (43055)
Rates: $44-$104;
Tel: (614) 522-3191

## NEW CALIFORNIA

SUPER 8 MOTEL
10220 US 42
(Marysville 43040)
Rates: $33-$47;
Tel: (614) 873-4100

## NEW PHILADELPHIA

BEST WESTERN-
VALLEY INN
131 Bluebell Dr SW (44663)
Rates: $49-$66;
Tel: (216) 339-7731

L-K MOTEL
1256 W High Ave (44663)
Rates: $29-$42;
Tel: (216) 339-6671

TRAVELODGE
P. O. Box 727 (44663)
Rates: $32-$52;
Tel: (216) 339-6671

## NEW RICHMOND

HOLLYHOCK
BED & BREAKFAST
1610 Altman Rd (45157)
Rates: N/A;
Tel: (513) 553-6585

## NILES

PARK INN INTERNATIONAL
1225 Youngstown-Warren Rd
(44446)
Rates: $39-$54;
Tel: (216) 652-1761

## NORTH BALTIMORE

CROWN INN
P. O. Box 82 (45872)
Rates: $35-$40;
Tel: (419) 257-3821

## NORTH CANTON

RED ROOF INN
5353 Inn Circle Ct NW
(44720)
Rates: N/A;
Tel: (800) 843-7663

## NORWALK

L-K MOTEL
283 Benedict Ave (44857)
Rates: $31-$64;
Tel: (419) 668-8255

## OXFORD

SCOTTISH INNS
5235 College Corner Rd
(45056)
Rates: $40-$48;
Tel: (513) 523-6306

## PAINESVILLE

RIDER'S 1812 INN
792 Mentor Ave (44077)
Rates: $70-$90;
Tel: (216) 354-8200

## PERRYSBURG

DAYS INN
10667 Fremont Pike (43551)
Rates: $45-$60;
Tel: (419) 874-8771

HOLIDAY INN-
FRENCH QUARTER
P. O. Box 268 (43551)
Rates: $66-$106;
Tel: (419) 874-3111

HOLIDAY INN-
PERRYSBURG I-75
10621 Fremont Pike (43551)
Rates: $52-$75;
Tel: (419) 874-3101

## PIQUA

COMFORT INN
987 E Ash St (45356)
Rates: $43-$53;
Tel: (513) 778-8100

## PORT CLINTON

L-K INN
1811 Harbor Rd (43452)
Rates: $45-$82;
Tel: (419) 732-2111

## PORTSMOUTH

HOLIDAY INN
P. O. Box 1190 (45662)
Rates: $55-$75;
Tel: (614) 354-2851

## REYNOLDSBURG

RED ROOF INN
2440 Brice Rd (43068)
Rates: N/A;
Tel: (800) 843-7663

## RIO GRANDE

COLLEGE HILL MOTEL
P. O. Box 172 (45674)
Rates: $28-$34;
Tel: (614) 245-5326

## ROSSFORD

**KNIGHTS INN**
1120 Buck Rd (43460)
Rates: N/A;
Tel: (800) 843-5644

## ST. CLAIRSVILLE

**DAYS INN
WHEELING WEST**
52601 Holiday Dr (43950)
Rates: $42-$59;
Tel: (614) 695-0100

**KNIGHTS INN
ST. CLAIRSVILLE/WHEELING**
51260 National Rd (43950)
Rates: $33-$42;
Tel: (614) 695-5038

**RED ROOF INN**
68301 Red Roof Ln (43950)
Rates: $27-$42;
Tel: (614) 695-4057

**TWIN PINES MOTEL**
46079 National Rd (43950)
Rates: N/A;
Tel: (614) 695-3720

## SANDUSKY

**RADISSON HARBOUR INN**
2001 Cleveland/Cedar Pt
Causeway (44870)
Rates: $45-$199;
Tel: (419) 627-2500

**TRAVELODGE
SANDUSKY/CEDAR POINT**
5906 Milan Rd (44870)
Rates: $29-$120;
Tel: (419) 627-8971

## SIDNEY

**COMFORT INN**
1959 W Michigan St (45365)
Rates: $41-$46;
Tel: (513) 492-3001

**DAYS INN**
420 Folkerth Ae (45365)
Rates: $32-$55;
Tel: (513) 492-1104

**HOLIDAY INN**
400 Folkerth Ave (45365)
Rates: $47-$57;
Tel: (513) 492-1131

## SPRINGFIELD

**DAYS INN WEST**
1715 W North St (45504)
Rates: $40-$47;
Tel: (513) 324-5561

**SPRINGFIELD INN**
100 S Fountain Ave (45502)
Rates: $74-$102;
Tel: (513) 322-3600

## STEUBENVILLE

**HOLIDAY INN**
1401 University Blvd (43952)
Rates: $40-$70;
Tel: (614) 282-0901

## STOW

**STOW INN**
4801 Darrow Rd (44224)
Rates: $40-$70;
Tel: (216) 688-3508

## TIFFIN

**TIFFIN MOTEL**
315 West Market St (44883)
Rates: N/A;
Tel: (419) 447-7411

## TOLEDO
(and Vicinity)

**BEST WESTERN
EXECUTIVE INN**
27441 Helen Dr
(Perrysburg 43551)
Rates: $43-$53;
Tel: (419) 874-9181

**THE CHARTER HOUSE
TOLEDO SOUTH**
I-280 & Hanley Rd
(Perrysburg 43551)
Rates: $25-$42;
Tel: (419) 827-5245

**COMFORT INN**
445 E Alexis Rd (43612)
Rates: $47-$62;
Tel: (419) 476-0170

**COMFORT INN EAST**
2930 Navarre Ave
(Oregon 43616)
Rates: $48-$69;
Tel: (419) 691-8911

**CROWN INN**
1727 S Alexis Rd (43613)
Rates: $31-$39;
Tel: (419) 473-1485

**DAYS INN**
150 Dussel Dr
(Maumee 43537)
Rates: $44-$58:
Tel: (419) 893 9960

**ECONO LODGE-TOLEDO**
1800 Miami St (43605)
Rates: $48-$59;
Tel: (419) 666-5120

**HAMPTON INN
TOLEDO SOUTH**
1409 Reynolds Rd
(Maumee 43537)
Rates: $48-$54;
Tel: (419) 893-1004

**HOLIDAY INN-
SOUTHWYCK**
2429 S Reynolds Rd (43614)
Rates: $50-$80;
Tel: (419) 381-8765)

**KNIGHTS INN-
TOLEDO WEST**
1520 S Holland-Sylvania Rd
(Maumee 43537)
Rates: $31-$38;
Tel: (419) 865-1380

**MARRIOTT HOTEL**
2 Seagate (43604)
Rates: $99-$190;
Tel: (419) 241-1411

**RAMADA INN SOUTHWYCK**
2340 S Reynolds Rd (43614)
Rates: $59-$77;
Tel: (419) 865-1361

**RED ROOF INN-HOLLAND**
1214 Corporate Dr
(Holland 43528)
Rates: $28-$42;
Tel: (419) 866-5512

**RED ROOF INN-MAUMEE**
1570 Reynolds Rd
(Maumee 43537)
Rates: $28-$48;
Tel: (419) 893-0292

**RED ROOF INN SECOR**
3530 Executive Pkwy (43606)
Rates: $53;
Tel: (419) 536-0118

**SECOR INN**
3560 Secor Rd (43606)
Rates: $41-$45;
Tel: (419) 531-2666

**SHERATON WESTGATE**
3536 Secor Rd (43606)
Rates: $56-$84;
Tel: (419) 535-7070

**WESTGATE MOTEL**
1115 S Reynolds Rd (43615)
Rates: N/A;
Tel: (419) 382-5843

# TROY

**DAYS INN OF TROY**
1610 W Main St (45373)
Rates: $34-$59;
Tel: (513) 339-7571

**KNIGHTS INN OF TROY**
30 Troy Town Dr (45373)
Rates: $33-$39;
Tel: (513) 339-1515

# UHRICHSVILLE

**COUNTRY HEARTH INN**
111 McCauley Dr (44683)
Rates: $27-$57;
Tel: (614) 922-0774

# URBANA

**LOGAN LODGE MOTEL**
2551 Rt 68S (43078)
Rates: $56-$61;
Tel: (513) 652-2188

# VAN WERT

**DAYS INN**
820 N Washington St (45891)
Rates: $35-$50;
Tel: (419) 238-5222

**TRAVELODGE**
875 N Washington St (45891)
Rates: $36-$53;
Tel: (419) 238-3700

# WADSWORTH

**KNIGHTS INN-
AKRON WEST**
810 High St (44281)
Rates: $35-$42;
Tel: (216) 336-6671

# WAPAKONETA

**DAYS INN**
1659 Wapak Fisher Rd
(45895)
Rates: $35-$49;
Tel: (419) 738-2184

**HOLIDAY INN**
P. O. Box 1980 (45895)
Rates: $46-$56;
Tel: (419) 728-8181

# WARREN

**BEST WESTERN
DOWNTOWN MOTOR INN**
777 Mahoning Ave (44483)
Rates: $43-$53;
Tel: (216) 392-2515

**PARK HOTEL**
136 N Park Ave (44481)
Rates: $60-$70;
Tel: (216) 393-1200

# WASHINGTON
# COURT HOUSE

**KNIGHTS INN**
1820 Columbus Ave (43160)
Rates: $34-$42;
Tel: (614) 335-9133

# WEST CHESTER

**CINCINNATI KNIGHTS INN**
7313 Kingsgate Way (45069)
Rates: N/A;
Tel: (800) 843-5644

# WESTERVILLE

**KNIGHTS INN**
32 Heatherdown Dr (43081)
Rates: N/A;
Tel: (614) 890-0426

# WESTLAKE

**RED ROOF INN**
29595 Clemens Rd (44145)
Rates: N/A;
Tel: (800) 843-7663

# WILLOUGHBY

**RED ROOF INN**
4166 OH 306 (44094)
Rates: $32-$46;
Tel: (216) 946-9872

# WILMINGTON

**L-K MOTEL**
264 W Curry Rd (45177)
Rates: $49-$55;
Tel: (513) 382-6605

# WOOSTER

**ECONO LODGE**
2137 E Lincolnway (44691)
Rates: $33-$43;
Tel: (216) 264-8883

**THE WOOSTER INN**
801 E Wayne Ave (44691)
Rates: $60-$90;
Tel: (216) 264-2341

## WORTHINGTON

**RED ROOF INN**
7474 N High St (43235)
Rates: N/A;
Tel: (800) 843-7663

## XENIA

**ALLENDALE INN**
38 S Allison Ave (45385)
Rates: $34-$39;
Tel: (513) 376-8124

**BEST WESTERN REGENCY INN**
600 Little Main St (45385)
Rates: $35-$49;
Tel: (513) 372-9954

## YOUNGSTOWN

**BEST WESTERN MEANDER INN**
870 N Canfield-Niles Rd (44515)
Rates: $46-$85;
Tel: (216) 544-2378

**DAYS INN-NORTH**
1610 Motor Inn Dr (Girard 44420)
Rates: $37-$49;
Tel: (216) 759-3410

**DAYSTOP**
8392 Market St (44512)
Rates: $34-$65;
Tel: (216) 758-2371

**ECONO LODGE**
1615 E Liberty St (Girard 44420)
Rates: $34 $40,
Tel: (216) 759-9820

**KNIGHTS INN-WEST**
5431 76th Dr (Austintown 44515)
Rates: $32-$40;
Tel: (216) 793-9305

**QUALITY INN-YOUNGSTOWN**
1051 N Canfield/Niles Rd (44515)
Rates: $40-$57;
Tel: (216) 793-9851

## ZANESVILLE

**HOLIDAY INN**
4645 E Pike (43701)
Rates: $55-$80;
Tel: (614) 453-0771

# OKLAHOMA

## ALTUS

**ECONO LODGE**
3203 N Main (73521)
Rates: $24-$32;
Tel: (405) 477-2300

**HOLIDAY INN**
2804 N Main (73521)
Rates: $42-$56;
Tel: (405) 482-9300

**RAMADA INN**
2515 E Broadway (73521)
Rates: $42-$91;
Tel: (405) 477-3000

## ALVA

**RANGER INN MOTEL**
420 E Oklahoma Blvd (73717)
Rates: $26-$32;
Tel: (405) 327-1981

**WHARTON'S VISTA MOTEL**
1330 W Oklahoma Blvd (73717)
Rates: $20-$29;
Tel: (405) 327-3232

## ARDMORE

**BEST WESTERN INN**
2519 W Hwy 142 (73401)
Rates: $32-$44;
Tel: (405) 223-1234

**HOLIDAY INN**
2705 Holiday Dr (73401)
Rates: $41-$57;
Tel: (405) 223-7130

**RAMADA INN**
2700 W Broadway (73401)
Rates: $42-$52;
Tel: (405) 226-1250

## ATOKA

**BEST WESTERN ATOKA INN**
2101 S Mississippi (74525)
Rates: $34-$42;
Tel: (405) 889-7381

## BARTLESVILLE

**HOLIDAY INN**
1410 SE Washington Blvd (74006)
Rates: $48-$55;
Tel: (918) 333-8320

## BOISE CITY

**TOWNSMAN MOTEL**
1205 E Main (73933)
Rates: $27-$35;
Tel: (405) 544-2506

## BROKEN BOW

**CHARLES WESLEY MOTOR LODGE**
302 N Park Dr (74728)
Rates: $30-$37;
Tel: (405) 584-3303

**END OF TRAIL MOTEL**
11 N Park Dr (74728)
Rates: N/A;
Tel: (405) 584-3350

## CHANDLER

**ECONOLODGE**
600 N Price (74834)
Rates: $30-$38;
Tel: (405) 258-2131

## CHECOTAH

**FOUNTAINHEAD RESORT HOTEL**
HC 60, Box 1533 (74426)
Rates: $55-$85;
Tel: (918) 689-9173

**I-40 INN**
Old 69 Hwy & I-40 (74426)
Rates: N/A;
Tel: (918) 473-2331

## CHICKASHA

**BEST WESTERN INN**
2101 S 4th (73018)
Rates: $37-$53;
Tel: (405) 224-4890

## CLAREMORE

**BEST WESTERN
WILL ROGERS MOTOR INN**
940 S Lynn Riggs Blvd (74017)
Rates: $32-$50;
Tel: (918) 341-4410

**MOTEL CLAREMORE**
812 E Will Rogers Blvd
(74017)
Rates: $32-$36;
Tel: (918) 341-3254

## CLINTON

**BUDGET HOST INN**
1413 Neptune Dr (73601)
Rates: $16-$26;
Tel: (405) 323-9333

## DUNCAN

**DUNCAN INN**
3402 N US 81 (73533)
Rates: $25-$36;
Tel: (405) 252-5210

**HOLIDAY INN**
1015 N Hwy 81 (73533)
Rates: $43-$53;
Tel: (405) 252-1500

**TRAVELODGE OF DUNCAN**
2335 Hwy 81N (73533)
Rates: $33-$41;
Tel: (405) 252-0810

## DURANT

**QUALITY INN**
2121 W Main St (74701)
Rates: $26-$35;
Tel: (405) 924-5432

## ELK CITY

**BEST WESTERN FLAMINGO
INN & RESTAURANT**
2000 W 3rd St (73644)
Rates: $26-$40;
Tel: (405) 225-1811

**DAYS INN**
1100 OK 34, I-40 Exit 41
(73644)
Rates: $26-$37;
Tel: (405) 225-9210

**ECONO LODGE**
108 Meadow Ridge (73644)
Rates: $24-$33;
Tel: (405) 225-5120

**ELK CITY TRAVELODGE**
301 Sleepy Hollow Ct (73644)
Rates: $25-$33;
Tel: (405) 243-0150

**HOLIDAY INN**
P. O. Box 782 (73648)
Rates: $46-$67;
Tel: (405) 225-6637

**QUALITY INN**
P.O. Box 1025 (73644)
Rates: $26-$36;
Tel: (405) 225-8140

**RED CARPET INN**
2604 E Hwy 66 (73644)
Rates: $24-$34;
Tel: (405) 225-2241

## ENID

**HOLIDAY INN**
2901 S Van Buren (73703)
Rates: $34-$58;
Tel: (405) 237-6000

**RAMADA INN**
3005 W Garriott Rd (73703)
Rates: $40-$55;
Tel: (405) 234-0440

## ERICK

**ECONO LODGE**
Rt 1, Box 605 (73645)
Rates: $26-$35;
Tel: (405) 526-3315

## GUTHRIE

**BEST WESTERN
TERRITORIAL INN**
2323 Territorial Tr (73044)
Rates: $40-$58;
Tel: (405) 282-8831

**HARRISON HOUSE
BED & BREAKFAST**
124 West Harrison (73044)
Rates: N/A;
Tel: (405) 282-1000

**TOWN HOUSE MOTEL**
221 E Oklahoma Ave (73044)
Rates: $25-$36;
Tel: (405) 282-2000

## GUYMON

**AMBASSADOR INN**
P. O. Box 5 (73942)
Rates: $36-$44;
Tel: (405) 338-5555

**BEST WESTERN
TOWNSMAN MOTEL**
P. O. Box 159 (73942)
Rates: $39-$55;
Tel: (405) 338-6556

## HENRYETTA

**HOLIDAY INN
HENRYETTA-OKMULGEE**
P. O. Box 789 (74437)
Rates: $61-$73;
Tel: (918) 652-2581

**LE BARON MOTEL**
Rt 2, Box 170 (74437)
Rates: $25-$35;
Tel: (918) 652-2531

## KINGSTON

**LAKE TEXOMA RESORT**
P. O. Box 41 (73439)
Rates: N/A;
Tel: (405) 564-2311

## LAKE MURRAY STATE PARK

**LAKE MURRAY RESORT**
P. O. Box 1329
(Ardmore 73402)
Rates: $49-$150;
Tel: (405) 223-6600

## LAWTON

**BEST WESTERN
SANDPIPER INN**
2202 N US Hwys 277 & 281
(73507)
Rates: $38-$52;
Tel: (405) 353-0310

**HOLIDAY INN**
3134 Cache Rd (73505)
Rates: $41-$54;
Tel: (405) 353-1682

**HOSPITALITY INN**
202 E Lee Blvd (73501)
Rates: $33-$40;
Tel: (405) 355-9765

**HOWARD JOHNSON
MOTEL**
1125 E Gore Blvd (73501)
Rates: $40-$139;
Tel: (405) 353-0200

**PARK INN INTERNATIONAL
EXECUTIVE**
3110 Cache Rd (73505)
Rates: $38-$48;
Tel: (405) 353-3104

**RAMADA INN**
601 N 2nd (73507)
Rates: $38-$49;
Tel: (405) 355-7155

## MCALESTER

**COMFORT INN**
P. O. Box 1532 (74502)
Rates: $34-$44;
Tel: (918) 426-0115

**DAYS INN**
Rt 0, Box 133 (74501)
Rates: $39-$44;
Tel: (918) 426-5050

**HOLIDAY INN**
1500 George Nigh Expwy
(74501)
Rates: $43-$50;
Tel: (918) 423-7766

## MIAMI

**BEST WESTERN
CONTINENTAL MOTOR INN**
2225 E Steve Owens Blvd
(74354)
Rates: $38-$58;
Tel: (918) 542-6681

## MUSKOGEE

**BEST WESTERN
TRADE WINDS INN**
534 S 32nd St (74401)
Rates: $42-$49;
Tel: (918) 683-2951

**DAYS INN**
900 S 32nd St (74401)
Rates: $38-$43;
Tel: (918) 683-3911

**RAMADA INN**
800 S 32nd St (74401)
Rates: $45-$52;
Tel: (918) 682-4341

## NORMAN

**HOLIDAY INN-NORMAN**
2600 W Main St (73069)
Rates: $44-$54;
Tel: (405) 329-1624

**THE RESIDENCE INN
BY MARRIOTT**
2681 Jefferson St (73072)
Rates: $80-$110;
Tel: (405) 366-0900

**SHERATON NORMAN**
1000 N Interstate Dr (73072)
Rates: $60-$90;
Tel: (405) 364-2882

## OKLAHOMA CITY
(and Vicinity)

**BEST WESTERN
SADDLEBACK INN**
4300 SW 3rd St (73108)
Rates: $53-$72;
Tel: (405) 947-7000

**BEST WESTERN
TRADEWINDS CENTRAL INN**
1800 East Reno St (73117)
Rates: N/A;
Tel: (405) 235-4531

**COACHMAN INN-
MIDWEST CITY**
5653 Tinker Diagonal
(Midwest City 73110)
Rates: $40-$45;
Tel: (405) 733-1339

**COMFORT INN**
4017 NW 39th Expwy
(73112)
Rates: $39-$47;
Tel: (405) 947-0038

**COMFORT INN-WEST**
321 N Mustange Rd
(Yukon 73099)
Rates: $40-$65;
Tel: (405) 324-1000

**DAYS INN
AIRPORT MERIDIAN**
4712 W I-40 (73128)
Rates: $30-$35;
Tel: (405) 947-8721

**DAYS INN NORTHWEST**
2801 NW 39th St (73112)
Rates: $36-$63;
Tel: (405) 946-0741

**DAYS INN SOUTH**
2616 I-35S (73129)
Rates: $38-$45;
Tel: (405) 677-0521

**ECONO LODGE**
7412 N Bryant (73111)
Rates: $26-$33;
Tel: (405) 478-0205

**ECONO LODGE**
820 S MacArthur Blvd
(73128)
Rates: $23-$32;
Tel: (405) 947-8651

**EMBASSY SUITES HOTEL**
1815 S Meridian Ave (73108)
Rates: $79-$124;
Tel: (405) 682-6000

**GOVERNORS SUITES HOTEL**
2308 S Meridian Ave (73108)
Rates: $54-$65;
Tel: (405) 682-5299

**HOLIDAY INN-AIRPORT WEST**
801 S Meridian Ave (73108)
Rates: $59-$76;
Tel: (405) 942-8511

**HILTON INN-NORTHWEST**
2945 NW Expwy (73112)
Rates: $69-$109;
Tel: (405) 848-4811

**HOLIDAY INN-EAST**
5701 Tinker Diagonal
(Midwest City 73110)
Rates: $52-$66;
Tel: (405) 737-4481

**HOLIDAY INN-NORTH**
12001 NE Expwy (73131)
Rates: $60-$65;
Tel: (405) 478-0400

**HOLIDAY INN-NORTHWEST**
3535 NW 39th Expwy
(73112)
Rates: $47-$56;
Tel: (405) 947-2351

**LA QUINTA
MOTOR INN-DEL CITY**
5501 Tinker Diagonal
(Del City 73115)
Rates: $43-$58;
Tel: (405) 672-0067

**LA QUINTA
MOTOR INN-SOUTH**
8315 I-35S (73149)
Rates: $41-$55;
Tel: (405) 631-8661

**MOTEL 6 WEST**
4200 I-40W (73108)
Rates: $25-$31;
Tel: (405) 947-6550

**OKLAHOMA CITY
MARRIOTT**
3233 NW Expwy (73112)
Rates: $75-$125;
Tel: (405) 842-6633

**RADISSON INN
OKLAHOMA CITY**
401 S Meridian Ave (73108)
Rates: $59-$89;
Tel: (405) 947-7681

**RAMADA INN-
AIRPORT SOUTH**
6800 I-35S (73149)
Rates: $46-$52;
Tel: (405) 631-3321

**RAMADA INN-
AIRPORT WEST**
800 S Meridian Ave (73108)
Rates: $42-$52;
Tel: (405) 942-0040

**RAMADA INN**
3709 NW 39th Expwy
(73112)
Rates: $36-$40;
Tel: (405) 942-7730

**RESIDENCE INN
BY MARRIOTT-WEST**
4361 W Reno (73107)
Rates: $85-$105;
Tel: (405) 942-4500

**RODEWAY INN**
4601 SW 3rd (73128)
Rates: $32-$125;
Tel: (405) 947-2400

**SEASONS INN**
1005 Waterwood Pkwy
(Edmond 73034)
Rates: $55-$150;
Tel: (800) 322-4686

**TRAVEL MASTER INN**
33 NE Expwy (73105)
Rates: $23-$30;
Tel: (405) 840-1824

**WALNUT GARDENS
APARTMENTS/SUITES**
6700 NW 16th St (73127)
Rates: $59-$69;
Tel: (405) 787-5151

**WILL ROGERS AIRPORT INN**
6300 E Terminal Dr (73159)
Rates: $35-$65;
Tel: (800) 583-2500

# PAULS VALLEY

**GARDEN INN MOTEL**
P. O. Box 931 (73075)
Rates: $21-$30;
Tel: (405) 238-7313

# PERRY

**BEST WESTERN
CHEROKEE STRIP MOTEL**
P. O. Box 529 (73077)
Rates: $40-$45;
Tel: (405) 336-2218

**DAN-D-MOTEL**
515 Fir St (73077)
Rates: $18-$24;
Tel: (405) 336-4463

**FIRST INTERSTATE INN**
P. O. Box 833 (73077)
Rates: $21-$32;
Tel: (405) 336-2277

## PONCA CITY

**B SQUARE INN**
1415 E Bradley (74604)
Rates: $29-$41;
Tel: (800) 749-1406

## PRYOR

**HOLIDAY MOTEL**
701 S Mill (74361)
Rates: $24-$34;
Tel: (918) 825-1204

**PRYOR HOUSE MOTOR INN**
123 S Mill St (74361)
Rates: $32-$42;
Tel: (918) 825-6677

## PURCELL

**ECONO LODGE**
2500 Hwy 74S (73080)
Rates: $27-$35;
Tel: (405) 527-5603

## SALLISAW

**BEST BET MOTOR INN**
Rt 2, Box 13 (74955)
Rates: $30-$40;
Tel: (918) 775-4406

**BEST WESTERN BLUE RIBBON MOTOR INN**
706 S Kerr Blvd (74955)
Rates: $40-$45;
Tel: (918) 775-6294

**GOLDEN SPUR INN**
P. O. Box 828 (74955)
Rates: $26-$34;
Tel: (918) 775-4443

**HOLIDAY INN EXPRESS**
1300 E Cherokee (74955)
Rates: $36-$38;
Tel: (918) 775-7791

**MCKNIGHT MOTEL**
1611 W Ruth St (74955)
Rates: $30-$49;
Tel: (800) 842-9442

## SAPULPA

**SUPER 8 OF SAPULPA**
1505 New Sapulpa Rd (74066)
Rates: $34-$39;
Tel: (918) 227-3300

## SAVANNA

**BUDGET HOST COLONIAL INN**
P. O. Box 323 (74565)
Rates: $22-$27;
Tel: (918) 548-3506

## SEQUOYAH STATE PARK

**INDIAN LODGE MOTEL**
Rt 2, Box 393
(Wagoner 74467)
Rates: $32-$70;
Tel: (918) 485-3184

## SHAWNEE

**BEST WESTERN CINDERELLA MOTOR HOTEL**
623 Kickapoo Spur (74801)
Rates: $42-$65;
Tel: (405) 273-7010

## STILLWATER

**BEST WESTERN STILLWATER**
600 E McElroy (74075)
Rates: $35-$49;
Tel: (405) 377-7010

**EXECUTIVE INN**
5010 W 6th St (74074)
Rates: $37-$44;
Tel: (405) 743-2570

**HOLIDAY INN**
2515 W 6th St (74074)
Rates: $43-$52;
Tel: (405) 372-0800

## STROUD

**BEST WESTERN STROUD MOTOR LODGE**
1200 N 8th Ave (74079)
Rates: $35-$43;
Tel: (918) 968-9515

## TONKAWA

**WESTERN INN**
Rt 1, Box 130 (74653)
Rates: $28-$34;
Tel: (405) 628-2577

## TULSA
(and Vicinity)

**ADAMS MARK-WILLIAMS CENTER HOTEL**
10 E 2nd St (74103)
Rates: $59 $975;
Tel: (918) 582-9000

**BEST WESTERN TRADE WINDS CENTRAL INN**
3141 E Skelly Dr (74105)
Rates: $50-$61;
Tel: (918) 749-5501

**BEST WESTERN TRADE WINDS EAST INN**
3337 E Skelly Dr (74135)
Rates: $38-$54;
Tel: (918) 743-7931

**CAMELOT HOTEL**
4956 S Peoria Ave (74105)
Rates: $54-$69;
Tel: (918) 747-8811

**COMFORT INN**
4717 S Yale Ave (74135)
Rates: $36-$45;
Tel: (918) 622-6776

**DAYS INN**
8201 E Skelly Dr (74129)
Rates: $36-$42;
Tel: (918) 665-6800

**DAYS INN TULSA AIRPORT**
1016 N Garnett Rd (74116)
Rates: $29-$34;
Tel: (918) 438-5050

**DOUBLETREE HOTEL
AT WARREN PLACE**
6110 S Yale Ave (74136)
Rates: $59-$148;
Tel: (918) 495-1000

**DOUBLETREE HOTEL
DOWNTOWN TULSA**
616 W 7th St (74127)
Rates: $55-$65;
Tel: (918) 587-8000

**EMBASSY SUITES HOTEL**
3332 S 79th E Ave (74145)
Rates: $79-$129;
Tel: (918) 622-4000

**GRANADA INN**
11521 E Skelly Dr (74128)
Rates: $45-$50;
Tel: (918) 438-7700

**THE GRANDVIEW HOTEL**
799 S Lewis Ave (74136)
Rates: $47-$57;
Tel: (918) 492-5000

**HAWTHORN SUITES**
3509 S 79th East Ave (74145)
Rates: $46-$102;
Tel: (918) 663-3900

**HOLIDAY INN HOLIDOME
TULSA-CENTRAL**
8181 E Skelly Dr (74129)
Rates: $56-$80;
Tel: (918) 663-4541

**HOLIDAY INN-
TULSA EAST AIRPORT**
1010 N Garnett Rd (74116)
Rates: $59-$70;
Tel: (918) 437-7660

**LA QUINTA
MOTOR INN 41st ST**
10829 E 41st St S (74146)
Rates: $41-$56;
Tel: (918) 665-0220

**LA QUINTA
MOTOR INN AIRPORT**
35 N Sheridan Rd (74115)
Rates: $43-$58;
Tel: (918) 836-3931

**LA QUINTA MOTOR INN-
TULSA SOUTH**
12525 E 52nd St S (74146)
Rates: $40-$52;
Tel: (918) 254-1626

**MARRIOTT HOTEL**
10918 East 31st St (74146)
Rates: N/A;
Tel: (918) 627-5000

**QUALITY INN AIRPORT**
222 N Garnett Rd (74116)
Rates: $38-$46;
Tel: (918) 438-0780

**THE RESIDENCE INN
BY MARRIOTT**
8181 E 41st St (74145)
Rates: $89-$109;
Tel: (918) 664-7241

**SHERATON INN-
TULSA AIRPORT**
2201 N 77th E Ave (74115)
Rates: $49-$94;
Tel: (918) 835-9911

**STRATFORD HOUSE INN**
1301 N Elm Pl
(Broken Arrow 74012)
Rates: $29-$34;
Tel: (918) 258-7556

**SUPER 8 MOTEL I-44**
1347 E Skelly Dr (74105)
Rates: $32-$88;
Tel: (918) 743-4431

**SW AIRPORT HOTEL**
11620 E Skelly Dr (74128)
Rates: $38-$57;
Tel: (918) 437-9200

**TULSA GRAND
MOTOR HOTEL**
5000 E Skelly Dr (74135)
Rates: $52-$250;
Tel: (918) 622-7000

## VINITA

**PARK HILLS MOTEL**
Rt 4, Box 292 (74301)
Rates: $20-$28;
Tel: (918) 256-5511

## WATONGA

**ROMAN NOSE RESORT**
Rt 1 (73772)
Rates: $40-$65;
Tel: (405) 623-7281

## WEATHERFORD

**BEST WESTERN MARK
MOTOR HOTEL**
525 E Main St (73096)
Rates: $32-$43;
Tel: (405) 772-3325

## WOODWARD

**BEST WESTERN
WAYFARER INN**
2901 Williams Ave (73801)
Rates: $32-$52;
Tel: (405) 256-5553

**NORTHWEST INN**
Hwy 270 & 1st St (73801)
Rates: N/A;
Tel: (405) 256-7600

# OREGON

## ALBANY

**BEST WESTERN PONY
SOLDIER MOTOR INN**
315 Airport Rd SE (97321)
Rates: $56-$73;
Tel: (503) 928-6322

**COMFORT INN**
251 Airport Way SE (97321)
Rates: $55-$79;
Tel: (503) 928 0921

**STARDUST MOTEL**
2735 E Pacific Blvd (97321)
Rates: N/A;
Tel: (503) 926-4233

## ASHLAND

**ASHLAND VALLEY INN**
1193 Siskiyou Blvd (97520)
Rates: $32-$78;
Tel: (503) 482-2641

**BEST WESTERN
BARD'S INN MOTEL**
132 N Main St (97521)
Rates: $48-$95;
Tel: (503) 482 0049

**BEST WESTERN
HERITAGE INN**
434 Valley View Rd (97520)
Rates: $37-$95;
Tel: (503) 482-6932

**KNIGHTS INN MOTEL**
2359 Hwy 66 (97520)
Rates: $29-$56;
Tel: (503) 482-5111

**QUALITY INN FLAGSHIP**
2520 Ashland St (97520)
Rates: $44-$79;
Tel: (503) 488-2330

**WINDMILL'S ASHLAND
HILLS INN**
2525 Ashland St (97520)
Rates: $39-$109;
Tel: (503) 482-2264

## ASTORIA

**CREST MOTEL**
5366 Leif Erickson Dr (97103)
Rates: $45-$78
Tel: (503) 325-3141

**RED LION INN**
400 Industry St (97103)
Rates: $60-$85;
Tel: (503) 325 7373

**ROSEBRIAR INN**
636 14th St (97103)
Rates: N/A;
Tel: (503) 325-7427

**SHILO INN**
1609 E Harbor Dr
(Warrenton 97146)
Rates: $64-$90;
Tel: (503) 861-2181

## BAKER CITY

**EL DORADO MOTEL**
695 E Campbell St (97814)
Rates: $30-$35;
Tel: (503) 523 6494

**QUALITY INN**
810 Campbell (97814)
Rates: $33-$39;
Tel: (503) 523-2242

**ROYAL MOTOR INN**
2205 Broadway (97814)
Rates: $25-$33;
Tel: (503) 523-6324

**THE WESTERN MOTEL**
3055 10th St (97814)
Rates: N/A;
Tel: (503) 523-3700

## BANDON

**BANDON WAYSIDE MOTEL**
Hwy 42 South (97411)
Rates: N/A;
Tel: (503) 347-3421

**CAPRICE MOTEL**
Rt 1, Box 530 (97411)
Rates: $24-$46;
Tel: (503) 347-4494

**THE INN
AT FACE ROCK MOTEL**
3225 Beach Loop Rd (97411)
Rates: $49-$79;
Tel: (503) 347-9441

## BEND

**BEST WESTERN
ENTRADA LODGE**
19221 Century Dr (97702)
Rates: $55-$89;
Tel: (503) 382-4080

**BEST WESTERN
WOODSTONE INN**
721 NE 3rd (97701)
Rates: $55-$89;
Tel: (503) 382-1515

**COMFORT INN**
61200 S Hwy 97 (97702)
Rates: $39-$83;
Tel: (503) 388-2227

**HAMPTON INN**
15 NE Butler Rd (97701)
Rates: $47-$59;
Tel: (503) 388 4114

**RED LION MOTEL**
849 NE 3rd St (97701)
Rates: $46-$68;
Tel: (503) 382-8384

**RED LION NORTH**
1415 NE 3rd St (97701)
Rates: $47-$65;
Tel: (503) 382-7011

**THE RIVERHOUSE
MOTOR INN**
3075 N Hwy 97 (97701)
Rates: $49-$67;
Tel: (503) 389-3111

**TOUCH OF CLASS INN
& CONVENTION CENTER**
3105 O B Riley Rd (97701)
Rates: $54-$89;
Tel: (503) 389-9600

**WESTWARD HO MOTEL**
904 Southeast Third St
(97702)
Rates: N/A;
Tel: (503) 382-2111

## BIGGS

**DINTY'S MOTOR INN**
P. O. Box 136 (Rufus 97050)
Rates: $30-$40;
Tel: (503) 739-2596

## BOARDMAN

**DODGE CITY INN**
1st Front St (97818)
Rates: N/A;
Tel: (503) 481-2451

**NUGGET INN**
P. O. Box 762 (97818)
Rates: $45-$55;
Tel: (503) 481-2375

## BROOKINGS

**HARBOR INN MOTEL**
15991 Hwy 101S (97415)
Rates: $36-$55;
Tel: (503) 469-3194

**PACIFIC SUNSET INN**
1144 Chetco Ave (97415)
Rates: $28-$53;
Tel: (503) 469-2141

## BURNS

**BEST WESTERN
PONDEROSA**
577 W Monroe (97720)
Rates: $32-$42;
Tel: (503) 573-2047

**ORBIT MOTEL**
P. O. Box 303 (97720)
Rates: $25-$39;
Tel: (800) 235-6155

**ROYAL INN**
999 Oregon Ave (97720)
Rates: $34-$46;
Tel: (503) 573-5295

## CANNON BEACH

**BEST WESTERN
SURFSAND RESORT**
P. O. Box 219 (97110)
Rates: $89-$129;
Tel: (503) 436-2274

**HALLMARK RESORT**
1400 S Hemlock (97110)
Rates: $49-$169;
Tel: (503) 436-1566

**MCBEE MOTEL**
Box 967 - 888 S Hemlock
(97110)
Rates: N/A;
Tel: (503) 436-2569

**QUIET CANNON LODGING**
372 N Spruce St (97110)
Rates: N/A;
Tel: (503) 436-1405

**TOLOVANA INN**
P. O. Box 165
(Tolovana Park 97145)
Rates: $61-$158;
Tel: (503) 436-2211

## CANYONVILLE

**LEISURE INN**
P. O. Box 869 (97417)
Rates: $31-$39;
Tel: (503) 839-4278

## CHEMULT

**CRATER LAKE MOTEL**
Hwy 97, P. O. Box 190
(97731)
Rates: N/A;
Tel: (503) 365-2241

## COOS BAY

**COOS BAY INN**
1445 N Bayshore Dr (97420)
Rates: $37-$75;
Tel: (503) 267-7171

**EDGEWATER INN**
275 E Johnson St (97420)
Rates: $67-$72;
Tel: (503) 267-0423

**RED LION INN**
1313 N Bayshore Dr (97420)
Rates: $58-$95;
Tel: (503) 267-4141

## COQUILLE

**MYRTLE LANE MOTEL**
787 N Central (97423)
Rates: $29-$39;
Tel: (503) 396-2102

## CORVALLIS

**SHANICO INN**
1113 NW 9th Ave (97330)
Rates: $42-$49;
Tel: (503) 754-7474

## COTTAGE GROVE

**BEST WESTERN VILLAGE
GREEN RESORT HOTEL**
725 Row River Rd (97424)
Rates: $54-$78;
Tel: (503) 942-2491

**COMFORT INN**
845 Gateway Blvd (97424)
Rates: $45-$52;
Tel: (503) 942-9747

## ELGIN

**CITY CENTRE MOTEL**
P. O. Box 207 (97827)
Rates: N/A;
Tel: (503) 437-2441

## ENTERPRISE

**PONDEROSA MOTEL**
102 SE Greenwood (97828)
Rates: $31-$39;
Tel: (503) 426-3186

**WILDERNESS INN**
301 W North St (97828)
Rates: $32-$42;
Tel: (503) 426-4535

## EUGENE

**BEST WESTERN
GREENTREE MOTEL**
1759 Franklin Blvd (97403)
Rates: $42-$68;
Tel: (503) 485-2727

**BEST WESTERN
NEW OREGON MOTEL**
P. O. Box 18 (97440)
Rates: $42-$68;
Tel: (503) 683-3669

**EUGENE HILTON**
66 E 6th & Oak Sts (97401)
Rates: $95-$185;
Tel: (503) 342-2000

**CAMPUS INN**
390 East Broadway (97401)
Rates: N/A;
Tel: (800) 888-6313

**HOLIDAY INN OF EUGENE**
225 Coburg Rd (97401)
Rates: $48-$61;
Tel: (503) 342-5181

**NENDEL'S MOTOR INN**
3540 Gateway Rd
(Springfield 97477)
Rates: $45-$59;
Tel: (503) 726-1212

**RED LION INN**
205 Coburg Rd (97401)
Rates: $62-$85;
Tel: (503) 342-5201

**RED LION INN/
EUGENE-SPRINGFIELD**
3280 Gateway Rd
(Springfield 97477)
Rates: $61-$85;
Tel: (503) 726-8181

**THE VALLEY RIVER INN**
P. O. Box 10088 (97440)
Rates: $98-$155;
Tel: (503) 687-0123

## FLORENCE

**PARK MOTEL**
85034 Hwy 101 (97439)
Rates: $26-$50;
Tel: (503) 997-2634

## GLENEDEN BEACH

**SALISHAN LODGE**
P. O. Box 118 (98388)
Rates: $104-$227;
Tel: (503) 764-2371

## GOLD BEACH

**BEST WESTERN INN
OF THE BEACHCOMBER**
1250 S Hwy 101 (97444)
Rates: $44-$87;
Tel: (503) 247-6691

**DRIFT IN MOTEL**
715 North Ellensburg (97444)
Rates: N/A;
Tel: (503) 247-4547

**INN AT GOLD BEACH**
P. O. Box 1030 (97444)
Rates: $26-$69;
Tel: (503) 247-6606

**IRELAND'S RUSTIC LODGES**
P. O. Box 774 (97444)
Rates: $30-$76;
Tel: (503) 247-7718

**JOT'S RESORT**
P. O. Box J (97444)
Rates: $45-$95;
Tel: (503) 247-6676

**RIVER BRIDGE INN**
P. O. Box 1336 (97444)
Rates: $32-$74;
Tel: (503) 247-4533

**WESTERN VILLAGE MOTEL**
P. O. Box 793 (97444)
Rates: $25-$59;
Tel: (503) 247-6611

## GOVERNMENT CAMP

**MT HOOD INN**
P. O. Box 400 (97028)
Rates: $70-$130;
Tel: (503) 272-3205

## GRANTS PASS

**FLAMINGO INN**
728 Northwest 6th St (97526)
Rates: N/A;
Tel: (503) 476-6601

**GOLDEN INN**
1950 Northwest Vine (97526)
Rates: N/A;
Tel: (503) 479-6611

**KNIGHTS INN**
104 Southeast 7th St (97526)
Rates: N/A;
Tel: (503) 479-5595

**REDWOOD MOTEL**
815 NE 6th St (97526)
Rates: $30-$50;
Tel: (503) 476-0878

**RIVERSIDE INN**
971 SE 6th St (97526)
Rates: $45-$80;
Tel: (503) 476-6873

**ROYAL VUE MOTEL**
110 NE Morgan Ln (97526)
Rates: $40-$66;
Tel: (503) 479-5381

**SHILO INN**
1880 Northwest 6th St
(97526)
Rates: N/A;
Tel: (503) 479-8391

## GRESHAM

**QUALITY INN**
1545 NE Burnside (97030)
Rates: $48-$55;
Tel: (503) 666-9545

## HERMISTON

**SANDS MOTEL**
835 North First (97838)
Rates: N/A;
Tel: (503) 567-5516

## HILLSBORO

**BEST WESTERN HALLMARK
INN-HILLSBORO AIRPORT**
3550 NE Cornell Rd (97124)
Rates: $58-$73;
Tel: (503) 648-3500

**PARK DUNES MOTEL**
622 SE 10th (97123)
Rates: $35-$48;
Tel: (800) 548-0163

## HOOD RIVER

**BEST WESTERN
HOOD RIVER INN**
1108 E Marina Way (97031)
Rates: $50-$95;
Tel: (503) 386-2200

**COLUMBIA GORGE HOTEL**
4000 Westcliff Dr (97031)
Rates: $175;
Tel: (503) 386-5566

**LOST LAKE RESORT**
Mt Hood National Forest
(97031)
Rates: N/A;
Tel: (503) 386-6366

**VAGABOND LODGE**
4070 Westcliff Dr (97031)
Rates: $33-$62;
Tel: (503) 386-2992

## HUNTINGTON

**FAREWELL BEND
MOTOR INN**
RR 2, Box 17, Exit 353 I-84
(97907)
Rates: $34-$42;
Tel: (503) 869-2211

## JOHN DAY

**BEST WESTERN INN**
315 W Main (97845)
Rates: $38-$58;
Tel: (503) 575-1700

**DREAMERS LODGE**
144 N Canyon Blvd (97845)
Rates: $32-$42;
Tel: (503) 575-0526

## KLAMATH FALLS

**CIMARRON MOTOR INN**
3060 S 6th St (97603)
Rates: $30-$40;
Tel: (800) 742-2648

**GOLDEN WEST MOTEL**
6402 South 6th (97603)
Rates: N/A;
Tel: (503) 882-1758

**OREGON MOTEL 8**
5225 Hwy 97 N (97601)
Rates: $24-$36;
Tel: (503) 883-3431

**RED LION INN**
2612 S 6th St (97603)
Rates: $54-$82;
Tel: (503) 882-8864

## LAKEVIEW

**BEST WESTERN
SKYLINE MOTOR LODGE**
414 N G St (97630)
Rates: $42-$58;
Tel: (503) 947-2194

**INTERSTATE 8 MOTEL**
354 North K St (97630)
Rates: N/A;
Tel: (503) 947-3341

**LAKEVIEW LODGE MOTEL**
301 Worth G (97630)
Rates: N/A;
Tel: (503) 947-2181

**RIM ROCK MOTEL**
727 South F St (97630)
Rates: N/A;
Tel: (503) 947-2185

## LA PINE

**MASTER HOST MOTOR INN**
P. O. Box 915 (97739)
Rates: $29-$37;
Tel: (503) 536-1737

## LEBANON

**LESITA MOTEL**
1830 S Main (97355)
Rates: N/A;
Tel: (503) 258-2434

## LINCOLN CITY

**BAY WEST DOCK
OF THE BAY MOTEL**
1116 SW 51st St (97367)
Rates: $45-$89;
Tel: (503) 996-3549

**BEACHFRONT MOTEL**
3313 NW Inlet Ave (97367)
Rates: N/A;
Tel: (503) 994-2324

**COHO INN**
1635 NW Harbor (97367)
Rates: $52-$66;
Tel: (503) 994-3684

**RED CARPET INN**
2645 NW Inlet Ave (97367)
Rates: $47-$79;
Tel: (503) 994-2134

**SEA ECHO MOTEL**
3510 NE Hwy 101 (97367)
Rates: N/A;
Tel: (503) 994-2575

**SHILO INN**
1501 NW 40th St (97367)
Rates: N/A;
Tel: (503) 994-3655

## MADRAS

**KAH-NEE-TA RESORT**
Box K (Warm Springs 97761)
Rates: $90-$250;
Tel: (800) 831-0100

**LEISURE INN**
12 SW 4th (97741)
Rates: $31-$39;
Tel (503) 475-6141

**SONNY'S MOTEL**
1539 SW Hwy 97 (97741)
Rates: $36-$42;
Tel. (503) 475-7217

## MCKENZIE BRIDGE

**THE COUNTRY PLACE**
56245 Delta Dr (97413)
Rates: N/A;
Tel: (503) 822-6008

## MCMINNVILLE

**FLYING M RANCH**
23029 NW Flying M Rd
(97128)
Rates: $50-$150;
Tel: (503) 662-3222

**PARAGON MOTEL**
2065 Hwy 99 West (97128)
Rates: N/A;
Tel: (503) 472-9493

## MEDFORD

**CEDAR LODGE MOTOR INN**
518 N Riverside (97501)
Rates: $37-$62;
Tel; (503) 773-7361

**HORIZON MOTOR INN**
1150 E Barnett Rd (97501)
Rates: $52-$64;
Tel: (503) 779-5085

**KNIGHTS INN**
500 N Riverside Ave (97501)
Rates: $26-$32;
Tel: (800) 626-1900

**NENDEL'S INN**
2300 Crater Lake Hwy
(97504)
Rates: $52-$72;
Tel: (503) 779-3141

**RED LION INN**
200 N Riverside (97501)
Rates: $79-$114;
Tel: (503) 779-5811

**SHILO INN**
2111 Biddle Rd (97504)
Rates: N/A;
Tel: (503) 770-5151

**WINDMILL INN
OF MEDFORD**
1950 Biddle Rd (97504)
Rates: $54-$70;
Tel: (503) 779-0050

## MILWAUKIE

**ECONO LODGE
SUITES INN**
17330 SE McLoughlin Blvd
(97222)
Rates: $42-$64;
Tel: (503) 654-2222

## MYRTLE POINT

**MYRTLE TREES MOTEL**
1010 8th St (97458)
Rates: $30-$39;
Tel: (503) 572-5811

## NEWBERG

**SHILO INN**
501 Sitka Ave (97132)
Rates: $58-$64;
Tel: (503) 537-0303

## NEWPORT

**BEST WESTERN
HALLMARK RESORT**
744 SW Elizabeth St (97365)
Rates: $70-$105;
Tel: (503) 265-8853

**THE HOTEL NEWPORT**
3019 N Coast Hwy (97365)
Rates: $72-$92;
Tel: (503) 265-9411

**SHILO INN**
536 SW Elizabeth (97365)
Rates: N/A;
Tel: (503) 265-7701

**VAL-U INN**
531 SW Fall St (97365)
Rates: $40-$75;
Tel: (503) 265-6203

**WEST WIND MOTEL**
747 SW Coast Hwy (97365)
Rates: N/A;
Tel: (503) 265-5388

## NORTH BEND

**PONY VILLAGE MOTOR LODGE**
Virginia Ave (97459)
Rates: $41-$59;
Tel: (503) 756-3191

## ONTARIO

**BEST WESTERN INN**
251 Goodfellow St (97914)
Rates: $45-$60;
Tel: (503) 889-2600

**COLONIAL MOTOR INN**
761 Tapadera Ave (97914)
Rates: $21-$48;
Tel· (800) 727-5014

**HOLIDAY BUDGET MOTEL**
615 E Idaho (97914)
Rates: $28-$36;
Tel: (503) 889-9188

**HOWARD JOHNSON
LODGE**
1249 Tapadera Ave (97914)
Rates: $41-$59;
Tel: (503) 889-8621

**MOTEL 6**
275 Butler St (97914)
Rates: $22-$28;
Tel: (503) 889-6617

**OREGON TRAIL MOTEL**
92 E Idaho Ave (97914)
Rates: N/A;
Tel: (503) 889-8633

## OREGON CITY

**VAL-U INN**
1900 Clackamette Dr (97045)
Rates: $51-$65;
Tel: (503) 655-7141

## PENDLETON

**CHAPARRAL MOTEL**
P. O. Box 331 (97801)
Rates: $37-$47;
Tel: (503) 276-8654

**ECONO LODGE**
201 SW Court Ave (97801)
Rates: $28-$41;
Tel: (503) 276-5252

**RED LION INN/
INDIAN HILLS**
P. O. Box 1556 (97801)
Rates: $60-$78;
Tel: (503) 276-6111

**TAPADERA MOTOR INN**
105 SE Court (97801)
Rates: $33-$43;
Tel: (503) 276-3231

## PHILOMATH

**GALAXIE MOTEL**
104 South 20th St (97370)
Rates: N/A;
Tel: (503) 929-4334

## PORTLAND
(and Vicinity)

**THE BENSON HOTEL**
309 SW Broadway at Oak
(97205)
Rates: $145-$205;
Tel: (503) 228-2000

**BEST WESTERN
HERITAGE INN**
4319 NW Yeon (97210)
Rates: $53-$79;
Tel: (503) 497-9044

**BEST WESTERN INN
AT THE CONVENTION CTR**
420 NE Holladay (97232)
Rates: $60-$67;
Tel: (503) 233-6331

**BEST WESTERN INN
AT THE MEADOWS**
1215 N Hayden Meadows Dr
(97217)
Rates: $68-$74;
Tel: (503) 286-9600

**BEST WESTERN-
SHERWOOD INN**
15700 SW Upper Boones Ferry
Rd (Lake Oswego 97035)
Rates: $47-$53;
Tel: (503) 620-2980

**THE CLACKAMAS INN**
16010 SE 82nd (97015)
Rates: $54-$64;
Tel: (503) 650-5340

**COMFORT INN-
LLOYD CENTER**
431 NE Multnomah St (97232)
Rates: $56-$82;
Tel: (503) 233-7933

**DAYS HOTEL-
PORTLAND AIRPORT**
11550 NE Airport Way
(97220)
Rates: $75-$95;
Tel: (503) 252-3200

**DELTA INN**
9930 N Whitaker (97217)
Rates: $43-$53;
Tel: (503) 289-1800

**EMBASSY SUITES
HOTEL-PORTLAND
WASHINGTON SQ**
9000 SW Washington Square
Rd (Tigard 97223)
Rates: $117-$132;
Tel: (503) 644-4000

**GREENWOOD INN**
10700 SW Allen Blvd
(Beaverton 97005)
Rates: $72-$97;
Tel: (503) 643-7444

**HOLIDAY INN-AIRPORT**
8439 NE Columbia Blvd
(97220)
Rates: $78-$93;
Tel: (503) 256-5000

**HOWARD JOHNSON
PLAZA HOTEL**
14811 Kruse Oaks Blvd
(Lake Oswego 97035)
Rates: $80-$120;
Tel: (503) 624-8400

**IMPERIAL HOTEL**
400 SW Broadway & Stark St
(97205)
Rates: $55-$75;
Tel: (503) 228-7221

**MALLORY HOTEL**
729 SW 15th (97205)
Rates: $45-$90;
Tel: (503) 223-6311

**PORTLAND
MARRIOTT HOTEL**
1401 SW Front Ave (97201)
Rates: $99-$160;
Tel: (503) 226-7600

**PORTLAND-ROSE MOTEL**
8920 SW Barbur (97219)
Rates: N/A;
Tel: (503) 244-0107

**QUALITY INN
PORTLAND AIRPORT**
8247 NE Sandy Blvd (97220)
Rates: $57-$82;
Tel: (503) 256-4111

**RED LION HOTEL/
COLUMBIA RIVER**
1401 N Hayden Island Dr
(97217)
Rates: $99-$134;
Tel: (503) 283-2111

**RED LION HOTEL/
DOWNTOWN**
310 SW Lincoln (97201)
Rates: $88-$115;
Tel: (503) 221-0450

**RED LION HOTEL-
JANTZEN BEACH**
909 N Hayden Island Dr
(97217)
Rates: $96-$127;
Tel: (503) 283-4466

**RED LION HOTEL/
LLOYD CENTER**
1000 NE Multnomah St
(97232)
Rates: $110-$150;
Tel: (503) 281-6111

**RED LION INN/COLISEUM**
1224 N Thunderbird Way
(97227)
Rates: $58-$85;
Tel: (503) 235-8311

**RESIDENCE INN BY
MARRIOTT PORTLAND
DOWTOWN**
1710 NE Multnomah St
(97232)
Rates: $104-$170;
Tel: (503) 288-1400

**RESIDENCE INN BY MARRIOTT
PORTLAND SOUTH**
P. O. Box 1110
(Lake Oswego 97035)
Rates: $102-$138;
Tel: (503) 684-2603

**RIVER PLACE
ALEXIS HOTEL**
1510 SW Harbor Way
(97201)
Rates: $150-$180;
Tel: (503) 228-3233

**SHILO INN**
3828 NE 82nd Ave (97220)
Rates: N/A;
Tel: (503) 256-2550

**SHILO INN**
11600 SW Barnes Rd (97225)
Rates: N/A;
Tel: (503) 641-6565

**SHILO INN-LLOYD CENTER**
1506 NE 2nd Ave (97232)
Rates: $52-$66;
Tel: (503) 231-7665

**SHILO INN-
WASHINGTON SQUARE**
10830 SW Greenburg Rd
(97223)
Rates: $51-$61;
Tel: (503) 620-4320

**SWEETBRIER INN**
7125 SW Nyberg Rd
(Tualatin 97062)
Rates: $54-$74;
Tel: (503) 692-5800

**TRAVELODGE SUITES**
7740 SE Powell Blvd (97206)
Rates: $49-$60;
Tel: (503) 788-9394

## PORT ORFORD

**SEA CREST MOTEL**
P. O. Box C (97465)
Rates: $30-$55;
Tel: (503) 332-3040

## PRINEVILLE

**OCHOCO INN**
123 E 3rd St (97754)
Rates: $32-$42;
Tel: (503) 447-6231

## REDMOND

**REDMOND INN**
1545 Hwy 97S (97756)
Rates: $42-$51;
Tel: (503) 548-1091

## REEDSPORT

**TROPICANA MOTEL**
1593 Highway Ave (97467)
Rates: $35-$60;
Tel: (503) 271-3671

**WESTERN HILLS MOTEL**
1821 Winchester Ave (97467)
Rates: $36-$50;
Tel: (503) 271-2149

## ROCKAWAY BEACH

**OCEAN LOCOMOTION
MOTEL**
19130 Alder Ave (97136)
Rates: N/A;
Tel: (503) 355-2093

**SILVER SANDS MOTEL**
P. O. Box 161 (97136)
Rates: $60-$75;
Tel: (503) 355-2206

**TRADEWINDS MOTEL**
523 N Pacific St (97136)
Rates: $45-$85;
Tel: (503) 355-2112

## ROSEBURG

**BEST WESTERN
DOUGLAS INN MOTEL**
511 SE Stephens St (97470)
Rates: N/A;
Tel: (503) 673-6625

**BEST WESTERN
GARDEN VILLA MOTEL**
760 NW Garden Valley
(97470)
Rates: N/A;
Tel: (503) 672-1601

**WINDMILL INN**
1450 NW Mulholland Dr
(97470)
Rates: $52-$82;
Tel: (503) 673-0901

## SALEM

**CITY CENTRE MOTEL**
510 Liberty St SE (97301)
Rates: N/A;
Tel: (503) 364-0121

**PHOENIX INN**
4370 Commercial SE (97308)
Rates: $42-$63;
Tel: (503) 588-9220

**QUALITY INN**
3301 Market St NE (97301)
Rates: $59-$69;
Tel: (503) 370-7888

**SALEM GRAND MOTEL**
1555 State St (97301)
Rates: N/A;
Tel: (503) 581-2466

**SHILO INN**
1855 Hawthorne NE (97303)
Rates: N/A;
Tel: (503) 581-9410

**TIKI LODGE MOTEL**
3705 Market St NE (97301)
Rate: $45-$56;
Tel: (503) 581-4441

## SEASIDE

**EBB TIDE MOTEL**
300 N Promenade (97138)
Rates: $70-$135;
Tel: (800) 468-6232

**HUNTLEY INN**
441 2nd Ave (97138)
Rates: $46-$74;
Tel: (800) 448-5544

## SPRINGFIELD

**SHILO INN**
3350 Gateway (97477)
Rates: N/A;
Tel: (503) 747-0332

**VILLAGE INN MOTEL**
1875 Mohawk Blvd (97477)
Rates: $42-$47;
Tel: (503) 747-4546

## THE DALLES

**BEST WESTERN
TAPADERA MOTOR INN**
112 W Second (97058)
Rates: $42-$62;
Tel: (503) 296-9107

**HUNTLEY INN**
2500 W 6th (97058)
Rates: $41-$49;
Tel: (503) 296-1191

**SHILO INN**
3223 NE Frontage Rd (97058)
Rates: $50-$99;
Tel: (503) 298-5502

## TIGARD

**SHILO INN**
7300 Hazel Fern Rd (97223)
Rates: N/A;
Tel: (503) 620-3460

## TILLAMOOK

**SHILO INN/TILLAMOOK**
2515 N Main (97141)
Rates: $63-$79;
Tel: (503) 842-7971

## TROUTDALE

**PHOENIX INN**
477 NW Phoenix Dr (97060)
Rates: $50-$61;
Tel: (503) 669-6500

## UMATILLA

**HEATHER INN**
705 Willamette Ave (97882)
Rates: $46-$51;
Tel: (503) 922-4871

## WALDPORT

**SUNDOWN MOTEL**
5050 SW PCH 101 (97394)
Rates: N/A;
Tel: (800) 535-0192

## WARM SPRINGS

**KAH-NEE-TA VILLAGE**
P. O. Box K (97761)
Rates: $80-$120;
Tel: (503) 553-1112

## WARRENTON

**SHILO INN**
1609 E Harbor Dr (97146)
Rates: N/A;
Tel: (503) 861-2181

## WILSONVILLE

**SUPER 8 MOTEL**
25438 SW Pkwy Ave (97070)
Rates: N/A;
Tel: (503) 682-2088

## WOODBURN

**COMFORT INN WOODBURN**
120 NE Arney Rd (97071)
Rates: $52-$82;
Tel: (503) 982-1727

## WOOD VILLAGE

**SHILO INN**
2522 NE 238th Dr (97060)
Rates: N/A;
Tel: (503) 667-1414

## YACHATS

**FIRESIDE MOTEL**
P. O. Box 313 (97498)
Rates: $42-$72;
Tel: (503) 547-3636

**ROCK PARK COTTAGES**
431 West 2nd St (97498)
Rates: N/A;
Tel: (503) 547-3214

**SHAMROCK LODGETTES**
P. O. Box 346 (97498)
Rates: $65-$90;
Tel: (503) 547-3312

# PENNSYLVANIA

## ADAMSTOWN

**BLACK FOREST INN**
Rt 272 (19501)
Rates: N/A;
Tel: (215) 484-4801

## ALLENTOWN

**ALLENWOOD MOTEL**
1058 Hausman Rd (18104)
Rates: $39;
Tel: (215) 395-3707

**CENTER VALLEY
MOTOR LODGE**
4942 Rt 209
(Center Valley 18034)
Rates: $35-$50;
Tel: (215) 797-0128

**COMFORT INN**
7625 Imperial Way (18106)
Rates: $35-$80;
Tel: (215) 091-0544

**DAYS INN
CONFERENCE CENTER**
1151 Bulldog Dr (18104)
Rates: $48-$79;
Tel: (215) 395-3731

**RED ROOF INN**
1846 Catasauqua Rd (18103)
Rates: $36-$54;
Tel: (215) 264-5404

## ALTOONA

**ECONO LODGE**
2906 Pleasant Valley Blvd
(16602)
Rates: $36-$43;
Tel: (814) 944-3555

**HOJO INN**
1500 Sterling St (16602)
Rates: $41-$46;
Tel: (814) 946-7601

**RAMADA MOTOR HOTEL**
1 Sheraton Dr (16601)
Rates: $60-$140;
Tel: (814) 946-1631

## BARKEYVILLE

**DAYS INN**
P. O. Box 98A (16038)
Rates: $42-$58;
Tel: (814) 786-7910

## BEAVER FALLS

**BEAVER VALLEY MOTEL**
SR 18 (15010)
Rates: $37-$52;
Tel: (412) 843-0630

**HOLIDAY INN**
P. O.Box 696 (15010)
Rates: $68-$86;
Tel: (412) 846 2700

## BEDFORD

**BEST WESTERN HOSS'S INN**
RD 2, Box 33B (15522)
Rates: $38-$62;
Tel: (814) 623-9006

**JANEY LYNN MOTEL**
RD 5, Box 367 (15522)
Rates: $24-$39;
Tel: (814) 623-9515

**QUALITY INN**
RD 2, Box 171 (15522)
Rates: $54-$66;
Tel: (814) 623-5188

**SUPER 8 MOTEL**
RD 2, Box 32A (15522)
Rates: $37-$43;
Tel: (814) 623-5880

## BETHLEHEM

**COMFORT INN**
3191 Highfield Dr (18017)
Rates: $49-$74;
Tel: (215) 865-6300

**COMFORT SUITES**
120 W 3rd St (18015)
Rates: $55-$99;
Tel: (215) 882-9700

## BLOOMSBURG

**ECONO LODGE
AT BLOOMSBURG**
189 Columbia Mall Dr
(17815)
Rates: $40-$58;
Tel: (717) 387-0490

**THE INN AT TURKEY HILL**
991 Central Rd (17815)
Rates: $55-$150;
Tel: (717) 387-1500

**MAGEE'S MAIN STREET**
20 W Main St (17815)
Rates: $48-$77;
Tel: (800) 331-9815

**QUALITY INN-
BUCKHORN PLAZA**
1 Buckhorn Rd (17815)
Rates: $44-$69;
Tel: (717) 784-5300

## BOYERTOWN

**MEL-DOR MOTEL**
P. O. Box 349
(New Berlinville 19545)
Rates: $35-$43;
Tel: (215) 367-2626

## BREEZEWOOD

**ECONO LODGE**
RD 1, Box 101A (15533)
Rates: $29-$61;
Tel: (814) 735-4341

**PENN AIRE MOTEL**
P.O. Box 156 (15533)
Rates: $33-$80;
Tel: (814) 735-4351

**WILTSHIRE MOTEL**
Star Rt 2, Box 1 (15533)
Rates: $28-$36;
Tel: (814) 735-4361

## BRIDGEVILLE

**KNIGHTS INN**
111 Hickory Grade Rd
(15017)
Rates: N/A;
Tel: (800) 843-5644

## BRISTOL

**COMFORT INN**
6401 Bristol Pk
(Levittown 19057)
Rates: $48-$58;
Tel: (215) 547-5000

## BROOKVILLE

**BUDGET HOST
GOLD EAGLE INN**
RD 3, Box 358 (15825)
Rates: $25-$54;
Tel: (814) 849-7344

**ECONO LODGE**
RD 5, Box 151 (15825)
Rates: $29-$60;
Tel: (814) 849-8381

## BUTLER

**DAYS INN**
139 Pittsburgh Rd (16001)
Rates: $42-$72;
Tel: (412) 287-6761

**SUPER 8 MOTEL**
128 Pittsburgh Rd (16001)
Rates: $36-$43;
Tel: (412) 287-8888

## CARLISLE

**ALBRIGHT MOTEL**
1165 Harrisburg Pike (17013)
Rates: $25-$28;
Tel: (717) 249-4380

**BEST WESTERN INN
OF THE BUTTERFLY**
1245 Harrisburg Pike (17013)
Rates: $50-$73;
Tel: (717) 243-5411

**COAST TO COAST
BUDGET HOST INN**
1252 Harrisburg Pike (17013)
Rates: $31-$48;
Tel: (717) 243-8585

**ECONO LODGE**
1460 Harrisburg Pike (17013)
Rates: $37-$64;
Tel: (717) 249-7775

**HOLIDAY INN**
1450 Harrisburg Pike (17013)
Rates: $55-$72;
Tel: (717) 245-2400

**HOWARD JOHNSON
MOTOR LODGE**
1255 Harrisburg Pike (17013)
Rates: $39-$80;
Tel: (717) 243-6000

**KNIGHTS INN**
1153 Harrisburg Pike (17013)
Rates: $36-$43;
Tel: (717) 249-7622

**RODEWAY INN**
1239 Harrisburg Pike (17013)
Rates: $34-$70;
Tel: (717) 249-2800

## CHAMBERSBURG

**CHAMBERSBURG
TRAVELODGE**
565 Lincoln Way E (17201)
Rates: $46-$56;
Tel: (717) 264-4187

**HOLIDAY INN**
1095 Wayne Ave (17201)
Rates: $55-$72;
Tel: (717) 263-3400

## CLARION

**DAYS INN OF CLARION**
Rt 68 & I-80 (16214)
Rates: $35-$65;
Tel: (814) 226-8682

**HOLIDAY INN**
Rt 68 & I-80; Tel: (16214)
Rates: $58-$77;
Tel: (814) 226-8850

**KNIGHTS INN**
Rt 3 (16214)
Rates: $37-$40;
Tel: (814) 226-4550

## CLEARFIELD

**BEST WESTERN
MOTOR INN**
P. O. Box 286 (16830)
Rates: $51-$68;
Tel: (814) 765-2441

**DAYS INN**
RR 2, Box 245B (16830)
Rates: $39-$60;
Tel: (814) 765-5381

**ROYAL NINE MOTOR INN**
Rt 322 E, P. O. Box 297
(16830)
Rates: N/A;
Tel: (814) 765-2639

## COOKSBURG

**FOREST VIEW CABINS**
Box 105 (16217)
Rates: N/A;
Tel: (814) 744-8413

## DANVILLE

**HOWARD JOHNSON
MOTEL**
15 Valley West Rd (17821)
Rates: $40-$65;
Tel: (717) 275-5100

**RED ROOF INN**
RD 2, Box 88 (17821)
Rates: $34-$53;
Tel: (717) 275-7600

## DENVER

**BLACK FOREST INN**
P. O. Box 457
(Adamstown 19501)
Rates: $33-$68;
Tel: (215) 484-4801

**BLACK HORSE LODGE
AND SUITES**
P. O. Box 343 (17517)
Rates: $57-$149;
Tel: (215) 267-7563

**ECONO LODGE**
RD 3, Box 132 (17517)
Rates: $34-$89;
Tel: (215) 267-4649

**HOLIDAY INN-
LANCASTER COUNTY**
P. O. Box 129 (17517)
Rates: $48-$96;
Tel: (215) 267-7541

**PENNSYLVANIA
DUTCH MOTEL**
2275 N Reading Rd (17517)
Rates: $32-$46;
Tel: (215) 267-5559

## DUBOIS

**HOLIDAY INN**
US 219 (15801)
Rates: $55-$72;
Tel: (814) 371-5100

## EASTON

**DAYS INN**
2555 Nazareth Rd (18042)
Rates: $39-$59;
Tel: (215) 253-0546

**EASTON INN
MOTOR HOTEL**
S 3rd St & Larry Holmes Dr
(18042)
Rates: $60-$98;
Tel: (800) 882-0113

## EBENSBURG

**THE COTTAGE
RESTAURANT & INN**
RD 4, Box 50 (15931)
Rates: $48-$64;
Tel: (814) 472-8002

## EDINBORO

**EDINBORO INN**
Rt 6N (16412)
Rates: $56-$82;
Tel: (814) 734-5650

## ERIE

**DAYS INN**
7400 Schultz Rd (16509)
Rates: $46-$89;
Tel: (814) 868-8521

**HOLIDAY INN-DOWNTOWN**
18 W 18th St (16501)
Rates: $64-$82;
Tel: (814) 456-2961

**HOLIDAY INN-SOUTH**
8040 Perry Hwy (16509)
Rates: $64-$73;
Tel: (814) 864-4911

**HOWARD JOHNSON**
7575 Peach St (16509)
Rates: $54-$96;
Tel: (814) 864-4811

**KNIGHTS INN**
7455 Schultz Rd (16509)
Rates: $35-$45;
Tel: (814) 868-0879

**RAMADA INN**
6101 Wattsburg Rd (16509)
Rates: $40-$75;
Tel: (814) 825-3100

**RED ROOF INN**
7865 Perry Hwy (16509)
Rates: $29-$69;
Tel: (814) 868-5246

## EXTON

**HOLIDAY INN EXPRESS**
120 N Pottstown Pike (19341)
Rates: $60-$70;
Tel: (215) 524-9000

**HOLIDAY INN
EXTON/IONVILLE**
815 N Pottstown Pike (19341)
Rates: $56-$95;
Tel: (215) 363-1100

## FAYETTEVILLE

**RITE SPOT MOTEL**
5651 Lincoln Way E (17222)
Rates: $31-$40;
Tel: (717) 352-2144

## FRACKVILLE

**ECONO LODGE**
501 S Middle St (17931)
Rates: $29-$65;
Tel: (717) 874-3838

## FRANKLIN

**FRANKLIN MOTEL**
1421 Liberty St (16323)
Rates: N/A;
Tel: (814) 437-3061

## FRYSTOWN

**MOTEL OF FRYSTOWN**
90 Fort Motel Dr
(Myerstown 17067)
Rates: $30-$40;
Tel: (717) 933-4613

## GALETON

**OX YOKE INN**
RD 1, Route 6 (16922)
Rates: N/A;
Tel: (814) 435-6522

**PINE LOG MOTEL**
P. O. Box 151 (16922)
Rates: $30-$36;
Tel: (814) 435-6400

## GETTYSBURG

**HERITAGE MOTOR LODGE**
64 Steinwehr Ave (17325)
Rates: N/A;
Tel: (717) 334-9281

**HOLIDAY INN-
BATTLEFIELD**
516 Baltimore St (17325)
Rates: $40-$98;
Tel: (717) 334-6211

**HOWARD JOHNSON
LODGE**
301 Steinwehr Ave (17325)
Rates: $34-$71;
Tel: (717) 334-1188

**QUALITY INN GETTYSBURG
MOTOR LODGE**
380 Steinwehr Ave (17325)
Rates: $35-$75;
Tel: (717) 334-1103

## GRANTVILLE

**ECONO LODGE**
RD 1, Box 5005 (17028)
Rates: $35-$65;
Tel: (717) 469-0631

**HOLIDAY INN HARRISBURG-
HERSHEY AREA, I-81**
P. O. Box 179 (17028)
Rates: $86-$170;
Tel: (717) 469-0661

## GREENSBURG

**KNIGHTS INN MOTEL**
1215 S Main St (15601)
Rates: $31-$47;
Tel: (800) 722-7220

## HAMLIN

**COMFORT INN**
RD 5 (Lake Ariel 18436)
Rates: $47-$84;
Tel: (717) 689-4148

## HARRISBURG

**BEST WESTERN
COUNTRY OVEN**
300 N Mountain Rd (17112)
Rates: $48-$81;
Tel: (717) 652-7180

**BEST WESTERN
HOTEL CROWN PARK**
765 Eisenhower Blvd (17111)
Rates: $75-$95;
Tel: (717) 558-9500

**BUDGETEL INN**
990 Eisenhower Blvd (17111)
Rates: $38-$59;
Tel: (717) 939-8000

**BUDGETEL INN**
200 N Mountain Rd (17112)
Rates: $45-$59;
Tel: (717) 540-9339

**COMFORT INN EAST**
4021 Union Deposit Rd
(17109)
Rates: $49-$74;
Tel: (717) 561-8100

**DAYS INN**
353 Lewisberry Rd
(New Cumberland 17070)
Rates: $39-$60;
Tel: (717) 774-4156

**ECONO LODGE**
150 Nationwide Dr (17110)
Rates: $38-$46;
Tel: (717) 545-9089

**THE HARRISBURG HOTEL**
23 S 2nd St (17101)
Rates: $49-$110;
Tel: (717) 234-5021

**HARRISBURG MARRIOTT**
4650 Lindle Rd (17111)
Rates: $84;
Tel: (717) 564-5511

**HILTON AND TOWERS**
1 N 2nd St (17101)
Rates: $121-$185;
Tel: (717) 233-6000

**HOLIDAY INN
HARRISBURG-WEST**
5401 Carlisle Pike
(Mechanicsburg 17055)
Rates: $75-$85;
Tel: (717) 697-0321

**KEYSTONE INN**
353 Lewisberry Rd
(New Cumberland 17070)
Rates: $23-$54;
Tel: (717) 774-1310

**KNIGHTS INN**
300 Commerce Dr
(New Cumberland 17070)
Rates: $25-$35;
Tel: (717) 774-5990

**PENN HARRIS HOTEL
& CONVENTION CENTER**
P. O. Box 839
(Camp Hill 17001)
Rates: $60-$80;
Tel: (717) 763-7117

**QUALITY INN SUMMERDALE**
501 N Enola Rd (Enola 17025)
Rates: $50-$73;
Tel: (717) 732-0785

**RED ROOF INN-NORTH**
400 Corporate Cir (17110)
Rates: $37-$52;
Tel: (717) 657-1445

**RED ROOF INN-SOUTH**
950 Eisenhower Blvd (17111)
Rates: $37-$46;
Tel: (717) 939-1331

**RESIDENCE INN
BY MARRIOTT**
4480 Lewis Rd (17111)
Rates: $98-$134;
Tel: (717) 561-1900

**SHERATON INN
HARRISBURG**
800 East Park Dr (17111)
Rates: $75-$135;
Tel: (717) 561-2800

**SUPER 8 MOTEL-NORTH**
4125 N Front St (17110)
Rates: $38-$56;
Tel: (717) 233-5891

# HAZLETON

**COMFORT INN-
WEST HAZLETON**
RR 1, Box 301 (18201)
Rates: $51-$80;
Tel: (717) 455-9300

**FOREST HILL INN**
RD 1, Box 262 (18201)
Rates: $44-$49;
Tel: (717) 459-2730

**HOLIDAY INN**
Rt 209 (18201)
Rates: $66-$75;
Tel: (717) 455-2061

**MOUNT LAUREL MOTEL**
Rt 309 South (18201)
Rates: N/A;
Tel: (717) 455-6391

# HERMITAGE

**ROYAL MOTEL**
301 S Hermitage Rd (16148)
Rates: N/A;
Tel: (412) 347-5546

# HERSHEY

**DAYS INN HERSHEY**
350 W Chocolate Ave (17033)
Rates: $45-$100;
Tel: (717) 534-2162

# HUNTINGDON

**DAYS INN-
RAYSTOWN LAKE**
RD 1, Box 353 (16652)
Rates: $38-$54;
Tel: (814) 643-3934

# INDIANA

**BEST WESTERN
UNIVERISTY INN**
1545 Wayne Ave (15701)
Rates: $50-$55;
Tel: (412) 349-9620

# JOHNSTOWN

**COMFORT INN**
455 Theatre Dr (15904)
Rates: $50-$61;
Tel: (814) 266-3678

**DAYS INN**
1540 Scalp Ave (15904)
Rates: $40-$80;
Tel: (814) 269-3366

**HOLIDAY INN-DOWNTOWN**
250 Market St (15901)
Rates: $59-$79;
Tel: (814) 535-7777

**SUPER 8 MOTEL**
1440 Scalp Ave (15904)
Rates: $39-$54;
Tel: (814) 266-8789

# KANE

**KANE VIEW MOTEL**
RD 1, Box 91A (16735)
Rates: $32-$45;
Tel: (814) 837-8600

# KEMPTON

**HAWK MT. INN
BED & BREAKFAST**
RD 1, Box 186 (19529)
Rates: N/A;
Tel: (215) 756-4224

# KING OF PRUSSIA

**COMFORT INN
VALLEY FORGE**
550 W Dekalb Pike (19406)
Rates: $49-$75;
Tel: (215) 962-0700

**HOLIDAY INN
OF KING OF PRUSSIA**
260 Goddard Blvd (19406)
Rates: $89-$107;
Tel: (215) 265-7500

**RESIDENCE INN
BY MARRIOTT**
600 W Swedesford Rd
(Berwyn 19312)
Rates: $120-$160;
Tel: (215) 640-9494

# KRUMSVILLE

**TOP MOTEL**
RD 1, Box 834
(Lenhartsville 19534)
Rates: N/A;
Tel: (215) 756-6021

# KULPSVILLE

**HOLIDAY INN**
1750 Sumneytown Pike
(19443)
Rates: $71-$95;
Tel: (215) 368-3800

# KUTZTOWN

**LINCOLN MOTEL**
RD 4, Box 171 (19530)
Rates: $38-$45;
Tel: (215) 683-3456

# LAMAR

**COMFORT INN
OF LAMAR-LOCK HAVEN**
RR3, Box 600 (Mill Hall 17751)
Rates: $39-$80;
Tel: (717) 726-4901

# LANCASTER

**BEST WESTERN EDEN
RESORT INN & CONF CTR**
222 Eden Rd (17601)
Rates: $85-$114;
Tel: (717) 569-6444

**BRUNSWICK HOTEL**
P. O. Box 749 (17603)
Rates: $48-$68;
Tel: (717) 397-4801

**CAMERON ESTATE INN**
RD 1, Box 305
(Mount Joy 17552)
Rates: $65-$110;
Tel: (717) 653-1773

**DUTCH FAMILY INN MOTEL**
2250 Lincoln Hwy E (17602)
Rates: $68-$77;
Tel: (717) 393-5499

**LANCASTER HOST RESORT**
2300 Lincoln Hwy E (17602)
Rates: $59-$159;
Tel: (717) 299-5500

## LEWISTOWN

**HOLIDAY INN
OF LEWISTOWN**
Rt 322 (Burnham 17009)
Rates: $39-$65;
Tel: (717) 248-4961

## LIONVILLE

**EXTON COMFORT INN**
5 N Pottstown Pike (19341)
Rates: $58-$64;
Tel: (215) 524-8811

**HAMPTON INN**
Jct SR 113 & 100 (19341)
Rates: $52-$69;
Tel: (215) 363-5555

## LITITZ

**GENERAL SUTTER INN**
14 E Main St (17543)
Rates: $60-$90;
Tel: (717) 626-2115

## LOCK HAVEN

**DAYS INN**
101 E Walnut St (17745)
Rates: $47-$52;
Tel: (717) 748-3297

## MANSFIELD

**COMFORT INN**
300 Gateway Dr (16933)
Rates: $39-$75;
Tel: (717) 662-3000

**MANSFIELD INN**
26 S Main St (16933)
Rates: $45-$65;
Tel: (717) 662-2136

**OASIS MOTEL**
RD 1, Box 90 (16933)
Rates: $27-$40;
Tel: (717) 659-5576

**WEST'S DELUXE MOTEL**
RD 1, Box 97 (16933)
Rates: $30-$40;
Tel: (717) 659-5141

## MATAMORAS

**BEST WESTERN INN
AT HUNT'S LANDING**
900 Rt 6 & 209 (18336)
Rates: $52-$78;
Tel: (717) 491-2400

## MEADVILLE

**DAVID MEAD INN**
455 Chestnut St (16335)
Rates: N/A;
Tel: (814) 336-1692

**DAYS INN OF MEADVILLE**
240 Conneaut Lake Rd
(16335)
Rates: $40-$72;
Tel: (814) 337-4264

**SUPER 8 MOTEL**
845 Conneaut Lake Rd
(16335)
Rates: $38-$45;
Tel: (814) 333-8883

## MERCER

**COLONIAL INN MOTEL**
Rt 19N (16137)
Rates: $27-$36;
Tel: (412) 662-5600

**HOWARD JOHNSON
MOTOR LODGE**
RD 6 (16137)
Rates: $60-$67;
Tel: (412) 748-3030

## MILESBURG

**DAYS INN**
P. O. Box 538 (16853)
Rates: $36-$45;
Tel: (814) 355-7521

## MILFORD

**MYER MOTEL**
RD 4, Box 8030 (18337)
Rates: $40-$70;
Tel: (717) 296-7223

**TOURIST VILLAGE MOTEL**
P. O. Box 487 (18337)
Rates: $32-$46;
Tel: (717) 491-4414

## MONTGOMERYVILLE

**COMFORT INN**
P. O. Box 88 (18936)
Rates: $64-$93;
Tel: (215) 361-3600

## MOOSIC

**DAYS INN-MONTAGE**
4130 Birney Ave (18507)
Rates: $40-$55;
Tel: (717) 457-6713

## MORGANTOWN

**CONESTOGA
WAGON MOTEL**
Rt 23 East (19543)
Rates: N/A;
Tel: (215) 286-5061

**HOLIDAY INN-HOLIDOME**
N of Exit 22 off P'A Tpk
(19543)
Rates: $65-$95;
Tel: (215) 286-3000

## MYERSTOWN

**MOTEL OF FRYSTOWN**
90 Fort Motel Dr (17067)
Rates: N/A;
Tel: (717) 933-4613

## NEW CASTLE

**COMFORT INN**
1740 New Butler Rd (16101)
Rates: $47-$59;
Tel: (412) 658-7700

## NEW COLUMBIA

**NEW COLUMBIA COMFORT INN**
P. O. Box 62 (17856)
Rates: $49-$63;
Tel: (717) 568-8000

## NEW CUMBERLAND

**HARRISBURG SOUTH KNIGHTS INN**
300 Commerce Dr (17070)
Rates: N/A;
Tel: (800) 843-5644

## NEW HOPE

**HOLIDAY INN**
P. O. Box 419 (18938)
Rates: $79-$95;
Tel: (215) 862-5221

**WEDGEWOOD INN**
111 W Bridge St (18938)
Rates: $60-$160;
Tel: (215) 862-2570

## NEW STANTON

**HOWARD JOHNSON LODGE**
P. O. Box 214 (15672)
Rates: $40-$66;
Tel: (412) 925-3511

## OIL CITY

**HOLIDAY INN**
1 Seneca St (16301)
Rates: $59-$76;
Tel: (814) 677-1221

## PHILADELPHIA
(and Vicinity)

**BARCLAY HOTEL**
237 S 18th St (19103)
Rates: $135-$400;
Tel: (800) 421-6662

**CHESTNUT HILL HOTEL**
8229 Germantown Ave (19118)
Rates: $80-$120;
Tel: (800) 628-9744

**COMFORT INN**
3660 Street Rd
(Bensalem 19020)
Rates: $54-$95;
Tel: (215) 245-0100

**FOUR SEASONS HOTEL PHILADELPHIA**
1 Logan Sq (19103)
Rates: $145-$295;
Tel: (215) 963-1500

**HAMPTON INN-WILLOW GROVE**
Rt 611 (Willow Grove 19090)
Rates: $68-$74;
Tel: (215) 659-3535

**HOLIDAY INN-AIRPORT**
45 Industrial Hwy
(Essington 19029)
Rates: $93-$103;
Tel: (215) 521-2400

**HOLIDAY INN-CENTER CITY**
18th & Market Sts (19103)
Rates: $69-$152;
Tel: (215) 561-7500

**KNIGHTS INN-AIRPORT**
43 Industrial Hwy
(Essington 19029)
Rates: N/A;
Tel: (800) 843-5644

**MARRIOTT PHILADELPHIA AIRPORT**
4509 Island Ave (19153)
Rates: $74-$140;
Tel: (215) 365-4150

**PHILADELPHIA COURT HOTEL**
10th and Packer Ave (19158)
Rates: $79-$450;
Tel: (215) 755-9500

**QUALITY INN HISTORIC DOWNTOWN SUITES**
1010 Race St (19107)
Rates: $75-$99;
Tel: (215) 922-1730

**RAMADA HOTEL & CONFERENCE CENTER**
2400 Old Lincoln Hwy
(Trevose 19053)
Rates: $80-$120;
Tel: (215) 638-8300

**RED ROOF INN**
3100 Lincoln Hwy
(Trevose 19053)
Rates: $41-$52;
Tel: (215) 244-9422

**RED ROOF INN-AIRPORT**
49 Industrial Hwy
(Essington 19029)
Rates: $39-$49;
Tel: (215) 521-5090

**RED ROOF INN-OXFORD VALLEY**
3100 Cabot Blvd W
(Langhorne 19047)
Rates: $47-$66;
Tel: (215) 750-6200

**RESIDENCE INN BY MARRIOTT-WILLOW GROVE**
3 Walnut Grove Dr
(Horsham 19044)
Rates: $105-$133;
Tel: (215) 443-7330

**THE RITTENHOUSE HOTEL & CONDO RESIDENCE**
210 W Rittenhouse Sq (19103)
Rates: $150-$260;
Tel: (215) 546-9000

**THE WARWICK HOTEL**
1701 Locust St (19103)
Rates: $105-$170;
Tel: (215) 735-6000

## PHILIPSBURG

**MAIN LINER MOTEL**
RD 3, Box 115 (16866)
Rates: $26-$38;
Tel: (814) 342-2004

## PINE GROVE

**ECONO LODGE**
RD 1, Box 581 (17963)
Rates: $35-$60;
Tel: (717) 345-4099

# PITTSBURGH
(and Vicinity)

**BEST WESTERN-
PARKWAY CENTER INN**
875 Greentree Rd (15220)
Rates: $59-$99;
Tel: (412) 922-7070

**COMFORT INN-
PARKWAY WEST**
RD 1 (Oakdale 15071)
Rates: $48-$65;
Tel: (412) 787-2600

**DAYS INN**
100 Kisow Dr (15205)
Rates: $35-$50;
Tel: (412) 922-0120

**DAYS INN**
909 Sheraton Dr
(Mars 16046)
Rates: $48-$67;
Tel: (412) 772-2700

**DAYS INN-MONROEVILLE**
2727 Mosside Blvd
(Monroeville 15146)
Rates: $47-$61;
Tel: (412) 856-1610

**DAYS INN
OF NEW KENSINGTON**
300 Tarentum Bridge Rd
(New Kensington 15068)
Rates: $50-$75;
Tel: (412) 335-9171

**DAYS INN-
PITTSBURGH AIRPORT**
1170 Thorn Run Rd Ext
(Coraopolis 15108)
Rates: $52-$56;
Tel: (412) 269-0990

**EMBASSY SUITES-
CORAOPOLIS**
550 Cherrington Pkwy
(Coraopolis 15108)
Rates: $89-$135;
Tel: (412) 269-9070

**HAMPTON INN**
3315 Hamlet St (15213)
Rates: $69-$87;
Tel: (412) 681-1000

**HAMPTON INN
HOTEL AIRPORT**
1420 Beers School Rd
(Coraopolis 15108)
Rates: $55-$65;
Tel: (412) 264-0020

**HAMPTON INN HOTEL
GREENTREE**
555 Trumbull Dr (15205)
Rates: $60-$68;
Tel: (412) 992-0100

**HAMPTON INN
WARRENDALE**
210 Executive Dr
(Mars 16046)
Rates: $47-$65;
Tel: (412) 776-1000

**HILTON AIRPORT INN**
P. O. Box 12411 (15231)
Rates: $59-$125;
Tel: (412) 262-3800

**HOLIDAY INN-
MCKNIGHT ROAD**
4859 McKnight Rd (15237)
Rates: $69-$127;
Tel: (412) 366-5200

**HOLIDAY INN-
PITTSBURGH CENTRAL**
401 Holiday Dr (15220)
Rates: $79-$122;
Tel: (412) 922-8100

**HOLIDAY INN
AT UNIVERSITY CENTER**
100 Lytton Ave (15213)
Rates: $119-$141;
Tel: (412) 682-6200

**KNIGHTS INN-
PITTSBURGH/BRIDGEVILLE**
111 Hickory Grade Rd
(Bridgeville 15017)
Rates: $32-$45;
Tel: (412) 221-8110

**LA QUINTA
MOTOR INN-AIRPORT**
1433 Beers School Rd
(Coraopolis 15108)
Rates: $50-$64;
Tel: (412) 269-0400

**MARRIOTT GREEN TREE**
101 Marriott Dr (15205)
Rates: $65-$99;
Tel: (412) 922-8400

**OAK LEAF MOTEL**
US Rt 19, Perry Int #3
(Mars 16046)
Rates: N/A;
Tel: (412) 776-1551

**THE PITTSBURGH
PLAZA HOTEL**
1500 Beers School Rd
(Coraopolis 15108)
Rates: $49-$64;
Tel: (412) 264-7900

**RAMADA INN-AIRPORT**
1412 Beers School Rd
(Coraopolis 15108)
Rates: $65-$85;
Tel: (412) 264-8950

**RED ROOF INN-CRANBERRY**
20009 Rt 19
(Cranberry 16046)
Rates: $35-$54;
Tel: (412) 776-5670

**RED ROOF INN-
MONROEVILLE**
2729 Mosside Blvd
(Monroeville 15146)
Rates: $41-$59;
Tel: (412) 856-4738

**RED ROOF INN
PITTSBURGH**
6404 Steubenville Pike
(15205)
Rates: $41-$48;
Tel: (412) 787-7870

**RED ROOF INN
PITTSBURGH AIRPORT**
1454 Beers School Rd
(Coraopolis 15108)
Rates: $39-$47;
Tel: (412) 264-5678

**RESIDENCE IN
BY MARRIOTT GREENTREE**
700 Mansfield Ave (15205)
Rates: $114-$144;
Tel: (412) 279-6300

**SHERATON HOTEL
AT STATION SQUARE**
7 Station Square Dr (15219)
Rates: $135-$170;
Tel: (412) 261-2000

306

**SHERATON INN
PITTSBURGH SOUTH**
164 Ft Couch Rd (15241)
Rates: $50-$59;
Tel: (412) 343-4600

**TRAVELODGE**
4800 Steubenville Pike
(15205)
Rates: $32-$38;
Tel: (412) 922-6900

**WM PENN MOTEL**
4139 Wm Penn Hwy
(Monroeville 15146)
Rates: $36-$47;
Tel: (412) 373-0700

## PLEASANTVILLE

**WEST VU MOTEL**
RD 1, Box 366
(Alum Bank 15521)
Rates: $25-$34;
Tel: (814) 839-2632

## POTTSTOWN

**MODERN MOTEL**
1417 S Hanover St (19464)
Rates: N/A;
Tel: (215) 323-6650

**COMFORT INN**
99 Robinson St (19464)
Rates: $49-$72;
Tel: (215) 326-5000

## POTTSVILLE

**QUALITY HOTEL**
100 S Center St (17901)
Rates: $68-$78;
Tel: (717) 622-4600

## PUNXSUTAWNEY

**PANTALL HOTEL**
135 E Mahoning (15767)
Rates: $39-$77;
Tel: (814) 938-6600

## QUAKERTOWN

**ECONO LODGE**
1905 Rt 663 (18951)
Rates: $36-$75;
Tel: (215) 538-3000

## READING

**COUNTRY INN**
330 E Wyomissing Ave
(19607)
Rates: N/A;
Tel: (215) 777-2579

**DUTCH COLONY
MOTOR INN**
4635 Perkiomen Ave (19606)
Rates: $48-$59;
Tel: (215) 779-2345

**ECONO LODGE**
Spring & Papermill Rds
(Wyomissing 19610)
Rates: $46-$56;
Tel: (215) 378-5101

**HOLIDAY INN-NORTH**
2545 5th St (19605)
Rates: $64-$129;
Tel: (215) 929-4741

**THE INN AT READING**
1040 Park Rd
(Wyomissing 19610)
Rates: $47-$103;
Tel: (215) 372-7811

**WELLESLEY INN**
910 Woodland Ave
(Wyomissing 19610)
Rates: $35-$69;
Tel: (215) 374-1500

## SCRANTON

**BEST WESTERN
UNIVERSITY INN**
Franklin & Mulberry Sts
(18503)
Rates: $45-$60;
Tel: (717) 346-7061

**DAYS INN**
1226 O'Neill Hwy
(Dunmore 18512)
Rates: $49-$69;
Tel: (717) 348-6101

**ECONO LODGE**
1027 O'Neill Hwy
(Dunmore 18512)
Rates: $35-$59;
Tel: (717) 346-8782

**ECONO LODGE**
1175 Kane St (18505)
Rates: $39-$97;
Tel: (717) 348-1000

**HOLIDAY INN-EAST**
200 Tique St (Dunmore 18512)
Rates: $62-$78;
Tel: (717) 343-4771

**LACKAWANNA
STATION HOTEL**
70 Lackawanna Ave (18503)
Rates: $84-$300;
Tel: (800) 347-6888

**SUMMIT INN**
649 Northern Blvd
(Clarks Summit 18411)
Rates: $34-$50;
Tel: (717) 586-1211

## SELINSGROVE

**COMFORT INN**
P. O. Box 299 (17870)
Rates: $48-$58;
Tel: (717) 374-8880

**DAYS INN-
SUNBURY/SELINSGROVE**
P. O. Box 487
(Shamokin Dam 17876)
Rates: $39-$60;
Tel: (717) 743-1111

## SHARON

**ROYAL MOTEL**
301 S Hermitage Rd
(Hermitage 16148)
Rates: $32-$38;
Tel: (412) 347-5546

## SHARTLESVILLE

**DUTCH MOTEL**
P. O. Box 25 (19554)
Rates: $30-$45;
Tel: (215) 488-1479

307

## SOMERSET

**DAYS INN-SOMERSET**
220 Waterworks Rd (15501)
Rates: $42-$64;
Tel: (814) 445-9200

**HIGHLANDER MOTEL**
799 N Center Ave (15501)
Rates: $30-$34;
Tel: (814) 445-7988

**KNIGHTS INN**
I-76 & I-70, Exit 10 (15501)
Rates: $37-$47;
Tel: (814) 445-8933

**RAMADA INN**
P. O. Box 511 (15501)
Rates: $56-88;
Tel: (814) 443-4646

## STATE COLLEGE

**AUTOPORT MOTEL**
1405 S Atherton St (16801)
Rates: $50-$75;
Tel: (814) 237-7666

**DAYS INN-PENN STATE**
240 S Pugh St (16801)
Rates: $55-$91;
Tel: (814) 238-8454

**HAMPTON INN**
1101 E College Ave (16801)
Rates: $49-$75;
Tel: (814) 231-1590

**HOLIDAY INN-PENN STATE**
1450 S Atherton St (16801)
Rates: $50-$75;
Tel: (814) 238-3001

## STRASBURG

**HISTORIC STRASBURG INN**
SR 896 (17579)
Rates: $45-$85;
Tel: (717) 687-7691

## STROUDSBURG

**BUDGET MOTEL**
P. O. Box 216 (18301)
Rates: $33-$56;
Tel: (717) 424-5451

**SHERATON POCONO INN**
1220 W Main St (18360)
Rates: $75-$109;
Tel: (717) 424-1930

## TOWANDA

**TOWANDA MOTEL**
383 York Ave (18848)
Rates: $39-$70;
Tel: (717) 265-2178

## UNIONTOWN

**HOLIDAY INN**
700 W Main St (15401)
Rates: $70-$175;
Tel: (412) 437-2816

**THE LODGE AT CHALK HILL**
Rt 40E, Box 240
(Chalk Hill 15421)
Rates: $45-$60;
Tel: (412) 438-8880

**SUMMIT INN RESORT**
2 Skyline Dr
(Farmington 15437)
Rates: $51-$89;
Tel: (412) 438-8594

## WASHINGTON

**BEST WESTERN MOTEL**
1385 W Chestnut St (15301)
Rates: $34-$70;
Tel: (412) 222-6500

**CENTURY PLAZA MOTEL**
1880 W Chestnut St (15301)
Rates: N/A;
Tel: (412) 225-9290

**HOLIDAY INN-MEADOWLANDS**
340 Race Track Rd (15301)
Rates: $76-$95;
Tel: (412) 222-6200

**KNIGHTS INN**
125 Knights Inn Dr (15301)
Rates: $32-$46;
Tel: (800) 772-7220

**RED ROOF INN**
1399 W Chestnut St (15301)
Rates: $33-$46;
Tel: (412) 228-5750

## WAYNESBORO

**BEST WESTERN WAYNESBORO**
239 W Main St (17268)
Rates: $49-$58;
Tel: (717) 762-9113

## WAYNESBURG

**ECONO LODGE**
350 Miller Ln (15370)
Rates: $37-$50;
Tel: (412) 627-5544

**SUPER 8 MOTEL**
80 Miller Ln (15370)
Rates: $34-$41;
Tel: (412) 627-8880

## WELLSBORO

**CANYON MOTEL**
18 East Ave (16901)
Rates: $28-$48;
Tel: (717) 724-1681

**SHERWOOD MOTEL**
2 Main St (16901)
Rates: $28-$48;
Tel: (717) 724-3424

## WEST CHESTER

**ABBEY GREEN MOTOR LODGE**
1036 Wilmington Pike (19382)
Rates: $39-$57;
Tel: (215) 692-3310

## WEST MIDDLESEX

**HOLIDAY INN-
SHARON/HERMITAGE**
3200 S Hermitage Rd
(Hermitage 16159)
Rates: $62-$75;
Tel: (412) 981-1530

**RAMADA INN SHENANGO**
P. O. Box 596 (16159)
Rates: $57-$72;
Tel: (412) 528-2501

**SHENANGO VALLEY
COMFORT INN**
Rt 18 & Wilson Rd (16159)
Rates: $45-$55;
Tel: (412) 342-7200

## WEST READING

**PENN VIEW MOTEL**
250 Penn Ave (19611)
Rates: N/A;
Tel: (215) 376-8011

## WHITE HAVEN

**POCONO DAYS INN**
Rt 940, HCR 1, Box 35
(18661)
Rates: $50-$115;
Tel: (717) 443-0391

## WILKES-BARRE

**HAMPTON INN WILKES-
BARRE/CROSS CRK PT**
1063 Hwy 315 (18702)
Rates: $46-$67;
Tel: (717) 825-3838

**HOLIDAY INN**
800 Kidder St (18702)
Rates: $49-$89;
Tel: (717) 824-8901

**HOWARD JOHNSON
HOTEL**
500 Kidder St (18702)
Rates: $38-$52;
Tel: (717) 824-2411

**HOWARD JOHNSON
MOTOR LODGE**
307 Rt 315 (18640)
Rates: $42-$60;
Tel: (717) 654-3301

**KNIGHTS INN**
310 SR 315 (Pittston 18640)
Rates: $32-$42;
Tel: (717) 654-6020

**RED ROOF INN**
1035 Hwy 315 (18702)
Rates: $31-$43;
Tel: (717) 829-6422

**WOODLANDS INN
& RESORT**
1073 PA 315 (18702)
Rates: $62-$110;
Tel. (717) 824-9831

## WILLIAMSPORT

**BING'S MOTEL**
2961 Lycoming Creek Rd
(17701)
Rates: $28-$34;
Tel: (717) 494-0601

**CITY VIEW INN**
RD 4, Box 550 (17701)
Rates: $42-$48;
Tel: (717) 326-2601

**DAYS INN**
1840 E 3rd St (17701)
Rates: $39-$65;
Tel: (717) 326-1981

**RIDGEMONT MOTEL**
RD 4, Box 536 (17701)
Rates: $32-$34;
Tel: (717) 321-5300

**SHERATON
WILLIAMSPORT**
100 Pine St (17701)
Rates: $77-$95;
Tel: (717) 327-8231

## WIND GAP

**TRAVEL INN OF WIND GAP**
RD 1, Box 163 (18091)
Rates: $38-$52;
Tel: (215) 863-4146

## YORK

**ECONO LODGE-YORK**
125 Arsenal Rd (17404)
Rates: $30-$57;
Tel: (717) 846-6260

**HAMPTON INN**
1550 Mt Zion Rd (17402)
Rates: $64-$76;
Tel: (717) 840-1500

**HOLIDAY INN**
2600 E Market St (17402)
Rates: $69-$79;
Tel: (717) 755-1966

**HOLIDAY INN-RT 30E**
334 Arsenal Rd (17402)
Rates: $69-$79;
Tel: (717) 845-5671

**HOLIDAY INN YORK**
2000 Loucks Rd (17404)
Rates: $79-$99;
Tel: (717) 846-9500

**HOWARD JOHNSON
MOTOR LODGE**
I-83 Exit 9E (17402)
Rates: $49-$89;
Tel: (717) 843-9971

**RAMADA INN**
1650 Toronita St (17402)
Rates: $49-$89;
Tel: (717) 846-4940

**RED ROOF INN**
323 Arsenal Rd (17402)
Rates: $29-$57;
Tel: (717) 843-8181

**SPIRIT OF 76 MOTEL**
1162 Haines Rd (17402)
Rates: $30-$45;
Tel: (717) 755-1068

**YORKTOWNE HOTEL**
48 E Market St at Duke St
(17401)
Rates: $53-$89;
Tel: (717) 848-1111

# RHODE ISLAND

## EAST PROVIDENCE

**NEW YORKER MOTOR LODGE**
400 Newport Ave (02916)
Rates: N/A;
Tel: (401) 434-8000

## KINGSTON

**COACHMAN MOTOR INN**
3199 Tower Hill Rd
(S Kingstown 02874)
Rates: N/A;
Tel: (401) 783-2516

**QUALITY INN**
3009 Tower Hill Rd
(S Kingstown 02874)
Rates: $70-$105;
Tel: (401) 789-1051

## MIDDLETOWN

**BUDGET INN**
1185 W Main Rd (02840)
Rates: $36-$86;
Tel: (401) 849-4700

**COMFORT INN OF NEWPORT**
936 W Main Rd (02840)
Rates: $45-$105;
Tel: (401) 846-7600

**HOWARD JOHNSON
LODGE-NEWPORT**
351 W Main Rd (02840)
Rates: $39-$129;
Tel: (401) 849-2000

## NEWPORT

**ANNA'S VICTORIAN
CONNECTION**
5 Fowler Ave (02840)
Rates: N/A;
Tel: (401) 849-2489

**JOHN BANISTER HOUSE**
56 Pelham St (02840)
Rates: N/A;
Tel: (401) 846-0050

**MOTEL 6**
249 J T Connell Hwy (02840)
Rates: $32-$48;
Tel: (401) 848-0600

**NEWPORT MARRIOTT HOTEL**
25 America's Cup Ave (02840)
Rates: $95-$219;
Tel: (401) 849-1000

## PORTSMOUTH

**FOUNDER'S BROOK
MOTEL & SUITES**
314 Boyd's Ln (02871)
Rates: $40-$100;
Tel: (401) 683-1244

## PROVIDENCE
(and Vicinity)

**HOLIDAY INN
DOWNTOWN**
21 Atwells Ave (02903)
Rates: $75-$115;
Tel: (401) 831-3900

**PROVIDENCE MARRIOTT
HOTEL**
Charles & Orms Sts (02904)
Rates: $79-$156;
Tel: (401) 272-2400

## SAUNDERSTOWN

**QUALITY INN**
3009 Tower Hill Rd
(RFD 1 02874)
Rates: $55-$105;
Tel: (401) 789-1051

## WAKEFIELD

**LARCHWOOD INN
& HOLLY HOUSE**
520-521 Main St (02879)
Rates: $30-$90;
Tel: (401) 783-5454

## WARWICK

**HOLIDAY INN
AT THE CROSSINGS**
800 Greenwich Ave (02886)
Rates: $115-$165;
Tel: (401) 732-6000

**HOWARD JOHNSON
MOTEL**
20 Jefferson Blvd (02888)
Rates: $59-$94;
Tel: (401) 467-9800

**PROVIDENCE
AIRPORT/WARWICK
ECONO LODGE**
2138 Post Rd (02886)
Rates: $55-$65;
Tel: (401) 737-7400

## WYOMING

**THE WAY STOP**
161 New London Tpke
(02898)
Rates: N/A;
Tel: (401) 539-7233

# SOUTH CAROLINA

## AIKEN

**BEST WESTERN
EXECUTIVE INN**
3560 Augusta Rd (29801)
Rates: $42-$44;
Tel: (803) 649-3968

**DAYS INN**
1204 Richland Ave W (29801)
Rates: $30-$38;
Tel. (803) 649-5524

**DELUXE INN-AIKEN**
P. O. Box 2875 (29801)
Rates: $27 $44;
Tel: (803) 642 2840

## ANDERSON

**HOLIDAY INN**
3025 N Main St (29621)
Rates: $52-$57;
Tel: (803) 226 6051

**PARK INN INTERNATIONAL**
3430 N Main St (29621)
Rates: N/A;
Tel: (803) 225-3721

**QUALITY INN**
3509 Clemson Blvd (29621)
Rates: $59-$65;
Tel: (803) 226-1000

**ROYAL AMERICAN
MOTOR INN**
4515 Clemson Blvd (29621)
Rates: $28-$32;
Tel: (803) 226-7236

## BEAUFORT

**DAYS INN-BEAUFORT**
1809 S Ribaut
(Port Royal 29935)
Rates: $41-$45;
Tel: (803) 524-1551

**HOLIDAY INN
OF BEAUFORT**
P. O. Box 1008 (29902)
Rates: $45-$51;
Tel: (803) 524-2144

**HOWARD JOHNSON
LODGE**
3127 Boundary St (29902)
Rates: $40-$48;
Tel: (803) 524-6020

## CAMDEN

**COLONY INN**
P. O. Box 131 (29020)
Rates: $32-$41;
Tel: (803) 342-5508

**GREENLEAF INN**
1310 N Broad St (29020)
Rates. $45-$70;
Tel: (803) 425-1806

**PARKVIEW MOTEL**
1039 W DeKalb St (29020)
Rates: $21-$27;
Tel: (803) 432-7687

## CHARLESTON
(and Vicinity)

**BEST WESTERN INN**
1540 Savannah Hwy (29407)
Rates: $42-$69;
Tel: (803) 571-6100

**BEST WESTERN
NAVAL CENTER**
2070 McMillian St (29406)
Rates: $42-$53;
Tel: (803) 554-1600

**BEST WESTERN
RIVERS AVENUE INN**
P. O. Box 71113 (29415)
Rates: $39-$43;
Tel; (803) 554-4982

**COMFORT INN**
5055 N Arco Ln (29418)
Rates: $40-$55;
Tel: (803) 554-6485

**DAYS INN-AIRPORT**
2998 W Montague Ave
(N Charleston 29405)
Rates: $37-$52;
Tel: (803) 747-4101

**DAYS INN
PATRIOT'S POINT**
261 Hwy 17 Bypass (29464)
Rates: $37-$56;
Tel: (803) 881-1800

**ECONO LODGE-
SAVANNAH HWY**
2237 Savannah Hwy (29414)
Rates: $27-$49;
Tel: (803) 571-1880

**GUILDS INN**
101 Pitt St
(Mt. Pleasant 29464)
Rates: $70-$100;
Tel: (803) 881-0510

**HAMPTON INN-AIRPORT**
4701 Arco Ln
(N Charleston 29418)
Rates: $41-$53;
Tel: (803) 554-7154

**HAMPTON INN-
CHARLESTON/
MT. PLEASANT**
255 Johnnie Dodds Blvd
(Mt. Pleasant 29464)
Rates: $44-$55;
Tel: (803) 881-3300

**HAMPTON INN-RIVERVIEW**
11 Ashley Point Dr (29407)
Rates: $48-$68;
Tel: (803) 556-5200

**HEART OF CHARLESTON-
QUALITY INN**
125 Calhoun St (29401)
Rates: $40-$89;
Tel: (803) 722-3391

**HOJO INN**
3640 Dorchester Rd (29405)
Rates: $35-55;
Tel: (803) 554-4140

**HOLIDAY INN CHARLESTON/MT. PLEASANT**
250 Hwy 17 Bypass (29464)
Rates: $49-$81;
Tel: (803) 884-6000

**HOLIDAY INN-INTERNATIONAL AIRPORT**
6099 Fain St (29418)
Rates: $55;
Tel: (803) 744-1621

**HOLIDAY INN-RIVERVIEW**
301 Savannah Hwy (29407)
Rates: $71-$86;
Tel: (803) 556-7100

**HOWARD JOHNSON RIVERFRONT**
250 Spring St (29403)
Rates: $51-$79;
Tel: (803) 722-4000

**INDIGO INN**
1 Maiden Ln (29401)
Rates: $70-$120;
Tel: (803) 577-5900

**LA QUINTA MOTOR INN**
2499 La Quinta Ln (29418)
Rates: $42-$57;
Tel: (803) 797-8181

**MARRIOTT HOTEL-CHARLESTON**
4770 Marriott Dr
(N Charleston 29418)
Rates: $115-$135;
Tel: (803) 747-1900

**MASTERS INN**
300 Wingo Way
(Mt. Pleasant 29464)
Rates: $33-$48;
Tel: (800) 633-3434

**MIDDLETON INN AT MIDDLETON PLACE**
Ashley River Rd (29414)
Rates: $79-$109;
Tel: (803) 446-0500

**MILLS HOUSE HOTEL**
115 Meeting St (29401)
Rates: $105-$170;
Tel: (803) 577-2400

**RAMADA INN**
Johnnie Dodds Blvd
(Mt. Pleasant 29464)
Rates: $36-$54;
Tel: (803) 884-1411

**RED ROOF INN**
7480 Northwoods Blvd
(N Charleston 29418)
Rates: $31-$39;
Tel: (803) 572-9100

**RESIDENCE INN BY MARRIOTT**
7645 Northwoods Blvd
(29418)
Rates: $90-$110;
Tel: (803) 572-5757

**SHERATON AIRPORT INN**
5991 Rivers Ave
(N Charleston 29418)
Rates: $74-$90;
Tel: (803) 744-2501

**SHERATON CHARLESTON HOTEL**
170 Lockwood Dr (29403)
Rates: $79-$130;
Tel: (803) 723-3000

**SUPER 8 MOTEL**
2311 Ashley Phosphate
(N Charleston 29418)
Rates: N/A;
Tel: (803) 572-2228

**TOWN & COUNTRY INN**
2008 Savannah Hwy (29407)
Rates: $56-$64;
Tel: (803) 571-1000

## CHERAW

**INN CHERAW**
321 Second St (29520)
Rates: $28-$42;
Tel: (803) 537-2011

## CLEMSON

**HOLIDAY INN**
P. O. Box 512 (29631)
Rates: $46-$54;
Tel: (803) 654-4450

## CLINTON

**DAYS INN**
SR 56 & I-26 (29325)
Rates: $33-$39;
Tel: (803) 833-6600

## COLUMBIA

**BUDGETEL INN-COLUMBIA EAST**
1538 Horseshoe Dr (29204)
Rates: $30-$46;
Tel: (803) 736-6400

**BUDGETEL INN WEST**
911 Bush River Rd (29210)
Rates: $33-$49;
Tel: (803) 798-3222

**COMFORT INN**
499 Piney Grove Rd (29210)
Rates: $33-$49;
Tel: (803) 798-0500

**DAYS INN**
7128 Parkland Rd (29223)
Rates: $34-$49;
Tel: (803) 736-0000

**ECONO LODGE**
494 Piney Grove Rd (29210)
Rates: $28-$33;
Tel: (803) 731-4060

**ECONO LODGE NORTHEAST**
7700 Two Notch Rd (29223)
Rates: $29-$39;
Tel: (803) 788-5544

**ECONOMY INNS OF AMERICA**
1776 Burning Tree Rd (29210)
Rates: $26-$33;
Tel: (803) 798-9210

**EMBASSY SUITES HOTEL COLUMBIA**
200 Stoneridge Dr (29210)
Rates: $74-$109;
Tel: (803) 252-8700

**HAMPTON INN**
1094 Chris Dr
(W Columbia 29169)
Rates: $44-$56;
Tel: (803) 791-8940

**HOLIDAY INN-COLISEUM AT USC**
630 Assembly St (29201)
Rates: $39-$49;
Tel: (803) 799-7800

**HOLIDAY INN-NORTHEAST**
7510 Two Notch Rd (29223)
Rates: $59-$75;
Tel: (803) 738-3000

**HOLIDAY INN-NORTHWEST (EXPRESS)**
773 St. Andrews Rd (29210)
Rates: $41-$56;
Tel: (803) 772-7275

**KNIGHTS INN COLUMBIA/AIRPORT**
1987 Airport Blvd (29033)
Rates: $30-$38;
Tel: (803) 794-0222

**KNIGHTS INN-COLUMBIA NORTHWEST**
1803 Bush River Rd (29210)
Rates: $24-$36;
Tel: (803) 772-0022

**LA QUINTA MOTOR INN**
1335 Garner Ln (29210)
Rates: $38-$51;
Tel: (803) 798-9590

**MARRIOTT HOTEL-COLUMBIA**
1200 Hampton St (29201)
Rates: $69-$109;
Tel: (803) 771-7000

**QUALITY INN-NORTHEAST**
1539 Horseshoe Dr (29223)
Rates: $42-$56;
Tel: (803) 736-1600

**RAMADA HOTEL**
8105 Two Notch Rd (29223)
Rates: $54-$60;
Tel: (803) 736-5600

**RAMADA INN WEST**
113 McSwain Dr
(W Columbia 29169)
Rates: $49-$79;
Tel: (803) 796-2700

**RED ROOF INN-EAST**
7580 Two Notch Rd (29223)
Rates: $28-$38;
Tel: (803) 736-0850

**RED ROOF INN-WEST**
10 Berryhill Rd (29210)
Rates: $24-$39;
Tel: (803) 798-9220

**RESIDENCE INN BY MARRIOTT**
150 Stoneridge Dr (29221)
Rates: $85-$115;
Tel: (803) 779-7000

**SHERATON HOTEL & CONVENTION CENTER**
2100 Bush River Rd (29210)
Rates: $55-$79;
Tel: (803) 731-0300

**SUPER 8 MOTEL**
2516 Augusta Rd (29169)
Rates: $28-$36;
Tel: (803) 796-4833

**TREMONT INN**
111 Knox Abbott Dr
(Cayce 29033)
Rates: $30-$38;
Tel: (803) 796-6240

## DILLON

**DAYS INN**
Rt 1, Box 70 (29536)
Rates: $45-$49;
Tel: (803) 774-6041

**ECONO LODGE**
Rt 1, Box 76 (29536)
Rates: $29-$45;
Tel: (803) 774-4181

**HOWARD JOHNSON MOTOR LODGE**
Rt 1, Box 73 (29536)
Rates: $36-$65;
Tel: (803) 774-5111

**TRAVELODGE**
P. O. Box 309 (29536)
Rates: $35-$40;
Tel: (803) 774-4161

## EASLEY

**DAYS INN**
1711 Bypass 123 (29649)
Rates: $33-$37;
Tel: (803) 859-9902

## FLORENCE

**DAYS INN**
2111 W Lucas St (29501)
Rates: $40-$58;
Tel: (803) 665-4444

**DAYS INN SOUTH**
I-95 Exit 157 & US 76 (29502)
Rates: $25-$39;
Tel: (803) 665-8550

**ECONO LODGE**
P. O. Box 5688 (29502)
Rates: $33-$43;
Tel: (803) 665-8558

**ECONO LODGE-SOUTH**
Rt 5, Box 58F (29501)
Rates: $29-$35;
Tel: (803) 662-7712

**HAMPTON INN**
1826 W Lucas St (29501)
Rates: $42-$56;
Tel: (803) 662-7000

**HOJO INN**
P. O. Box 905 (29503)
Rates: $34-$58;
Tel: (803) 669-1921

**KNIGHTS INN**
1834 W Lucas St (29501)
Rates: $29-$36;
Tel: (803) 667-6100

**PARK INN INTERNATIONAL**
831 S Irby St (29501)
Rates: $30-$35;
Tel: (803) 662-9421

**QUALITY INN/I-95**
P. O. Box 1512 (29503)
Rates: $35-$45;
Tel: (803) 669-1715

**RAMADA INN**
2038 W Lucas St (29501)
Rates: $46-$52;
Tel: (803) 689-4241

**RED ROOF INN**
2690 David McLeod Blvd (29501)
Rates: $29-$65;
Tel: (803) 678-9000

Vacation with Your Pet!

**SUPER 8 MOTEL**
1832 W Lucas St (29502)
Rates: $34-$37;
Tel: (803) 661-7267

**THUNDERBIRD MOTOR INN**
P. O. Box 3909 (29502)
Rates: $30-$37;
Tel: (803) 669-1611

**YOUNG'S PLANTATION INN**
P. O. Box 3806 (29502)
Rates: $28-$38;
Tel: (803) 669-4171

## FOLLY BEACH

**HOLIDAY INN-FOLLY BEACH**
1 Center St (29439)
Rates: $51-$79;
Tel: (803) 588-6464

## FORT MILL

**BEST WESTERN-CAROWINDS**
3482 US 21 (29715)
Rates: $44-$49;
Tel: (803) 548-8000

## GAFFNEY

**COMFORT INN**
143 Corona Dr (29341)
Rates: $34-$45;
Tel: (803) 487-4200

## GEORGETOWN

**CAROLINIAN MOTOR INN/CLARION HOUSE INN**
706 Church St (29440)
Rates: $39-$60;
Tel: (803) 546-5191

**DESEASONS MOTEL**
412 St. James St (29440)
Rates: N/A;
Tel: (803) 546-4117

## GREENVILLE

**COLONIAL INN**
P. O. Box 2323 (29602)
Rates: $25-$39;
Tel: (803) 233-5393

**COMFORT INN/I-85**
412 Mauldin Rd (29605)
Rates: $35-$44;
Tel: (803) 277-6730

**DAYS INN**
P. O. Box 8375 Sta A (29604)
Rates: $29-$36;
Tel: (803) 277-4010

**HOWARD JOHNSON LODGE & SUITES**
2756 Laurens Rd (29607)
Rates: $39-$49;
Tel: (803) 288-6900

**LA QUINTA MOTOR INN**
31 Old Country Rd (29607)
Rates: $40-$53;
Tel: (803) 297-3500

**THE PHOENIX INN**
P. O. Box 5064 Sta B (29606)
Rates: $42-$67;
Tel: (803) 233-4651

**QUALITY INN**
50 Orchard Park Dr (29615)
Rates: $35-$61;
Tel: (803) 297-9000

**RAMADA HOTEL & CONVENTION CENTER**
1001 S Church St (29601)
Rates: $49-$61;
Tel: (803) 232-7666

**RED ROOF INN**
2801 Laurens Rd (29607)
Rates: $25-$41;
Tel: (803) 297-4458

**REGENCY INN**
27 S Pleasantburg Dr (29607)
Rates: $27-$40;
Tel: (803) 232-3339

**RESIDENCE INN BY MARRIOTT**
48 McPrice Ct (29615)
Rates: $78-$98;
Tel: (803) 297-0099

**TRAVELODGE**
830 Congaree Rd (29607)
Rates: $43-$65;
Tel: (803) 288-6221

## HARDEEVILLE

**DAYS INN**
P. O. Box 613 (29927)
Rates: $30-$48;
Tel: (803) 784-2221

**ECONO LODGE**
P. O. Box (29927)
Rates: $26-$36;
Tel: (803) 784-2201

**HOLIDAY INN**
P. O. Box 1109 (29927)
Rates: $40-$50;
Tel: (803) 784-2151

**HOWARD JOHNSON MOTOR LODGE**
P. O.Box 568 (29927)
Rates: $37-$41;
Tel: (803) 784-2271

## HARTSVILLE

**LANDMARK INN**
P. O. Drawer 370 (29550)
Rates: $41-$51;
Tel: (803) 332-2611

## HILTON HEAD ISLAND

**BEST WESTERN OCEANWALK SUITES**
36 S Forest Beach Dr (29938)
Rates: $40-$110;
Tel: (803) 842-3100

**DAYS INN RESORT**
2 Tanglewood Dr (29928)
Rates: $39-$80;
Tel: (803) 842-6662

**HOLIDAY INN EXPRESS**
40 Waterside Dr (29928)
Rates: $29-$69;
Tel: (803) 842-8888

**RED ROOF INN**
5 Regency Pkwy (29928)
Rates: $29-$50;
Tel: (803) 686-6808

314

**THE WESTIN RESORT-PORT ROYAL PLANTATION**
2 Grass Lawn Ave (29928)
Rates: $85-$290;
Tel: (803) 681-4000

## LADSON

**DAYS INN**
119 Gateway Dr (29456)
Rates: $35-$45;
Tel: (803) 797-1214

## LITTLE RIVER

**HARBOR INN**
P. O. Box 548 (29566)
Rates: $33-$63;
Tel: (803) 249-3535

## MANNING

**DAYS INN OF MANNING**
Rt 5,I-95 & US 301 (29102)
Rates: $24-$47;
Tel: (803) 473-2596

**MANNING ECONOMY INN**
P. O. Box 97 (29102)
Rates: $28-$38;
Tel: (803) 473-4021

## MOUNT PLEASANT

**MASTERS ECONOMY INN**
300 Wingo Way (29464)
Rates: N/A;
Tel: (803) 884-2814

## MURRELLS INLET

**BROCKWOOD INN**
P. O. Box 544 (29576)
Rates: $25-$50;
Tel: (803) 651-2550

## MYRTLE BEACH

**BEST WESTERN LANDMARK RESORT HOTEL**
1501 S Ocean Blvd (29577)
Rates: $45-$129;
Tel: (803) 448-9441

**CARAVAN MOTEL**
2600 S Ocean Blvd (29577)
Rates: N/A;
Tel: (803) 448-6388

**CATOE VILLA**
P. O. Box 1017 (29578)
Rates: $22-$98;
Tel: (803) 448-5706

**CORAL REEF RESORT**
2706 S Ocean Blvd (29577)
Rates: $15-$65;
Tel: (803) 448-8471

**ECONO LODGE NORTHGATE**
3450 Hwy 17S Bypass (29577)
Rates: $28-$69;
Tel: (803) 293-6100

**EL DORADO MOTEL**
P. O. Box 36 (29577)
Rates: $25-$59;
Tel: (803) 626-3559

**KNIGHTS INN**
3622 Hwy 501 (29577)
Rates: $22-$59;
Tel: (803) 236-7400

**PELICAN MOTEL**
2310 N Ocean Blvd
(N Myrtle Beach 29582)
Rates: N/A;
Tel: (803) 249-1416

**THE PILOT HOUSE**
2606 N Ocean Blvd (29577)
Rates: $22-$86;
Tel: (803) 448-3533

**SPORTSMAN MOTOR INN**
1405 S Ocean Blvd (29577)
Rates: N/A;
Tel: (803) 334-5547

**SUMMER WIND RESORT INN**
1903 S Ocean Blvd (29577)
Rates: $22-$83;
Tel: (803) 626-7464

## NEWBERRY

**DAYS INN**
Rt 1, Box 407B (29108)
Rates: $29-$43;
Tel: (803) 276-2294

**NEWBERRY INN BEST WESTERN**
Rt 1, Box 405 (29108)
Rates: $28-$35;
Tel: (803) 276-5850

## ORANGEBURG

**HOLIDAY INN**
415 John C Calhoun Dr (29115)
Rates: $50-$70;
Tel: (803) 531-4600

**RUSSELL STREET INN**
491 N Russell St (29115)
Rates: $35-$64;
Tel: (803) 531-2030

## POINT SOUTH

**DAYS INN**
Jct US 17 & I-95
(Yemassee 29945)
Rates: $39-$46;
Tel: (803) 726-8156

**POINT SOUTH BEST WESTERN**
P. O. Drawer AA
(Ridgeland 29936)
Rates: $36-$48;
Tel: (803) 726-8101

## RIDGEWAY

**RIDGEWAY MOTEL**
P. O. Box 472 (29130)
Rates: $26-$29;
Tel: (803) 337-3238

## ROCK HILL

**THE BOOK & THE SPINDLE**
626 Oakland Ave (29730)
Rates: $48-$63;
Tel: (803) 328-1913

**DAYS INN**
914 Riverview Rd (29730)
Rates: $36-$60;
Tel: (803) 329-6581

**HOLIDAY INN**
2640 N Cherry Rd (29730)
Rates: $49-$64;
Tel: (803) 329-1122

**HOWARD JOHNSON LODGE**
2625 Cherry Rd (29730)
Rates: $46-$52;
Tel: (803) 329-3121

## ST. GEORGE

**BEST WESTERN- ST. GEORGE**
P. O. Box 386 (29477)
Rates: $29-$45;
Tel: (803) 563-2277

**COTTON PLANTERS INN**
P. O. Box 2 (29477)
Rates: $27-$32;
Tel: (803) 563-5551

**ECONO LODGE**
P. O. Box 132 (29477)
Rates: $24-$34;
Tel: (803) 563-4027

**ECONOMY INN OF AMERICA**
P. O. Box 666 (29477)
Rates: $19-$31;
Tel: (803) 563-4195

**HOLIDAY INN**
Jct I-95 & US 78 (29477)
Rates: $40-$46;
Tel: (803) 563-4581

**ST. GEORGE ECONOMY MOTEL**
P. O. Box 757 (29477)
Rates: $26-$31;
Tel: (803) 563-2360

**ST. GEORGE MOTOR INN**
215 S Parler Ave (29477)
Rates: $15-$19;
Tel: (803) 563-3029

**SOUTHERN INN II**
P. O.Box 375 (29477)
Rates: $20-$29;
Tel: (803) 563-3775

## SANTEE

**DAYS INN**
P. O. Box 9 (29142)
Rates: $30-$44;
Tel: (803) 854-2175

**HOLIDAY INN**
P. O. Box 27 (29142)
Rates: $47;
Tel: (803) 854-2121

## SIMPSONVILLE

**COMFORT INN**
600 Fairview Rd (29681)
Rates: $44-$75;
Tel: (803) 963-2777

## SPARTANBURG

**DAYS INN**
1355 Boiling Springs Rd (29303)
Rates: $32-$39;
Tel: (803) 585-2413

**ECONO LODGE**
710 Sunbeam Rd (29303)
Rates: $25-$33;
Tel: (803) 578-9450

**HAMPTON INN**
4930 College Dr (29301)
Rates: $36-$47;
Tel: (803) 576-6080

**HOLIDAY INN-NORTH**
Boiling Springs Rd (29303)
Rates: $46-$59;
Tel: (803) 578-5400

**RADISSON INN & CONFERENCE CENTER**
7136 Asheville Hwy (29303)
Rates: $39;
Tel: (803) 578-5530

**RAMADA INN**
1000 Hearon Cir (29303)
Rates: $45-$62;
Tel: (803) 578-7170

**RESIDENCE INN BY MARRIOTT**
P. O. Box 4156 (29305)
Rates: $65-$125;
Tel: (803) 576-3333

**WILSON WORLD HOTEL**
9027 Fairforest Rd (29301)
Rates: $41-$74;
Tel: (803) 574-2111

## SUMMERTON

**SUMMERTON INN**
P. O. Box 640 (29148)
Rates: $17-$39;
Tel: (803) 485-2635

## SUMMERVILLE

**HOLIDAY INN- SUMMERVILLE**
120 Holiday Inn Dr (29483)
Rates: $44-$55;
Tel: (803) 875-3300

## SUMTER

**DAYS INN**
P. O. Box 2731 (29151)
Rates: $35-$40;
Tel: (803) 469-9210

**PARK INN INTERNATIONAL**
226 N Washington (29151)
Rates: N/A;
Tel: (800) 457-6884

**RAMADA INN**
P. O. Box 520 (29150)
Rates: $39-$56;
Tel: (803) 775-2323

**SUMTER ECONOMY INN**
P. O. Box 704 (29150)
Rates: $35-$39;
Tel: (803) 469-4740

## TURBEVILLE

**COMFORT INN**
P. O. Box 289 (29162)
Rates: $29-$45;
Tel: (803) 659-8282

## WALTERBORO

**BEST WESTERN
WALTERBORO INN**
1140 Snider's Hwy (29488)
Rates: $28-$40;
Tel: (803) 538-3600

**COMFORT INN**
1109 Snider's Hwy (29488)
Rates: $33-$53;
Tel: (803) 538-5403

**ECONO LODGE**
I-95 & SC 63 (29488)
Rates: $24-$34;
Tel: (803) 538-3830

**HOLIDAY INN**
1120 Snider's Hwy (29488)
Rates: $42-$54;
Tel: (803) 538-5473

**HOWARD JOHNSON
MOTOR LODGE**
1139 Snider's Hwy (29488)
Rates: $35-$45;
Tel: (803) 538-5911

**RICE PLANTERS INN**
P. O. Box 529 (29488)
Rates: $21-$30;
Tel: (803) 538-8964

**SUPER 8 MOTEL**
Rt 3, Box 760 (29488)
Rates: $29-$50;
Tel: (803) 538-5383

**THUNDERBIRD INN**
P. O. Box 815 (29488)
Rates: $21-$30;
Tel: (803) 538-2503

## WINNSBORO

**FAIRFIELD MOTEL**
US 321 Bypass (29180)
Rates: $25-$29;
Tel: (803) 635-4681

## YEMASSEE

**PALMETTO LODGE**
P. O. Box 218 (29945)
Rates: $18-$26;
Tel: (803) 589-2361

**SOUTHERN COMFORT INN**
P. O. Box 574 (29945)
Rates: $18-$25;
Tel: (803) 589-2015

# SOUTH DAKOTA

## ABERDEEN

**BEST WESTERN
RAMKOTA INN ABERDEEN**
1400 8th Ave NW (57401)
Rates: $45-$59;
Tel: (605) 229-4040

**BREEZE-INN MOTEL**
1216 6th Ave SW (57401)
Rates: $23-$30;
Tel: (605) 225-4222

**BUDGET SAVER MOTEL**
1409 6th Ave SE (57401)
Rates: N/A;
Tel: (605) 225-5300

**CEDAR PASS LODGE**
P. O. Box 5 (Interior 57750)
Rates: $31-$41;
Tel: (605) 433-5460

**HOLIDAY INN**
P. O.Box 1007 (57401)
Rates: $40-$70;
Tel: (605) 225-3600

**WHITE HOUSE INN**
500 6th Ave SW (57401)
Rates: N/A;
Tel: (800) 225-6000

## BELLE FOURCHE

**ACE MOTEL**
109 6th Ave (57717)
Rates: $19-$52;
Tel: (605) 892-2612

**MOTEL LARIAT**
1033 Elkhorn (57717)
Rates: $22-$46;
Tel: (605) 892-2601

**SUNSET MOTEL**
HCR 30, Box 65 (57717)
Rates: $22-$48;
Tel: (605) 892-2508

## BERESFORD

**CROSSROADS MOTEL**
Hwys 29 & 46 (57004)
Rates: $22-$32;
Tel: (605) 763-2020

## BROOKINGS

**BEST WESTERN
STAUROLITE INN**
P. O. Box 522 (57006)
Rates: $45-$75;
Tel: (605) 692-9421

**HOLIDAY INN**
2500 E 6th St (57006)
Rates: $49-$99;
Tel: (605) 692-9471

**WAYSIDE MOTEL**
1430 6th St (57006)
Rates: N/A;
Tel: (800) 658-4577

## BUFFALO

**TIPPERARY LODGE**
P. O. Box 247 (57720)
Rates: $25-$36;
Tel: (605) 375-3721

## CANISTOTA

**BEST WESTERN
U-BAR MOTEL**
P. O. Box 97 (57012)
Rates: $23-$39;
Tel: (605) 296-3466

## CHAMBERLAIN

**BEL AIRE MOTEL**
312 E King St (57325)
Rates: $35-$48;
Tel: (605) 734-5595

**COMFORT INN**
P. O.Box 38 (Oacoma 57365)
Rates: $28-$69;
Tel: (605) 734-5593

**LAKE SHORE MOTEL**
115 N River St (57325)
Rates: $30-$44;
Tel: (605) 734-5566

**OASIS INN**
P. O. Box 128 (57325)
Rates: $35-$60;
Tel: (605) 734-6061

## CUSTER

**ALLEN'S ROCKET MOTEL**
211 Mt Rushmore Rd (57730)
Rates: $30-$58;
Tel: (605) 673-4401

**BAVARIAN INN MOTEL**
P. O. Box 152 (57730)
Rates: $50-$106;
Tel: (800) 351-1477

**BLUE BELL
LODGE & RESORT**
HCR 83, Box 63 (57730)
Rates: $60-$95;
Tel: (605) 255-4531

**BUZZARD'S ROOST**
HCR 83, Box 120 (57730)
Rates: $34-$58;
Tel: (605) 673-2326

**CHIEF MOTEL**
120 Mt Rushmore Rd (57730)
Rates: $26-$65;
Tel: (605) 673-2318

**DAKOTA COWBOY INN**
208 W Mt Rushmore Rd
(57730)
Rates: $28-$70;
Tel: (605) 673-4659

## CUSTER STATE PARK

**LEGION LAKE RESORT**
HCR 83, Box 67
(Custer 57730)
Rates: $55-$100;
Tel: (800) 658-3530

**STATE GAME LODGE**
HCR 83, Box 74
(Custer 57730)
Rates: $70-$175;
Tel: (800) 658-3530

## DEADWOOD

**DEADWOOD
GULCH RESORT**
P. O. Box 643 (57732)
Rates: $48-$85;
Tel: (605) 578-1294

**FIRST GOLD HOTEL**
270 Main St (57732)
Rates: $47-$77;
Tel: (605) 578-9777

## DESMET

**COTTAGE INN MOTEL**
101 5th St SE Hwy 14 (57231)
Rates: N/A;
Tel: (800) 848-0251

## EUREKA

**LAKEVIEW MOTEL**
RR 1, Box 49 (57437)
Rates: N/A;
Tel: (605) 284-2681

## FAITH

**PRAIRIE VISTA INN**
P. O. Box 575 (57626)
Rates: $34-$48;
Tel: (605) 967-2343

## FREEMAN

**FENSEL'S MOTEL**
Hwy 81 (57029)
Rates: N/A;
Tel: (605) 925-4204

## GETTYSBURG

**HARER LODGE B & B**
RR 1, Box 87A (57442)
Rates: N/A;
Tel: (605) 765-2167

## HILL CITY

**LANTERN INN MOTEL**
P. O. Box 744 (57745)
Rates: $32-$60;
Tel: (605) 574-2582

**PALMER GULCH LODGE**
Box 295, Hwy 244 (57745)
Rates: N/A;
Tel: (800) 233-4331

**ROBINS ROOST CABINS**
HCR 87, Box 62 (57745)
Rates: N/A;
Tel: (605) 574-2252

## HOT SPRINGS

**BATTLE MOUNTAIN MOTEL**
402 Battle Mtn Ave (57747)
Rates: N/A;
Tel: (800) 888-1304

**BEST WESTERN
INN BY THE RIVER**
602 W River St (57747)
Rates: $30-$78;
Tel: (605) 745-4292

**BISON MOTEL**
646 South 5th St (57747)
Rates: N/A;
Tel: (605) 745-5191

**SUPER 8 MOTEL**
800 Mammoth St (57747)
Rates: N/A;
Tel: (605) 745-3888

## HURON

**CROSSROADS MOTEL**
P. O. Box 833 (57350)
Rates: $49-$130;
Tel: (605) 352-3204

**TRAVELER MOTEL**
241 Lincoln NW (57350)
Rates: N/A;
Tel: (605) 352-6401

## INTERIOR

**BADLANDS INN**
Box 103 (57750)
Rates: N/A;
Tel: (605) 433-5401

**CEDAR PASS LODGE**
#1 Cedar St (57750)
Rates: N/A;
Tel: (605) 433-5460

## KADOKA

**BEST WESTERN
H & H EL CENTRO MOTEL**
P. O. Box 37 (57543)
Rates: $28-$70;
Tel: (605) 837-2287

**CUCKLEBURR MOTEL**
P. O. Box 575 (57543)
Rates: $22-$45;
Tel: (605) 837-2151

**WEST MOTEL**
P. O. Box 247 (57543)
Rates: $21-$36;
Tel: (605) 837-2427

## KEYSTONE

**BED AND BREAKFAST INN**
P. O. Box 154 (57751)
Rates: $35-$60;
Tel: (605) 666-4490

**BEST WESTERN
FOUR PRESIDENTS MOTEL**
P. O. Box 690 (57751)
Rates: $75-$85;
Tel: (605) 666-4472

**THE FIRST LADY INN**
P. O. Box 677 (57751)
Rates: $40-$74;
Tel: (605) 666-4990

**GOLD NUGGET MOTEL**
HC 33, Box 1605
(Rapid City 57701)
Rates: $25-$46;
Tel: (605) 348-2082

**KELLY INN**
P. O. Box 654 (57751)
Rates: $25-$69;
Tel: (605) 666-4483

**POWDER HOUSE LODGE**
P. O. Box 714 (57751)
Rates: $30-$72;
Tel: (605) 666-4646

**TRIPLE R RANCH**
Hwy 16A (57751)
Rates: N/A;
Tel: (605) 666-4605

## KIMBALL

**TRAVLERS MOTEL**
P. O. Box 457 (57355)
Rates: $27-$42;
Tel: (605) 778-6215

## LEAD

**BEST WESTERN
GOLDEN HILLS RESORT**
900 Miners Ave (57754)
Rates: $69-$99;
Tel: (605) 584-1800

## MADISON

**LAKE PARK MOTEL**
P. O. Box 47 (57042)
Rates: $27-$37;
Tel: (605) 256-3524

**SUPER 8 MOTEL**
P. O. Box 5 (57042)
Rates: $27-$33;
Tel: (605) 256-6931

## MILBANK

**MANOR MOTEL**
P. O. Box 26 (57252)
Rates: $28-$40;
Tel: (605) 432-4527

**SUPER 8 MOTEL**
P. O. Box 86 (57252)
Rates: $28-$42;
Tel: (605) 432-9288

## MITCHELL

**BEST WESTERN
MOTOR INN**
P. O. Box 849 (57301)
Rates: $27-$52;
Tel: (605) 996-5536

**BUDGET HOST INN**
1313 S Ohlman (57301)
Rates: $33-$43;
Tel: (605) 996-6647

**COACHLIGHT MOTEL**
P. O. Box 416 (57301)
Rates: $28-$35;
Tel: (605) 996-5686

**HOLIDAY INN**
P. O. Box 458 (57301)
Rates: $45-$75;
Tel: (605) 996-6501

**HOLIDAY INN**
1525 W Havens St (57301)
Rates: $60-$70;
Tel: (605) 996-3145

**MOTEL 6**
1309 S Ohlman St (57301)
Rates: $29-$35;
Tel: (605) 996-0530

**SIESTA MOTEL**
1210 W Havens St (57301)
Rates: $35-$45;
Tel: (605) 996-5544

**THUNDERBIRD MOTEL**
P. O. Box 984 (57301)
Rates: $35-$45;
Tel: (605) 996-6645

## MOBRIDGE

**WRANGLER MOTOR INN**
820 West Grand Circle
(57601)
Rates: N/A;
Tel: (605) 845-3641

## MURDO

**ANDERSON MOTEL**
408 Lincoln (57559)
Rates: N/A;
Tel: (605) 669-2448

**HOSPITALITY INN**
P. O. Box 464 (57559)
Rates: $25-$68;
Tel: (605) 669-2425

## PICKSTOWN

**FORT RANDALL INN**
P. O. Box 122 (57367)
Rates: $28-$37;
Tel: (605) 487-7801

## PIERRE

**BEST WESTERN KINGS INN**
220 S Pierre St (57501)
Rates: $42-$55;
Tel: (605) 224-5951

**BEST WESTERN
RAMKOTA INN**
920 W Sioux (57501)
Rates: $49-$64;
Tel: (605) 224-6877

**CAPITOL INN MOTEL**
815 Wells Ave (57501)
Rates: $26-$30;
Tel: (800) 658-3055

**DAYS INN**
520 W Sioux Ave (57501)
Rates: $27-$42;
Tel: (605) 224-0411

**GOVERNOR'S INN**
700 W Sioux Ave (57501)
Rates: $32-$49;
Tel: (605) 224-4200

**STATE MOTEL**
640 N Euclid Ave (57501)
Rates: $25-$45;
Tel: (605) 224-5896

**SUPER 8 MOTEL**
720 West Capitol (57501)
Rates: N/A;
Tel: (605) 224-1617

## PLATTE

**KINGS INN**
P. O. Box 54 (57369)
Rates: $22-$34;
Tel: (605) 337-3385

## PRESHO

**HUTCH'S MOTEL**
P. O. Box 449 (57568)
Rates: $24-$42;
Tel: (605) 895-2591

## RAPID CITY

**AVANTI MOTEL**
102 North Maple (57701)
Rates: N/A;
Tel: (800) 658-5464

**CASTLE INN**
15 E North St (57701)
Rates: $24-$79;
Tel: (800) 658-5464

**ECONO LODGE
OF RAPID CITY**
625 E Disk Dr (57701)
Rates: $29-$199;
Tel: (605) 342-6400

**ELK CREEK
RESORT & LODGE**
HC 80, Box 767
(Piedmont 57769)
Rates: $26-$79;
Tel: (605) 787-4884

**FOOTHILLS INN**
1625 N La Crosse St (57701)
Rates: $19-$99;
Tel: (605) 348-5640

**HILTON INN**
445 Mt. Rushmore Rd (57701)
Rates: $75-$250;
Tel: (605) 348-8300

**HOLIDAY INN-
MT. RUSHMORE AREA**
P. O. Box 7008 (57709)
Rates: $75-$95;
Tel: (605) 348-1230

**HOWARD JOHNSON
LODGE**
P. O. Box 1795 (57709)
Rates: $48-$88;
Tel: (605) 343-8550

**LAZY U MOTOR LODGE**
2215 Mt Rushmore Rd (57701)
Rates: $19-$54;
Tel: (605) 343-4242

**RAMADA INN RAPID CITY**
1721 N La Crosse St (57701)
Rates: $49-$139;
Tel: (605) 342-1300

**ROCKERVILLE TRADING
POST & MOTEL**
HCR 33, Box 1607 (57701)
Rates: $22-$58;
Tel: (605) 341-4880

**SUPER 8 MOTEL**
2124 LaCrosse St (57701)
Rates: N/A;
Tel: (605) 348-8070

**TIP-TOP MOTOR HOTEL**
405 St Joseph St (57701)
Rates: $28-$65;
Tel: (605) 343-3901

**TRADEWINDS MOTEL**
420 East North St (57701)
Rates: N/A;
Tel: (605) 342-4153

## REDFIELD

**COACHMAN INN**
826 4th St (57469)
Rates: $23-$38;
Tel: (800) 382-8000

## SIOUX FALLS

**BEST WESTERN RAMKOTA INN**
2400 N Louise Ave (57107)
Rates: $57-$73;
Tel: (605) 336-0650

**BUDGET HOST PLAZA INN**
2620 E 10th St (57103)
Rates: $27-$47;
Tel: (605) 336-1550

**COMFORT INN**
3216 S Carolyn Ave (57106)
Rates: $36-$60;
Tel: (605) 361-2822

**COMFORT SUITES**
3208 S Carolyn Ave (57106)
Rates: $53-$68;
Tel: (605) 362-9711

**EMPIRE INN**
4208 W 41st St (57106)
Rates: $27-$49;
Tel: (605) 361-2345

**EXEL INN OF SIOUX FALLS**
1300 W Russell St (57104)
Rates: $24-$39;
Tel: (605) 331-5800

**HOLIDAY INN (AIRPORT)**
1301 W Russell St (57104)
Rates: $60-$76;
Tel: (605) 335-1020

**HOLIDAY INN-CITY CENTRE**
100 W 8th St (57102)
Rates: $60-$66;
Tel: (605) 339-2000

**KELLY INN**
P. O. Box 84711 (57107)
Rates: $38-$48;
Tel: (605) 338-6242

**MOTEL 6**
3009 W Russell St (57104)
Rates: $29-$35;
Tel: (605) 336-7800

**RAMKOTA INN**
2400 N Louise Ave (57107)
Rates: N/A;
Tel: (605) 336-0650

**SELECT INN**
3500 S Gateway Blvd (57106)
Rates: $27-$36;
Tel: (605) 361-1864

**SUBURBAN MOTEL**
3308 E 10th St (57103)
Rates: $22-$32;
Tel: (605) 336-3668

**SUNSET MOTEL**
5213 W 12th St (57106)
Rates: N/A;
Tel: (605) 336-3050

**TRAVELODGE**
809 West Ave N (57104)
Rates: $32-$44;
Tel: (605) 336-0230

**WESTWICK MOTEL**
5801 West 12th St (57106)
Rates: N/A;
Tel: (800) 658-5464

## SISSETON

**HOLIDAY MOTEL**
1 1/2 Mi E at JCT US 127 (57262)
Rates: $22-$30;
Tel: (605) 698-7644

**I-29 MOTEL**
Just off I-29 Jct SD 10E (57262)
Rates: $25-$37;
Tel: (800) 341-8000

**VIKING MOTEL**
West Hwy 10 (57262)
Rates: N/A;
Tel: (605) 698-7663

## SPEARFISH

**ANTLER MOTEL**
517 West Jackson Blvd (57783)
Rates: N/A;
Tel: (605) 642-5753

**KELLY INN**
P. O. Box 989 (57583)
Rates: $35-$62;
Tel: (605) 642-7795

**L RANCHO MOTEL**
334 West Jackson Blvd (57783)
Rates: N/A;
Tel: (605) 642-2061

**QUEEN'S MOTEL**
305 Main St (57783)
Rates: $20-$42;
Tel: (605) 642-2631

**ROYAL REST MOTEL**
444 Main St (57783)
Rates: N/A;
Tel: (605) 642-3842

**SHADY PINES CABINS**
514 Mason St (57783)
Rates: N/A;
Tel: (800) 551-8920

**SHERWOOD LODGE**
231 West Jackson Blvd (57783)
Rates: N/A;
Tel: (605) 642-4688

## STURGIS

**BEST WESTERN PHIL-TOWN INN**
P. O. Box 777 (57785)
Rates: $39-$79;
Tel: (605) 347-3604

**JUNCTION INN**
1802 S Junction Ave (57785)
Rates: $27-$51;
Tel: (605) 347-5675

**SUPER 8 MOTEL**
P. O. Box 703 (57785)
Rates: $48-$55;
Tel: (605) 347-4447

## VERMILLION

**SUPER 8 LODGE**
1208 E Cherry St (57069)
Rates: $28-$48;
Tel: (605) 624-8005

## WALL

**BEST WESTERN
PLAINS MOTEL**
P. O. Box 393 (57790)
Rates: $36-$78;
Tel: (605) 279-2145

**HITCHING POST MOTEL**
10th Ave (57790)
Rates: N/A;
Tel: (605) 279-2133

**KINGS INN MOTEL**
P.O. Box 440 (57790)
Rates: $48-$52;
Tel: (605) 279-2178

## WATERTOWN

**BEST WESTERN
RAMKOTA INN**
P. O. Box 346 (57201)
Rates: $45-$56;
Tel: (605) 886-8011

**DRAKE MOTOR INN**
P. O. Box 252 (57201)
Rates: $27-$37;
Tel: (800) 821-8695

**GUEST HOUSE
MOTOR INN**
P. O. Box 1147 (57201)
Rates: $32-$37;
Tel: (605) 886-8061

**SUPER 8 MOTEL**
P. O. Box 876 (57201)
Rates: $28-38;
Tel: (605) 882-1900

**TRAVEL HOST MOTEL**
1714 9th Ave SW (57201)
Rates: $27-$35;
Tel: (605) 886-6120

## WHITE LAKE

**WHITE LAKE MOTEL**
RR 2, Box 72 (57383)
Rates: N/A;
Tel: (605) 249-2320

## WINNER

**BUFFALO TRAIL MOTEL**
1030 W US 18 (57580)
Rates: $28-$75;
Tel: (605) 842-2212

**WARRIOR INN MOTEL**
Hwys 44 & 118 (57580)
Rates: $32-$60;
Tel: (605) 842-3121

## YANKTON

**BROADWAY MOTEL**
1210 Broadway (57078)
Rates: $25-$33;
Tel: (605) 665-7805

**COMFORT INN**
2118 Broadway (57078)
Rates: $33-$40;
Tel: (605) 665-8053

**LEWIS & CLARK RESORT**
P.O. Box 754 (57078)
Rates: $35-$70;
Tel: (605) 665-2680

**MULBERRY INN**
512 Mulberry St (57078)
Rates: $25-$48;
Tel: (605) 665-7116

**YANKTON INN
& CONVENTION CENTER**
P. O. Box 157 (57078)
Rates: $40-$56;
Tel: (605) 665-2906

# TENNESSEE

## ATHENS

**DAYS INN OF ATHENS**
2541 Decatur Pike (37302)
Rates: $28-$40;
Tel: (615) 745-5800

**HOLIDAY INN ATHENS I-75**
Rt 3, Box 32 (37303)
Rates: $32-$42;
Tel: (615) 745-1212

**HOMESTEAD INN**
1827 Holiday Dr (37303)
Rates: $28-$33;
Tel: (615) 744-9002

**HOMESTEAD INN WEST**
2808 Decatur Pike (37303)
Rates: $29-$34;
Tel: (615) 745-9002

**SCOTTISH INNS**
2620 Decatur Pike (37303)
Rates: $26-$36;
Tel: (615) 744-8200

## BRISTOL

**HOJO INN**
975 Volunteer Pkwy (37620)
Rates: $36-$42;
Tel: (615) 968-9474

**HOLIDAY INN I-81**
111 Holiday Dr (37620)
Rates: $44-$62;
Tel: (615) 968-1101

## BROWNSVILLE

**DAYS INN**
2530 Anderson Ave (38012)
Rates: $32-$37;
Tel: (615) 772-3297

## BUCKSNORT

**BUDGET HOST INN
AT BUCKSNORT**
Rt 1 (Only 37140)
Rates: $25-$33;
Tel: (615) 729-5450

## BUFFALO

**DAYS INN
OF HURRICANE MILLS**
Rt 1, Box 53A
(Hurricane Mills 37078)
Rates: $32-$45;
Tel: (615) 296-7647

**ECONO LODGE**
Rt 1, Box 79
(Hurricane Mills 37078)
Rates: $27-$45;
Tel: (615) 296-2432

## CARYVILLE

**BUDGET HOST INN**
P. O.Box 16 (37714)
Rates: $24 $31;
Tel: (615) 562-9595

**HOLIDAY INN COVE LAKE**
Rt 1, Box 14 (37714)
Rates: $40-$51;
Tel: (615) 562-8476

**LAKE VIEW INN**
P. O. Box 250 (37714)
Rates: $19-$44;
Tel: (615) 562-9456

## CHATTANOOGA

**BEST WESTERN-
HERITAGE INN**
7641 Lee Hwy (37421)
Rates: $35-$45;
Tel: (615) 899-3311

**BEST WESTERN
MOTOR INN SOUTH**
6710 Ringgold Rd (37412)
Rates: $48-$63;
Tel: (615) 894-6820

**BEST WESTERN ROYAL INN**
3644 Cummings Hwy (37419)
Rates: $32-$54;
Tel: (615) 821-6840

**CASCADES MOTEL**
3625 Ringgold Rd (37412)
Rates: $18-$25;
Tel: (615) 698-1571

**CHATTANOOGA MARRIOTT
AT THE CONV CTR**
2 Carter Plaza (37402)
Rates: $60;
Tel: (615) 756-0002

**COMFORT HOTEL
RIVER CENTRE**
407 Chestnut St (37402)
Rates: $45-$52;
Tel: (615) 756-5150

**COMFORT INN**
7717 Lee Hwy (37421)
Rates: $36-$48;
Tel: (615) 894-5454

**DAYS INN & LODGE**
1401 N Mack Smith Rd
(East Ridge 37412)
Rates: $33-$45;
Tel: (615) 894-7480

**DAYS INN CHATTANOOGA
LOOKOUT MOUNTAIN**
101 E 20th St (37408)
Rates: $36-$40;
Tel: (615) 267-9761

**DAYS INN-
LOOKOUT MOUNTAIN**
3801 Cummings Hwy (37419)
Rates: $38-$48;
Tel: (615) 821-6044

**ECONO LODGE**
1417 St. Thomas St (37412)
Rates: $26-$39;
Tel: (615) 894-1417

**FRIENDSHIP INN**
7725 Lee Hwy (37421)
Rates: $28-$36;
Tel: (615) 899-2288

**HOLIDAY INN-SOUTHEAST**
6700 Ringgold Rd (37412)
Rates: $55-$71;
Tel: (615) 892-8100

**KINGS LODGE MOTEL**
2400 Westside Dr (37404)
Rates: $29-$45;
Tel: (615) 698-8944

**QUALITY INN
& CONVENTION CTR**
1400 N Mack Smith Rd
(37411)
Rates: $40-$48;
Tel: (615) 894-0440

**RAMADA INN AIRPORT**
6639 Capehart Ln (37412)
Rates: $38-$44;
Tel: (615) 894-6110

**RED CARPET INN**
5111 Hunter Rd (37363)
Rates: $30-$39;
Tel: (615) 238-5838

**RED ROOF INN**
7014 Shallowford Rd (37421)
Rates: $28 $47;
Tel: (615) 899-0143

## CLARKSVILLE

**COMFORT INN**
1112 SR 76 & I-24 Exit 11
(37043)
Rates: $30-$50;
Tel: (615) 358-2020

**DAYS INN**
3065 Guthrie Hwy (37040)
Rates: $34-$48;
Tel: (615) 552-1155

**DAYS INN OF CLARKSVILLE**
1100 Hwy 76 Connector Rd
(37043)
Rates: $27-$40;
Tel: (615) 358-3194

**HOLIDAY INN
DOWNTOWN**
803 N 2nd St (37040)
Rates: $41-$51;
Tel: (615) 645-9084

**HOLIDAY INN I-24**
3095 Guthrie Hwy (37040)
Rates: $42-$55;
Tel: (615) 648-4848

## CLEVELAND

**BEST WESTERN
CLEVELAND INN**
156 James Asberry Dr (37311)
Rates: $38-$47;
Tel: (615) 472-5566

**BUDGETEL INN**
107 Interstate Dr NW (37312)
Rates: $34-$47;
Tel: (615) 339-1000

**DAYS INN OF CLEVELAND**
2550 Georgetown Rd (37311)
Rates: $30-$45;
Tel: (615) 476-2112

**HOLIDAY INN I-75 SOUTH**
P. O. Box 3896 (37320)
Rates: $39-$46;
Tel: (615) 479-4531

**HOLIDAY INN NORTH**
P. O. Box 3360 (37320)
Rates: $45-$65;
Tel: (615) 472-1504

**TRAVEL INN**
3000 Valley Hills Tr NW
(37311)
Rates: $28-$33;
Tel: (615) 472-2185

## COLLIERVILLE

**PLANTATION INN**
1230 W Poplar (38017)
Rates: $32-$42;
Tel: (615) 853-1235

## COLUMBIA

**ECONO LODGE**
1548 Bear Creek Pkwy
(38401)
Rates: $34-$42;
Tel: (615) 381-1410

**JAMES K POLK MOTEL**
1111 Nashville Hwy (38401)
Rates: $29-$39;
Tel: (615) 388-4913

## COOKEVILLE

**BEST WESTERN
THUNDERBIRD MOTEL**
900 S Jefferson (38501)
Rates: $27-$45;
Tel: (615) 526-7115

**COMFORT INN**
1100 S Jefferson Ave (38501)
Rates: $27-$42;
Tel: (615) 528-1040

**HOLIDAY INN**
970 S Jefferson Ave (38501)
Rates: $54-$168;
Tel: (615) 526-7125

**HOWARD JOHNSON
MOTOR LODGE**
2021 E Sprikng St (38501)
Rates: $30-$45;
Tel: (615) 526-3333

**STAR MOTOR INN**
1115 S Willow (38501)
Rates: $24-$39;
Tel: (615) 526-9511

**SUPER 8 MOTEL**
1330 Bunker Hill Rd (38501)
Rates: $25-$38;
Tel: (615) 528-2020

## CORNERSVILLE

**ECONO LODGE**
P. O. Box 266 (Pulaski 38478)
Rates: $34-$45;
Tel: (615) 293-2111

## CROSSVILLE

**RAMADA INN**
P. O. Box 626 (38555)
Rates: $44-$59;
Tel: (615) 484-7581

## CUMBERLAND GAP

**HOLIDAY INN**
P. O. Box 37 (37724)
Rates: $45-$64;
Tel: (615) 869-3631

## DAYTON

**BEST WESTERN OF DAYTON**
Hwy 27N (37321)
Rates: $35-$65;
Tel: (615) 775-6560

**DAYS INN**
1702 Hwy 27S (37321)
Rates: $32-$55;
Tel: (615) 775-9718

## DICKSON

**ECONO LODGE**
2338 Hwy 46 (37055)
Rates: $32-$44;
Tel: (615) 446-0541

**HOLIDAY INN**
2420 Hwy 46S (37055)
Rates: $38-$60;
Tel: (615) 446-9081

## DUCKTOWN

**BEST WESTERN
COPPER INN**
P. O. Box 98 (37326)
Rates: $33-$59;
Tel: (615) 496-5541

## DYERSBURG

**HOLIDAY INN DYERSBURG**
P. O. Box 490 (38024)
Rates: $45-$66;
Tel: (615) 285-8601

## ELIZABETHTON

**COMFORT INN**
1515 US 19E Bypass (37643)
Rates: $38-$52;
Tel: (615) 542-4466

## FRANKLIN

**BEST WESTERN
GOOSE CREEK INN**
2404 Goos Creek Bypass
(37064)
Rates: $34-$48;
Tel: (615) 794 7200

**BEST WESTERN
MAXWELL'S INN**
Jct I-65 & SR 96, Exit 65
(37064)
Rates: $41-$46;
Tel: (615) 790-0570

## GALLATIN

**SHONEY'S INN**
221 W Main St (37066)
Rates: $36-$42;
Tel: (615) 452-5433

## GATLINBURG

**ALTO MOTEL**
P. O. Box 1277 (37738)
Rates: $60-$70;
Tel: (615) 436-5175

**BON AIR MOUNTAIN INN**
P. O.Box 36 (37738)
Rates: $43-$95;
Tel: (800) 848-4857

**COX'S GATEWAY MOTEL**
1100 Parkway (37738)
Rates: $48-$150;
Tel: (615) 436-5656

**CREEKSTONE MOTEL**
104 Oglewood Ln (37738)
Rates: $32-$50;
Tel: (615) 436-4628

**HIGHLAND MOTOR INN**
131 Parkway (37738)
Rates: $30-$68;
Tel: (615) 436-4110

**HOLIDAY INN-
RESORT COMPLEX**
P. O. Box 1130 (37738)
Rates: $79-$99;
Tel: (615) 436-9201

**MIDTOWN LODGE**
805 Parkway (37738)
Rates: $65-$95;
Tel: (800) 633-2446

**PARK VISTA HOTEL**
P. O. Box 30 (37738)
Rates: $55-$230;
Tel: (615) 436-9211

## HARRIMAN

**BEST WESTERN SUNDANCER
MOTOR LODGE**
P. O. Box 1421 (37748)
Rates: $30-$40;
Tel· (615) 882 6200

## HURRICANE MILLS

**DAYS INN**
Rt 1, Box 83A (37078)
Rates: $38-$56;
Tel: (615) 296-7647

## JACKSON

**ADMIRAL BENBOW
EXECUTIVE INN**
2295 N Highland Ave (38305)
Rates: $27-$33;
Tel; (901) 668-1145

**BUDGETEL INN**
2370 N Highland Ave (38305)
Rates: $28-$43;
Tel: (901) 664-1800

**CASEY JONES STATION INN**
1943 Hwy 45 Bypass (38305)
Rates: $27-$33;
Tel: (901) 668-3636

**DAYS INN-WEST**
2239 Hollywood Dr (38305)
Rates: $30-$48;
Tel: (901) 668-4840

**ECONO LODGE**
2318 N Highland Ave (38305)
Rates: $31-$37;
Tel: (901) 668-0490

**ECONO LODGE
JACKSON WEST**
196 Providence Rd
(Denmark 38391)
Rates: $25-$44;
Tel: (901) 427-2778

**GARDEN PLAZA HOTEL**
1770 Hwy 45 Bypass (38305)
Rates: $54-$77;
Tel: (901) 664-6900

**RAMADA INN**
1849 Hwy 45 Bypass (38305)
Rates: $30-$42;
Tel: (901) 668-4222

**TRAVELERS MOTEL**
2247 N Highland Ave (38305)
Rates: $19-$28;
Tel: (901) 668-0542

**WILSON WORLD HOTEL**
541 Carriage House Dr
(38301)
Rates: $34-$59;
Tel: (901) 668-6000

## JELLICO

**DAYS INN**
P. O. Box 299 (37762)
Rates: $31-$36;
Tel: (615) 784-7281

**JELLICO MOTEL**
P. O. Box 177 (37762)
Rates: $24-$36;
Tel: (615) 784-7211

## JOHNSON CITY

**GARDEN PLAZA HOTEL**
211 Mockingbird Ln (37604)
Rates: $68-$79;
Tel: (615) 929-2000

**HOLIDAY INN**
2406 N Roan St (37601)
Rates: $50-$65;
Tel: (615) 282-2161

**RED ROOF INN**
210 Broyles Dr (37601)
Rates: $28-$37;
Tel: (615) 282-3040

# KIMBALL

## SCOTTISH INNS
I-24 Exit 152, Hwy 72 (37347)
Rates: N/A;
Tel: (615) 837-7933

# KINGSPORT

## COMFORT INN
100 Indian Center Ct (37660)
Rates: $48-$80;
Tel: (615) 378-4418

## HOLIDAY INN
700 Lynn Garden Dr (37660)
Rates: $46-$52;
Tel: (615) 247-3133

## RAMADA INN
2005 La Masa Dr (37660)
Rates: $56-$66;
Tel: (615) 245-0271

## TRAVELER'S INN
I-81 at Exit 59 (37663)
Rates: N/A;
Tel: (615) 239-9137

# KINGSTON

## DAYS INN
I-40 & Gallaher Rd (37763)
Rates: $34-$48;
Tel: (615) 376-2069

## ECONO LODGE
905 N Kentucky St (37763)
Rates: $28-$38;
Tel: (615) 376-4965

# KINGSTON SPRINGS

## FRIENDSHIP INN
P. O. Box 260 (37082)
Rates: $32-$50;
Tel: (615) 952-2900

# KNOXVILLE

## CAMPUS INN
1706 W Cumberland Ave
(37916)
Rates: $39-$55;
Tel: (615) 521-5000

## COMFORT INN
5334 Central Ave Pike
(37912)
Rates: $38-$54;
Tel: (615) 688-1010

## COMFORT INN
323 Emory Rd (37949)
Rates: $35-$56;
Tel: (615) 938-5500

## COMFORT INN-WEST
11748 Snyder Rd (37922)
Rates: $36-$59;
Tel: (615) 675-5566

## DAYS INN EAST
5423 Asheville Hwy (37914)
Rates: $34-$59;
Tel: (615) 637-3511

## DAYS INN-KNOXVILLE WEST/LOVELL RD
200 Lovell Rd (37922)
Rates: $33-$50;
Tel: (615) 966-5801

## ECONO LODGE
402 Lovell Rd (37922)
Rates: $29-$49;
Tel: (615) 675-7200

## ECONO LODGE
6200 Papermill Rd (37919)
Rates: $43-$50;
Tel: (615) 584-8511

## HAMPTON INN-EAST
814 Brakebill Rd (37914)
Rates: $44-$69;
Tel: (615) 525-3511

## HAMPTON INN KNOXVILLE AIRPORT
148 International Ave
(Alcoa 37701)
Rates: $46-$54;
Tel: (615) 983-1101

## HAMPTON INN-KNOXVILLE WEST
9128 Executive Park Blvd
(37923)
Rates: $49-$59;
Tel: (615) 693-1101

## HAMPTON INN NORTH
119 Cedar Ln (37912)
Rates: $45-$60;
Tel: (615) 689-1011

## HOLIDAY INN-CEDAR BLUFF
304 Cedar Bluff Rd (37923)
Rates: $59-$79;
Tel: (615) 693-1011

## HOLIDAY INN-NORTHWEST
5335 Central Ave Pike
(37912)
Rates: $54-$62;
Tel: (615) 688-9110

## HOLIDAY INN-WEST
1315 Kirby Rd (37909)
Rates: $59-$89;
Tel: (615) 584-3911

## HOWARD JOHNSON MOTOR LODGE
118 Merchants Dr (37912)
Rates: $45-$75;
Tel: (615) 688-3141

## HYATT REGENCY KNOXVILLE
500 Hill Ave SE (37915)
Rates: $110-$125;
Tel: (615) 637-1234

## LA QUINTA MOTOR INN
258 Peters Rd N (37923)
Rates: $42-$55;
Tel: (615) 690-9777

## LUXBURY HOTEL
420 Peters Rd N (37922)
Rates: $49-$54;
Tel: (615) 539-0058

## THE MIDDLETON
800 W Hill Ave (37902)
Rates: $60-$65;
Tel: (615) 524-8100

## QUALITY INN WEST
7621 Kingston Pike (37919)
Rates: $46-$64;
Tel: (615) 693-8111

## RAMADA INN KNOXVILLE AIRPORT
P. O. Box 120 (Alcoa 37701)
Rates: $44-$48;
Tel: (615) 970-3060

## RED ROOF INN-NORTH
5640 Merchants Center Blvd
(37912)
Rates: $36-$44;
Tel: (615) 689-7100

**RED ROOF INN-WEST**
209 Advantage Pl (37922)
Rates: $34-$48;
Tel: (615) 691-1664

**WEST PARK INN**
11320 Outlet Dr (37922)
Rates: $25-$29;
Tel: (615) 966-7500

## LAKE CITY

**THE LAMB'S INN**
P. O. Box 381 (37769)
Rates: $24-$42;
Tel: (615) 426-2171

## LEBANON

**BUDGET HOST INN**
903 US 231S (37087)
Rates: $24-$39;
Tel: (615) 449-2900

**COMFORT INN**
829 S Cumberland St (37087)
Rates: $25-$40;
Tel: (615) 444-1001

**DAYS INN**
914 Murfreesboro Rd (37087)
Rates: $25-$48;
Tel: (615) 444-5635

**HAMPTON INN**
US 231, 1/2 Mi N Jct I-40
(37087)
Rates: $34-$46;
Tel: (615) 444-7400

## LENOIR CITY

**ECONO LODGE**
1211 Hwy 321N (37771)
Rates: $30-$37;
Tel: (615) 986-0295

## LEWISBURG

**BEST WESTERN WALKING
HORSE LODGE**
255 Ellington Pkwy (37091)
Rates: $50-$60;
Tel: (615) 359-4005

## LOUDON

**HOLIDAY INN EXPRESS**
12452 Hwy 72N (37774)
Rates: $28-$38;
Tel: (615) 458-5668

## MANCHESTER

**AMBASSADOR INN**
Rt 6, Box 6022 (37355)
Rates: $29-$33;
Tel: (615) 728-2200

**BEST WESTERN-
OLD FORT MOTOR INN**
Rt 8, Box 8143 (37355)
Rates: $24-$40;
Tel: (615) 728-9720

**ECONO LODGE**
Rt 8, Box 8131 (37355)
Rates: $19-$28;
Tel: (615) 728-9530

**HAMPTON INN**
I-24 & SR 53 (37355)
Rates: $38-$48;
Tel: (615) 728-3300

**HOLIDAY INN**
I-24 & US 41 (37355)
Rates: $39-$46;
Tel: (615) 728-9651

**SCOTTISH INN**
Rt 8, Box 8580 (37355)
Rates: $18-$49;
Tel: (615) 728-0506

## MARTIN

**ECONO LODGE**
853 University St (38237)
Rates: $36-$45;
Tel: (901) 587-4241

**UNIVERSITY LODGE**
P. O. Box 50 (38237)
Rates: $36-$41;
Tel: (901) 587-9577

## MCMINNVILLE

**SHONEYS INN**
118 Sunnyside Heights
(37110)
Rates: $38-$51;
Tel: (615) 473-4446

## MEMPHIS
(and Vicinity)

**BUDGETEL INN**
6020 Shelby Oaks Dr (38134)
Rates: $34-$50;
Tel: (901) 377-2233

**BUDGETEL INN
MEMPHIS AIRPORT**
3005 Millbranch Rd (38116)
Rates: $33-$49;
Tel: (901) 396-5411

**COMFORT INN**
2889 Austin Peay Hwy
(38128)
Rates: $52-$75;
Tel: (901) 386-0033

**COMFORT INN
AIRPORT/GRACELAND**
1561 E Brook Rd (38116)
Rates: $38-$55;
Tel: (901) 345-3344

**DAYS INN POPLAR EAST**
5877 Poplar Ave (38119)
Rates: $50-$56;
Tel: (901) 767-6300

**DAYS INN WEST/PYRAMID**
1100 Ingram Blvd
(West Memphis 72301)
Rates: $40-$50;
Tel: (501) 735-8600

**ECONO LODGE AIRPORT**
3456 Lamar Ave (38118)
Rates: $33-$49;
Tel: (901) 365-7335

**ECONO LODGE GRACELAND**
3280 Elvis Presley Blvd
(38116)
Rates: $35-$48;
Tel: (901) 345-1425

**EMBASSY SUITES**
1022 S Shady Grove Rd
(38119)
Rates: $109-$124;
Tel: (901) 684-1777

**THE FRENCH QUARTER
SUITES HOTEL**
2144 Madison Ave (38104)
Rates: $85-$130;
Tel: (901) 728-4000

**HAMPTON INN**
1585 Sycamore View Rd
(38134)
Rates: $38-$55;
Tel: (901) 388-4881

**HOLIDAY INN EAST**
5795 Poplar Ave (38119)
Rates: $77-$90;
Tel: (901) 682-7881

**HOLIDAY INN-
OVERTON SQUARE AREA**
1837 Union Ave (38104)
Rates: $58-$85;
Tel: (901) 278-4100

**HOMEWOOD SUITES**
5811 Poplar Ave (38119)
Rates: $89-$149;
Tel: (901) 763-0500

**LA QUINTA
MOTOR INN-AIRPORT**
2745 Airways Blvd (38132)
Rates: $40-$53;
Tel: (901) 396-1000

**LA QUINTA
MOTOR INN-EAST**
6068 Macon Cove (38134)
Rates: $43-$56;
Tel: (901) 382-2323

**LA QUINTA MOTOR INN-
MEDICAL CENTER**
42 S Camilla St (38104)
Rates: $40-$53;
Tel: (901) 526-1050

**MARRIOTT RESIDENCE INN**
6141 Poplar Pike (38119)
Rates: $89-$115;
Tel: (901) 685-9595

**MEMPHIS AIRPORT HOTEL**
2240 Democrat Rd (38132)
Rates: $50-$275;
Tel: (901) 332-1130

**THE MEMPHIS INN**
4879 American Way (38118)
Rates: $27-$38;
Tel: (901) 794-8300

**QUALITY INN
MEMPHIS AIRPORT**
2959 Airways Blvd (38116)
Rates: $35-$45;
Tel: (901) 345-1250

**RAMADA CONVENTION
CENTER HOTEL**
160 Union Ave (38103)
Rates: $51-$61;
Tel: (901) 525-5491

**RAMADA HOTEL I-240
AT MT. MORIAH**
2490 Mt. Moriah Rd (38115)
Rates: $54-$69;
Tel: (901) 362-8010

**RED ROOF INN-EAST**
6055 Shelby Oaks Dr (38134)
Rates: $27-$41;
Tel: (901) 388-6111

**RED ROOF INN
MEDICAL CENTER**
210 S Pauline (38104)
Rates: $27-$39;
Tel: (901) 528-0650

**RED ROOF INN-SOUTH**
3875 American Way (38118)
Rates: $29-$39;
Tel: (901) 363-2335

**WILSON INN-
MEMPHIS CENTRAL**
2705 Cherry Rd (38116)
Rates: $37-$58;
Tel: (901) 366-9300

**WILSON INN-MEMPHIS EAST**
8635 Hwy 64 (38133)
Rates: $37-$53;
Tel: (901) 372-0000

## MILLINGTON

**BEST WESTERN INN**
7726 Hwy 51N (38053)
Rates: $40-$45;
Tel: (901) 873-2222

## MONTEAGLE

**COUNTRY INN**
P. O. Box 188 (37356)
Rates: $24-$32;
Tel: (800) 468-6580

**JIM OLIVER'S SMOKE
HOUSE MOTOR LODGE**
P. O. Box 579 (37356)
Rates: $24-$125;
Tel: (800) 678-0997

## MORRISTOWN

**RAMADA INN**
P. O. Box 190 (37815)
Rates: $46-$75;
Tel: (615) 587-2400

## MURFREESBORO

**BEST WESTERN
WAYSIDE INN**
US 231 & I-24 (37130)
Rates: $32-$44;
Tel: (615) 896-2320

**DAYS INN**
1855 S Church St (37130)
Rates: $35-$50;
Tel: (615) 896-5080

**GARDEN PLAZA HOTEL**
1850 Old Fort Pkwy (37129)
Rates: $62-$73;
Tel: (615) 895-5555

**HAMPTON INN**
2230 Old Fort Pkwy (37129)
Rates: $42-$52;
Tel: (615) 896-1172

**HOJO INN**
US 231 & I-24 (37130)
Rates: $30-$54;
Tel: (615) 896-5522

**HOLIDAY INN HOLIDOME**
2227 Old Fort Pkwy (37130)
Rates: $53-$66;
Tel: (615) 896-2420

**MURFREESBORO MOTEL**
1150 NW Broad St (37129)
Rates: $23-$34;
Tel: (615) 893-2100

**SHONEY'S INN**
1954 S Church St (37130)
Rates: $37-$43;
Tel: (800) 222-2222

# NASHVILLE
(and Vicintiy)

**THE BELVEDERE INN**
2403 Brick Church Pike
(37207)
Rates: $28-$44;
Tel: (615) 226-9805

**BEST WESTERN
CALUMET INN**
701 Stewart Ferry Pike
(37214)
Rates: $42-$68;
Tel: (615) 889-9199

**BEST WESTERN METRO INN**
99 Spring St (37207)
Rates: $24-$57,
Tel: (615) 259-9160

**BUDGETEL INN**
531 Donelson Pike (37214)
Rates: $32-$57;
Tel: (615) 885-3100

**BUDGETEL INN
NASHVILLE NORTH**
120 Cartwright Ct
(Goodletsville 37072)
Rates: $32-$45;
Tel: (615) 851-1891

**BUDGETEL INN
NASHVILLE WEST**
5612 Lenox Ave (37209)
Rates: $40-$55;
Tel: (615) 353-0700

**COMFORT INN SOUTHEAST**
97 Wallace Rd (37211)
Rates: $30-$49;
Tel: (615) 833-6860

**DAYS INN BELL ROAD**
501 Collins Park Dr
(Antioch 37013)
Rates: $27-$59;
Tel: (615) 731-7800

**DAYS INN
NASHVILLE CENTRAL**
211 N First St (37213)
Rates: $30-$69;
Tel: (615) 254-1551

**DAYS INN
WEST TRINITY LANE**
1400 Brick Church Pike
(37207)
Rates: $25-$60;
Tel: (615) 228-5977

**DAYS INN WHITEHOUSE**
P. O. Box 49
(Whitehouse 37188)
Rates: $25-$49;
Tel: (615) 672-3746

**DRURY INN-AIRPORT**
837 Briley Pkwy (37217)
Rates: $43-$57;
Tel: (615) 361-6999

**DRURY INN-NORTH**
2306 Brick Church Pike
(37207)
Rates: $41-$48;
Tel: (615) 226-9560

**DRURY INN-SOUTH**
343 Harding Pl (37211)
Rates: $41-$48;
Tel: (615) 834-7170

**ECONO LODGE-OPRYLAND**
2460 Music Valley Dr (37214)
Rates: $32-$59;
Tel: (615) 889-0090

**ECONO LODGE RIVERGATE**
320 Long Hollow Pike
(Goodlettesville 37072)
Rates: $30-45;
Tel: (615) 859-4988

**EMBASSY SUITES**
10 Century Blvd (37214)
Rates: $109-$119;
Tel: (615) 871-0033

**FRIENDSHIP INN**
650 Wade Cir
(Goodlettesville 37072)
Rates: $26-$38;
Tel: (615) 859-1416

**FRIENDSHIP INN**
625 N Gallatin
(Madison 37115)
Rates: $24-$40;
Tel: (615) 865-2323

**HAMPTON INN**
2350 Elm Hill Pike (37214)
Rates: $46-$61;
Tel: (615) 871-0222

**HAMPTON INN
HOTEL-NORTH**
P. O. Box 70029 (37207)
Rates: $40-$60;
Tel: (615) 226-3300

**HILTON SUITES-BRENTWOOD**
9000 Overlook Blvd
(Brentwood 37027)
Rates: $99-$109;
Tel: (615) 370-0111

**HOLIDAY INN-
BRILEY PARKWAY**
2200 Elm Hill Pike (37210)
Rates: $89-$99;
Tel: (615) 883-9770

**HOLIDAY INN
EXPRESS-AIRPORT**
1111 Airport Center Dr
(37214)
Rates: $55-$61;
Tel: (615) 883-1366

**HOLIDAY INN EXPRESS
NASHVILLE SE AIRPORT**
981 Murfreesboro Rd (37217)
Rates: $51-$57;
Tel: (615) 367-9150

**HOLIDAY INN-NORTH**
230 W Trinity Ln (37207)
Rates: $50-$57;
Tel: (615) 226-0111

**HOLIDAY INN-VANDERBILT**
2613 W End Ave (37203)
Rates: $66-$90;
Tel: (615) 327-4707

**HOWARD JOHNSON-
NORTH**
P. O. Box 70029 (37207)
Rates: $40-$68;
Tel: (615) 226-4600

**HOWARD JOHNSON
LODGE AT OPRYLAND**
2600 Music Valley Dr (37214)
Rates: $36-$75;
Tel: (615) 889-8235

**LA QUINTA MOTOR INN-
METRO CENTER**
2001 Metro Center Blvd
(37228)
Rates: $42-$55;
Tel: (615) 259-2130

**LA QUINTA
MOTOR INN-SOUTH**
4311 Sidco Dr (37204)
Rates: $39-$50;
Tel: (615) 834-6900

**NASHVILLE MED
CENTER INN**
1909 Hayes St (37203)
Rates: $48-$66;
Tel: (615) 329-1000

**QUALITY INN AIRPORT**
1 International Plaza (37217)
Rates: $42-$52;
Tel: (615) 361-7666

**QUALITY INN
EXECUTIVE PLAZA**
823 Murfreesboro Rd (37217)
Rates: $38-$54;
Tel: (615) 367-1234

**RAMADA INN SOUTHEAST/
HICKORY HOLLOW MALL**
P. O. Box 110693 (37211)
Rates: $29-$59;
Tel: (615) 731-8540

**RED ROOF INN**
110 Northgate Dr
(Goodlettesville 37072)
Rates: $29-$47;
Tel: (615) 859-2537

**RED ROOF INN
NASHVILLE EAST**
510 Claridge Dr (37214)
Rates: $25-$47;
Tel: (615) 872-0735

**RED ROOF INN SOUTH**
4271 Sidco Dr (37204)
Rates: $27-$47;
Tel: (615) 832-0093

**RESIDENCE INN BRENTWOOD**
206 Ward Cir
(Brentwood 37027)
Rates: $89-$129;
Tel: (615) 371-0100

**RODEWAY INN
MUSIC CITY HOTEL**
797 Briley Pkwy (37217)
Rates: $48-$173;
Tel: (615) 361-5900

**THE SAVE INN**
323 Harding Pl (37211)
Rates: $32-$45;
Tel: (615) 834-0570

**SCOTTISH INNS**
893 Murfreesboro Rd (37217)
Rates: $28-$40;
Tel: (615) 361-6830

**SHERATON
MUSIC CITY HOTEL**
777 McGavock Pike (37214)
Rates: $115-$140;
Tel: (615) 885-2200

**SHONEY'S INN OF NASHVILLE**
1521 Demonbraun St (37203)
Rates: $49-$59;
Tel: (615) 255-9977

**STOUFFER NASHVILLE HOTEL**
611 Commerce St (37203)
Rates: $139-$189;
Tel: (615) 255-8400

**SUPER 8 MOTEL**
412 Robertson Ave (37209)
Rates: $39-$66;
Tel: (615) 356-0888

**THRIFTY INN-NORTH**
1516 Hampton St (37207)
Rates: $33-$45;
Tel: (615) 228-5513

**THRIFTY INN-SOUTH**
I-24 & Harding Pl (37211)
Rates: $31-$38;
Tel: (615) 834-4242

**TRAVELODGE-NASHVILLE
AIRPORT SOUTH**
1274 Murfreesboro Rd
(37217)
Rates: $29-$48;
Tel: (615) 366-9000

## NEWPORT

**BEST WESTERN INN**
P. O. Box 382 (37821)
Rates: $29-$42;
Tel: (615) 623-8713

**HOLIDAY INN**
P. O. Box 250 (37821)
Rates: $39-$64;
Tel: (615) 623-8622

**RAMSEY MOTEL**
P. O. Box 1148 (37821)
Rates: $20-$40;
Tel: (615) 625-1521

## OAK RIDGE

**COMFORT INN**
433 S Rutgers Ave (37830)
Rates: $54-$71;
Tel: (615) 481-8200

**DAYS INN**
206 S Illinois Ave (37830)
Rates: $47-$51;
Tel: (615) 483-5615

**GARDEN PLAZA HOTEL**
215 S Illinois (37830)
Rates: $75-$87;
Tel: (615) 481-2468

**HOLIDAY INN**
420 S Illinois Ave (37830)
Rates: $45-$52;
Tel: (615) 483-4371

## ONEIDA

**THE GALLOWAY INN**
P. O. Box 585 (37841)
Rates: $23-$29;
Tel: (615) 569-8835

## PIGEON FORGE

**THE GRAND HOTEL &
CONVENTION CENTER**
3171 N Parkway (37863)
Rates: $29-$99;
Tel: (615) 453-1000

**PINE GROVE LODGE**
2440 Parkway (37863)
Rates: $30-$75;
Tel: (615) 428-1231

**QUALITY INN**
2385 Parkway (37863)
Rates: $30-$89;
Tel: (615) 453-4106

## PORTLAND

**BUDGET HOST INN**
5339 Long Rd (37148)
Rates: $29-$42;
Tel: (615) 325-2005

## PULASKI

**BEST WESTERN SANDS MOTOR HOTEL**
P. O. Box 376 (38478)
Rates: $34-$42;
Tel: (615) 363-4501

## RICEVILLE

**BEST INN**
P. O. Box 3125 (37370)
Rates: $16-$20·
Tel: (615) 462-2224

## SEVIERVILLE

**BEST WESTERN DUMPLIN VALLEY INN**
3426 Winfield Dunn Pkwy (37764)
Rates: $27-$89;
Tel: (615) 933-3467

## SHELBYVILLE

**SHELBYVILLE INN**
317 N Cannon Blvd (37160)
Rates: $44-$59;
Tel: (615) 684-6050

## SMYRNA

**DAYS INN**
1300 Plaza Dr (37167)
Rates: $41-$75;
Tel: (615) 355-6161

## SPRINGFIELD

**BEST WESTERN SPRINGFIELD**
2001 Memorial Blvd (37172)
Rates: $43-$50;
Tel: (615) 384-1234

## SWEETWATER

**COMFORT INN**
P. O. Box 48 (37874)
Rates: $29-$45;
Tel: (615) 337-6646

**COMFORT INN**
Rt 5, Box 48 (37874)
Rates: $34-$55;
Tel: (615) 337-3353

**DAYS INN**
Rt 5, Box 46 (37874)
Rates: $29-$45;
Tel: (615) 337-4200

**QUALITY INN SWEETWATER**
P. O. Box 6655 (37874)
Rates: $34-$45;
Tel: (615) 337-3541

## TOWNSEND

**BEST WESTERN VALLEY VIEW LODGE**
P.O. Box 148 (37882)
Rates: $27-$69;
Tel: (615) 448-2237

## WHITE PINE

**DAYS INN**
3670 Roy Messer Hwy (37890)
Rates: $39 $44,
Tel: (615) 674-2573

**HILLCREST INN**
3683 Roy Messer Hwy (37890)
Rates: $27-$30;
Tel: (615) 674-2561

## WILDERSVILLE

**BEST WESTERN CROSSROADS INN**
Rt 1, Box 3955 (38388)
Rates: $32-$42;
Tel: (901) 968-2532

# TEXAS

## ABILENE

**BEST WESTERN COLONIAL INN**
3210 Pine St (79601)
Rates: $35-$49;
Tel: (915) 677-2683

**CLASSIC INN**
3950 Ridgemont Dr (79606)
Rates: $36-$46;
Tel: (915) 695-1262

**ECONO LODGE**
1633 W Stamford (79601)
Rates: $24-$38;
Tel: (915) 673-5424

**ECONOMY INN**
1525 E I-20 (79601)
Rates: $24-$32;
Tel: (915) 673-5251

**EMBASSY SUITES HOTEL**
4250 Ridgemont Dr (79606)
Rates: $75-$85;
Tel: (915) 698-1234

**HOLIDAY INN EXPRESS**
1625 SR 351 (79601)
Rates: $45-$49;
Tel: (915) 673-5271

**KIVA MOTEL**
5403 S 1st St (79605)
Rates: $41-$115;
Tel: (915) 695-2150

**LA QUINTA MOTOR INN**
3501 W Lake Rd (79601)
Rates: $44-$56;
Tel: (915) 676-1676

**QUALITY INN**
505 Pine St (79601)
Rates: $41-$150;
Tel: (915) 676-0222

**ROYAL INN**
5695 S 1st St (79605)
Rates: $29-$40;
Tel: (915) 692-3022

## ALICE

**DAYS INN**
555 N Johnson St (78332)
Rates: $35-$45;
Tel: (512) 664-6616

**KINGS INN MOTEL**
815 Hwy 281S (78332)
Rates: $30-$35;
Tel: (512) 664-4351

## ALPINE

**SUNDAY HOUSE
INN MOTEL**
P. O. Box 578 (79830)
Rates: $42-$53;
Tel: (915) 837-3363

## ALVIN

**HOMEPLACE INN**
1588 S Hwy 35 Bypass
(77511)
Rates: $48-$59;
Tel: (713) 331-0335

## AMARILLO

**AMARILLO EAST
TRAVELODGE**
3205 I-40E/Tee Anchor Blvd
(79104)
Rates: $32-$38;
Tel: (806) 372-8171

**AMARILLO WEST
TRAVELODGE**
2035 Paramount Blvd (79109)
Rates: $32-$42;
Tel: (806) 353-3541

**BEST WESTERN
AMARILLO INN**
1610 Coulter Dr (79106)
Rates: $49-$61;
Tel: (806) 358-7861

**THE BIG TEXAS MOTEL**
P. O. Box 37000 (79120)
Rates: $35-$45;
Tel: (806) 372-5000

**COMFORT INN**
2100 S Coulter Dr (79106)
Rates: $38-$54;
Tel: (806) 358-6141

**COMFORT INN-AIRPORT**
1515 I-40E (79102)
Rates: $45-$59;
Tel: (806) 376-9993

**FRIENDSHIP INN-
BRONCO MOTEL**
6005 Amarillo Blvd W (79106)
Rates: $25-$32;
Tel: (806) 355-3321

**HAMPTON INN**
1700 I-40E (79103)
Rates: $40-$56;
Tel: (806) 372-1425

**HARVEY HOTEL-AMARILLO**
3100 I-40W (79102)
Rates: $49-$99;
Tel: (806) 358-6161

**LA QUINTA INN-AIRPORT**
1708 I-40E (79103)
Rates: $41-$56;
Tel: (806) 373-7486

**LA QUINTA INN-
MEDICAL CENTER**
2108 S Coulter Dr (79106)
Rates: $43-$58;
Tel: (806) 352-6311

**TRAVELODGE-WEST**
2035 Paramount (79109)
Rates: $27-$40;
Tel: (806) 353-3541

## ARANSAS PASS

**HOMEPORT INN**
1515 Wheeler Ave (78336)
Rates: $30-$36;
Tel: (512) 758-3213

## ARLINGTON

**ARLINGTON TRAVELODGE**
1181 N Watson Rd (76006)
Rates: $32-$46;
Tel: (817) 649-0993

**BEST WESTERN-
GREAT SOUTHWEST INN**
3501 E Division St (76011)
Rates: $38-$60;
Tel: (817) 640-7722

**COMFORT INN**
1601 E Division St (76011)
Rates: $42-$58;
Tel: (817) 261-2300

**COUNTRY SUITES
BY CARLSON**
1075 West 'N Wild Way
(76011)
Rates: $69-$89;
Tel: (817) 261-8900

**DAYS INN AIRPORT
SOUTH/SIX FLAGS**
1195 N Watson Rd (76011)
Rates: $30-$58;
Tel: (817) 649-8881

**DAYS INN-
DOWNTOWN/SIX FLAGS**
910 N Collins St (76011)
Rates: $31-$55;
Tel: (817) 261-8444

**HAWTHORN SUITES HOTEL**
2401 Brookhollow Plaza Dr
(76011)
Rates: $70-$120;
Tel: (817) 640-1188

**HOWARD JOHNSON
HOTEL**
903 N Collins St (76011)
Rates: $65-$75;
Tel: (817) 261-3621

**LA QUINTA MOTOR INN-
ARLINGTON**
825-A N Watson Rd (76011)
Rates: $53-$86;
Tel: (817) 640-4142

**OASIS MOTEL**
818 W Division St (76012)
Rates: $23-$40;
Tel: (817) 274-1616

# ATHENS

**SPANISH TRACE
INN MOTEL**
716 E Tyler St (75751)
Rates: $39-$75;
Tel: (903) 675-5173

# ATLANTA

**BEST WESTERN
TRAVEL INN**
801 Loop 59N (75551)
Rates: $30-$40;
Tel: (903) 796-7121

**THE BUTLER'S INN**
1100 W Main St (75551)
Rates: $29-$37;
Tel: (903) 796-8235

# AUSTIN
(and Vicinity)

**BEST WESTERN
SEVILLE PLAZA INN**
4323 I-35S (78744)
Rates: $40-$45;
Tel: (512) 447-5511

**BEST WESTERN SOUTH**
3909 I-35S (78741)
Rates: $38-$42;
Tel: (512) 444-0531

**COMFORT INN**
7928 Gessner Dr (78753)
Rates: $40-$65;
Tel: (512) 339-7311

**DRURY INN AUSTIN-
HIGHLAND MALL**
919 E Koenig Ln (78751)
Rates: $47-$52;
Tel: (512) 454-1144

**DRURY INN AUSTIN NORTH**
6511 I-35N (78752)
Rates: $46-$64;
Tel: (512) 467-9500

**EMBASSY SUITES-
DOWNTOWN**
300 S Congress Ave (78704)
Rates: $109-$129;
Tel: (512) 469-9000

**EXEL INN OF AUSTIN**
2711 IH-35S (78741)
Rates: $28-$41;
Tel: (512) 462-9201

**FOUR SEASONS
HOTEL AUSTIN**
98 San Jacinto Blvd (78701)
Rates: $128-$158;
Tel: (512) 478-4500

**GUEST QUARTERS SUITE
HOTEL-AUSTIN**
303 W 15th St (78701)
Rates: $89-$135;
Tel: (512) 478-7000

**HABITAT SUITES HOTEL**
500 Highland Mall Blvd
(78752)
Rates: $89-$119;
Tel: (512) 467-6000

**HAWTHORN SUITES-
AUSTIN CENTRAL**
935 La Posada Dr (78752)
Rates: $69-$123;
Tel: (512) 459-3335

**HAWTHORN SUITES-
AUSTIN SOUTH**
4020 I-35S (78704)
Rates: $89-$129;
Tel: (512) 440-7722

**HAWTHORN SUITES-
NORTHWEST**
8888 Tallwood Dr (78759)
Rates: $95-$155;
Tel: (512) 343-0008

**HOLIDAY INN-
AIRPORT/HIGHLAND MALL**
6911 I-35N (78752)
Rates: $63-$73;
Tel: (512) 459-4251

**HOLIDAY INN NORTH-
WEST PLAZA**
8901 Business Park Dr
(78759)
Rates: $75-$80;
Tel: (512) 343-0888

**HOLIDAY INN-TOWNLAKE**
20 N IH-35 (78701)
Rates: $69-$95;
Tel: (512) 472-8211

**HOWARD JOHNSON
PLAZA HOTEL-NORTH**
7800 I-35 (78753)
Rates: $58-$74;
Tel: (512) 836-8520

**HOWARD JOHNSON
PLAZA HOTEL-SOUTH**
3401 I-35S (78741)
Rates: $52-$93;
Tel: (512) 448-2444

**LA QUINTA MOTOR INN-
BEN WHITE**
4200 I-35S (78745)
Rates: $48-$60;
Tel: (512) 443-1774

**LA QUINTA MOTOR INN-
HIGHALND MALL/AIRPORT**
5812 I-35N (78751)
Rates: $49-$62;
Tel: (512) 459-4381

**LA QUINTA
MOTOR INN-NORTH**
7100 I-35N (78752)
Rates: $48-$60;
Tel: (512) 452-9401

**LA QUINTA
MOTOR INN OLTORF**
1603 E Oltorf (78741)
Rates: $48-$60;
Tel: (512) 447-6661

**QUALITY INN-SOUTH**
2200 I-35S (78704)
Rates: $47-$60;
Tel: (512) 444-0561

**RAMADA AIRPORT &
CONFERENCE CENTER**
5660 I-35N (78751)
Rates: $79-$89;
Tel: (512) 458-2340

**RED LION HOTEL-
AUSTIN AIRPORT**
6121 I-35N (78752)
Rates: $73-$128;
Tel: (512) 323-5466

**RODEWAY INN I-35 AIRPORT**
5526 I-35N (78751)
Rates: $42-$56;
Tel: (512) 451-7001

**WYNDHAM AUSTIN HOTEL**
4140 Governor's Row (78744)
Rates: $119-$350;
Tel: (512) 448-2222

# BANDERA

**ECONO LODGE**
1900 Hwy 16S (78003)
Rates: $49-$58;
Tel: (210) 796-3093

# BAY CITY

**CATTLEMEN'S MOTEL**
905 Ave F (77414)
Rates: $29-$39;
Tel: (409) 245-1751

# BAYTOWN

**LA QUINTA MOTOR INN**
4911 I-10E (77521)
Rates: $50-$64;
Tel: (713) 421-5566

# BEAUMONT

**BEAUMONT HILTON HOTEL**
2355 I-10S (77705)
Rates: $80-$100;
Tel: (409) 842-3600

**BEST WESTERN
BEAUMONT INN**
2155 N 11th St (77703)
Rates: $36-$42;
Tel: (409) 898-8150

**BEST WESTERN
JEFFERSON INN**
1610 I-10S (77707)
Rates: $38-$44;
Tel: (409) 842-0037

**DAYS INN**
30 North I-10 (77702)
Rates: $29-$32;
Tel: (409) 838-0581

**HOLIDAY INN
BEAUMONT PLAZA**
3950 I-10S (77705)
Rates: $73-$91;
Tel: (409) 842-5995

**HOLIDAY INN I-10
MIDTOWN**
2095 N 11th St (77703)
Rates: $50-$67;
Tel: (409) 892-2222

**LA QUINTA MOTOR INN**
220 I-10N (77702)
Rates: $41-$56;
Tel: (409) 838-9991

**QUALITY INN**
P. O. Box 5295 (77702)
Rates: $43-$48;
Tel: (409) 892-7722

# BEDFORD

**LA QUINTA
MOTOR INN-BEDFORD**
1450 W Airport Frwy (76022)
Rates: $43-$55;
Tel: (817) 267-5200

# BEEVILLE

**BEST WESTERN
DRUMMERS INN**
P. O. Box 1748 (78102)
Rates: $36-$44;
Tel: (512) 358-4000

# BIG BEND
# NATIONAL PARK

**CHISOS MOUNTAINS LODGE**
Chisos Basin
(Basin Rural Sta. 79834)
Rates: $53-$70;
Tel: (915) 477-2291

# BIG SPRING

**BEST WESTERN
MOTEL BIG SPRING**
P. O. Box 1444 (79720)
Rates: $38-$46;
Tel: (915) 267-1601

**DAYS INN BIG SPRING**
300 Tulane Ave (79720)
Rates: $42-$48;
Tel: (915) 263-7621

**GREAT WESTERN MOTEL**
2900 E I-20 (79720)
Rates: $30-$50;
Tel: (915) 267-4553

**PONDEROSA MOTOR INN**
2701 S Gregg St (79720)
Rates: $23-$30;
Tel: (915) 267-5237

# BORGER

**THE INN PLACE OF BORGER**
100 Bulldog Blvd (79007)
Rates: $39-$46;
Tel: (806) 273-9556

# BOWIE

**BOWIE INN MOTEL**
P. O. Box 163 (76230)
Rates: $30-$53;
Tel: (817) 872-5426

**PARK LODGE**
708 Park Ave (76230)
Rates: $28-$46;
Tel: (817) 872-1111

# BRADY

**PLATEAU MOTEL**
P. O. Box 1348 (76825)
Rates: $27-$38;
Tel: (915) 597-2185

**SUNSET INN**
2108 S Bridge (76825)
Rates: $40-$44;
Tel: (915) 597-0789

# BROOKSHIRE

**BRAZOS VALLEY INN**
217 Waller Ave (77423)
Rates: $36-$49;
Tel: (713) 934-3122

# BROWNSVILLE

**FORT BROWN
HOTEL & RESORT**
P. O. Box 2255 (78520)
Rates: $69-$200;
Tel: (800) 582-3333

**HOLIDAY INN**
1945 N Expwy (78520)
Rates: $38-$66;
Tel: (210) 546-4591

**LA QUINTA MOTOR INN**
55 Sam Perl Blvd (78520)
Rates: $41-$53;
Tel: (210) 546-0381

**SHERATON INN
PLAZA ROYALE**
3777 N Expwy (78520)
Rates: $73-$93;
Tel: (210) 350-9191

## BROWNWOOD

**COMFORT INN**
410 E Commerce (76801)
Rates: $38-$49;
Tel: (915) 646-3511

**HOLIDAY INN**
P. O. Box 699 (76801)
Rates: $37-$54;
Tel: (915) 646-2551

**POST OAK INN MOTEL**
606 Early Blvd (76801)
Rates: $23-$45;
Tel: (915) 643-5621

## BUFFALO

**BEST WESTERN
CRAIG'S INN**
P. O. Box 667 (75831)
Rates: $37-$41;
Tel: (903) 322-5831

## CANTON

**BEST WESTERN
CANTON INN**
Rt 3, Box 6B (75103)
Rates: $39-$74;
Tel: (903) 567-6591

## CASTROVILLE

**BEST WESTERN
ALSATIAN INN**
1650 Hwy 90W (78009)
Rates: $43-$59;
Tel: (210) 538-2282

## CENTER

**BEST WESTERN
CENTER INN**
1005 Hurst St (75935)
Rates: $35-$45;
Tel: (409) 598-3384

## CHILDRESS

**BEST WESTERN
CLASSIC INN**
1805 Avenue F NW (79201)
Rates: $43-$46;
Tel: (817) 937-6353

**CHATEAU INN**
1612 Ave F NW Hwy 287
(79201)
Rates: $32-$40;
Tel: (817) 937-3695

## CISCO

**OAK MOTEL**
300 I-20E (76437)
Rates: $20-$29;
Tel: (817) 442-2100

## CLAUDE

**L A MOTEL**
200 E 1st St (79019)
Rates: $22-$35;
Tel: (806) 226-4981

## CLUTE

**LA QUINTA MOTOR INN**
1126 SR 332 (77531)
Rates: $44-$57;
Tel: (409) 265-7461

## COLDSPRING

**SAN JACINTO INN**
P. O. Box 459 (77331)
Rates: $33-$36;
Tel: (409) 653-3008

## COLLEGE STATION

**COLLEGE STATION
HILTON & CONF CTR**
801 University Dr E (77840)
Rates: $56-$104;
Tel: (409) 693-7500

**COMFORT INN**
104 Texas Ave S (77840)
Rates: $42-$70;
Tel: (409) 846-7333

**HAMPTON INN**
320 Texas Ave S (77840)
Rates: $44-$58;
Tel: (409) 846 0184

**HOLIDAY INN-
COLLEGE STATION**
1503 Texas Ave S (77840)
Rates: $47-$59;
Tel: (409) 693-1736

**LA QUINTA MOTOR INN**
607 Texas Ave S (77840)
Rates: $47-$61;
Tel: (409) 696-7777

**MANOR HOUSE
MOTOR INN**
2504 Texas Ave S (77840)
Rates: $52-$57;
Tel: (409) 764-9540

**RAMADA INN
MOTOR HOTEL**
1502 Texas Ave S (77840)
Rates: $38-$100;
Tel: (409) 693-9891

## COLUMBUS

**HOMEPLACE**
2436 Hwy 71S (78934)
Rates: $44-$57;
Tel: (409) 732-6293

## CONROE

**HOLIDAY INN**
1601 I-45S (77301)
Rates: $59-$65;
Tel: (409) 756-8941

## CONWAY

**S & S MOTOR INN**
Rt 2, Box 58
(Panhandle 79068)
Rates: $24-$30;
Tel: (806) 537-5111

## CORPUS CHRISTI

**BEST WESTERN
GARDEN INN**
11217 IH-37 (78410)
Rates: $49-$65;
Tel: (512) 241-6675

**COMFORT INN AIRPORT**
6301 I-37 (78409)
Rates: $35-$51;
Tel: (512) 289-6925

**CORPUS CHRISTI INN**
2838 S Padre Island Dr
(78415)
Rates: $45-$55;
Tel: (512) 854-0005

**DAYS INN**
901 Navigation (78408)
Rates: $35-$54;
Tel: (512) 888-8599

**DRURY INN**
2021 N Padre Island Dr
(78408)
Rates: $49-$56;
Tel: (512) 289-8200

**EMBASSY SUITES HOTEL**
4337 S Padre Island Dr
(78411)
Rates: $95-$105;
Tel: (512) 853-7899

**GULF BEACH-II
LUXURY MOTOR INN**
3500 Surfside Blvd (78402)
Rates: $39-$69;
Tel: (512) 882-3500

**HOLIDAY INN-AIRPORT**
5549 Leopard St (78408)
Rates: $69-$80;
Tel: (512) 289-5100

**HOLIDAY INN-
EMERALD BEACH**
1102 S Shoreland Dr (78401)
Rates: $73-$115;
Tel: (512) 883-5731

**HOLIDAY INN NORTH
PADRE ISLAND RESORT**
15202 Windward Dr (78418)
Rates: $49-$135;
Tel: (512) 949-8041

**LA QUINTA
MOTOR INN-NORTH**
5155 I-37N (78408)
Rates: $52-$62;
Tel: (512) 888-5721

**LA QUINTA
MOTOR INN-SOUTH**
6225 S Padre Island Dr
(78412)
Rates: $58-$70;
Tel: (512) 991-5730

**RADISSON MARINA HOTEL**
300 N Shoreline Blvd (78403)
Rates: $61-$83;
Tel: (512) 883-5111

**SURFSIDE CONDOMINIUM
APARTMENTS**
15005 Windward Dr (78418)
Rates: $65-$100;
Tel: (512) 949-8128

**VAL-U-INN**
5224 I-37 at Navigation Blvd
(78407)
Rates: $37-$45;
Tel: (512) 883-2951

## CROCKETT

**EMBERS MOTOR INN**
1401 Loop 304E (75835)
Rates: $24-$33;
Tel: (409) 544-5681

## DALHART

**BEST WESTERN
NURSANICKEL MOTEL**
Hwy 87S (79022)
Rates: $31-$51;
Tel: (806) 249-5637

**BEST WESTERN SKIES
MOTOR INN**
623 Denver Ave (79022)
Rates: $33-$42;
Tel: (806) 249-4538

**COMFORT INN**
HCR 2, Box 22 (79022)
Rates: $32-$52;
Tel: (806) 249-8585

**SANDS MOTEL**
301 Liberal St (79022)
Rates: $19-$35;
Tel: (806) 249-4568

## DALLAS
(and Vicinity)

**ADDISON INN**
4103 Belt Line Rd (75244)
Rates: $40-$53;
Tel: (214) 991-8888

**BEST WESTERN-
OAKTREE INN**
13333 N Stemmons Frwy
(75234)
Rates: $44-$59;
Tel: (214) 241-8521

**BRISTOL SUITES**
7800 Alpha Rd (75204)
Rates: $79-$114;
Tel: (214) 233-7600

**CLARION HOTEL**
1241 W Mockingbird Ln
(75247)
Rates: $79-$450;
Tel: (800) 442-7547

**COUNTRY SUITES
BY CARLSON**
4100 W John Carpenter Frwy
(Irving 75063)
Rates: $49-$79;
Tel: (214) 929-4008

**CRESCENT COURT HOTEL**
400 Crescent Court (75210)
Rates: $205-$1200;
Tel: (800) 654-6541

**DALLAS GRAND HOTEL**
1914 Commerce St (75201)
Rates: $75-$135;
Tel: (214) 747-7000

**DAYS INN-
DALLAS/GARLAND**
6222 Belt Line Rd
(Garland 75043)
Rates: $29-$40;
Tel: (214) 226-7621

**DAYS INN-MESQUITE**
3601 Hwy 80E (75150)
Rates: $30-$40;
Tel: (214) 279-6561

**DAYS INN REGAL ROW**
1575 Regal Row (75247)
Rates: $40-$55;
Iel: (214) 638-6100

**DOUBLETREE HOTEL
AT CAMPBELL CENTRE**
8250 N Central Expwy
(75206)
Rates: $49-$99;
Tel: (214) 691-8700

**DRURY INN-
DALLAS NORTH**
2421 Walnut Hill Ln (75229)
Rates: $55 $61;
Tel: (214) 484-3330

**DRURY INN-DFW AIRPORT**
4210 W Airport Frwy
(Irving 75062)
Rates: $51-$57;
Tel. (214) 986-1200

**EMBASSY SUITES DALLAS-
MARKET CENTER**
2727 Stemmons Frwy (75207)
Rates: $139-$149·
Tel: (214) 630-5332

**EMBASSY SUITES HOTEL-
DALLAS/PARK CENTRAL**
13131 N Central Expwy
(75243)
Rates: $109-$149;
Tel: (214) 234-3300

**EXEL INN OF DALLAS EAST**
8510 East R L Thornton Frwy
(75228)
Rates: $26-$39;
Tel: (214) 328-8500

**EXEL INN OF DFW AIRPORT**
8205 Esters Rd (Irving 75063)
Rates: $35-$44;
Tel: (214) 929-0066

**FOUR SEASONS
RESORT & CLUB**
4150 N MacArthur Blvd
(Irving 75038)
Rates: $109-$220;
Tel: (214) 717-0700

**HAMPTON INN-ADDISON**
4555 Beltway Dr (75244)
Rates: $51-$62;
Tel: (214) 991-2800

**HAMPTON INN-
DALLAS/DUNCANVILLE**
4154 Preferred Place (75237)
Rates: $47-$49;
Tel: (214) 298-4747

**HAMPTON INN-GARLAND**
12670 E Northwest Hwy
(75228)
Rates: $40-$51;
Tel: (214) 613-5000

**HAMPTON INN-
DALLAS NORTH**
11069 Composite Dr (75229)
Rates: $54-$61;
Tel: (214) 484-6557

**THE HARVEY HOTEL-
ADDISON**
14315 Midway Rd (75244)
Rates: $55-$109·
Tel· (214) 980-8877

**THE HARVEY HOTEL-
DALLAS**
7815 LBJ Frwy at Colt Rd
(75240)
Rates: $49-$79·
Tel: (214) 960-7000

**THE HARVEY HOTEL-
DFW AIRPORT**
4545 W John Carpenter Frwy
(Irving 75063)
Rates: $49-$130;
Tel: (214) 929-4500

**HARVEY SUITES**
4550 W John Carpenter Frwy
(Irving 75063)
Rates: $59-$120;
Tel: (800) 922-9222

**HAWTHORN SUITES
HOTEL-DALLAS**
7900 Brookriver Dr (75247)
Rates: $89-$119;
Tel: (214) 688-1010

**HAWTHORN SUITES
HOTEL RICHARDSON**
250 Municipal Dr
(Richardson 75080)
Rates: $59-$120;
Tel: (214) 669-1000

**HOLIDAY INN-
BROOKHOLLOW/
LOVE FIELD**
7050 Stemmons Frwy (75247)
Rates: $82-$108;
Tel: (214) 630-8500

**HOLIDAY INN
CROWNE PLAZA**
4099 Valley View Ln (75244)
Rates: $55-$79;
Tel: (214) 385-9000

**HOLIDAY INN-
DFW AIRPORT-NORTH**
4441 Hwy 114 (Irving 75063)
Rates: $49-$98;
Tel: (214) 929-8181

**HOLIDAY INN LBJ
NORTHEAST (GARLAND)**
11350 LBJ Frwy (75238)
Rates: $49 $72;
Tel: (214) 341-5400

**HOLIDAY INN
NORTH PARK PLAZA**
10650 N Central Expwy
(75231)
Rates: $55;
Tel. (214) 373-6000

**HOLIDAY INN-
PARK CENTRAL**
8102 LBJ Frwy (75251)
Rates: $58-$78;
Tel: (214) 239-7211

**HOMEWOOD SUITES
LAS COLINAS**
4300 Wingren Rd
(Irving 75039)
Rates: $69-$129;
Tel: (214) 556-0665

**LA QUINTA
MOTOR INN-CENTRAL**
4440 N Central Expwy
(75206)
Rates: $50-$62;
Tel: (214) 821-4220

**LA QUINTA MOTOR INN-
DFW AIRPORT EAST**
4105 W Airport Frwy
(Irving 75062)
Rates: $42-$55;
Tel: (214) 252-6546

**LA QUINTA
MOTOR INN-EAST**
8303 R L Thornton Frwy
(75228)
Rates: $41-$53;
Tel: (214) 324-3731

**LA QUINTA
MOTOR INN-GARLAND**
12721 I-635 (Garland 75041)
Rates: $43-$55;
Tel: (214) 271-7581

**LA QUINTA
MOTOR INN-NORTHPARK**
10001 N Central Expwy
(75231)
Rates: $48-$60;
Tel: (214) 361-8200

**LA QUINTA
MOTOR INN-NORTHWEST**
13235 Stemmons Frwy
(75234)
Rates: $42-$54;
Tel: (214) 620-7333

**LA QUINTA
MOTOR INN-REGAL ROW**
1625 Regal Row (75247)
Rates: $53-$65;
Tel: (214) 630-5701

**LA QUINTA
MOTOR INN-RICHARDSON**
13685 N Central Expwy
(75243)
Rates: $47-$57;
Tel: (214) 234-1016

**LE BARON HOTEL
& CONVENTION CTR**
1055 Regal Row (75247)
Rates: $52-$62;
Tel: (214) 634-8550

**THE MANSION
ON TURTLE CREEK**
2821 Turtle Creek Blvd
(75219)
Rates: $230-$370;
Tel: (214) 559-2100

**MARRIOTT HOTEL-
DFW AIRPORT**
8440 Freeport Pkwy
(Irving 75063)
Rates: $75-$145;
Tel: (214) 929-8800

**MARRIOTT HOTEL QUORUM**
14901 Dallas Pkwy (75240)
Rates: $79-$145;
Tel: (214) 661-2800

**MARRIOTT PARK CENTRAL**
7750 LBJ Frwy (75251)
Rates: $70-$104;
Tel: (214) 233-4421

**OMNI MANDALAY
HOTEL AT LAS COLINAS**
221 E Las Colinas Blvd
(Irving 75039)
Rates: $155-$170;
Tel: (214) 556-0800

**PLAZA
OF THE AMERICAS HOTEL**
650 N Pearl St (75201)
Rates: $150-$190;
Tel: (214) 979-9000

**PRESTON SUITES HOTEL**
6104 LBJ Frwy (75240)
Rates: $90-$220;
Tel: (214) 458-2626

**RADISSON-CENTRAL**
6060 N Central Expy (75206)
Rates: $79-$300;
Tel: (214) 750-6060

**RADISSON HOTEL
& SUITES DALLAS**
2330 W Northwest Hwy
(75220)
Rates: $89-$129;
Tel: (214) 351-4477

**RAMADA HOTEL
DOWNTOWN CONV CTR**
1011 S Akard St (75215)
Rates: $45-$125;
Tel: (214) 421-1083

**RAMADA INN
DFW AIRPORT SOUTH**
4110 W Airport Frwy
(Irving 75062)
Rates: $56-$90;
Tel: (214) 399-2005

**RED ROOF INN-CARROLLTON**
1720 S Broadway
(Carrollton 75006)
Rates: $26-$36;
Tel: (214) 245-1700

**RED ROOF INN-
DALLAS EAST**
8108 East R L Thornton Frwy
(75228)
Rates: $26-$37;
Tel: (214) 388-8741

**RED ROOF INN/
DFW AIRPORT**
8150 Esters Blvd
(Irving 75063)
Rates: $28-$43;
Tel: (214) 929-0020

**RED ROOF INN-
MARKET CENTER**
1550 Empire Central Dr
(75235)
Rates: $24-$35;
Tel: (214) 638-5151

**RED ROOF INN-
NORTHWEST**
10335 Gardner Rd (75220)
Rates: $24-$35;
Tel: (214) 506-8100

**RESIDENCE INN
BY MARRIOTT/CENTRAL-
NORTHPARK**
10333 N Central Expwy
(75231)
Rates: $69-$119;
Tel: (214) 750-8220

**RESIDENCE INN
BY MARRIOTT-
DALLAS MARKET CENTER**
6950 N Stemmons Frwy
(75247)
Rates: $98-$128;
Tel: (214) 631-2472

**RESIDENCE INN
BY MARRIOTT-NORTH**
13636 Goldmark Dr (75240)
Rates: $80-$130;
Tel: (214) 669-0478

**SHERATON-
MOCKINGBIRD WEST**
1893 W Mockingbird Ln
(75235)
Rates: $66-$115;
Tel: (214) 634-8850

**SHERATON PARK CENTRAL**
12720 Merit Dr (75251)
Rates: $109-$119;
Tel: (214) 385-3000

**SOUTHLAND CENTER HOTEL**
400 N Olive St (75201)
Rates: $79-$129;
Tel: (214) 922-8000

**STOUFFER DALLAS HOTEL-MARKET CENTER**
2222 Stemmons Frwy (75207)
Rates: $89-$184;
Tel: (214) 631-2222

**TERRA COTTA INN**
6101 LBJ Frwy (75240)
Rates: $39-$45;
Tel: (214) 387-2525

**TRAVELODGE HOTEL-DALLAS MARKET CTR**
4500 Harry Hines Blvd
(75219)
Rates: $58;
Tel: (214) 522-6650

**THE WESTIN HOTEL-GALLERIA DALLAS**
13340 Dallas Pkwy (75240)
Rates: $160-$240;
Tel. (214) 934-9494

**WILSON WORLD MOTOR HOTEL**
4600 W Airport Frwy
(Irving 75062)
Rates: $50-$70;
Tel. (214) 513-0800

## DEL RIO

**BEST WESTERN INN OF DEL RIO**
810 Ave F (78840)
Rates: $43-$61;
Tel: (210) 775-7511

**REMINGTON INN**
3808 Hwy 90W (78840)
Rates: $25-$32;
Tel: (210) 775-0585

**TWIN CITY INN**
2005 Avenue F (78840)
Rates: $39 $52;
Tel: (210) 775-7591

## DENTON

**EXEL INN OF DENTON**
4211 I-35E North (76201)
Rates: $24-$37;
Tel: (817) 383 1471

**HOLIDAY INN**
1500 Dallas Dr (76205)
Rates: $45-$115;
Tel: (817) 387-3511

**LA QUINTA MOTOR INN**
700 Fort Worth Dr (76201)
Rates: $42-$48;
Tel: (817) 387-5840

**QUALITY INN**
820 I-35E (76205)
Rates: $39-$46;
Tel: (817) 387-0591

**SHERATON DENTON & CONFERENCE CENTER**
2211 I-35E North (76205)
Rates: $70 $88;
Tel: (817) 565-8499

## DUMAS

**BEST WESTERN DUMAS INN MOTEL**
1712 S Dumas Ave (79029)
Rates: $48-$68;
Tel: (806) 935-6441

**MOORE REST INN MOTEL**
119 W 17th St (79029)
Rates: $25-$35;
Tel: (806) 935-6222

**PHILLIPS MANOR MOTEL**
18721 S Dumas Ave (79029)
Rates: $28-$44;
Tel: (806) 935-9281

## EAGLE PASS

**EAGLE PASS INN**
2150 N Hwy 277 (78852)
Rates: $28-$45;
Tel: (210) 773-9531

**LA QUINTA MOTOR INN**
2525 Main St (78852)
Rates: $45-$62;
Tel: (210) 773-7000

## EASTLAND

**EASTLAND BUDGET HOST INN**
P. O. Box 108 (76448)
Rates: $32-$38;
Tel: (817) 629-2655

**ECONO LODGE OF EASTLAND**
2001 I-20W (76448)
Rates: $32-$38;
Tel: (817) 629-3324

## EL CAMPO

**EL CAMPO INN**
210 West Hwy 59 (77437)
Rates: $34-$48;
Tel: (409) 543-1110

## EL PASO

**ALLSTAR INN**
1330 Lomaland Dr (79935)
Rates: $25-$31;
Tel: (915) 592-6386

**BEVERLY CREST MOTOR INN**
8709 Dyer St (79904)
Rates: $28-$35;
Tel: (915) 755-7631

**COMFORT INN**
900 N Yarborough St (79915)
Rates: $42-$46;
Tel: (915) 594-9111

**DAYS INN EL PASO**
9125 Gateway W (79925)
Rates: $44-$57;
Tel: (915) 593-8400

**ECONO LODGE**
6363 Montana St (79925)
Rates: $32-$36;
Tel: (915) 778-3311

**EL PASO AIRPORT HILTON**
2027 Airway Blvd (79925)
Rates: $85-$95;
Tel: (915) 778-4241

**EL PASO CITY CENTER TRAVELODGE**
409 E Missouri St (79901)
Rates: $42-$47;
Tel: (915) 544-3333

**EMBASSY SUITES HOTEL**
6100 Gateway E (79905)
Rates: $75-$114;
Tel: (915) 779-6222

**HOLIDAY INN-SUNLAND PARK**
900 Sunland Park Dr (79922)
Rates: $63-$72;
Tel: (915) 833-2900

**HOWARD JOHNSON LODGE**
8887 Gateway W (79925)
Rates: $45-$52;
Tel: (915) 591-9471

**LA QUINTA MOTOR INN-AIRPORT**
6140 Gateway E (79905)
Rates: $46-$61;
Tel: (915) 778-9321

**LA QUINTA MOTOR INN-LOMALAND**
11033 Gateway W (79935)
Rates: $44-$57;
Tel: (915) 591-2244

**LA QUINTA MOTOR INN-WEST**
7550 Remcon Cir (79912)
Rates: $45-$60;
Tel: (915) 833-2522

**MARRIOTT-EL PASO**
1600 Airway Blvd (79925)
Rates: $64-$114;
Tel: (915) 779-3300

**QUALITY INN**
6201 Gateway W (79925)
Rates: $45-$50;
Tel: (915) 778-6611

**RAMADA INN EL PASO**
113 W Missouri St (79901)
Rates: $58;
Tel: (915) 544-3300

## EULESS

**LA QUINTA MOTOR INN-AIRPORT WEST**
1001 W Airport Frwy (76040)
Rates: $45-$60;
Tel: (817) 540-0233

## FORT DAVIS

**LIMPIA HOTEL**
P. O. Box 822 (79734)
Rates: $49-$62;
Tel: (915) 426-3237

## FORT STOCKTON

**BEST WESTERN SUNDAY HOUSE INN**
3201 W Dickinson (79735)
Rates: $38-$52;
Tel: (915) 336-8521

**COMFORT INN**
2601 I-10W (79735)
Rates: $40-$46;
Tel: (915) 336-9781

**ECONO LODGE OF FORT STOCKTON**
800 E Dickinson Blvd (79735)
Rates: $30-$46;
Tel: (915) 336-9711

**HOWARD JOHNSON**
3200 W Dickinson Blvd (79735)
Rates: $35-$43;
Tel: (915) 336-8531

**SANDS MOTEL**
1801 W Dickinson Blvd (79735)
Rates: $26-$30;
Tel: (915) 336-2274

## FORT WORTH
(and Vicinity)

**BEST WESTERN-WEST BRANCH INN**
7301 W Frwy (76116)
Rates: $38-$58;
Tel: (817) 244-7444

**CARAVAN MOTOR HOTEL**
P. O. Box 10128 (76114)
Rates: $28-$42;
Tel: (817) 626-1951

**THE CLARION HOTEL & CONFERENCE CTR**
2000 Beach St (76103)
Rates: $65-$104;
Tel: (817) 534-4801

**COMFORT INN**
I-30 at Beach St (76103)
Rates: $36-$42;
Tel: (817) 535-2591

**COUNTRY SUITES BY CARLSON**
8401 I-30 W (76116)
Rates: $39-$44;
Tel: (817) 560-0060

**DAYS INN WEST**
8500 I-30W & Las Vegas Tr (76108)
Rates: $38-$48;
Tel: (817) 246-4961

**GREEN OAKS INN & CONFERENCE CENTER**
6901 W Frwy (76116)
Rates: $68-$195;
Tel: (800) 433-2174

**HAMPTON INN FORT WORTH-WEST**
2700 Cherry Ln (76116)
Rates: $48-$54;
Tel: (817) 560-4180

**HOLIDAY INN NORTH/ CONFERENCE CTR**
2540 Meacham Blvd (76106)
Rates: $72-$75;
Tel: (817) 625-9911

**HOLIDAY INN SOUTH/ CONFERENCE CTR**
100 Alta Mesa Blvd E (76134)
Rates: $75-$80;
Tel: (817) 293-3088

**LA QUINTA MOTOR INN-FORT WORTH WEST**
7888 I-30W (76108)
Rates: $44-$56;
Tel: (817) 246-5511

**LA QUINTA
MOTOR INN-NORTHEAST**
7920 Bedford-Euless Rd
(76180)
Rates: $42-$52;
Tel: (817) 485-2750

**LEXINGTON HOTEL SUITES**
8401 W I-30 (76116)
Rates: $49-$67;
Tel: (817) 560-0060

**LEXINGTON INN-
DFW WEST**
8709 Airport Frwy
(N Richland Hills 76180)
Rates: $39-$45;
Tel: (817) 656-8881

**RADISSON PLAZA
HOTEL FORT WORTH**
815 Main St (76102)
Rates: $79-$107;
Tel: (817) 870-2100

**RAMADA INN-MIDTOWN**
1401 S University Dr (76107)
Rates: $50-$55;
Tel: (817) 336-9311

**RAMADA INN-NORTHEAST**
125 NE Loop 820
(Hurst 76053)
Rates: $42-$62;
Tel: (817) 284-9461

**RESIDENCE INN
BY MARRIOTT FT WORTH**
1701 S University Dr (76107)
Rates: $80-$100;
Tel: (817) 870-1011

**THE WORTHINGTON
HOTEL**
200 Main St (76102)
Rates: $129-$159;
Tel: (817) 870-1000

## FREDERICKSBURG

**COMFORT INN**
908 S Adams St (78624)
Rates: $49-$54;
Tel: (210) 997-9811

**DIETZEL MOTEL**
P. O. Box 266 (78624)
Rates: $29-$39;
Tel: (210) 997-3330

## FREEPORT

**HOMEPLACE INN**
1015 W 2nd at Velasco
(77541)
Rates: $46-$58;
Tel: (409) 239-1602

## GAINESVILLE

**BEST WESTERN
SOUTHWINDS MOTEL**
Star Rt (76240)
Rates: $32-$39;
Tel: (817) 665-7737

**HOLIDAY INN**
600 Fair Pk Blvd (76240)
Rates: $45-$50;
Tel: (817) 665-8800

## GALVESTON

**LA QUINTA MOTOR INN**
1402 Seawall Blvd (77550)
Rates: $49-$107;
Tel: (409) 763-1224

**RAMADA INN RESORT**
600 Strand St (77550)
Rates: $85-$95;
Tel: (409) 765-5544

## GEORGETOWN

**RAMADA GEORGETOWN**
333 I-35N (78628)
Rates: $45-$55;
Tel: (512) 869-2541

## GIDDINGS

**BEST WESTERN
CLASSIC INN-GIDDINGS**
3556 E Austin (78942)
Rates: $34-$44;
Tel: (409) 542-5791

**ECONO LODGE**
Rt 3, Box 461 (78942)
Rates: $27-$39;
Tel: (409) 542-9666

**GIDDINGS SANDS MOTEL**
1600 E Austin (78942)
Rates: $31-$46;
Tel: (409) 542-3111

## GRANBURY

**BEST WESTERN
CLASSIC INN**
1204 E Hwy 377 (76048)
Rates: $44-$59;
Tel: (817) 573-8874

## GRAND PRAIRIE

**LA QUINTA MOTOR INN**
1410 NW 19th St (75050)
Rates: $39-$69;
Tel: (214) 641-3021

**RAMADA INN-
GRAND PRAIRIE**
402 E Safari Pkwy (75050)
Rates: $50-$75;
Tel: (214) 263-4421

## GREENVILLE

**BEST WESTERN INN**
1216 I-30W (75401)
Rates: $36-$65;
Tel: (903) 454-1792

**BUDGET HOST INN**
5118 I-30 (75401)
Rates: $25-$32;
Tel: (903) 455-8462

**HOLIDAY INN**
1215 E I-30 (75401)
Rates: $41-$46;
Tel: (903) 454-7000

**ROYAL INN**
I-30 & US 69 (75401)
Rates: $27-$41;
Tel: (903) 455-9600

## HARLINGEN

**HOLIDAY INN**
1901 W Tyler St (78550)
Rates: $55-$81;
Tel: (210) 425-1810

**LA QUINTA MOTOR INN**
1002 US 83S Expwy (78552)
Rates: $48-$63;
Tel: (210) 428-6888

# HENDERSON

**DAYS INN**
P. O. Box 1064 (75653)
Rates: $36-$44;
Tel: (903) 657-9561

# HEREFORD

**BEST WESTERN
RED CARPET INN**
830 W 1st St (79045)
Rates: $32-$48;
Tel: (806) 364-0540

# HILLSBORO

**BEST WESTERN
HILLSBORO INN**
P. O. Box 632 (76645)
Rates: $34-$46;
Tel: (817) 582-8465

**RAMADA INN**
P. O. Box 1205 (76645)
Rates: $36-$49;
Tel: (817) 582-3493

# HOUSTON
(and Vicintiy)

**BEST WESTERN-
HOUSTON WEST**
22455 I-10, Katy Frwy
(Katy 77450)
Rates: $43-$51;
Tel: (713) 392-9800

**DAYS INN-AIRPORT**
17607 Eastex Frwy (77396)
Rates: $39-$45;
Tel: (713) 446-4611

**DAYS INN I-10 EAST**
10155 E Frwy (77029)
Rates: $46;
Tel: (713) 675-2711

**DAYS INN-WEST**
9799 Katy Frwy (77024)
Rates: $42-$51;
Tel: (713) 468-7801

**DOUBLETREE HOTEL**
15747 John F Kennedy Blvd
(77032)
Rates: $98-$300;
Tel: (713) 442-8000

**DOUBLETREE HOTEL
AT ALLEN CENTER**
400 Dallas St (77002)
Rates: $96;
Tel: (713) 759-0202

**FOUR SEASONS HOTEL-
HOUSTON CENTER**
1300 Lamar St (77010)
Rates: $85-$240;
Tel: (713) 650-1300

**GRUMPY'S MOTOR INN**
4222 Spencer Hwy
(Pasadena 77504)
Rates: $28-$35;
Tel: (713) 944-6652

**GUEST QUARTERS
SUITE HOTEL**
5353 Westheimer Rd (77056)
Rates: $154-$174;
Tel: (713) 961-9000

**HILTON-HOUSTON
HOBBY AIRPORT**
8181 Airport Blvd (77061)
Rates: $65-$132;
Tel: (713) 645-3000

**HOLIDAY INN
HOBBY AIRPORT**
9100 Gulf Frwy (77017)
Rates: $96-$116;
Tel: (713) 943-7979

**HOLIDAY INN HOUSTON
INTERCONTINENTAL
AIRPORT**
3702 N Sam Houston Pkwy E
(77032)
Rates: $49-$86;
Tel: (713) 449-2311

**HOLIDAY INN
SOUTHWEST FREEWAY**
11160 Southwest Frwy
(77031)
Rates: $65-$88;
Tel: (713) 530-1400

**HOLIDAY INN-WEST**
14703 Park Row (77078)
Rates: $85-$350;
Tel: (713) 558-5580

**HOLIDAY INN-WEST LOOP
NEAR GALLERIA**
3131 W Loop S (77027)
Rates: $54;
Tel: (713) 621-1900

**HYATT REGENCY
HOUSTON**
1200 Louisiana St (77002)
Rates: $150-$206;
Tel: (713) 654-1234

**HYATT REGENCY
WEST HOUSTON**
13210 Katy Frwy (77079)
Rates: $129-$154;
Tel: (713) 558-8338

**INTERSTATE
MOTOR LODGE**
13213 I-10E (77015)
Rates: $31-$40;
Tel: (713) 453-6353

**J W MARRIOTT HOUSTON**
5150 Westheimer Rd (77056)
Rates: $139-$149;
Tel: (713) 961-1500

**THE LANCASTER**
701 Texas at Louisiana
(77002)
Rates: $95-$185;
Tel: (713) 228-9500

**LA QUINTA-ASTRODOME**
9911 Buffalo Speedway
(77054)
Rates: $56-$80;
Tel: (713) 668-8082

**LA QUINTA INN-INTER-
CONTINENTAL AIRPORT**
6 N Belt E (77060)
Rates: $51-$66;
Tel: (713) 447-6888

**LA QUINTA INN-
LOOP 1960**
17111 N Frway (77090)
Rates: $45-$58;
Tel: (713) 444-7500

**LA QUINTA MOTOR INN-BROOK HOLLOW**
11002 Northwest Frwy (77092)
Rates: $51-$64;
Tel: (713) 688-2581

**LA QUINTA MOTOR INN-CY-FAIR**
13290 FM 1960W (77065)
Rates: $55-$70;
Tel: (713) 469-4018

**LA QUINTA MOTOR INN-GREENWAY PLAZA**
4015 Southwest Frwy (77027)
Rates: $57-$72;
Tel: (713) 623-4750

**LA QUINTA MOTOR INN-HOBBY AIRPORT**
9902 Gulf Frwy (77034)
Rates: $58-$73;
Tel: (713) 941-0900

**LA QUINTA MOTOR INN-HOUSTON EAST**
11999 E Frwy (77029)
Rates: $46-$59;
Tel: (713) 453-5425

**LA QUINTA MOTOR INN-SHARPSTOWN**
8201 Southwest Frwy (77074)
Rates: $48-$61;
Tel: (713) 772-3626

**LA QUINTA MOTOR INN-SOUTHWEST FRWY/DELTWAY**
10552 Southwest Frwy (77074)
Rates: $48-$62;
Tel: (713) 270-9559

**LA QUINTA MOTOR INN-WILCREST**
11113 Katy Frwy (77079)
Rates: $55-$70;
Tel: (713) 932-0808

**LA QUINTA MOTOR INN-WIRT RD**
8017 Katy Frwy (77024)
Rates: $54-$67;
Tel: (713) 688-8941

**THE LOVETT INN**
501 Lovett Blvd (77006)
Rates: $50-$100;
Tel: (713) 522-5224

**MARRIOTT AIRPORT-HOUSTON**
18700 JFK Blvd
(Intercontinental Airport 77032)
Rates: $65-$150;
Tel: (713) 443-2310

**MARRIOTT ASTRODOME-HOUSTON**
2100 S Braeswood Blvd/Greenbrier (77030)
Rates: $59-$109;
Tel: (713) 797-9000

**MARRIOTT NORTH AT GREENSPOINT**
255 N Sam Houston Pkwy E (77060)
Rates: $69-$119;
Tel: (713) 875-4000

**MARRIOTT-WEST LOOP-BY THE GALLERIA**
1750 W Loop S (77027)
Rates: $89-$169;
Tel: (713) 960-0111

**MOTEL 6**
16884 Northwest Frwy (77040)
Rates: $30-$36;
Tel: (713) 937-7056

**QUALITY INN-INTERCONTINENTAL AIRPORT**
P. O. Box 60135 (77205)
Rates: $55-$70;
Tel: (713) 446-9131

**RADISSON SUITE HOTEL HOUSTON**
1400 Old Spanish Tr (77054)
Rates: $62;
Tel: (713) 796-1000

**RAMADA HOTEL NEAR THE GALLERIA**
7787 Katy Frwy (77024)
Rates: $49-$81;
Tel: (713) 681-5000

**RAMADA HOTEL NORTHWEST**
12801 Northwest Frwy (77040)
Rates: $78-$98;
Tel: (713) 462-9977

**RAMADA INN SOUTH/NASA**
1301 NASA Rd One (77058)
Rates: $72-$77;
Tel: (713) 488-0220

**RESIDENCE INN BY MARRIOTT-ASTRODOME**
7710 S Main St (77030)
Rates: $110-$160;
Tel: (713) 660-7993

**RESIDENCE INN BY MARRIOTT-SOUTHWEST**
6910 Southwest Frwy (77074)
Rates: $100-$125·
Tel: (713) 785-3415

**RESIDENCE INN-HOUSTON CLEAR LAKE**
525 Bay Area Blvd (77058)
Rates: $130-$175;
Tel: (713) 486-2424

**THE RITZ-CARLTON, HOUSTON**
1919 Briar Oaks Ln (77027)
Rates: $95-$295;
Tel: (713) 840-7600

**RODEWAY INN-SOUTHWEST FREEWAY**
3135 Southwest Frwy (77098)
Rates: $41-$47;
Tel: (713) 526-1071

**SHERATON ASTRODOME HOTEL**
8686 Kirby Dr (77054)
Rates: $59-$89;
Tel: (713) 748-3221

**STOUFFER PRESIDENTE HOTEL-HOUSTON**
6 Greenway Plaza E (77046)
Rates: $79-$159;
Tel: (713) 629-1200

**SUPER 8 MOTEL INTERCONTINENTAL**
15350 JFK Blvd (77032)
Rates: $35-$44;
Tel: (713) 442-1830

**TRAVELODGE GREENWAY PLAZA HOTEL**
2828 Southwest Frwy (77098)
Rates: $49;
Tel: (713) 526-4571

**THE WESTIN GALLERIA**
5060 W Alabama St (77056)
Rates: $77-$185;
Tel: (713) 960-8100

**THE WESTIN OAKS**
P. O. Box 4486 (77056)
Rates: $82-$215;
Tel: (713) 960-8100

## HUNTSVILLE

**PARK INN INTERNATIONAL**
1407 I-45 (77340)
Rates: $42-$57;
Tel: (409) 295-6454

**SAN HOUSTON INN**
3296 I-45S Exit 114 (77340)
Rates: $42-$48;
Tel: (409) 295-9151

## INGRAM

**HUNTER HOUSE
MOTOR INN**
P. O. Box 920 (78025)
Rates: $42-$55;
Tel: (210) 367-2377

## JACKSBORO

**JACKSBORO INN**
Rt 1, Box 12A (76056)
Rates: $30-$38;
Tel: (817) 567-3751

## JACKSONVILLE

**CHEROKEE INN**
P. O. Box 1229 (75766)
Rates: $39-$50;
Tel: (903) 586-9841

## JASPER

**RAMADA INN**
239 E Gibson (75951)
Rates: $54-$58;
Tel: (409) 384-9021

## JUNCTION

**CAROUSEL INN**
P. O. Box 311 (76849)
Rates: $24-$38;
Tel: (915) 446-3301

**DAYS INN**
111 St. Martinez St (76849)
Rates: $45-$60;
Tel: (915) 446-3730

**THE HILLS MOTEL**
1520 Main St (76849)
Rates: $27-$34;
Tel: (915) 446-2567

**LA VISTA MOTEL**
2040 N Main St (76849)
Rates: $18-$26;
Tel: (915) 446-2191

## KERRVILLE

**BEST WESTERN
SUNDAY INN**
2124 Sidney Baker St (78028)
Rates: $56-$88;
Tel: (210) 896-1313

**ECONO LODGE**
2145 Sidney Baker St (78028)
Rates: $32-$58;
Tel; (210) 896-1711

**HILTON Y.O. RANCH**
2033 Sidney Baker St (78028)
Rates: $65-$230;
Tel: (210) 257-4440

**INN OF THE HILLS
RIVER RESORT**
1001 Junction Hwy (78028)
Rates: $50-$85;
Tel: (210) 895-5000

**SAVE INN MOTEL**
1804 Sidney Baker St (78028)
Rates: $25-$45;
Tel: (210) 896-8200

## KILLEEN

**HILTON MOTOR HOTEL**
803 E Central Texas Expy
(76541)
Rates: $50-$125;
Tel: (817) 526-4343

**HOLIDAY INN**
1100 S Ft Hood St (76541)
Rates: $40-$51;
Tel: (817) 634-3101

**LA QUINTA MOTOR INN**
1112 Ft Hood St (76541)
Rates: $40-$60;
Tel: (817) 526-8331

## KINGSVILLE

**BEST WESTERN
KINGSVILLE INN**
2402 E King Ave (78363)
Rates: $41-$53;
Tel: (512) 595-5656

**ECONO LODGE**
2502 E Kenedy (78363)
Rates: $34-$39;
Tel: (512) 592-5251

**LA CUPULA MOTOR INN**
P. O. Box 1440 (78363)
Rates: $41-$46;
Tel: (512) 595-5753

## LAJITAS

**LAJITAS ON THE RIO GRANDE**
Star Rt 70, Box 400
(Terlingua 79852)
Rates: $48-$65;
Tel: (915) 424-3471

## LAKE JACKSON

**HILTON INN MOTEL**
925 TX 332W (77566)
Rates: $44-$150;
Tel: (409) 297-1161

## LA PORTE

**LA QUINTA MOTOR INN**
1105 Hwy 146S (77571)
Rates: $54-$69;
Tel: (713) 470-0760

# LAREDO

**FAMILY GARDENS INN**
5830 San Bernardo (78041)
Rates: $46-$52;
Tel: (210) 723-5300

**FIESTA INN**
P. O. Box 1036 (78040)
Rates: $49-$64;
Tel: (210) 723-3603

**HOWARD JOHNSON HOTEL**
1 S Main Ave (78040)
Rates: $59-$110;
Tel: (210) 722-2411

**LA QUINTA MOTOR INN**
3610 Santa Ursula Ave (78041)
Rates: $56-$75;
Tel: (210) 722-0511

**MONTEREY INN**
4820 San Bernardo Ave (78040)
Rates: $35-$37;
Tel: (210) 722-7631

# LEWISVILLE

**HAMPTON INN**
200 N Stemmons Frwy (75067)
Rates: $46-$53;
Tel: (214) 434-1000

**LA QUINTA MOTOR INN**
1657 N Stemmons Frwy (75067)
Rates: $38-$50;
Tel: (214) 221-7525

# LIVINGSTON

**PARK INN INTERNATIONAL**
2500 Hwy 59S (77351)
Rates: $34-$40;
Tel: (409) 327-2525

# LONGVIEW

**BEST WESTERN LONGVIEW INN**
605 Access Rd (75602)
Rates: $40-$54;
Tel: (903) 753-0350

**COMFORT INN**
203 N Spur 63 (75601)
Rates: $39-$48;
Tel: (903) 757-7858

**DAYS INN OF LONGVIEW**
3103 Estes Pkwy (75602)
Rates: $45;
Tel: (903) 758-1113

**ECONO LODGE**
3120 Estes Pkwy (75607)
Rates: $29-$38;
Tel: (903) 753-4884

**HOLIDAY INN**
P. O. Box 7758 (75607)
Rates: $50-$66;
Tel: (903) 758-0700

**LA QUINTA MOTOR INN**
502 S Access Rd (75602)
Rates: $44-$57;
Tel: (903) 757-3663

**SHILO INN**
3304 S Eastman Rd (75602)
Rates: $32-$38;
Tel: (903) 758-0711

**STRATFORD HOUSE INN**
3100 Estes Pkwy (75602)
Rates: N/A;
Tel: (903) 758-4322

# LUBBOCK

**HOLIDAY INN CIVIC CENTER**
801 Ave Q (79401)
Rates: $70-$95;
Tel: (806) 763-1200

**HOLIDAY INN- LUBBOCK SOUTH**
6624 I-27 (79404)
Rates: $58-$73;
Tel: (806) 745-2208

**LA QUINTA MOTOR INN**
601 Ave Q (79401)
Rates: $46-$61;
Tel: (806) 763-9441

**LUBBOCK PLAZA HOTEL**
3201 S Loop 289 (79423)
Rates: $72-$85;
Tel: (806) 797-3241

**MOTEL VILLAGE INN**
4925 Brownfield Rd (79407)
Rates: $31-$38;
Tel: (806) 795-5281

**PARAGON HOTEL**
4115 Brownfield Hwy (79407)
Rates: N/A;
Tel: (806) 792-0065

**RESIDENCE INN BY MARRIOTT LUBBOCK**
2551 S Loop 289 (79423)
Rates: $90-$120;
Tel: (806) 745-1963

# LUFKIN

**DAYS INN**
2130 S 1st St (75901)
Rates: $41-$49;
Tel: (409) 639-3301

**EXPO INN**
3200 N Medford Dr (75901)
Rates: $29-$35;
Tel: (409) 632-7300

**HOLIDAY INN**
4306 S 1st St (75901)
Rates: $29-$48;
Tel: (409) 639-3333

**LA QUINTA MOTOR INN**
2119 S 1st St (75901)
Rates: $45-$60;
Tel: (409) 634-3351

# MARSHALL

**BEST WESTERN OF MARSHALL**
5555 E End Blvd S (75670)
Rates: $40-$46;
Tel: (903) 935-1941

**ECONOMY INN**
6002 E End Blvd S (75670)
Rates: $30-$36;
Tel: (903) 935-1184

**HOLIDAY INN EXPRESS**
100 I-20W (75670)
Rates: $48;
Tel: (903) 935-7923

**RAMADA INN**
5301 E End Blvd S (75670)
Rates: $48-$57;
Tel: (903) 938-9261

## MCALLEN

**DRURY INN-MCALLEN**
612 W Expwy (78501)
Rates: $58-$64;
Tel: (210) 687-5100

**FAIRWAY RESORT**
P. O. Box 1690 (78503)
Rates: $56-$101;
Tel: (210) 682-2445

**HAMPTON INN**
300 W Expwy US 83 (78501)
Rates: $58-$64;
Tel: (210) 682-4900

**HOLIDAY INN AIRPORT**
P. O. Box 1660 (78502)
Rates: $55-$67;
Tel: (210) 686-1741

**HOLIDAY INN
CIVIC CENTER**
P. O. Box 2978 (78502)
Rates: $58-$86;
Tel: (210) 686-2471

**LA QUINTA MOTOR INN**
1100 S 10th St (78501)
Rates: $56-$68;
Tel: (210) 687-1101

**THRIFTY-INN**
620 Expwy 83W (78501)
Rates: $39-$51;
Tel: (210) 631-6700

## MCKINNEY

**COMFORT INN**
2104 N Central Expy (75070)
Rates: $36-$45;
Tel: (214) 548-8888

## MEMPHIS

**BEST WESTERN
DE VILLE MOTEL**
P. O. Box 339 (79245)
Rates: $38-$42;
Tel: (806) 259-3583

## MIDLAND

**BEST WESTERN
AIRPORT HOTEL**
P. O. Box 60017 (79711)
Rates: $40-$44;
Tel: (915) 561-8000

**HAMPTON INN-MIDLAND**
3904 W Wall St (79703)
Rates: $42-$50;
Tel: (915) 694-7774

**HILTON & TOWERS-MIDLAND**
Wall & Loraine Sts (79701)
Rates: $75-$90;
Tel: (915) 683-6131

**LA QUINTA MOTOR INN**
4130 W Wall St (79703)
Rates: $43-$55;
Tel: (915) 697-9900

**PLAZA INN**
4108 N Big Spring St (79705)
Rates: $54;
Tel: (915) 686-8733

**RAMADA HOTEL**
3100 W Wall St (79701)
Rates: $38-$50;
Tel: (915) 699-4144

## MINERAL WELLS

**DAYS INN**
3701 E Hubbard (76067)
Rates: $42-$75;
Tel: (817) 325-6961

**12 OAKS INN**
4103 Hwy 180E (76067)
Rates: $27-$36;
Tel: (817) 325-6956

## MISSION

**MISSION INN**
P. O. Box 1786 (78572)
Rates: $32-$36;
Tel: (210) 581-7451

## MONAHANS

**BEST WESTERN
COLONIAL INN**
702 W I-20 (79756)
Rates: $32-$46;
Tel: (915) 943-4345

## MOUNT PLEASANT

**BEST WESTERN MOTEL**
I-30 & US 271 Business
(75455)
Rates: $36-$40;
Tel: (903) 572-4303

**LAKEWOOD MOTEL**
2214 Lakewood Dr (75455)
Rates: $27-$35;
Tel: (903) 572-9808

## MULESHOE

**HERITAGE HOUSE INN**
2301 W American Blvd
(79347)
Rates: $36-$46;
Tel: (806) 272-7575

## NACOGDOCHES

**ECONO LODGE**
2020 NW Stallings Dr (75961)
Rates: $34-$46;
Tel: (409) 569-0880

**THE FREDONIA HOTEL**
200 N Fredonia St (75961)
Rates: $56-$81;
Tel: (409) 564-1234

**HOLIDAY INN**
3400 South St (75961)
Rates: $55-$61;
Tel: (409) 569-8100

**LA QUINTA MOTOR INN**
3215 South St (75961)
Rates: $43-$56;
Tel: (409) 560-5453

## NAVASOTA

**BEST WESTERN
NAVASOTA INN**
818 Hwy 6 Loop S (77868)
Rates: $34-$44;
Tel: (409) 825-7775

## NEW BRAUNFELS

**HOLIDAY INN**
1051 I-35 E (78130)
Rates: $58-$150;
Tel: (210) 625-8017

**RODEWAY INN**
1209 I-35S (78130)
Rates: $35-$65;
Tel: (210) 629-6991

## ODEM

**DAYS INN-ODEM**
P. O. Box 1296 (78370)
Rates: $30-$62;
Tel: (512) 368-2166

## ODESSA

**BEST WESTERN
GARDEN OASIS**
110 W I-20 (79761)
Rates: $35-$85;
Tel: (915) 337-3006

**HOLIDAY INN CENTRE**
P. O. Box 4891 (79760)
Rates: $55-$150;
Tel: (915) 362-2311

**LA QUINTA MOTOR INN**
5001 Hwy 80E (79761)
Rates: $43-$55;
Tel: (915) 333-2820

**LEXINGTON SUITES**
3031 E US 80 (79761)
Rates: $35-$42;
Tel: (915) 333-9676

**ODESSA EXECUTIVE INN**
2505 E 2nd St (79761)
Rates: $24-$34;
Tel: (915) 333-1528

**VILLA WEST INN**
P. O. Box 2265 (79760)
Rates: $19-$29;
Tel: (915) 335-5055

## ORANGE

**BEST WESTERN INN**
P. O. Box 1839 (77630)
Rates: $38-$46;
Tel: (409) 883-6616

**DAYS INN**
P. O. Box 1668 (77630)
Rates: $34-$39;
Tel: (409) 883-9981

**RAMADA INN**
P. O. Box 1839 (77630)
Rates: $30-$125;
Tel: (409) 883-0231

## OZONA

**FLYING W LODGE**
P. O. Box 985 (76943)
Rates: $25-$31;
Tel: (915) 392-2656

## PALESTINE

**BEST WESTERN
PALESTINE INN**
1601 W Palestine Ave (75801)
Rates: $35-$39;
Tel: (903) 723-4655

**DAYS INN**
1100 E Palestine Ave (75801)
Rates: $39-$45;
Tel: (903) 729-3151

## PARIS

**BEST WESTERN
INN OF PARIS**
3755 NE Loop 286 (75460)
Rates: $28-$34;
Tel: (903) 785-5566

**HOLIDAY INN**
3560 NE Loop 285 (75460)
Rates: $46-$65;
Tel: (903) 785-5545

## PECOS

**BEST WESTERN
SUNDAY HOUSE**
900 W Palmer (79772)
Rates: $34-$48;
Tel: (915) 447-2215

**PARK INN**
P. O. Box 1777 (79772)
Rates: $39-$47;
Tel: (915) 445-5404

## PLAINVIEW

**BEST WESTERN
CONESTOGA INN**
600 N I-27 (79072)
Rates: $40-$48;
Tel: (806) 293-9454

**HOLIDAY INN**
P. O. Box 1925 (79072)
Rates: $35-$51;
Tel: (806) 293-4181

## PLANO

**COMFORT INN**
621 Central Pkwy E (75074)
Rates; $35-$46;
Tel: (214) 424-5568

**THE HARVEY HOTEL-
PLANO**
1600 N Central Expwy
(75074)
Rates: $49-$83;
Tel: (214) 578-8555

**HOLIDAY INN**
700 Central Pkwy E (75074)
Rates: $69-$79;
Tel: (214) 881-1881

**LA QUINTA MOTOR INN**
1820 N Central Expwy
(75074)
Rates: $39-$51;
Tel: (214) 423-1300

## PORT ARKANSAS

**EL CORTES VILLAS**
Hwy 361 (78373)
Rates: $45-$107;
Tel: (512) 749-6206

**EXECUTIVE KEYS**
P. O. Box 1087 (78373)
Rates: $38-$172;
Tel: (512) 749-6272

## PORT ARTHUR

**RAMADA INN**
P. O. Box 2826 (77643)
Rates: $50-$135;
Tel: (409) 962-9858

## PORT ISABEL

**PADRE VISTA MOTEL**
P. O. Box 546 (78578)
Rates: $30-$120;
Tel: (210) 943-7866

**YACHT CLUB HOTEL**
700 Yturria St (78578)
Rates: $35-$99;
Tel: (210) 943-1301

## PORT LAVACA

**DAYS INN**
2100 N Bypass 35 (77979)
Rates: $46-$58;
Tel: (512) 552-4511

**SHELL FISH INN**
Bypass Hwy 35N (77979)
Rates: $30-$42;
Tel: (512) 552-3393

## QUANAH

**CASA ROYALE MOTEL**
1500 W 11th St (79252)
Rates: $35-$45;
Tel: (817) 663-6341

## ROBSTOWN

**ROYAL MOTOR INN**
Hwy 77S (78380)
Rates: $27-$35;
Tel: (512) 387-9416

## ROCKPORT

**BEST WESTERN
ROCKPORT REBEL**
3902 N Hwy 35 (78358)
Rates: $39-$60;
Tel: (512) 729-8351

**LAGUNA REEF**
1021 Water St (78382)
Rates: $39-$155;
Tel: (512) 729-1742

**THE VILLAGE INN**
503 N Austin St (78382)
Rates: $32-$44;
Tel: (512) 729-6370

## ROSENBERG

**BEST WESTERN
SUNDOWNER MOTOR INN**
28382 Southwest Frwy
(77471)
Rates: $34-$50;
Tel: (713) 342-6000

## ROUND ROCK

**BEST WESTERN
TRAVELERS INN**
1400 I-35N (78681)
Rates: $37-$40;
Tel: (512) 255-4437

**LA QUINTA INN**
2004 I-35N (78681)
Rates: $49-$61;
Tel: (512) 255-6666

## SAN ANGELO

**BEST WESTERN
INN OF THE WEST**
415 W Beauregard (76901)
Rates: $35-$37;
Tel: (915) 653-2995

**DAYS INN**
4613 S Jackson (76903)
Rates: $30-$38;
Tel: (915) 658-6594

**EL PATIO MOTEL**
1901 W Beauregard St
(76901)
Rates: $20-$35;
Tel: (915) 655-5711

**HOLIDAY INN
CONVENTION CENTER
HOTEL**
441 Rio Concho Dr (76903)
Rates: $48-$67;
Tel: (915) 658-2828

**INN OF THE CONCHOS**
2021 N Bryant Blvd (76903)
Rates: $36-$46;
Tel: (915) 658-2811

**LA QUINTA MOTOR INN**
2307 Loop 306 (76904)
Rates: $46-$58;
Tel: (915) 949-0515

**LAS BRISAS MOTEL**
1601 Bryant Blvd (76903)
Rates: $23-$36;
Tel: (915) 653-1323

**OLE COACH MOTOR INN**
4205 S Bryant Blvd (76903)
Rates: $29-$39;
Tel: (915) 653-6966

**RIVER VIEW INN**
333 Rio Concho Dr (76903)
Rates: $37-$45;
Tel: (915) 655-8151

## SAN ANTONIO
(and Vicinity)

**ALOHA INN**
1435 Austin Hwy (78209)
Rates: $28-$38;
Tel: (210) 828-0933

**BEST WESTERN INGRAM PARK INN**
6855 NW Loop 410 (78238)
Rates: $45-$65;
Tel: (210) 520-8080

**BEST WESTERN TOWN HOUSE MOTEL**
942 NE Loop 410 (78209)
Rates: $35-$56;
Tel: (210) 826-6311

**COACHMAN INN-BROOKS FIELD**
3180 Gollard Rd (78223)
Rates: $36-$52;
Tel. (210) 337-7171

**COMFORT INN I-10 EAST**
4403 I-10E (78219)
Rates: $38-$60;
Tel: (210) 333-9430

**DAYS INN EAST**
4039 E Houston St (78220)
Rates: $35-$90;
Tel: (210) 337-6753

**DAYS INN NORTHEAST**
32443 I-35 North (78219)
Rates: $45-$90;
Tel: (210) 225-4521

**DRURY INN AIRPORT**
143 NE Loop 410 (78216)
Rates: $56-$64;
Tel: (210) 366-4300

**DRURY INN EAST**
8300 IH-35N (78239)
Rates: $53-$62;
Tel: (210) 654-1144

**DRURY SUITES**
8811 Jones Maltsberger (78216)
Rates: N/A;
Tel: (210) 308-8100

**EMBASSY SUITES NORTHWEST**
7750 Briaridge (78230)
Rates: $109-$169;
Tel: (210) 340-5421

**EMILY MORGAN HOTEL-ALAMO PLAZA**
705 E Houston St (78205)
Rates: $85-$95;
Tel: (210) 225-8486

**EXECUTIVE GUESTHOUSE HOTEL**
12828 US Hwy 281N (78216)
Rates: $74-$124;
Tel: (210) 494-7600

**HAMPTON INN-AIRPORT**
8818 Jones Maltsberger (78216)
Rates: $61-$70;
Tel: (210) 366-1800

**HAWTHORNE SUITES**
4041 Bluemel Rd (78240)
Rates: $79-$109;
Tel: (210) 561-9660

**HILTON PALACIO DEL RIO**
200 S Alamo St (78205)
Rates: $154-$216;
Tel: (210) 222-1400

**HOLIDAY INN-AIRPORT**
77 NE Loop 410 (78216)
Rates: $92-$145;
Tel: (210) 349-9900

**HOLIDAY INN-DOWNTOWN-MARKET SQUARE**
318 W Durango (78204)
Rates: $69-$99;
Tel: (210) 225-3211

**HOLIDAY INN EXPRESS**
6023 NW Expwy I-10 (78201)
Rates: $49-$59;
Tel: (210) 736-1900

**HOLIDAY INN-NORTHEAST**
3855 N Pan Am Hwy (78219)
Rates: $55-$65;
Tel: (210) 226-4361

**HOLIDAY INN-NORTHWEST**
3233 NW Loop 410 (78213)
Rates: $59-$84;
Tel: (210) 377-3900

**HOLIDAY INN RIVERWALK**
217 N St. Mary's St (78205)
Rates: $95-$129;
Tel: (210) 224-2500

**KNIGHTS COURT WINDSOR PARK**
6370 IH-35N (78218)
Rates: $42-$67;
Tel: (210) 646-6336

**LA QUINTA MOTOR INN-AIRPORT EAST**
333 NE Loop 410 (78216)
Rates: $59-$77;
Tel: (210) 828-0781

**LA QUINTA MOTOR INN-AIRPORT WEST**
219 NE Loop 410 (78216)
Rates: $56-$73;
Tel: (210) 342-4291

**LA QUINTA MOTOR INN-CONVENTION CTR**
1001 E Commerce St (78205)
Rates: $83-$90;
Tel: (210) 222-9181

**LA QUINTA MOTOR INN-INGRAM PARK**
7134 NW Loop 410 (78238)
Rates: $65-$72;
Tel: (210) 680-8883

**LA QUINTA MOTOR INN-LACKLAND**
6511 Military Dr W (78227)
Rates: $58-$65;
Tel: (210) 674-3200

**LA QUINTA MOTOR INN-MARKET SQUARE**
900 Dolorosa (78207)
Rates: $74-$81;
Tel: (210) 271-0001

**LA QUINTA MOTOR INN-TOEPPERWEIN**
12822 I-35N (78233)
Rates: $45-$67;
Tel: (210) 657-5500

**LA QUINTA MOTOR INN-VANCE JACKSON**
5922 NW Expwy (78201)
Rates: $50-$67;
Tel: (210) 734-7931

**LA QUINTA MOTOR INN-WURZBACH**
9542 I-10W (78230)
Rates: $52-$73;
Tel: (210) 593-0338

**MARRIOTT RIVERCENTER**
101 Bowie St (78205)
Rates: $160-$180;
Tel: (210) 223-1000

**MARRIOTT RIVERWALK**
711 E Riverwalk (78205)
Rates: $135-$170;
Tel: (210) 224-4555

**OAK HILLS MOTOR INN**
7401 Wurzbach Rd (78229)
Rates: $50-$58;
Tel: (210) 696-9900

**OAK MOTOR LODGE**
150 Humphreys Ave (78209)
Rates: $25-$50;
Tel: (210) 826-6368

**PLAZA SAN
ANTONIO HOTEL**
555 S Alamo St (78205)
Rates: $140-$200;
Tel: (210) 229-1000

**RAMADA HOTEL AIRPORT**
1111 NE Loop 410 (78209)
Rates: $59-$113;
Tel: (210) 828-9031

**RODEWAY INN-
CROSSROADS**
6804 Northwest Expwy
(78201)
Rates: $35-$53;
Tel: (210) 734-7111

**RODEWAY INN-
DOWNTOWN LAREDO ST**
1500 IH-35S/IH-10 (78204)
Rates: $46-$85;
Tel: (210) 271-3334

**RODEWAY INN-
FIESTA PARK**
19793 I-10W (78257)
Rates: $48-$85;
Tel: (210) 698-3991

**ST. ANTHONY HOTEL**
P. O. Box 2411 (78298)
Rates: $106-$150;
Tel: (210) 227-4392

**SAN ANTONIO AIRPORT
HILTON & CONF CTR**
611 NW Loop 410 (78216)
Rates: $99-$104;
Tel: (210) 340-6060

**SHERATON FIESTA HOTEL**
37 NE Loop 410 (78216)
Rates: $119-$149;
Tel: (210) 366-2424

**SHERATON
GUNTHER HOTEL**
205 E Houston St (78205)
Rates: $105-$135;
Tel: (210) 227-3241

**SUPER 8 MOTEL**
11021 I-35 N (78233)
Rates: N/A;
Tel: (800) 843-1991

**TEXAS-GUESTEL SUITES**
13101 E Loop 1604N (78233)
Rates: $59-$84;
Tel: (210) 655-9491

**THRIFTY-INN NORTHWEST**
9806 I-10 West (78230)
Rates: $38-$61;
Tel: (210) 696-0810

**SANDERSON**

**DESERT AIR MOTEL**
P. O. Box 326 (79848)
Rates: $22-$34;
Tel: (915) 345-2572

**SAN MARCOS**

**DAYS INN**
1005 IH-35N (78666)
Rates: $38-$75;
Tel: (512) 353-5050

**EXECUTIVE HOUSE HOTEL**
1433 I-35N (78666)
Rates: $24-$51;
Tel: (512) 353-7770

**HOLIDAY INN**
1635 Aquarena Springs Dr
(78666)
Rates: $46-$60;
Tel: (512) 353-8011

**HOMEPLACE INN**
1429 I-35N (78666)
Rates: $40-$62;
Tel: (512) 396-0400

**SEGOVIA**

**BEST WESTERN
RIVER VALLEY INN**
HC 10, Box 138
(Junction 76849)
Rates: $46-$50;
Tel: (915) 446-3331

**SEGUIN**

**HOLIDAY INN-SEGUIN**
2950 N 123 Bypass (78155)
Rates: $53-$80;
Tel: (210) 372-0860

**SHAMROCK**

**BEST WESTERN IRISH INN**
301 I-40E (79079)
Rates: $38-$55;
Tel: (806) 256-2106

**BUDGET INN**
711 E 12th St (Rt 66 79079)
Rates: N/A;
Tel: (806) 256-3257

**ECONO LODGE**
1006 E 12th St (79079)
Rates: $27-$46;
Tel: (806) 256-2111

**THE WESTERN MOTEL**
104 E 12th St (79079)
Rates: $20-$32;
Tel: (806) 256-3244

**SHERMAN**

**RAMADA INN**
2105 Texoma Pkwy (75090)
Rates: $43-$61;
Tel: (903) 892-2161

**SHERATON INN-SHERMAN**
3605 Hwy 75S (75090)
Rates: $49-$63;
Tel: (903) 868-0555

## SNYDER

**GREAT WESTERN MOTEL**
800 E Coliseum Dr (79549)
Rates: $27-$45;
Tel: (915) 573-1166

**PURPLE SAGE MOTEL**
Rt 2, Box 201 (79549)
Rates: $32-$50;
Tel: (915) 573-5491

## SONORA

**DEVIL'S RIVER MOTEL**
I-10 & Golf Course Rd (76950)
Rates: $32-$42;
Tel: (915) 387-3516

**HOLIDAY HOST MOTEL**
Hwy 290E (76950)
Rates: $24-$31;
Tel: (915) 387-2532

**TWIN OAKS MOTEL**
907 Crockett Ave (76950)
Rates: $28-$40;
Tel: (915) 387-2551

## SOUTH PADRE ISLAND

**BEST WESTERN
FIESTA ISLES**
P. O. Box 3079 (78597)
Rates: $48-$118;
Tel: (512) 761-4913

**BRIDGEPOINT**
334 Padre Blvd (78597)
Rates: N/A;
Tel: (512) 761-7969

**RADISSON RESORT
SOUTH PADRE ISLAND**
500 Padre Blvd (78597)
Rates: $89-$330;
Tel: (512) 761-6511

**THE TIKI
APARTMENT HOTEL**
6608 Padre Blvd (78597)
Rates: $54-$114;
Tel: (512) 761-2694

## STEPHENVILLE

**BEST WESTERN
CROSS TIMBERS**
1625 S Loop (76401)
Rates: $39-$45;
Tel: (817) 968-2114

**BUDGET HOST
TEXAN MOTOR INN**
3030 W Washington (76401)
Rates: $33-$48;
Tel: (817) 968-5003

**HOLIDAY INN MOTEL**
2865 W Washington (76401)
Rates: $36-$150;
Tel: (817) 968-5256

**RAINTREE INN MOTEL**
701 S Loop (76401)
Rates: $33-$46;
Tel: (817) 968-3392

## STUDY BUTTE

**LONGHORN RANCH
MOTEL**
P. O. Box 267, HC 65
(Alpine 79830)
Rates: $32-$54;
Tel: (915) 371-2541

## SULPHUR SPRINGS

**BEST WESTERN
TRAIL DUST INN**
P. O. Box 789 (75482)
Rates: $38-$65;
Tel: (903) 885-7515

**HOLIDAY INN**
1495 E Industrial (75482)
Rates: $43-$54;
Tel: (903) 885-0562

## SWEETWATER

**BEST WESTERN
SUNDAY HOUSE**
701 SW Georgia St (79556)
Rates: $36-$46;
Tel: (915) 235-4853

**HOLIDAY INN**
P. O. Box 157 (79556)
Rates: $44-$58;
Tel: (915) 236-6887

**MOTEL 6**
510 NW Georgia (79556)
Rates: $21-$27;
Tel: (915) 235-4387

**RANCH HOUSE MOTEL**
301 SW Georgia (79556)
Rates: $26-$38;
Tel: (915) 236-6341

## TEMPLE

**HOLIDAY INN**
802 N General Bruce Dr
(76504)
Rates: $46-$64;
Tel: (817) 778-4411

**LA QUINTA MOTOR INN**
1604 W Barton Ave (76504)
Rates: $46-$53;
Tel: (817) 771-2980

**RAMADA INN**
400 SW HK Dodgen Loop 363
(76504)
Rates: $46-$59;
Tel: (817) 773-1515

## TERRELL

**BEST WESTERN-
LA PIEDRA INN**
309 IH-20E (75160)
Rates: $32-$48;
Tel: (214) 563-2676

## TEXARKANA

**BEST WESTERN
KINGS ROW INN**
4200 N State Line Ave
(75502)
Rates: $41-$46;
Tel: (501) 774-3851

**BUDGETEL INN**
5012 N State Line Ave
(75502)
Rates: $33-$49;
Tel: (501) 773-1000

**FOUR STATES INN**
4300 N State Line Ave
(75502)
Rates: $34-$42;
Tel: (501) 773-3144

**HOLIDAY INN EXPRESS**
5401 N State Line Ave
(75503)
Rates: $42-$49;
Tel: (903) 792-3366

**HOLIDAY INN TEXARKANA**
5100 N State Line Ave
(75502)
Rates: $61-$82;
Tel: (501) 774-3521

**LA QUINTA
MOTOR INN-TEXARKANA**
5201 N State Line Ave
(75503)
Rates: $39-$51;
Tel: (903) 794-1900

**RAMADA INN**
P. O. Box 5190 (75503)
Rates: $36-$54;
Tel: (903) 794-3131

**SHERATON INN HOTEL**
5301 N State Line Ave
(77503)
Rates: $64-$200;
Tel: (903) 792-3222

**SHONEY'S INN**
P. O. Box 866 (75504)
Rates: $38-$60;
Tel: (501) 772-0070

## TEXAS CITY

**LA QUINTA MOTOR INN**
1121 Hwy 146N (77590)
Rates: $46-$77;
Tel: (409) 947-3101

## THE WOODLANDS

**LA QUINTA MOTOR INN**
28673 I-45N (77381)
Rates: $55-$68;
Tel: (713) 367-7722

## TYLER

**BEST WESTERN
INN & SUITES**
2828 W NW Loop 323
(75702)
Rates: $39-$52;
Tel: (903) 595-2681

**DAYS INN**
3300 Mineola Hwy (75712)
Rates: $36-$47;
Tel: (903) 595-2451

**ECONO LODGE**
3209 W Gentry Pkwy (75702)
Rates: $29-$36;
Tel: (214) 593-0103

**HOLIDAY INN-
SOUTHEAST CROSSING**
3310 Troup Hwy (75701)
Rates: $52-$67;
Tel: (903) 583-3600

**LA QUINTA MOTOR INN**
1601 W SW Loop 323
(75701)
Rates: $49-$61;
Tel: (903) 561-2223

**QUALITY HOTEL
& CONFERENCE CENTER**
2843 W NW Loop 323
(75712)
Rates: $42-$57;
Tel: (903) 597-1301

**RESIDENCE INN
BY MARRIOTT**
3303 Troup Hwy (75701)
Rates: $66-$102;
Tel: (903) 595-5188

**SHERATON HOTEL**
5701 S Broadway (75703)
Rates: $58-$86;
Tel: (903) 561-5800

**STRATFORD HOUSE
INN MOTEL**
2600 W NW Loop 323
(75702)
Rates: $31-$35;
Tel: (903) 597-2756

## UVALDE

**BEST WESTERN
CONTINENTAL INN**
701 E Main St (78801)
Rates: $30-$40;
Tel: (210) 278-5671

**HOLIDAY INN**
920 E Main St (78801)
Rates: $45-$61;
Tel: (210) 278-4511

**INN OF UVALDE**
810 E Main St (78801)
Rates: $25-$32;
Tel: (210 ) 278-9173

## VAN HORN

**BEST WESTERN
AMERICAN INN**
P. O. Box 626 (79855)
Rates: $28-$46;
Tel: (915) 283-2030

**BEST WESTERN
INN OF VAN HORN**
P. O. Box 1179 (79855)
Rates: $37-$44;
Tel: (915) 283-2410

**COMFORT INN**
1601 W Broadway (79855)
Rates: $34-$46;
Tel: (915) 283-2211

**DAYS INN**
600 E Broadway St (79855)
Rates: $33-$43;
Tel: (915) 283-2401

**PLAZA INN**
P. O. Box 776 (79855)
Rates: $31-$42;
Tel: (915) 283-2780

## VEGA

**BEST WESTERN
SANDS MOTEL**
P. O. Box 350 (79092)
Rates: $38-$50;
Tel: (806) 267-2131

**BONANZA MOTEL**
607 Vega Blvd, Hwy 66E
(79092)
Rates: N/A;
Tel: (806) 267-2158

## VERNON

**BEST WESTERN
VILLAGE INN**
1615 Expressway (76384)
Rates: $34-$46;
Tel: (817) 552-5417

**GREENTREE INN**
3029 Morton (76384)
Rates: $32-$35;
Tel: (817) 552-5421

**SUNDAY HOUSE INN**
3110 Frontage Rd (76384)
Rates: $32-$48;
Tel: (817) 552-9982

**WESTERN MOTEL**
715 Wilbarger St (76384)
Rates: $21-$30;
Tel: (817) 552- 2531

## VICTORIA

**HAMPTON INN**
3112 E Houston Hwy (77901)
Rates: $39-$47;
Tel: (512) 578-2030

**HOLIDAY INN**
2705 E Houston Hwy (77901)
Rates: $45-$50;
Tel: (512) 575-0251

**LA QUINTA MOTOR INN**
7603 N Navarro St (77904)
Rates: $45-$52;
Tel: (512) 572-3585

**RAMADA INN**
3901 E Houston Hwy (77901)
Rates: $44-$49;
Tel: (512) 578-2723

## WACO

**BEST WESTERN
CLASSIC INN**
6624 Hwy 84W (76712)
Rates: $39-$47;
Tel: (817) 776-3194

**HOLIDAY INN-WACO I-35**
1001 Lake Brazos Dr (76704)
Rates: $55-$69;
Tel: (817) 753-0261

**LA QUINTA MOTOR INN**
1110 S 9th St (76706)
Rates: $48-$62;
Tel: (817) 752-9741

**RAMADA INN**
4201 Franklin Ave (76710)
Rates: $44-$52;
Tel: (817) 772-9440

**RIVERPLACE INN**
101 I-35N (76704)
Rates: $28-$46;
Tel: (817) 752-8222

**WACO HILTON INN**
113 S University Parks Dr
(76701)
Rates: $75-$85;
Tel: (817) 754-8484

## WEATHERFORD

**BEST WESTERN
SANTA FE INN**
1927 Santa Fe Dr (76086)
Rates: $39-$48;
Tel: (817) 594-7401

## WEST COLUMBIA

**HOMEPLACE INN**
714 Columbia Dr (77486)
Rates: $44-$55;
Tel: (409) 345-2399

## WHARTON

**HOMEPLACE INN**
1808 FM 102 (77488)
Rates: $42-$52;
Tel: (409) 532-1152

## WICHITA FALLS

**BEST WESTERN
TOWNE CREST INN**
1601 8th St (76301)
Rates: $29-$35;
Tel: (817) 322-1182

**ECONO LODGE**
1700 Fifth St (76301)
Rates: $39-$43;
Tel: (817) 761-1889

**HAMPTON INN**
1317 Kenley (76305)
Rates: $39-$53;
Tel: (817) 766-3300

**LA QUINTA MOTOR INN**
1128 Central Frwy N (76305)
Rates: $42-$57;
Tel: (817) 322-6971

**RAMADA HOTEL
WICHITA FALLS**
401 Broad St (76301)
Rates: $44-$49;
Tel: (817) 766-6000

**SHERATON INN**
100 Central Frwy (76303)
Rates: $69-$79;
Tel: (817) 761-6000

## WOODVILLE

**WOODVILLE INN**
201 N Magnolia (75979)
Rates: $34-$40;
Tel: (409) 283-3741

## ZAPATA

**BEST WESTERN
INN BY THE LAKE**
Star Rt 1, Box 252 (78076)
Rates: $35-$42;
Tel: (512) 765-8403

# UTAH

## BEAVER

**BEST WESTERN PAICE INN**
161 S Main St (84713)
Rates: $32-$48;
Tel: (801) 438-2438

**BEST WESTERN PARADISE INN**
1451 N 300 West (84713)
Rates: $38-$46;
Tel: (801) 438-2455

**COUNTRY INN**
1450 N 300 W (84713)
Rates: $28-$42;
Tel: (801) 438-2484

**DELANO MOTEL**
480 N Main St (84713)
Rates: $28-$34;
Tel: (801) 438-2418

## BICKNELL

**AQUARIUS MOTEL AND RESTAURANT**
240 W Main St (84715)
Rates: $19-$42;
Tel: (801) 425-3835

## BLANDING

**PROSPECTOR MOTOR LODGE**
591 S Hwy 191 (84511)
Rates: $27-$41;
Tel: (801) 678-3231

## BLUFF

**KOKOPELLI INN**
Hwy 191 (84512)
Rates: $38-$42;
Tel: (801) 672-2322

**RECAPTURE LODGE**
P. O. Box 309 (84512)
Rates: $30-$44;
Tel: (801) 672-2281

## BRIGHAM CITY

**HOJO INN**
1167 S Main St (84302)
Rates: $35-$44;
Tel: (801) 723-8511

## BRYCE CANYON NATIONAL PARK

**BEST WESTERN RUBY'S INN**
On SR 12 & 63 (84764)
Rates: $39-$70;
Tel: (801) 834-5341

**BRYCE VALLEY INN**
P. O. Box A (Tropic 84776)
Rates: $45-$62;
Tel: (801) 679-8811

## CAPITAL REEF NATIONAL PARK

**CAPITOL REEF INN & CAFE**
P. O. Box 100 (Torrey 84775)
Rates: $32-$36;
Tel: (801) 425-3271

**SUNGLOW MOTEL**
63 E Main St (Bicknell 84715)
Rates: $25-$34;
Tel: (801) 425-3821

## CEDAR CITY

**ASTRO BUDGET INN**
323 S Main St (84720)
Rates: $22-$50;
Tel: (801) 586-6557

**COMFORT INN**
250 N 1100 West (84720)
Rates: $33-$75;
Tel: (801) 586-2082

**HOLIDAY INN-CONVENTION CTR**
1575 W 200 North (84720)
Rates: $46-$95;
Tel: (801) 586-8888

**QUALITY INN**
18 S Main St (84720)
Rates: $45-$68;
Tel: (801) 586-2433

**RAYCAP MOTEL**
2555 N Main St (84720)
Rates: $32-$43;
Tel: (801) 586-7435

**RODEWAY INN**
281 S Main St (84720)
Rates: $36-$70;
Tel: (801) 586-9916

**THRIFTY MOTEL**
344 S Main St (84720)
Rates: $20-$48;
Tel: (801) 586-9114

## DELTA

**BEST WESTERN MOTOR INN**
527 E Topaz Blvd (84624)
Rates: $40-$50;
Tel: (801) 864-3882

## FILLMORE

**BEST WESTERN PARADISE INN**
800 N Main St (84631)
Rates: $38-$48;
Tel: (801) 743-6895

**SPINNING WHEEL MOTEL**
65 S Main (84631)
Rates: N/A;
Tel: (801) 743-6260

## GREEN RIVER

**BOOKCLIFF LODGE**
395 E Main (84525)
Rates: $30-$70;
Tel: (801) 564-3406

## HATCH

**GALAXY MOTEL**
216 North Main (84735)
Rates: N/A;
Tel: (801) 735-4327

## HURRICANE

**BEST WESTERN
WESTON LAMPLIGHTER**
280 W State (84737)
Rates: $38-$55;
Tel: (801) 635-4647

**PARK VILLA**
650 W State (84737)
Rates: $25-$50;
Tel: (801) 635-4010

## KANAB

**AIKENS LODGE**
79 W Center St (84741)
Rates: $27-$40;
Tel: (801) 644-2625

**BRANDON MOTEL**
223 West Center St (84741)
Rates: N/A;
Tel: (801) 644-2631

**FOUR SEASONS
MOTOR INN**
P. O. Box 308 (84741)
Rates: $56-$63;
Tel: (801) 644-2635

**PARRY LODGE**
89 E Center St (84741)
Rates: $41-$62;
Tel: (801) 644-2601

**QUAIL PARK LODGE**
125 N 300 West (84741)
Rates: $28-$45;
Tel: (801) 644-2639

**SHILO INN**
296 West 100 North (84741)
Rates: $49-$68;
Tel: (801) 644-2562

## MEXICAN HAT

**SAN JUAN INN**
P. O. Box 535 (84531)
Rates: $38-$52;
Tel: (801) 683-2220

## MOAB

**BOWEN MOTEL**
169 N Main St (84532)
Rates: $27-$55;
Tel: (801) 259-7132

**PACK CREEK RANCH**
P. O. Box 1270 (84532)
Rates: $90-$200;
Tel: (801) 259-5505

**RED ROCK MOTEL**
51 N 100 St W (84532)
Rates: $34-$48;
Tel: (801) 259-5431

**THE VIRGINIAN MOTEL**
70 E 200 St S (84532)
Rates: $25-$45;
Tel: (801) 259-5951

## MONTICELLO

**CANYONLANDS
MOTOR INN**
P. O. Box 1142 (84535)
Rates: $18-$48;
Tel: (801) 587-2266

## MONUMENT VALLEY

**GOULDING'S TRADING
POST & LODGE**
P. O. Box 1 (84536)
Rates: $52-$92;
Tel: (801) 727-3231

## MOUNT CARMEL JUNCTION

**GOLDEN HILLS MOTEL**
P. O. Box 34
(Mount Carmel 84755)
Rates: $19-$40;
Tel: (801) 648-2268

## OGDEN

**BEST WESTERN
HIGH COUNTRY INN**
1335 W 12th St (84404)
Rates: $44-$57;
Tel: (801) 394-9474

**BEST WESTERN
OGDEN PARK HOTEL**
247 24th St (84401)
Rates: $69-$101;
Tel: (801) 627-1190

**FLYING J INN**
1206 W 21st St (84404)
Rates: $40;
Tel: (801) 393-8644

**MILLSTREAM**
1450 Washington Blvd
(84404)
Rates: N/A;
Tel: (801) 394-9425

**OGDEN TRAVELODGE**
2110 Washington Blvd
(84401)
Rates: $40-$52;
Tel: (801) 394-4563

**SUPER 8 MOTEL**
1508 W 2100 South (84401)
Rates: $30-$38;
Tel: (801) 731-7100

## PANGUITCH

**COLOR COUNTRY MOTEL**
P. O. Box 163 (84759)
Rates: $22-48;
Tel: (801) 676-2386

**HORIZON MOTEL**
730 N Main (84759)
Rates: $30-$69;
Tel: (801) 676-2651

**MARIANNA INN MOTEL**
P. O. Box 150 (84759)
Rates: $25-$55;
Tel: (801) 676-8844

# PARK CITY

**BEST WESTERN
LANDMARK INN**
6560 N Landmark Dr (84060)
Rates: $48-$107;
Tel: (801) 649-7300

**OLYMPIA RESORT HOTEL
AND CONVENTION CTR**
1895 Sidewinder Dr (84060)
Rates: $69-$154;
Tel: (801) 649-2900

# PAROWAN

**BEST WESTERN
SWISS VILLAGE INN**
580 N Main St (84761)
Rates: $39-$67;
Tel: (801) 477-3391

**JEDEDIAH'S INN
& RESTAURANT**
625 West 200 South (84761)
Rates: $54-$59;
Tel: (801) 477-3326

# PAYSON

**COMFORT INN**
830 N Main (84651)
Rates: $50-$63;
Tel: (801) 465-4861

# PRICE

**DAYS INN-PRICE**
838 Westwood Blvd (84501)
Rates: $40-$56;
Tel: (801) 637-8880

**GREEN WELL MOTEL**
655 E Main (84501)
Rates: $23-$44;
Tel: (801) 637-3520

**MR SLEEP**
641 W Price River Dr (84501)
Rates: $29-$34;
Tel: (801) 637-7000

**NATIONAL 9**
720 E Main St
(Wellington 84542)
Rates: $25-$45;
Tel: (801) 637-7980

# PROVO

**COLONY INN SUITES**
1380 S University Ave (84601)
Rates: $26-$58;
Tel: (801) 374-6800

**COMFORT INN UNIVERSITY**
1555 Canyon Rd (84604)
Rates: $49-$85;
Tel: (801) 374-6020

**DAYS INN**
1675 N 200W (84604)
Rates: $46-$57;
Tel: (801) 375-8600

**HORNES' EAST BAY INN**
1292 S University Ave (84601)
Rates: $28-$59;
Tel: (800) 326-0025

**UPTOWN MOTEL**
469 W Center St (84601)
Rates: $22-$38;
Tel: (801) 373-8248

# RICHFIELD

**BEST WESTERN
APPLE TREE INN**
145 S Main ST (84701)
Rates: $38-$95;
Tel: (801) 896-5481

**BUDGET HOST
KNIGHTS INN**
69 S Main St (84701)
Rates: $28-38;
Tel: (801) 896-8228

**NEW WEST MOTEL**
447 S Main St (84701)
Rates: $24-$34;
Tel: (801) 896-4076

**ROMANICO INN**
1170 S Main St (84701)
Rates: $26-$42;
Tel: (801) 896-8471

# ROOSEVELT

**BEST WESTERN INN**
Rt 2, Box 2860 (84066)
Rates: $38-$42;
Tel: (801) 722-4644

# ST. GEORGE

**COLORADO FAMILY INN**
559 E St. George Blvd (84770)
Rates: N/A;
Tel: (801) 628-4436

**HOLIDAY INN/HOLIDOME**
850 S Bluff St (84770)
Rates: $58-$100;
Tel: (801) 628-4235

**REGENCY INN**
770 E St George Blvd (84770)
Rates: $28-$40;
Tel: (801) 673-6119

**TRAVELODGE EAST**
175 N 1000 East St (84770)
Rates: $32-$74;
Tel: (801) 673-4621

# SALINA

**BUDGET HOST
SCENIC HILLS MOTEL**
75 East 1500S (84654)
Rates: $27-$47;
Tel: (801) 529-7483

**CEDAR CREEK INN**
60 N State St (84654)
Rates: $33-$50;
Tel: (801) 529-7467

**LONE STAR MOTEL**
785 W Main (84654)
Rates: $24-$36;
Tel: (801) 529-3642

**RANCH MOTEL**
80 N State St (84654)
Rates: N/A;
Tel: (801) 529-7789

**SAFARI MOTEL**
1425 S State St (84654)
Rates: $32-$56;
Tel: (801) 529-7447

## SALT LAKE CITY
(and Vicinity)

**BONNEVILLE INN MOTEL**
315 W 3300 South (84115)
Rates: $39-$49;
Tel: (801) 486-8780

**COMFORT INN-
SALT LAKE CITY AIRPORT**
200 N Admiral Byrd Rd
(84116)
Rates: $55-$75;
Tel: (801) 537-7444

**DAYS INN AIRPORT**
1900 W North Temple St
(84116)
Rates: $46-$75;
Tel: (801) 539-8538

**ECONO LODGE**
715 W N Temple (84116)
Rates: $44-$58;
Tel: (801) 363-0062

**EMBASSY SUITES HOTEL**
600 S W Temple (84101)
Rates: $99-$109;
Tel: (801) 359-7800

**HILTON AIRPORT**
5151 Wiley Post Wmy (84116)
Rates: $69-$79;
Tel: (801) 539-1515

**HILTON HOTEL-
SALT LAKE CITY**
150 W 5th St (84101)
Rates: $90-$122;
Tel: (801) 532-3344

**HOLIDAY INN-AIRPORT**
1659 W N Temple (84116)
Rates: $65-$71;
Tel: (801) 533-9000

**HOLIDAY INN-
DOWNTOWN**
230 W 600 South St (84101)
Rates: $66-$76;
Tel: (801) 532-7000

**HOWARD JOHNSON**
122 W S Temple (84101)
Rates: $53-$89;
Tel: (801) 521-0130

**MARRIOTT HOTEL**
75 S W Temple (84101)
Rates: $69-$139;
Tel: (801) 531-0800

**NENDELS INN**
2080 West North Temple
(84116)
Rates: N/A;
Tel: (801) 355-0088

**QUALITY INN-CITY CENTER**
154 W 6th S (84101)
Rates: $58-$84;
Tel: (801) 521-2930

**QUALITY INN-SOUTH**
4465 Century Dr (84123)
Rates: $39-$79;
Tel: (801) 268-2533

**RADISSON HOTEL-
SALT LAKE CITY AIRPORT**
2177 West N Temple (84116)
Rates: $59-$119;
Tel: (801) 364-5800

**THE RESIDENCE INN
BY MARRIOTT**
765 East 400 S (84102)
Rates: $125-$176;
Tel: (801) 532-5511

**ROYAL EXECUTIVE INN**
121 N 3rd W (84103)
Rates: $36-$49;
Tel: (801) 521-3450

**SHILO INN**
206 Southwest Temple
(84101)
Rates: N/A;
Tel: (801) 521-9500

**THE SKYLINE INN**
2475 E 17th S (84108)
Rates: $39-$48;
Tel: (801) 582-5350

## SPRINGDALE

**BUMBLEBERRY INN**
897 Zion Park Blvd (84767)
Rates: $39-$54;
Tel: (801) 772-3224

**UNDER THE EAVES
BED & BREAKFAST**
980 Zion Park Blvd (84767)
Rates: $35-$75;
Tel: (801) 772-3457

## TORREY

**CAPITOL REEF INN**
360 West Main St (84775)
Rates: N/A;
Tel: (801) 425-3271

## TREMONTON

**SANDMAN MOTEL**
585 W Main (84337)
Rates: $29-$37;
Tel: (801) 257-5675

## ZION NATIONAL PARK

**BEST WESTERN
DRIFTWOOD LODGE**
P. O. Box 98
(Springdale 84767)
Rates: $52-$62;
Tel: (801) 772-3262

# VERMONT

## ALBURG

**YE OLDE GRAYSTONE
BED & BREAKFAST**
RFD 1, Box 76 (05440)
Rates: $50-$55;
Tel: (802) 796-3911

## ARLINGTON

**THE ARLINGTON INN**
P. O. Box 369 (05250)
Rates: $75-$160;
Tel: (802) 375-6532

**CUTLEAF MAPLES**
Rt 7A (05250)
Rates: N/A;
Tel: (802) 375-2725

**HILL FARM INN**
RR 2, Box 2015 (05250)
Rates: N/A;
Tel: (800) 882-2545

**VALHALLA MOTEL**
Historic Rt 7A (05250)
Rates: N/A;
Tel: (800) 258-2212

## BARRE

**THE HOLLOW INN
& MOTEL**
278 S Main St (05641)
Rates: $55-$94;
Tel: (802) 479-9313

## BELLOWS FALLS

**WHIPPOWIL COTTAGES**
US Rt 5 (05101)
Rates: N/A;
Tel: (802) 463-3442

## BENNINGTON

**BAYBERRY MOTEL**
P. O. Box 137
(Shaftsbury 05262)
Rates: $36-$65;
Tel: (802) 447-7180

**BENNINGTON MOTOR INN**
143 W Main St (05201)
Rates: $48-$90;
Tel: (802) 442-5479

**FIFE 'N DRUM MOTEL**
Rt 7S, RR 1, Box 4340 (05201)
Rates: $34-$69;
Tel: (802) 442-4074

**KNOTTY PINE MOTEL**
130 Northside Dr (05201)
Rates: $38-$62;
Tel: (802) 442-5487

**PLEASANT VALLEY MOTEL**
Pleasant Valley Rd (05201)
Rates: $40-$48;
Tel: (802) 442-6222

**SOUTH GATE MOTEL**
P. O. Box 1073 (05201)
Rates: $32-$64;
Tel: (802) 447-7525

**VERMONTER MOTOR
LODGE**
RR 1, Box 2377 (05201)
Rates: $35-$75;
Tel: (802) 442-2529

## BETHEL

**GREENHURST INN**
River St, RD 2 Box 60 (05032)
Rates: N/A;
Tel: (802) 234-9474

## BRADFORD

**BRADFORD MOTEL**
P. O. Box 250 (05033)
Rates: $35-$70;
Tel: (802) 222-4467

## BRANDON

**BRANDON MOTOR LODGE**
Rt 7 South (05733)
Rates: N/A;
Tel: (802) 247-3802

## BRATTLEBORO

**CHESTERFIELD INN**
Rt 9 (West Chesterfield, NH
03466)
Rates: $99-$159;
Tel: (603) 256-3211

**COLONIAL MOTEL & SPA**
VT 9, I-91 exit 3 to VT 9W
(05301)
Rates: $32-$65;
Tel: (802) 257-7733

**MOLLY STARK MOTEL**
RD 4, Box 53
(West Brattleboro 05301)
Rates: $30-$56;
Tel: (802) 254-2440

**QUALITY INN**
Putney Rd (05301)
Rates: $56-$92;
Tel: (802) 254-8701

## BROWNSVILLE

**MILL BROOK
BED & BREAKFAST**
P. O. Box 410, Rt 44 (05037)
Rates: N/A;
Tel: (802) 484-7283

## BURLINGTON

**ANCHORAGE INNS**
108 Dorset St
(So Burlington 05403)
Rates: $36-$66;
Tel: (802) 863-7000

**ECONO LODGE**
1076 E Williston Rd
(So Burlington 05403)
Rates: $52-$82;
Tel: (802) 863-1125

**FRIENDSHIP LAKE
VIEW INN**
1860 Shelburne Rd (05403)
Rates: $34-$84;
Tel: (802) 862-0230

**HOLIDAY INN
BURLINGTON**
1068 Williston Rd
(So Burlington 05403)
Rates: $65-$102;
Tel: (802) 863-6363

**HOWARD JOHNSON
MOTOR LODGE**
P. O. Box 993 (05402)
Rates: $52 $90;
Tel: (802) 863-5541

**RADISSON HOTEL
BURLINGTON**
60 Battery St (05401)
Rates: $89-$119;
Tel: (802) 658-6500

**RAMADA INN**
P. O. Box 2306
(So Burlington 05407)
Rates: $54-$99;
Tel: (802) 658-0250

**SHERATON-BURLINGTON
HOTEL & CONF CTR**
870 Williston Red
(So Burlington 05403)
Rates: $79-$137;
Tel: (802) 865-6600

**TOWN & COUNTRY MOTEL**
490 Shelburne Rd (05401)
Rates: $43-$65;
Tel: (802) 862-5786

## CANAAN

**LAKE WALLACE MOTEL**
Rt 114 (05903)
Rates: N/A;
Tel: (802) 266-3311

## COLCHESTER

**DAYS INN**
23 College Pkwy (05446)
Rates: $55-$65;
Tel: (802) 655-0900

**HAMPTON INN HOTEL
& CONFRENCE CTR**
8 Mountain View Dr (05446)
Rates: $62-$86;
Tel: (802) 655-6177

## CRAFTSBURY COMMON

**THE INN
ON THE COMMON**
P. O. Box 75 (05827)
Rates: $130-$260;
Tel: (802) 586-9619

## DANBY

**TUCKER INN**
RFD 1, Box 100 (05739)
Rates: $35-$60;
Tel: (802) 293-5835

## DORSET

**BARROWS HOUSE**
Rt 30 (05251)
Rates: $85-$210;
Tel: (802) 867-4455

## ESSEX JUNCTION

**THE WILSON INN**
10 Kellog Rd (05452)
Rates: N/A;
Tel: (802) 879-1515

## FAIRLEE

**SILVER MAPLE LODGE
& COTTAGES**
RR 1, Box 8 (05045)
Rates: $46-$64;
Tel: (802) 333-4326

## FRANKLIN

**FAIR MEADOWS FARM
BED & BREAKFAST**
Box 430, Rt 235 (05457)
Rates: N/A;
Tel: (802) 285-2132

## GRAFTON

**THE HAYES HOUSE**
Bear Hill Rd (05146)
Rates: N/A;
Tel: (802) 843-2461

## HIGHGATE SPRINGS

**THE TYLE PLACE
ON LAKE CHAMPLAIN**
US 7 off I-89 (05460)
Rates: $36 $140;
Tel: (802) 868-4291

## ISLAND POND

**LAKEFRONT MOTEL**
P. O. Box 161 (05846)
Rates: $55-$60;
Tel: (802) 723-6507

## JEFFERSONVILLE

**THE HIGHLANDER MOTEL**
RR 1, Box 436 (05464)
Rates: $42-$64;
Tel: (802) 644-2725

**THE JEFFERSON HOUSE**
Main St, P. O.Box 288 (05464)
Rates: N/A;
Tel: (802) 644-2030

# KILLINGTON

**CEDARBROOK
MOTOR INN/SUITES**
HCR 34 (05751)
Rates: $30-$99;
Tel: (802) 422-9666

**CORTINA INN**
US Rte 4 (05751)
Rates: N/A;
Tel: (800) 451-6108

**ECONO LODGE-
MOUNTAINSIDE**
RD 2, Box 7650
(Mendon 05701)
Rates: $38-$95;
Tel: (802) 773-6644

**INN OF THE
SIX MOUNTAINS**
Killington Rd (05751)
Rates: N/A;
Tel: (800) 228-4676

**KILLINGTON PICO
MOTOR INN**
On US 4 (05751)
Rates: $48-$120;
Tel: (802) 773-4088

**RED CLOVER INN**
RR 2, Box 7450
(Mendon 05701)
Rates: $120-$165;
Tel: (802) 775-2290

**VAL ROC MOTEL**
SR 100S (05751)
Rates: $39-$92;
Tel: (802) 422-3881

# LONDONDERRY

**WHITE PINE LODGE**
Rt 11 West (05148)
Rates: N/A;
Tel: (802) 824-3909

# LUDLOW

**THE COMBES FAMILY INN**
RFD 1, Box 275A (05149)
Rates: $61-$86;
Tel: (802) 228-8799

**TIMBER INN MOTEL**
RR 1, Box 1003 (05149)
Rates: $40-$95;
Tel: (802) 228-8666

# LYNDONVILLE

**LYNBURKE MOTEL**
SR 114 (05851)
Rates: $35-$50;
Tel: (802) 626-3346

**OLD CUTTER INN**
RR 1, Box 52
(East Burke 05832)
Rates: $42-$140;
Tel: (802) 626-5152

# MANCHESTER

**BRITTANY INN MOTEL**
Rt 7A, Box 760 (05255)
Rates: $45-$65;
Tel: (802) 362-1033

**WEDGEWOOD NORTH
MOTEL**
RR 1, Box 2295
(Manchester Center 05255)
Rates: $45-$100;
Tel: (802) 362-2145

# MARLBORO

**WHETSTONE INN**
1/2 Mi off VT 9 (05344)
Rates: $30-$85;
Tel: (802) 254-2500

# MIDDLEBURY

**THE MIDDLEBURY INN**
P. O. Box 631 (05753)
Rates: $68-$156;
Tel: (802) 388-4961

**OCTOBER PUMPKIN
BED & BREAKFAST**
P. O. Box 226, Rt 125 E
(05740)
Rates: N/A;
Tel: (800) 237-2007

# MONTPELIER

**ECONO LODGE**
101 Northfield St (05602)
Rates: $44-$89;
Tel: (802) 223-5258

**INN ON THE COMMON**
Main St
(Craftsbury Common 05827)
Rates: $100-$220;
Tel: (800) 521-2233

# MT. TABOR

**TUCKER INN**
RR 1, Box 100, Old Rt 7
(05739)
Rates: N/A;
Tel: (802) 293-5835

# NEWFANE

**THE FOUR COLUMNS INN**
P. O. Box 278 (05345)
Rates: $100-$275;
Tel: (802) 365-7713

# NEWPORT

**NEWPORT CITY MOTEL**
974 East Main St (05855)
Rates: N/A;
Tel: (802) 334-6558

**TOP OF THE HILLS
MOTEL & COUNTRY INN**
HCR 61, Box 14 (05855)
Rates: $43-$62;
Tel: (802) 334-6748

# NORTH HERO

**SHORE ACRES INN**
RR 1, Box 3, US Rt 2 (05475)
Rates: N/A;
Tel: (802) 372-8722

## PUTNEY

**PUTNEY INN**
P. O. Box 181 (05346)
Rates: $58-$78;
Tel: (802) 387-5517

## QUECHEE

**FRIENDSHIP INN
AT QUECHEE GORGE**
P. O. Box Q (05059)
Rates: $54-$82;
Tel: (802) 295-7600

## RUTLAND

**GREEN-MONT MOTEL**
138 North Main St (05701)
Rates: N/A;
Tel: (802) 775-2575

**HIGHLANDER MOTEL**
203 North Main St (05701)
Rates: N/A;
Tel: (802) 773-6069

**HOLIDAY INN**
S Main St (05701)
Rates: $75-$169;
Tel. (802) 775-1911

**HOWARD JOHNSON INN**
S Main St (05701)
Rates: $40-$118;
Tel: (802) 775-4303

## SHELBURNE

**ECONO LODGE**
1961 Shelburne Rd (05482)
Rates: $35-$70;
Tel: (802) 985-3377

## SOUTH BURLINGTON

**ETHAN ALLEN MOTEL**
1611 Williston Rd (05403)
Rates: N/A;
Tel: (802) 863-4573

## SPRINGFIELD

**THE ABBY LYN MOTEL**
RD 1, Box 80
(No Springfield 05150)
Rates: $38-$60;
Tel: (802) 886-2223

**HOWARD JOHNSON
LODGE**
818 Charlestown Rd (05156)
Rates: $53-$89;
Tel: (802) 885-4516

**PA-LO-MAR MOTEL**
2 Linhale Dr (05156)
Rates: N/A;
Tel: (802) 885-4142

## STOWE

**COMMODORE'S INN**
P. O. Box 970 (05672)
Rates: $52-$122;
Tel: (802) 253-7131

**GREEN MOUNTAIN INN**
P. O. Box 60 (05672)
Rates: $69-$205;
Tel: (802) 253-7301

**HONEYWOOD INN**
4527 Mountain Rd (05672)
Rates: N/A;
Tel: (802) 253-4124

**INNSBRUCK INN**
4361 Mountain Rd (05672)
Rates: $45-$119;
Tel: (802) 253-8582

**MOUNTAIN ROAD RESORT**
P. O. Box 8 (05672)
Rates: $50-$325;
Tel: (800) 367-6873

**MOUNTAINEER INN**
3343 Mountain Rd (05672)
Rates: $35-$75;
Tel: (802) 253-7525

**NOTCH BROOK RESORT**
1229 Notch Brook Rd (05672)
Rates: $53-$68;
Tel: (802) 253-4882

**THE SNOWDRIFT MOTEL**
2135 Mountain Rd (05672)
Rates: N/A;
Tel: (802) 253-7305

**TEN ACRES LODGE**
14 Barrows Rd (05672)
Rates: $45-$160;
Tel: (802) 253-7638

**TOPNOTCH
AT STOWE RESORT & SPA**
P. O. Box 1458 (05672)
Rates: $108-$650;
Tel: (802) 253-8585

## WAITSFIELD

**MILLBROOK INN**
RFD Box 62 (05673)
Rates: N/A;
Tel: (802) 496-2405

## WARREN

**GOLDEN LION
RIVERSIDE INN**
P. O. Box 336 (05674)
Rates: $60;
Tel: (802) 496-3084

**POWDERHOUND RESORT**
Rt 100, Box 369 (05674)
Rates: $50-$130;
Tel: (802) 496-5100

## WATERBURY

**HOLIDAY INN
OF WATERBURY-STOWE**
P. O. Box 149 (05676)
Rates: $65-$128;
Tel: (802) 244-7822

## WEATHERSFIELD

**INN AT WEATHERSFIELD**
Rt 106, P. O. Box 165 (05151)
Rates: N/A;
Tel: (802) 263-9217

## WHITE RIVER JUNCTION

**HOLIDAY INN**
P. O. Box 1010 (05001)
Rates: $70-$125;
Tel: (802) 295-3000

**HOWARD JOHNSON MOTEL**
1 Blk E of Jct I-89, I-91 (05001)
Rates: $55-$99;
Tel: (802) 295-3015

## WILDER

**WILDER MOTEL**
319 Hartford Ave (05088)
Rates: N/A;
Tel: (802) 295-9793

## WOODSTOCK

**BRAESIDE MOTEL**
P. O. Box 411 (05091)
Rates: $48-$88;
Tel: (802) 457-1366

**KEDRON VALLEY INN**
SR 106 (So Woodstock 05071)
Rates: $93-$244;
Tel: (802) 457-1473

**THE WINSLOW HOUSE**
38 US 4 (05091)
Rates: $55-$85;
Tel: (802) 457-1820

# VIRGINIA

## ABINGDON

**EMPIRE MOTEL**
887 Empire Dr (24210)
Rates: $33-$41;
Tel: (703) 628-7131

## ALEXANDRIA

**BEST WESTERN OLD COLONY INN**
625 1st St (22314)
Rates: $79-$185;
Tel: (703) 548-6300

**COMFORT INN**
5716 S Van Dorn St (22310)
Rates: $56-$85;
Tel: (703) 922-9200

**COMFORT INN-MT VERNON**
7212 Richmond Hwy (22306)
Rates: $50-$80;
Tel: (703) 765-9000

**ECONO LODGE OLD TOWN**
700 N Washington St (22314)
Rates: $54-$63;
Tel: (703) 836-5100

**GUEST QUARTERS HOTEL**
100 S Reynolds St (22304)
Rates: $79-$250;
Tel: (703) 370-9600

**HOLIDAY INN OLD TOWN**
480 King St (22314)
Rates: $99-$250;
Tel: (703) 549-6080

**HOWARD JOHNSON-OLD TOWN**
5821 Richmond Hwy (22303)
Rates: $55-$98;
Tel: (703) 329-1400

**RAMADA HOTEL-OLD TOWN**
901 N Fairfax St (22314)
Rates: $106-$250;
Tel: (703) 683-6000

**RED ROOF INN**
5975 Richmond Hwy (22303)
Rates: $49-$62;
Tel: (703) 960-5200

## ALTAVISTA

**COMFORT SUITES HOTEL**
P. O. Box 714 (24517)
Rates: $50-$59;
Tel: (804) 369-4000

## ASHLAND

**COMFORT INN**
101 Cottage Greene Dr (23005)
Rates: $42-$60;
Tel: (804) 752-7777

**HOJO INN**
101 S Carter Rd (23005)
Rates: $46-$52;
Tel: (804) 798-9291

## BASYE

**SKY CHALET COUNTRY INN**
P. O. Box 300 (22810)
Rates: $49-$75;
Tel: (703) 856-2147

## BEDFORD

**BEST WESTERN TERRACE HOUSE INN**
921 Blue Ridge Ave (24523)
Rates: $39-$47;
Tel: (703) 586-8286

## BLACKSBURG

**BEST WESTERN
RED LION INN**
900 Plantation Rd (24060)
Rates: $42-$53;
Tel: (703) 552-7770

**BLACKSBURG MARRIOTT**
900 Prices Fork Rd (24060)
Rates: $69-$79;
Tel: (703) 552-7001

**COMFORT INN**
3705 S Main St (24060)
Rates: $51-$65;
Tel. (703) 951-1530

**HICKORY INN
BLACKSBURG**
3503 Holiday Ln (24060)
Rates: $48-$60;
Tel: (703) 951-1330

**HOJO INN**
3333 S Main St (24060)
Rates: $29-$32;
Tel: (703) 951-4242

**HOLIDAY INN**
3503 Holiday Ln (24060)
Rates: $48-$100;
Tel: (703) 951-1330

## BLAND

**BIG WALKER MOTEL**
P. O. Box 155 (24315)
Rates: $26-$33;
Tel: (703) 688-3331

## BRISTOL

**DAYS INN**
P. O. Box 1746 (24203)
Rates: $38-$55;
Tel: (703) 669-9353

**ECONO LODGE**
912 Commonwealth Ave
(24201)
Rates: $30-$44;
Tel: (703) 466-2112

**RODEWAY INN
OF TRI-CITY AIRPORT**
P. O. Box 1153
(Blountville, TN 37617)
Rates: $35-$58;
Tel: (615) 323-4155

**SKYLAND MOTEL**
4748 Lee Hwy (24201)
Rates: $20-$32;
Tel: (703) 669-0166

## BUENA VISTA

**BUENA VISTA MOTEL**
P. O. Box 947 (24416)
Rates: $34-$40;
Tel: (703) 261-2138

## CAPE CHARLES

**HOLIDAY MOTEL**
RFD 1, Box 131 S (23310)
Rates: N/A;
Tel: (804) 331-1000

## CARMEL CHURCH

**COMFORT INN-CARMEL
CHURCH/KINGS DOMINION**
P. O. Box 105
(Ruther Glen 22546)
Rates: $43-$70;
Tel: (804) 448-2828

## CHARLOTTESVILLE

**BEST WESTERN-
CAVALIER INN**
P. O. Box 5647 (22905)
Rates: $49;
Tel: (804) 296-8111

**BEST WESTERN-
MOUNT VERNON**
P. O. Box 72854 (22906)
Rates: $48-$56;
Tel: (804) 296-5501

**THE BOARDS HEAD INN
& SPORTS CLUB**
P. O. Box 5307 (22905)
Rates: $100-$155;
Tel: (804) 296-2181

**COMFORT INN**
1807 Emmet St, US 27 N
(22901)
Rates: $45-$59;
Tel: (804) 293-6188

**DAYS HOTEL
OF CHARLOTTESVILLE**
1901 Emmet St (22901)
Rates: $42-$76;
Tel: (804) 977-7700

**ENGLISH INN-
BED & BREAKFAST**
2000 Morton Dr (22901)
Rates: $58-$89;
Tel: (804) 971-9900

**HOLIDAY INN-
CHARLOTTESVILLE
MONTICELLO**
I-64 & 5th St (22901)
Rates: $58-$73;
Tel: (804) 977-5100

**HOLIDAY INN-NORTH**
1600 Emmet St (22901)
Rates: $58-$68;
Tel: (804) 293-9111

**KNIGHTS INN
OF CHARLOTTESVILLE**
1300 Seminole Tr (22901)
Rates: $41-$58;
Tel: (804) 973-8133

**OMNI CHARLOTTESVILLE
HOTEL**
235 W Main St (22901)
Rates: $99-$150;
Tel: (804) 971-5500

## CHESAPEAKE

**COMFORT INN**
4433 S Military Hwy 23321)
Rates: $41-$65;
Tel: (804) 488-7900

**ECONO LODGE
CHESAPEAKE**
2222 Military Hwy S (23320)
Rates: $32-$49;
Tel: (804) 543-2200

**RED ROOF INN**
724 Woodlake Dr (23320)
Rates: $32-$42;
Tel: (804) 523-0123

**TRAVELODGE**
701 Woodlake Dr (23320)
Rates: $33-$46;
Tel: (804) 420-2976

**WELLESLEY INN**
1750 Sara Dr (23320)
Rates: $40-$70;
Tel: (804) 366-0100

## CHESTER

**DAYS INN-CHESTER**
P. O. Box AN (23831)
Rates: $33-$53;
Tel: (804) 748-5871

## CHRISTIANBURG

**DAYS INN**
P. O. Box 768 (24073)
Rates: $40-$50;
Tel: (703) 382-0261

**ECONO LODGE**
2430 Roanoke St (24073)
Rates: $31-$39;
Tel: (703) 382-6161

## COVINGTON

**COMFORT INN**
Rt 5, Mallow Rd (24426)
Rates: $53-$66;
Tel: (703) 962-2141

**HOLIDAY INN**
P. O. Box 920 (24426)
Rates: $50-$68;
Tel: (703) 962-4951

**KNIGHTS COURT**
Rt 2, Box 417 (24426)
Rates: $41-$48;
Tel: (703) 962-7600

## CULPEPER

**COMFORT INN**
890 Willis Ln (22701)
Rates: $44-$54;
Tel: (703) 825-4900

**GRAVES' MOUNTAIN LODGE GUEST RANCH**
VA 670 (Syria 22743)
Rates: $75-$200;
Tel: (703) 923-4231

**SCOTTISH INNS**
By Pass Rt 29 Exit 15 (22701)
Rates: N/A;
Tel: (703) 829-6700

## DANVILLE

**STRATFORD INN**
2500 Riverside Dr (24540)
Rates: $42-$52;
Tel: (804) 793-2500

## DOSWELL

**BEST WESTERN-KINGS QUARTERS**
P. O. Box 100 (23047)
Rates: $32-$88;
Tel: (804) 876-3321

## DUFFIELD

**RAMADA INN**
P. O. Box 260 (24244)
Rates: $48-$62;
Tel: (703) 431-4300

## DULLES INTL AIRPORT AREA

**HOLIDAY INN WASHINGTON DULLES**
1000 Sully Rd (Sterling 22170)
Rates: $90-$120;
Tel: (703) 471-7411

**RAMADA RENAISSANCE-WASHINGTON DULLES**
13869 Park Center Rd
(Herndon 22071)
Rates: $109-$126;
Tel: (703) 478-2900

**WELLESLEY INN**
485 Elden St (Herndon 22070)
Rates: $47-$75;
Tel: (703) 478-9777

## DUMFRIES

**QUALITY INN**
17133 Dumfries Rd (22026)
Rates: $53-$60;
Tel: (703) 221-1141

## EMPORIA

**BEST WESTERN EMPORIA**
1100 W Atlantic Ave (23847)
Rates: $40-$49;
Tel: (804) 634-3200

**COMFORT INN**
1411 Skippers Rd (23847)
Rates: $38-$42;
Tel: (804) 348-3282

**EMPORIA TRAVELODGE**
3175 Sussex Dr (23847)
Rates: $26-$38;
Tel: (804) 535-8535

**HAMPTON INN**
1207 W Atlantic St (23847)
Rates: $43-$56;
Tel: (804) 634-9200

**HOLIDAY INN**
P. O. Box 827 (23847)
Rates: $46-$57;
Tel: (804) 634-4191

**RESTE' MOTEL**
3190 Sussex Dr (23847)
Rates: $21-$27;
Tel: (804) 535-8505

## FAIRFAX

**COMFORT INN-UNIVERSITY CENTER**
11180 Main St (22030)
Rates: $54-$95;
Tel: (703) 591-5900

**HOLIDAY INN FAIRFAX CITY**
3535 Chain Bridge Rd (22030)
Rates: $59-$89;
Tel: (703) 591-5500

**WELLESLEY INN**
10327 Lee Hwy (22030)
Rates: N/A;
Tel: (703) 359-2888

# FALLS CHURCH

**MARRIOTT-FAIRVIEW PARK**
3111 Fairview Park Dr
(22042)
Rates: $142-$500;
Tel: (703) 849-9400

# FANCY GAP

**CASCADE MOUNTAIN INN**
Rt 2, Box 36 (24328)
Rates: $30-$45;
Tel: (703) 728-2300

**DOC RUN LODGE**
Rt 2, Box 338 (Hillsville 24343)
Rates: $80-$105;
Tel: (703) 398-2212

# FORT CHISWELL

**GATEWAY MOTEL #2**
Rt 3, Box 488
(Max Meadows 24360)
Rates: $23-$32;
Tel: (703) 637-3119

# FREDERICKSBURG

**BEST WESTERN FREDERICKSBURG**
2205 William St (22401)
Rates: $35-$49;
Tel: (703) 371-5050

**BEST WESTERN-JOHNNY APPLESEED**
543 Warrenton Rd (22405)
Rates: $35-$46;
Tel: (703) 373-0000

**BEST WESTERN-THUNDERBIRD INN**
3000 Plank Rd (22401)
Rates: $35-$49;
Tel: (703) 786-7404

**DAYS INN FREDERICKSBURG NORTH**
14 Simpson Rd (22405)
Rates: $36-$43;
Tel: (703) 373-5340

**DAYS INN FREDERICKSBURG SOUTH**
5316 Jefferson Davis Hwy
(22401)
Rates: $36-$43;
Tel: (703) 898-6800

**DUNNING MILLS INN**
2305 C Jefferson Davis Hwy
(22401)
Rates: $55-$90;
Tel: (703) 373-1256

**HAMPTON INN**
2310 William St (22401)
Rates: $46-$55·
Tel: (703) 371-0330

**HOLIDAY INN FREDERICKSBURG SOUTH**
5324 Jefferson Davis Hwy
(22401)
Rates: $43-$58;
Tel: (703) 898-1102

**HOLIDAY INN-NORTH**
564 Warrenton Rd (22405)
Rates: $35-$55;
Tel: (703) 371-5550

**RAMADA INN-SPOTSYLVANIA MALL**
P. O. Box 36 (22404)
Rates: $45-$59;
Tel: (703) 786-8361

**ROYAL INN MOTEL**
5309 Jefferson Davis Hwy
(22401)
Rates: $32-$35;
Tel: (703) 891-2700

# FRONT ROYAL

**FRONT ROYAL MOTEL**
1400 Shenandoah Ave
(22630)
Rates: N/A;
Tel: (703) 635-4114

**SUPER 8 MOTEL**
111 South St (22630)
Rates: $37-$47;
Tel: (703) 636-4888

# GLADE SPRING

**GLADE ECONOMY INN**
P. O. Box 453 (24340)
Rates: $24-$32;
Tel; (703) 429-5131

# HAMPTON

**ARROW INN**
7 Semple Farm Rd (23666)
Rates: $37-$59;
Tel· (804) 865-0300

**DAYS INN-HAMPTON**
1918 Coliseum Dr (23666)
Rates: $37-$51;
Tel: (804) 826-4810

**HAMPTON INN**
1813 W Mercury Blvd (23666)
Rates. $40-$65;
Tel: (804) 838-8484

**HOLIDAY INN**
1815 W Mercury Blvd (23666)
Rates· $68-$88;
Tel: (804) 838-0200

**LA QUINTA MOTOR INN**
2138 W Mercury Blvd (23666)
Rates: $38-$55;
Tel: (804) 827-8680

**RED ROOF INN**
1925 Coliseum Dr (23666)
Rates: $34-$45;
Tel: (804) 838-1870

**SHERATON INN-COLISEUM**
1215 W Mercury Blvd (23666)
Rates: $59-$99;
Tel: (804) 838-5011

**STRAWBERRY BANKS MOTOR INN**
P. O. Box 3268 (23663)
Rates: $36-$55;
Tel: (804) 723-6061

# HARRISONBURG

**COMFORT INN**
1440 E Market St (22801)
Rates: $43-$55;
Tel: (703) 433-6066

## HARRISONBURG

**ECONO LODGE**
1703 E Market St (22801)
Rates: $35-$41;
Tel: (703) 433-2576

**HOJO INN
BY HOWARD JOHNSON**
P. O. Box 68 (22801)
Rates: $39-$49;
Tel: (703) 434-6771

**HOLIDAY INN**
1 Pleasant Valley Rd (22801)
Rates: $55-$59;
Tel: (703) 434-9981

**MOTEL 6**
10 Linda Ln (22801)
Rates: $25-$31;
Tel: (703) 433-6939

**REBEL'S ROOST MOTEL**
3317 S Main St (22801)
Rates: $28-$36;
Tel: (703) 434-9696

**ROCKINGHAM MOTEL**
4035 S Main St (22801)
Rates: $29-$35;
Tel: (703) 433-2538

**SCOTTISH INN**
Rt 11 N, Exit 65 on I-81
(22801)
Rates: N/A;
Tel: (703) 434-5301

**SHERATON
HARRISONBURG INN**
1400 E Market St (22801)
Rates: $57-$80;
Tel: (703) 433-2521

**VILLAGE INN**
Rt 1, Box 76 (22801)
Rates: $34-$50;
Tel: (703) 434-7355

## HILLSVILLE

**ECONO LODGE**
P. O. Box 275 (24343)
Rates: $32-$42;
Tel: (703) 728-9118

## HOPEWELL

**COMFORT INN**
5380 Oaklawn Blvd
(Prince George 23875)
Rates: $43-$63;
Tel: (804) 452-0022

## HOT SPRINGS

**CASCADES INN**
P. O. Drawer U (24445)
Rates: $125-$220;
Tel: (703) 839-5355

**HILLCREST MOTEL**
P. O. Box 656 (24445)
Rates: $32-$42;
Tel: (703) 839-5316

**ROSELOE MOTEL**
Rt 2, Box 590 (24445)
Rates: $34-$44;
Tel: (703) 839-5373

## IRVINGTON

**THE TIDES INN RESORT**
P. O. Box 480 (22480)
Rates: $120-$272;
Tel: (804) 438-5000

**TIDES LODGE RESORT**
P. O. Box 309 (22480)
Rates: $108-$240;
Tel: (804) 438-6000

## LEXINGTON

**BEST WESTERN KEYDET-
GENERAL MOTEL**
RFD 6, Box 31 (24450)
Rates: $36-$64;
Tel: (703) 463-2143

**COMFORT INN-
VIRGINIA HORSE CENTER**
P. O. Box 905 (24450)
Rates: $45-$65;
Tel: (703) 463-7311

**HOLIDAY INN**
P. O. Box 1108 (24450)
Rates: $48-$67;
Tel: (703) 463-7351

**HOWARD JOHNSON
MOTOR HOTEL**
6 Mi N on US 11 (24450)
Rates: $39-$73;
Tel: (703) 463-9181

**RAMADA INN LEXINGTON**
Rt 5, Box 381 (24450)
Rates: $46-$57;
Tel: (703) 463-6666

**THRIFTY INN**
820 S Main St (24450)
Rates: $29-$42;
Tel: (703) 463-2151

## LURAY

**INTOWN MOTEL**
410 W Main St (22835)
Rates: $32-$74;
Tel: (703) 743-6511

**RAMADA INN LURAY/
SHENANDOAH VALLEY**
P. O. Box 389 (22835)
Rates: $40-$86;
Tel: (703) 743-4521

## LYNCHBURG

**COMFORT INN**
P. O. Box 10729 (24506)
Rates: $53-$85;
Tel: (804) 847-9041

**ECONO LODGE**
P. O. Box 2028 (24501)
Rates: $33-$43;
Tel: (804) 847-1045

**HOLIDAY INN**
P. O. Box 10729 (24506)
Rates: $54-$64;
Tel: (804) 847-4424

**HOWARD JOHNSON
MOTEL**
P. O. Box 10729 (24506)
Rates: $46-$63;
Tel: (804) 845-7041

**RADISSON HOTEL
LYNCHBURG**
601 Main St (24504)
Rates: $60-$85;
Tel: (804) 528-2500

## MANASSAS

**BEST WESTERN MANASSAS**
8640 Mathis Ave (22110)
Rates: $43-$53;
Tel: (703) 368-7070

**HOJO INN**
7249 New Market Ct (22110)
Rates: $39-$51;
Tel: (703) 369-1700

**HOLIDAY INN MANASSAS**
10800 Van Dor Ln (22110)
Rates: $55-$59;
Tel: (703) 335-0000

**OLDE TOWNE INN**
9403 Main St (22110)
Rates: $29-$39;
Tel: (703) 368-9191

**RAMADA INN**
10820 Balls Ford Rd (22110)
Rates: $54-$75;
Tel: (703) 361-8000

**RED ROOF INN-
MANASSAS**
10610 Automotive Dr (22110)
Rates: $38-$47;
Tel: (703) 335-9333

## MARION

**ECONO LODGE-
MOUNT ROGERS**
P. O. Drawer R
(Chilhowie 24319)
Rates: $32-$48;
Tel: (703) 646-8981

**HOLIDAY INN**
1424 N Main St (24354)
Rates: $46-$53;
Tel: (703) 783-3193

## MARTINSVILLE

**BEST WESTERN MOTEL**
P. O. Box 1183 (24114)
Rates: $38-$48;
Tel: (703) 632-5611

**DUTCH INN MOTEL**
633 Virginia Ave
(Collinsville 24078)
Rates: $43-$95;
Tel: (703) 647-3721

**ECONO LODGE**
800 S Virginia Ave
(Collinsville 24078)
Rates: $32-$40;
Tel: (703) 647-3941

**FAIRYSTONE MOTEL**
P. O. Box 727 (24114)
Rates: $34-$45;
Tel: (703) 647-3941

## MOUNT JACKSON

**BEST WESTERN-
MT. JACKSON**
P. O. Box 777 (22842)
Rates: $44-$52;
Tel: (703) 477-2911

**THE WIDOW KIP'S**
Rt 1, Box 117 (22842)
Rates: $55-$70;
Tel: (703) 477-2400

## NATURAL BRIDGE

**THE NATURAL BRIDGE
RESORT & CONF CTR**
P. O. Box 57 (24578)
Rates: $39-$82;
Tel: (703) 291-2121

**WATTSTULL INN**
Rt 1 (Buchanan 24066)
Rates: $38-$44;
Tel: (703) 254-1551

## NEW MARKET

**BATTLEFIELD MOTEL**
Rt 1, Box 127 (22844)
Rates: $20-$48;
Tel: (703) 740-3105

**DAYS INN**
9360 George C Collins Pkwy
(22844)
Rates: $39-$65;
Tel: (703) 740-4100

**SHENVALEE MOTEL**
P. O. Box 930 (22844)
Rates: $36-$58;
Tel: (703) 740-3181

## NEWPORT NEWS

**AMERICAN TUDOR INN**
15540 Warwick Rd (23602)
Rates: $26-$49;
Tel: (804) 887-0180

**COMFORT INN**
12330 Jefferson Ave (23602)
Rates: $49-$60;
Tel: (804) 249-0200

**DAYS INN**
14747 Warwick Blvd (23602)
Rates: $34-$53;
Tel: (804) 874-0201

**DAYS INN-OYSTER POINT**
11829 Fishing Point Dr
(23606)
Rates: $42-$59;
Tel: (804) 873-6700

**HOLIDAY INN**
6128 Jefferson Ave (23605)
Rates: $52-$75;
Tel: (804) 826-4500

**HOST INN**
985 J Clyde Morris Blvd
(23601)
Rates: $30-$39;
Tel: (804) 599-3303

**KING JAMES
MOTOR HOTEL**
6045 Jefferson Ave (23605)
Rates: $30-$50;
Tel: (804) 245-2801

**KNIGHTS INN**
797 J Clyde Morris Blvd
(23601)
Rates: $29-$43;
Tel: (804) 595-6336

**RAMADA INN**
950 J Clyde Morris Blvd
(23601)
Rates: $40-$67;
Tel: (804) 599-4460

**REGENCY INN MOTEL**
13700 Warwick Blvd (23602)
Rates: $24-$39;
Tel: (804) 874-4100

**ROYAL INN**
12340 Warwick Blvd (23606)
Rates: $23-$38;
Tel: (804) 599-6035

# NORFOLK
(and Vicinity)

**COMFORT INN
TOWN POINT**
930 Virginia Beach Blvd
(23504)
Rates: $35-$70;
Tel: (804) 623-5700

**DAYS INN MILITARY CIRCLE**
5701 Chambers St (23502)
Rates: $36-$62;
Tel: (804) 461-0100

**ECONO LODGE
W. OCEAN VIEW BEACH**
9601 4th View St (23503)
Rates: $38-$53;
Tel: (804) 480-9611

**HOWARD JOHNSON
HOTEL NORFOLK
DOWNTOWN**
700 Monticello Ave (23510)
Rates: $65-$87;
Tel: (804) 627-5555

**LODGE AT LITTLE CREEK**
7969 Shore Dr (23518)
Rates: N/A;
Tel: (804) 588-3600

**MARRIOTT-
WATERSIDE HOTEL**
235 E Main St (23510)
Rates: $124-$600;
Tel: (804) 627-4200

**QUALITY INN-
LAKE WRIGHT**
6280 Northampton Blvd
(23502)
Rates: $47-$70;
Tel: (804) 461-6251

**RAMADA INN NORFOLK**
345 Granby St (23510)
Rates: $45-$75;
Tel: (804) 622-6682

**SCOTTISH INN**
1001 N Military Hwy (23502)
Rates: N/A;
Tel: (804) 461-4391

# PETERSBURG

**AMERICAN INN**
2209 County Dr (23803)
Rates: $31-$37;
Tel: (804) 733-2800

**BEST WESTERN
OF PETERSBURG**
405 E Washington St (23803)
Rates: $47-$65;
Tel: (804) 733-1776

**DAYS INN**
12208 S Crater Rd (23805)
Rates: $35-$49;
Tel: (804) 733-4400

**ECONO LODGE-SOUTH**
16905 Parkdale Rd (23805)
Rates: $28-$41;
Tel: (804) 862-2717

**ECONO LODGE WEST**
11974 S Crater Rd (23805)
Rates: $36-$45;
Tel: (804) 732-2900

**FLAGSHIP INN**
815 S Crater Rd (23803)
Rates: $32-$52;
Tel: (804) 861-3470

**HOLIDAY INN NORTH-
FT. LEE AREA**
I-95 & Washington St (23803)
Rates: $49-$67;
Tel: (804) 733-0730

**PETERSBURG NORTH
TRAVELODGE**
P. O. Box 126 (23834)
Rates: $27-$38;
Tel: (804) 526-4611

**QUALITY INN-
PETERSBURG SOUTH**
P. O. Box 1836 (23805)
Rates: $30-$48;
Tel: (804) 733-1152

**QUALITY INN-
STEVEN KENT**
P. O. Box 1536 (23805)
Rates: $35-$49;
Tel: (804) 733-0600

**TRAVELODGE**
16600 Sunnybrook Rd, Exit 12
(23805)
Rates: N/A;
Tel: (804) 733-5522

# PORTSMOUTH

**ECONO LODGE
OLDE TOWNE**
1031 London Blvd (23704)
Rates: $29-$49;
Tel: (804) 399-4414

**HOLIDAY INN-
PORTSMOUTH
WATERFRONT**
8 Crawford Pkwy (23704)
Rates: $69-$84;
Tel: (804) 393-2573

# RADFORD

**BEST WESTERN
RADFORD INN**
P. O. Box 1008 (24141)
Rates: $44-$64;
Tel: (703) 639-3000

**COMFORT INN**
P. O. Box 1008 (24141)
Rates: $39-$59;
Tel: (703) 639-4800

**DOGWOOD LODGE**
Rt 2, Box 257 (24141)
Rates: $24-$34;
Tel: (703) 639-9338

**EXECUTIVE MOTEL**
P. O. Box 708 (24141)
Rates: $27-$34;
Tel: (703) 639-1664

# RICHMOND

**ALPINE MOTEL**
7009 Brook Rd (23227)
Rates: $28-$42;
Tel: (804) 262-4798

**BEST WESTERN
GOVERNOR'S INN**
9848 Midlothian Tpke (23235)
Rates: $44-$58;
Tel: (804) 323-0007

**COMFORT INN**
2100 W Hundred Rd
(Chester 23831)
Rates: $53-$60;
Tel: (804) 751-0000

**COMFORT INN
CONFERENCE CENTER**
3200 W Broad St (23230)
Rates: $39-$45;
Tel: (804) 359-4061

**CRICKET INN**
7300 W Broad St (23294)
Rates: $39-$54;
Tel: (804) 672-8621

**DAYS INN**
1600 Robin Hood Rd (23220)
Rates: $38-$55;
Tel: (804) 353-1287

**DAYS INN**
2100 Dickens Rd (23230)
Rates: $52-$58;
Tel: (804) 282-3300

**DAYS INN-SOUTH**
6346 Midlothian Tpke (23225)
Rates: $40-$50;
Tel: (804) 276-6450

**ECONO LODGE-NORTH**
5221 Brook Rd (23227)
Rates: $38-$45;
Tel: (804) 266-7603

**HAMPTON INN**
5300 Airport Sq Ln
(Sandston 23150)
Rates: $69-$78;
Tel: (804) 222-8200

**HOJO INN**
801 E Parham Rd (23227)
Rates: $39-$79;
Tel: (804) 266-8753

**HOLIDAY INN-AIRPORT**
5203 Williamsburg Rd
(Sandston 23150)
Rates: $65-$75;
Tel: (804) 222-6450

**HOLIDAY INN-BELLS ROAD**
4303 Commerce Rd (23234)
Rates: $61-$80;
Tel: (804) 275-7891

**HOLIDAY INN CENTRAL**
3207 N Blvd (23230)
Rates: $49-$65;
Tel: (804) 359-9441

**HOLIDAY INN-
CROSSROADS**
2000 Staples Mill Rd (23230)
Rates: $55;
Tel: (804) 359-6061

**HOLIDAY INN-DOWNTOWN**
301 W Franklin St (23220)
Rates: $65-$75;
Tel: (804) 644-9871

**HOLIDAY INN
KOGER CENTER SOUTH**
1021 Koger Center Blvd
(23235)
Rates: $74-$84;
Tel: (804) 379-3800

**HOWARD JOHNSON
LODGE & SUITES-
DIAMOND STADIUM**
1501 Robin Hood Rd (23220)
Rates: $37-$39;
Tel: (804) 353-0116

**JAMES RIVER INN**
8008 W Broad St (23229)
Rates: $36-$49;
Tel: (804) 346-0000

**KNIGHTS INN**
5252 Airport Sq Ln (23150)
Rates: N/A;
Tel: (804) 226-4519

**LA QUINTA MOTOR INN**
6910 Midlothian Tpke (23225)
Rates: $42-$55;
Tel: (804) 745-7100

**MARRIOTT HOTEL-
DOWNTOWN**
500 E Broad St (23219)
Rates: $99-$700;
Tel: (804) 643-3400

**RED ROOF INN-BELLS RD**
4350 Commerce Rd (23234)
Rates: $31-$43;
Tel: (804) 271-7240

**RED ROOF INN-
CHIPPENHAUM**
100 Greshamwood Pl (23225)
Rates: $31-$41;
Tel: (804) 745-0600

**RESIDENCE INN**
2121 Dickens Rd (23230)
Rates: $99-$119;
Tel: (804) 285-8200

**RICHMOND
MARRIOTT HOTEL**
500 E Broad St (23219)
Rates: $89-$135;
Tel: (804) 643-3400

**SHERATON INN-AIRPORT**
4700 S Labumum Ave (23231)
Rates: $62-$95;
Tel: (804) 226-4300

**SHERATON PARK SOUTH**
9901 Midlothian Tpke (23235)
Rates: $59-$99;
Tel: (804) 323-1144

**SHONEY'S INN**
7007 West Broad St (23294)
Rates: N/A;
Tel: (804) 672-7007

## ROANOKE

**BEST WESTERN
COACHMAN INN**
235 Roanoke Rd
(Daleville 24083)
Rates: $39-$55;
Tel: (703) 992-1234

**COMFORT INN-AIRPORT**
3695 Thirlane Rd NW (24019)
Rates: $38-$50;
Tel: (703) 563-0229

**COMFORT INN TROUTVILLE**
2654 Lee Hwy
(Troutville 24175)
Rates: $39-$59;
Tel: (703) 992-5600

**HOLIDAY INN-AIRPORT**
6626 Thirlane Rd (24019)
Rates: $56-$79;
Tel: (703) 366-8861

369

**HOLIDAY INN-
CENTRAL/FRANKLIN RD**
1927 Franklin Rd SW (24014)
Rates: $38-$65;
Tel: (703) 343-0121

**HOLIDAY INN-
TANGLEWOOD**
4468 Starkey Rd SW (24014)
Rates: $54-$104;
Tel: (703) 774-4400

**HOWARD JOHNSON
LODGE-TROUTVILLE**
P. O. Box 100
(Troutville 24175)
Rates: $38-$70;
Tel: (703) 992-3000

**MARRIOTT-
ROANOKE AIRPORT**
2801 Hershberger Rd NW
(24017)
Rates: $58-$120;
Tel: (703) 563-9300

**OLYMPIA INN**
7120 Willliamson Rd (24019)
Rates: N/A;
Tel: (703) 366-7681

**ROANOKER
MOTOR LODGE**
7645 Williamson Rd (24019)
Rates: $22-$29;
Tel: (703) 362-3344

**SHERATON INN
ROANOKE AIRPORT**
2727 Ferndale Dr NW (24017)
Rates: $60;
Tel: (703) 372-4500

**TRAVELODGE**
2444 Lee Hwy S
(Troutville 24175)
Rates: $38-$45;
Tel: (703) 992-6700

## SALEM

**ARBORGATE INN**
301 Wildwood Rd (24153)
Rates: $23-$41;
Tel: (703) 389-0280

**BLUE JAY
BUDGET HOST INN**
5399 W Main St (24153)
Rates: $28-$36;
Tel: (703) 380-2080

**HOLIDAY INN**
1671 Skyview Rd (24153)
Rates: $52-$78;
Tel: (703) 389-7061

**QUALITY INN**
179 Sheraton Dr (24153)
Rates: $44-$57;
Tel: (703) 562-1912

## SOUTH HILL

**COMFORT INN MOTEL**
918 E Atlantic St (23970)
Rates: $34-$48;
Tel: (804) 447-2600

**ECONO LODGE**
623 E Atlantic St (23970)
Rates: $32-$44;
Tel: (804) 447-7116

**HOLIDAY INN**
P. O. Box 594 (23970)
Rates: $52-$62;
Tel: (804) 447-3123

## SPERRYVILLE

**THE CONYERS HOUSE**
Rt 1, Box 157 (22740)
Rates: $90-$195;
Tel: (703) 987-8025

## STAFFORD

**DAYS INN**
2868 Jefferson Davis Hwy
(22554)
Rates: $42-$55;
Tel: (703) 659-0022

## STAUNTON

**COMFORT INN**
1302 Richmond Ave (24401)
Rates: $38-$57;
Tel: (703) 886-5000

**DAYS INN**
Rt 2, Box 414 (24401)
Rates: $38-$50;
Tel: (703) 337-3031

**ECONO LODGE-
HESSIAN HOUSE**
Rt 2, Box 364 (24401)
Rates: $30-$49;
Tel: (703) 337-1231

**ECONO LODGE STAUNTON**
1031 Richmond Rd (24401)
Rates: $31-$47;
Tel: (703) 885-5158

**HOLIDAY INN OF STAUNTON**
P. O. Box 2526 (24401)
Rates: $46-$63;
Tel: (703) 248-5111

## SUFFOLK

**HOLIDAY INN-SUFFOLK**
2864 Pruden Blvd (23434)
Rates: $44-$58;
Tel: (804) 934-2311

## TROUTVILLE

**TRAVELODGE**
2444 Lee Hwy S (24175)
Rates: N/A;
Tel: (703) 992-6700

## VIRGINIA BEACH

**CRICKET INN**
5745 Northampton Blvd
(23455)
Rates: $28-$50;
Tel: (804) 460-3414

**ECONO LODGE
NORTHAMPTON**
5819 Northampton Blvd
(23455)
Rates: $34-$57;
Tel: (804) 464-9306

**EXECUTIVE INN**
717 S Military Hwy (23464)
Rates: N/A;
Tel: (800) 678-3466

**HOLIDAY INN AIRPORT**
5725 Northampton Blvd
(23455)
Rates: $48-$60;
Tel: (804) 464-9351

**LA QUINTA MOTOR INN**
192 Newtown Rd (23462)
Rates: $41-$58;
Tel: (803) 497-6620

**OCEAN HOLIDAY HOTEL**
2417 Atlantic Ave (23451)
Rates: $40-$120;
Tel: (804) 425-6920

**OCEAN ONE**
1801 Atlantic Ave (23451)
Rates: $48-$125;
Tel: (804) 437-9100

**PRINCESS ANNE INN**
2501 Atlantic Ave (23451)
Rates: $70-$125;
Tel: (804) 428-5611

**RED ROOF INN**
196 Ballard Ct (23462)
Rates: $26-$48;
Tel: (804) 490-0225

**THE THUNDERBIRD
MOTOR LODGE**
P. O. Box 506 (23451)
Rates: $30-$110;
Tel: (804) 428-3024

**TRAVELODGE/
VIRGINIA BEACH**
4800 Bonney Rd (23462)
Rates: $34-$53;
Tel: (804) 473-9745

## WARRENTON

**COMFORT INN**
6633 Lee Hwy (22186)
Rates: $39-$62;
Tel: (703) 349-8900

**HAMPTON INN**
501 Blackwell Rd (22186)
Rates: $47-$67;
Tel: (703) 349-4200

**HOJO INN**
6 Broadview Ave (22186)
Rates: $29-$34;
Tel: (703) 347-4141

## WAYNESBORO

**COMFORT INN-
WAYNESBORO**
6540 W Broad St (22980)
Rates: $40-$50;
Tel: (703) 942-1171

**DAYS INN-WAYNESBORO**
2060 Rosser Ave (22980)
Rates: $42-$62;
Tel: (703) 943-1101

**HOLIDAY INN**
P. O. Box 849 (22980)
Rates: $55-$62,
Tel: (703) 942-5201

## WILLIAMSBURG

**BEST WESTERN-
PATRICK HENRY INN**
P. O. Drawer S (23187)
Rates: $49-$99;
Tel: (804) 229-9540

**BEST WESTERN
WILIAMSBURG
WESTPARK HOTEL**
1600 Richmond Rd (23185)
Rates: $34-$50;
Tel: (804) 229-1134

**COMFORT INN-
HISTORIC AREA**
120 Bypass Rd (23185)
Rates: $35-$70;
Tel: (804) 229-2000

**THE COMMONWEALTH
INN**
1233 Richmond Rd (23185)
Rates: $25-$59;
Tel: (804) 253-1087

**FAMILY INNS OF AMERICA**
5413 Airport Rd (23185)
Rates: $49-$129;
Tel: (804) 253-0999

**GEORGE WASHINGTON
INN**
500 Merrimac Tr (23185)
Rates: $39-$79;
Tel: (804) 220-1410

**GOVERNOR'S INN**
P. O. Box 1776 (23185)
Rates: $39-$80;
Tel: (804) 229-1000

**HERITAGE INN**
1324 Richmond Rd (23185)
Rates: $32-$66;
Tel: (804) 229-6220

**HOLIDAY INN-
DOWNTOWN**
814 Capitol Landing Rd
(23185)
Rates: $51-$99;
Tel: (804) 229-0200

**HOWARD JOHNSON
LODGE-HISTORIC AREA**
7135 Pocahontas Tr (23185)
Rates: $39-$99;
Tel: (804) 229-6900

**QUARTERPATH INN**
620 York St (23185)
Rates: $33-$62;
Tel: (804) 220-0960

**RAMADA INN-
HISTORIC AREA**
351 York St (23185)
Rates: $50-$100
Tel: (804) 229-4100

**WILLAIMSBURG CENTER**
600 Bypass Rd (23185)
Rates: $39-$79;
Tel: (804) 220-2800

**YORK STREET
HOTEL SUITES**
351 York St (23187)
Rates: $115-$159;
Tel: (804) 229-4100

## WINCHESTER

**BEST WESTERN LEE-
JACKSON MOTOR INN**
711 Millwood Ave (22601)
Rates: $37-$49;
Tel: (703) 662-4154

**BUDGETEL INN**
800 Millwood Ave (22601)
Rates: $38-$47;
Tel: (703) 678-0800

**HOLIDAY INN**
1050 Millwood Pike (22601)
Rates: $49-$69;
Tel: (703) 667-3300

**MOHAWK MOTEL**
RR 9, Box 48 (22603)
Rates: $23-$30;
Tel: (703) 667-1410

**QUALITY INN EAST**
603 Millwood Ave (22601)
Rates: $40-$55;
Tel: (703) 667-2250

**TOURIST CITY MOTEL**
214 Millwood Ave (22601)
Rates: $23-$31;
Tel: (703) 662-9011

**TRAVELODGE**
160 Front Royal Pike (22601)
Rates: $35-$95;
Tel: (703) 665-0685

**TRAVELODGE
OF WINCHESTER**
1825 Dominion Ave (22601)
Rates: $39-$53;
Tel: (703) 665-0865

## WOODBRIDGE

**DAYS INN
POTOMAC MILLS**
14619 Potomac Mills Rd
(22192)
Rates: $63-$80;
Tel: (703) 494-443

## WOODSTOCK

**HAMILTON MOTEL**
Rt 2, US 11 (22664)
Rates: $29-$40;
Tel: (703) 459-4086

## WYTHEVILLE

**BEST WESTERN
WYTHEVILLE INN**
355 Nye Rd (24382)
Rates: $42-$105;
Tel: (703) 228-7300

**DAYS INN**
150 Malin Dr (24382)
Rates: $36-$49;
Tel: (703) 228-5500

**ECONO LODGE**
P. O. Box 530 (24382)
Rates: $28-$46;
Tel: (703) 228-5517

**HOJO INN**
P. O. Box 552 (24382)
Rates: $30-$55;
Tel: (703) 228-3188

**HOLIDAY INN**
P. O. Box 697 (24382)
Rates: $43-$65;
Tel: (703) 228-5483

**INTERSTATE
MOTOR LODGE**
705 Chapman Rd (24382)
Rates: $23-$29;
Tel: (703) 228-8618

**JOHNSON'S MOTEL**
US Hwy, 11 S (24382)
Rates: N/A;
Tel: (703) 228-4812

**MACWYTHE INN**
P. O. Box 442 (24382)
Rates: $27-$32;
Tel: (800) 445-9601

**RAMADA INN**
955 Peppers Ferry Rd (24382)
Rates: $35-$52;
Tel: (703) 228-6000

**SUPER 8 MOTEL**
130 Nye Cir (24382)
Rates: $35-$39;
Tel: (703) 228-6620

## YORKTOWN

**YORKTOWN
MOTOR LODGE**
8829 George Washington Hwy
(23692)
Rates: $24-$40;
Tel: (804) 898-5451

# WASHINGTON

## ABERDEEN

**CENTRAL PARK MOTEL**
6504 Olympic Hwy (98520)
Rates: N/A;
Tel: (206) 533-1210

**FLAMINGO MOTEL**
1120 E Wishkah (98520)
Rates: $29-$69;
Tel: (206) 532-4103

**NORDIC INN**
1700 S Boone St (98520)
Rates: $30-$52;
Tel: (206) 533-0100

**OLYMPIC INN**
616 W Heron St (98520)
Rates: $40-$70,
Tel: (206) 533-4200

**RED LION MOTEL**
521 W Wishkah (98520)
Rates: $50-$75;
Tel: (206) 532-5210

**THUNDERBIRD MOTEL**
410 West Wishkah (98520)
Rates: N/A;
Tel: (206) 532-3153

**TRAVELURE MOTEL**
623 W Wishkah (98520)
Rates: $31-$40;
Tel: (206) 532-3280

## ANACORTES

**ANACORTES INN**
3006 Commercial Ave
(98221)
Rates: $40-$58;
Tel: (206) 293-3153

**ISLANDS INN**
3401 Commercial Ave
(98221)
Rates: $54-$95;
Tel: (206) 293-4644

**SAN JUAN MOTEL**
1103 6th St (98221)
Rates: N/A;
Tel: (206) 293-5105

**SHIP HARBOR INN**
5316 Ferry Terminal Rd
(98221)
Rates: $38-$72;
Tel: (206) 293-5177

## ARLINGTON

**SMOKEY POINT
MOTOR INN**
17329 Smokey Point Dr
(98223)
Rates: $36-$47;
Tel: (206) 659-8561

## ASHFORD

**CABIN AT THE BERRY**
37221 Hwy 706 East (98304)
Rates: N/A;
Tel: (206) 569-2628

## AUBURN

**VAL-U INN**
9 14th Ave NW (98001)
Rates: $56-$69;
Tel: (206) 735-9600

## BAINBRIDGE ISLAND

**BAINBRIDGE INN**
9200 Hemlock Ave NE (98110)
Rates: N/A;
Tel: (206) 842-7564

## BELLEVUE

**BELLEVUE MOTEL**
1657 Bellevue Way NE
(98004)
Rates: N/A;
Tel: (206) 454-3042

**BEST WESTERN
GREENWOOD HOTEL**
625 116th Ave NE (98004)
Rates: $69;
Tel: (206) 455-9444

**HOLIDAY INN-BELLEVUE**
11211 Main St (98004)
Rates: $80-$95;
Tel: (206) 455-5240

**KANES MOTEL**
14644 SE Eastgate Way
(98007)
Rates: N/A;
Tel: (206) 746-8201

**PACIFIC GUEST SUITES**
915 118th Ave SE (98005)
Rates: N/A;
Tel: (206) 454-7888

**RED LION HOTEL**
300 112th Ave SE (98004)
Rates: $132-$168,
Tel: (206) 455-1300

**RED LION INN/
BELLEVUE CENTER**
818 112th Ave NE (98004)
Rates: $87-$129;
Tel: (206) 455-1515

**THE RESIDENCE INN
BY MARRIOTT SEATTLE EAST**
14455 NE 29th Pl (98007)
Rates: $129-$189;
Tel: (206) 882-1222

## BELLINGHAM

**ANDERSON CREEK LODGE**
5602 Mission Rd (98226)
Rates: $85-$125;
Tel: (206) 966-2126

**COACHMAN INN**
120 Samish Way (98225)
Rates: $54-$63;
Tel: (206) 671-9000

**KEY MOTEL**
212 N Samish Way (98225)
Rates: $36-$54;
Tel: (206) 733-4060

**VAL-U INN**
805 Lakeway Dr (98226)
Rates: $44-$63;
Tel: (206) 671-9600

## BINGEN

**BINGEN SCHOOL INN**
Humboldt & Cedar Sts (98605)
Rates: N/A;
Tel: (509) 493-3363

## BOTHELL

**WAGON WHEEL MOTEL**
8042 NE Bothell Way (98011)
Rates: N/A;
Tel: (206) 486-6631

## BREMERTON

**DUNES MOTEL**
3400 11th St (98312)
Rates: $36-$44;
Tel: (206) 377-0093

**FLAGSHIP INN**
4320 Kitsap Way (98312)
Rates: $49-$59;
Tel: (206) 479-6566

**MIDWAY INN**
2909 Wheaton Way (98310)
Rates: $45-$48;
Tel: (206) 479-2909

**NENDELS SUITES**
4303 Kitsap Way (98312)
Rates: $49-$84;
Tel: (206) 377-4402

## BREWSTER

**BREWSTER MOTEL**
806 Bridge St (98812)
Rates: N/A;
Tel: (509) 689-2625

## BRIDGEPORT

**STIRLING MOTEL**
1717 Foster Ave (98813)
Rates: N/A;
Tel: (509) 686-4821

## BURLINGTON

**STERLING MOTOR INN**
866 S Burlington Blvd (98233)
Rates: $35-$55;
Tel: (206) 757-0071

## CASHMERE

**VILLAGE INN MOTEL**
229 Cottage Ave (98815)
Rates: $25-$62;
Tel: (206) 782-3522

## CASTLE ROCK

**TIMBERLAND MOTOR INN**
1271 Mt St. Helens Way
(98611)
Rates: $35-$48;
Tel: (206) 274-6002

## CATHLAMET

**CATHLAMET HOTEL**
69 Main St (98612)
Rates: N/A;
Tel: (800) 446-0454

**GALLERY B & B**
At Little Cape Horn (98612)
Rates: N/A;
Tel: (206) 425-7395

## CENTRALIA

**FERRYMAN'S INN**
1003 Eckerson Rd (98531)
Rates: $34-$39;
Tel: (206) 330-2094

**HUNTLEY INN**
702 W Harrison Ave (98531)
Rates: $39-$46;
Tel: (206) 736-2875

**PARK MOTEL**
1011 Belmont Ave (98531)
Rates: $29-$38;
Tel: (206) 736-9333

**PEPPERTREE WEST MOTOR INN**
1208 Alder St (98531)
Rates: $30-$38;
Tel: (206) 736-1124

## CHELAN

**BRICKHOUSE INN BED & BREAKFAST**
304 Wapato St (98816)
Rates: N/A;
Tel: (509) 682-4791

**LAKE CHELAN MOTEL**
2044 West Woodin Ave (98816)
Rates: N/A;
Tel: (509) 682-2742

## CHENEY

**WILLOW SPRINGS MOTEL**
5 B St (99004)
Rates: $35-$41;
Tel: (509) 235-5138

## CHEWELAH

**NORDLIG MOTEL**
101 W Grant St (99109)
Rates: $33-$39;
Tel: (509) 935-6704

## CLARKSTON

**NENDELS VALU INN**
222 Bridge St (99403)
Rates: $35-$45;
Tel: (509) 758-1631

**SUNSET MOTEL**
1200 Bridge St, US Hwy 12 (99403)
Rates: N/A;
Tel: (800) 845-5223

# CLE ELUM

**BONITA MOTEL**
906 E First St (98922)
Rates: N/A;
Tel: (509) 674-2380

**CEDARS MOTEL**
1001 E 1st St (98922)
Rates: $29-$40;
Tel: (509) 674-5535

**STEWART LODGE**
805 W First St (98922)
Rates: $40-$53;
Tel: (509) 674-4548

**TIMBER LODGE MOTEL**
301 W First St (98922)
Rates: $40-$50;
Tel: (509) 674-5966

# COLVILLE

**BEAVER LODGE RESORT**
2430 Hwy 20 East (99114)
Rates: N/A;
Tel: (509) 684-5657

**BENNY'S PANORAMA MOTEL**
915 South Main St (99114)
Rates: N/A;
Tel: (509) 684-2517

# CONNELL

**TUMBLEWOOD MOTEL**
433 South Columbia (99326)
Rates: N/A;
Tel: (509) 234-2081

# COPALIS BEACH

**BEACHWOOD RESORT**
P. O. Box 116 (98536)
Rates: N/A;
Tel: (206) 289-2177

# COULEE CITY

**BLUE TOP MOTEL**
109 N 6th St (99115)
Rates: $25-$45;
Tel: (509) 632-5596

**LAKEVIEW MOTEL**
HCR 1, Box 11 (99115)
Rates: N/A;
Tel: (509) 632-5792

# COULEE DAM

**COULEE HOUSE MOTEL**
110 Roosevelt Way (99116)
Rates: $44-$58;
Tel: (509) 633-1101

**PONDEROSA MOTEL**
10 Lincoln St (99116)
Rates: $36-$56;
Tel: (509) 633-2100

# DEER PARK

**LOVE'S VICTORIAN BED & BREAKFAST**
North 31317 Cedar Rd (99006)
Rates: N/A;
Tel: (509) 276-6939

# EASTSOUND

**NORTH BEACH INN**
P. O. Box 80 (98245)
Rates: N/A;
Tel: (206) 376-4793

# EATONVILLE

**LAGRANDE MOTEL**
46719 Mt Hwy East (98348)
Rates: N/A;
Tel: (206) 832-4912

# EDMONDS

**ANDY'S MOTEL**
22201 Hwy 99 (98020)
Rates: N/A;
Tel: (206) 776-6080

**K & E MOTOR INN**
23921 Hwy 99 (98020)
Rates: $39-$54;
Tel: (206) 778-2181

# ELLENSBURG

**BEST WESTERN ELLENSBURG INN**
1700 Canyon Rd (98926)
Rates: $40-$55;
Tel: (509) 925-9801

**ELLENSBURG REGAL LODGE**
300 W 6th St (98926)
Rates: $35-$155;
Tel: (509) 925-3116

**HAROLDS MOTEL**
601 N Water (98926)
Rates: $29-$46;
Tel: (509) 925-4141

**I-90 INN MOTEL**
1390 Dollar Way Rd (98926)
Rates: $30-$44;
Tel: (509) 925-9844

**NITES INN**
1200 S Ruby (98926)
Rates: $34-$41;
Tel: (509) 962-9600

# EPHRATA

**LARIAT MOTEL**
1639 Basin St SW (98823)
Rates: N/A;
Tel: (509) 754-2437

# EVERETT

**NENDEL'S INN**
2800 Pacific Ave (98201)
Rates: $46-$60;
Tel: (206) 258-4141

**NORTHWEST MOTOR INN**
9602 19th Ave SE (98208)
Rates: $39-$60;
Tel: (206) 337-9090

**QUALITY INN HOTEL & CONFERENCE CENTER**
101 128th St SE (98208)
Rates: $59-$75;
Tel: (206) 745-2555

**ROYAL MOTOR INN**
952 N Broadway (98201)
Rates: N/A;
Tel: (206) 259-5177

**TOPPER MOTEL**
1030 N Broadway (98201)
Rates: N/A;
Tel: (206) 259-3151

## FEDERAL WAY

**SUPER 8 MOTEL**
1688 S 348th St (98003)
Rates: N/A;
Tel: (206) 838-8808

## FORKS

**KALALOCH LODGE**
HC 80, Box 1100 (98331)
Rates: $55-$125;
Tel: (206) 962-2271

**MANITOU LODGE**
P. O. Box 600 (98331)
Rates: $35-$65;
Tel: (206) 374-6295

**TOWN MOTEL**
HC 80, Box 350 (98331)
Rates: N/A;
Tel: (206) 374-6231

## FREELAND

**HARBOUR INN MOTEL**
1606 Main St (98249)
Rates: $35-$62;
Tel: (206) 321-6900

## FRIDAY HARBOR

**ISLANDS WEST
ALL SUITES INN**
680 Spring St (98250)
Rates: $68-$198;
Tel: (206) 378-3031

**SAN JUAN INN**
P. O. Box 776 (98250)
Rates: N/A;
Tel: (206) 378-2070

**WHARFSIDE
BED & BREAKFAST**
P. O. Box 1212 (98250)
Rates: N/A;
Tel: (206) 378-5661

## GIG HARBOR

**NO CABBAGES MOTEL**
7712 Goodman Dr NW
(98332)
Rates: N/A;
Tel: (206) 858-7797

**THE PARSONAGE
BED & BREAKFAST**
4107 Burnham Dr (98332)
Rates: N/A;
Tel: (206) 851-8654

**WESTWYND MOTEL**
6703 144 St NW (98332)
Rates: N/A;
Tel: (206) 857-4047

## GLACIER

**MT BAKER CHALET**
9857 Mt Baker Hwy (98244)
Rates: N/A;
Tel: (206) 599-2405

## GOLDENDALE

**PONDEROSA MOTEL**
775 E Broadway St (98620)
Rates: $32-$41;
Tel: (509) 773-5842

## HOME VALLEY

**HOME VALLEY
BED & BREAKFAST**
P. O. Box 377 (98648)
Rates: N/A;
Tel: (509) 427-7070

## HOQUIAM

**NENDELS VALU INN**
910 Simpson Ave (98550)
Rates: $40-$75;
Tel: (206) 532-8161

**SNORE & WHISKER MOTEL**
3031 Simpson Ave (98550)
Rates: N/A;
Tel: (206) 532-5060

## ILWACO

**101 HACIENDAS**
101 Brumbach (98624)
Rates: N/A;
Tel: (206) 642-8459

## IONE

**PORTER'S PLAZA MOTEL**
103 S 2nd Ave (99139)
Rates: N/A;
Tel: (509) 442-3534

## KALAMA

**COLUMBIA INN MOTEL**
602 NE Frontage Rd (98625)
Rates: $30-$39;
Tel: (206) 673-2855

## KELSO

**KELSO INN MOTEL**
505 N Pacific (98626)
Rates: $29-$38;
Tel: (206) 636-4610

**MOTEL 6**
106 Minor Rd (98626)
Rates: $31-$37;
Tel: (206) 425-3229

**RED LION INN**
510 Kelso Dr (98626)
Rates: $80-$97;
Tel: (206) 636-4400

## KENNEWICK

**CAVANAUGH'S
AT COLUMBIA CENTER**
1101 N Columbia Center Blvd
(99336)
Rates: $58-$88;
Tel: (509) 783-0611

**NENDEL'S MOTOR INN**
2811 W 2nd Ave (99336)
Rates: $43-$51;
Tel: (509) 735-9511

**SHANIKO INN**
321 N Johnson St (99336)
Rates: $45-$53;
Tel: (509) 735-6385

**TAPADERA BUDGET INN**
300A N Ely (99336)
Rates: $35-$55;
Tel: (509) 783-6191

## KENT

**DAYS INN OF KENT**
1711 W Meeker St (98032)
Rates: $45-$50;
Tel; (206) 854-1950

**HOMECOURT
ALL SUITE HOTEL**
6329 S 212th (98032)
Rates: $70-$85;
Tel: (206) 395-3800

**VAL U INN**
22420 84th Ave S (98032)
Rates $48-$66;
Tel. (206) 872-5525

## KIRKLAND

**BEST WESTERN
ARNOLD'S MOTOR INN**
12223 NE 116th (98034)
Rates: $53-$79;
Tel: (206) 822-2300

**LA QUINTA MOTOR INN**
10530 NE Northup Way
(98033)
Rates: $51-$74;
Tel: (206) 828-6585

## LAKE STEVENS

**PEONY HOUSE
BED & BREAKFAST**
1602 E Lakeshore (98258)
Rates: N/A;
Tel: (206) 334-1046

## LANGLEY

**STRAWBRIDGE INN**
4667 S Strawbridge Ln
(98260)
Rates: N/A;
Tel: (206) 321-6567

## LEAVENWORTH

**CANYONS INN**
185 Hwy 2 (98826)
Rates: $56-$70;
Tel: (800) 537-9382

**DER RITTERHOF
MOTOR INN**
190 Hwy 2 (98826)
Rates: $59-$65;
Tel: (800) 255-5845

**THE EVERGREEN INN**
1117 Front St (98826)
Rates: $35-$90;
Tel: (509) 548-5515

**INGALLS TRADING POST**
3057 US Hwy 97 (98826)
Rates: N/A;
Tel: (509) 548-5142

**OBERTAL MOTOR INN**
922 Commercial St (98826)
Rates: $61-$75;
Tel. (800) 537-9382

**PHIPPEN'S
BED & BREAKFAST**
1226 Front St (98826)
Rates: N/A;
Tel: (800) 666-9806

**RIVER'S EDGE LODGE**
8401 Hwy 2 (98826)
Rates: $35-$70;
Tel: (509) 548-7612

## LONG BEACH

**ANCHORAGE
MOTOR COURT**
Rt 1, Box 581 (98631)
Rates: $52-$98;
Tel: (206) 642-2351

**CHAUTAUQUA LODGE**
304 North 14th (98631)
Rates: N/A;
Tel: (206) 642-4401

**LONG BEACH MOTEL**
12th South & Pacific (98631)
Rates: N/A;
Tel: (206) 642-3500

**NENDEL'S EDGEWATER INN**
P. O. Box 793 (98631)
Rates: $42-$85;
Tel: (206) 642-2311

**O'CONNOR'S
SHAMAN MOTEL**
115 3rd St SW (98631)
Rates: $34-$84;
Tel: (206) 642-3714

**OUR PLACE AT THE BEACH**
P. O. Box 266 (98631)
Rates: $45-$55;
Tel; (206) 642-3793

**SAND LO MOTEL**
1910 Pacific Hwy (98631)
Rates: N/A;
Tel: (206) 642-2600

**THE SANDS MOTEL**
Box 531, Hwy 103 (98631)
Rates: N/A;
Tel: (206) 642-2100

## LONGVIEW

**HUDSON MANOR MOTEL**
1616 Hudson St (98632)
Rates: $26-$38;
Tel: (206) 425-1100

**LEWIS & CLARK
MOTOR INN**
838 15th Ave (98632)
Rates: $32-$41;
Tel: (206) 423-6460

**TOWN CHALET MOTEL**
1722 Washington Way
(98632)
Rates: $29-$41;
Tel: (206) 423-2020

**THE TOWNHOUSE**
744 Washington Way (98632)
Rates: $26-$38;
Tel: (206) 423-7200

## LYNNWOOD

**THE RESIDENCE INN
BY MARRIOTT-SEATTLE**
18200 Alderwood Mall Blvd
(98037)
Rates: $120-$170;
Tel: (206) 771-1100

## MARYSVILLE

**BEST WESTERN TULALIP INN**
P. O. Box 426 (98270)
Rates: $61-$71;
Tel: (206) 659-4488

**THE VILLAGE MOTOR INN**
235 Beech St (98270)
Rates: $45-$59;
Tel: (206) 659-0005

## MAZAMA

**LOST RIVER RESORT**
Harts Pass Hwy (98833)
Rates: N/A;
Tel: (509) 996-2537

## METALINE FALLS

**CIRCLE MOTEL**
HCZ Box 616, Hwy 31
(99153)
Rates: N/A;
Tel: (509) 446-4343

## MOCLIPS

**HI TIDE
OCEAN BEACH RESORT**
P. O. Box 308 (98562)
Rates: $64-$149;
Tel: (206) 276-4142

## MONROE

**BROOKSIDE MOTEL**
19930 Hwy 2 (98272)
Rates: N/A;
Tel: (206) 794-8832

## MONTESANO

**MONTE SQUARE MOTEL**
518 1/2 South 1st St (98563)
Rates: N/A;
Tel: (206) 249-4424

## MORTON

**ROY'S MOTEL**
161 2nd St, Hwy 7 (98356)
Rates: N/A;
Tel: (206) 496-5000

## MOSES LAKE

**EL RANCHO MOTEL**
1214 S Pioneer Way (98837)
Rates: N/A;
Tel: (800) 341-8000

**HALLMARK INN**
3000 Marina Dr (98837)
Rates: N/A;
Tel: (800) 235-4255

**INTERSTATE INN**
2801 West Broadway (98837)
Rates: N/A;
Tel: (509) 765-1777

**LAKESIDE MOTEL**
802 West Broadway (98837)
Rates: N/A;
Tel: (509) 765-8651

**NENDEL'S INN**
2801 W Broadway (98837)
Rates: $38-$50;
Tel: (509) 765-1777

**SAGE "N" SAND MOTEL**
1011 S Pioneer Way (98837)
Rates: N/A;
Tel: (800) 336-0454

**SHILO INN**
1819 E Kittleson (98837)
Rates: $62-$77;
Tel: (509) 765-9317

**SUNLAND MOTOR INN**
309 E Third Ave (98837)
Rates: N/A;
Tel: (509) 765-1170

## MOUNT RAINIER

**RAINIER COUNTRY CABINS**
P. O. Box IRS (98304)
Rates: N/A;
Tel: (206) 569-2355

## MOUNT VERNON

**BEST WESTERN
COTTONTREE INN**
2300 Market Pl (98273)
Rates: $59-$72;
Tel: (206) 428-5678

**BEST WESTERN
MOTOR INN**
300 W College Way (98273)
Rates: $42-$67;
Tel: (206) 424-4287

**MOUNT VERNON
TRAVELODGE**
1910 Freeway Dr (98273)
Rates: $45-$68;
Tel: (206) 428-7020

**TOWN & COUNTRY
MOTOR INN**
2009 Riverside Dr (98273)
Rates: $40-$57;
Tel: (206) 424-4141

**WEST WINDS MOTEL**
2020 Riverside Dr (98273)
Rates: N/A;
Tel: (206) 424-4224

**WHISPERING FIRS**
1957 Kanako Ln (98273)
Rates: N/A;
Tel: (206) 428-1990

**THE WHITE SWAN INN**
1388 Moore Rd (98273)
Rates: N/A;
Tel: (206) 445-6805

## NEWPORT

**NEWPORT CITY INN**
220 N Washington, Box 9
(99156)
Rates: N/A;
Tel: (509) 447-3436

# OAK HARBOR

**ACORN MOTOR INN**
8066 State Hwy 20 (98277)
Rates: $41-$62;
Tel: (206) 675-6646

**THE AULD HOLLAND INN**
5861 N SR 20 (98277)
Rates: $45-$78;
Tel: (206) 675-2288

**MARANATHA SEAHORSE
BED & BREAKFAST**
4487 N Moran Beach Ln
(98277)
Rates: N/A,
Tel: (206) 679-2075

# OCEAN CITY

**WEST WINDS
RESORT MOTEL**
Rt 4, Box 160 (98569)
Rates: N/A;
Tel: (206) 289-3448

# OCEAN PARK

**OCEAN PARK RESORT**
P. O. Box 339 (98640)
Rates: $40-$61;
Tel: (206) 665-4585

**SUNSET VIEW RESORT**
256th & Park Ave (98640)
Rates: N/A;
Tel: (206) 665-4494

**SHAKTI COVE COTTAGES**
P. O. Box 385 (98640)
Rates: N/A;
Tel: (206) 665-4000

# OCEAN SHORES

**THE CANTERBURY INN**
643 Ocean Shores Blvd
(98569)
Rates: $64-$160;
Tel: (206) 289-3317

**CASA DEL ORO MOTEL**
667 Point Brown Ave NW
(98569)
Rates: N/A;
Tel: (206) 289-2281

**DISCOVERY INN**
1031 Discovery Ave SE
(98569)
Rates: $40-$76;
Tel: (206) 289-3371

**GIRCHE GUMEE MOTEL**
648 Ocean Shores Blvd NW
(98569)
Rates: $35-$75;
Tel: (206) 289-3323

**GREY GULL
CONDOMINIUM MOTEL**
651 Ocean Shores Blvd
(98569)
Rates: $75-$143;
Tel: (206) 289-3381

**THE POLYNESIAN
CONDOMINIUM RESORT**
615 Ocean Shores Blvd
(98569)
Rates: $42-$149;
Tel: (206) 289-3361

**POLYNESIAN RESORT**
291 Ocean Shores Blvd
(98569)
Rates: N/A;
Tel: (800) 562-4836

**ROYAL PACIFIC MOTEL**
781 Ocean Shores Blvd
(98569)
Rates: N/A;
Tel: (206) 289-3306

# OKANOGAN

**CEDARS INN**
One Apple Way (98840)
Rates: N/A;
Tel: (509) 422-6431

**PONDEROSA
MOTOR LODGE**
1034 S 2nd Ave (98840)
Rates: $27-$37;
Tel: (509) 422-0400

# OLYMPIA

**BEST WESTERN-
ALADDIN MOTOR INN**
900 Capitol Way (98501)
Rates: $52-$68;
Tel: (206) 352-7200

**BEST WESTERN
TUMWATER INN**
5188 Capitol Blvd (98501)
Rates: $48-$62;
Tel: (206) 956-1235

**CAPITAL INN MOTEL**
120 College St SE (98503)
Rates: $47-$62;
Tel: (206) 493-1991

**GOLDEN GAVEL
MOTOR HOTEL**
909 Capitol Way (98501)
Rates: $29-$42;
Tel: (206) 352-8533

**LEE STREET SUITES**
348 Lee St SW (98501)
Rates: N/A;
Tel: (206) 943-8391

**QUALITY INN**
2300 Evergreen Park Dr
(98502)
Rates: $69-$89;
Tel: (206) 943-4000

**SHALIMAR SUITES**
5895 Capital Blvd S (98501)
Rates: N/A;
Tel: (206) 943-8391

**TYEE HOTEL**
500 Tyee Dr
(Tumwater 98502)
Rates: $62-$71;
Tel: (206) 352-0511

# OLYMPIC
NATIONAL PARK

**LOG CABIN RESORT**
6540 E Beach Rd (98362)
Rates: $50-$75;
Tel: (206) 928-3325

# OMAK

**LEISURE VILLAGE MOTEL**
630 Okoma Dr (98841)
Rates: $33-$44;
Tel: (509) 826-4442

## OROVILLE

**RED APPLE INN**
1815 Main St (98844)
Rates: N/A;
Tel: (509) 476-3694

## OTHELLO

**ALADDIN MOTOR INN**
1020 E Cedar (99344)
Rates: $33-$50;
Tel: (509) 488-5671

## PACKWOOD

**MOUNTAIN VIEW
LODGE MOTEL**
P. O. Box 525 (98361)
Rates: $28-$70;
Tel: (206) 494-5555

**WOODLAND MOTEL**
11890 US 12 (Randle 98377)
Rates: $20-$40;
Tel: (206) 494-6766

## PASCO

**HALLMARK MOTEL**
720 W Lewis St (99301)
Rates: $27-$36;
Tel: (509) 547-7766

**RED LION MOTOR INN**
2525 N 20th Ave (99301)
Rates: $70-$90;
Tel: (509) 547-0701

**VAL-U INN**
1800 W Lewis St (99301)
Rates: $46-$59;
Tel: (509) 547-0791

## POMEROY

**PIONEER MOTEL**
1201 Main St, Box 579
(99347)
Rates: N/A;
Tel: (509) 843-9960

## PORT ANGELES

**AGGIE'S INN**
602 E Front St (98362)
Rates: $46-$68;
Tel: (206) 457-0471

**DAN DEE MOTEL**
132 E Lauridsen Blvd (98362)
Rates: N/A;
Tel: (206) 457-5404

**INDIAN VALLEY MOTEL**
7020 Hwy 101 West (98362)
Rates: N/A;
Tel: (206) 928-3266

**LAKE CRESCENT
LODGE RESORT**
HC 62, Box 11 (98362)
Rates: $64-$114;
Tel: (206) 928-3211

**THE POND MOTEL**
196 Hwy 101W (98362)
Rates: $28-$54;
Tel: (206) 452-8422

**RED LION BAYSHORE INN**
221 N Lincoln St (98362)
Rates: $83-$122;
Tel: (206) 452-9215

## PORT HADLOCK

**PORT HADLOCK INN**
201 Alcohol Loop Rd (98339)
Rates: N/A;
Tel: (206) 385-5801

## PORT TOWNSEND

**BISHOP VICTORIA
GUEST SUITES**
714 Washington St (98368)
Rates: $54-$98;
Tel: (206) 385-6122

**HARBORSIDE INN**
330 Benedict St (98368)
Rates: $45-$94;
Tel: (206) 385-7909

**PORT TOWNSEND MOTEL**
2020 Washington St (98368)
Rates: $48-$90;
Tel: (206) 385-2211

**THE TIDES INN**
1807 Water St (98368)
Rates: $58-$135;
Tel: (206) 385-0595

**THE WATER STREET HOTEL**
Quincy St Dock (98368)
Rates: $40-$55;
Tel: (206) 385-5467

## POULSBO

**POULSBO'S
EVERGREEN MOTEL**
18680 Hwy 305 (98370)
Rates: $42-$54;
Tel: (206) 779-3921

## PROSSER

**PROSSER MOTEL**
206 6th St (99350)
Rates: $24-$35;
Tel: (509) 786-2555

## PULLMAN

**AMERICAN TRAVEL INN**
515 S Grand (99163)
Rates: $32-$42;
Tel: (509) 334-3500

**NENDELS INN**
915 SE Main (99163)
Rates: N/A;
Tel: (509) 332-2646

**QUALITY INN PARADISE
CREEK MOTOR INN**
SE 1050 Johnson Ave (99163)
Rates: $57-$82;
Tel: (509) 332-0500

## PYUALLUP

**NORTHWEST MOTOR INN**
1409 S Meridian (98371)
Rates: $42-$51;
Tel: (206) 841-2600

## QUILCENE

**MAPLE GROVE MOTEL**
61 Maple Grove Rd (98376)
Rates: N/A;
Tel: (206) 765-3410

## QUINAULT

**LAKE QUINAULT LODGE**
P. O. Box 7 (98575)
Rates: $55-$105;
Tel: (206) 288-2571

## RANDLE

**MEDICI MOTEL**
661 Cispus Rd (98377)
Rates: N/A;
Tel: (206) 497-7700

**TALL TIMBER**
10023 Hwy 12 (98377)
Rates: N/A;
Tel: (206) 497-5908

**WOODLAND MOTEL**
11890 US Hwy 12 (98377)
Rates: N/A;
Tel: (206) 494-5298

## RAYMOND

**MAUNU'S MOUNTCASTLE MOTEL**
524 3rd St (98577)
Rates: $32-$40;
Tel: (206) 942-5571

## RENTON

**TRAVELERS INN**
7710 Lake Washington Blvd (98056)
Rates: N/A;
Tel: (206) 228-2858

## RICHLAND

**BALI HI MOTEL**
1201 George Washington Way (99352)
Rates: $35-$42;
Tel: (509) 943-3101

**COLUMBIA CENTER DUNES MOTEL**
1751 Fowler Ave (99352)
Rates: $29-$37;
Tel: (509) 783-8181

**NENDEL'S INN**
615 Jadwin Ave (99352)
Rates: $37-$43;
Tel: (509) 943-4611

**RED LION INN- HANFORD HOUSE**
802 George Washington Way (99352)
Rates: $62-$90;
Tel: (509) 946-7611

**SHILO INN-RIVERSHORE**
50 Comstock St (99352)
Rates: $52-$70;
Tel: (509) 946-4661

## RITZVILLE

**BEST WESTERN HERITAGE INN**
1405 Smitty's Blvd (99169)
Rates: $47-$65;
Tel: (509) 659-1007

**COLWELL MOTOR INN**
501 W 1st Ave (99169)
Rates: $38-$48;
Tel: (509) 659-1620

**COTTAGE MOTEL**
508 E 1st Ave (99169)
Rates: N/A;
Tel: (509) 569-0721

## ROCKPORT

**DIABLO LAKE RESORT**
Hwy 20 Mile 127 1/2 (98283)
Rates: N/A;
Tel: (206) 386-4429

## ROSLYN

**THE ROSLYN INNS**
P. O. Box 386 (98941)
Rates: N/A;
Tel: (509) 649-2936

## SEABECK

**SUMMER SONG BED & BREAKFAST**
P. O. Box 82 (98380)
Rates: N/A;
Tel: (206) 830-5089

## SEATTLE
(and Vicinity)

**AIRPORT PLAZA HOTEL**
18601 Pacific Hwy S (98188)
Rates: $44-$75;
Tel: (206) 433-0400

**THE ALEXIS HOTEL**
1007 First Ave (98104)
Rate: $155-$325;
Tel: (206) 624-4844

**AURORA SEAFAIR INN**
9100 Aurora Ave N (98103)
Rates: $38-$65;
Tel: (206) 522-3754

**BEECH TREE MANOR INN**
1405 Queen Anne Ave N (98109)
Rates: N/A;
Tel: (206) 281-7037

**BEST WESTERN EXECUTIVE INN**
200 Taylor Ave N (98109)
Rates: $78-$126;
Tel: (206) 448-9444

**DOUBLETREE INN**
205 Strander Blvd (98188)
Rates: $79-$99;
Tel: (206) 246-8220

**DOUBLETREE SUITES**
16500 Southcenter Pkwy (98188)
Rates: $99-$140;
Tel: (206) 575-8220

**ECONO LODGE**
325 Aurora N (98109)
Rates: $59-$69;
Tel: (206) 441-0400

**GEISHA MOTOR INN**
9613 Aurora Ave N (98103)
Rates: N/A;
Tel: (206) 524-8880

**HAMPTON INN-
SEATTLE SOUTHCENTER**
7200 S 156th St
(Tukwila 98188)
Rates: $59-$77;
Tel: (206) 228-5800

**HOJO INN**
20045 International Blvd
(Sea-Tac 98198)
Rates: $38-$60;
Tel: (206) 878-3310

**HOMEWOOD SUITES**
6955 Southcenter Blvd
(98188)
Rates: $119-$129;
Tel: (206) 433-8000

**INN AT THE MARKET**
86 Pine St (98101)
Rates: $95-$170;
Tel: (206) 443-3600

**LA QUINTA MOTOR INN-
SEA TAC INTL**
2824 S 188th St (98188)
Rates: $51-$67;
Tel: (206) 241-5211

**LEGEND MOTEL**
22204 Pacific Hwy S (98198)
Rates: N/A;
Tel: (206) 878-0366

**MARRIOTT RESIDENCE INN-
SEATTLE SOUTH**
16201 W Valley Hwy (98188)
Rates: $104-$185;
Tel: (206) 226-5500

**MARRIOTT SEA-
TAC AIRPORT**
3201 S 176th St (98188)
Rates: $111-$123;
Tel: (206) 241-2000

**PARK INN CLUB**
225 Aurora Ave N (98109)
Rates: N/A;
Tel: (206) 728-7666

**PENSIONE NICHOLAS**
9123 First Ave (98101)
Rates: N/A;
Tel: (206) 441-7125

**QUALITY INN CITY CENTER**
2224 8th Ave (98121)
Rates: $66-$98;
Tel: (206) 624-6820

**RAMADA INN SEATTLE
AT NORTHGATE**
2140 N Northgate Way
(98133)
Rates: $80-$104;
Tel: (206) 365-0700

**RED LION
SEATTLE AIRPORT HOTEL**
18740 Pacific Hwy S (98188)
Rates: $115-$145;
Tel: (206) 246-8600

**RESIDENCE INN
BY MARRIOTT
SEATTLE DOWNTOWN**
800 Fairview Ave N (98109)
Rates: $125-$200;
Tel: (206) 624-6000

**RODESIDE LODGE**
12501 Aurora Ave N (98133)
Rates: $39-$75;
Tel: (206) 364-7771

**SEATTLE AIRPORT HILTON**
17620 Pacific Hwy S (98188)
Rates: $105-$140;
Tel: (206) 244-4800

**SHERATON SEATTLE
HOTEL & TOWERS**
6th Ave & Pike (98101)
Rates: $155-$215;
Tel: (206) 621-9000

**STOUFFER MADISON
HOTEL**
515 Madison St (98104)
Rates: $154-$234;
Tel: (206) 583-0300

**TOWNE & COUNTRY SUITES**
14800 Interurban Ave S
(98168)
Rates: N/A;
Tel: (206) 246-2323

**UNIVERSITY MOTEL**
4731 12th Ave NE (98105)
Rates: $47-$59;
Tel: (206) 522-4724

**WARWICK HOTEL**
401 Lenora (98121)
Rates: $140-$185;
Tel: (206) 443-4300

**WEST COAST
PLAZA PARK SUITES**
1011 Pike St (98101)
Rates: $126-$280;
Tel: (206) 682-8282

## SEAVIEW

**SOUTHWESTER LODGE**
Beach Access Rd - 38 Pl
(98664)
Rates: N/A;
Tel: (206) 642-2542

## SEKIU

**OLSON'S RESORT**
Front (98381)
Rates: N/A;
Tel: (206) 963-2311

## SEQUIM

**BEST WESTERN
SEQUIM BAY LODGE**
1788 Hwy 101E (98382)
Rates: $48-$130:
Tel: (206) 683-0691

**GREATHOUSE MOTEL**
740 E Washington St (98382)
Rates: N/A;
Tel: (206) 683-7272

**GROVELAND COTTAGE**
1673 Sequim-Dungeness Way
(98382)
Rates: N/A;
Tel: (206) 683-3565

**SUNDOWNER MOTEL**
364 W Washington St (98382)
Rates: $45-$69;
Tel: (206) 683-5532

## SHELTON

**HALLMARK MOTEL**
628 Railroad Ave (98584)
Rates: $37-$52;
Tel: (206) 426-4468

## SILVER LAKE

**SILVER LAKE RESORT**
3201 Spirit Lake Hwy (98645)
Rates: N/A;
Tel: (206) 274-6141

## SKYKOMISH

**SKYRIVER INN**
P. O. Box 280 (98288)
Rates: $45-$55;
Tel: (206) 677-2261

## SNOHOMISH

**COUNTRYMAN
BED & BREAKFAST**
119 Cedar (98290)
Rates: N/A;
Tel: (206) 568-9622

## SNOQUALMIE

**THE OLD HONEY FARM
BED & BREAKFAST**
8910 384th Ave SE (98065)
Rates: $45-$55;
Tel: (206) 000-1037

## SNOQUALMIE FALLS

**SALISH LODGE**
37807 SE Fall City (98065)
Rates: $155-$730;
Tel: (800) 826-6124

## SNOQUALMIE PASS

**WARDHOLM WEST
BED & BREAKFAST**
P. O. Box 143 (98068)
Rates: N/A;
Tel: (206) 434-6540

## SOAP LAKE

**NOTARAS LODGE**
P. O. Box 987 (98851)
Rates: $32-$45;
Tel: (509) 246-0462

## SOUTH BEND

**H & H MOTEL**
Hwy 101 Water (98586)
Rates: N/A;
Tel: (206) 875-5523

**SEAQUEST MOTEL**
801 West First St (98586)
Rates: N/A;
Tel: (800) 624-7006

## SPOKANE

**THE ALPENHAUS**
West 2834 Sunset Blvd
(99204)
Rates: N/A;
Tel: (509) 747-0102

**CARROLL'S MOTEL**
East 1234 Sprague Ave
(99202)
Rates: N/A;
Tel: (509) 534-0669

**CAVANAUGH'S INN-
FOURTH AVENUE**
110 E 4th Ave (99202)
Rates: $41-$74;
Tel: (509) 838-6101

**CAVANAUGH'S RIVER INN**
N 700 Division St (99202)
Rates: $85-$99;
Tel: (509) 326-5577

**CEDAR VILLAGE MOTEL**
West 5415 Sunset Hwy
(99204)
Rates: N/A;
Tel: (509) 838-8558

**COMFORT INN BROADWAY**
6309 E Broadway (99212)
Rates: $51-$75;
Tel: (509) 535-7185

**COMFORT INN NORTH**
7111 N Division St (99208)
Rates: $55-$105;
Tel: (509) 467-7111

**COMFORT INN-VALLEY**
P. O. Box 141152 (99214)
Rates: $52-$95;
Tel: (509) 924-3838

**DAYS INN**
1919 N Hutchinson Rd (99212)
Rates: $39-$55;
Tel: (509) 926-5399

**LIBERTY MOTEL**
6801 N Division (99208)
Rates: $33-$48;
Tel: (509) 467-6000

**QUALITY INN VALLEY SUITES**
8923 E Mission (99212)
Rates: $75-$150;
Tel: (509) 928-5218

**RAMADA INN**
P. O. Box 19228 (99219)
Rates: $56-$72;
Tel: (509) 838-5211

**RED LION INN**
P. O. Box 3385 (99220)
Rates: $78-$98;
Tel: (509) 924-9000

**RED TOP MOTEL**
East 7217 Trent (99212)
Rates: N/A;
Tel: (509) 926-5728

**SHANGRI-LA MOTEL**
2922 W Government Way
(99204)
Rates: $29-$40;
Tel: (509) 747-2066

**SHILO INN**
E 923 3rd Ave (99202)
Rates: N/A;
Tel: (509) 535-9000

**SUNTREE INN**
211 S Division St (99202)
Rates: $49-$54;
Tel: (509) 838-6630

## STEVENSON

**RIVER VIEW MOTOR INN**
MPO 02L Frank Johns Rd
(98648)
Rates: $30-$47;
Tel: (509) 427-5628

**SKAMANIA LODGE**
1131 SW Skamania Lodge Dr
(98648)
Rates: $85-$145;
Tel: (509) 427-7700

## SULTAN

**DUTCH CUP MOTEL**
918 Main St (98294)
Rates: $37-$51;
Tel: (206) 793-2215

## SUNNYSIDE

**NENDEL'S MOTOR INN**
408 Yakima Valley Hwy
(98944)
Rates: $37-$42;
Tel: (509) 837-7878

**RED APPLE MOTEL**
412 Yakima Valley Hwy
(98944)
Rates: N/A;
Tel: (509) 839-2100

**TOWN HOUSE MOTEL**
509 Yakima Valley Hwy
(98944)
Rates: $35-$41;
Tel: (509) 837-5500

## TACOMA

**BEST WESTERN
EXECUTIVE INN**
5700 Pacific Hwy E (98424)
Rates: $51-$69;
Tel: (206) 922-0080

**BEST WESTERN
LAKEWOOD MOTOR INN**
6125 Motor Ave SW (98499)
Rates: $50-$69;
Tel: (206) 584-2212

**BEST WESTERN
TACOMA INN**
8726 S Hosmer St (98444)
Rates: $56-$76;
Tel: (206) 535-2880

**DAYS INN**
6802 Tacoma Mall Blvd
(98409)
Rates: $53-$62;
Tel: (206) 475-5900

**ECONO LODGE**
3518 Pacific Hwy E (98424)
Rates: $32-$41;
Tel: (206) 922-0550

**HOMETEL INN**
3518 Pacific Hwy E (98424)
Rates: $29-$39;
Tel: (206) 922-0555

**LA QUINTA MOTOR INN**
1425 E 27th St (98421)
Rates: $56-$71;
Tel: (206) 383-0146

**NENDELS-TACOMA**
8702 S Hosmer St (98444)
Rates: $59-$67;
Tel: (206) 535-3100

**QUALITY HOTEL-
TACOMA DOME**
2611 East E St (98421)
Rates: $66-$71;
Tel: (206) 572-7272

**ROYAL COACHMAN INN**
5805 Pacific Hwy E (98424)
Rates: $54-$67;
Tel: (206) 922-2500

**SHERATON-
TACOMA HOTEL**
1320 Broadway Plaza
(98402)
Rates: $99-$135;
Tel: (206) 572-3200

**SHERWOOD INN**
8402 S Hosmer St (98444)
Rates: $43-$59;
Tel: (206) 535-2800

**SHILO INN**
7414 S Hosmer St (98408)
Rates: $64-$69;
Tel: (206) 475-4020

**TACOMA COMFORT INN**
5601 Pacific Hwy E (98424)
Rates: $46-$56;
Tel: (206) 926-2301

## TOKELAND

**TOKELAND HOTEL**
100 Hotel (98590)
Rates: N/A;
Tel: (206) 267-7006

## TOLEDO

**COWLITZ MOTEL**
162 Cowlitz Loop Rd (98591)
Rates: N/A;
Tel: (206) 864-6611

## TONASKET

**RAINBOW RESORT**
761 Loomis Hwy (98855)
Rates: N/A;
Tel: (509) 223-3700

## TOPPENISH

**OXBOW MOTOR INN**
511 S Elm (98948)
Rates: $31-$37;
Tel: (509) 865-5800

## TWISP

**IDLE-A-WHILE MOTEL**
505 North Hwy 20 (98856)
Rates: N/A;
Tel: (509) 997-3222

## UNION

**ALDERBROOK INN**
E 7101 Hwy 106 (98592)
Rates: $47-$85;
Tel: (206) 898-2200

**ROBIN HOOD VILLAGE**
E 6780 Hwy 106 (98592)
Rates: N/A;
Tel: (206) 898-2163

## VANCOUVER

**BEST WESTERN
FERRYMAN'S INN**
7901 NE 6th Ave (98665)
Rates: $49-$58;
Tel: (206) 574-2151

**COMFORT INN**
13207 NE 20th Ave (98686)
Rates: $45-$56;
Tel: (206) 574-6000

**NENDEL'S SUITES**
7001 NE Hwy 99 (98665)
Rates: $40-$54;
Tel: (206) 696-0516

**RED LION INN
AT THE QUAY**
100 Columbia St (98660)
Rates: $73-$110;
Tel: (206) 694-8341

**RESIDENCE INN-
PORTLAND NORTH**
8005 NE Parkway Dr (98662)
Rates: $100-$150;
Tel: (206) 253-4800

**SALMON CREEK MOTEL**
11901 NE Hwy 99 (98686)
Rates: $35-$55;
Tel: (206) 573-0751

**SHILO INN DOWNTOWN-
VANCOUVER**
401 E 13th St (98660)
Rates: $55-$67;
Tel: (206) 696-0411

**SHILO INN-HAZEL DELL**
13206 Hwy 99 (98686)
Rates: $46-$57;
Tel: (206) 573-0511

**SUNNYSIDE MOTEL**
12200 NE Hwy 99 (98686)
Rates: N/A;
Tel: (206) 573-4141

**VANCOUVER LODGE**
601 Broadway (98660)
Rates: $40-$55;
Tel: (206) 693-3668

## WALLA WALLA

**CITY CENTER MOTEL**
627 W Main St (99362)
Rates: N/A;
Tel: (509) 529-2660

**COMFORT INN**
520 N 2nd Ave (99362)
Rates: $51-$69;
Tel: (509) 525-2522

**SICYON GALLERY
BED & BREAKFAST**
1283 Star (99362)
Rates: N/A;
Tel: (509) 525-2964

## WENATCHEE

**AVENUE MOTEL**
720 N Wenatchee Ave
(98801)
Rates: $40-$44;
Tel: (509) 663-7161

**CHIEFTAN MOTEL**
P. O. Box 1905 (98801)
Rates: $41-$75;
Tel: (509) 663-8141

**ECONO LODGE**
700 N Wenatchee Ave
(98801)
Rates: $33-$53;
Tel: (509) 663-8133

**FORGET ME NOT
BED & BREAKFAST**
1133 Washington St (98801)
Rates: N/A;
Tel. (509) 663-6114

**HOLIDAY LODGE**
610 N Wenatchee Ave
(98801)
Rates: $36-$65;
Tel: (800) 722-0852

**LYLES MOTEL**
924 N Wenatchee Ave
(98801)
Rates: $28-$48;
Tel: (800) 582-3788

**ORCHARD INN**
1401 N Miller St (98801)
Rates: $37-$51;
Tel: (509) 662-3443

**RED LION INN**
1225 N Wenatchee Ave
(98801)
Rates: $64-$84;
Tel: (509) 663-0711

**WEST COAST WENATCHEE
CENTER HOTEL**
201 N Wenatchee Ave
(98801)
Rates: $68-$78;
Tel: (509) 662-1234

## WESTPORT

**COHO MOTEL**
P. O. Box 1087 (98595)
Rates: $34-$57;
Tel: (206) 268-0111

**ISLANDER MOTEL**
West Haven Dr (98595)
Rates: N/A;
Tel: (206) 268-9166

**PACIFIC MOTEL**
330 S Forrest (98595)
Rates: N/A;
Tel: (206) 268-9325

**SANDS MOEL**
1416 Montesano (98595)
Rates: N/A;
Tel: (800) 654-5250

**SPORTSMAN RESORT**
P. O. Box 2027 (98595)
Rates: N/A;
Tel: (206) 268-0055

## WILBUR

**SETTLE INN**
Brace & Main (99185)
Rates: N/A;
Tel: (509) 647-5812

## WINTHROP

**BEST WESTERN MARIGOT**
P. O. Box 813 (98862)
Rates: $48-$65;
Tel: (509) 996-3100

**PINEY WOODS INN**
Hwy 20 (98862)
Rates: N/A;
Tel: (509) 996-2616

**THE VIRGINIAN RESORT**
P. O. Box 237 (98862)
Rates: $35-$75;
Tel: (509) 996-2535

## WOODLAND

**LEWIS RIVER INN**
1100 Lewis River Rd (98674)
Rates: $41-$49;
Tel: (206) 225-6257

**SCANDIA MOTEL**
1123 Hoffman St (98674)
Rates: $30-$42;
Tel: (206) 225-8006

**WOODLANDER INN**
1500 Atlantic (98674)
Rates: $38-$50;
Tel: (206) 225-6548

## YAKIMA

**BALI HAI MOTEL**
710 N 1st St (98901)
Rates: $18-$35;
Tel: (509) 452-7178

**CAVANAUGH'S
AT YAKIMA CENTER**
607 E Yakima Ave (98901)
Rates: $58-$92;
Tel: (509) 248-5900

**COLONIAL MOTOR INN**
1405 N 1st St (98901)
Rates: N/A;
Tel: (509) 453-8981

**DAYS INN**
2408 Rudkin Rd (98903)
Rates: $38-$60;
Tel: (509) 248-9700

**ECONO LODGE**
510 N 1st St (98901)
Rates: $33-$38;
Tel: (509) 457-6155

**HOLIDAY INN OF YAKIMA**
9 N 9th St (98901)
Rates: $51-$75;
Tel: (509) 452-6511

**HUNTLEY INN**
12 E Valley Mall Blvd (98903)
Rates: $39-$59;
Tel: (509) 248-6924

**RED CARPET MOTOR INN**
1608 Fruitvale Blvd (98902)
Rates: $26-$39;
Tel: (509) 457-1131

**RED LION INN/
YAKIMA VALLEY**
1507 N 1st St (98901)
Rates: $60-$78;
Tel: (509) 248-7850

**RED LION MOTEL**
818 N 1st St (98901)
Rates: $47-$75;
Tel: (509) 453-0391

# WEST VIRGINIA

## BECKLEY

**BECKLEY HOTEL
& CONFERENCE CTR**
1940 Harper Rd (25801)
Rates: $65-$200;
Tel: (800) 274-6010

**BEST WESTERN
MOTOR LODGE**
1939 Harper Rd (25801)
Rates: $36-$49;
Tel: (304) 252-0671

**CHARLES HOUSE MOTEL**
223 S Heber St (25801)
Rates: N/A;
Tel: (304) 253-8318

**COMFORT INN**
1909 Harper Rd (25801)
Rates: $43-$53;
Tel: (304) 255-2161

## BERKELEY SPRINGS

**PARK HAVEN
MOTOR LODGE**
Rt 1, Box 298, Rt 522 S
(25411)
Rates: N/A;
Tel: (304) 258-1734

## BLUEFIELD

**ECONO LODGE**
3400 Cumberland Rd (24701)
Rates: $29-$40;
Tel: (304) 327-8171

**HOLIDAY INN**
US 460, 52 Bypass (24701)
Rates: $53-$120;
Tel: (304) 325-6170

## BRIDGEPORT

**HEDGES MOTEL**
Rt 50 East (26330)
Rates: N/A;
Tel: (304) 842-2811

## BUCKHANNON

**BAXA HOTEL-MOTEL**
21 N Kanawha St (26201)
Rates: N/A;
Tel: (304) 472-2500

**COLONIAL MOTEL**
24 N Kanawha St (26201)
Rates: N/A;
Tel: (304) 472-3000

# WEST VIRGINIA

## CHAPMANVILLE

**FRIENDSHIP INN**
P. O. Box 4545 (25508)
Rates: N/A;
Tel: (304) 855 7182

## CHARLESTON

**DAYS INN**
6210 MacCorkle Ave SW
(St Albans 25177)
Rates: $33-$45;
Tel: (304) 766-6231

**HOLIDAY INN DOWNTOWN CHARLESTON HOUSE**
600 Kanawah Blvd E (25301)
Rates: $78-$92;
Tel: (304) 344-4092

**HOLIDAY INN HEART-O-TOWN**
1000 Washington St (25301)
Rates: $50-$63;
Tel: (304) 343-4661

**KNIGHTS INN**
6401 MacCorkle Ave SE
(25304)
Rates: N/A;
Tel: (800) 843-5644

**RED ROOF INN-KANAWHA CITY**
6305 MacCorkle Ave SE
(25304)
Rates: $33-$46;
Tel: (304) 925-6953

**RED ROOF INN-S CHARLESTON**
4006 MacCorkle Ave SW
(S Charleston 25309)
Rates: $33-$48;
Tel: (304) 744-1500

## CLARKSBURG

**HOLIDAY INN-CLARKSBURG- BRIDGEPORT**
100 Lodgeville Rd
(Bridgeport 26330)
Rates: $44-$69;
Tel: (304) 842-5411

**KNIGHTS INN CLARKSBURG**
1235 W Main St
(Bridgeport 26330)
Rates: $36-$40;
Tel: (304) 842-7115

**TERRACE MOTEL**
1202 E Pike St (26301)
Rates: N/A;
Tel: (304) 622-6161

## DAVIS

**DEERFIELD VILLAGE RESORT**
Rt 1, Box 152 (26260)
Rates: $90-$175;
Tel: (304) 866-4698

## ELKINS

**BEST WESTERN MOTEL**
P. O. Box 1878 (26241)
Rates: $36 $77;
Tel: (304) 636-7711

**CHEAT RIVER LODGE**
Rt 1, Box 115 (26241)
Rates: N/A;
Tel: (304) 636-2301

**ECONO LODGE**
US 33E (26241)
Rates: $34-$59;
Tel: (304) 636-5311

**ELKINS MOTOR LODGE**
P. O. Box 46 (26241)
Rates: $33-$50;
Tel: (800) 245-5074

**MOUNTAIN SPLENDOR INN**
P. O. Box 1802 (26241)
Rates: N/A;
Tel: (304) 636-8111

## FAIRMONT

**COUNTRY CLUB MOTOR LODGE**
1499 Locust Ave (26554)
Rates: $20-$26;
Tel: (304) 366-4141

**HOLIDAY INN**
I-79 & E Grafton Rd (26554)
Rates: $42-$65;
Tel: (304) 366-5500

**RED ROOF INN**
Rt 1, Box 602 (26554)
Rates: $27-$40;
Tel: (304) 366-6800

## FAYETTEVILLE

**COMFORT INN-NEW RIVER**
P. O. Box 929 (25840)
Rates: $32-$58;
Tel: (304) 574-3443

## FRANKLIN

**MT. STATE MOTEL**
Rt 220 North (26807)
Rates: N/A;
Tel: (304) 358-2084

## HILLSBORO

**THE CURRENT**
Denmar Rd (24946)
Rates: N/A;
Tel: (304) 653-4722

## HINTON

**PENCE SPRINGS HOTEL**
P. O. Box 90
(Pence Springs 24962)
Rates: $45-$300;
Tel: (304) 445-2606

## HUNTINGTON

**COLONIAL INN**
4644 Rt 60 E (25705)
Rates: N/A;
Tel: (304) 736-3466

**HOLIDAY INN-DOWNTOWN/ UNIVERSITY**
1415 4th Ave (25701)
Rates: $55-$100;
Tel: (304) 525-7741

**RADISSON HOTEL HUNTINGTON**
1001 3rd Ave (25701)
Rates: $96-$106;
Tel: (304) 525-1001

**RAMADA INN**
P. O. Box 999 (25713)
Rates: $42-$60;
Tel: (304) 736-3451

**RED ROOF INN**
5190 US Rt 60 East (25705)
Rates: N/A;
Tel: (800) 843-7663

## HURRICANE

**RED ROOF INN**
P. O. Box 468 (25526)
Rates: $26-$33;
Tel: (304) 757-6392

**SMILEY'S MOTEL**
419 Hurricane Creek Rd
(25526)
Rates: $33-$39;
Tel: (304) 562-3346

## JANE LEW

**WILDERNESS PLANTATION INN & RESTAURANT**
P. O. Drawer 96 (26378)
Rates: $35-$46;
Tel: (304) 884-7806

## LEWISBURG

**BRIER INN**
540 N Jefferson St (24901)
Rates: $42-$47;
Tel: (304) 645-7722

**BUDGET HOST FORT SAVANNAH INN**
204 N Jefferson St (24901)
Rates: $32-$52;
Tel: (304) 645-3055

**GENERAL LEWIS INN**
301 E Washington St (24901)
Rates: $50-$85;
Tel: (304) 645-2600

## MARTINSBURG

**ARBORGATE INN**
1599 Edwin Miller Blvd
(25401)
Rates: $33-$47;
Tel: (304) 267-2211

**ECONO LODGE**
Rt 2, Box 208N (25401)
Rates: $39-$49;
Tel: (304) 274-2181

**HERITAGE MOTOR INN**
1024 Winchester Ave (25401)
Rates: N/A;
Tel: (304) 267-2935

**PIKESIDE MOTEL**
2138 Winchester Pike (25401)
Rates: N/A;
Tel: (304) 263-5189

## MORGANTOWN

**EURO-SUITES HOTEL**
501 Chestnut Ridge Rd
(26505)
Rates: $80-$100;
Tel: (304) 598-1000

**FRIENDSHIP INN-MOUNTAINEER**
452 Country Club Rd (26505)
Rates: $29-$41;
Tel: (304) 599-4850

**HOLIDAY INN**
1400 Saratoga Ave (26505)
Rates: $42-$72;
Tel: (304) 599-1680

**RAMADA INN**
P. O. Box 1242 (26505)
Rates: $50-$60;
Tel: (304) 296-3431

## NITRO

**BEST WESTERN MOTOR INN**
4115 1st Ave (25143)
Rates: $36-$41;
Tel: (304) 755-8341

## OCEANA

**OCEANA MOTEL**
Cook Parkway (24870)
Rates: N/A;
Tel: (304) 682-6186

## PARKERSBURG

**BEST WESTERN INN**
Jct I-177 & US 50 (26101)
Rates: $32-$46;
Tel: (304) 485-6551

**ECONO LODGE**
Jct I-77 & US 50 (26101)
Rates: $34-$41;
Tel: (304) 422-5401

**RED ROOF INN**
3714 7th St (26101)
Rates: $37-$48;
Tel: (304) 485-1741

## PRINCETON

**DAYS INN**
P. O. Box 830 (24740)
Rates: $51-$60;
Tel: (304) 425-8100

**TOWN-N-COUNTRY MOTEL**
P. O. Box 1329 (24740)
Rates: $25-$36;
Tel: (304) 425-8156

## RICHWOOD

**FOUR SEASONS LODGE**
39-55 Rt Marlinton Rd
(26261)
Rates: N/A;
Tel: (304) 846-4605

**OAKFORD INN**
29 Oakford Ave (26261)
Rates: N/A;
Tel: (800) 834-9161

## SUMMERSVILLE

**BEST WESTERN
SUMMERSVILLE LAKE**
1203 Broad St (26651)
Rates: $35-$43;
Tel: (304) 872-6900

**COMFORT INN**
903 Industrial Dr N (26651)
Rates: $43-$63;
Tel: (304) 872-6500

**SUPER 8 MOTEL**
306 Merchants Walk (26651)
Rates: N/A·
Tel: (304) 872-4888

## SUTTON

**ELK MOTOR COURT**
35 Camden Ave (26601)
Rates: N/A;
Tel: (304) 765-7173

## WEIRTON

**BEST WESTERN INN-
WEIRTON**
350 Three Springs Dr (26062)
Rates: $49-$58;
Tel: (304) 723-5522

## WESTON

**COMFORT INN**
P. O. Box 666 (26452)
Rates: $40-$50;
Tel: (304) 269-7000

## WHEELING

**COMFORT INN**
RD 1, Box 258
(Triadelphia 26059)
Rates: $33-$59;
Tel: (304) 547-1380

**DAYS INN**
RD 1, Box 292
(Triadelphia 26059)
Rates: $42-$47;
Tel: (304) 547-0610

**MCLURE HOUSE**
1200 Market St (26003)
Rates: $53-$65;
Tel: (304) 232-0300

## WHITE SULPHUR SPRINGS

**OLD WHITE MOTEL**
P. O. Box 58 (24986)
Rates: $30-$60;
Tel: (304) 536-2441

**SUPERIOR COLONIAL
COURT MOTEL**
P. O. Box 188 (24986)
Rates: $35-$42;
Tel: (304) 536-2121

## WILLOW ISLAND

**WILLOW ISLAND MOTEL**
717 Riverview Dr (26134)
Rates: N/A;
Tel: (304) 665-2418

# WISCONSIN

## ALGOMA

**RIVER HILLS MOTEL**
WI 42N (54201)
Rates: $35-$60;
Tel: (800) 236-3451

## ANTIGO

**CUTLASS MOTOR LODGE**
915 S Superior St (54409)
Rates: $44-$159;
Tel: (800) 288-5277

## APPLETON

**BEST WESTERN
MIDWAY HOTEL**
3033 W College Ave (54914)
Rates: $74-$84;
Tel: (414) 731-4141

**BUDGETEL INN**
3920 W College Ave (54914)
Rates: $36-$52;
Tel: (414) 734-6070

**COMFORT SUITES
COMFORT DOME**
3809 W Wisconsin Ave
(54915)
Rates: $59-$95;
Tel: (414) 730-3800

**EXEL INN OF APPLETON**
210 N Westhill Blvd (54914)
Rates: $31-$45;
Tel: (414) 733-5551

**PAPER VALLEY HOTEL
& CONF CTR**
P. O.Box 8000 (54911)
Rates: $72-$105;
Tel: (414) 733-8000

**WOODFIELD SUITES**
3730 W College Ave (54914)
Rates: $64-$69;
Tel: (414) 734-9231

## ASHLAND

**ANDERSON'S
CHEQUAMEGON MOTEL**
2200 W Lakeshore Dr (54806)
Rates: $24-$56;
Tel: (715) 682-4658

**ASHLAND MOTEL**
2300 W Lakeshore Dr (54806)
Rates: $26-$54;
Tel: (715) 682-5503

**BEST WESTERN
HOLIDAY HOUSE**
Rt 3, Box 24 (54806)
Rates: $37-$72;
Tel: (715) 682-5235

## BAILEYS HARBOR

**PARENT MOTEL
& COTTAGES**
8404 Hwy 57 (54202)
Rates: $45-$65;
Tel: (414) 839-2218

**SANDS RESORT MOTEL**
2371 Ridges Dr (54202)
Rates: $50-$110;
Tel: (414) 839-2401

## BARABOO

**BEST WESTERN
BARABOO INN**
725 W Pine St (53913)
Rates: $48-$82;
Tel: (608) 356-1100

**QUALITY INN**
P. O. Box 84 (53913)
Rates: $70-$160;
Tel: (608) 356-6422

**SPINNING WHEEL MOTEL**
809 8th St (53913)
Rates: $26-$55;
Tel: (608) 356-3933

**THUNDERBIRD
MOTOR INN**
1013 8th St (53913)
Rates: $57;
Tel: (608) 356-7757

## BAYFIELD

**BAY VILLA MOTEL**
Rte 1 Box 33 (54814)
Rates: $40-$80;
Tel: (715) 779-3252

## BEAVER DAM

**GRAND VIEW MOTEL**
1510 N Center (53916)
Rates: $24-$39;
Tel: (414) 885-9208

**SUPER 8 MOTEL**
711 Park Ave (53916)
Rates: $38-$60;
Tel: (414) 887-8880

## BELGIUM

**AMERICINN MOTEL**
120 Lakeview Dr (53004)
Rate: $36-$46;
Tel: (414) 285-3566

## BELOIT

**COMFORT INN OF BELOIT**
2786 Milwaukee Rd (53511)
Rates: $44-$80;
Tel: (608) 362-2666

## BLACK RIVER FALLS

**AMERICAN BUDGET INN**
919 Hwy 54 (54615)
Rates: $39-$55;
Tel: (715) 284-4333

**ARROWHEAD LODGE**
I-94 & Hwy 54 (54615)
Rates: N/A;
Tel: (800) 284-9471

**BEST WESTERN-
ARROWHEAD LODGE**
600 Oasis Rd (54615)
Rates: $52-$63;
Tel: (715) 284-9471

**PINES MOTOR LODGE**
Rt 4, Box 297 (54615)
Rates: $29-$42;
Tel: (715) 284-5311

## BOULDER JUNCTION

**WHITE BIRCH
VILLAGE COTTAGES**
P. O. Box 284 (54512)
Rates: $400-$700;
Tel: (715) 385-2182

**WILDCAT LODGE**
P. O. Box 138 (54512)
Rates: $60-$150;
Tel: (715) 385-2421

**ZASTROW'S
LYNX LAKE LODGE**
P. O. Box 277 (54512)
Rates: $249;
Tel: (800) 882-5969

## BURLINGTON

**RAINBOW MOTEL**
733 Milwaukee Ave (53105)
Rates: $40-$57;
Tel: (414) 763-2491

## CAMP DOUGLAS

**K & K MOTEL**
Rt 2, Box 242A (54618)
Rates: $25-$38;
Tel: (608) 427-3100

## CHIPPEWA FALLS

**INDIANHEAD MOTEL**
501 Summit Ave (54729)
Rates: $37-$46;
Tel: (715) 723-9171

**LAKE AIRE MOTEL**
5732 Sandburst Ln (54729)
Rates: $24-$36;
Tel: (715) 723-2231

# COON VALLEY

**COULEE INN MOTEL**
703 Central Ave (54623)
Rates: N/A;
Tel: (608) 452-3510

# CRIVITZ

**SHAFFER PARK MOTEL**
Rt 3 (54114)
Rates: $42-$45;
Tel: (715) 854-2186

# DODGEVILLE

**SUPER 8 MOTEL
OF DODGEVILLE**
1308 Johns St (53533)
Rates: $35-$53;
Tel: (608) 935-3888

# DRESSER

**VALLEY MOTEL**
Hwy 35 (54009)
Rates: N/A;
Tel: (715) 755 2701

# DUNBAR

**RICHARDS' MOTEL**
On US 8 (54119)
Rates: $26-$34;
Tel: (715) 324-5444

# EAGLE RIVER

**THE EDGEWATER INN**
5054 Hwy 70W (54521)
Rates: $24-$36;
Tel: (715) 479-4011

**GYPSY VILLA RESORT**
950 Circle Dr (54521)
Rates: $275-$1358;
Tel: (800) 232-9714

**HIAWATHA MOTOR INN**
1982 Hwy 45 North (54521)
Rates: N/A;
Tel: (715) 479-6431

**RIVERSIDE MOTEL RESORT**
5012 Hwy 70 West (54521)
Rates: N/A;
Tel: (800) 530-0019

**WHITE EAGLE MOTEL**
4948 Hwy 70 (54521)
Rates: $30-$46;
Tel: (715) 479-4426

# EAU CLAIRE

**COMFORT INN**
3117 Craig Rd (54701)
Rates: $36-$47;
Tel: (715) 833-9798

**DAYS INN-
UNIVERSITY SOUTH**
2703 Craig Rd (54701)
Rates: $52-$61;
Tel: (715) 835-2211

**DAYS INN-WEST**
6319 Traux Ln (54703)
Rates: $35-$44;
Tel: (715) 874-5550

**EXEL INN OF EAU CLAIRE**
2305 Craig Rd (54701)
Rates: $29-$45;
Tel: (715) 834-3193

**HEARTLAND INN**
4075 Commonwealth Ave
(54701)
Rates: $39-$52;
Tel: (715) 839-7100

**HOLIDAY INN
CONVENTION CENTER**
205 S Barstow St (54701)
Rates: $54-$69;
Tel: (715) 835-6121

**HOLIDAY INN
GATEWAY & CONF PLAZA**
1202 W Clairemont Ave
(54701)
Rates: $55-$79;
Tel: (715) 834-3181

**HOWARD JOHNSON
LODGE**
809 W Clairemont Ave
(54701)
Rates: $47-$64;
Tel: (715) 834-6611

**MAPLE MANOR MOTEL**
2507 S Hastings Way (54701)
Rates: $29-$44;
Tel: (715) 834-2618

**ROADSTAR INN**
1151 W MacArthur Ave
(54701)
Rates: $30-$40;
Tel: (715) 832-9731

# ELLISON BAY

**ANDERSON'S RETREAT**
12621 Woodland Dr (54210)
Rates: N/A;
Tel: (414) 854-2746

# FENNIMORE

**FENNIMORE HILLS MOTEL**
5814 Hwy 18W (53809)
Rates: $41-$53;
Tel: (608) 822-3281

# FOND DU LAC

**BUDGETEL INN**
77 Holiday Ln (54937)
Rates: $36-$58;
Tel: (414) 921-4000

**DAYS INN**
107 N Pioneer Rd (54937)
Rates: $29-$44;
Tel: (414) 923-6790

**HOLIDAY INN**
625 Rolling Meadows Dr
(54937)
Rates: $49-$80;
Tel: (414) 923-1440

**TRAVELERS INN**
1325 S Main St (54935)
Rates: N/A;
Tel: (414) 923-0223

# FOUNTAIN CITY

**FOUNTAIN MOTEL**
810 S Main St (54629)
Rates: $30-$40;
Tel: (608) 687-3111

# FREDERIC

**FREDERIC MOTEL**
Hwy 35 (54837)
Rates: N/A;
Tel: (715) 327-4496

# GERMANTOWN

**SUPER 8 MOTEL-
GERMANTOWN/
MILWAUKEE**
N96 W17490 County Line Rd
(53022)
Rates: $36-$65;
Tel: (414) 255-0880

# GILLS ROCK

**HARBOR HOUSE INN**
12666 SR 42 (54210)
Rates: $29-$79;
Tel: (414) 854-5196

# GREEN BAY

**BARTH'S TOWER MOTEL**
2625 Humboldt Rd (54311)
Rates: N/A;
Tel: (414) 468-1242

**BAY MOTEL**
1301 S Military Ave (54304)
Rates: $28-$50;
Tel: (414) 494-3441

**BEST WESTERN
DOWNTOWNER**
321 S Washington St (54301)
Rates: $38-$69;
Tel: (414) 437-8771

**BUDGETEL INN**
2840 S Oneida (54304)
Rates: $45-$53;
Tel: (414) 494-7887

**COMFORT INN**
2841 Ramada Way (54304)
Rates: $38-$65;
Tel: (414) 498-2060

**DAYS INN-DOWNTOWN**
406 N Washington St (54301)
Rates: $50-$75;
Tel: (414) 435-4484

**DAYS INN-WEST**
1978 Gross Ave (54304)
Rates: $39-$51;
Tel: (414) 498-8088

**EXEL INN**
2870 Ramada Way (54304)
Rates: $31-$45;
Tel: (414) 499-3599

**GREEN BAY AIRPORT
HOLIDAY INN**
2580 S Ashland Ave (54304)
Rates: $63-$73;
Tel: (414) 499-5121

**HOLIDAY INN-CITY CENTER**
200 Main St (54301)
Rates: $62-$95;
Tel: (414) 437-5900

**SKY LIT MOTEL**
2120 S Ashland Ave (54304)
Rates: $27-$37;
Tel: (414) 494-5641

**SUPER 8 MOTEL**
2868 S Oneida St (54304)
Rates: $44-$55;
Tel: (414) 494-2042

**VALLEY MOTEL**
116 N Military Ave
(Shawano 54303)
Rates: $33-$40;
Tel: (414) 494-3455

# HAYWARD

**LAKE HAYWARD MOTEL**
Rt 6, Box 6248 (54843)
Rates: $31-$52;
Tel: (715) 634-2646

**ROSS' TEAL LAKE LODGE**
Rt 7A (54843)
Rates: $90-$250;
Tel: (715) 462-3631

# HUDSON

**COMFORT INN**
811 Dominion Dr (54016)
Rates: $42-$70;
Tel: (715) 386-6355

**FAIRFIELD INN BY MARRIOTT**
2400 Center Dr (54016)
Rates: $45-$72;
Tel: (715) 386-6688

# HURLEY

**AMERICAN BUDGET INN**
850 10th Ave N (54534)
Rates: $35-$75;
Tel: (715) 561-3500

**HOLIDAY INN**
1000 10th Ave (54534)
Rates: $48-$62;
Tel: (715) 561-3030

# IRON RIDGE

**IRON RIDGE INN MOTEL**
P. O. Box 308 (53035)
Rates: $38-$44;
Tel: (414) 387-4090

# IRON RIVER

**THE LUMBERMENS INN**
P. O. Box 127 (54847)
Rates: $36-$46;
Tel: (715) 372-4515

# JANESVILLE

**RAMADA INN**
3431 Milton Ave (53545)
Rates: $55-$61;
Tel: (608) 756-2341

**SELECT INN**
3520 Milton Ave (53545)
Rates: $29-$37;
Tel: (608) 754-0251

# JOHNSON CREEK

**COLONIAL INN MOTEL**
Hwy 26 & B (53038)
Rates: N/A;
Tel: (414) 699-3518

## KENOSHA

**BUDGETEL INN**
7540 118th Ave (53142)
Rates: $38-$48;
Tel: (414) 857-7911

**HOLIDAY INN
HARBORSIDE**
5125 6th Ave (53140)
Rates: $69-$85;
Tel: (414) 658-3281

**HOWARD JOHNSON
MOTEL**
12121 75th St (53142)
Rates: $46-$71;
Tel: (414) 857-2311

**KNIGHTS INN**
7221 122nd Ave (53142)
Rates: $38-$47;
Tel: (414) 857-2622

## LA CROSSE

**BEST WESTERN-
MIDWAY HOTEL**
1835 Rose St (54601)
Rates: $64-$74;
Tel: (608) 781 7000

**BLUFF VIEW INN**
3715 Mormon Coulee Rd
(54601)
Rates: $27-$75;
Tel: (608) 788-0600

**DAYS INN**
2325 Bainbridge St (54603)
Rates: $51-$84;
Tel: (608) 785-0420

**EXEL INN OF LA CROSSE**
2150 Rose St (54603)
Rates: $28-$44;
Tel: (608) 781-0400

**THE RADISSON HOTEL
LA CROSSE**
200 Harborview Plaza
(54601)
Rates: $73;
Tel: (608) 784-6680

**ROADSTAR INN**
2622 Rose St (54603)
Rates: $34-$46;
Tel: (608) 781-3070

**SUPER 8 OF LA CROSSE**
1625 Rose St (54603)
Rates: $43-$51;
Tel: (608) 781-8880

## LAC DU FLAMBEAU

**DILLMAN'S LODGE**
P. O. Box 98 (54538)
Rates: N/A;
Tel: (715) 588-3143

## LADYSMITH

**BEST WESTERN
EL RANCHO MOTEL**
8500 W Flambeau Ave
(54848)
Rates: $40-$48;
Tel: (715) 532-6666

**EVERGREEN MOTEL**
1201 W Lake Ave (54848)
Rates: $30-$38;
Tel: (715) 532-5611

## LAKE GENEVA

**LAKEWOOD INN MOTEL**
1150 Wells St (53147)
Rates: N/A;
Tel: (414) 248-6773

**T C SMITH HISTORIC INN
BED & BREAKFAST**
865 Main St (53147)
Rates: $55-$185;
Tel: (414) 248-1097

## LAND O' LAKES

**SUNRISE LODGE**
West Shore Dr (54540)
Rates: $47-$64;
Tel: (715) 547-3684

## LA POINTE

**MADELINE ISLAND MOTEL**
P. O. Box 51 (54850)
Rates: $31-$54;
Tel: (715) 747-3000

## LODI

**LODI VALLEY SUITES**
N 1440 Hwy 113 (53555)
Rates: $35-$59;
Tel: (608) 592-7331

## LUCK

**LUCK COUNTRY INN**
P. O. Box 179 (54853)
Rates: $40-$72;
Tel: (715) 472-2000

## MADISON
(and Vicinity)

**BEST WESTERN INN
ON THE PARK**
22 S Carroll (53703)
Rates: $63-$109;
Tel: (608) 257-8811

**BUDGETEL BUDGET DOME
OF MADISON**
8102 Excelsior Dr (53717)
Rates: $44-$79;
Tel: (608) 831-7711

**CONCOURSE HOTEL**
1 W Dayton St (53703)
Rates: $69-$350;
Tel: (800) 356-8293

**EAST TOWNE SUITES**
4801 Annamark Dr (53704)
Rates: $57-$77;
Tel: (608) 244 2020

**EDGEWATER HOTEL**
P. O. Box 490 (53701)
Rates: $85-$375;
Tel: (608) 256-9071

**EXEL INN OF MADISON**
4202 E Towne Blvd (53704)
Rates: $28-$42;
Tel: (608) 241-3861

**HOLIDAY INN EAST TOWNE**
4402 E Washington Ave
(53704)
Rates: $77-$85;
Tel: (608) 244-4703

## HOMEWOOD SUITES-MADISON
501 D'Onofrio Dr (53719)
Rates: $99-$109;
Tel: (608) 833-8333

## QUALITY INN SOUTH
4916 E Broadway (53716)
Rates: $50-$65;
Tel: (608) 222-5501

## RED ROOF INN
4830 Hayes Rd (53704)
Rates: $31-$53;
Tel: (608) 241-1787

## RESIDENCE INN BY MARRIOTT
501 D'Onofrio Dr (53719)
Rates: $90-$140;
Tel: (608) 833-8333

## ROADSTAR INN
3535 Evan Acres Rd (53704)
Rates: $29-$37;
Tel: (608) 221-3331

## SELECT INN
4845 Hayes Rd (53704)
Rates: $29-$42;
Tel: (608) 249-1815

## WEST TOWNE ROAD STAR
6900 Seybold Rd (53719)
Rates: $34-$45;
Tel: (608) 274-6900

# MANITOWISH WATERS

## VOSS' BIRCHWOOD LODGE
P. O. Box 456 (54545)
Rates: $52-$790;
Tel: (715) 543-8441

# MANITOWOC

## BUDGETEL INN
908 Washington St (54220)
Rates: $32-$45;
Tel: (414) 682-8271

# MARINETTE

## SUPER 8 MOTEL
1508 Marinette Ave (54143)
Rates: $38-45;
Tel: (715) 735-7887

# MARSHFIELD

## BEST WESTERN MARSHFIELD INNKEEPER
2700 S Roddis Ave (54449)
Rates: $44-$49;
Tel: (715) 387-1761

## DOWNTOWN MOTEL
750 S Central Ave (54449)
Rates: $29-$56;
Tel: (715) 387-1111

## MARSHFIELD INN
116 W Ives (54449)
Rates: $37-$42;
Tel: (715) 387-6381

# MAUSTON

## COUNTRY INN BY CARLSON
P. O. Box 25 (53948)
Rates: $42-$64;
Tel: (608) 847-5959

# MAZOMANIE

## BEL AIRE MOTEL
10291 Hwy 14 (53560)
Rates: $30-$40;
Tel: (608) 795-2806

# MEDFORD

## KRAMER MOTEL
321 N 8th St (54451)
Rates: $29-$38;
Tel: (715) 748-4420

# MENOMONIE

## BOLO COUNTRY INN
207 Pine Ave W (54751)
Rates: $45-$80;
Tel: (715) 235-5596

## SUPER 8 MOTEL
1622 N Broadway (54751)
Rates: $39-$50;
Tel: (715) 235-8889

# MERCER

## GREAT NORTHERN MOTEL
Hwy 51S (54547)
Rates: $35-$49;
Tel: (715) 476-2440

# MILWAUKEE
(and Vicinity)

## ARBORGATE INN
8698 N Servite Dr (53223)
Rates: $35-$44;
Tel: (414) 354-5354

## BEST WESTERN MIDWAY HOTEL-BROOKFIELD
1005 S Moorland Rd (53005)
Rates: $70-$107;
Tel: (414) 786-9540

## BREEZE INN TO THE CHALET MOTEL
10401 N Port Washington Rd
(Mequon 53092)
Rates: $39-$59;
Tel: (414) 241-4510

## BUDGETEL INN
7141 S 13th St (53154)
Rates: $35-$51;
Tel: (414) 762-2266

## BUDGETEL INN-BROOKFIELD
20391 W Bluemound Rd
(Waukesha 53186)
Rates: $37-$53;
Tel: (414) 782-9100

## BUDGETEL INN MILWAUKEE NORTH EAST
5110 N Port Washington Rd
(53217)
Rates: $37-$53;
Tel: (414) 964-8484

## BUDGETEL INN N.W.
5442 N Lovers Ln (53225)
Rates: $36-$52;
Tel: (414) 531-1300

## DAYS INN
N88 W14776 Main St
(Menomonee Falls 53051)
Rates: $45-$65;
Tel: (414) 255-1700

**EXEL INN OF MILWAUKEE NORTHEAST**
5485 N Port Washington Rd (53217)
Rates: $35-$49;
Tel: (414) 961-7272

**EXEL INN OF MILWAUKEE SOUTH**
1201 W College Ave (53221)
Rates: $31-$45;
Tel: (414) 764-1776

**EXEL INN OF MILWAUKEE WEST**
115 N Mayfair Rd
(Wauwatosa 53226)
Rates: $33-$47;
Tel: (414) 257-0140

**HOLIDAY INN-MILWAUKEE WEST**
201 N Mayfair Rd (53226)
Rates: $64-$97;
Tel: (414) 771-4400

**HOLIDAY INN-SOUTH**
6331 S 13th St (53221)
Rates: $65-$95;
Tel: (414) 764-1500

**HOTEL WISCONSIN**
720 N Old World Third St (53202)
Rates: $59-$75;
Tel: (414) 271-4900

**HOWARD JOHNSON LODGE-AIRPORT**
1716 W Layton Ave (53221)
Rates: $29-$68;
Tel: (414) 282-7000

**KNIGHTS INN**
9420 S 20th St
(Oak Creek 53154)
Rates: $35-$46;
Tel: (414) 761-3807

**MILWAUKEE MARRIOTT**
375 S Moorland Rd
(Brookfield 53005)
Rates: $94-$109;
Tel: (414) 786-1100

**PORT MOTEL**
9717 W Appleton Ave (53225)
Rates: N/A;
Tel: (414) 466-4728

**PORT ZEDLER MOTEL**
10036 N Port Washington Rd
(Mequon 53092)
Rates: $32-$45;
Tel: (414) 241-5850

**RAMADA INN-AIRPORT**
6401 S 13th St (53221)
Rates: $68-$85;
Tel: (414) 764-5300

**RED ROOF INN**
6360 S 13th St
(Oak Creek 53154)
Rates: $34-$48;
Tel: (414) 764-3500

**RESIDENCE INN BY MARRIOTT**
7275 N Port Washington Rd (53217)
Rates: $131-$156;
Tel: (414) 352-0070

**RESIDENCE INN BY MARRIOTT-BROOKFIELD**
950 S Pinehurst Ct
(Brookfield 53005)
Rates: $131-$156;
Tel: (414) 782-5990

**SHERATON MAYFAIR**
2303 N Mayfair Rd (53226)
Rates: $85-$100;
Tel: (414) 257-3400

**SUPER 8-MILWAUKEE AIRPORT**
5253 S Howell Ave (53207)
Rates: $46-$53;
Tel: (414) 481-8488

## MINOCQUA

**AQUA AIRE MOTEL**
806 Hwy 51 N (54548)
Rates: N/A;
Tel: (715) 356-3433

**BEST WESTERN LAKEVIEW MOTOR LODGE**
P. O. Box 575 (54548)
Rates: $60-$87;
Tel: (715) 356-5208

**CROSS TRAILS MOTEL**
8644 US 51 N (54548)
Rates: $50-$67;
Tel: (800) 842-5261

**SUPER 8 MOTEL**
P. O. Box 325 (54548)
Rates: $36-$57;
Tel: (715) 356-9541

## NEKOOSA

**SHERMALOT MOTEL**
1148 Queensway (54457)
Rates: N/A;
Tel: (715) 325-2626

## NEW GLARUS

**CHALET LANDHAUS**
P. O. Box 878 (53574)
Rates: $49-$99;
Tel: (608) 527-5234

**SWISS-AIRE MOTEL**
P. O. Box 253 (53574)
Rates: $28-$48;
Tel: (608) 527-2138

## NEW LISBON

**EDGE O' THE WOOD MOTEL**
W 7396 Frontage Rd (53950)
Rates: $29-$43;
Tel: (608) 562-3705

## NEW RICHMOND

**AMERICINN MOTEL**
1020 S Knowles (54017)
Rates: $35-$62;
Tel: (715) 246-3993

## OAK CREEK

**KNIGHTS INN**
942 S 20th St (53154)
Rates: N/A;
Tel: (414) 761-3807

**RED ROOF INN**
6360 South 13th St (53154)
Rates: N/A;
Tel: (800) 843-7663

## OCONOMOWOC

**OLYMPIA RESORT
& CONFERENCE CENTER**
1350 Royale Mile Rd (53066)
Rates: $69-$109;
Tel: (414) 567-0311

## ONALASKA

**COMFORT INN**
1223 Crossing Meadows Dr
(54650)
Rates: $45-$69;
Tel: (608) 781-7500

## OSHKOSH

**BUDGETEL INN**
1950 Omro Rd (54901)
Rates: $33-$43;
Tel: (414) 233-4190

**HOLIDAY INN
HOLIDOME & MEETING CTR**
500 S Koeller Rd (54901)
Rates: $55-$80;
Tel: (414) 233-1511

**HOWARD JOHNSON
MOTEL**
1919 Omro Rd (54901)
Rates: $36-$60;
Tel: (414) 233-1200

**MOTEL 6**
1015 S Washburn St (54904)
Rates: $21-$29;
Tel: (414) 235-0265

**OSHKOSH HILTON
& CONVENTION CTR**
1 N Main St (54901)
Rates: $77-$88;
Tel: (414) 231-5000

## OSSEO

**BUDGET HOST
TEN-SEVEN INN**
Rt 4, Box 219 (54758)
Rates: $27-$42;
Tel: (715) 597-3114

**FRIENDSHIP INN
ALAN HOUSE MOTEL**
P. O. Box 7 (54758)
Rates: $38-$48;
Tel: (715) 597-3175

## PARK FALLS

**NORTHWAY
MOTOR LODGE**
Hwy 13S (54552)
Rates: $39-$45;
Tel: (715) 762-2406

**SUPER 8 PARK FALLS**
1212 Hwy 13S (54552)
Rates: $37-$49;
Tel: (715) 762-3383

## PEMBINE

**GRAND MOTEL**
P. O. Box 67 (54156)
Rates: $24-$35;
Tel: (715) 324-5417

## PHILLIPS

**SKYLINE MOTEL**
804 North Lake Ave (54555)
Rates: N/A;
Tel: (715) 339-3086

## PLATTEVILLE

**BEST WESTERN GOVERNOR
DODGE MOTOR INN**
P. O. Box 658 (53818)
Rates: $57-$68;
Tel: (608) 348-2301

**MOUND VIEW MOTEL**
1455 E Hwy 151 (53818)
Rates: $30-$43;
Tel: (608) 348-9518

## PORTAGE

**RIDGE MOTOR INN**
Hwy 51 N (53901)
Rates: $40-$80;
Tel: (608) 742-5306

## PORT WASHINGTON

**BEST WESTERN
HARBORSIDE MOTOR INN**
135 E Grand Ave (53074)
Rates: $53-$85;
Tel: (414) 284-9461

## PRAIRIE DU CHIEN

**BEST WESTERN
QUIET HOUSE**
Hwy 18/35S (53821)
Rates: $55-$125;
Tel: (608) 326-4777

**BRIDGEPORT INN**
P. O. Box 436 (53821)
Rates: $49-$65;
Tel: (608) 326-6082

**BRISBOIS MOTOR INN**
P. O. Box 37 (53821)
Rates: $29-$69;
Tel: (608) 326-8404

**DELTA MOTEL**
1733 1/2 S Marquette Rd
(53821)
Rates: $28-$55;
Tel: (608) 326-4951

**HOLIDAY MOTEL**
1010 S Marquette Rd (53821)
Rates: $24-$55;
Tel: (608) 326-2448

**PRAIRIE MOTEL**
1616 S Marquette Rd (53821)
Rates: $24-$55;
Tel: (608) 326-6461

**SUPER 8 MOTEL**
Hwy 18/35/60S (53821)
Rates: $39-$59;
Tel: (608) 326-8777

## PRAIRIE DU SAC

**SKYVIEW MOTEL**
Rt 1, Box 165 (53578)
Rates: $29-$45;
Tel: (608) 643-4344

## PRENTICE

**COUNTRYSIDE MOTEL**
P. O. Box 286 (54556)
Rates: $34-$42;
Tel: (715) 428-2333

## RACINE

**FAIRFIELD INN BY MARRIOTT**
6421 Washington Ave (53406)
Rates: $44-$58;
Tel: (414) 886-5000

**HOLIDAY INN-RIVERSIDE**
3700 Northwestern Ave
(53405)
Rates: $39-$90;
Tel: (414) 637-9311

**KNIGHTS INN**
1149 Oakes Rd (53406)
Rates: $41-$45;
Tel: (414) 886-6667

**RACINE MARRIOTT HOTEL**
7111 Washington Ave (53406)
Rates: $69-$118;
Tel: (414) 886-6100

## REEDSBURG

**MOTEL REEDSBURG**
1133 E Main St (53959)
Rates: $30-$58;
Tel: (608) 524-2306

## RHINELANDER

**CLARIDGE MOTOR INN-
BEST WESTERN**
70 N Stevens St (54501)
Rates: $48-$69;
Tel: (715) 362-7100

**HOLIDAY ACRES RESORT**
P. O. Box 460 (54501)
Rates: $58-$188;
Tel: (800) 261-1500

**HOLIDAY INN**
P. O. Box 675 (54501)
Rates: $48-$68;
Tel: (715) 369-3600

**KAFKA'S RESORT**
4281 W Lake George Rd
(54501)
Rates: $380-$590;
Tel: (800) 426-6674

## RIB LAKE

**OLKIVES
LAKEVIEW RESORT**
N9503 Spirit Lake Rd (54470)
Rates: N/A;
Tel: (715) 427-3344

## RICE LAKE

**CURRIER'S LAKEVIEW
RESORT MOTEL**
2010 E Sawyer St (54868)
Rates: $29-$72;
Tel: (715) 234-7474

## RICHLAND CENTER

**STARLITE MOTEL**
Rt 2 Hwy 14 East (53581)
Rates: N/A;
Tel: (608) 647-6159

## RIPON

**BEST WESTERN
WELCOME INN**
240 E Fond Du Lac St (54971)
Rates: $39-$52;
Tel: (414) 748-2821

## ST. CROIX FALLS

**DALLES HOUSE MOTEL**
P. O. Box 664 (54024)
Rates: $37-$66;
Tel: (800) 341-8000

## ST. GERMAIN

**ST. GERMAIN MOTEL**
P. O. Box 268 (54558)
Rates: N/A;
Tel: (715) 542-3535

## SAYNER

**FROELICH'S SAYNER
LODGE**
P. O. Box 100-MO (54560)
Rates: $69-$79;
Tel: (800) 553-9695

## SHAWANO

**SUPER 8 MOTEL**
211 Waukechon St (54166)
Rates: $40-$150·
Tel: (715) 526-6688

## SHEBOYGAN

**BUDGETEL INN**
2932 Kohler Memorial Dr
(53081)
Rates: $35-$45;
Tel: (414) 457-2321

**COMFORT INN**
4332 N 40th St (53083)
Rates: $36-$61;
Tel: (414) 457-7724

**PARKWAY MOTEL**
3900 Motel Rd (53081)
Rates: $27-$42;
Tel: (414) 458-8338

**SUPER 8 MOTEL**
3402 Wilgus Rd (53081)
Rates: $37-$44;
Tel: (414) 458-8080

## SIREN

**PINE WOOD MOTEL**
23862 Hwy 35S (54872)
Rates: $30-$42;
Tel: (715) 349-5225

## SPARTA

**BEST NIGHTS INN**
303 Wisconsin St (54656)
Rates: $26-$69;
Tel: (608) 269-3066

**COUNTRY INN BY CARLSON**
737 Avon Rd (54656)
Rates: $40-$52;
Tel: (608) 269-3110

**DOWNTOWN MOTEL**
509 S Water St (54656)
Rates: $25-$35;
Tel: (608) 269-3138

**HERITAGE MOTEL**
704 W Wisconsin St (54656)
Rates: $32-$42;
Tel: (608) 269-6991

## SPOONER

**GREEN ACRES MOTEL**
P. O. Box 28 (54801)
Rates: $35-$79;
Tel: (715) 635-2177

## STEVENS POINT

**BUDGETEL INN**
4917 Main St (54481)
Rates: $33-$49;
Tel: (715) 344-1900

**HOLIDAY INN**
P. O. Box 97 (54481)
Rates: $65-$97;
Tel: (715) 341-1340

**POINT MOTEL**
209 Division St (54481)
Rates: $31-$36;
Tel: (715) 344-6455

**TRAVELER MOTEL**
3350 Church (54481)
Rates: $32-$43;
Tel: (800) 341-8000

## STODDARD

**WATER'S EDGE MOTEL**
201 N Pearl St (54658)
Rates: N/A;
Tel: (608) 457-2126

## STOUGHTON

**CHOSE FAMILY INN**
1124 W Main St (53589)
Rates: $34-$45;
Tel: (608) 872-0330

## STURGEON BAY

**HOLIDAY MOTEL**
29 N 2nd Ave (54235)
Rates: $49-$56;
Tel: (414) 743-5571

## SUPERIOR

**BEST WESTERN
BRIDGEVIEW MOTOR INN**
415 Hammond Ave (54880)
Rates: $40-$82;
Tel: (715) 392-8174

**DAYS INN-BAYFRONT**
110 E 2nd St (54880)
Rates: $38-$108;
Tel: (715) 392-4783

**DRIFTWOOD INN**
2200 E 2nd St (54880)
Rates: $24-$62;
Tel: (715) 398-6661

**SUPERIOR INN**
525 Hammond Ave (54880)
Rates: $35-$62;
Tel: (715) 394-7706

## THREE LAKES

**ONEIDA VILLAGE INN**
P. O. Box C (54562)
Rates: $35-$48;
Tel: (715) 546-3373

## TOMAH

**BUDGET HOST
DAYBREAK MOTEL**
Hwys 12 & 16 (54660)
Rates: $30-$53;
Tel: (608) 372-5946

**ECONO LODGE**
2005 N Superior Ave (54660)
Rates: $32-$52;
Tel: (608) 372-9100

**HOLIDAY INN**
P. O. Box 745 (54660)
Rates: $60-$66;
Tel: (608) 372-3211

**LARK INN**
229 N Superior Ave (54660)
Rates: $30-$55;
Tel: (608) 372-5981

**RED GABLES MOTEL**
Hwy 12 N, Box 23 (54660)
Rates: N/A;
Tel: (608) 372-6868

**SUPER 8 MOTEL**
P. O. Box 48 (54660)
Rates: $35-$54;
Tel: (608) 372-3901

**TOMAH COMFORT INN**
305 Wittig Rd (54660)
Rates: $44-$64;
Tel: (608) 372-6600

## TREVOR

**STATE LINE MOTEL**
23610 128th St (53179)
Rates: N/A;
Tel: (414) 396-9561

## TWO RIVERS

**COOL CITY MOTEL**
3009 Lincoln Ave (54241)
Rates: N/A;
Tel: (414) 793-2244

## WASHBURN

**LAKE SUPERIOR INN**
P. O. Box 626 (54891)
Rates: $52-$62;
Tel: (715) 373-5671

**REDWOOD
MOTEL & CHALETS**
P. O. Box 385 (54891)
Rates: $28-$48;
Tel: (715) 373-5512

## WASHINGTON ISLAND

**VIKING VILLAGE MOTEL**
P. O. Box 135 (54246)
Rates: $48-$85;
Tel: (414) 847-2551

## WATERTOWN

**FLAGS INN MOTEL**
N627 Hwy 26 (53094)
Rates: N/A;
Tel: (414) 261-9400

**HERITAGE INN**
700 E Main St (53094)
Rates: $44-$49;
Tel: (414) 261-9010

## WAUKESHA

**HOLIDAY INN**
2417 Bluemound Rd (53186)
Rates: $56-$69;
Tel: (414) 786-0460

**SELECT INN**
2510 Plaza Ct (53186)
Rates: $32-$44;
Tel: (414) 786-6015

**SUPER 8 MOTEL**
2501 Plaza Ct (53186)
Rates: $32-$49;
Tel: (414) 785-1590

## WAUPACA

**BEST WESTERN
GRAND SEASONS HOTEL**
110 Grand Season Dr (54981)
Rates: $49-$61;
Tel: (715) 258-9212

**VILLAGE INN MOTEL**
1060 W Fulton (54981)
Rates: $37-$47;
Tel: (800) 626-6391

## WAUSAU

**ACE MOTEL**
2211 W Stewart Ave (54401)
Rates: N/A;
Tel: (715) 845-4261

**BEST WESTERN
MIDWAY HOTEL**
2901 Martin Ave (54401)
Rates: $64-$93;
Tel: (715) 842-1616

**BUDGETEL INN**
1910 Stewart Ave (54401)
Rates: $32-$41;
Tel: (715) 842-0421

**EXEL INN OF WAUSAU**
116 S 17th Ave (54401)
Rates: $29-$43;
Tel: (715) 842-0641

**HOLIDAY INN**
P. O. Box 1224 (54401)
Rates: $48-$76;
Tel: (715) 845-4341

**HOWARD JOHNSON
LODGE**
2001 N Mountain Rd (54401)
Rates: $55-$63;
Tel: (715) 842-0711

**MARLENE MOTEL**
2010 Stewart Ave (54401)
Rates: $27-$34;
Tel: (715) 845-6248

**RIB MOUNTAIN INN**
2900 Rib Mountain Way
(54401)
Rates: $43-$62;
Tel: (715) 848-2802

**SUPER 8 MOTEL**
2006 Stewart Ave (54401)
Rates: $41-$51;
Tel: (715) 848-2888

## WEYERHAEUSER

**COUNTRY VIEW MOTEL**
W14691 Hwy 8 (54895)
Rates: $24-$30;
Tel: (715) 353-2780

## WHITEWATER

**BLACK STALLION INN**
Rt 1 US Hwy 12 (53190)
Rates: N/A;
Tel: (414) 473-7700

**SUPER 8 MOTEL**
917 E Milwaukee St (53190)
Rates: $39-$46;
Tel: (414) 473-8818

## WISCONSIN DELLS

**HOLIDAY INN**
P. O. Box 236 (53965)
Rates: $52-$89;
Tel: (608) 254-8306

**INN OF THE DELLS**
611 Wisconsin Dells Pkwy
(53965)
Rates: $40-$115;
Tel: (608) 253-1511

**KINGS INN MOTEL**
Jct Hwy 12 & 23 (53965)
Rates: N/A;
Tel: (608) 254-2043

# WYOMING

## AFTON

**BEST WESTERN
HI COUNTRY INN**
P. O. Box 907 (83110)
Rates: $35-$50;
Tel: (307) 886-3856

**LAZY B MOTEL**
P. O. Box 430 (83110)
Rates: $30-$42;
Tel: (307) 886-3187

**MOUNTAIN INN**
US 89, Rt 1 (83110)
Rates: $35-$52;
Tel: (307) 886-3156

## ALPINE

**ALPEN HAUS
MOTOR HOTEL**
P. O.Box 258 (83128)
Rates: $30-$60;
Tel: (307) 654-7545

**BEST WESTERN
FLYING SADDLE LODGE**
P. O. Box 227 (83128)
Rates: $48-$130;
Tel: (307) 654-7561

## BUFFALO

**ARROWHEAD MOTEL**
749 Fort St (82834)
Rates: $20-$35;
Tel: (307) 684-9453

**CANYON MOTEL**
997 Fort St (82834)
Rates: $27-$36;
Tel: (307) 684-2957

**CROSS ROADS HOJO INN**
P. O. Box 639 (82834)
Rates: $38-$71;
Tel: (307) 684-2256

**ECONO LODGE**
333 Hart St (82834)
Rates: $31-$56;
Tel: (307) 684-2219

**MANSION HOUSE MOTEL**
313 North Main (82834)
Rates: N/A;
Tel: (307) 684-2218

**MOUNTAIN VIEW MOTEL**
585 Fort St (82834)
Rates: $26-$32;
Tel: (307) 684-2881

**SUPER 8 MOTEL**
Clearmont Rt, Box 10 (82834)
Rates: $27-$53;
Tel: (307) 684-2531

**WYOMING MOTEL**
610 E Hart (82834)
Rates: $21-$68;
Tel: (307) 684-5505

**Z-BAR MOTEL, IMA**
626 Fort St (82834)
Rates: $24-$40;
Tel: (307) 684-5535

## CASPER

**CASPER HILTON INN**
P. O. Box 224 (82602)
Rates: $56-$78;
Tel: (307) 266-6000

**DAYS INN**
400 West F (82601)
Rates: $43-$57;
Tel: (307) 235-6668

**FIRST INTERSTATE INN**
P. O. Box 9047 (82601)
Rates: $26-$35;
Tel: (307) 234-9125

**HILTON INN
MOTOR HOTEL**
P. O. Box 224 (82602)
Rates: $58-$175;
Tel: (307) 266-6000

**HOLIDAY INN**
P. O. Box 3500 (82602)
Rates: $48-$68;
Tel: (307) 235-2531

**KELLY INN**
821 N Poplar (82601)
Rates: $34-$38;
Tel: (307) 266-2400

**LA QUINTA MOTOR INN**
301 East E St (82601)
Rates: $33-$38;
Tel: (307) 234-1159

**SHILO INN**
P. O. Box 246
(Evansville 82636)
Rates: $39-$49;
Tel: (307) 237-1335

## CHEYENNE

**ATLAS MOTEL**
1524 W Lincoln Way (82001)
Rates: N/A;
Tel: (307) 632-9214

**BEST WESTERN
HITCHING POST INN**
P. O. Box 1769 (82001)
Rates: $52-$75;
Tel: (307) 638-3301

**COMFORT INN**
2245 Etchepare Dr (82007)
Rates: $28-$42;
Tel: (307) 638-7202

**DRUMMOND'S RANCH
BED & BREAKFAST**
399 Happy Jack Rd (82007)
Rates: $60-$75;
Tel: (307) 634-6042

**HOLIDAY INN**
204 W Fox Farm Rd (82007)
Rates: $65-$95;
Tel: (307) 638-4466

**LA QUINTA MOTOR INN**
2410 W Lincolnway (82001)
Rates: $45-$59;
Tel: (307) 632-7117

**LINCOLN COURT**
1720 Lincolnway (82001)
Rates: $45-$60;
Tel: (307) 638-3302

**RODEWAY INN**
3839 E Lincolnway (82001)
Rates: N/A;
Tel: (307) 634-2171

## CODY

**ABSAROKA
MOUNTAIN LODGE**
1231 E Yellowstone Hwy
(Wapiti 82450)
Rates: $42-$70;
Tel: (307) 587-3963

**BIG BEAR MOTEL**
139 W Yellowstone Hwy
(82414)
Rates: $24-$48;
Tel: (307) 587-3117

**ELEPHANT HEAD LODGE**
1170 Yellowstone Hwy
(Wapiti 82450)
Rates: $44-$50;
Tel: (307) 587-3980

**GOFF CREEK
LODGE RESORT**
P. O. Box 155A (82414)
Rates: $50-$78;
Tel: (307) 587-3753

**HALF MILE CREEK RANCH**
P. O. Box 48 (Wapiti 82450)
Rates: $60;
Tel: (307) 587-9513

**KELLY INN OF CODY**
P. O. Box 216 (82414)
Rates: $40-$75;
Tel: (307) 527-5505

**SHOSHONE LODGE**
P. O. Box 790T (82414)
Rates: $36-$70;
Tel: (307) 587-4044

**TROUT CREEK INN**
North Fork Rt (82414)
Rates: $26-$60;
Tel: (307) 587-6288

**YELLOWSTONE
VALLEY INN**
3324 Yellowstone Park Hwy
(82414)
Rates: $29-$54;
Tel: (307) 587-3961

## DOUGLAS

**CHIEFTAIN MOTEL**
815 E. Richards (82633)
Rates: $25-$34;
Tel: (307) 358-2673

**HOLIDAY INN**
1450 Riverbend Dr (82633)
Rates: $51-$59;
Tel: (307) 358-9790

## DUBOIS

**BLACK BEAR
COUNTRY INN**
P. O. Box 595 (82513)
Rates: $24-$38;
Tel: (307) 455-2344

**BRANDING IRON MOTEL**
P. O. Box 705 (82513)
Rates: $26-$35;
Tel: (307) 455-2893

**LAZY L & B RANCH**
Route 66 (82513)
Rates: $595-$825;
Tel: (307) 455-2839

**PINNACLE MOTOR LODGE**
3577 UW Hwy 26 (82513)
Rates: $25-$39;
Tel: (307) 455-2506

**STAGECOACH
MOTOR INN**
P. O. Box 216 (82513)
Rates: $30-$46;
Tel: (307) 455-2303

**WIND RIVER MOTEL**
519 W Ramshorn (82513)
Rates: N/A;
Tel: (307) 455-2611

## EVANSTON

**BIG HORN
MOTEL & APARTMENTS**
202 Bear River Dr (82930)
Rates: $20-$40;
Tel: (307) 789-6830

**DUNMAR INN**
P. O. Box 0786 (82931)
Rates: $54-$84;
Tel: (307) 789-3770

**PRAIRIE INN MOTEL**
264 Bear River Dr (82930)
Rates: $34-$42;
Tel: (307) 789-2920

**SUPER 8 MOTEL**
70 Bear River Dr (82930)
Rates: $26-$34;
Tel: (307) 789-7510

**WESTON PLAZA**
1983 Harrison Dr (82930)
Rates: $44-$49;
Tel: (307) 789-0783

## EVANSVILLE

**SHILO INN**
I-25 & Curtis Rd (82636)
Rates: N/A;
Tel: (307) 237-1335

## GILLETTE

**ARROWHEAD MOTEL**
202 Emerson (82716)
Rates: N/A;
Tel: (307) 686-0909

**BEST WESTERN
TOWER WEST LODGE**
109 N Hwy 14-16 (82716)
Rates: $47-$58;
Tel: (307) 686-2210

**DAYS INN GILLETTE**
910 E Boxelder (82716)
Rates: $38-$45;
Tel: (307) 682-3999

**GILLETTE SUPER 8**
208 S Decker Ct (82716)
Rates: $30-$42;
Tel: (307) 682-8078

**HOLIDAY INN OF GILLETTE**
2009 S Douglas Hwy 59
(82716)
Rates: $50-$58;
Tel: (307) 686-3000

**RAMADA LIMITED**
608 E 2nd St (82716)
Rates: $29-$53;
Tel: (307) 682-9341

**RODEWAY INN**
1020 Hwy 51E (82716)
Rates: $36-$56;
Tel: (307) 682-5111

## GLENROCK

**ALL AMERICAN INN-GLENROCK**
500 W Aspen (82637)
Rates: $19-$42;
Tel: (307) 436-2772

## GRAND TETON NATIONAL PARK

**COLTER BAY VILLAGE**
P. O. Box 240 (Moran 83013)
Rates: $48-$94;
Tel: (307) 543-2855

**FLAGG RANCH VILLAGE**
P. O. Box 187 (83013)
Rates: $65-$82;
Tel: (307) 543-2861

**JACKSON LAKE LODGE**
P. O. Box 240 (Moran 83013)
Rates: $79-$150;
Tel: (307) 543-2855

**SIGNAL MOUNTAIN LODGE**
P. O. Box 50 (Moran 83013)
Rates: $60-$140;
Tel: (307) 543-2831

**TOGWOTEE MOUNTAIN LODGE**
P. O. Box 91 (Moran 83013)
Rates: $59-$236;
Tel: (307) 543-2847

## GREEN RIVER

**COACHMAN INN MOTEL**
470 E Flaming Gorge Way
(82935)
Rates: $25-$34;
Tel: (307) 875-3681

**DESMOND MOTEL**
140 N 7th W (82935)
Rates: $26-$36;
Tel: (307) 875-3701

**SUPER 8 MOTEL**
280 W Flaming Gorge Way
(82935)
Rates: N/A;
Tel: (307) 875-9330

## GREYBULL

**ANTLER MOTEL**
1116 N 6th St (82426)
Rates: $25-$32;
Tel: (307) 765-4404

**K-BAR MOTEL**
300 Greybull Ave (82426)
Rates: $28-$32;
Tel: (307) 765-4426

**SAGE MOTEL**
1135 N 6th St (82426)
Rates: $28-$32;
Tel: (307) 765-4443

**YELLOWSTONE MOTEL**
247 Greybull Ave (82426)
Rates: $30-$60;
Tel: (307) 765-4456

## HELL'S HALF ACRE

**HELL'S HALF ACRE MOTEL**
Hwys 20 & 26 (82648)
Rates: N/A;
Tel: (307) 472-0018

## HULETT

**MOTEL PIONEER**
P. O. Box 389 (82720)
Rates: $24-$39;
Tel: (307) 467-5656

## JACKSON

**CRYSTAL SPRINGS INN**
P. O. Box 250
(Teton Village 83025)
Rates: $42-$84;
Tel: (307) 733-4423

**FLAT CREEK MOTEL**
1935 N US 89 (83001)
Rates: $65-$95;
Tel: (307) 733-5276

**THE 49'ER INN**
330 W Pearl (83001)
Rates: $46-$96;
Tel: (307) 733-7550

**FRIENDSHIP INN-ANTLER**
P. O. Box 575 (83001)
Rates: $56-$86;
Tel: (307) 733-2535

**SNOW KING RESORT**
400 Snow King Ave (83001)
Rates: $75-$330;
Tel: (307) 733-5200

**VIRGINIAN LODGE**
750 W Broadway (83001)
Rates: $40-$75;
Tel: (307) 733-2792

## KEMMERER

**FAIRVIEW MOTEL**
1429 1st West Ave (83101)
Rates: $30-$54;
Tel: (307) 877-3938

## LANDER

**BUDGET HOST PRONGHORN LODGE**
150 E Main St (82520)
Rates: $27-$46;
Tel: (307) 332-3940

**HOLIDAY LODGE**
210 McFarlane Dr (82520)
Rates: $26-$45;
Tel: (307) 332-2511

**SILVER SPUR MOTEL**
340 N 10th (82520)
Rates: $24-$42;
Tel: (307) 332-5189

# LARAMIE

**BEST WESTERN
FOSTER'S COUNTRY INN**
1561 Jackson St (82070)
Rates: $48-$62;
Tel: (307) 742-8371

**BEST WESTERN GAS LITE**
960 N 3rd St (82070)
Rates: $29-$59;
Tel: (307) 742-6616

**DOWNTOWN MOTEL**
165 N 3rd St (82070)
Rates: $23-$49;
Tel. (307) 742-6671

**HOLIDAY INN OF LARAMIE**
2313 Soldier Springs (82070)
Rates: $46-$66;
Tel: (307) 742-6611

**LARAMIE INN**
421 Boswell (82070)
Rates: $48-$58;
Tel: (307) 742-3721

**SUNSET INN**
1104 S 3rd St (82070)
Rates: $28-$60;
Tel: (307) 742-3741

# LOVELL

**HORSESHOE BEND MOTEL**
375 E Main St (82431)
Rates: $30-$36;
Tel: (307) 548-2221

**SUPER 8 MOTEL**
P. O. Box 235 (82431)
Rates: $32-$40;
Tel: (307) 548-2725

# LUSK

**TRAIL MOTEL**
305 W 8th St (82225)
Rates: $32-$50;
Tel: (307) 334-2530

# MOORCROFT

**MOORCOURT MOTEL**
P. O. Box 195 (82721)
Rates: $35-$58;
Tel: (307) 756-3411

# NEWCASTLE

**FOUNTAIN INN-
CRYSTAL PARK RESORT**
2 Fountain Plaza (82701)
Rates: $42-$62;
Tel: (307) 746-4426

**HILL TOP MOTEL**
1121 S Summit (82701)
Rates: N/A;
Tel: (307) 746-4494

**THE PINES MOTEL**
248 E Wentworth (82701)
Rates: N/A;
Tel: (307) 746-4334

# PINEDALE

**BOULDER LAKE LODGE**
Box 1100 (82941)
Rates: N/A;
Tel: (307) 537-4300

**LAKESIDE LODGE**
99 FSR 111 Fremont Lake
(82941)
Rates: N/A;
Tel: (307) 367-2221

**SUN DANCE MOTEL**
148 E Pine (82941)
Rates: $34-$55;
Tel: (307) 367-4336

**THE ZZZZ INN**
P. O. Box 1076 (82941)
Rates: $40-$65;
Tel: (307) 367-2121

# POWELL

**BEST WESTERN KINGS INN**
777 E 2nd St (82435)
Rates: $36-$67;
Tel: (307) 754-5117

# RANCHESTER

**RANCHESTER
WESTERN MOTEL**
350 Dayton St (82839)
Rates: $19-$40;
Tel: (307) 655-2212

# RAWLINS

**BEST WESTERN
BEL AIR INN**
P. O. Box 387 (82301)
Rates: $49-$75;
Tel: (307) 324-2737

**BRIDGER INN**
1904 E Cedar St (82301)
Rates: $26-$34;
Tel: (307) 328-1401

**DAYS INN**
2222 E Cedar St (82301)
Rates: $45-$68;
Tel: (307) 324-5063

**RAWLINS MOTEL**
905 W Spruce St (82301)
Rates: $28-$42;
Tel: (307) 324-3456

**SLEEP INN**
1400 Higley Blvd (82301)
Rates: $39-$44;
Tel: (307) 328-1732

**SUNSET MOTEL**
1302 W Spruce St (82301)
Rates: $22-$35;
Tel: (307) 324-3448

# RIVERTON

**HI-LO MOTEL**
414 N Federal Blvd (82501)
Rates: $24-$33;
Tel: (307) 856-9223

**HOLIDAY INN**
900 E Sunset (82501)
Rates: $47-$56;
Tel: (307) 856-8100

**SUNDOWNER
STATION MOTEL**
1616 N Federal Blvd (82501)
Rates: $39-$45;
Tel: (800) 874-1116

**SUPER 8 MOTEL**
1040 N Federal Blvd (82501)
Rates: $30-$44;
Tel: (307) 857-2400

**THUNDERBIRD MOTEL**
302 E Fremont (82501)
Rates: $25-$40;
Tel: (307) 856-9201

## ROCK SPRINGS

**AMERICAN FAMILY INN**
1625 N Elk St (82901)
Rates: $24-$44;
Tel: (307) 382-4217

**COMFORT INN**
1670 Sunset Dr (82901)
Rates: $38-$55;
Tel: (307) 382-9490

**FRIENDSHIP INN**
1004 Dewar Dr (82901)
Rates: $29-$36;
Tel: (307) 362-6673

**HOLIDAY INN**
1675 Sunset Dr (82901)
Rates: $53-$66;
Tel: (307) 382-9200

**THE INN
AT ROCK SPRINGS**
2518 Foothill Blvd (82901)
Rates: $48-$71;
Tel: (307) 362-9600

**LA QUINTA MOTOR INN**
2717 Dewar Dr (82901)
Rates: $39-$54;
Tel: (307) 362-1770

**NOMAD INN**
1545 Elk St (82901)
Rates: $29-$43;
Tel: (307) 362-5646

## SARATOGA

**HACIENDA MOTEL**
P. O. Box 960 (82331)
Rates: $29-$52;
Tel: (307) 326-5751

## SHERIDAN

**BEST WESTERN SHERIDAN
CENTER MOTOR INN**
612 N Main St (82801)
Rates: $46-$54;
Tel: (307) 674-7421

**GUEST HOUSE MOTEL**
2007 N Main St (82801)
Rates: $26-$36;
Tel: (307) 674-7496

**HOLIDAY INN**
1809 Sugarland Dr (82801)
Rates: $48-$125;
Tel: (307) 672-8931

**THE MILL INN MOTEL**
2161 Coffeen Ave (82801)
Rates: $32-$41;
Tel: (307) 672-6401

**TRAILS END MOTEL**
2125 N Main St (82801)
Rates: $30-$52;
Tel: (307) 672-2477

**TRIANGLE MOTEL**
540 Coffeen Ave (82801)
Rates: N/A;
Tel: (307) 674-8031

## SUNDANCE

**BEST WESTERN INN
AT SUNDANCE**
121 S 6th St (82729)
Rates: $35-$67;
Tel: (307) 283-2800

**HAWKEN GUEST RANCH**
P. O. Box 863 (82729)
Rates: N/A;
Tel: (307) 756-9319

## THERMOPOLIS

**BEST WESTERN
MOONLIGHTER MOTEL**
600 Broadway (82443)
Rates: $30-$54;
Tel: (307) 864-2321

**EL RANCHO MOTEL**
924 Shoshoni Rd (82443)
Rates: $21-$40;
Tel: (307) 864-2341

**HOLIDAY INN
OF THE WATERS**
P. O. Box 1323 (82443)
Rates: $40-$81;
Tel: (307) 864-3131

## TORRINGTON

**MAVERICK MOTEL**
Rt 1, Box 354 (82240)
Rates: $27-$32;
Tel: (307) 532-4064

**OREGON TRAIL LODGE**
710 East Valley Blvd (82240)
Rates: N/A;
Tel: (307) 532-2101

## WHEATLAND

**BEST WESTERN
TORCHLITE MOTOR INN**
1809 N 16th St (82201)
Rates: $37-$52;
Tel: (307) 322-4070

**MOTEL WEST WINDS**
1756 South Rd (82201)
Rates: $26-$36;
Tel: (307) 322-2705

**VIMBO'S MOTEL**
203 16th St (82201)
Rates: $32-$41;
Tel: (307) 322-3842

## WORLAND

**BEST WESTERN
SETTLERS INN**
2200 Big Horn Ave (82401)
Rates: $42-$52;
Tel: (307) 347-8201

**SUN VALLEY MOTEL**
500 N 10th St (82401)
Rates: $24-$48;
Tel: (307) 347-4251

## YELLOWSTONE
## NATIONAL PARK

**CANYON LODGE**
Yellowstone, Montana (82190)
Rates: $43-$80;
Tel: (307) 344-7311

**LAKE LODGE & CABINS**
Yellowstone, Montana (82190)
Rates: $39-$79;
Tel: (307) 344-7311

# Toll-Free '800' Numbers:

## Car Rental Toll-Free '800' Numbers

Advantage Rent-A-Car
800-777-5500

Agency Rent-A-Car
800-321-1972

Airways Rent-A-Car
800-937-3748
800-669-1588 CT
800-952-9200 O'Hare

Alamo Rent-A-Car
800-327-9633

Allstate Rent-A-Car
800-634-6186

American Intl Rent-A-Car
800-527-0202

Autoglobe Intl Car Rentals
800-858-1515

Avis-Reservations Center
800-331-1212

Aztec Rent-A-Car
800-231-0400

Brooks Rent-A-Car
800-634-6721

Budget Rent-A-Car
800-527-0700

Dollar Rent-A-Car
800-421-6868

Enterprise Rent-A-Car
800-325-8007

Fairway Rent-A-Car
800-634-3476

General Rent-A-Car
800-327-7607

Hertz Corporation
800-654-3131

Inter American Car Rental
800-327-1278

National Car Rental
800-227-7368

Payless Rent-A-Car Inc
800-237-2804

Rent Rite
Reservation Network
800-554-7483

Rent-A-Vette
800-372-1981 (except NV)

Rent-A-Wreck
800-535-1391

Sears Rent-A-Car
800-527-0770

Showcase Rental Car
800-421-6808

Thrifty Rent-A-Car
800-367-2277

Tilden (National Car)
800-227-7368

U-Haul Intl RV Rentals
800-468-4285

U-Save Auto Rental
of America
800-272-8728

USA Rent-A-Car
System Inc
800-872-2277

Ugly Duckling Rent-A-Car
800-843-3825

Value Rent-A-Car
800-327-2501

Viva Van & Car Rentals
800-926-6926

## STATE DEPARTMENTS OF TOURISM
### Toll-Free '800' Numbers

Alabama
800-252-2262

Alaska
800-426-0082

Arizona
800-842-8257

Arkansas
800-628-8725

California
800-862-2543

Colorado
800-627-3766

Connecticut
800-282-6863

Delaware
800-441-8846

Dist. of Columbia
202-789-7000

Florida
800-868-7476

Georgia
404-656-3590

Hawaii
800-257-2999

Idaho
800-635-7820

Illinois
800-233-0121

Indiana
800-289-6646

Iowa
800-345-4692

Kansas
800-252-6727

Kentucky
800-225-8747

Louisiana
800-334-8626

Maine
800-533-9595

Maryland
800-543-1036

Massachusetts
800-447-6277

| | | |
|---|---|---|
| **Michigan**<br>800-543-2937 | **Utah**<br>801-538-1030 | **Drury Inn**<br>800-325-8300 |
| **Minnesota**<br>800-657-3700 | **Vermont**<br>802-828-3236 | **Econo Lodges of America**<br>800-446-6900 |
| **Mississippi**<br>800-927-6378 | **Virginia**<br>800-847-4882 | **Economy Inns of America**<br>800-826-0778 |
| **Missouri**<br>800-877-1234 | **Washington**<br>800-544-1800 | **Embassy Suites**<br>800-362-2779 |
| **Montana**<br>800-541-1447 | **West Virginia**<br>800-225-5982 | **Exel Inns of America**<br>800-356-8013 |
| **Nebraska**<br>800-228-4307 | **Wisconsin**<br>800-432-8747 | **Fairfield Inn by Marriott**<br>800 228 2000 |
| **Nevada**<br>800-638-2328 | **Wyoming**<br>800-225-5996 | **Fairmont Hotels**<br>800-527-4727 |
| **New Hampshire**<br>603-271-2343 | | **Four Seasons Hotel**<br>800-332-3442 |

**New Jersey**
800-537-7397

## HOTEL/MOTEL
## Toll-Free '800' Numbers

**Friendship Inns
of America**
800-453-4511

**New Mexico**
800 545 2040

**Auberges Wandlyn Inns**
800-561-0006

**Guest Quarters**
800-424-2900

**New York**
800-225-5692

**Best Western Intl Inc**
800-528-1234

**Hampton Inn**
800-426-7866

**North Carolina**
000 047-4802

**Budget Host**
800-283-4678

**Harley Hotels**
800-321-2323

**North Dakota**
800-435-5063

**Budgetel Inn**
800-428-3438

**Hawthorn Suites**
800-527-1133

**Ohio**
800-282-5393

**Clarion Hotels**
800-252-7466

**Helmsley Hotels**
800-221-4982

**Oklahoma**
800-654-8240

**Comfort Inns**
800-228-5150

**Hilton Hotels Corp**
800-445-8667

**Oregon**
800-547-7852

**Compri Hotels**
800-426-6774

**Holiday Inns**
800-465-4329

**Pennsylvania**
800-847-4872

**Courtyard by Marriott**
800-321-2211

**Howard Johnson Hotels**
800-654-2000

**Rhode Island**
800-556-2484

**Crown Sterling Suites**
800-433-4600

**Hyatt Corp**
800-238-9000

**South Carolina**
800-872-3505

**Davis Bros Motor Lodges**
800-841-9480

**Inter-Continental Hotels**
800-327-0200

**South Dakota**
800-732-5682

**Days Inn**
800-325-2525

**L-K Motels Inc**
800-282-5711

**Tennessee**
615-741-2158

**Dillon Inn**
800-253-7503

**La Quinta Motor Inns**
800-531-5900

**Texas**
800-888-8839

**Doubletree Hotels**
800-528-0444

Lexington Hotel Suites
800-537-8483

Loews Hotel
800-223-0888

Marriott Hotels
800-228-9290

Master Hosts Inn
800-251-1962

Meridien
800-543-4300

Motel 6
800-437-7486

Omni Hotels
800-843-6664

Parks Inns International
800-437-7275

Princess Resorts
800-227-5650

Quality Inns
800-228-5151

Ramada Inns
800-228-2828

Red Carpet/Scottish Inns
800-251-1962

Red Lion-Thunderbird
800-547-8010

Red Roof Inns
800-843-7663

Residence Inn by Marriott
800-331-3131

Ritz-Carlton
800-241-3333

Rodeway Inns
International
800-228-2000

Sheraton Hotels & Inns
800-325-3535

Shilo Inns
800-222-2244

Signature Inns
800-822-5252

Sonesta Hotels
800-766-3782

Stouffer Hotels & Resorts
800-468-3571

Super 8 Motels
800-800-8000

Susse Chalet
Motor Lodges/Inns
800-258-1980

Travelodge Intl/
Viscount Hotel
800-255-3050

Treadway Inns Corp
800-873-2392

Trusthouse Forts Hotels
800-225-5843

Vagabond Hotels Inc
800-522-1555

Westin Hotels
800-228-3000

Wyndham Hotels
800-822-4200

# ORDER EXTRA COPIES
## OF VACATIONING WITH YOUR PET!

## For Your Organization or as Gifts
## For Friends and Relatives!

*(See Following Page for Special Pricing.)*

Fill out the coupon below and mail it to:

### VACATIONING WITH YOUR PET!
PET-FRIENDLY PUBLICATIONS • P.O. BOX 8459 • SCOTTSDALE, AZ 85252

---

### PET-FRIENDLY PUBLICATIONS
### P.O. BOX 8459
### SCOTTSDALE, AZ 85252

PLEASE SEND ME _____ COPIES OF VACATIONING WITH YOUR PET!

NAME _____

ADDRESS _____ APT#/STE# _____

CITY _____ STATE _____ ZIP _____

NUMBER OF BOOKS _____ @ $ _____ = $ _____

SHIPPING & HANDING CHARGES = $ 3.75

TOTAL AMOUNT OF ORDER (INCLUDING SHIPPING & HANDLING) = $ _____

ENCLOSED IS MY CHECK OR MONEY ORDER _____

PLEASE BILL MY (CHECK ONE) MASTERCARD ____ VISA ____

CREDIT CARD # _____ EXP. DATE _____

SIGNATURE _____

# ORDER EXTRA COPIES
## OF VACATIONING WITH YOUR PET!

### For Your Organization or as Gifts
### For Friends and Relatives!

You know how much fun you have vacationing and travelling with your pet...why not help your pet-owning friends share these new experiences with their pets?

**VACATIONING WITH YOUR PET** is the perfect gift. Additional copies can be purchased directly from the publisher at the following prices:

| | |
|---|---|
| 1 to 3 copies: | $14.95 each<br>plus $3.75 shipping and handling per order. |
| 4 to 10 copies: | (20% discount) $12 each<br>plus $3.75 shipping and handling per order. |
| 11 copies or more: | Call publisher at<br>**1 (800) 496-2665**<br>for volume discount pricing. |